THE SOURCES OF THE HEXATEUCH

J, E, and P, in the text of the American Standard Edition, according to the consensus of scholarship, edited with introductions and notes

By

EDGAR SHEFFIELD BRIGHTMAN, Ph.D.
Professor of Ethics and Religion in Wesleyan University

WIPF & STOCK · Eugene, Oregon

Wipf and Stock Publishers
199 W 8th Ave, Suite 3
Eugene, OR 97401

The Sources of the Hexateuch
By Brightman, Edgar Sheffield
ISBN 13: 978-1-5326-3761-2
Publication date 7/19/2017
Previously published by The Abingdon Press, 1918

To
ALBERT CORNELIUS KNUDSON, Ph.D.
TO WHOM THIS BOOK AND ITS WRITER
OWE MUCH

TABLE OF CONTENTS

CHAPTER		PAGE
	PREFACE....................................	7
	INTRODUCTION...............................	9
I	J: THE JAHVISTIC OR JUDÆAN NARRATIVE........	19
II	E: THE ELOHISTIC OR EPHRAIMITIC NARRATIVE...	112
III	P: THE PRIESTLY CODE	203
	BIBLIOGRAPHY...............................	387
	ABBREVIATIONS..............................	390
	INDEX......................................	391

PREFACE

EXPERIENCE in the classroom at Nebraska Wesleyan and Wesleyan Universities has shown that there is need for an edition of the documents constituting the main sources of the Hexateuch. It is impossible to teach the Old Testament historically without frequent reference to J, E, and P. Students become interested in the problem and wish to read the sources, only to discover that the desired documents are not available.

The Sources of the Hexateuch is an attempt to supply this need by editing the documents J, E, and P according to the consensus of English, Scotch, Dutch, German, French, Swiss, and American scholarship. Every Bible student, whether he accepts the results of criticism or not, will find here a conspectus presenting the critical view in concrete form, and thus be able more accurately to estimate the truth or error in the theory presented.

No new translation and no new theories are presented here. This is a synthesis with no new thesis. The aim is not polemic, although the writer frankly accepts the critical position. The purpose of the book will have been attained if the outcome be a more intensive scientific and religious study of the Hexateuch.

The writer desires to express his thanks for encouragement and suggestions bearing on various aspects of the book to numerous colleagues at Wesleyan University, notably to Professors Heidel, Armstrong, and Conley; and, among other scholars, in particular to Professors Knudson, of Boston; Fowler, of Brown; Bacon, of Yale; Paton and Nourse, of Hartford; and Eiselen of Garrett.

EDGAR SHEFFIELD BRIGHTMAN.

Middletown, Connecticut.

INTRODUCTION

1. EXPLANATION OF THE GENERAL PLAN OF THE BOOK.

Scholars have been at work now for over a century on the problem of the analysis of the Hexateuch—the first six books of the Old Testament. An enormous amount has been written, and many widely varying opinions expressed. But out of the debate there has arisen a gradually increasing body of results on which scholars in general agree, based on the view that the Hexateuch as we now have it is made up of an interweaving of various older writings (called documents or sources).

There is no doubt that such interweaving as this theory presupposes did actually occur in Bible times. It is proven by a comparison of Chronicles with its sources in Samuel and Kings; or of Matthew and Luke with their source, Mark; or of Tatian's Diatessaron with the four Gospels. The case of the Hexateuch, however, differs in one respect from the instances cited: whereas in the illustrations we still have both the compilation (Chronicles, Matthew, the Diatessaron) and some at least of the earlier sources on which they are based (Samuel, Kings, Mark), in the case of the Hexateuch the earlier sources no longer exist as separate writings. The sources must be reconstructed by criticism.

It is not within the province of the present book to give an account of the methods used in determining the analysis into sources. Some hints will be found in the later outline of the history of criticism; but for a full discussion the reader is referred to Eiselen, The Books of the Pentateuch, or Driver, Introduction to the Literature of the Old Testament. We confine ourselves to the exposition of results rather than methods.

The generally accepted results designate by letters* the various sources of the Hexateuch as follows:

J (the Jahvistic or Judæan Narrative), written 850 B. C.

E (the Elohistic or Ephraimitic narrative), written 750 B. C.

---
* The letters are used indifferently to indicate either the documents or their authors.

10 SOURCES OF THE HEXATEUCH

D (Deuteronomy in its original form), written 650, published 621 B. C.

P (the Priestly Code), 500 B. C.

It is agreed that J and E were combined by Rje (a redactor, reviser, or editor), about 650 (his finished work being called JE); that JE and D were combined by Rd, who also made additions to D, about 600-550 (his finished work being called JED); and that the Pentateuch was put into substantially its present form by Rp, who united JED with P, about 400. Since 400 only one important addition was made, namely, Gn. 14, perhaps about 300, or even later.

Such in main outline is the critical view of the Hexateuch on which scholars the world over are in general agreed.

It is the aim of this book to present in usable form the restored documents, J, E, and P, distinguishing in each document the work of the various redactors. D is omitted because the book of Dt. may be read consecutively in any Bible, whereas J, E, and P stand in such intricate relations to each other that it is all but impossible to form any conception of their connection or their unity without such editing as is here undertaken. An attempt is made to represent objectively and accurately the consensus of scholarship, the assured results of criticism.

2. DEFINITION OF THE TERM "CONSENSUS OF SCHOLARSHIP."

Statements made in the previous section need further definition. There are many intelligent and educated Christians—even some scholars—who do not accept the critical analysis, with its denial of the Mosaic authorship of the Pentateuch. How, then, can it be said that "all scholars agree" on the results?

By a scholar or a critic in this book is meant one who (1) has made an expert and intensive study of the problem of the Hexateuch, being familiar both with the Hebrew text itself and with the range of scholarly discussion on all sides of debated questions, and (2) has published his results in monographs that have been recognized by scholars in general as worthy of attention.* Practically no such monographs have been recently

---

* It is to be noted that practically all the men fulfilling this description are to be found in the ranks of Protestant Christianity. Roman Catholics have not made any significant contributions in recent years; Greek Catholics and non-Christians, never.

published by scholars that do not accept the critical standpoint.

By the expression "all scholars agree" is meant that the scholars whose works have been consulted (except Eerdmans and his school) are at one in support of the opinion in question save perhaps for possible variations in minor matters that do not affect the significant content of the documents. Practically all the important critics since Wellhausen have been consulted.

3. THE EXISTENCE OF A CONSENSUS AMONG SCHOLARS.

Many might be inclined to deny the existence of any substantial agreements among critics. It is true that if one is centering attention on differences in minor detail, a bewildering array of contradictions might be marshaled. So too a non-Christian approaching the writings of Christian theologians and philosophers in a prejudiced and polemic mood, might easily discover so many differences that he would be tempted to say, "I cannot be a Christian, for there is no agreement among Christians as to what Christianity is." But there is a fundamental thread of unity binding together all Christians, despite differences. So too is there among scholars a remarkable consensus.

To the existence of such a consensus scholars themselves testify. In 1887 Briggs wrote, "I doubt whether there is any question of scholarship whatever in which there is greater agreement among scholars than in this question of the literary analysis of the Hexateuch." Bacon quotes Briggs with evident approval (Genesis of Genesis, pp. 24, 25). George Foote Moore, in 1892, wrote to Bacon (op. cit.), "There is no reason to think that the general results on which critics now agree will be overturned." In 1893 Addis reported (p. x) that he had worked out his analysis independently, and that when Kautzsch's work appeared in Germany the two were found in "constant agreement even in minute detail."

A. Lods, in the new French Bible, 1916, speaks of the critical results as "conclusions which have forced themselves on Hebraists of every school."

It is sometimes said that the present debate between the so-called "Wellhausen School" and the "History of Religion School" presupposes the rejection of the critical view of the Hexateuch. Such is not the case.

In 1910, Sellin, a leader of the conservative wing of the "History of Religion School," introduced his account of J with the statement, "Without going into a hair-splitting analysis, we present the sections of the Pentateuch which, with almost complete agreement, are assigned to J." Gressmann, another critic of the newer school, said in 1911, introducing his lectures in OT Theology: "We are in the main at one with Wellhausen in the criticism of the Pentateuch. The matter is in principle settled. There remain only the problems regarding the history of the material itself."

In 1912, Smend, in his important and suggestive study of the narrative portions of the Hexateuch, asserts that "the main outlines of Wellhausen's Hexateuchal criticism will in the future, as in the past, be shown to be valid; . . . his results have been almost unanimously accepted."

Even Eerdmans, the successor of Kuenen at Leyden, free lance among critics, destroyer and radical, admits that the consensus of scholars was so complete as to cause him to hesitate long before raising his protest; while Kittel has now become a convert to the Grafian view.

The consensus exists. It is not a matter of nationality, or theological prejudice, or "schools," or religion, or irreligion, but simply of the overwhelming and convincing weight of the evidence. It is a consensus that is not merely "in general" or "on the whole," but extends, with surprising agreement, into the detailed analysis of verses and half verses. *A priori* it seems inconceivable that such accurate division of sources could be made; or that any number of scholars would agree on the same analysis. A study of the present volume will show the unwarranted character of such assumptions.

It is obvious that the agreement would not be equally unanimous at every point. In general, the separation of J and E is not so certain as the separation of JE and P; the analysis in Ex. and Nu. is more complicated and difficult than

INTRODUCTION 13

in Gn. Even now it is not yet safe to separate J and E in detail all through Josh. But in spite of these difficulties, the agreements, even in hotly debated passages, greatly outweigh the differences.

4. How the Consensus Is Indicated in the Text.

In the following pages the text of each document (according to the American Standard Version: used by permission) is printed consecutively, and is divided into sections for convenience of reference.

In cases where "all scholars agree" as to the analysis, the text is printed without remark. In cases where there are any significant differences, footnotes usually mention the differences only, implying that "all" scholars not mentioned accept the analysis as printed. Occasionally in much debated passages the full list of authorities consulted is given. Reference to the bibliography will indicate what critics have been taken into account.

Redactional material (Rje, Rd, Rp, or merely R when the identification is not certain) is indicated by the use of smaller type. Less attention is paid to giving a complete account of differences with respect to this material.

5. A Brief Outline of the History of the Criticism of the Hexateuch.

Astruc, physician to Louis XIV, in 1753 discovered variations in the use of the names "Jehovah" and "Elohim," that led him to distinguish two main documents in the Pentateuch (the first, or Elohistic, our P and E; the second, or Jahvistic, our J); but he did not question the Mosaic authorship.

Ilgen 1798 was the first to separate P and E in the Elohistic source.

Vater 1802ff., abandoning the documentary theory in favor of a "fragmentary hypothesis," raised doubts regarding the Mosaic authorship.

De Wette 1806 established the date of the publication of Dt. as 621 on the basis of 2K. 22-23, and regarded the entire Pentateuch as a development. His view is still accepted.

Stähelin 1830 offered the "supplementary hypothesis," which made his "Elohist" (P), the oldest material, and viewed "J" and "E" as later supplementations thereto.

Hupfeld 1853 held that J, E, and P are independent sources, and that J in particular did not know P. This view is still held.

Graf 1866 showed that P was postexilic. This discovery was epoch-making.

Kuenen 1869 accepted Graf's ideas, and carried them further.

Wellhausen 1876 built still further on the same foundation, and created a systematic interpretation of Israelitic history and religion on the basis of the analysis of the Hexateuch into J, E, D, and P (following Knobel and Nöldeke in his analysis of P).

Since Wellhausen no essentially new contribution has been made. Wellhausen's historical and religious interpretations have been subjected to vigorous attack, but, with few exceptions, scholars agree that he was usually right in his analysis and in his dating of the documents.

6. PRESENT DEBATE AMONG CRITICS.

In the main there is agreement among critics on the subjects taken up in this volume.

There is, however, a certain amount of difference due to varying opinions on—

a. The exact nature and amount of the redactional material. Smend, for example, holds that Rje rewrote his sources less extensively than Wellhausen had thought.

b. The question as to whether J and E as restored by criticism are unified and consistent, or whether they are the work of several hands. Most critics lay stress on at least two strata in E, E^1 and E^2; but Smend holds to the unity of E and separates J into J^1 and J^2, a separation already recognized by most scholars in Gn. 1-11. But these stratifications within the documents are relatively unimportant in comparison with the larger problems, and little account is taken of them in the present volume.

c. Differences on the part of a few with reference to the dat-

INTRODUCTION 15

ing of the documents. Proksch and Sellin put J in the United Kingdom; Smend dates E 700-650. In some measure such differences will affect a critic's conception of the nature and scope of a document.

Over against these relatively nonessential differences there have been some scholars that have made a more fundamental attack on the critical position. Dillmann, while agreeing on the whole in analysis, long dissented with reference to P; he defended the preexilic date of P. But he finally came to doubt his position (so Smend). Still more negative was Klostermann's result; but his counter-analysis has found almost no approval among scholars, and we may leave it out of account in our present study.

Certain conservative theologians, fearing in the analysis an irreverent attack on inspiration, also oppose it (e. g., in the articles on the various books of the Hexateuch in The International Standard Bible Encyclopædia). Such polemic attacks do not lend themselves to fruitful correlation with the plan of this work.

Specific mention should be made of Wiener and Dahse, who hold that the analysis is impossible on account of the uncertainty of the MT (Hebrew text of the OT) as compared with the LXX (Greek translations). They insist that the LXX proves the use of the divine name to be no safe criterion for the separation of the sources (which critics would generally admit). But Wiener and Dahse have not published a systematic study of the analysis, so that their views are not accessible for the present purpose.

Eerdmans is the most important opponent of the critical position. Wiener has said, "The year 1908 saw the beginning of a new critical development which makes it very difficult to speak positively of modern critical views." Wiener apparently has little regard for the works of McNeile 1908, Sellin 1910, Skinner 1910, Steuernagel 1912, Smend 1912, Driver (new ed.) 1914, and Eichrodt 1916—all in substantial agreement on the critical analysis; but he had in mind the influence exerted by Eerdmans since 1908, when the first "Alttestamentliche Studien" appeared.

It is sometimes said that Eerdmans has overthrown the Wellhausen position. He agrees with the critical school in only one or two points. He recognizes that the Code of the Covenant (Ex. 20^{22}-23^{33}) is a separate and ancient collection of laws; he accepts De Wette's view of Dt. as introducing centralization of worship in 621; and he regards the Pentateuch as composite and mostly late. But he denies the unity of either J, E, or P in any sense; holds that many passages universally regarded as composite are really unified; denies the existence of stylistic and literary differences among the "documents"; and for his general conception returns to a sort of combination of Vater's Fragmentary Hypothesis and Stähelin's Supplementary Hypothesis.

According to Eerdmans, the word "Elohim" (God) is to be treated as a plural (esp. in Gn.), and is indicative of polytheism in Israel down to 621. He is in no sense a defender of the traditional view, except that the "E" Decalogue and CC may be Mosaic. He attacks everyone that has preceded him. No one is on the right track. In almost every direction previous thought must be abandoned and entirely new hypotheses created.

On the surface such a view has little to commend it. Nevertheless, Eerdmans repays careful study. He makes many brilliant and suggestive exegetical conjectures, and, after all, is not so utterly far from the established view as one might infer. In many passages he agrees with the critical analysis both as to the fact of composition and as to grouping of verses. For example, in Genesis, he separates all of the "P" material from "JE" except 14 verses and 6 half verses (cf. Eichrodt). This is a remarkable tribute to the correctness of the critical results. In the latter part of Gn. and the first of Ex. he finds a "Jacob recension" which is polytheistic (dated 933-700), and an "Israel recension," which has pre-Deuteronomic, post-Deuteronomic and postexilic elements. These recensions do not correspond to J, E, or P, but the subdivisions of each often follow the lines of cleavage agreed on by criticism.

"P" he subdivides into "learned," postexilic glosses (here agreeing with the critical dating in many cases) and valuable

INTRODUCTION 17

preexilic tradition (which many, if not most, critics are disposed to recognize in P).

Eerdmans is a great scholar, and at many points his views are taken into account. But the frequent expression "all scholars agree" in this volume *always makes a tacit exception of Eerdmans, unless he is specifically mentioned.*

Note on the Spelling of the Divine Name "Jehovah."

The name of God in Hebrew consists of four consonants, JHVH or YHWH. This "tetragrammaton" was viewed by the Jews as too holy to pronounce, and instead they said "The Lord" (hence the usage of the King James Version). This led them to spell JHVH with the vowels belonging to the word "Lord" (in Hebrew Adonai); thus arose the traditional vocalization, Jehovah.

Scholars are agreed that the name never was pronounced thus in Hebrew, and an attempt is generally made to spell it more nearly in accordance with ancient Hebrew practice. Many English and American scholars prefer Yahweh; others, Jahweh; Peters uses Yahaweh; many others, including most Germans, write Jahwe or Jahve. This last form, Jahve, is probably to be preferred. J should be retained because there is not sufficient original distinction between J and Y to warrant a change from the traditional initial consonant of Jehovah; the final h should be dropped because it is silent, and has no true consonantal function.

Nevertheless, in order to avoid inconsistency with the American Standard Version, the form "Jehovah" will be retained in this book; except that in the derivatives, the forms "Jahvist" and "Jahvistic" will be used, to avoid confusion with Wellhausen's "Jehovist," who is Rje, not J.

CHAPTER I

J: THE JAHVISTIC OR JUDÆAN NARRATIVE

1. LITERARY CHARACTERISTICS.
   a. Is J a Literary Unity?

There is substantial agreement with reference to the chief contents of J. But there is difference among scholars as to whether the J literature was all written by one man at one time, or whether it was written by different men animated, on the whole, by similar ideals, and using closely related forms of expression.

It is obvious that J as it stands in the following text is not a smooth, perfectly connected, unified narrative. This fact is in a large measure accounted for by the various processes of editing ("redaction") through which the document has passed. Most critics agree that J experienced certain changes before it was united with E; and, in particular, Rje, while preserving a remarkably large proportion of the material of J and E as they lay before him, naturally made harmonistic changes in each (some of which we can no longer detect) and omitted portions now of J, and now of E, where the two documents ran parallel, or where their material did not suit his purpose. Hence we should not expect to find a perfect unity in the J that criticism has restored. We have now only a fragmentary, incomplete J (though remarkably connected and unified!); the problem is: Does this J presuppose that it came from one original book, written by one man, or does it represent the work of several hands?

All are agreed that J did not compose his narrative out of his imagination. He certainly drew on ancient oral tradition (as Gunkel in particular has emphasized); and probably also used certain literary sources.

All are also agreed that there are many more or less important variations and inconsistencies within J (cf. Gn. 4^{26} with $4^{3.13}$).

Some insist that these variations are wholly due to the fact that the author was drawing on different traditions. These critics are so impressed by the unity of J that they believe it easier to account for one man's using varying traditions (sagas) than for a school's writing with such remarkable unanimity of spirit and literary style. Kittel has been the great advocate of the unity of J, whom he regards as "a personality of the first rank, a man of decided moral and religious uniqueness." So also Sellin, who says that J as a whole is the work of "a quite definitely stamped literary and absolutely artistic personality." B. Luther shares this opinion. Smend approximates closely to it, for his J^2 is the great literary personality that dominates the present form of the J material. Eichrodt also agrees; he says, "We must (in order to give greater consistency to the source theory) bring out more clearly the picture of the authors standing behind the various books, and thus reveal each source as the purposive work of a literary personality."

But the majority of critics lay more stress on the complexity of J and its apparent contradictions. Especially in Gn. 2-11 do most scholars (since Kuenen and Budde) trace a J^2 distinguished from J^1. This leads Budde to call J and E "comprehensive, contemporaneous, literary schools." Gunkel believes that in so far as any one man gave the document its present form, he has been guided by the tradition more than he has shaped it independently. J for Gunkel is a collection of cognate traditions, not a free composition stamped in every part with the author's own spirit and ideas. Cornill says that the unity of J must be unconditionally denied; and Steuernagel declares that J consists of a large number of relatively independent sections. A. Lods speaks of a school, not an author (SB.).

However, the acceptance of the second view does not exclude the possibility of some one personality as the dominating spirit in the school, either at its outset (so Wellhausen) or at its climax (Smend).

Summarizing the situation with reference to the problem of unity, we may say that J is not a completely smooth and consecutive narrative, written at one time, but it is (with certain qualifications) a unity in main type of thought, expression, religious mood, social and ethical outlook and historical background; so that the J literature as a whole plainly belongs together, as contrasted with the E, D, and P types.

b. The Extent of J.

All are agreed that J material may be found in Gn., Ex., Nu., and Josh. There is no J in Lv. and probably none in Dt. Some of the J in Josh. is found, with other related material, in Jg. 1^1-2^5, which is also assigned to J.

Critics disagree as to whether J originally closed with this account of the conquest of Canaan, or whether it continued down to the founding of the kingdom, or even beyond that event. There is ancient material in Jg., S., and K. that has marked affinity with J, and is attributed to that source by Budde (to times of David), Bacon, Cornill, Sellin (J ending with 1 K. 2^{46}) et al. Most critics treat Jg. 2^5 as the last trace of J. Steuernagel and Kittel, for example, note the close relation between the older narratives in Jg. and J, but decline to identify the two.

c. The Literary Style of J.

In spite of the fact that the form of the traditions which J incorporates had in many instances been fixed long before his time (1200, Gunkel) by oral or written tradition (so also Steuernagel, E. Meyer, Smend), J has a remarkable and characteristic literary style. The agreement among critics is unanimous (always excepting the school of Eerdmans). "J is," says Kittel, "an artist in form and language such as few before or after him." All describe his style as picturesque, vivid, concrete (often specifying the time of day, Bacon) living, naïve, natural, robust; as a story-teller he is unsurpassed.

A few especially happy accounts of J's style may be noted. Driver says that he "excels in the power of delineating life and character. His touch is singularly light: with a few strokes he paints a scene which, before he has finished, is impressed indelibly upon his reader's memory. . . . His dialogues especially (which are frequent) are remarkable for the delicacy and truthfulness with which character and emotions find expression in them."

Proksch finds something "sunny" in J's work, and charm and beauty in his characters in spite of the survival of primitive traits. Smend, thinking particularly of his J^2, calls him "a poet who composes on a grand and connected scale; a fascinating narrator and an eloquent orator," combining the highest national enthusiasm with human feeling and spiritual outlook.

d. J's Peculiarities in the Use of Proper Names.

Turning to more specific traits of J, we find all critics agreeing that his usage with reference to proper names is marked by certain peculiarities.

Outstanding is the name "Jehovah" (Jahve). Through his entire narrative, beginning with Gn. 2^4, J uses, almost exclusively, the divine name "Jehovah," that E mentions first in Ex. 3, and P first in Ex. 6 (except that editors have introduced it in a few earlier passages). J does not, however, confine himself to this name; he says "God" (Elohim) "(1) When God is spoken of by those not in covenant with Jehovah, as by Adam and Eve before the time of Seth . . . , and by the Serpent. . . . (2) When emphasis is laid on God's abstract nature, especially in contrast to man, Gn. 16^{13}32^{30}. (3) In the construct state,* when, with a following word, it is used descriptively of God, as 'God of Abraham,' 'of heaven and earth,' etc." (Woods in HDB).

It follows that the use of the divine names is by no means an infallible, or the chief, criterion for separation of the sources. Steuernagel says that there is no compulsion for a Jahvistic writer always to use the name "Jehovah." Eichrodt rightly calls dependence on this criterion the "baby-shoes" of criticism, that need to be taken off.

Other proper names used by J in contrast to E are: Israel (as a later name of Jacob), Canaanite (for E's Amorite), Sinai (vs. Horeb E), and Hobab son of Reuel (as father-in-law of Moses). The absence of Aaron from J in its original form is asserted by Wellhausen, Cornill, Holzinger, Stade, Gressmann, White, Addis, Cook, Kent, et al., vs. Kittel only, who finds Aaron original in J.

---

* A noun followed by another noun in the "possessive" is said to be in the construct state.

JAHVISTIC OR JUDÆAN NARRATIVE

e. Other Characteristic Words and Expressions.

There are numerous words and expressions that are used either by J only or by him much more frequently than by other writers. Examples are: break forth, call on the name of, find favor in the eyes of, land flowing with milk and honey, three days' journey.

Many of the most striking stylistic peculiarities are apparent only to the reader of Hebrew. J employs characteristic Hebrew words for: before, beget, entreat, from the time that, ground, harden (of Pharaoh's heart), hasten, know, language, Lord (Adonai), maid, man and wife, oath, parts, this time, until.

Lists of such expressions may be found in Bacon, Driver, Carpenter and Harford, McNeile, Sellin, Woods, and in most introductions.

2. CHARACTERISTIC IDEAS.

a. Aim of J.

The aim of J is recognized to have been wholly ethical and religious: to elevate and purify the ideals of the nation.

Although a skillful story-teller, "he does not aim to entertain, but, rather, to solve problems" (Kittel)—such as sin, evil, pain, labor, sickness, death, language, the antithesis of agriculturalist and nomad.

B. Luther draws an instructive parallel between the aims and characteristics of J and of the great literary prophets that followed him (from Amos on). J was a spectator of history; the prophets intervened in the life of their times. J was an optimist; the prophets inclined to pessimism regarding the nation. J's art was idealistic, portraying things and persons as they ought to be; the art of the prophets was realistic, portraying things and persons as they are.

b. Characteristic Religious Ideas.

The outstanding characteristic of J's religious thought is his anthropomorphic and anthropopathic conception of Jehovah. The Jehovah of the creation story walks in the garden in the cool of the day, and is very human. He comes down from heaven to observe the tower of Babel. He shuts Noah into the ark. He (or his angel) visits earth in visible form Gn. 18-19.

He meets Moses and seeks to slay him Ex. 4^{24}. He descends to Mount Sinai and is seen by Moses Ex. $24^{9-11}33^{17-23}$. He is grieved, repents, covenants, makes oaths, is angry, and has many of the other traits of man's consciousness, as well as his form (so Driver, Carpenter, and Harford, et al.).

There are certain attempts on the part of J to modify or weaken this anthropomorphism (so Steuernagel). God appears as a flame of fire, Gn. 15^{17} Ex. 3^2; in a dream—somewhat more spiritual than an actual theophany, Gn. 26^{24} 28^{13ff}; through the mediation of angels—emphasizing the transcendence of Jehovah Gn. $16^{7ff}\cdot19^{1ff}\cdot24^7$ Ex. 3^2. But such passages are relatively rare.

The predominance of the anthropomorphic is now very generally attributed either to the ancient sagas used by J (so Kittel), or to the earliest writer in the J school (so all who distinguish a J^1 and J^2). For, with all his anthropomorphism, J has many signs of an exalted and transcendent conception of Deity. Jehovah dwells in heaven, and usually rules from above; he is Lord of all the world, almighty, seeing into the hearts of men (Kittel). He is holy, unapproachable, perhaps even more majestic than in E (Eichrodt).

J's standpoint is very nearly monotheistic. He does not, indeed, deny that other gods than Jehovah exist; but "He tolerates no god beside himself in Israel" (cf. Nu. $25^{1...5}$). J prepares the way for the "moral monotheism" of Amos (Smend). This monotheistic (more correctly henotheistic) tendency is revealed especially in the story of the plagues. Such monotheism is a naïve mood, not a theory (Kittel).

J's spiritual faith is revealed further in the fact that he bases his religion to a surprisingly small degree on divine interventions or miracles. In fact, B. Luther says flatly that J "rejects miracles and substitutes for them natural events" (contrast J's with E's account of the crossing of the Red Sea or the plagues). In harmony with this conception (not unrelated to the modern philosophy of the divine immanence, which sees God in every natural event), J holds to an "unbroken continuity of revelation of Jehovah, from Gn. 4^{26} on" (Carpenter and Harford).

There is a question whether J looked forward to a future

JAHVISTIC OR JUDÆAN NARRATIVE

Messiah or to an eschatological Messianic future. Most scholars, especially those of the "Wellhausen School," believe that J knew nothing of this hope. Three passages have a possible bearing, Gn. $3^{15} 49^{10}$ Nu. 24^{17}. Gn. 3^{15} has been viewed traditionally as a Messianic prophecy, and has been called the *Protevangelium*, the first Gospel. But modern scholars agree in denying such exegesis; the verse speaks only of enmity between serpents and men—an allegory of the moral struggle of humanity. Perhaps there is a hint at the final victory of good (Dillmann, Driver, Kautzsch), but this is not clearly implied (Mitchell, Skinner, et al.). Gn. 49^{10} is regarded as Messianic by all except Skinner, who refers it to David and his dynasty. Many view it as an interpolation—Wellhausen, Stade, Dillmann, Holzinger, Driver, Kautzsch, Cornill(10b), Mitchell et al.—because it interrupts 9 and 11, because it would be the only case of a personal Messiah before the eighth century, and because Ez. 21^{27} seems to be the original from which v. 10 is taken. But many others hold with Skinner and Steuernagel that the interruption of vv. 9 and 11 is not evident (Cornill retains 10a); and that the other two arguments are inconclusive. Hence v. 10 (taken in connection with 11 and 12) is regarded as Messianic by Gunkel, Gressmann, Sellin, et al. Nu. 24^{17} is generally treated as a *vaticinium ex eventu* referring to David. Holzinger holds that it originally referred to David, but in its present form, to the Messiah. Sellin reverses the order and makes it originally Messianic, but Davidic in its present form. Gn. 49^{10} is then the only surely Messianic passage in J, and it may be an interpolation.

J's attitude toward the cultus is noteworthy. He reverences the ancient shrines at Hebron, Beersheba, Bethel, Shechem, Peniel, etc. He keeps the three annual feasts (Ex. 34). He recognizes the function of sacrifice (Abel, Noah, Ex. 34). But "his altars are more for prayer than for sacrifice" (Kittel, B. Luther). Like the great prophets, he is more interested in righteousness than in ritual. He "never mentions massebahs, asherahs, or images of any kind" (Luther). In contrast to P, he derives sacrifice and the distinction of clean and unclean not from God's command to Moses, but from the practice of antiquity.

In general, the religious atmosphere of J is recognized as prophetic or "pre-prophetic" (prior to the literary prophets, from Amos 760-750 on). Driver's statement that "the prophetic element is conspicuously prominent," and Steuernagel's that "the prophetic movement finds no traceable echo here," mean that J represents the prophetic movement at a time before its literary exponents had arisen. To find its author or authors among the priests (Bacon, Smend) does not commend itself to the majority of critics.

c. Characteristic Ethical Ideas.

On the whole, J makes religion ethical (Kittel), but the patriarchs do not live on a high moral plane; they deceive and have very primitive ideas about the family and sex relations in general.

Carpenter and Harford emphasize J's friendliness to non-Hebrews. Esau's (i. e., Edom's) magnanimity is described; Joseph takes an Egyptian wife; Jehovah is worshiped in other nations, as by Nimrod, Laban, Balaam, etc.

d. Attitude toward Culture.

Budde, B. Luther, and Kittel find in J an adherent of the nomadic ideal represented by the Nazirites and the Rechabites, and so an opponent of culture. But most scholars agree with Carpenter and Harford in the view that J is especially interested in civilization and its history. He narrates "the development of the arts, cattle-breeding and agriculture, music, metal-working, husbandry, and culture of the vine"; and he gives a classification of all nations and an account of the origin of language.

e. Attitude toward History.

J conceives human history as working out the divine purposes. His historical outlook is also colored by a strong national consciousness, "a broad and comprehensive patriotism" (Bacon). He treats of all the tribes. He thinks of Israel as related to the other great nations of the world.

J represents the work of Moses as very important, and yet not something entirely novel (in contrast to E and especially to P). For J, the religion of Moses was organically connected with the religion of the patriarchs.

JAHVISTIC OR JUDÆAN NARRATIVE

As far as we may judge from the fragments that remain, J pictures the conquest of Canaan as a slow, painful process, only gradually accomplished by more or less isolated bands of Hebrews, under no centralized leadership (in contrast to E and P, where Joshua is a completely victorious general).

3. HOME OF AUTHOR.

A very few have held that J originated in the northern kingdom, e. g., Schrader, Reuss, Kuenen, and, more recently, B. Luther. But it is one of the assured results of criticism that J was written in the southern kingdom (Judah); so think Wellhausen, Dillmann, Cornill, Budde, Kittel, E. Meyer, Stade, Holzinger, Steuernagel, Baudissin, Gunkel, Proksch, Sellin, Smend, Eichrodt, Driver, Carpenter and Harford, Bacon, George Foote Moore, Mitchell, and countless others. Kautzsch suspects that the first form of J may have been written in Israel, but he admits that in its present form it must come from Judah.

The reasons for this agreement are evident. J is interested in the sacred places of the south, especially Hebron. The tribe of Judah receives special attention as in Gn. 38, 49, and Jg. 1. Judah (not Reuben E) takes the lead in the Joseph story. Nu. 24^{17-18} refers to the reign of David, according to most critics (Smend). Joshua, the Ephraimitic hero, is very inconspicuous in J (Cornill). Steuernagel asserts that all of the specifically Judahite material in the Pentateuch is to be found in J.

J was not a narrow partisan of the southern kingdom. He mentions with friendliness and reverence persons and places connected with North Israel. This is due to the fact that he was drawing on a tradition older than the division of the kingdom. But the characteristic interest and distinguishing features of J all point to the southern kingdom as his home.

4. THE DATE OF J—850.

Professor Eiselen's excellent work, The Books of the Pentateuch, pp. 63-120, gives a thorough and dispassionate examination of the traditional view that Moses wrote the Pentateuch. Critics have for a long time ceased to hold the Mosaic authorship, and seek to discover clues to the dating of J (and the other documents) by examining the material in order to find a *terminus ad quem* later than which the document in question could not have been written, and a *terminus a quo* earlier than which it could not have been written.

a. Evidence for the *Terminus ad quem* of the Composition of J.

i. All critics agree that J was written before Dt. The date of Dt. (published 621, composed 650) is an assured result of criticism, accepted even by Eerdmans. J and E both precede Dt.; in theological ideas, ritual, conception of the priesthood, place of worship, etc., they show no trace of the ideas of Dt.; whereas all extensive post-Deuteronomic writings do show such traces in abundance. This yields 650 as *terminus ad quem*.

ii. Most critics agree that J is older than the earliest literary prophets, Amos and Hosea. On the one hand, J does not reach the ethical and religious heights of these prophets, but seems to represent a less advanced stage, where the burning prophetic sense of social injustice and individual sin is just dawning. On the other hand, the historical allusions in Amos 2^9 and Hosea $12^{3-4, 12-13}$ and other passages are all to events mentioned in J and E (Kittel, Carpenter and Harford, et al.). They knew J and E; J and E did not know them. This yields 760-750 (Amos) as a more accurate *terminus ad quem*.

iii. The overwhelming majority of critics agree that J is older than E. Dillmann defended for a long time with great tenacity the priority of E; but his view was largely based on his analysis which included in J numerous passages now generally ascribed to later writers (Dr.). The relatively higher antiquity of J is accepted by scholars of widely varying theological opinions, and diverse nationality. Among those that hold this view are Wellhausen, Kuenen, H. Schultz, Bacon, E. Meyer, Stade, Wildeboer, Kautzsch, Gunkel, Budde, Cornill, Sellin, Driver, McNeile, Mitchell, George Foote Moore, Smend, and Eichrodt.

Reasons for this consensus are abundant. The style and ideas of J are more primitive than those of E. The reader may convince himself of this fact by a comparison of the introductions to each document with each other and with the documents themselves. Hence we have as *terminus ad quem* for J 750 (the date of E).

iv. Smend uses another fact to fix the *terminus ad quem* at about 750. J mentions the Assyrians (cf. Gn. 10), but shows no trace of conflict with them. The Assyrians appeared on the Israelitic horizon as a foe in 854, at the battle of Karkar. Jehu paid tribute to them, 842. They became involved in the affairs of the southern kingdom at the time of the Syro-Ephraimitic war (735-734). This confirms the other results.

v. There is no clear reference to the division of the kingdom (for Gn. 49^{26b} need not read "separation," but may refer to the Nazirite vow). Hence Sellin and Proksch would make the rebellion of Jeroboam I the *terminus ad quem* (937 or 933). But most critics hold that such use of the *argumentum e silentio* is not legitimate. Steuernagel, for example, would account for this silence on the ground that the sagas on which J and E are founded doubtless took shape in the period of the united kingdom. Further, we may add that J was dominated by the idea of the spiritual unity of the nation, and might therefore purposely refrain from alluding to its political division.

b. Evidence for the *Terminus a quo* of the Composition of J.

We have seen that J was written not later than 750. How much earlier than this could it have been composed? Critics agree on certain general considerations.

i. References to the complete conquest and enslavement of the Canaanites presuppose the [time of Solomon. Such expressions as "the Canaanite was then in the land" Gn. 12^{6}13^7 Jg. 1$^{21.28}$, imply that at the time of the writer the Canaanite was no longer a factor. Gn. 9$^{25-27}$ must have been written at a time when Canaan was already enslaved; an event which occurred in the reign of Solomon 1K. 9$^{20-21}$. Cornill views this as furnishing an absolutely certain *terminus a quo* (so also, Kautzsch, Carpenter and Harford, A. Lods, et al.).

ii. References to the kingdom presuppose at least the times of David or Solomon. Sellin calls attention to Gn. 36^{31}49$^{8-12}$ Nu. 24$^{18-19}$.

iii. Gn. 49 is unanimously regarded as an ancient poem incorporated by J into his work. While it is very difficult to date this poem exactly, all agree that in its present form it contains allusions to the united kingdom; and many hold that it presupposes the time of Ahab (d. 854); see J19 below.

iv. The nations mentioned in Gn. 10 (Proksch) and the boundaries of Israel Gn. 15^{18} correspond to the national and international situation during the reign of Solomon.

v. The use of the divine name "Jehovah" points to a period after the time of David. Gray, König, Carpenter and Harford find that proper names compounded with "Jah" or "Jahve" do not occur among the patriarchs, are exceedingly rare in the Mosaic age, and emerge freely only in the time of David. This evidence would suggest the time of David as a *terminus a quo* for a document that uses the name "Jehovah" almost uniformly.

vi. Gn. 27^{40a} presupposes that the conquest of Edom by David is past.

c. The Closer Determination of the Date of J.

If Gn. 27^{40b} were original, we should probably have a reference to the revolt of Edom from Joram of Judah, 840, but the passage is probably a later gloss.

i. All recognize, with Driver, that the language of J "belongs to the golden period of Hebrew literature and resembles the best parts of Jg. and Sm," betraying no trace of an archaic flavor.

ii. All agree that J was written in a time of national peace and prosperity. This leaves open the reigns of Solomon and Jehoshaphat. The former is preferred by Schultz, Sellin, and Proksch. The latter, the reign of Jehoshaphat, is accepted by the vast majority of scholars. So, with little variation from the year 850, Wellhausen, Kuenen, Stade, Riehm, Kittel, B. Luther, McNeile, Cornill, Kautzsch, Gunkel, George Foote Moore, Mitchell, Steuernagel, Staerk, Smend(J^1), and "the overwhelming majority of scholars" (Eichrodt).

The chief reason for the all but unanimous verdict lies in the relation of the religious and moral ideas of J to the development pictured in the books of Samuel and Kings. J is believed to have more affinity with Elijah (so Kittel, B. Luther

JAHVISTIC OR JUDÆAN NARRATIVE

et al.) than with the type of morals and religion that existed in the reign of Solomon. Some scholars detect in 2 Ch. 17^9 an allusion to the existence of J in the times of Jehoshaphat.

By way of conclusion we may quote Sellin's estimate of J: "From all this material a work with a quite definite theme was created, a work of breadth of view and religious inwardness and depth, a work transfused with the Spirit of the living God that saves, punishes sin, but is gracious and merciful to all. No nation of antiquity has anything equal to it. In this writing, which despite its apparently quite particularistic tendency is transfused with the assurance of a unity in the human race and the dream of a kingdom of God on this earth full of wonder, a writing which comes from the first youthful period of Israel, a spring bubbles up from which humanity will always be able to draw the strength of youth for its religious life."

THE TEXT OF J

1. THE CREATION OF MAN. P1.
Gn. 2⁴ᵇ⁻⁷

4b. In the day that Jehovah God made earth and heaven, 5 and no plant of the field was yet in the earth, and no herb of the field had yet sprung up; for Jehovah God had not caused it to rain upon the earth: and there was not a man to till the ground; 6 but there went up a mist from the earth, and watered the whole face of the ground. 7 And Jehovah God formed man of the dust of the ground, and breathed into his nostrils the breath of life; and man became a living soul.

2. THE GARDEN OF EDEN.
Gn. 2⁸⁻¹⁷

8 And Jehovah God planted a garden eastward, in Eden; and there he put the man whom he had formed. 9 And out of the ground made Jehovah God to grow every tree that is pleasant to the sight, and good for food; the tree of life also in the midst of the garden, and the tree of the knowledge of good and evil.

10 And a river went out of Eden to water the garden; and from thence it was parted, and became four heads. 11 The name of the first is Pishon: that is it which compasseth the whole land of Havilah, where there is gold; 12 and the gold of that land is good: there is bdellium and the onyx stone. 13 And the name of the second river is Gihon: the same is it that compasseth the whole land of Cush. 14 And the name of the third river is Hiddekel: that is it which goeth in front of Assyria. And the fourth river is the Euphrates.

15 And Jehovah God took the man, and put him into the garden of Eden to dress it and to keep it. 16 And Jehovah God commanded the man, saying, Of every tree of the garden thou mayest freely eat: 17 but of the tree of the knowledge of good and evil, thou shalt not eat of it: for in the day that thou eatest thereof thou shalt surely die.

3. THE CREATION OF WOMAN.
Gn. 2¹⁸⁻²⁵

18 And Jehovah God said, It is not good that the man should

[The numbered footnotes refer to the corresponding division of J (E or P) and not to anything in the text.]
¹ The word "God" after "Jehovah" is not original in J; so most critics except Eerd. and Eichr.
² Gloss in 2⁹: Bu., Co., Ka.? (and many), Sk., Kent., Smend, SB.; St., Ba., Ka.? view entire verse as J². 2¹⁰⁻¹⁴ R: most critics since Ewald (Sk.), esp., Ka., Gu., GFM., Kent, Sk., Co., St., Smend. J³: SB.

be alone; I will make a help meet for him. 19 And out of the ground Jehovah God formed every beast of the field, and every bird of the heavens; and brought them unto the man to see what he would call them: and whatsoever the man called every living creature, that was the name thereof. 20 And the man gave names to all cattle, and to the birds of the heavens, and to every beast of the field; but for man there was not found a help meet for him. 21 And Jehovah God caused a deep sleep to fall upon the man, and he slept; and he took one of his ribs, and closed up the flesh instead thereof: 22 and the rib which Jehovah God had taken from the man, made he a woman, and brought her unto the man. 23 And the man said, This is now bone of my bones, and flesh of my flesh: she shall be called Woman, because she was taken out of Man. 24 Therefore shall a man leave his father and his mother, and shall cleave unto his wife: and they shall be one flesh. 25 And they were both naked, the man and his wife, and were not ashamed.

4. THE FALL.
Gn. 3^{1-24}

3^1 Now the serpent was more subtle than any beast of the field which Jehovah God had made. And he said unto the woman, Yea, hath God said, Ye shall not eat of any tree of the garden? 2 And the woman said unto the serpent, Of the fruit of the trees of the garden we may eat: 3 but of the fruit of the tree which is in the midst of the garden, God hath said, Ye shall not eat of it, neither shall ye touch it, lest ye die. 4 And the serpent said unto the woman, Ye shall not surely die: 5 for God doth know that in the day ye eat thereof, then your eyes shall be opened, and ye shall be as God, knowing good and evil. 6 And when the woman saw that the tree was good for food, and that it was a delight to the eyes, and that the tree was to be desired to make one wise, she took of the fruit thereof, and did eat; and she gave also unto her husband with her, and he did eat. 7 And the eyes of them both were opened, and they knew that they were naked; and they sewed fig-leaves together, and made themselves aprons. 8 And they heard the voice of Jehovah God walking in the garden in the cool of the day: and the man and his wife hid themselves from the presence of Jehovah God amongst the trees of the garden.

9 And Jehovah God called unto the man, and said unto him, Where art thou? 10 And he said, I heard thy voice in the garden, and I was afraid, because I was naked; and I hid my-

---

[4] Many view 3^{20} as late: so Co., Gu., Mi., St. $3^{22.24}$ are regarded as J^2 by Bu., Ba., Ka.?, Gu., Mi., Kent, St., Sk., Co., et al.

self. 11 And he said, Who told thee that thou wast naked? Hast thou eaten of the tree, whereof I commanded thee that thou shouldest not eat? 12 And the man said, The woman whom thou gavest to be with me, she gave me of the tree, and I did eat. 13 And Jehovah God said unto the woman, What is this thou hast done? And the woman said, The serpent beguiled me, and I did eat.

14 And Jehovah God said unto the serpent, Because thou hast done this, cursed art thou above all cattle, and above every beast of the field; upon thy belly shalt thou go, and dust shalt thou eat all the days of thy life: 15 and I will put enmity between thee and the woman, and between thy seed and her seed: he shall bruise thy head, and thou shalt bruise his heel. 16 Unto the woman he said, I will greatly multiply thy pain and thy conception; in pain thou shalt bring forth children; and thy desire shall be to thy husband, and he shall rule over thee. 17 And unto Adam he said, Because thou hast hearkened unto the voice of thy wife, and hast eaten of the tree, of which I commanded thee, saying, Thou shalt not eat of it: cursed is the ground for thy sake; in toil shalt thou eat of it all the days of thy life; 18 thorns also and thistles shall it bring forth to thee; and thou shalt eat the herb of the field; 19 in the sweat of thy face shalt thou eat bread, till thou return unto the ground; for out of it wast thou taken: for dust thou art, and unto dust shalt thou return.

20 And the man called his wife's name Eve; because she was the mother of all living. 21 And Jehovah God made for Adam and for his wife coats of skins, and clothed them.

22 And Jehovah God said, Behold, the man is become as one of us, to know good and evil; and now, lest he put forth his hand, and take also of the tree of life, and eat, and live forever—23 therefore Jehovah God sent him forth from the garden of Eden, to till the ground from whence he was taken. 24 So he drove out the man; and he placed at the east of the garden of Eden the Cherubim, and the flame of a sword which turned every way, to keep the way of the tree of life.

5. CAIN AND HIS DESCENDANTS. P2.

Gn. 4¹⁻²⁴

4¹ And the man knew Eve his wife; and she conceived, and bare Cain, and said, I have gotten a man with *the help of* Jehovah.

2 And again she bare his brother Abel. And Abel was a keeper of sheep, but Cain was a tiller of the ground. 3 And in process of time it

---

§ 4²⁻¹⁶ J²: so all critics who recognize a J², as We., Bu., Ba., Ka., CH., GFM., Mi., Gu., Co., Kent, Sk., St., Smend, and Di. J³: SB.—"Cain" is identified with the Kenites by most critics (so Ka., Smend); cf. J 35, 45 (R) Nu. 24²², J 58, Jg. 4¹¹, 1S. 27¹⁰ 30²⁹.

came to pass, that Cain brought of the fruit of the ground an offering unto Jehovah. 4 And Abel, he also brought of the firstlings of his flock and of the fat thereof. And Jehovah had respect unto Abel and to his offering: 5 but unto Cain and to his offering he had not respect. And Cain was very wroth, and his countenance fell. 6 And Jehovah said unto Cain, Why art thou wroth? and why is thy countenance fallen? 7 If thou doest well, shall it not be lifted up? and if thou doest not well, sin coucheth at the door; and unto thee shall be its desire; but do thou rule over it. 8 And Cain told Abel his brother. And it came to pass, when they were in the field, that Cain rose up against Abel his brother, and slew him.

9 And Jehovah said unto Cain, Where is Abel thy brother? And he said, I know not: am I my brother's keeper? 10 And he said, What hast thou done? the voice of thy brother's blood crieth unto me from the ground. 11 And now cursed art thou from the ground, which hath opened its mouth to receive thy brother's blood from thy hand; 12 when thou tillest the ground, it shall not henceforth yield unto thee its strength; a fugitive and a wanderer shalt thou be in the earth. 13 And Cain said unto Jehovah, My punishment is greater than I can bear. 14 Behold, thou hast driven me out this day from the face of the ground; and from thy face shall I be hid; and I shall be a fugitive and a wanderer in the earth; and it will come to pass, that whosoever findeth me will slay me. 15 And Jehovah said unto him, Therefore whosoever slayeth Cain, vengeance shall be taken on him sevenfold. And Jehovah appointed a sign for Cain, lest any finding him should smite him. 16 And Cain went out from the presence of Jehovah, and dwelt in the land of Nod, on the east of Eden.

17 And Cain knew his wife; and she conceived, and bare Enoch: and he builded a city, and called the name of the city, after the name of his son, Enoch. 18 And unto Enoch was born Irad: and Irad begat Mehujael; and Mehujael begat Methushael; and Methushael begat Lamech.

19 And Lamech took unto him two wives: the name of the one was Adah, and the name of the other Zillah. 20 And Adah bare Jabal: he was the father of such as dwell in tents and *have* cattle. 21 And his brother's name was Jubal: he was the father of all such as handle the harp and pipe. 22 And Zillah, she also bare Tubal-cain, the forger of every cutting instrument of brass and iron: and the sister of Tubal-cain was Naamah. 23 And Lamech said unto his wives:
    Adah and Zillah, hear my voice;
    Ye wives of Lamech, hearken unto my speech:
    For I have slain a man for wounding me,
    And a young man for bruising me:
24 If Cain shall be avenged sevenfold,
    Truly Lamech seventy and seven fold.

6. SETH AND ENOSH. E11iii. P2, 17.
Gn. 4²⁵⁻²⁶ (J²)

25 And Adam knew his wife again; and she bare a son, and called his name Seth: For, *said she*, God hath appointed me another seed instead of Abel; for Cain slew him. 26 And to Seth, to him also there was born a son; and he called his name Enosh. Then began men to call upon the name of Jehovah.

7. THE NAMING OF NOAH. P 3i.
Gn. 5²⁹

29 And he called his name Noah, saying, This same shall comfort us in our work and in the toil of our hands, *which cometh* because of the ground which Jehovah hath cursed.

8. "SONS OF GOD AND DAUGHTERS OF MEN."
Gn. 6¹⁻⁴

6¹ And it came to pass, when men began to multiply on the face of the ground, and daughters were born unto them, 2 that the sons of God saw the daughters of men that they were fair; and they took them wives of all that they chose. 3 And Jehovah said, My Spirit shall not strive with man forever, for that he also is flesh: yet shall his days be a hundred and twenty years. 4 The Nephilim were in the earth in those days, and also after that, when the sons of God came in unto the daughters of men, and they bare children to them: the same were the mighty men that were of old, the men of renown.

9. THE STORY OF THE DELUGE. P 3ii, iii, iv.
Gn. 6⁵⁻⁸ 7¹⁻⁵.⁷⁻¹⁰.¹²·¹⁶ᵇ·¹⁷ᵇ·²²⁻²³ 8²ᵇ⁻³ᵃ·⁶⁻¹²·¹³ᵇ·²⁰⁻²² (all J²)

5 And Jehovah saw that the wickedness of man was great in the earth, and that every imagination of the thoughts of his heart was only evil continually. 6 And it repented Jehovah that he had made man on the earth, and it grieved him at his heart. 7 And Jehovah said, I will destroy man whom I have created from the face of the ground; both man, and beast, and creeping things, and birds of the heavens; for it repenteth me that I have made them. 8 But Noah found favor in the eyes of Jehovah.

7¹ And Jehovah said unto Noah, Come thou and all thy house into the ark; for thee have I seen righteous before me in this generation. 2 Of every clean beast thou shalt take to thee seven and seven, the male and his female; and of the beasts that are not clean two, the male and his female: 3 of the birds also of the heavens, seven and seven, male and female, to keep

---

⁷ There is evidently an omission in J before 5²⁹. Eerd. alone views this v. as R.
⁸ This passage is evidently one of the oldest in J, going back to a mythological and polytheistic origin. In 6³ for "strive in," read "rule in," as Am. Rev., margin; or "remain in," SB.
⁹ There is some confusion in the text. Bu., followed by many, suggests as the original order 7¹⁰·⁷·¹⁶ᵇ·¹²·¹⁷ᵇ·²²·²³. In 7⁹, Sam., Targ. Onk., Vulg. read "Jehovah" instead of "God."

...8^{22}]   J 6–9   37

seed alive upon the face of all the earth. 4 For yet seven days, and I will cause it to rain upon the earth forty days and forty nights; and every living thing that I have made will I destroy from off the face of the ground. 5 And Noah did according unto all that Jehovah commanded him.

7 And Noah went in, and his sons, and his wife, and his sons' wives with him, into the ark, because of the waters of the flood. 8 Of clean beasts, and of beasts that are not clean, and of birds, and of everything that creepeth upon the ground, 9 there went in two and two unto Noah into the ark, male and female, as God commanded Noah.

10 And it came to pass after the seven days, that the waters of the flood were upon the earth. 12 And the rain was upon the earth forty days and forty nights. 16b And Jehovah shut him in. 17b And the waters increased, and bare up the ark, and it was lifted up above the earth.

22 All in whose nostrils was the breath of the spirit of life, of all that was on the dry land, died. 23 And every living thing was destroyed that was upon the face of the ground, both man, and cattle, and creeping things, and birds of the heavens; and they were destroyed from the earth: and Noah only was left, and they that were with him in the ark.

8^{2b} And the rain from heaven was restrained; 3a and the waters returned from off the earth continually.

6 And it came to pass at the end of forty days, that Noah opened the window of the ark which he had made: 7 and he sent forth a raven, and it went forth to and fro, until the waters were dried up from off the earth. 8 And he sent forth a dove from him, to see if the waters were abated from off the face of the ground; 9 but the dove found no rest for the sole of her foot, and she returned unto him to the ark; for the waters were on the face of the whole earth: and he put forth his hand, and took her, and brought her in unto him into the ark. 10 And he stayed yet other seven days; and again he sent forth the dove out of the ark; 11 and the dove came in to him at eventide; and, lo, in her mouth an olive-leaf plucked off; so Noah knew that the waters were abated from off the earth. 12 And he stayed yet other seven days, and sent forth the dove; and she returned not again unto him any more.

13b And Noah removed the covering of the ark, and looked, and, behold, the face of the ground was dried.

20 And Noah builded an altar unto Jehovah, and took of every clean beast, and of every clean bird, and offered burnt-offerings on the altar. 21 And Jehovah smelled the sweet savor; and Jehovah said in his heart, I will not again curse the ground any more for man's sake, for that the imagination of man's heart is evil from his youth; neither will I again smite any more everything living, as I have done. 22 While the earth remaineth, seedtime and harvest, and cold and heat, and summer and winter, and day and night shall not cease.

For Gn. $9^{18\text{-}19}$ cf. J^{11}

10. NOAH'S CURSE ON CANAAN.
Gn. 9²⁰⁻²⁷

9²⁰ And Noah began to be a husbandman, and planted a vineyard: 21 and he drank of the wine, and was drunken; and he was uncovered within his tent. 22 And Ham, the father of Canaan, saw the nakedness of his father, and told his two brethren without. 23 And Shem and Japheth took a garment, and laid it upon both their shoulders, and went backward, and covered the nakedness of their father; and their faces were backward, and they saw not their father's nakedness. 24 And Noah awoke from his wine, and knew what his youngest son had done unto him. 25 And he said,
    Cursed be Canaan;
    A servant of servants shall he be unto his brethren.
26 And he said,
    Blessed be Jehovah, the God of Shem;
    And let Canaan be his servant.
27 God enlarge Japheth,
    And let him dwell in the tents of Shem;
    And let Canaan be his servant.

11. A FRAGMENTARY GENEALOGY OF THE SONS OF NOAH. P4, 5.
Gn. 9¹⁸⁻¹⁹10⁸⁻¹⁹·²¹·²⁴·²⁵⁻³⁰ (J²)

18 And the sons of Noah, that went forth from the ark, were Shem, and Ham, and Japheth: and Ham is the father of Canaan. 19 These three were the sons of Noah: and of these was the whole earth overspread.

10⁸ And Cush begat Nimrod: he began to be a mighty one in the earth. 9 He was a mighty hunter before Jehovah: wherefore it is said, Like Nimrod a mighty hunter before Jehovah. 10 And the beginning of his kingdom was Babel and Erech, and Accad, and Calneh, in the land of Shinar. 11 Out of that land he went forth into Assyria, and builded Nineveh, and Rehoboth-Ir, and Calah, 12 and Resen between Nineveh and Calah (the same is the great city).

13 And Mizraim begat Ludim, and Anamim, and Lehabim, and Naphtuhim, 14 and Pathrusim, and Casluhim (whence went forth the Philistines), and Caphtorim.

15 And Canaan begat Sidon his first-born, and Heth, 16 and the Jebusite, and the Amorite, and the Girgashite, 17 and the Hivite, and the Arkite, and the Sinite, 18 and the Arvadite, and the Zemarite, and the Hamathite: and afterwards were the families of the Canaanite spread abroad. 19 And the border of the Canaanite was from Sidon, as thou goest toward Gerar, unto Gaza; as thou goest toward Sodom and Gomorrah and Admah and Zeboiim, unto Lasha.

---

[10] The passage reflects the history of the early kingdom: We., Bu., E. Meyer, Smend, et al.—Eerd. finds polytheism in 9²⁷.

[11] There is general agreement on the redactional material, except 10⁹ J: Bu., Ba., Dr. (vs. We., Di., Sk., Gu., St., et al.), and 10¹⁶⁻¹⁸ᵃ, J: Co., Ki.

21 And unto Shem, the father of all the children of Eber, the elder brother of Japheth, to him also were children born. 24 And Arpachshad begat Shelah; and Shelah begat Eber.

25 And unto Eber were born two sons: the name of the one was Peleg; for in his days was the earth divided; and his brother's name was Joktan. 26 And Joktan begat Almodad, and Sheleph, and Hazarmaveth, and Jerah, 27 and Hadoram, and Uzal, and Diklah, 28 and Obal, and Abimael, and Sheba, 29 and Ophir, and Havilah, and Jobab: all these were the sons of Joktan. 30 And their dwelling was from Mesha, as thou goest toward Sephar, the mountain of the east.

12. THE TOWER OF BABEL.

Gn. 11^{1-9}

11^1 And the whole earth was of one language and of one speech. 2 And it came to pass, as they journeyed east, that they found a plain in the land of Shinar; and they dwelt there. 3 And they said one to another, Come, let us make brick, and burn them thoroughly. And they had brick for stone, and slime had they for mortar. 4 And they said, Come, let us build us a city, and a tower, whose top *may reach* unto heaven, and let us make us a name; lest we be scattered abroad upon the face of the whole earth.

5 And Jehovah came down to see the city and the tower, which the children of men builded. 6 And Jehovah said, Behold, they are one people, and they have all one language; and this is what they begin to do: and now nothing will be witholden from them, which they purpose to do. 7 Come, let us go down, and there confound their language, that they may not understand one another's speech. 8 So Jehovah scattered them abroad from thence upon the face of all the earth: and they left off building the city. 9 Therefore was the name of it called Babel; because Jehovah did there confound the language of all the earth: and from thence did Jehovah scatter them abroad upon the face of all the earth.

13. THE STORY OF ABRAHAM. E1. P7.

13i. ABRAM'S MARRIAGE.

Gn. 11^{28-30}

28 And Haran died before his father Terah in the land of his nativity, in Ur of the Chaldees. 29 And Abram and Nahor took them wives: the name of Abram's wife was Sarai; and the name of Nahor's wife, Milcah, the daughter of Haran, the father of Milcah, and the father of Iscah. 30 And Sarai was barren; she had no child.

---

[12] The anthropomorphisms in vv. 5 and 7, and the plural in v. 7 lead many to detect a polytheistic origin for this story: so, e. g., Stade, Gu, Ho., Pr., Eerd., (Eichr.).
[13i] In 11^{28} Rp, because Ur as home of Abraham is peculiar to P.

13ii. THE CALL OF ABRAM.
Gn. 12¹⁻⁴ᵃ

12¹ Now Jehovah said unto Abram, Get thee out of thy country, and from thy kindred, and from thy father's house, unto the land that I will show thee: 2 and I will make of thee a great nation, and I will bless thee, and make thy name great; and be thou a blessing: 3 and I will bless them that bless thee, and him that curseth thee will I curse: and in thee shall all the families of the earth be blessed. 4a So Abram went, as Jehovah had spoken unto him; and Lot went with him.

13iii. ABRAM IN CANAAN. P7i.
Gn. 12⁶⁻⁹

6 And Abram passed through the land unto the place of Shechem, unto the oak of Moreh. And the Canaanite was then in the land. 7 And Jehovah appeared unto Abram, and said, Unto thy seed will I give this land: and there builded he an altar unto Jehovah, who appeared unto him. 8 And he removed from thence unto the mountain on the east of Beth-el, and pitched his tent, having Beth-el on the west, and Ai on the east: and there he builded an altar unto Jehovah, and called upon the name of Jehovah. 9 And Abram journeyed, going on still toward the South.

13iv. ABRAM'S DECEPTION REGARDING SARAI IN EGYPT. J14iv. E1ii.
Gn. 12¹⁰⁻²⁰

10 And there was a famine in the land: and Abram went down into Egypt to sojourn there; for the famine was sore in the land. 11 And it came to pass, when he was come near to enter into Egypt, that he said unto Sarai his wife, Behold now, I know that thou art a fair woman to look upon: 12 and it will come to pass when the Egyptians shall see thee, that they will say, This is his wife: and they will kill me, but they will save thee alive. 13 Say, I pray thee, thou art my sister; that it may be well with me for thy sake, and that my soul may live because of thee. 14 And it came to pass, that, when Abram was come into Egypt, the Egyptians beheld the woman that she was very fair. 15 And the princes of Pharaoh saw her, and praised her to Pharaoh: and the woman was taken into Pharaoh's house. 16 And he dealt well with Abram for her sake: and he had sheep, and oxen, and he-asses, and men-servants, and maid-servants, and she-asses, and camels. 17 And Jehovah plagued Pharaoh and his house with great plagues because of Sarai, Abram's wife. 18 And Pharaoh called Abram, and said, What is this that thou

---
¹³ⁱᵛ While this passage belongs in the Jahvistic school, it is generally regarded, by most scholars since We., as later than J14iv. So CH., Ba., Smend, "an excerpt from a separate Jahvistic collection" Gu., Sk., SB.—In 12¹⁷ LXX reads "God" for "Jehovah."

hast done unto me? why didst thou not tell me that she was thy wife? 19 why saidst thou, She is my sister, so that I took her to be my wife? now therefore behold thy wife, take her, and go thy way. 20 And Pharaoh gave men charge concerning him: and they brought him on the way, and his wife, and all that he had.

13v. SEPARATION OF ABRAM AND LOT. P7ii.
Gn. 13$^{1-5.7-11a.12b-18}$

13^1 And Abram went up out of Egypt, he, and his wife, and all that he had, and Lot with him, into the South. 2 And Abram was very rich in cattle, in silver, and in gold. 3 And he went on his journeys from the South even to Beth-el, unto the place where his tent had been at the beginning, between Beth-el and Ai, 4 unto the place of the altar, which he had made there at the first: and there Abram called on the name of Jehovah. 5 And Lot also, who went with Abram, had flocks, and herds, and tents.

7 And there was a strife between the herdsmen of Abram's cattle and the herdsmen of Lot's cattle: and the Canaanite and the Perizzite dwelt then in the land. 8 And Abram said unto Lot, Let there be no strife, I pray thee, between me and thee, and between my herdsmen and thy herdsmen; for we are brethren. 9 Is not the whole land before thee? separate thyself, I pray thee, from me: if *thou wilt take* the left hand, then I will go to the right; or if *thou take* the right hand, then I will go to the left. 10 And Lot lifted up his eyes, and beheld all the Plain of the Jordan, that it was well watered everywhere, before Jehovah destroyed Sodom and Gomorrah, like the garden of Jehovah, like the land of Egypt, as thou goest unto Zoar. 11a So Lot chose him all the Plain of the Jordan; and Lot journeyed east, 12b and moved his tent as far as Sodom. 13 Now the men of Sodom were wicked and sinners against Jehovah exceedingly.

14 And Jehovah said unto Abram, after that Lot was separated from him, Lift up now thine eyes, and look from the place where thou art, northward and southward and eastward and westward: 15 for all the land which thou seest, to thee will I give it, and to thy seed for ever. 16 And I will make thy seed as the dust of the earth: so that if a man can number the dust of the earth, then may thy seed also be numbered. 17 Arise, walk through the land in the length of it and in the breadth of it; for unto thee will I give it.

18 And Abram moved his tent, and came and dwelt by the oaks of Mamre, which are in Hebron, and built there an altar unto Jehovah.

[13v] In 13^{10} gloss: Olshausen, Di., Ka., Gu., Sk., SB.; for "Zoar," Pesh. reads "Zoan" (in Egypt).—Some regard 13$^{14-17}$ as J: so Di., Dr., Ad.—In vv. 10, 13, 14 LXX reads "God," which is perhaps correct (Gu., Eerd., Eichr.), but this change would not affect the analysis (Gu., Eichr., vs. Eerd.).

42   SOURCES OF THE HEXATEUCH   [Gn. 15¹

13vi. JEHOVAH PROMISES AN HEIR (AND THE LAND) TO ABRAM. E1i. P7iv.
Gn. 15¹ᵃ·²ᵃ·³ᵇ⁻⁴·⁶⁻¹²·¹⁷⁻²¹

15¹ᵃ After these things the word of Jehovah came unto Abram. 2a And Abram said, O Lord Jehovah, what wilt thou give me, seeing I go childless, 3b and, lo, one born in my house is mine heir? 4 And, behold, the word of Jehovah came unto him, saying, This man shall not be thine heir; but he that shall come forth out of thine own bowels shall be thine heir. 6 And he believed in Jehovah; and he reckoned it to him for righteousness.
7 And he said unto him, I am Jehovah that brought thee out of Ur of the Chaldees, to give thee this land to inherit it. 8 And he said, O Lord Jehovah, whereby shall I know that I shall inherit it?
9 And he said unto him, Take me a heifer three years old, and a she-goat three years old, and a ram three years old, and a turtle-dove, and a young pigeon. 10 And he took him all these, and divided them in the midst, and laid each half over against the other; but the birds divided he not. 11 And the birds of prey came down upon the carcasses, and Abram drove them away. 12 And when the sun was going down . . . lo, a horror of great darkness fell upon him. 17 And it came to pass, that, when the sun went down, and it was dark, behold, a smoking furnace, and a flaming torch that passed between these pieces. 18 In that day Jehovah made a covenant with Abram, saying, Unto thy seed have I given this land, from the river of Egypt unto the great river, the river Euphrates: 19 the Kenite, and the Kenizzite, and the Kadmonite, 20 and the Hittite, and the Perizzite, and the Rephaim, 21 and the Amorite, and the Canaanite, and the Girgashite, and the Jebusite.

13vii. SARAI AND HAGAR: PROMISE OF ISHMAEL'S BIRTH. E1iv.
Gn. 16¹ᵇ⁻²·⁴⁻¹⁴

16¹ᵇ And she had an handmaid, an Egyptian, whose name was Hagar. 2 And Sarai said unto Abram, Behold now, Jehovah hath restrained me from bearing; go in, I pray thee, unto my handmaid; it may be that I shall obtain children by her. And Abram hearkened to the voice of Sarai.
4 And he went in unto Hagar, and she conceived: and when she saw that she had conceived, her mistress was despised in

---

¹³ᵛⁱ The separation of J and E in 15¹⁻² is "highly precarious" Sk. There is a general consensus regarding the other vv., except as to the precise limits of the R. But Smend makes vv. 3-4 E, and Co., Gu., Sk. assign 11 to E. Eerd. regards vv. 1-6 as late. SB. accepts above analysis, except "after these things" in 1a, and v. 6: E; and vv. 13-15a are added to J.
¹³ᵛⁱⁱ vv. 8-10 Rje: "generally acknowledged" (Ad.); but SB. assigns v. 8 to J. v. 14, Beer-lahai-roi means, "The well of the living one who seeth me" (Am. Rev., margin).

her eyes. 5 And Sarai said unto Abram, My wrong be upon thee: I gave my handmaid into thy bosom; and when she saw that she had conceived, I was despised in her eyes: Jehovah judge between me and thee. 6 But Abram said unto Sarai, Behold, thy maid is in thy hand; do to her that which is good in thine eyes. And Sarai dealt hardly with her, and she fled from her face.

7 And the angel of Jehovah found her by a fountain of water in the wilderness, by the fountain in the way to Shur. 8 And he said, Hagar, Sarai's handmaid, whence camest thou? and whither goest thou? And she said, I am fleeing from the face of my mistress Sarai. 9 And the angel of Jehovah said unto her, Return to thy mistress, and submit thyself under her hands. 10 And the angel of Jehovah said unto her, I will greatly multiply thy seed, that it shall not be numbered for multitude. 11 And the angel of Jehovah said unto her, Behold, thou art with child, and shalt bear a son; and thou shalt call his name Ishmael, because Jehovah hath heard thy affliction. 12 And he shall be *as* a wild ass among men; his hand *shall be* against every man, and every man's hand against him; and he shall dwell over against all his brethren. 13 And she called the name of Jehovah that spake unto her, Thou art a God that seeth: for she said, Have I even here looked after him that seeth me? 14 Wherefore the well was called Beer-lahai-roi; behold, it is between Kadesh and Bered.

13viii. JEHOVAH AND THE THREE MEN AT MAMRE: PROMISE OF ISAAC'S BIRTH.

Gn. 18$^{1\text{-}15}$

18^1 And Jehovah appeared unto him by the oaks of Mamre, as he sat in the tent door in the heat of the day; 2 and he lifted up his eyes and looked, and, lo, three men stood over against him: and when he saw them, he ran to meet them from the tent door, and bowed himself to the earth, 3 and said, My lord, if now I have found favor in thy sight, pass not away, I pray thee, from thy servant: 4 let now a little water be fetched, and wash your feet, and rest yourselves under the tree: 5 and I will fetch a morsel of bread, and strengthen ye your heart; after that ye shall pass on: forasmuch as ye are come to your servant. And they said, So do, as thou hast said. 6 And Abraham hastened into the tent unto Sarah, and said, Make ready quickly three measures of fine meal, knead it, and make cakes. 7 And Abraham ran unto the herd, and fetched a calf tender and good, and gave it unto the servant; and he hasted to dress it. 8 And he took butter, and milk,

---

[13viii] The passage is entirely unified J, in spite of efforts by Kraetzschmar and Smend to find two narratives. The story reflects polytheistic ideas (Eerd., Pr., Gu.).

and the calf which he had dressed, and set it before them; and he stood by them under the tree, and they did eat. 9 And they said unto him, Where is Sarah thy wife? And he said, Behold, in the tent. 10 And he said, I will certainly return unto thee when the season cometh round; and, lo, Sarah thy wife shall have a son. And Sarah heard in the tent door, which was behind him. 11 Now Abraham and Sarah were old, *and* well stricken in age; it had ceased to be with Sarah after the manner of women. 12 And Sarah laughed within herself, saying, After I am waxed old shall I have pleasure, my lord being old also? 13 And Jehovah said unto Abraham, Wherefore did Sarah laugh, saying, Shall I of a surety bear a child, who am old? 14 Is anything too hard for Jehovah? At the set time I will return unto thee, when the season cometh round, and Sarah shall have a son. 15 Then Sarah denied, saying, I laughed not; for she was afraid. And he said, Nay; but thou didst laugh.

13ix. WICKEDNESS OF SODOM AND ITS DESTRUCTION. P7vi. Gn. 18^{16}-19^{28}

16 And the men rose up from thence, and looked toward Sodom: and Abraham went with them to bring them on the way. 17 And Jehovah aid, Shall I hide from Abraham that which I do; 18 seeing that Abraham shall surely become a great and mighty nation, and all the nations of the earth shall be blessed in him? 19 For I have known him, to the end that he may command his children and his household after him, that they may keep the way of Jehovah, to do righteousness and justice; to the end that Jehovah may bring upon Abraham that which he hath spoken of him. 20 And Jehovah said, Because the cry of Sodom and Gomorrah is great, and because their sin is very grievous; 21 I will go down now, and see whether they have done altogether according to the cry of it, which is come unto me; and if not, I will know.

22 And the men turned from thence, and went toward Sodom: but Abraham stood yet before Jehovah. 23 And Abraham drew near, and said, Wilt thou consume the righteous with the wicked? 24 Peradventure there are fifty righteous within the city: wilt thou consume and not spare the place for the fifty righteous that are therein? 25 That be far from thee to do after this manner, to slay the righteous with the wicked, that so the righteous should be as the wicked; that be far from thee: shall not the Judge of all the earth do right? 26 And Jehovah said, If I find in Sodom fifty righteous within the city, then I will spare all the place for their sake. 27 And Abraham answered and said, Behold now, I have taken upon me to speak unto the Lord, who am but dust and ashes:

---

[13]ix 18^{17-19} R: We., Gu., Ka.? J[2]: Ku., CH., Mi., St. J: Di., Ad., Dr., Se. v. 17J, vv. 18-19 R: SB. $18^{22b-33a}$, "viewed by most as a later addition" Ka. So We., Co., Gu., SB. (J[3]), or J[2]: Ku., CH., Mi., St., Smend: but J: Pr. only.

28 peradventure there shall lack five of the fifty righteous: wilt thou destroy all the city for lack of five? And he said, I will not destroy it, if I find there forty and five. 29 And he spake unto him yet again, and said, Peradventure there shall be forty found there. And he said, I will not do it for the forty's sake. 30 And he said, Oh let not the Lord be angry and I will speak: peradventure there shall thirty be found there. And he said, I will not do it, if I find thirty there. 31 And he said, Behold now, I have taken upon me to speak unto the Lord: peradventure there shall be twenty found there. And he said, I will not destroy it for the twenty's sake. 32 And he said, Oh let not the Lord be angry, and I will speak yet but this once: peradventure ten shall be found there. And he said, I will not destroy it for the ten's sake. 33 And Jehovah went his way, as soon as he had left off communing with Abraham: and Abraham returned unto his place.

19 And the two angels came to Sodom at even; and Lot sat in the gate of Sodom: and Lot saw them, and rose up to meet them; and he bowed himself with his face to the earth; 2 and he said, Behold now, my lords, turn aside, I pray you, into your servant's house, and tarry all night, and wash your feet, and ye shall rise up early, and go on your way. And they said, Nay; but we will abide in the street all night. 3 And he urged them greatly; and they turned in unto him, and entered into his house; and he made them a feast, and did bake unleavened bread, and they did eat. 4 But before they lay down, the men of the city, *even* the men of Sodom, compassed the house round, both young and old, all the people from every quarter; 5 and they called unto Lot, and said unto him, Where are the men that came in to thee this night? bring them out unto us, that we may know them. 6 And Lot went out unto them to the door, and shut the door after him. 7 And he said, I pray you, my brethren, do not so wickedly. 8 Behold now, I have two daughters that have not known man; let me, I pray you, bring them out unto you, and do ye to them as is good in your eyes; only unto these men do nothing, forasmuch as they are come under the shadow of my roof. 9 And they said, Stand back. And they said, This one fellow came in to sojourn, and he will needs be a judge: now will we deal worse with thee, than with them. And they pressed sore upon the man, even Lot, and drew near to break the door. 10 But the men put forth their hand, and brought Lot into the house to them, and shut to the door. 11 And they smote the men that were at the door of the house with blindness, both small and great, so that they wearied themselves to find the door.

12 And the men said unto Lot, Hast thou here any besides? son-in-law, and thy sons, and thy daughters, and whomsoever

thou hast in the city, bring them out of the place: 13 for we will destroy this place, because the cry of them is waxed great before Jehovah; and Jehovah hath sent us to destroy it. 14 And Lot went out, and spake unto his sons-in-law, who married his daughters, and said, Up, get you out of this place; for Jehovah will destroy the city. But he seemed unto his sons-in-law as one that mocked. 15 And when the morning arose, then the angels hastened Lot, saying, Arise, take thy wife, and thy two daughters that are here, lest thou be consumed in the iniquity of the city. 16 But he lingered; and the men laid hold upon his hand, and upon the hand of his wife, and upon the hand of his two daughters, Jehovah being merciful unto him: and they brought him forth, and set him without the city. 17 And it came to pass, when they had brought them forth abroad, that he said, Escape for thy life; look not behind thee, neither stay thou in all the Plain; escape to the mountain, lest thou be consumed. 18 And Lot said unto them, Oh, not so, my lord: 19 behold now, thy servant hath found favor in thy sight, and thou hast magnified thy lovingkindness, which thou hast showed unto me in saving my life; and I cannot escape to the mountain, lest evil overtake me, and I die: 20 behold now, this city is near to flee unto, and it is a little one. Oh let me escape thither (is it not a little one?), and my soul shall live. 21 And he said unto him, See, I have accepted thee concerning this thing also, that I will not overthrow the city of which thou hast spoken. 22 Haste thee, escape thither; for I cannot do anything till thou be come thither. Therefore the name of the city was called Zoar.

23 The sun was risen upon the earth when Lot came unto Zoar. 24 Then Jehovah rained upon Sodom and upon Gomorrah brimstone and fire from Jehovah out of heaven; 25 and he overthrew those cities, and all the Plain, and all the inhabitants of the cities, and that which grew upon the ground. 26 But his wife looked back from behind him, and she became a pillar of salt. 27 And Abraham gat up early in the morning to the place where he had stood before Jehovah: 28 and he looked toward Sodom and Gomorrah, and toward all the land of the Plain, and beheld, and, lo, the smoke of the land went up as the smoke of a furnace.

13x. LOT, THE ANCESTOR OF MOABITES AND AMMONITES.
Gn. 19$^{30-38}$

30 And Lot went up out of Zoar, and dwelt in the mountain, and his two daughters with him; for he feared to dwell in Zoar: and he dwelt in a cave, he and his two daughters. 31 And the first-born said unto the younger, Our father is old, and

there is not a man in the earth to come in unto us after the manner of all the earth: 32 come, let us make our father drink wine, and we will lie with him, that we may preserve seed of our father. 33 And they made their father drink wine that night: and the first-born went in, and lay with her father; and he knew not when she lay down, nor when she arose. 34 And it came to pass on the morrow, that the firstborn said unto the younger, Behold, I lay yesternight with my father: let us make him drink wine this night also; and go thou in, and lie with him, that we may preserve seed of our father. 35 And they made their father drink wine that night also: and the younger arose, and lay with him; and he knew not when she lay down, nor when she arose. 36 Thus were both the daughters of Lot with child by their father. 37 And the first-born bare a son, and called his name Moab: the same is the father of the Moabites unto this day. 38 And the younger, she also bare a son, and called his name Ben-ammi: the same is the father of the children of Ammon unto this day.

13xi. BIRTH OF ISAAC.   E1iii.   P7vii.
Gn. $21^{1a.2a.7.6b}$

21^{1a} And Jehovah visited Sarah as he had said. 2a And Sarah conceived, and bare Abraham a son in his old age. 7 And she said, Who would have said unto Abraham, that Sarah should give children suck? for I have borne him a son in his old age. 6b Every one that heareth will laugh with me.

13xii. ABRAHAM AT BEERSHEBA.
Gn. 21^{33-34}

33 And *Abraham* planted a tamarisk tree in Beer-sheba, and called there on the name of Jehovah, the Everlasting God. 34 And Abraham sojourned in the land of the Philistines many days.

13xiii. NAHOR'S CHILDREN.
Gn. 22^{20-24}

20 And it came to pass after these things, that it was told Abraham, saying, Behold, Milcah, she also hath borne children unto thy brother Nahor: 21 Uz his first-born, and Buz his brother, and Kemuel the father of Aram, 22 and Chesed, and Hazo, and Pildash, and Jidlaph, and Bethuel. 23 And Bethuel begat Rebekah: these eight did Milcah bear to Nahor, Abraham's brother. 24 And his concubine, whose name was

---

13xi 21^{2a} P*: Ku. only. 21^{6b} J: Bu., Ho., Ba., Co., Ka., Ki., Mi., Gu., GFM., SB., Sk. (6b after 7: Bu., Ho., Ki., Ka., Sk., SB.). E: We., Ku.?, Di., Dr., Ad., CH., St.
13xii v. 33 J: all exc. E: Ad., Mi., Smend. Eerd. finds here a polytheistic tree-cult, vs. all others! v. 34 R: We., Gu., Di., Dr., SB., Ka., Sk. E: CH., St. J: Co., Mi. (but out of place).
13xiii J: all, exc. We., E ("after these things" 20a).

Reumah, she also bare Tebah, and Gaham, and Tahash, and Maacah.

13xiv. ABRAHAM'S SERVANT SECURES REBEKAH AS WIFE FOR ISAAC. P9.

Gn. 24$^{1-67}$

24^1 And Abraham was old, *and* well stricken in age: and Jehovah had blessed Abraham in all things. 2 And Abraham said unto his servant, the elder of his house, that ruled over all that he had, Put, I pray thee, thy hand under my thigh: 3 and I will make thee swear by Jehovah, the God of heaven and the God of the earth, that thou wilt not take a wife for my son of the daughters of the Canaanites, among whom I dwell: 4 but thou shalt go unto my country, and to my kindred, and take a wife for my son Isaac. 5 And the servant said unto him, Peradventure the woman will not be willing to follow me unto this land: must I needs bring thy son again unto the land from whence thou camest? 6 And Abraham said unto him, Beware thou that thou bring not my son thither again. 7 Jehovah, the God of heaven, who took me from my father's house, and from the land of my nativity, and who spake unto me, and who sware unto me, saying, Unto thy seed will I give this land; he will send his angel before thee, and thou shalt take a wife for my son from thence. 8 And if the woman be not willing to follow thee, then thou shalt be clear from this my oath; only thou shalt not bring my son thither again. 9 And the servant put his hand under the thigh of Abraham his master, and sware to him concerning this matter.

10 And the servant took ten camels, of the camels of his master, and departed, having all goodly things of his master's in his hand: and he arose, and went to Mesopotamia, unto the city of Nahor. 11 And he made the camels to kneel down without the city by the well of water at the time of evening, the time that women go out to draw water. 12 And he said, O Jehovah, the God of my master Abraham, send me, I pray thee, good speed this day, and show kindness unto my master Abraham. 13 Behold, I am standing by the fountain of water; and the daughters of the men of the city are coming out to draw water: 14 and let it come to pass, that the damsel to whom I shall say, Let down thy pitcher, I pray thee, that I may drink; and she shall say, Drink, and I will give thy camels drink also: let the same be she that thou hast appointed for thy servant

---

 13xiv Pr., Gu., Smend find some E but do not agree. SB. finds J only. v. 10 "Mesopotamia," Hebrew, "Aram-naharaim," that is, "Aram of the two rivers" (Am. Rev., margin). v. 12 leads Eerd. to suspect polytheism here (but vv. 3, 7 disprove this, Eichr.). v. 61 was originally followed in J by the account of Abraham's death, and v. 67 read originally "father's" for "mother's," We., Ku., Di., Ad., Ka., Mi., Sk., St.

Isaac; and thereby shall I know that thou hast showed kindness unto my master. 15 And it came to pass, before he had done speaking, that, behold, Rebekah came out, who was born to Bethuel the son of Milcah, the wife of Nahor, Abraham's brother, with her pitcher upon her shoulder. 16 And the damsel was very fair to look upon, a virgin, neither had any man known her: and she went down to the fountain, and filled her pitcher, and came up. 17 And the servant ran to meet her, and said, Give me to drink, I pray thee, a little water from thy pitcher. 18 And she said, Drink, my lord: and she hasted, and let down her pitcher upon her hand, and gave him drink. 19 And when she had done giving him drink, she said, I will draw for thy camels also, until they have done drinking. 20 And she hasted, and emptied her pitcher into the trough, and ran again unto the well to draw, and drew for all his camels. 21 And the man looked stedfastly on her, holding his peace, to know whether Jehovah had made his journey prosperous or not. 22 And it came to pass, as the camels had done drinking, that the man took a golden ring of half a shekel weight, and two bracelets for her hands of ten shekels weight of gold, 23 and said, Whose daughter art thou? tell me, I pray thee. Is there room in thy father's house for us to lodge in? 24 And she said unto him, I am the daughter of Bethuel the son of Milcah, whom she bare unto Nahor. 25 She said moreover unto him, We have both straw and provender enough, and room to lodge in. 26 And the man bowed his head, and worshipped Jehovah. 27 And he said, Blessed be Jehovah, the God of my master Abraham, who hath not forsaken his lovingkindness and his truth toward my master: as for me, Jehovah hath led me in the way to the house of my master's brethren.

28 And the damsel ran, and told her mother's house according to these words. 29 And Rebekah had a brother, and his name was Laban: and Laban ran out unto the man, unto the fountain. 30 And it came to pass, when he saw the ring, and the bracelets upon his sister's hands, and when he heard the words of Rebekah his sister, saying, Thus spake the man unto me; that he came unto the man; and, behold, he was standing by the camels at the fountain. 31 And he said, Come in, thou blessed of Jehovah; wherefore standest thou without? for I have prepared the house, and room for the camels. 32 And the man came into the house, and he ungirded the camels; and he gave straw and provender for the camels, and water to wash his feet and the feet of the men that were with him. 33 And there was set food before him to eat: but he said, I will not eat, until I have told mine errand. And he said, Speak on. 34 And he said, I am Abraham's servant. 35 And Jehovah

hath blessed my master greatly; and he is become great: and he hath given him flocks and herds, and silver and gold, and men-servants and maid-servants, and camels and asses. 36 And Sarah my master's wife bare a son to my master when she was old: and unto him hath he given all that he hath. 37 And my master made me swear, saying, Thou shalt not take a wife for my son of the daughters of the Canaanites, in whose land I dwell: 38 but thou shalt go unto my father's house, and to my kindred, and take a wife for my son. 39 And I said unto my master, Peradventure the woman will not follow me. 40 And he said unto me, Jehovah, before whom I walk, will send his angel with thee, and prosper thy way; and thou shalt take a wife for my son of my kindred, and of my father's house: 41 then shalt thou be clear from my oath, when thou comest to my kindred; and if they give her not to thee, thou shalt be clear from my oath. 42 And I came this day unto the fountain, and said, O Jehovah, the God of my master Abraham, if now thou do prosper my way which I go: 43 behold, I am standing by the fountain of water; and let it come to pass, that the maiden that cometh forth to draw, to whom I shall say, Give me, I pray thee, a little water from thy pitcher to drink; 44 and she shall say to me, Both drink thou, and I will also draw for thy camels: let the same be the woman whom Jehovah hath appointed for my master's son. 45 And before I had done speaking in my heart, behold, Rebekah came forth with her pitcher on her shoulder; and she went down unto the fountain, and drew: and I said unto her, Let me drink, I pray thee. 46 And she made haste, and let down her pitcher from her shoulder, and said, Drink, and I will give thy camels drink also: so I drank, and she made the camels drink also. 47 And I asked her, and said, Whose daughter art thou? And she said, The daughter of Bethuel, Nahor's son, whom Milcah bare unto him: and I put the ring upon her nose, and the bracelets upon her hands. 48 And I bowed my head, and worshipped Jehovah, and blessed Jehovah, the God of my master Abraham, who had led me in the right way to take my master's brother's daughter for his son. 49 And now if ye will deal kindly and truly with my master, tell me: and if not, tell me; that I may turn to the right hand, or to the left.

50 Then Laban and Bethuel answered and said, The thing proceedeth from Jehovah: we cannot speak unto thee bad or good. 51 Behold, Rebekah is before thee, take her, and go, and let her be thy master's son's wife, as Jehovah hath spoken. 52 And it came to pass, that, when Abraham's servant heard their words, he bowed himself down to the earth unto Jehovah. 53 And the servant brought forth jewels of silver, and jewels

of gold, and raiment, and gave them to Rebekah: he gave also
to her brother and to her mother precious things. 54 And they
did eat and drink, he and the men that were with him, and tarried
all night; and they rose up in the morning, and he said, Send
me away unto my master. 55 And her brother and her mother
said, Let the damsel abide with us *a few* days, at the least ten;
after that she shall go. 56 And he said unto them, Hinder me
not, seeing Jehovah hath prospered my way; send me away
that I may go to my master. 57 And they said, We will call
the damsel, and inquire at her mouth. 58 And they called
Rebekah, and said unto her, Wilt thou go with this man? And
she said, I will go. 59 And they sent away Rebekah their
sister, and her nurse, and Abraham's servant, and his men.
60 And they blessed Rebekah, and said unto her, Our sister,
be thou *the mother* of thousands of ten thousands, and let thy
seed possess the gate of those that hate them.

61 And Rebekah arose, and her damsels, and they rode upon
the camels, and followed the man: and the servant took Rebekah, and went his way. 62 And Isaac came from the way of
Beer-lahai-roi; for he dwelt in the land of the South. 63 And
Isaac went out to meditate in the field at the eventide: and he
lifted up his eyes, and saw, and, behold, there were camels
coming. 64 And Rebekah lifted up her eyes, and when she
saw Isaac, she alighted from the camel. 65 And she said unto
the servant, What man is this that walketh in the field to meet
us? And the servant said, It is my master: and she took her
veil, and covered herself. 66 And the servant told Isaac all
the things that he had done. 67 And Isaac brought her into
his mother Sarah's tent, and took Rebekah, and she became
his wife; and he loved her: and Isaac was comforted after his
mother's death.

13xv. ABRAHAM AND KETURAH.
Gn. $25^{1-6.18}$. For Gn. 25^{11b}, cf. J13xv.

25^1 And Abraham took another wife, and her name was
Keturah. 2 And she bare him Zimran, and Jokshan, and
Medan, and Midian, and Ishbak, and Shuah. 3 And Jokshan
begat Sheba, and Dedan. And the sons of Dedan were As-
shurim, and Letushim, and Leummim. 4 And the sons of
Midian: Ephah, and Epher, and Hanoch, and Abida, and
Eldaah. All these were the children of Keturah.

5 And Abraham gave all that he had unto Isaac. 6 But unto
the sons of the concubines, that Abraham had, Abraham gave gifts; and
he sent them away from Isaac his son, while he yet lived, eastward, unto

---

[13xv] This narrative is almost surely out of place; it should come at an earlier point in
the life of Abraham.

the east country. 18 And they dwelt from Havilah unto Shur that is before Egypt, as thou goest toward Assyria: he abode over against all his brethren.

14. THE STORY OF ISAAC.

14i. ISAAC AT BEER-LAHAI-ROI.
Gn. 25^{11b}
11b And Isaac dwelt by Beer-lahai-roi.

14ii. BIRTH OF ESAU AND JACOB. J17: Gn. 38$^{27\text{-}30}$.
Gn. 25$^{21\text{-}26a}$

21 And Isaac entreated Jehovah for his wife, because she was barren: and Jehovah was entreated of him, and Rebekah his wife conceived. 22 And the children struggled together within her; and she said, If it be so, wherefore do I live? And she went to inquire of Jehovah. 23 And Jehovah said unto her,
  Two nations are in thy womb,
  And two peoples shall be separated from thy bowels:
  And the one people shall be stronger than the other people;
  And the elder shall serve the younger.
24 And when her days to be delivered were fulfilled, behold, there were twins in her womb. 25 And the first came forth red, all over like a hairy garment; and they called his name Esau. 26a And after that came forth his brother, and his hand had hold on Esau's heel; and his name was called Jacob.

14iii. ESAU SELLS HIS BIRTHRIGHT.
Gn. 25$^{27\text{-}34}$

27 And the boys grew: and Esau was a skilful hunter, a man of the field; and Jacob was a quiet man, dwelling in tents. 28 Now Isaac loved Esau, because he did eat of his venison: and Rebekah loved Jacob. 29 And Jacob boiled pottage: and Esau came in from the field, and he was faint: 30 and Esau said to Jacob, Feed me, I pray thee, with that same red *pottage*; for I am faint: therefore was his name called Edom. 31 And Jacob said, Sell me first thy birthright. 32 And Esau said, Behold, I am about to die: and what profit shall the birthright do to me? 33 And Jacob said, Swear to me first; and he sware unto him: and he sold his birthright unto Jacob. 34 And Jacob gave Esau bread and pottage of lentils; and he did eat and drink, and rose up, and went his way: so Esau despised his birthright.

14ii 25$^{24\text{-}26}$, perh. traces of E: We., CH., Gu., Ki., Pr., SB. (all . . . garment in v. 25).
14iii J: We., Di., Ku., Bu., Dr., Ka., Co., Se., Mi., St., Smend, et al. E: Gu., CH., Pr., Ki. vv. 29-34 E: SB.

14iv. ISAAC'S DECEPTION REGARDING REBEKAH IN GERAR. J13iv.

Gn. 26$^{1\text{-}33}$

26^1 And there was a famine in the land, besides the first famine that was in the days of Abraham. And Isaac went unto Abimelech king of the Philistines, unto Gerar. 2 And Jehovah appeared unto him, and said, Go not down into Egypt; dwell in the land which I shall tell thee of: 3 sojourn in this land, and I will be with thee, and will bless thee; for unto thee, and unto thy seed, I will give all these lands, and I will establish the oath which I sware unto Abraham thy father; 4 and I will multiply thy seed as the stars of heaven, and will give unto thy seed all these lands; and in thy seed shall all the nations of the earth be blessed; 5 because that Abraham obeyed my voice, and kept my charge, my commandments, my statutes, and my laws. 6 And Isaac dwelt in Gerar: 7 and the men of the place asked him of his wife; and he said, She is my sister: for he feared to say, My wife; lest, *said he,* the men of the place should kill me for Rebekah; because she was fair to look upon. 8 And it came to pass, when he had been there a long time, that Abimelech king of the Philistines looked out at a window, and saw, and, behold, Isaac was sporting with Rebekah his wife. 9 And Abimelech called Isaac, and said, Behold, of a surety she is thy wife: and how saidst thou, She is my sister? And Isaac said unto him, Because I said, Lest I die because of her. 10 And Abimelech said, What is this thou hast done unto us? one of the people might easily have lain with thy wife, and thou wouldest have brought guiltiness upon us. 11 And Abimelech charged all the people, saying, He that toucheth this man or his wife shall surely be put to death. 12 And Isaac sowed in that land, and found in the same year a hundredfold: and Jehovah blessed him. 13 And the man waxed great, and grew more and more until he became very great: 14 and he had possessions of flocks, and possessions of herds, and a great household: and the Philistines envied him. 15 Now all the wells which his father's servants had digged in the days of Abraham his father, the Philistines had stopped, and filled with earth. 16 And Abimelech said unto Isaac, Go from us; for thou art much mightier than we. 17 And Isaac departed thence, and encamped in the valley of Gerar, and dwelt there.

18 And Isaac digged again the wells of water, which they had digged in the days of Abraham his father; for the Philistines had stopped them after the death of Abraham: and he called their names after the names by which his father had called them. 19 And Isaac's servants digged

---

[14iv] 26^5: "the only clear case of Rd in Gn.," so all except 26$^{ab\text{-}5}$ E: Smend. vv. 15, 18 Rje.

in the valley, and found there a well of springing water. 20
And the herdsmen of Gerar strove with Isaac's herdsmen, saying, The water is ours: and he called the name of the well
Esek, because they contended with him. 21 And they digged
another well, and they strove for that also: and he called the
name of it Sitnah. 22 And he removed from thence, and digged
another well; and for that they strove not: and he called the
name of it Rehoboth; and he said, For now Jehovah hath made
room for us, and we shall be fruitful in the land.

23 And he went up from thence to Beer-sheba. 24 And Jehovah appeared unto him the same night, and said, I am the
God of Abraham thy father: fear not, for I am with thee, and
will bless thee, and multiply thy seed for my servant Abraham's
sake. 25 And he builded an altar there, and called upon the
name of Jehovah, and pitched his tent there: and there Isaac's
servants digged a well.

26 Then Abimelech went to him from Gerar, and Ahuzzath
his friend, and Phicol the captain of his host. 27 And Isaac
said unto them, Wherefore are ye come unto me, seeing ye
hate me, and have sent me away from you? 28 And they said,
We saw plainly that Jehovah was with thee: and we said, Let
there now be an oath betwixt us, even betwixt us and thee, and
let us make a covenant with thee, 29 that thou wilt do us no
hurt, as we have not touched thee, and as we have done unto
thee nothing but good, and have sent thee away in peace:
thou art now the blessed of Jehovah. 30 And he made them
a feast, and they did eat and drink. 31 And they rose up
betimes in the morning, and sware one to another: and Isaac
sent them away, and they departed from him in peace. 32 And
it came to pass the same day, that Isaac's servants came, and
told him concerning the well which they had digged, and said
unto him, We have found water. 33 And he called it Shibah:
therefore the name of the city is Beer-sheba unto this day.

14v. ISAAC DECEIVED BY REBEKAH AND JACOB WITH REFERENCE TO ESAU. E2.

Gn. 27[1a.2-10.14-15.17-18a.20.24-27.29*.30*.31-33a.35-36]

27[1a] And it came to pass, that when Isaac was old, and his
eyes were dim, so that he could not see, he called Esau his
elder son. 2 And he said, Behold now, I am old, I know not
the day of my death. 3 Now therefore take, I pray thee, thy
weapons, thy quiver and thy bow, and go out to the field, and
take me venison; 4 and make me savory food such as I love,

[14v] The analysis is difficult, and admittedly uncertain; many differences exist, and
Eerd. and Eichr. view analysis as impossible. Traces of E are found in parts of vv. 2-10,
14, 17-18a, 29, 31, 33a, 35-36 by Gu., CH., Pr., Co., St. Smend offers a new analysis with
J². SB. assigns to E. vv. 4a, 7-10, 14, 17-18a, 31a, 32, 35-36.

and bring it to me, that I may eat; that my soul may bless thee before I die.

5 And Rebekah heard when Isaac spake to Esau his son. And Esau went to the field to hunt for venison, and to bring it. 6 And Rebekah spake unto Jacob her son, saying, Behold, I heard thy father speak unto Esau thy brother, saying, 7 Bring me venison, and make me savory food, that I may eat, and bless thee before Jehovah before my death. 8 Now therefore, my son, obey my voice according to that which I command thee. 9 Go now to the flock, and fetch me from thence two good kids of the goats; and I will make them savory food for thy father, such as he loveth: 10 and thou shalt bring it to thy father, that he may eat, so that he may bless thee before his death.

14 And he went, and fetched, and brought them to his mother: and his mother made savory food, such as his father loved. 15 And Rebekah took the goodly garments of Esau her eldest son, which were with her in the house, and put them upon Jacob her younger son. 17 And she gave the savory food and the bread, which she had prepared, into the hand of her son Jacob. 18a And he came unto his father.

20 And Isaac said unto his son, How is it that thou hast found it so quickly, my son? And he said, Because Jehovah thy God sent me good speed. 24 And he said, Art thou my very son Esau? And he said, I am. 25 And he said, Bring it near to me, and I will eat of my son's venison, that my soul may bless thee. And he brought it near to him, and he did eat: and he brought him wine, and he drank. 26 And his father Isaac said unto him, Come near now, and kiss me, my son. 27 And he came near, and kissed him: and he smelled the smell of his raiment, and blessed him, and said,

See, the smell of my son
Is as the smell of a field which Jehovah hath blessed.
29 Let peoples serve thee,
And nations bow down to thee: . . .
Cursed be every one that curseth thee,
And blessed be every one that blesseth thee.

30 And it came to pass, as soon as Isaac had made an end of blessing Jacob, . . . that Esau his brother came in from his hunting. 31 And he also made savory food, and brought it unto his father; and he said unto his father, Let my father arise, and eat of his son's venison, that thy soul may bless me. 32 And Isaac his father said unto him, Who art thou? And he said, I am thy son, thy first-born, Esau. 33a And Isaac trembled very exceedingly, and said, Who then is he that hath taken venison, and brought it me?

35 And he said, Thy brother came with guile, and hath taken away thy blessing. 36 And he said, Is not he rightly named Jacob? for he hath supplanted me these two times: he took away my birthright; and, behold, now he hath taken away my blessing. And he said, hast thou not reserved a blessing for me?

14vi. ISAAC BLESSES ESAU. E2ii.
Gn. 27$^{37-38,40-45}$.

37 And Isaac answered and said unto Esau, Behold, I have made him thy lord, and all his brethren have I given to him for servants; and with grain and new wine have I sustained him: and what then shall I do for thee, my son? 38 And Esau said unto his father, Hast thou but one blessing, my father? bless me, even me also, O my father. And Esau lifted up his voice and wept.

40 And by thy sword shalt thou live, and thou shalt serve thy brother;
And it shall come to pass, when thou shalt break loose,
That thou shalt shake his yoke from off thy neck.

41 And Esau hated Jacob because of the blessing wherewith his father blessed him: and Esau said in his heart, The days of mourning for my father are at hand; then will I slay my brother Jacob. 42 And the words of Esau her elder son were told to Rebekah; and she sent and called Jacob her younger son, and said unto him, Behold, thy brother Esau, as touching thee, doth comfort himself, *purposing* to kill thee. 43 Now therefore, my son, obey my voice; and arise, flee thou to Laban my brother to Haran; 44 and tarry with him a few days, until thy brother's fury turn away; 45 until thy brother's anger turn away from thee, and he forget that which thou hast done to him: then will I send, and fetch thee from thence: why should I be bereaved of you both in one day?

15. THE STORY OF JACOB. E3. P10.

15i. JEHOVAH APPEARS TO JACOB AT BETHEL. E3i. P10iii.
Gn. 28$^{10.13-16.19}$.

10 And Jacob went out from Beer-sheba, and went toward Haran. 13 And, behold, Jehovah stood . . . and said, I am Jehovah, the God of Abraham thy father, and the God of Isaac: the land whereon thou liest, to thee will I give it, and

---
[14vi] Traces of E in vv. 37-38: Gu., CH., Pr., Sk., SB.; or in 41a, 42-43, 45: SB.; or in 45b: Co., CH., Ba. v. 40b is probably R: Ho., Gu., Ka., Se., Sk., SB.; in any case it is a prose allusion (in a poetical context) to Edom's revolt against Joram of Judah in 849, cf. 2K. 8$^{20-22}$. But v. 40 may be E: Gu., Mi., Ba., Smend, Ki., SB. (40a). SB. connects v. 40a with the conquest of Edom by David 2S. 8$^{13-14}$.
[15i] v. 10 E: We., Ku., Smend. vv. 13-16 R: Ku., Co., Ad., GFM. v. 14 R: Gu., Sk. In v. 13 after "stood," add, "beside him" (Am. Rev., margin).

to thy seed; 14 and thy seed shall be as the dust of the earth, and thou shalt spread abroad to the west, and to the east, and to the north, and to the south: and in thee and in thy seed shall all the families of the earth be blessed. 15 And, behold, I am with thee, and will keep thee whithersoever thou goest, and will bring thee again into this land; for I will not leave thee, until I have done that which I have spoken to thee of. 16 And Jacob awaked out of his sleep, and he said, Surely Jehovah is in this place; and I knew it not. 19 And he called the name of that place Beth-el: but the name of the city was Luz at the first.

15ii. JACOB MEETS RACHEL AND LABAN IN HARAN. E3ii. Gn. 29$^{2\text{-}14}$

2 And he looked, and, behold, a well in the field, and, lo, three flocks of sheep lying there by it; for out of that well they watered the flocks: and the stone upon the well's mouth was great. 3 And thither were all the flocks gathered: and they rolled the stone from the well's mouth, and watered the sheep, and put the stone again upon the well's mouth in its place. 4 And Jacob said unto them, My brethren, whence are ye? And they said, Of Haran are we. 5 And he said unto them, Know ye Laban the son of Nahor? And they said, We know him. 6 And he said unto them, Is it well with him? And they said, It is well: and, behold, Rachel his daughter cometh with the sheep. 7 And he said, Lo, it is yet high day, neither is it time that the cattle should be gathered together; water ye the sheep, and go and feed them. 8 And they said, We cannot, until all the flocks be gathered together, and they roll the stone from the well's mouth; then we water the sheep. 9 While he was yet speaking with them, Rachel came with her father's sheep; for she kept them. 10 And it came to pass, when Jacob saw Rachel the daughter of Laban his mother's brother, and the sheep of Laban his mother's brother, that Jacob went near, and rolled the stone from the well's mouth, and watered the flock of Laban his mother's brother. 11 And Jacob kissed Rachel, and lifted up his voice, and wept. 12 And Jacob told Rachel that he was her father's brother, and that he was Rebekah's son: and she ran and told her father.

13 And it came to pass, when Laban heard the tidings of Jacob his sister's son, that he ran to meet him, and embraced him, and kissed him, and brought him to his house. And he told Laban all these things. 14 And Laban said to him, Surely thou art my bone and my flesh. And he abode with him the space of a month.

15iii. JACOB MARRIES RACHEL AND LEAH. E3iii, v. P10i.
Gn. 29²⁶·³¹.

26 And Laban said, It is not so done in our place, to give the younger before the first-born. 31 And Jehovah saw that Leah was hated, and he opened her womb: but Rachel was barren.

15iv. BIRTH OF JACOB'S SONS. E3vi; P10iv.
Gn. 29³²⁻³⁵ 30³ᵇ⁻⁵·⁷·⁹⁻¹⁶·²⁰ᵇ⁻²¹·²⁴

32 And Leah conceived, and bare a son, and she called his name Reuben: for she said, Because Jehovah hath looked upon my affliction; for now my husband will love me. 33 And she conceived again, and bare a son: and said, Because Jehovah hath heard that I am hated, he hath therefore given me this *son* also: and she called his name, Simeon. 34 And she conceived again, and bare a son; and said, Now this time will my husband be joined unto me, because I have borne him three sons: therefore was his name called Levi. 35 And she conceived again, and bare a son: and she said, This time will I praise Jehovah: therefore she called his name Judah; and she left off bearing.

30³ᵇ And I also may obtain children by her. 4 And she gave him Bilhah her handmaid to wife: and Jacob went in unto her. 5 And Bilhah conceived and bare Jacob a son. 7 And Bilhah Rachel's handmaid conceived again, and bare Jacob a second son.

9 When Leah saw that she had left off bearing, she took Zilpah her handmaid, and gave her to Jacob to wife. 10 And Zilpah Leah's handmaid bare Jacob a son. 11 And Leah said, Fortunate! and she called his name Gad. 12 And Zilpah Leah's handmaid bare Jacob a second son. 13 And Leah said, Happy am I! for the daughters will call me happy: and she called his name Asher.

14 And Reuben went in the days of wheat harvest, and found mandrakes in the field, and brought them unto his mother Leah. Then Rachel said to Leah, Give me, I pray thee, of thy son's mandrakes. 15 And she said unto her, Is it a small matter that thou hast taken away my husband? and wouldest thou take away my son's mandrakes also? And Rachel said, Therefore he shall lie with thee to-night for thy son's mandrakes. 16 And Jacob came from the field in the evening, and Leah went out to meet him, and said, Thou must come in unto me; for I have surely hired thee with my son's mandrakes. And he lay with her that night.

---

¹⁵ⁱᵛ 30³ᵇ⁻⁵·⁷, uncertain. 30⁹ᵇ P: Dr.?, Co., Gu., Sk.; J: most critics, including SB.— The narrative is incomplete, due to omissions by Rje in combining with E; note that in 30³ᵇ Rachel speaks; in v. 20b, Leah; and v. 24, Rachel.

20b Now will my husband dwell with me, because I have borne him six sons: and she called his name Zebulun. 21 And afterwards she bare a daughter, and called her name Dinah.
24 And she called his name Joseph, saying, Jehovah add to me another son.

15v. Jacob Prepares to Leave Laban and Secures His Wages by a Trick. E3vii. P10ii.
Gn. 30$^{25.27.29\text{-}31.35\text{-}43}$ 31$^{1.3}$

25 And it came to pass, when Rachel had borne Joseph, that Jacob said unto Laban, Send me away, that I may go unto mine own place and to my country. 27 And Laban said unto him, If now I have found favor in thine eyes, *tarry*: *for* I have divined that Jehovah hath blessed me for thy sake. 29 And he said unto him, Thou knowest how I have served thee, and how thy cattle have fared with me. 30 For it was little which thou hadst before I came, and it hath increased unto a multitude; and Jehovah hath blessed thee whithersoever I turned: and now when shall I provide for mine own house also?

31 And he said, What shall I give thee? And Jacob said, Thou shalt not give me aught: if thou wilt do this thing for me, I will again feed thy flock and keep it.

35 And he removed that day the he-goats that were ringstreaked and spotted, and all the she-goats that were speckled and spotted, every one that had white in it, and all the black ones among the sheep, and gave them into the hand of his sons; 36 and he set three days' journey betwixt himself and Jacob: and Jacob fed the rest of Laban's flocks.

37 And Jacob took him rods of fresh poplar, and of the almond and of the plane-tree; and peeled white streaks in them, and made the white appear which was in the rods. 38 And he set the rods which he had peeled over against the flocks in the gutters in the watering-troughs where the flocks came to drink; and they conceived when they came to drink. 39 And the flocks conceived before the rods, and the flocks brought forth ringstreaked, speckled, and spotted. 40 And Jacob separated the lambs, and set the faces of the flocks toward the ringstreaked and all the black in the flock of Laban: and he put his own droves apart, and put them not unto Laban's flock. 41 And it came to pass, whensoever the stronger of the flock did conceive, that Jacob laid the rods before the eyes of the flock in the gutters, that they might conceive among the rods; 42 but when the flock were feeble, he put them not in: so the feebler were Laban's, and the stronger Jacob's. 43 And

the man increased exceedingly, and had large flocks, and maid-servants and men-servants, and camels and asses.

31¹ And he heard the words of Laban's sons, saying, Jacob hath taken away all that was our father's; and of that which was our father's hath he gotten all this glory.

3 And Jehovah said unto Jacob, Return unto the land of thy fathers, and to thy kindred; and I will be with thee.

15vi. LABAN FOLLOWS JACOB TO GALEED AND THEY MAKE A TREATY. E3viii.
Gn. 31^{25.27.46-53a}

25 And Laban came up with Jacob. Now Jacob had pitched his tent in the mountain: and Laban with his brethren encamped in the mountain of Gilead.

27 Wherefore didst thou flee secretly, and steal away from me, and didst not tell me, that I might have sent thee away with mirth and with songs, with tabret and with harp?

46 And Jacob said unto his brethren, Gather stones; and they took stones, and made a heap: and they did eat there by the heap. 47 And Laban called it Jegar-saha-dutha: but Jacob called it Galeed. 48 And Laban said, This heap is witness between me and thee this day. Therefore was the name of it called Galeed: 49 and Mizpah, for he said, Jehovah watch between me and thee, when we are absent one from another. 50 If thou shalt afflict my daughters, and if thou shalt take wives besides my daughters, no man is with us; see, God is witness betwixt me and thee.

51 And Laban said to Jacob, Behold this heap, and behold the pillar, which I have set betwixt me and thee. 52 This heap be witness and the pillar be witness, that I will not pass over this heap to thee, and that thou shalt not pass over this heap and this pillar unto me, for harm. 53a The God of Abraham, and the God of Nahor, the God of their father, judge betwixt us.

15vii. JACOB SUES FOR PEACE WITH ESAU. E3x.
Gn. 32^{3-13a}

3 And Jacob sent messengers before him to Esau his brother unto the land of Seir, the field of Edom. 4 And he commanded them, saying, Thus shall ye say unto my lord Esau: Thus saith thy servant Jacob, I have sojourned with Laban, and stayed until now: 5 and I have oxen, and asses, *and* flocks, and men-servants, and maid-servants: and I have sent to tell my lord,

---

^{15vi} Difficult and uncertain. v. 27, Laban speaks. v. 47 R: the two names mean "the heap of witness" in Aramaic and Hebrew, respectively (Am. Rev., margin). v. 49 R: CH., Ad., St., Mi., Gu. (49a); E: Gu., Ho., Sk., Smend. vv. 51-53a authorities divide— J: Ku., Co., Ka., Gu., Ho., Kent, Mi., Sk., SB.; E: We., Di., Ba., Dr., Ad., Pr., CH., St. In any case, the references to the pillar are not J (Sk.). There are other numerous traces of E found in 15vi by various scholars.

^{15vii} R: from 7b or 9 on, We., Co., Ba., Gu., Mi., St., Sk., Smend. vv. 9-12 J²: SB.

...32³²] J15v–ix 61

that I may find favor in thy sight. 6 And the messengers returned to Jacob, saying, We came to thy brother Esau, and moreover he cometh to meet thee, and four hundred men with him. 7 Then Jacob was greatly afraid and was distressed: and he divided the people that were with him, and the flocks, and the herds, and the camels, into two companies; 8 and he said, if Esau come to the one company, and smite it, then the company which is left shall escape. 9 And Jacob said, O God of my father Abraham, and God of my father Isaac, O Jehovah, who saidst unto me, Return unto thy country, and to thy kindred, and I will do thee good: 10 I am not worthy of the least of all the lovingkindnesses, and of all the truth, which thou hast showed unto thy servant; for with my staff I passed over this Jordan; and now I am become two companies. 11 Deliver me, I pray thee, from the hand of my brother, from the hand of Esau: for I fear him, lest he come and smite me, the mother with the children. 12 And thou saidst, I will surely do thee good, and make thy seed as the sand of the sea, which cannot be numbered for multitude.
13a And he lodged there that night.

15viii. JACOB CROSSES THE JABBOK. E3xi.
Gn. 32²²
22 And he rose up that night, and took his two wives, and his two handmaids, and his eleven children, and passed over the ford of the Jabbok.

15ix. JACOB WRESTLES WITH "A MAN" (GOD).
Gn. 32²⁴⁻³²
24 And Jacob was left alone; and there wrestled a man with him until the breaking of the day. 25 And when he saw that he prevailed not against him, he touched the hollow of his thigh; and the hollow of Jacob's thigh was strained, as he wrestled with him. 26 And he said, Let me go, for the day breaketh. And he said, I will not let thee go, except thou bless me. 27 And he said unto him, What is thy name? And he said, Jacob. 28 And he said, Thy name shall be called no more Jacob, but Israel: for thou hast striven with God and with men, and hast prevailed. 29 And Jacob asked him, and said, Tell me, I pray thee, thy name. And he said, Wherefore is it that thou dost ask after my name? And he blessed him there. 30 And Jacob called the name of the place Peniel: for, *said he*, I have seen God face to face, and my life is preserved. 31 And the sun rose upon him as he passed over Penuel, and he limped upon his thigh. 32 Therefore the children of Israel eat not the sinew of the hip which is upon the hollow of the

---
¹⁵ⁱˣ J (or JE) all, exc. Di., E. A few try to separate out an E narrative, vv. 26a, 27, 30-31; so Gu., Sk., Ka., Ho., Pr., E. Meyer (with slight differences). But the majority (and Eerd.) view it as unified. SB. assigns to E: vv. 24a, 25a, 26-28, 31-32a.

thigh, unto this day: because he touched the hollow of Jacob's thigh in the sinew of the hip.

15x. JACOB AND ESAU ARE RECONCILED. J15vii. E3xii. Gn. 33[1-5a.6-10a.11b-17]

33[1] And Jacob lifted up his eyes, and looked, and, behold, Esau was coming, and with him four hundred men. And he divided the children unto Leah, and unto Rachel, and unto the two handmaids. 2 And he put the handmaids and their children foremost, and Leah and her children after, and Rachel and Joseph hindermost. 3 And he himself passed over before them, and bowed himself to the ground seven times, until he came near to his brother. 4 And Esau ran to meet him, and embraced him, and fell on his neck, and kissed him: and they wept. 5 And he lifted up his eyes, and saw the women and the children; and said, Who are these with thee? 6 Then the handmaids came near, they and their children, and they bowed themselves. 7 And Leah also and her children came near, and bowed themselves: and after came Joseph near and Rachel, and they bowed themselves. 8 And he said, What meanest thou by all this company which I met? And he said, To find favor in the sight of my lord. 9 And Esau said, I have enough, my brother; let that which thou hast be thine. 10a And Jacob said, Nay, I pray thee, if now I have found favor in thy sight, then receive my present at my hand.

11b And he urged him, and he took it. 12 And he said, Let us take our journey, and let us go, and I will go before thee. 13 And he said unto him, My lord knoweth that the children are tender, and that the flocks and herds with me have their young: and if they overdrive them one day, all the flocks will die. 14 Let my lord, I pray thee, pass over before his servant: and I will lead on gently, according to the pace of the cattle that are before me and according to the pace of the children, until I come unto my lord unto Seir. 15 And Esau said, Let me now leave with thee some of the folk that are with me. And he said, What needeth it? let me find favor in the sight of my lord. 16 So Esau returned that day on his way unto Seir. 17 And Jacob journeyed to Succoth, and built him a house, and made booths for his cattle: therefore the name of the place is called Succoth.

15xi. THE OUTRAGE ON DINAH. J19 (Gn. 49[5-7]). E3xiv. Gn. 34[2b-3.5.7.11-12.14.19.25*-26.30-31]

2b And he took her, and lay with her, and humbled her.

[15xi] Agreement on the general result; differences in detail, esp. v. 25. Smend adds to J: vv. 13, 27-29 in part, and makes vv. 26, 30-31 E. Ki. also assigns v. 13 to J. In v. 14a J, read, "And they said unto him." The narrative is incomplete, and there is no indication as to "the thing" mentioned in v. 19.

3 And his soul clave unto Dinah the daughter of Jacob, and he loved the damsel, and spake kindly unto the damsel.
5 Now Jacob heard that he had defiled Dinah his daughter; and his sons were with his cattle in the field: and Jacob held his peace until they came. 7 And the sons of Jacob came in from the field when they heard it: and the men were grieved, and they were very wroth, because he had wrought folly in Israel in lying with Jacob's daughter; which thing ought not to be done.
11 And Shechem said unto her father and unto her brethren, Let me find favor in your eyes, and what ye shall say unto me I will give. 12 Ask me never so much dowry and gift, and I will give according as ye shall say unto me: but give me the damsel to wife.
14 And said unto them, We cannot do this thing, to give our sister to one that is uncircumcised; for that were a reproach unto us.
19 And the young man deferred not to do the thing, because he had delight in Jacob's daughter: and he was honored above all the house of his father.
25b Two of the sons of Jacob, Simeon and Levi, Dinah's brethren, took each man his sword. 26 And they slew Hamor and Shechem his son with the edge of the sword, and took Dinah out of Shechem's house, and went forth.
30 And Jacob said to Simeon and Levi, Ye have troubled me, to make me odious to the inhabitants of the land, among the Canaanites and the Perizzites: and, I being few in number, they will gather themselves together against me and smite me; and I shall be destroyed, I and my house. 31 And they said, Should he deal with our sister as with a harlot?

15xii. ISRAEL ENCAMPED BEYOND THE TOWER OF EDER: THE SIN OF REUBEN. J19 (Gn. 49⁴), 15xi, 17.

Gn. 35²¹⁻²²ᵃ

21 And Israel journeyed, and spread his tent beyond the tower of Eder. 22a And it came to pass, while Israel dwelt in that land, that Reuben went and lay with Bilhah his father's concubine: and Israel heard of it.

16. THE KINGS OF EDOM (ESAU). P11.

Gn. 36³¹⁻³⁹

31 And these are the kings that reigned in the land of Edom, before there reigned any king over the children of Israel.

---

[16] Generally ascribed to J (so SB.), but some doubt is expressed by We. (JE), Ku. (R), Ka., Co., Sk., St. (P). Whatever its source, the passage is ancient and trustworthy (E. Meyer, Gu.). Bela, v. 32, is probably the same name as Balaam J45 Nu. 24⁸⁻¹⁵.

32 And Bela the son of Beor reigned in Edom; and the name of his city was Dinhabah. 33 And Bela died, and Jobab the son of Zerah of Bozrah reigned in his stead. 34 And Jobab died, and Husham of the land of the Temanites reigned in his stead. 35 And Husham died, and Hadad the son of Bedad, who smote Midian in the field of Moab, reigned in his stead: and the name of his city was Avith. 36 And Hadad died, and Samlah of Masrekah reigned in his stead. 37 And Samlah died, and Shaul of Rehoboth by the River reigned in his stead. 38 And Shaul died, and Baal-hanan the son of Achbor reigned in his stead. 39 And Baal-hanan the son of Achbor died, and Hadar reigned in his stead: and the name of his city was Pau; and his wife's name was Mehetabel, the daughter of Matred, the daughter of Me-zahab.

Gn. $37^{3\ldots35}$, cf. J18. The order is changed here with a view to having the Joseph story printed consecutively.

17. JUDAH AND TAMAR THE CANAANITE.
Gn. 38^{1-30}

38^1 And it came to pass at that time, that Judah went down from his brethren, and turned in to a certain Adullamite, whose name was Hirah. 2 And Judah saw there a daughter of a certain Canaanite whose name was Shua; and he took her, and went in unto her. 3 And she conceived and bare a son; and he called his name Er. 4 And she conceived again, and bare a son; and she called his name Onan. 5 And she yet again bare a son, and called his name Shelah: and he was at Chezib, when she bare him. 6 And Judah took a wife for Er his first-born, and her name was Tamar. 7 And Er, Judah's first-born, was wicked in the sight of Jehovah; and Jehovah slew him. 8 And Judah said unto Onan, Go in unto thy brother's wife, and perform the duty of a husband's brother unto her, and raise up seed to thy brother. 9 And Onan knew that the seed would not be his; and it came to pass, when he went in unto his brother's wife, that he spilled it on the ground, lest he should give seed to his brother. 10 And the thing which he did was evil in the sight of Jehovah: and he slew him also. 11 Then said Judah to Tamar his daughter-in-law, Remain a widow in thy father's house, till Shelah my son be grown up; for he said, Lest he also die, like his brethren. And Tamar went and dwelt in her father's house.

12 And in the process of time Shua's daughter, the wife of

---
[17] Gn. 38, like Jg., presupposes a separation of the tribe of Judah from the other tribes (Smend). On Perez v. 29, cf. Ruth 4^{18}, 1 Ch. 2^{36}.

Judah, died; and Judah was comforted, and went up unto his sheep-shearers to Timnah, he and his friend Hirah the Adullamite. 13 And it was told Tamar, saying, Behold, thy father-in-law goeth up to Timnah to shear his sheep. 14 And she put off from her the garments of her widowhood, and covered herself with her veil, and wrapped herself, and sat in the gate of Enaim, which is by the way to Timnah; for she saw that Shelah was grown up, and she was not given unto him to wife. 15 When Judah saw her, he thought her to be a harlot; for she had covered her face. 16 And he turned unto her by the way, and said, Come, I pray thee, let me come in unto thee: for he knew not that she was his daughter-in-law. And she said, What wilt thou give me, that thou mayest come in unto me? 17 And he said, I will send thee a kid of the goats from the flock. And she said, Wilt thou give me a pledge, till thou send it? 18 And he said, What pledge shall I give thee? And she said, Thy signet and thy cord, and thy staff that is in thy hand. And he gave them to her, and came in unto her, and she conceived by him. 19 And she arose, and went away, and put off her veil from her, and put on the garments of her widowhood. 20 And Judah sent the kid of the goats by the hand of his friend the Adullamite, to receive the pledge from the woman's hand: but he found her not. 21 Then he asked the men of her place, saying, Where is the prostitute, that was at Enaim by the wayside? And they said, There hath been no prostitute here. 22 And he returned to Judah, and said, I have not found her; and also the men of the place said, There hath been no prostitute here. 23 And Judah said, Let her take it to her, lest we be put to shame: behold, I sent this kid, and thou hast not found her.

24 And it came to pass about three months after, that it was told Judah, saying, Tamar thy daughter-in-law hath played the harlot; and moreover, behold, she is with child by whoredom. And Judah said, Bring her forth, and let her be burnt. 25 When she was brought forth, she sent to her father-in-law, saying, By the man, whose these are, am I with child: and she said, Discern, I pray thee, whose are these, the signet, and the cords, and the staff. 26 And Judah acknowledged them, and said, She is more righteous than I, forasmuch as I gave her not to Shelah my son. And he knew her again no more. 27 And it came to pass in the time of her travail, that, behold, twins were in her womb. 28 And it came to pass, when she travailed, that one put out a hand: and the midwife took and bound upon his hand a scarlet thread, saying, This came out first. 29 And it came to pass, as he drew back his hand, that, behold, his brother came out: and she said, Wherefore hast thou made

a breach for thyself? therefore his name was called Perez. 30 And afterward came out his brother, that had the scarlet thread upon his hand: and his name was called Zerah.

18. THE STORY OF JOSEPH. E4. P12.

18i. JOSEPH SOLD TO THE ISHMAELITES. E4ii.
Gn. 37³⁻⁴·¹²⁻¹³ᵃᵇ·¹⁴ᶜ·¹⁸ᵇ·²¹·²³·²⁵⁻²⁷·²⁸ᵃ*·³²⁻³³·³⁵

3 Now Israel loved Joseph more than all his children, because he was the son of his old age: and he made him a coat of many colors. 4 And his brethren saw that their father loved him more than all his brethren; and they hated him, and could not speak peaceably unto him.

12 And his brethren went to feed their father's flock in Shechem. 13ab And Israel said unto Joseph, Are not thy brethren feeding the flock in Shechem? come, and I will send thee unto them. 14c So he sent him out of the vale of Hebron, and he came to Shechem.

18b And before he came near unto them, they conspired against him to slay him. 21 And Reuben heard it, and delivered him out of their hand, and said, Let us not take his life. 23 And it came to pass, when Joseph was come unto his brethren, that they stripped Joseph of his coat, the coat of many colors that was on him. 25 And they sat down to eat bread.

And they lifted up their eyes and looked, and, behold, a caravan of Ishmaelites was coming from Gilead, with their camels bearing spicery and balm and myrrh, going to carry it down to Egypt. 26 And Judah said unto his brethren, What profit is it if we slay our brother and conceal his blood? 27 Come, and let us sell him to the Ishmaelites, and let not our hand be upon him; for he is our brother, our flesh. And his brethren hearkened unto him, 28a* and sold Joseph to the Ishmaelites for twenty pieces of silver.

32 And they sent the coat of many colors, and they brought it to their father, and said, This have we found: know now whether it is thy son's coat or not. 33 And he knew it, and said, It is my son's coat; an evil beast hath devoured him; Joseph is without doubt torn in pieces. 35 And all his sons and all his daughters rose up to comfort him; but he refused to be comforted; and he said, For I will go down to Sheol to my son mourning. And his father wept for him.

Gn. 38¹⁻³⁰, cf. J17.

---

¹⁸ⁱ v. 21 "Reuben" is gloss by Rje, for original "Judah": Ka., Gu., Mi., Ba., Sk., Smend, et al. There are perhaps traces of E in v. 23 CH., Dr., Smend; in vv. 32b-33a Ba., CH., Gu.; in v. 35b Co., Gu., Pr., Sk., Smend, SB.

...39¹⁸]   J17–18ii   67

18ii. JOSEPH, THE SLAVE OF "AN EGYPTIAN," RESISTS THE
    TEMPTATION OF HIS MASTER'S WIFE.   E4iii.
    Gn. 39¹⁻⁴ᵃ·⁴ᶜᵈ⁻⁵·⁶ᵇ⁻¹⁹

39¹ And Joseph was brought down to Egypt; and Potiphar, an officer of Pharaoh's, the captain of the guard, an Egyptian, bought him of the hand of the Ishmaelites, that had brought him down thither. 2 And Jehovah was with Joseph, and he was a prosperous man; and he was in the house of his master the Egyptian. 3 And his master saw that Jehovah was with him, and that Jehovah made all that he did to prosper in his hand. 4acd And Joseph found favor in his sight: and he made him overseer over his house, and all that he had he put into his hand. 5 And it came to pass from the time that he made him overseer in his house, and over all that he had, that Jehovah blessed the Egyptian's house for Joseph's sake; and the blessing of Jehovah was upon all that he had, in the house and in the field.

6b And Joseph was comely, and well-favored. 7 And it came to pass after these things, that his master's wife cast her eyes upon Joseph; and she said, Lie with me. 8 But he refused, and said unto his master's wife, Behold, my master knoweth not what is with me in the house, and he hath put all that he hath into my hand: 9 he is not greater in this house than I; neither hath he kept back anything from me but thee, because thou art his wife: how then can I do this great wickedness, and sin against God? 10 And it came to pass, as she spake to Joseph day by day, that he hearkened not unto her, to lie by her, or to be with her. 11 And it came to pass about this time, that he went into the house to do his work; and there was none of the men of the house there within. 12 And she caught him by his garment, saying, Lie with me: and he left his garment in her hand, and fled, and got him out. 13 And it came to pass, when she saw that he had left his garment in her hand, and was fled forth, 14 that she called unto the men of her house, and spake unto them, saying, See, he hath brought in a Hebrew unto us to mock us: he came in unto me to lie with me, and I cried with a loud voice: 15 and it came to pass, when he heard that I lifted up my voice and cried, that he left his garment by me, and fled, and got him out. 16 And she laid up his garment by her, until his master came home. 17 And she spake unto him according to these words, saying, The Hebrew servant, whom thou hast brought unto us, came in unto me to mock me: 18 and it came to pass, as I lifted

---

¹⁸ⁱⁱ This story is remarkably similar to the ancient Egyptian tale, "The two Brothers." "There is no doubt of a connection" Ki., so Gu., Eerd., etc. For the text of the tale, see (in German), Gr. TB. 223-225; and (English) World's Best Literature, 5253ff, or Barton, Archæology and the Bible, 300-302.

up my voice and cried, that he left his garment by me, and fled out.

19 And it came to pass, when his master heard the words of his wife, which she spake unto him, saying, After this manner did thy servant to me; that his wrath was kindled.

18iii. JOSEPH IN PRISON (FRAGMENTARY ACCOUNT). E4iv.
Gn. 39²⁰⁻²³ 40^{1.3b.5.15b}

20 And Joseph's master took him, and put him into the prison, the place where the king's prisoners were bound: and he was there in the prison. 21 But Jehovah was with Joseph, and showed kindness unto him, and gave him favor in the sight of the keeper of the prison. 22 And the keeper of the prison committed to Joseph's hands all the prisoners that were in the prison; and whatsoever they did there, he was the doer of it. 23 The keeper of the prison looked not to anything that was under his hand, because Jehovah was with him; and that which he did, Jehovah made it to prosper.

40¹ And it came to pass after these things, that the butler of the king of Egypt and his baker offended their lord the king of Egypt . . . 3b into the prison, the place where Joseph was bound . . . 5b the butler and the baker of the king of Egypt, who were bound in the prison.

15b And here also have I done nothing that they should put me into the dungeon.

18iv. JOSEPH RELEASED FROM PRISON AND MADE RULER (FRAGMENTARY ACCOUNT). E4vi. P12ii.
Gn. 41^{14b.34-36.41.48}

14b And they brought him hastily out of the dungeon: and he shaved himself, and changed his raiment, and came in unto Pharaoh.

34 Let Pharaoh do *this*, and let him appoint overseers over the land, and take up the fifth part of the land of Egypt in the seven plenteous years. 35 And let them gather all the food of these good years that come, and lay up grain under the hand of Pharaoh for food in the cities, and let them keep it. 36 And the food shall be for a store against the seven years of famine, which shall be in the land of Egypt; that the land perish not through the famine.

41 And Pharaoh said unto Joseph, See, I have set thee over all the land of Egypt. 48 And he gathered up all the food

---

¹⁸ⁱⁱⁱ Rje has preserved only a few details from J's account of the imprisonment of Joseph. Note that Joseph is the speaker in 40^{15b}.
^{18iv} Joseph is the speaker in vv. 34-36. There is considerable difference as to the J vv. in this chapter, but the above analysis represents the consensus. vv. 34-36 J: Ba., Di., Co., Gu., Sk., Mi., St., Smend (35-36), CH. v. 41 J: same, and Pr., GFM., Ad., Ka. v. 48 J: Co., Ba., Gu., Sk., St., Mi., We., Smend. Others make these vv. E.

of the seven years which were in the land of Egypt, and laid up the food in the cities: the food of the field, which was round about every city, laid he up in the same.

18v. JOSEPH'S BROTHERS SEEK GRAIN IN EGYPT AND RETURN TO ISRAEL (FRAGMENTARY). E4viii.
Gn. 42²·⁴ᵇ⁻⁵·⁷*·²⁷⁻²⁸ᵃ·³⁸

2 And he said, Behold, I have heard that there is grain in Egypt: get you down thither, and buy for us from thence; that we may live, and not die; 4b . . . for he said, Lest peradventure harm befall him. 5 And the sons of Israel came to buy among those that came: for the famine was in the land of Egypt.
7 And Joseph saw his brethren, and he knew them, but made himself strange unto them . . . ; and he said unto them, Whence come ye? . . .
27 And as one of them opened his sack to give his ass provender in the lodging-place, he espied his money; and, behold, it was in the mouth of his sack. 28a And he said unto his brethren, My money is restored; and, lo, it is even in my sack: and their heart failed them, and they turned trembling one to another.
38 And he said, My son shall not go down with you; for his brother is dead, and he only is left: if harm befall him by the way in which ye go, then will ye bring down my gray hairs with sorrow to Sheol.

18vi. SECOND VISIT OF JOSEPH'S BROTHERS TO EGYPT. E4ix.
Gn. 43¹⁻¹³·¹⁵⁻²³ᵃ·²⁴⁻³⁴ 44¹⁻³⁴

43¹ And the famine was sore in the land. 2 And it came to pass, when they had eaten up the grain which they had brought out of Egypt, their father said unto them, Go again, buy us a little food. 3 And Judah spake unto him, saying, The man did solemnly protest unto us, saying, Ye shall not see my face, except your brother be with you. 4 If thou wilt send our brother with us, we will go down and buy thee food: 5 but if thou wilt not send him, we will not go down; for the man said unto us, Ye shall not see my face, except your brother be with you. 6 And Israel said, Wherefore dealt ye so ill with me, as to tell the man whether ye had yet a brother? 7 And they said, The man asked straitly concerning ourselves, and concerning our kindred, saying, Is your father yet alive? have

---

[18v] Israel (Jacob) is the speaker in v. 2. An account of the purchase of the grain is evidently omitted between 7 and 27. There is general agreement on the analysis (exc. vv. 2...7 E: Pr.). Even Eerd. admits that vv. 27-28 should be separated from their context. v. 38 is spoken by Israel after the return to Canaan; he refuses to permit Benjamin to leave him.

ye *another* brother? and we told him according to the tenor of these words: could we in any wise know that he would say, Bring your brother down? 8 And Judah said unto Israel his father, Send the lad with me, and we will arise and go; that we may live, and not die, both we, and thou, and also our little ones. 9 I will be surety for him; of my hand shalt thou require him: if I bring him not unto thee, and set him before thee, then let me bear the blame for ever: 10 for except we had lingered, surely we had now returned a second time. 11 And their father Israel said unto them, If it be so now, do this: take of the choice fruits of the land in your vessels, and carry down the man a present, a little balm, and a little honey, spicery and myrrh, nuts, and almonds; 12 and take double money in your hand; and the money that was returned in the mouth of your sacks carry again in your hand; peradventure it was an oversight: 13 take also your brother, and arise, go again unto the man. 15 And the men took that present, and they took double money in their hand, and Benjamin; and rose up, and went down to Egypt, and stood before Joseph.

16 And when Joseph saw Benjamin with them, he said to the steward of his house, Bring the men into the house, and slay, and make ready; for the men shall dine with me at noon. 17 And the man did as Joseph bade; and the man brought the men to Joseph's house. 18 And the men were afraid, because they were brought to Joseph's house; and they said, Because of the money that was returned in our sacks at the first time are we brought in; that he may seek occasion against us, and fall upon us, and take us for bondmen, and our asses. 19 And they came near to the steward of Joseph's house, and they spake unto him at the door of the house, 20 and said, Oh, my lord, we came indeed down at the first time to buy food: 21 and it came to pass, when we came to the lodging-place, that we opened our sacks, and, behold, every man's money was in the mouth of his sack, our money in full weight: and we have brought it again in our hand. 22 And other money have we brought down in our hand to buy food: we know not who put our money in our sacks. 23a And he said, Peace be to you, fear not: your God, and the God of your father, hath given you treasure in your sacks: I had your money. 24 And the man brought the men into Joseph's house, and gave them water, and they washed their feet; and he gave their asses provender. 25 And they made ready the present against Joseph's coming at noon: for they heard that they should eat bread there.

26 And when Joseph came home, they brought him the present which was in their hand into the house, and bowed

down themselves to him to the earth. 27 And he asked them of their welfare, and said, Is your father well, the old man of whom ye spake? Is he yet alive? 28 And they said, Thy servant our father is well, he is yet alive. And they bowed the head, and made obeisance. 29 And he lifted up his eyes, and saw Benjamin his brother, his mother's son, and said, Is this your youngest brother, of whom ye spake unto me? And he said, God be gracious unto thee, my son. 30 And Joseph made haste; for his heart yearned over his brother: and he sought where to weep; and he entered into his chamber, and wept there. 31 And he washed his face, and came out; and he refrained himself, and said, Set on bread. 32 And they set on for him by himself, and for them by themselves, and for the Egyptians, that did eat with him, by themselves: because the Egyptians might not eat bread with the Hebrews; for that is an abomination unto the Egyptians. 33 And they sat before him, the first-born according to his birthright, and the youngest according to his youth: and the men marvelled one with another. 34 And he took *and sent* messes unto them from before him: but Benjamin's mess was five times so much as any of theirs And they drank, and were merry with him.

44 And he commanded the steward of his house, saying, Fill the men's sacks with food, as much as they can carry, and put every man's money in his sack's mouth. 2 And put my cup, the silver cup, in the sack's mouth of the youngest, and his grain money. And he did according to the word that Joseph had spoken. 3 As soon as the morning was light, the men were sent away, they and their asses. 4 *And* when they were gone out of the city, and were not yet far off, Joseph said unto his steward, Up, follow after the men; and when thou dost overtake them, say unto them, Wherefore have ye rewarded evil for good? 5 Is not this that in which my lord drinketh, and whereby he indeed divineth? ye have done evil in so doing. 6 And he overtook them, and he spake unto them these words. 7 And they said unto him, Wherefore speaketh my lord such words as these? Far be it from thy servants that they should do such a thing. 8 Behold, the money, which we found in our sacks' mouths, we brought again unto thee out of the land of Canaan: how then should we steal out of thy lord's house silver or gold? 9 With whomsoever of thy servants it be found, let him die, and we also will be my lord's bondmen. 10 And he said, Now also let it be according unto your words: he with whom it is found shall be my bondman; and ye shall be blameless. 11 Then they hasted, and took down every man his sack to the ground, and opened every man his sack. 12 And he searched, *and* began at the eldest, and left off at the youngest: and the cup was found in Benjamin's sack. 13 Then they rent their clothes, and laded every man his ass, and returned to the city.

14 And Judah and his brethren came to Joseph's house; and he was yet there: and they fell before him on the ground. 15 And Joseph said unto them, What deed is this that ye have done? know ye not that such a man as I can indeed divine? 16 And Judah said, What shall we say unto my lord? what shall we speak? or how shall we clear ourselves? God hath found out the iniquity of thy servants: behold, we are my lord's bondmen, both we, and he also in whose hand the cup is found. 17 And he said, Far be it from me that I should do so: the man in whose hand the cup is found, he shall be my bondman; but as for you, get you up in peace unto your father.

18 Then Judah came near unto him, and said, Oh, my lord, let thy servant, I pray thee, speak a word in my lord's ears, and let not thine anger burn against thy servant; for thou art even as Pharaoh. 19 My lord asked his servants, saying, Have ye a father, or a brother? 20 And we said unto my lord, We have a father, an old man, and a child of his old age, a little one; and his brother is dead, and he alone is left of his mother; and his father loveth him. 21 And thou saidst unto thy servants, Bring him down unto me, that I may set mine eyes upon him. 22 And we said unto my lord, The lad cannot leave his father: for if he should leave his father, his father would die. 23 And thou saidst unto thy servants, Except your youngest brother come down with you, ye shall see my face no more. 24 And it came to pass when we came up unto thy servant my father, we told him the words of my lord. 25 And our father said, Go again, buy us a little food. 26 And we said, We cannot go down: if our youngest brother be with us, then will we go down; for we may not see the man's face, except our youngest brother be with us. 27 And thy servant my father said unto us, Ye know that my wife bare me two sons: 28 and the one went out from me, and I said, Surely he is torn in pieces; and I have not seen him since: 29 and if ye take this one also from me, and harm befall him, ye will bring down my gray hairs with sorrow to Sheol. 30 Now therefore when I come to thy servant my father, and the lad is not with us; seeing that his life is bound up in the lad's life; 31 it will come to pass, when he seeth that the lad is not *with us*, that he will die: and thy servants will bring down the gray hairs of thy servant our father with sorrow to Sheol. 32 For thy servant became surety for the lad unto my father, saying, If I bring him not unto thee, then shall I bear the blame to my father for ever. 33 Now therefore, let thy servant, I pray thee, abide instead of the lad

a bondman to my lord; and let the lad go up with his brethren.
34 For how shall I go up to my father, if the lad be not with
me? lest I see the evil that shall come on my father.

18vii. JOSEPH REVEALS HIMSELF TO HIS BROTHERS. E4ix.
Gn. 45$^{1a.4b-5a.10a.13-14.28}$

45^{1a} Then Joseph could not refrain himself before all them
that stood by him; and he cried, Cause every man to go out
from me. . . . 4b I am Joseph your brother, whom ye sold
into Egypt. 5a And now be not grieved, nor angry with
yourselves, that ye sold me hither. 10a And thou shalt dwell
in the land of Goshen. 13 And ye shall tell my father of all
my glory in Egypt, and of all that ye have seen: and ye shall
haste and bring down my father hither. 14 And he fell upon
his brother Benjamin's neck, and wept; and Benjamin wept
upon his neck.

28 And Israel said, It is enough; my son Joseph is yet alive:
I will go and see him before I die.

18viii. ISRAEL AND HIS SONS MOVE TO EGYPT. E4x, xi. P12iii.
Gn. 46$^{1a.28-34}$ 47$^{1-5a.6b}$

46^{1a} And Israel took his journey with all that he had, and
came to Beer-sheba. 28 And he sent Judah before him unto
Joseph, to show the way before him unto Goshen; and they
came into the land of Goshen.

29 And Joseph made ready his chariot, and went up to meet
Israel his father, to Goshen; and he presented himself unto
him, and fell on his neck, and wept on his neck a good while.
30 And Israel said unto Joseph, Now let me die, since I have
seen thy face, that thou art yet alive. 31 And Joseph said
unto his brethren, and unto his father's house, I will go up and
tell Pharaoh, and will say unto him, My brethren and my
father's house, who were in the land of Canaan, are come unto
me; 32 and the men are shepherds, for they have been keepers of cattle; and they have brought their flocks, and their
herds, and all that they have. 33 And it shall come to pass,
when Pharaoh shall call you, and shall say, What is your occupation? 34 that ye shall say, Thy servants have been keepers
of cattle from our youth even until now, both we, and our
fathers: that ye may dwell in the land of Goshen; for every
shepherd is an abomination unto the Egyptians.

47^1 Then Joseph went in and told Pharaoh, and said, My
father and my brethren, and their flocks, and their herds, and
all that they have, are come out of the land of Canaan; and,
behold, they are in the land of Goshen. 2 And from among
his brethren he took five men, and presented them unto Pha-

raoh. 3 And Pharaoh said unto his brethren, What is your occupation? And they said unto Pharaoh, Thy servants are shepherds, both we, and our fathers. 4 And they said unto Pharaoh, To sojourn in the land are we come; for there is no pasture for thy servants' flocks; for the famine is sore in the land of Canaan: now therefore, we pray thee, let thy servants dwell in the land of Goshen.

5a And Pharaoh spake unto Joseph, saying, 6b In the land of Goshen let them dwell: and if thou knowest any able man among them, then make them rulers over my cattle.

18ix. JOSEPH'S ADMINISTRATION IN FAMINE TIME. J18iv (Gn. 41^{34}). E4vii.

Gn. 47$^{13\text{-}26}$

13 And there was no bread in all the land; for the famine was very sore, so that the land of Egypt and the land of Canaan fainted by reason of the famine. 14 And Joseph gathered up all the money that was found in the land of Egypt, and in the land of Canaan, for the grain which they bought: and Joseph brought the money into Pharaoh's house. 15 And when the money was all spent in the land of Egypt, and in the land of Canaan, all the Egyptians came unto Joseph, and said, Give us bread: for why should we die in thy presence? for *our* money faileth. 16 And Joseph said, Give your cattle; and I will give you for your cattle, if money fail. 17 And they brought their cattle unto Joseph; and Joseph gave them bread in exchange for the horses, and for the flocks, and for the herds, and for the asses: and he fed them with bread in exchange for all their cattle for that year. 18 And when that year was ended, they came unto him the second year, and said unto him, We will not hide from my lord, how that our money is all spent; and the herds of cattle are my lord's; there is nought left in the sight of my lord, but our bodies, and our lands: 19 Wherefore should we die before thine eyes, both we and our land? buy us and our land for bread, and we and our land will be servants unto Pharaoh: and give us seed, that we may live, and not die, and that the land be not desolate.

20 So Joseph bought all the land of Egypt for Pharaoh; for the Egyptians sold every man his field, because the famine was sore upon them: and the land became Pharaoh's. 21 And as for the people, he removed them to the cities from one end of the border of Egypt even to the other end thereof. 22 Only the land of the priests bought he not: for the priests had a

---

$^{18\text{viii}}$ 47^{5} in LXX combines vv. 5a and 6b as above, thus confirming the critical analysis.

$^{18\text{ix}}$ All agree that the passage is out of its proper context, and is confused. Rje: Ki. SB. finds E in vv. 13b, 14a, 15a, 20b, 26b.

portion from Pharaoh, and did eat their portion which Pharaoh gave them; wherefore they sold not their land. 23 Then Joseph said unto the people, Behold, I have bought you this day and your land for Pharaoh: lo, here is seed for you, and ye shall sow the land. 24 And it shall come to pass at the ingatherings, that ye shall give a fifth unto Pharaoh, and four parts shall be your own, for seed of the field, and for your food, and for them of your households, and for food for your little ones. 25 And they said, Thou hast saved our lives: let us find favor in the sight of my lord, and we will be Pharaoh's servants. 26 And Joseph made it a statute concerning the land of Egypt unto this day, that Pharaoh should have the fifth; only the land of the priests alone became not Pharaoh's.

19. THE BLESSING OF JACOB. E5, 51. P13.
    Gn. 47$^{27a.29-31}$ 48$^{2b.9b-10a.13-14.17-19}$ 49^{1b-28a}

Introductory Note—The blessing in 49^{1b-28a} is generally recognized as one of the most ancient pieces of Hebrew poetry in the OT. Its parts were probably not all written at the same time (although Co., 1912, views it as a unity on metrical grounds). All agree that some of the blessings (Dan, Gad, Benjamin, Joseph?) date from the period of the Judges; others (Judah) from the time of David or Solomon. It assumed its present form either (a) in the period of the Judges (except for very brief additions: Se., Gr., Ki.), or (b) in the United Kingdom (Co., Mi., CH., Dr., Sk., St.), or (c) in the reign of Ahab (We., Ku., Ad., Stade, Ka.). The question as to date turns largely on 49$^{22-26}$; some hold that it presupposes the Divided Kingdom (Ba., We., Smend, and Ka., who says that it is almost universally assigned to the period of struggle between Ephraim and the Aramæans of Damascus in the ninth century); but many date it in the period of the Judges or the United Kingdom (Se., St. 22-24a, Mi., Gr., Co., Dr., Sk., et al.). All agree that Gn. 49 is older than Dt. 33, which it resembles (E49, q. v.).

Se. suggests that the twelve blessings may be connected with the Babylonian zodiac schema.

27a And Israel dwelt in the land of Egypt, in the land of Goshen.

29 And the time drew near that Israel must die: and he called his son Joseph, and said unto him, If now I have found favor in thy sight, put, I pray thee, thy hand under my thigh, and deal kindly and truly with me: bury me not, I pray thee, in Egypt; 30 but when I sleep with my fathers, thou shalt carry me out of Egypt, and bury me in their burying-place.

And he said, I will do as thou hast said. 31 And he said, Swear unto me: and he sware unto him. And Israel bowed himself upon the bed's head.

48 2b And Israel strengthened himself, and sat upon the bed. 9b And he said, Bring them, I pray thee, unto me, and I will bless them. 10a Now the eyes of Israel were dim for age, so that he could not see. 13 And Joseph took them both, Ephraim in his right hand toward Israel's left hand, and Manasseh in his left hand toward Israel's right hand, and brought them near unto him. 14 And Israel stretched out his right hand, and laid it upon Ephraim's head, who was the younger, and his left hand upon Manasseh's head, guiding his hands wittingly; for Manasseh was the first-born.

17 And when Joseph saw that his father laid his right hand upon the head of Ephraim, it displeased him; and he held up his father's hand, to remove it from Ephraim's head unto Manasseh's head. 18 And Joseph said unto his father, Not so, my father; for this is the first-born; put thy right hand upon his head. 19 And his father refused, and said, I know *it*, my son, I know *it*; he also shall become a people, and he also shall be great: howbeit his younger brother shall be greater than he, and his seed shall become a multitude of nations.

49 1b Gather yourselves together, that I may tell you that which shall befall you in the latter days.

2 Assemble yourselves, and hear, ye sons of Jacob;
   And hearken unto Israel your father.
3   Reuben, thou art my first-born, my might, and the beginning of my strength;
   The pre-eminence of dignity, and the pre-eminence of power.
4 Boiling over as water, thou shalt not have the pre-eminence;
   Because thou wentest up to thy father's bed;
   Then defiledst thou it: he went up to my couch.
5   Simeon and Levi are brethren;
   Weapons of violence are their swords.
6 O my soul, come not thou into their council;
   Unto their assembly, my glory, be not thou united;
   For in their anger they slew a man,
   And in their self-will they hocked an ox.

---

19 49⁴ refers to J15xii. 49¹⁰: the text is corrupt, translation uncertain, exegesis doubtful; it is, however, surely Messianic, and is regarded as genuine by Pr., Gu., Se., Gr., Sk., St., SB., Co. (10b gloss): as redactional, by We., Stade, Di., Dr., Ho. vv. 11-12 are regarded as "eschatological-Messianic" by Gr., Gu., Se. Cf. 49²⁵⁻²⁶ with Dt. 33¹³⁻¹⁶, from which this may be taken, CH., Co., Ka., St. v. 26 "that was separate from": read, as in Am. Rev., margin, "that is prince among." "Prince" means probably "the consecrated one" rather than "the crowned one"—and so may refer to the Nazirite vow rather than to political conditions, Se., Gu., Mi., Co.?

7 Cursed be their anger, for it was fierce;
  And their wrath, for it was cruel:
  I will divide them in Jacob,
  And scatter them in Israel.
8   Judah, thee shall thy brethren praise:
  Thy hand shall be on the neck of thine enemies;
  Thy father's sons shall bow down before thee.
9 Judah is a lion's whelp;
  From the prey, my son, thou art gone up:
  He stooped down, he couched as a lion,
  And as a lioness; who shall rouse him up?
10 The sceptre shall not depart from Judah,
  Nor the ruler's staff from between his feet,
  Until Shiloh come;
  And unto him shall the obedience of the peoples be.
11 Binding his foal unto the vine,
  And his ass's colt unto the choice vine;
  He hath washed his garments in wine,
  And his vesture in the blood of grapes:
12 His eyes shall be red with wine,
  And his teeth white with milk.
13   Zebulun shall dwell at the haven of the sea;
  And he shall be for a haven of ships;
  And his border shall be upon Sidon.
14   Issachar is a strong ass,
  Couching down between the sheepfolds:
15 And he saw a resting-place that it was good,
  And the land that it was pleasant;
  And he bowed his shoulder to bear,
  And became a servant under task-work.
16   Dan shall judge his people,
  As one of the tribes of Israel.
17 Dan shall be a serpent in the way,
  An adder in the path,
  That biteth the horse's heels,
  So that his rider falleth backward.
18 I have waited for thy salvation, O Jehovah.
19   Gad, a troop shall press upon him;
  But he shall press upon their heel.
20   Out of Asher his bread shall be fat,
  And he shall yield royal dainties.
21   Naphtali is a hind let loose:
  He giveth goodly words.
22   Joseph is a fruitful bough,
  A fruitful bough by a fountain;
  His branches run over the wall.

23 The archers have sorely grieved him,
   And shot at him, and persecuted him:
24 But his bow abode in strength,
   And the arms of his hands were made strong,
   By the hands of the Mighty One of Jacob
   (From thence is the shepherd, the stone of Israel),
25 Even by the God of thy father, who shall help thee.
   And by the Almighty, who shall bless thee,
   With blessings of heaven above,
   Blessings of the deep that coucheth beneath,
   Blessings of the breasts, and of the womb.
26 The blessings of thy father
   Have prevailed above the blessings of my progenitors
   Unto the utmost bound of the everlasting hills:
   They shall be on the head of Joseph,
   And on the crown of the head of him that was separate from
      his brethren.
27   Benjamin is a wolf that raveneth:
   In the morning he shall devour the prey,
   And at even he shall divide the spoil.
28 All these are the twelve tribes of Israel: and this is it that their father spake unto them and blessed them.

20. THE DEATH AND BURIAL OF JACOB. E6. P14.
   Gn. 49^{33a*} 50$^{1-11.14}$

33a* He gathered up his feet into his bed. 50^1 And Joseph fell upon his father's face, and wept upon him, and kissed him. 2 And Joseph commanded his servants the physicians to embalm his father: and the physicians embalmed Israel. 3 And forty days were fulfilled for him; for so are fulfilled the days of embalming: and the Egyptians wept for him threescore and ten days.
   4 And when the days of weeping for him were past, Joseph spake unto the house of Pharaoh, saying, If now I have found favor in your eyes, speak, I pray you, in the ears of Pharaoh, saying, 5 My father made me swear, saying, Lo, I die: in my grave which I have digged for me in the land of Canaan, there shalt thou bury me. Now therefore let me go up, I pray thee, and bury my father, and I will come again. 6 And Pharaoh said, Go up, and bury thy father, according as he made thee swear.
   7 And Joseph went up to bury his father; and with him went up all the servants of Pharaoh, the elders of his house, and all the elders of the land of Egypt, 8 and all the house of Joseph, and his brethren, and his father's house: only their little ones, and their flocks, and their herds, they left in the land of Goshen.

[20] Uncertain traces of E in 50$^{1-4a.7b.9-10a}$, Co., Gu., Pr., Smend, SB. (2a, 3a, 9, 10b-11).

9 And there went up with him both chariots and horsemen: and it was a very great company. 10 And they came to the threshing-floor of Atad, which is beyond the Jordan, and there they lamented with a very great and sore lamentation: and he made a mourning for his father seven days. 11 And when the inhabitants of the land, the Canaanites, saw the mourning in the floor of Atad, they said, This is a grievous mourning to the Egyptians: wherefore the name of it was called Abel-Mizraim, which is beyond the Jordan.

14 And Joseph returned into Egypt, he, and his brethren, and all that went up with him to bury his father, after he had buried his father

21. THE DEATH OF JOSEPH. E6.

Ex. 1^6

6 And Joseph died, and all his brethren, and all that generation.

22. THE ISRAELITES OPPRESSED BY PHARAOH.

Ex. 1$^{8-12.20b}$

8 Now there arose a new king over Egypt, who knew not Joseph. 9 And he said unto his people, Behold, the people of the children of Israel are more and mightier than we: 10 come, let us deal wisely with them, lest they multiply, and it come to pass, that, when there falleth out any war, they also join themselves unto our enemies, and fight against us, and get them up out of the land. 11 Therefore they did set over them taskmasters to afflict them with their burdens. And they built for Pharaoh store-cities, Pithom and Raamses. 12 But the more they afflicted them, the more they multiplied and the more they spread abroad. And they were grieved because of the children of Israel. 20b And the people multiplied, and waxed very mighty.

23. MOSES MURDERS AN EGYPTIAN.

Ex. 2$^{11-14}$

11 And it came to pass in those days, when Moses was grown up, that he went out unto his brethren, and looked on their burdens: and he saw an Egyptian smiting a Hebrew, one of his brethren. 12 And he looked this way and that way, and when he saw that there was no man, he smote the Egyptian, and hid him in the sand.

---

[22] vv. 8-10 E: Ku., Di., Ad. only. But vv. 9-10 are stylistically similar to Gn. 11$^{6-7}$ J. vv. 11-12 J: Dr., Ho., Se., CH., Ba., GFM., McN., Smend, SB., et al. E: We., Co., Gr., Pr., Bä., St., Ki., et al. v. 20b om. Targums, Sam. Pent.; R: Ho; E: SB. (after v. 17).
[23] J: We., Co., CH., Gr., Se., Bä., Ki., Pr., Meyer, St.?, McN., Smend; E: Di., Ba., Ho., Dr., GFM., St.?, SB.

13 And he went out on the second day, and, behold, two men of the Hebrews were striving together: and he said to him that did the wrong, Wherefore smitest thou thy fellow? 14 And he said, Who made thee a prince and a judge over us? thinkest thou to kill me, as thou killedst the Egyptian? And Moses feared, and said, Surely the thing is known.

24. MOSES IN THE LAND OF MIDIAN. E11. Vs. P69, 77.

24i. HIS FLIGHT.
Ex. 2^{15}
15 Now when Pharaoh heard this thing, he sought to slay Moses. But Moses fled from the face of Pharaoh, and dwelt in the land of Midian: and he sat down by a well.

24ii. MOSES MARRIES ZIPPORAH, DAUGHTER OF REUEL, PRIEST OF MIDIAN. E11i.
Ex. 2$^{16-22}$
16 Now the priest of Midian had seven daughters: and they came and drew water, and filled the troughs to water their father's flock. 17 And the shepherds came and drove them away; but Moses stood up and helped them, and watered their flock. 18 And when they came to Reuel their father, he said, How is it that ye are come so soon to-day? 19 And they said, An Egyptian delivered us out of the hand of the shepherds, and moreover he drew water for us, and watered the flock. 20 And he said unto his daughters, And where is he? why is it that ye have left the man? call him, that he may eat bread. 21 And Moses was content to dwell with the man: and he gave Moses Zipporah his daughter. 22 And she bare a son, and he called his name Gershom; for he said, I have been a sojourner in a foreign land.

24iii. MOSES COMMISSIONED TO FREE THE HEBREWS: THE BURNING BUSH. E11ii, iv. P18.
Ex. 2^{23a} 3$^{2-4a.5.7-8.16-18}$ 4$^{1-16.19-20a.22-23}$

2^{23a} And it came to pass in the course of those many days, that the king of Egypt died.

3^{2} And the angel of Jehovah appeared unto him in a flame of fire out of the midst of a bush: and he looked, and, behold, the bush burned with fire, and the bush was not consumed. 3 And Moses said, I will turn aside now, and see this great sight, why the bush is not burnt. 4 And when Jehovah saw that he turned aside to see. 5 And he said, Draw not nigh

---

[24iii] The lists of Canaanitic nations (3^{8b,17} and often in J and E) have generally been regarded as Rd since We. and E. Meyer (1881); but Smend holds that they are original here and frequently in J^{2} and E.

hither: put off thy shoes from off thy feet, for the place whereon thou standest is holy ground.

7 And Jehovah said, I have surely seen the affliction of my people that are in Egypt, and have heard their cry by reason of their taskmasters; for I know their sorrows; 8 and I am come down to deliver them out of the hand of the Egyptians, and to bring them up out of that land unto a good land and a large, unto a land flowing with milk and honey; unto the place of the Canaanite, and the Hittite, and the Amorite, and the Perizzite, and the Hivite, and the Jebusite. 16 Go, and gather the elders of Israel together, and say unto them, Jehovah, the God of your fathers, the God of Abraham, of Isaac, and of Jacob, hath appeared unto me, saying, I have surely visited you, and *seen* that which is done to you in Egypt: 17 and I have said, I will bring you up out of the affliction of Egypt unto the land of the Canaanite, and the Hittite, and the Amorite, and the Perizzite, and the Hivite, and the Jebusite, unto a land flowing with milk and honey. 18 And they shall hearken to thy voice: and thou shalt come, thou and the elders of Israel, unto the king of Egypt, and ye shall say unto him, Jehovah, the God of the Hebrews, hath met with us: and now let us go, we pray thee, three days' journey into the wilderness, that we may sacrifice to Jehovah our God.

4^1 And Moses answered and said, But, behold, they will not believe me, nor hearken unto my voice; for they will say, Jehovah hath not appeared unto thee.

2 And Jehovah said unto him, What is that in thy hand? And he said, A rod. 3 And he said, Cast it on the ground. And he cast it on the ground, and it became a serpent; and Moses fled from before it.

4 And Jehovah said unto Moses, Put forth thy hand, and take it by the tail (and he put forth his hand, and laid hold of it, and it became a rod in his hand); 5 that they may believe that Jehovah, the God of their fathers, the God of Abraham, the God of Isaac, and the God of Jacob, hath appeared unto thee.

6 And Jehovah said furthermore unto him, Put now thy hand into thy bosom. And he put his hand into his bosom: and when he took it out, behold, his hand was leprous, as *white as* snow. 7 And he said, Put thy hand into thy bosom again. (And he put his hand into his bosom again; and when he took it out of his bosom, behold, it was turned again as his *other* flesh). 8 And it shall come to pass, if they will not believe thee, neither hearken to the voice of the first sign, that they will believe the voice of the latter sign. 9 And it shall come to pass, if they will not believe even these two signs, neither hearken unto thy voice, that thou shalt take of the

water of the river, and pour it upon the dry land: and the water which thou takest out of the river shall become blood upon the dry land.

10 And Moses said unto Jehovah, Oh, Lord, I am not eloquent, neither heretofore, nor since thou hast spoken unto thy servant; for I am slow of speech, and of a slow tongue. 11 And Jehovah said unto him, Who hath made man's mouth? or who maketh *a man* dumb, or deaf, or seeing, or blind? is it not I, Jehovah? 12 Now therefore go, and I will be with thy mouth, and teach thee what thou shalt speak.

13 And he said, Oh, Lord, send, I pray thee, by the hand of him whom thou wilt send. 14 And the anger of Jehovah was kindled against Moses, and he said, Is there not Aaron thy brother the Levite? I know that he can speak well. And also, behold, he cometh forth to meet thee: and when he seeth thee, he will be glad in his heart. 15 And thou shalt speak unto him, and put the words in his mouth: and I will be with thy mouth, and with his mouth, and will teach you what ye shall do. 16 And he shall be thy spokesman unto the people; and it shall come to pass, that he shall be to thee a mouth, and thou shalt be to him as God.

19 And Jehovah said unto Moses in Midian, Go, return into Egypt; for all the men are dead that sought thy life. 20a And Moses took his wife and his sons, and set them upon an ass, and he returned to the land of Egypt.

22 And thou shalt say unto Pharaoh, Thus saith Jehovah, Israel is my son, my first-born: 23 and I have said unto thee, Let my son go, that he may serve me; and thou hast refused to let him go: behold, I will slay thy son, thy first-born.

25. THE INSTITUTION OF CIRCUMCISION. E54.

Ex. $4^{24\text{-}26}$

24 And it came to pass on the way at the lodging-place, that Jehovah met him, and sought to kill him. 25 Then Zipporah took a flint, and cut off the foreskin of her son, and cast it at his feet; and she said, Surely a bridegroom of blood art thou to me. 26 So he let him alone. Then she said, A bridegroom of blood *art thou*, because of the circumcision.

26. MOSES IN EGYPT.

26i. APPEAL TO PHARAOH: BRICKS WITHOUT STRAW; MOSES'S PRAYER ANSWERED. E13i; P20, 22.

Ex. $4^{29\text{-}31}\ 5^{3.5\text{-}23}\ 6^1$

4^{29} And Moses and Aaron went and gathered together all the

---

[25] "One of the oldest sections in the Hexateuch" Addis et al.
[26i] $4^{29\text{-}31}$ entire R: Ho., GFM., et al. 5^3 E: Pr. Traces of E in $5^{4\text{-}21}$: Pr., Gr., Bä., Ho., Smend.—Almost all critics agree that Aaron was probably unknown to the oldest J tradition. Aaron in a J context is superfluous, and R; in Dt. he is mentioned only 9^{20}, 10^6, 32^{50}; and in the prophets only Micah 6^4 (We., Gr., Ad., McN., Ho., White in HBD., SB., et al.).

elders of the children of Israel: 30 and Aaron spake all the words which Jehovah had spoken unto Moses, and did the signs in the sight of the people. 31 And the people believed: and when they heard that Jehovah had visited the children of Israel, and that he had seen their affliction, then they bowed their heads and worshipped.

5³ And they said, The God of the Hebrews hath met with us: let us go, we pray thee, three days' journey into the wilderness, and sacrifice unto Jehovah our God, lest he fall upon us with pestilence or with the sword.

5 And Pharaoh said, Behold, the people of the land are now many, and ye make them rest from their burdens. 6 And the same day Pharaoh commanded the taskmasters of the people, and their officers, saying, 7 Ye shall no more give the people straw to make brick, as heretofore: let them go and gather straw for themselves. 8 And the number of the bricks, which they did make heretofore, ye shall lay upon them; ye shall not diminish aught thereof: for they are idle; therefore they cry, saying, Let us go and sacrifice to our God. 9 Let heavier work be laid upon the men, that they may labor therein; and let them not regard lying words.

10 And the taskmasters of the people went out, and their officers, and they spake to the people, saying, Thus saith Pharaoh, I will not give you straw. 11 Go yourselves, get you straw where ye can find it; for nought of your work shall be diminished. 12 So the people were scattered abroad throughout all the land of Egypt to gather stubble for straw. 13 And the taskmasters were urgent, saying, Fulfil your works, *your* daily tasks, as when there was straw. 14 And the officers of the children of Israel, whom Pharaoh's taskmasters had set over them, were beaten, and demanded, Wherefore have ye not fulfilled your task both yesterday and to-day, in making brick as heretofore?

15 Then the officers of the children of Israel came and cried unto Pharaoh, saying, Wherefore dealest thou thus with thy servants? 16 There is no straw given unto thy servants, and they say to us, Make brick: and, behold, thy servants are beaten; but the fault is in thine own people. 17 But he said, Ye are idle, ye are idle: therefore ye say, Let us go and sacrifice to Jehovah. 18 Go therefore now, and work; for there shall no straw be given you, yet shall ye deliver the number of bricks. 19 And the officers of the children of Israel did see that they were in evil case, when it was said, Ye shall not diminish aught from your bricks, *your* daily tasks. 20 And they met Moses and Aaron, who stood in the way, as they came forth from Pharaoh: 21 and they said unto them, Jehovah look upon you, and judge; because ye have made our savor to be ab-

horred in the eyes of Pharaoh, and in the eyes of his servants, to put a sword in their hand to slay us.

22 And Moses returned unto Jehovah, and said, Lord, wherefore hast thou dealt ill with this people? why is it that thou hast sent me? 23 For since I came to Pharaoh to speak in thy name, he hath dealt ill with this people; neither hast thou delivered thy people at all.

6^1 And Jehovah said unto Moses, Now shalt thou see what I will do to Pharaoh: for by a strong hand shall he let them go, and by a strong hand shall he drive them out of his land.

26ii. THE FIRST PLAGUE: NILE BECOMES FOUL. E13ii. P23i. Ex. 7$^{14-15a.16-17a.18.21a.24-25}$

14 And Jehovah said unto Moses, Pharaoh's heart is stubborn, he refuseth to let the people go. 15a Get thee unto Pharaoh in the morning; lo, he goeth out unto the water. 16 And thou shalt say unto him, Jehovah, the God of the Hebrews, hath sent me unto thee, saying, Let my people go, that they may serve me in the wilderness: and, behold, hitherto thou hast not hearkened. 17a Thus saith Jehovah, In this shalt thou know that I am Jehovah. 18 And the fish that are in the river shall die, and the river shall become foul; and the Egyptians shall loathe to drink water from the river.

21a And the fish that were in the river died; and the river became foul, and the Egyptians could not drink water from the river. 24 And all the Egyptians digged round about the river for water to drink; for they could not drink of the water of the river. 25 And seven days were fulfilled, after that Jehovah had smitten the river.

26iii. THE SECOND PLAGUE: FROGS. P23ii. Ex. 8$^{1-4.8-15a}$

1 And Jehovah spake unto Moses, Go in unto Pharaoh, and say unto him, Thus saith Jehovah, Let my people go, that they may serve me. 2 And if thou refuse to let them go, behold, I will smite all thy borders with frogs: 3 and the river shall swarm with frogs, which shall go up and come into thy house, and into thy bedchamber, and upon thy bed, and into the house of thy servants, and upon thy people, and into thine ovens, and into thy kneading-troughs: 4 and the frogs shall come up both upon thee, and upon thy people, and upon all thy servants.

8 Then Pharaoh called for Moses and Aaron, and said, Entreat

26ii 7^{17a} R: "many critics" Dr.; so Ho., Kent. But J: McN., Gr., Smend, et al.
26iii v. 10b Rd or Rje. In v. 15a, J's word for "hardened" means "made heavy" (Am. Rev., margin). E's word, e.g., 10^{27}, means "to make strong"; P's, e. g., 7^{22}, means "to be strong." The translation in the text obscures these differences.

Jehovah, that he take away the frogs from me, and from my people; and I will let the people go, that they may sacrifice unto Jehovah. 9 And Moses said unto Pharaoh, Have thou this glory over me: against what time shall I entreat for thee, and for thy servants, and for thy people, that the frogs be destroyed from thee and thy houses, and remain in the river only? 10 And he said, Against to-morrow. And he said, Be it according to thy word; that thou mayest know that there is none like unto Jehovah our God. 11 And the frogs shall depart from thee, and from thy houses, and from thy servants, and from thy people; they shall remain in the river only. 12 And Moses and Aaron went out from Pharaoh: and Moses cried unto Jehovah concerning the frogs which he had brought upon Pharaoh. 13 And Jehovah did according to the word of Moses; and the frogs died out of the houses, out of the courts, and out of the fields. 14 And they gathered them together in heaps; and the land stank. 15 But when Pharaoh saw that there was respite, he hardened his heart.

26iv. THE THIRD PLAGUE: FLIES. (J only).

Ex. 8^{20-32}

20 And Jehovah said unto Moses, Rise up early in the morning, and stand before Pharaoh; lo, he cometh forth to the water; and say unto him, Thus saith Jehovah, Let my people go, that they may serve me. 21 Else, if thou wilt not let my people go, behold, I will send swarms of flies upon thee, and upon thy servants, and upon thy people, and into thy houses: and the houses of the Egyptians shall be full of swarms of flies, and also the ground whereon they are. 22 And I will set apart in that day the land of Goshen, in which my people dwell, that no swarms of flies shall be there; to the end thou mayest know that I am Jehovah in the midst of the earth. 23 And I will put a division between my people and thy people: by to-morrow shall this sign be. 24 And Jehovah did so; and there came grievous swarms of flies into the house of Pharaoh, and into his servants' houses: and in all the land of Egypt the land was corrupted by reason of the swarms of flies.

25 And Pharaoh called for Moses and for Aaron, and said, Go ye, sacrifice to your God in the land. 26 And Moses said, It is not meet so to do; for we shall sacrifice the abomination of the Egyptians to Jehovah our God: lo, shall we sacrifice the abomination of the Egyptians before their eyes, and will they not stone us? 27 We will go three days' journey into the wilderness, and sacrifice to Jehovah our God, as he shall command us. 28 And Pharaoh said, I will let you go, that ye may sacri-

fice to Jehovah your God in the wilderness; only ye shall not go very far away: entreat for me. 29 And Moses said, Behold, I go out from thee, and I will entreat Jehovah that the swarms of flies may depart from Pharaoh, from his servants, and from his people, to-morrow: only let not Pharaoh deal deceitfully any more in not letting the people go to sacrifice to Jehovah. 30 And Moses went out from Pharaoh, and entreated Jehovah. 31 And Jehovah did according to the word of Moses; and he removed the swarms of flies from Pharaoh, from his servants, and from his people; there remained not one. 32 And Pharaoh hardened his heart this time also, and he did not let the people go.

26v. THE FOURTH PLAGUE: MURRAIN. (J only).
Ex. 9$^{1-7}$

1 Then Jehovah said unto Moses, Go in unto Pharaoh, and tell him, Thus saith Jehovah, the God of the Hebrews, Let my people go, that they may serve me. 2 For if thou refuse to let them go, and wilt hold them still, 3 behold, the hand of Jehovah is upon thy cattle which are in the field, upon the horses, upon the asses, upon the camels, upon the herds, and upon the flocks: *there shall be* a very grievous murrain. 4 And Jehovah shall make a distinction between the cattle of Israel and the cattle of Egypt; and there shall nothing die of all that belongeth to the children of Israel. 5 And Jehovah appointed a set time, saying, To-morrow Jehovah shall do this thing in the land. 6 And Jehovah did that thing on the morrow; and all the cattle of Egypt died; but of the cattle of the children of Israel died not one. 7 And Pharaoh sent, and, behold, there was not so much as one of the cattle of the Israelites dead. But the heart of Pharaoh was stubborn, and he did not let the people go.

26vi. THE FIFTH PLAGUE: HAIL. E13iii.
Ex. 9$^{13-21.23b.24b.25b-34}$

13 And Jehovah said unto Moses, Rise up early in the morning, and stand before Pharaoh, and say unto him, Thus saith Jehovah, the God of the Hebrews, Let my people go, that they may serve me. 14 For I will this time send all my plagues upon thy heart, and upon thy servants, and upon thy people; that thou mayest know that there is none like me in all the earth. 15 For now I had put forth my hand, and smitten thee and thy people with pestilence, and thou hadst been cut off from the earth: 16 but in very deed for this cause have I made thee to stand, to show thee my power, and that my name may

---

²⁵ᵛⁱ vv. 31-32 J: Dr., Ba., McN., Smend.

be declared throughout all the earth. 17 As yet exaltest thou thyself against my people, that thou wilt not let them go? 18 Behold, to-morrow about this time I will cause it to rain a very grievous hail, such as hath not been in Egypt since the day it was founded even until now. 19 Now therefore send, hasten in thy cattle and all that thou hast in the field; *for* every man and beast that shall be found in the field, and shall not be brought home, the hail shall come down upon them, and they shall die. 20 He that feared the word of Jehovah among the servants of Pharaoh made his servants and his cattle flee into the houses: 21 and he that regarded not the word of Jehovah left his servants and his cattle in the field.

23b And Jehovah sent thunder and hail, and fire ran down unto the earth; and Jehovah rained hail upon the land of Egypt,—24b very grievous, such as had not been in all the land of Egypt since it became a nation. 25b And the hail smote every herb of the field, and brake every tree of the field. 26 Only in the land of Goshen, where the children of Israel were, was there no hail.

27 And Pharaoh sent, and called for Moses and Aaron, and said unto them, I have sinned this time: Jehovah is righteous, and I and my people are wicked. 28 Entreat Jehovah; for there hath been enough of *these* mighty thunderings and hail; and I will let you go, and ye shall stay no longer. 29 And Moses said unto him, As soon as I am gone out of the city, I will spread abroad my hands unto Jehovah; the thunders shall cease, neither shall there be any more hail; that thou mayest know that the earth is Jehovah's. 30 But as for thee and thy servants, I know that ye will not yet fear Jehovah God. 31 And the flax and the barley were smitten: for the barley was in the ear, and the flax was in bloom. 32 But the wheat and the spelt were not smitten: for they were not grown up. 33 And Moses went out of the city from Pharaoh, and spread abroad his hands unto Jehovah: and the thunders and hail ceased, and the rain was not poured upon the earth. 34 And when Pharaoh saw that the rain and the hail and the thunders were ceased, he sinned yet more, and hardened his heart, he and his servants. 35 And the heart of Pharaoh was hardened, and he did not let the children of Israel go; as Jehovah had spoken by Moses.

26vii. THE SIXTH PLAGUE: LOCUSTS. E13iv.
Ex. $10^{1-11.13b.14b.15a.15c-19}$

1 And Jehovah said unto Moses, Go in unto Pharaoh: for I have hardened his heart, and the heart of his servants, that I may show these my signs in the midst of them, 2 and that thou mayest tell in the ears of thy son, and of thy son's son, what things I have wrought upon

Egypt, and my signs which I have done among them; that ye may know that I am Jehovah. 3 And Moses and Aaron went in unto Pharaoh, and said unto him, Thus saith Jehovah, the God of the Hebrews, How long wilt thou refuse to humble thyself before me? let my people go, that they may serve me. 4 Else, if thou refuse to let my people go, behold, to-morrow will I bring locusts into thy border: 5 and they shall cover the face of the earth, so that one shall not be able to see the earth: and they shall eat the residue of that which is escaped, which remaineth unto you from the hail, and shall eat every tree which groweth for you out of the field: 6 and thy houses shall be filled, and the houses of all thy servants, and the houses of all the Egyptians; as neither thy fathers nor thy fathers' fathers have seen, since the day that they were upon the earth unto this day. And he turned, and went out from Pharaoh.

7 And Pharaoh's servants said unto him, How long shall this man be a snare unto us? let the men go, that they may serve Jehovah their God: knowest thou not yet that Egypt is destroyed? 8 And Moses and Aaron were brought again unto Pharaoh: and he said unto them, Go, serve Jehovah your God; but who are they that shall go? 9 And Moses said, We will go with our young and with our old; and with our sons and with our daughters, with our flocks and with our herds will we go; for we must hold a feast unto Jehovah. 10 And he said unto them, So be Jehovah with you, as I will let you go, and your little ones: look to it; for evil is before you. 11 Not so: go now ye that are men, and serve Jehovah; for that is what ye desire. And they were driven out from Pharaoh's presence.

13b And Jehovah brought an east wind upon the land all that day, and all the night; and when it was morning, the east wind brought the locusts; 14b and rested in all the borders of Egypt; very grievous were they; before them there were no such locusts as they, neither after them shall be such. 15a For they covered the face of the whole earth, so that the land was darkened. 15c And there remained not any green thing, either tree or herb of the field, through all the land of Egypt.

16 Then Pharaoh called for Moses and Aaron in haste; and he said, I have sinned against Jehovah your God, and against you. 17 Now therefore forgive, I pray thee, my sins only this once, and entreat Jehovah your God, that he may take away from me this death only. 18 And he went out from Pharaoh, and entreated Jehovah. 19 And Jehovah turned an exceeding strong west wind, which took up the locusts, and drove them into the Red Sea; there remained not one locust in all the border of Egypt.

26viii. THE SEVENTH PLAGUE THREATENED: THE FIRST-BORN.
J24iii. E13vi. P23v.
Ex. 10$^{24-26.28-29}$ 11$^{4-8}$

10^{24} And Pharaoh called unto Moses, and said, Go ye, serve Jehovah; only let your flocks and your herds be stayed: let your little ones also go with you. 25 And Moses said, Thou must also give into our hand sacrifices and burnt-offerings, that we may sacrifice unto Jehovah our God. 26 Our cattle also shall go with us; there shall not a hoof be left behind; for thereof must we take to serve Jehovah our God; and we know not with what we must serve Jehovah, until we come thither.

28 And Pharaoh said unto him, Get thee from me, take heed to thyself, see my face no more; for in the day thou seest my face thou shalt die. 29 And Moses said, Thou hast spoken well; I will see thy face again no more.

11^{4} And Moses said, Thus saith Jehovah, About midnight will I go out into the midst of Egypt: 5 and all the first-born in the land of Egypt shall die, from the first-born of Pharaoh that sitteth upon his throne, even unto the first-born of the maid-servant that is behind the mill; and all the first-born of cattle. 6 And there shall be a great cry throughout all the land of Egypt, such as there hath not been, nor shall be any more. 7 But against any of the children of Israel shall not a dog move his tongue, against man or beast: that ye may know how that Jehovah doth make a distinction between the Egyptians and Israel. 8 And all these thy servants shall come down unto me, and bow down themselves unto me, saying, Get thee out, and all the people that follow thee: and after that I will go out. And he went out from Pharaoh in hot anger.

26ix. PASSOVER INSTITUTED IN CONNECTION WITH THE SLAYING OF THE FIRST-BORN. P23v.
Ex. 12$^{21-27.29-34}$

21 Then Moses called for all the elders of Israel, and said unto them, Draw out, and take you lambs according to your families, and kill the passover. 22 And ye shall take a bunch of hyssop, and dip it in the blood that is in the basin, and strike the lintel and the two side-posts with the blood that is in the basin; and none of you shall go out of the door of his house until the morning. 23 For Jehovah will pass through to smite

---

26viii 10$^{24-26.28-29}$. E: Ad., Pr. only.—We., Jül., Smend, et al., believe that the origin of this plague lies in an ancient custom of offering the first-born to Jehovah at Easter time.
26ix 12^{24-27a} Rd: Ba., Bä., St., Kent, Smend; Rje: Ho.—vv. 21-27 entire R: Jül., Co., Bu., Gr.; later than JE, but before P: We.—v. 31a E: Dr., Ba., Co., Bä., Smend.—vv. 31b-34 E: Dr., Se., St.

the Egyptians; and when he seeth the blood upon the lintel, and on the two side-posts, Jehovah will pass over the door, and will not suffer the destroyer to come in unto your houses to smite you. 24 And ye shall observe this thing for an ordinance to thee and to thy sons for ever. 25 And it shall come to pass, when ye are come to the land which Jehovah will give you, according as he hath promised, that ye shall keep this service. 26 And it shall come to pass, when your children shall say unto you, What mean ye by this service? 27 that ye shall say, It is the sacrifice of Jehovah's passover, who passed over the houses of the children of Israel in Egypt, when he smote the Egyptians, and delivered our houses. And the people bowed the head and worshipped.
29 And it came to pass at midnight, that Jehovah smote all the first-born in the land of Egypt, from the first-born of Pharaoh that sat on his throne unto the first-born of the captive that was in the dungeon; and all the first-born of cattle. 30 And Pharaoh rose up in the night, he, and all his servants, and all the Egyptians; and there was a great cry in Egypt; for there was not a house where there was not one dead. 31 And he called for Moses and Aaron by night, and said, Rise up, get you forth from among my people, both ye and the children of Israel; and go, serve Jehovah, as ye have said. 32 Take both your flocks and your herds, as ye have said, and be gone; and bless me also. 33 And the Egyptians were urgent upon the people, to send them out of the land in haste; for they said, We are all dead men. 34 And the people took their dough before it was leavened, their kneading-troughs being bound up in their clothes upon their shoulders.

26x. EXODUS FROM EGYPT. E13viii. P24.
Ex. 12^{37b-39} 13$^{3-16.21-22}$

12^{37b} . . . about six hundred thousand on foot that were men, besides children. 38 And a mixed multitude went up also with them; and flocks, and herds, even very much cattle.
39 And they baked unleavened cakes of the dough which they brought forth out of Egypt; for it was not leavened, because they were thrust out of Egypt, and could not tarry, neither had they prepared for themselves any victuals.
13^3 And Moses said unto the people, Remember this day, in which ye came out from Egypt, out of the house of bondage; for by strength of hand Jehovah brought you out from this place: there shall no leavened bread be eaten. 4 This day ye go forth in the month Abib. 5 And it shall be, when Jehovah shall bring thee into the land of the Canaanite, and the Hittite, and the Amorite, and the Hivite, and the Jebusite, which he sware unto thy fathers to give thee, a land flowing with milk and honey,

26x 12^{39} E: Dr., Co., Ho., Se,—13$^{3-16}$ R: all, except Di., J (cf. Dr. 123).

...14¹¹] J26ix–27 91

that thou shalt keep this service in this month. 6 Seven days thou shalt eat unleavened bread, and in the seventh day shall be a feast to Jehovah. 7 Unleavened bread shall be eaten throughout the seven days; and there shall no leavened bread be seen with thee, neither shall there be leaven seen with thee, in all thy borders. 8 And thou shalt tell thy son in that day, saying, It is because of that which Jehovah did for me when I came forth out of Egypt. 9 And it shall be for a sign unto thee upon thy hand, and for a memorial between thine eyes, that the law of Jehovah may be in thy mouth: for with a strong hand hath Jehovah brought thee out of Egypt. 10 Thou shalt therefore keep this ordinance in its season from year to year.

11 And it shall be, when Jehovah shall bring thee into the land of the Canaanite, as he sware unto thee and to thy fathers, and shall give it thee, 12 that thou shalt set apart unto Jehovah all that openeth the womb, and every firstling which thou hast that cometh of a beast; the males shall be Jehovah's. 13 And every firstling of an ass thou shalt redeem with a lamb; and if thou wilt not redeem it, then thou shalt break its neck: and all the first-born of man among thy sons shalt thou redeem. 14 And it shall be, when thy son asketh thee in time to come, saying, What is this? that thou shalt say unto him, By strength of hand Jehovah brought us out from Egypt, from the house of bondage: 15 and it came to pass, when Pharaoh would hardly let us go, that Jehovah slew all the first-born in the land of Egypt, both the first-born of man, and the first-born of beast: therefore I sacrifice to Jehovah all that openeth the womb, being males; but all the first-born of my sons I redeem. 16 And it shall be for a sign upon thy hand, and for frontlets between thine eyes: for by strength of hand Jehovah brought us forth out of Egypt.

21 And Jehovah went before them by day in a pillar of cloud, to lead them the way, and by night in a pillar of fire, to give them light; that they might go by day and by night: 22 the pillar of cloud by day, and the pillar of fire by night, departed not from before the people.

27. ESCAPE BY CROSSING THE RED SEA. E14, 16.
    Ex. 14$^{5-6.10a.11-14.19b-20.21b.24.25b.27b.28b.30-31}$

5 And it was told the king of Egypt that the people were fled: and the heart of Pharaoh and of his servants was changed towards the people, and they said, What is this we have done, that we have let Israel go from serving us? 6 And he made ready his chariot and took his people with him.

10a And when Pharaoh drew nigh, the children of Israel lifted up their eyes, and, behold, the Egyptians were marching after them; and they were sore afraid. 11 And they said unto Moses, Because there were no graves in Egypt, hast thou taken us away to die in the wilderness? wherefore hast thou dealt

---
[27] v. 20 JE: analysis uncertain.—v. 31 E: Ba.?, Pr.; R: Gr., CH., Bä., McN.

thus with us, to bring us forth out of the land of Egypt? 12 Is not this the word that we spake unto thee in Egypt, saying, Let us alone, that we may serve the Egyptians? For it were better for us to serve the Egyptians, than that we should die in the wilderness. 13 And Moses said unto the people, Fear ye not, stand still, and see the salvation of Jehovah, which he will work for you to-day: for the Egyptians whom ye have seen to-day, ye shall see them again no more for ever. 14 Jehovah will fight for you, and ye shall hold your peace.

19b And the pillar of cloud removed from before them, and stood behind them: 20 and it came between the camp of Egypt and the camp of Israel; and there was the cloud and the darkness, yet gave it light by night: and the one came not near the other all the night.

21b And Jehovah caused the sea to go *back* by a strong east wind all the night, and made the sea dry land. 24 And it came to pass in the morning watch, that Jehovah looked forth upon the host of the Egyptians through the pillar of fire and of cloud, and discomfited the host of the Egyptians; 25b so that the Egyptians said, Let us flee from the face of Israel; for Jehovah fighteth for them against the Egyptians.

27b And the sea returned to its strength when the morning appeared; and the Egyptians fled against it; and Jehovah overthrew the Egyptians in the midst of the sea. 28b There remained not so much as one of them.

30 Thus Jehovah saved Israel that day out of the hand of the Egyptians; and Israel saw the Egyptians dead upon the sea-shore. 31 And Israel saw the great work which Jehovah did upon the Egyptians, and the people feared Jehovah: and they believed in Jehovah, and in his servant Moses.

28. Waters of Marah and Elim. E18.

Ex. 15$^{22\text{-}25a.27}$

22 And Moses led Israel onward from the Red Sea, and they went out into the wilderness of Shur; and they went three days in the wilderness, and found no water. 23 And when they came to Marah, they could not drink of the waters of Marah, for they were bitter: therefore the name of it was called Marah. 24 And the people murmured against Moses, saying, What shall we drink? 25a And he cried unto Jehovah; and Jehovah showed him a tree, and he cast it into the waters, and the waters were made sweet.

27 And they came to Elim, where were twelve springs of

---

[28] The analysis in Ex. 15$^{22\text{-}18}$ is unusually difficult and doubtful.—v. 27 P: Nöldeke, Di., Ki., Gr., St.; E: Co., Ki. (in part).

water, and threescore and ten palm-trees: and they encamped there by the waters.

29. BREAD FROM HEAVEN. J36. P29.
Ex. 16⁴⁻⁵·¹³ᵇ⁻¹⁵ᵃ·²¹

4 Then said Jehovah unto Moses, Behold, I will rain bread from heaven for you; and the people shall go out and gather a day's portion every day, that I may prove them, whether they will walk in my law, or not. 5 And it shall come to pass on the sixth day, that they shall prepare that which they bring in, and it shall be twice as much as they gather daily. 13b And in the morning the dew lay round about the camp. 14 And when the dew that lay was gone up, behold, upon the face of the wilderness a small round thing, small as the hoarfrost on the ground. 15a And when the children of Israel saw it, they said one to another, What is it? for they knew not what it was. 21 And they gathered it morning by morning, every man according to his eating: and when the sun waxed hot, it melted.

30. MASSAH: TEMPTING JEHOVAH. J42. E18. P66.
Ex. 17¹ᵇ⁻²·⁷

1b And there was no water for the people to drink. 2 Wherefore the people strove with Moses, and said, Give us water that we may drink. And Moses said unto them, Why strive ye with me? wherefore do ye tempt Jehovah? 7 And he called the name of the place Massah, and Meribah, because of the striving of the children of Israel, and because they tempted Jehovah, saying, Is Jehovah among us, or not?

31. APPEARANCE OF JEHOVAH ON SINAI. E22. P31.
Ex. 19³ᵇ⁻⁹·¹¹ᵇ⁻¹³·¹⁸·²⁰⁻²⁵

3ᵇ And Jehovah called unto him out of the mountain, saying, Thus shalt thou say to the house of Jacob, and tell the children of Israel: 4 Ye have seen what I did unto the Egyptians, and how I bare you on eagles' wings, and brought you unto myself. 5 Now therefore, if ye will obey my voice indeed, and keep my covenant, then ye shall be mine own possession from among all peoples: for all the earth is mine: 6 and ye shall be unto me a kingdom of priests, and a holy nation. These are the words which thou shalt speak unto the children of Israel.

7 And Moses came and called for the elders of the people, and set be-

---

[29] There is no consensus regarding the analysis of Ex. 16. However, Co., Gr., Bä., St., Smend, Ki., agree on the above J verses (except for slight variations regarding possible redactional elements).
[30] E: Ba., CH., Ho., St.—Meribah is Kadesh (Smend); and the scene of this story should be in the context of Numbers.
[31] There are great difficulties in the analysis of 19-34. No attempt is made to note every minor difference among critics.

fore them all these words which Jehovah commanded him. 8 And all the people answered together, and said, All that Jehovah hath spoken we will do. And Moses reported the words of the people unto Jehovah.

9 And Jehovah said unto Moses, Lo, I come unto thee in a thick cloud, that the people may hear when I speak with thee, and may also believe thee for ever. And Moses told the words of the people unto Jehovah.

11b Jehovah will come down in the sight of all the people upon mount Sinai. 12 And thou shalt set bounds unto the people round about, saying, Take heed to yourselves, that ye go not up into the mount, or touch the border of it: whosoever toucheth the mount shall be surely put to death: 13 no hand shall touch him, but he shall surely be stoned, or shot through; whether it be beast or man, he shall not live: when the trumpet soundeth long, they shall come up to the mount.

18 And mount Sinai, the whole of it, smoked, because Jehovah descended upon it in fire; and the smoke thereof ascended as the smoke of a furnace, and the whole mount quaked greatly.

20 And Jehovah came down upon mount Sinai, to the top of the mount: and Jehovah called Moses to the top of the mount; and Moses went up. 21 And Jehovah said unto Moses, Go down, charge the people, lest they break through unto Jehovah to gaze, and many of them perish. 22 And let the priests also, that come near to Jehovah, sanctify themselves, lest Jehovah break forth upon them.

23 And Moses said unto Jehovah, The people cannot come up to mount Sinai: for thou didst charge us, saying, Set bounds about the mount, and sanctify it. 24 And Jehovah said unto him, Go, get thee down; and thou shalt come up, thou, and Aaron with thee: but let not the priests and the people break through to come up unto Jehovah, lest he break forth upon them.

25 So Moses went down unto the people, and told them.

32. Appearance of Jehovah to Moses (Aaron, Nadab and Abihu) and Seventy Elders. E31.

Ex. 24[1-2.9-11]

24[1] And he said unto Moses, Come up unto Jehovah, thou, and Aaron, Nadab, and Abihu, and seventy of the elders of Israel; and worship ye afar off: 2 and Moses alone shall come near unto Jehovah; but they shall not come near; neither shall the people go up with him.

---

[32] There is much difference of opinion regarding the assignment to J or E. J: Di., Ba., Dr., CH., Se., Sten., Ho., McN., Nourse, Smend, Ki., Paton. E: Ku., We., Ad., Co., GFM., Bä., Gr., St., Eiselen. P: Pr. only. The primitive anthropomorphisms, the name "Jehovah" in vv. 1 and 2, and the fact that vv. 3-8 are surely E point to J. "God of Israel" in v. 10 and "God" in v. 11 point to E (but "God" in the construct as in v. 10, or referring to his abstract nature as exalted above and contrasted to man as in v. 11 are usages frequent in J). Pr. thinks that the similarity to Ezekiel points to P (but all others find this far-fetched).

9 Then went up Moses, and Aaron, Nadab, and Abihu, and seventy of the elders of Israel: 10 and they saw the God of Israel; and there was under his feet as it were a paved work of sapphire stone, and as it were the very heaven for clearness. 11 And upon the nobles of the children of Israel he laid not his hand: and they beheld God, and did eat and drink.

33. APPEARANCE OF JEHOVAH TO MOSES "UPON THE ROCK."
J34 (vv. 6-7). 1K. 19.
Ex. 33^{1-3a} Nu. $11^{11-12.15}$ Ex. 33^{12-23}

33^1 And Jehovah spake unto Moses, Depart, go up hence, thou and the people that thou hast brought up out of the land of Egypt, unto the land of which I sware unto Abraham, to Isaac, and to Jacob, saying, Unto thy seed will I give it: 2 and I will send an angel before thee; and I will drive out the Canaanite, the Amorite, and the Hittite, and the Perizzite, the Hivite, and the Jebusite: 3a unto a land flowing with milk and honey.

Nu. 11^{11} And Moses said unto Jehovah, Wherefore hast thou dealt ill with thy servant? and wherefore have I not found favor in thy sight, that thou layest the burden of all this people upon me? 12 Have I conceived all this people? have I brought them forth, that thou shouldest say unto me, Carry them in thy bosom, as a nursing-father carrieth the sucking child, unto the land which thou swarest unto their fathers? 15 And if thou deal thus with me, kill me, I pray thee, out of hand, if I have found favor in thy sight; and let me not see my wretchedness.

Ex. 33^{12} And Moses said unto Jehovah, See, thou sayest unto me, Bring up this people: and thou hast not let me know whom thou wilt send with me. Yet thou hast said, I know thee by name, and thou hast also found favor in my sight. 13 Now therefore, I pray thee, if I have found favor in thy sight, show me now thy ways, that I may know thee, to the end that I may find favor in thy sight: and consider that this nation is thy people. 14 And he said, My presence shall go *with thee,* and I will give thee rest. 15 And he said unto him, If thy presence go not *with me,* carry us not up hence. 16 For wherein now shall it be known that I have found favor in thy sight, I and thy people? is it not in that thou goest with us, so that we are separated, I and thy people, from all the people that are upon the face of the earth?

17 And Jehovah said unto Moses, I will do this thing also that thou hast spoken; for thou hast found favor in my sight, and I know thee by name. 18 And he said, Show me, I pray

---

[33] Nu. $11^{11-12.15}$ in this connection: Ba., GFM., Gray. These vv. E?: Ho., Gr., St.— "Moses desired to see the face of God. . . . No man felt this longing so deeply as he; hence he is the genius of his age," Pr.

thee, thy glory. 19 And he said, I will make all my goodness pass before thee, and will proclaim the name of Jehovah before thee; and I will be gracious to whom I will be gracious, and will show mercy on whom I will show mercy. 20 And he said, Thou canst not see my face; for man shall not see me and live. 21 And Jehovah said, Behold, there is a place by me, and thou shalt stand upon the rock: 22 and it shall come to pass, while my glory passeth by, that I will put thee in a cleft of the rock, and will cover thee with my hand until I have passed by: 23 and I will take away my hand, and thou shalt see my back; but my face shall not be seen.

34. THE SO-CALLED J DECALOGUE: COVENANT ON SINAI. E23, 24, 25, 26.
Ex. 34$^{1-28}$

Introductory Note.—Ex. 34^{28} in its present form suggests that the Ten Commandments are to be found in the preceding context vv. 1-27. Hence, the majority of critics since We. see here a J Decalogue, older than the E Decalogue of Ex. 20. But there are more than ten commandments, and critics disagree as to which were the original ten.

Knudson has shown the differences among critics in an investigation of which the following is a summary: The views of We. 1889, Bertholet 1899, Ho. 1900, Bä. 1903, Stade 1905, and Bu. 1906 are given. Smend 1912 has declared his agreement with We. The Roman numerals indicate the hypothetical commandments in order.

    I—v. 14a. All agree.
    II—v. 17. All agree.
    III—v. 18a (We., Ho.); 19a (Bertholet, Bä., Bu.); 21a (Stade).
    IV—v. 18a (Stade); 19a (We.); 20b (Bertholet); 21a (Bä., Bu.); 22a (Ho.).
    V—v. 18a (Bu.); 22a (We., Bertholet, Bä., Stade); 22b (Ho.).
    VI—v. 19a (Ho.); 22 (Bu.); 22b (We., Bertholet, Bä., Stade).
    VII—v. 25a. All agree.
    VIII—v. 25b. All agree.
    IX—v. 26a. All agree.
    X—v. 26b. All agree.

[34] 34^{1,4,28} if not worked over by R as indicated above (according to most critics since We.), must be E (so Ku., Bä., St., Nourse). For analogous reasons Ki. takes vv. 1-5.28 together as a J narrative continuing the J account that he finds in Ex. 32. In any event it is worthy of note that Dt. 10$^{1ff.}$ uses only vv. 1.4.28. There is great difference as to the nature and amount of the revision in v. 28. If the verse is not E, and if there is no true J Decalogue, then the words "the ten commandments" are doubtless a gloss by Rje, referring to the new copy of the E Decalogue. The expression is regarded as a gloss by Ba., Se., McN., Marti, Bä., Eerd., et al. Others (as Ki., Ho., et al.) excise the expression "the words of the covenant."

* A large minority of scholars are inclined, on various grounds, to doubt the existence of a J Decalogue, e. g., Se., St., Knudson, Nourse, Pr., Marti, Baudissin, Eerd., and Kittel (who regards Ex. 34 as an abbreviated analagon of CC). Gr. finds a "dodecalogue." Eerd. sees in Ex. 34 a post-exilic copy of Ex. 23.

1 And Jehovah said unto Moses, Hew thee two tables of stone like unto the first: and I will write upon the tables the words that were on the first tables, which thou brakest. 2 And be ready by the morning, and come up in the morning unto mount Sinai, and present thyself there to me on the top of the mount. 3 And no man shall come up with thee; neither let any man be seen throughout all the mount; neither let the flocks nor herds feed before that mount. 4 And he hewed two tables of stone like unto the first; and Moses rose up early in the morning, and went up unto mount Sinai, as Jehovah had commanded him, and took in his hand two tables of stone. 5 And Jehovah descended in the cloud, and stood with him there, and proclaimed the name of Jehovah. 6 And Jehovah passed by before him, and proclaimed, Jehovah, Jehovah, a God merciful and gracious, slow to anger, and abundant in lovingkindness and truth; 7 keeping lovingkindness for thousands, forgiving iniquity and transgression and sin; and that will by no means clear *the guilty*, visiting the iniquity of the fathers upon the children, and upon the children's children, upon the third and upon the fourth generation. 8 And Moses made haste, and bowed his head toward the earth, and worshipped. 9 And he said, If now I have found favor in thy sight, O Lord, let the Lord, I pray thee, go in the midst of us; for it is a stiffnecked people; and pardon our iniquity and our sin, and take us for thine inheritance.

10 And he said, Behold, I make a covenant: before all thy people I will do marvels, such as have not been wrought in all the earth, nor in any nation; and all the people among which thou art shall see the work of Jehovah; for it is a terrible thing that I do with thee. 11 Observe thou that which I command thee this day: behold, I drive out before thee the Amorite, and the Canaanite, and the Hittite, and the Perizzite, and the Hivite, and the Jebusite. 12 Take heed to thyself, lest thou make a covenant with the inhabitants of the land whither thou goest, lest it be for a snare in the midst of thee: 13 but ye shall break down their altars, and dash in pieces their pillars, and ye shall cut down their Asherim 14 (for thou shalt worship no other god: for Jehovah, whose name is Jealous, is a jealous God); 15 lest thou make a covenant with the inhabitants of the land, and they play the harlot after their gods, and sacrifice unto their gods, and one call thee and thou eat of his sacrifice; 16 and thou take of their daughters unto thy sons, and their daughters play the harlot

after their gods, and make thy sons play the harlot after their gods. 17 Thou shalt make thee no molten gods.

18 The feast of unleavened bread shalt thou keep. Seven days thou shalt eat unleavened bread, as I commanded thee, at the time appointed in the month Abib; for in the month Abib thou camest out from Egypt. 19 All that openeth the womb is mine; and all thy cattle that is male, the firstlings of cow and sheep. 20 And the firstling of an ass thou shalt redeem with a lamb: and if thou wilt not redeem it, then thou shalt break its neck. All the first-born of thy sons thou shalt redeem. And none shall appear before me empty.

21 Six days thou shalt work, but on the seventh day thou shalt rest: in plowing time and in harvest thou shalt rest. 22 And thou shalt observe the feast of weeks, *even* of the firstfruits of wheat harvest, and the feast of ingathering at the year's end. 23 Three times in the year shall all thy males appear before the Lord Jehovah, the God of Israel. 24 For I will cast out nations before thee, and enlarge thy borders: neither shall any man desire thy land, when thou goest up to appear before Jehovah thy God three times in the year.

25 Thou shalt not offer the blood of my sacrifice with leavened bread; neither shall the sacrifice of the feast of the passover be left unto the morning. 26 The first of the first-fruits of thy ground thou shalt bring unto the house of Jehovah thy God. Thou shalt not boil a kid in its mother's milk.

27 And Jehovah said unto Moses, Write thou these words: for after the tenor of these words I have made a covenant with thee and with Israel. 28 And he was there with Jehovah forty days and forty nights; he did neither eat bread nor drink water. And he wrote upon the tables the words of the covenant, the ten commandments.

35. Moses Invites Hobab the Midianite to Join Him. E20. Nu. 10$^{29\text{-}32}$

29 And Moses said unto Hobab, the son of Reuel the Midianite, Moses' father-in-law, We are journeying unto the place of which Jehovah said, I will give it you: come thou with us, and we will do thee good; for Jehovah hath spoken good concerning Israel. 30 And he said unto him, I will not go; but I will depart to mine own land, and to my kindred. 31 And he said, Leave us not, I pray thee; forasmuch as thou knowest how we are to encamp in the wilderness, and thou shalt be to us instead of eyes. 32 And it shall be, if thou go with us, yea, it shall be, that what good soever Jehovah shall do unto us, the same will we do unto thee.

---

[35] GFM. notes Hobab's consent implied in Jg. 1^{16} and 4^{11}.

36. THE STORY OF THE QUAILS. J29. P29.
Nu. 11[4-10.13.18-23.24a.31-34]

4 And the mixed multitude that was among them lusted exceedingly: and the children of Israel also wept again, and said, Who shall give us flesh to eat? 5 We remember the fish, which we did eat in Egypt for nought; the cucumbers, and the melons, and the leeks, and the onions, and the garlic: 6 but now our soul is dried away; there is nothing at all save this manna to look upon. 7 And the manna was like coriander seed, and the appearance thereof as the appearance of bdellium. 8 The people went about, and gathered it, and ground it in mills, or beat it in mortars, or boiled it in pots, and made cakes of it: and the taste of it was as the taste of fresh oil. 9 And when the dew fell upon the camp in the night the manna fell upon it.

10 And Moses heard the people weeping throughout their families, every man at the door of his tent: and the anger of Jehovah was kindled greatly; and Moses was displeased. 13 Whence should I have flesh to give unto all this people? for they weep unto me, saying, Give us flesh, that we may eat.

18 And say thou unto the people, Sanctify yourselves against to-morrow, and ye shall eat flesh; for ye have wept in the ears of Jehovah, saying, Who shall give us flesh to eat? for it was well with us in Egypt: therefore Jehovah will give you flesh, and ye shall eat. 19 Ye shall not eat one day, nor two days, nor five days, neither ten days, nor twenty days, 20 but a whole month, until it come out at your nostrils, and it be loathsome unto you; because that ye have rejected Jehovah who is among you, and have wept before him, saying, Why came we forth out of Egypt?

21 And Moses said, The people, among whom I am, are six hundred thousand footmen; and thou hast said, I will give them flesh, that they may eat a whole month. 22 Shall flocks and herds be slain for them, to suffice them? or shall all the fish of the sea be gathered together for them, to suffice them? 23 And Jehovah said unto Moses, Is Jehovah's hand waxed short? now shalt thou see whether my word shall come to pass unto thee or not.

24a And Moses went out, and told the people the words of Jehovah.

31 And there went forth a wind from Jehovah, and brought quails from the sea, and let them fall by the camp, about a day's journey on this side, and a day's journey on the other side, round about the camp, and about two cubits above the face of the earth. 32 And the people rose up all that day, and all the night, and all the next day, and gathered the quails:

he that gathered least gathered ten homers: and they spread them all abroad for themselves round about the camp. 33 While the flesh was yet between their teeth, ere it was chewed, the anger of Jehovah was kindled against the people, and Jehovah smote the people with a very great plague. 34 And the name of that place was called Kibroth-hattaavah, because there they buried the people that lusted.

Nu. 11$^{11\text{-}12.15}$, cf. J^{33}

37. The Journey to the Wilderness of Paran. E39.
Nu. 11^{35} 12^{16}

35 From Kibroth-hattaavah the people journeyed unto Hazeroth; and they abode at Hazeroth. 12^{16} And afterward the people journeyed from Hazeroth, and encamped in the wilderness of Paran.

38. The Commission and Report of the Spies. E39. P55.
Nu. 13$^{17b.19.22.27\text{-}29}$

17b And said unto them, Get you up this way by the South, 19 and what the land is that they dwell in, whether it is good or bad; and what cities they are that they dwell in, whether in camps, or in strongholds.

22 And they went up by the South, and came unto Hebron; and Ahiman, Sheshai, and Talmai, the children of Anak, were there. (Now Hebron was built seven years before Zoan in Egypt).

27 And they told him, and said, We came unto the land whither thou sentest us; and surely it floweth with milk and honey; and this is the fruit of it. 28 Howbeit the people that dwell in the land are strong, and the cities are fortified, *and* very great: and moreover we saw the children of Anak there. 29 Amalek dwelleth in the land of the South: and the Hittite, and the Jebusite, and the Amorite, dwell in the hill-country; and the Canaanite dwelleth by the sea, and along by the side of the Jordan.

39. The Fear of the People. E35. P56.
Nu. 14$^{1c.3}$

1c And the people wept that night. 3 And wherefore doth Jehovah bring us unto this land to fall by the sword? Our wives and our little ones will be a prey: were it not better for us to return into Egypt?

---

[38] There is disagreement as to the analysis. Co., St., Gray find some E in v. 27, and Ba., CH., Di., GFM., Smend regard v. 28 as E vs. Co., St., Bu., E. Meyer, Bä., Ki.: J and Pr. and Ew.: P. Gr., Gray and Ka. regard it as wholly or in part R.

[39] All are agreed in assigning these passages to J (or JE), except v. 1c E: Ba., Ku., and St. (J or E?).

40. THE ANSWER OF THE SPIES. E34. P55, 56.
Nu. 14⁸⁻⁹

8 If Jehovah delight in us, then he will bring us into this land, and give it unto us; a land which floweth with milk and honey. 9 Only rebel not against Jehovah, neither fear ye the people of the land; for they are bread for us: their defence is removed from over them, and Jehovah is with us: fear them not.

41. JEHOVAH'S REBUKE OF THE PEOPLE. E36. P58.
Nu. 14¹¹⁻²¹·³¹⁻³³

11 And Jehovah said unto Moses, How long will this people despise me? and how long will they not believe in me, for all the signs which I have wrought among them? 12 I will smite them with the pestilence, and disinherit them, and will make of thee a nation greater and mightier than they.

13 And Moses said unto Jehovah, Then the Egyptians will hear it; for thou broughtest up this people in thy might from among them; 14 and they will tell it to the inhabitants of this land. They have heard that thou Jehovah art in the midst of this people; for thou Jehovah art seen face to face, and thy cloud standeth over them, and thou goest before them, in a pillar of cloud by day, and in a pillar of fire by night. 15 Now if thou shalt kill this people as one man, then the nations which have heard the fame of thee will speak, saying, 16 Because Jehovah was not able to bring this people into the land which he sware untq them, therefore he hath slain them in the wilderness. 17 And now, I pray thee, let the power of the Lord be great, according as thou hast spoken, saying, 18 Jehovah is slow to anger, and abundant in lovingkindness, forgiving iniquity and transgression; and that will by no means clear *the guilty*, visiting the iniquity of the fathers upon the children, upon the third and upon the fourth generation. 19 Pardon, I pray thee, the iniquity of this people according unto the greatness of thy lovingkindness, and according as thou hast forgiven this people, from Egypt even until now.

20 And Jehovah said, I have pardoned according to thy word: 21 but in very deed, as I live, and as all the earth shall be filled with the glory of Jehovah . . .

31 But your little ones, that ye said should be a prey, them will I bring in, and they shall know the land which ye have rejected. 32 But as for you, your dead bodies shall fall in this wilderness. 33 And your children shall be wanderers in the wilderness forty years, and shall bear your whoredoms, until your dead bodies be consumed in the wilderness.

---

⁴¹ vv. 11b-21: Rje. vv. 31-33 may be P: CH., Co., Gray or Rp: Ku., Bä., Gr., Smend, or JE: Dr., Ho., St.? There is a question whether the forty years appeared at all in J or E; there is no doubt in D and P. The early prophets (Am. 2⁹ᶠᶠ·⁵²⁵ᶠ· Ho. 2¹⁴) regarded the sojourn in the wilderness as a period of divine favor; while D and P view it as a term of punishment. Cf. Gray, Numbers 161.

42. THE PEOPLE STRIVE WITH MOSES. J30.
Nu. 20³ᵃ·⁵

3a And the people strove with Moses, and spake, saying, 5 And wherefore have ye made us to come up out of Egypt, to bring us in unto this evil place? it is no place of seed, or of figs, or of vines, or of pomegranates; neither is there any water to drink.

43. THE BAN AGAINST THE KING OF ARAD.
Nu. 21¹⁻³

1 And the Canaanite, the king of Arad, who dwelt in the South, heard tell that Israel came by the way of Atharim; and he fought against Israel, and took some of them captive. 2 And Israel vowed a vow unto Jehovah, and said, If thou wilt indeed deliver this people into my hand, then I will utterly destroy their cities. 3 And Jehovah hearkened to the voice of Israel, and delivered up the Canaanites; and they utterly destroyed them and their cities: and the name of the place was called Hormah.

44. THE STORY OF BALAAM. E 45.
Nu. 22⁵* ⁶⁻⁷·¹¹·¹⁷⁻¹⁸·²²⁻³⁵·³⁷·³⁹ 24¹⁻²

5 And he sent messengers unto Balaam, the son of Beor, . . . to the land of the children of his people, to call him, saying, Behold, there is a people come out from Egypt: behold they cover the face of the earth, and they abide over against me. 6 Come now therefore, I pray thee, curse me this people; for they are too mighty for me: peradventure I shall prevail, that we may smite them, and that I may drive them out of the land; for I know that he whom thou blessest is blessed, and he whom thou cursest is cursed.

7 And the elders of Moab and the elders of Midian departed with the rewards of divination in their hand; and they came unto Balaam, and spake unto him the words of Balak. 11 Behold, the people that is come out of Egypt, it covereth the face of the earth: now, come curse me them; peradventure I shall be able to fight against them, and shall drive them out. 17 For I will promote thee unto very great honor, and whatsoever thou sayest unto me I will do: come therefore, I pray thee, curse me this people.

18 And Balaam answered and said unto the servants of Balak, If Balak would give me his house full of silver and gold,

---
⁴² Perhaps E: Dr., St., Gr.
⁴³ J: Ku., Co., CH., Ba., Ho., Ad., Bä., St., Dr., Gr. E: Pr., Se. only.
⁴⁴ v. 5: for "his people" read, "Ammon" with LXX, Sam. Pent., Syr., Vulg.; so Ba., Ho., Gray, Gr., Smend, Ki., et al.—vv. 6, 11, 17-18, 37 E: Ba., Ad., Pr., St., Gr., Ki.—v. 39 may be E: Gr. or R: Di., Gray.—vv. 22-35 J: all exc. St.: E. The speaking ass (cf. serpent in J4) and the occurrence of the name "Jehovah" thirteen times point strongly to J.

...24¹] J42–44 103

I cannot go beyond the word of Jehovah my God, to do less or more. 22 And God's anger was kindled because he went; and the angel of Jehovah placed himself in the way for an adversary against him. Now he was riding upon his ass, and his two servants were with him. 23 And the ass saw the angel of Jehovah standing in the way, with his sword drawn in his hand; and the ass turned aside out of the way, and went into the field: and Balaam smote the ass, to turn her into the way. 24 Then the angel of Jehovah stood in a narrow path between the vineyards, a wall being on this side, and a wall on that side. 25 And the ass saw the angel of Jehovah, and she thrust herself unto the wall, and crushed Balaam's foot against the wall: and he smote her again. 26 And the angel of Jehovah went further, and stood in a narrow place, where was no way to turn either to the right hand or to the left. 27 And the ass saw the angel of Jehovah, and she lay down under Balaam: and Balaam's anger was kindled, and he smote the ass with his staff. 28 And Jehovah opened the mouth of the ass, and she said unto Balaam, What have I done unto thee, that thou hast smitten me these three times? 29 And Balaam said unto the ass, Because thou hast mocked me: I would there were a sword in my hand, for now I had killed thee. 30 And the ass said unto Balaam, Am not I thine ass, upon which thou hast ridden all thy life long unto this day? was I ever wont to do so unto thee? And he said, Nay.

31 Then Jehovah opened the eyes of Balaam, and he saw the angel of Jehovah standing in the way, with his sword drawn in his hand; and he bowed his head, and fell on his face. 32 And the angel of Jehovah said unto him, Wherefore hast thou smitten thine ass these three times? behold, I am come forth for an adversary, because thy way is perverse before me: 33 and the ass saw me, and turned aside before me these three times: unless she had turned aside from me, surely now I had even slain thee, and saved her alive. 34 And Balaam said unto the angel of Jehovah, I have sinned; for I knew not that thou stoodest in the way against me: now therefore, if it displease thee, I will get me back again. 35 And the angel of Jehovah said unto Balaam, Go with the men; but only the word that I shall speak unto thee, that thou shalt speak. So Balaam went with the princes of Balak.

37 And Balak said unto Balaam, Did I not earnestly send unto thee to call thee? wherefore camest thou not unto me? am I not able indeed to promote thee to honor? 39 And Balaam went with Balak, and they came unto Kiriath-huzoth.

24¹ And when Balaam saw that it pleased Jehovah to bless Israel, he went not, as at the other times, to meet with enchantments, but he set his face toward the wilderness.

2 And Balaam lifted up his eyes, and he saw Israel dwelling according to their tribes; and the Spirit of God came upon him.

45. THE PARABLES OF BALAAM.   J16.   E46.
Nu. 24³⁻²⁵

Introductory Note.—It is generally agreed that these parables are among the oldest elements in J, and were not composed by J himself, but were taken from earlier sources. In particular, vv. 17-19 show that the writer probably had David in mind (Co., Gr., St., Ho., Gray, et al.) unless we have here a pre-Davidic eschatology (Se., and cf. Rev. 22¹⁶) or unless the "star" is Omri (cf. Moabite Stone, Gray?). Gall's post-exilic dating of the entire passage, based on Messianic exegesis, is generally rejected, as is the Messianic interpretation of v. 17 (so Gray, and even Gr.).

3 And he took up his parable, and said,
    Balaam the son of Beor saith,
    And the man whose eye was closed saith;
4 He saith, who heareth the words of God,
    Who seeth the vision of the Almighty,
    Falling down, and having his eyes open:
5 How goodly are thy tents, O Jacob,
    Thy tabernacles, O Israel!
6 As valleys are they spread forth,
    As gardens by the river-side,
    As lign-aloes which Jehovah hath planted,
    As cedar-trees beside the waters.
7 Water shall flow from his buckets,
    And his seed shall be in many waters,
    And his king shall be higher than Agag,
    And his kingdom shall be exalted.
8 God bringeth him forth out of Egypt;
    He hath as it were the strength of the wild-ox:
    He shall eat up the nations his adversaries,
    And shall break their bones in pieces,
    And smite *them* through with his arrows.

---

[45] v. 4, tr. for "God," "El"; for "the Almighty," "Shaddai" (cf. J19, Gn. 49²⁵; E4viii, Gn. 43¹⁴; P17, Ex. 6²).—v. 7, for "Agag" LXX reads "Gog" (eschatological king).—v. 16, names of God, "El," "Elyon" (here, Dt. 32⁸ and Gn. 14 only in Pentateuch), "Shaddai," cf. v. 4.—vv. 20-24 are generally regarded as ₄R, on account of v. 22 (Assyrian captivity) and v. 24 (Greek rule, cf. Dn. 11³⁰). So: We., Ku., Co., Ho. (but Asshur is Syria), Di., Ad. (who, however, does not admit the reference to the Greek period), Eiselen, St., Gray, Smend, Ki. (R, yet not very late). But Hommel, Gr., Se. insist that the vv. are Davidic; for them, "Asshur" is Arabian "Shur" (cf. J13xv, Gn. 25³·¹⁰). Gr. emends vv. 23-24 to refer to Ishmael, and eliminate Kittim.

9 He couched, he lay down as a lion,
  And as a lioness; who shall rouse him up?
  Blessed be every one that blesseth thee,
  And cursed be every one that curseth thee.
10 And Balak's anger was kindled against Balaam, and he smote his hands together; and Balak said unto Balaam, I called thee to curse mine enemies, and, behold, thou hast altogether blessed them these three times. 11 Therefore now flee thou to thy place: I thought to promote thee unto great honor; but, lo, Jehovah hath kept thee back from honor. 12 And Balaam said unto Balak, Spake I not also to thy messengers that thou sentest unto me, saying, 13 If Balak would give me his house full of silver and gold, I cannot go beyond the word of Jehovah, to do either good or bad of mine own mind; what Jehovah speaketh that will I speak? 14 And now, behold, I go unto my people: come, *and* I will advertise thee what this people shall do to thy people in the latter days. 15 And he took up his parable, and said,
  Balaam the son of Beor saith,
  And the man whose eye was closed saith;
16 He saith, who heareth the words of God,
  And knoweth the knowledge of the Most **High**,
  Who seeth the vision of the Almighty,
  Falling down, and having his eyes open:
17 I see him, but not now;
  I behold him, but not nigh:
  There shall come forth a star out of Jacob,
  And a sceptre shall rise out of Israel,
  And shall smite through the corners of Moab,
  And break down all the sons of tumult.
18 And Edom shall be a possession,
  Seir also shall be a possession, *who were* his enemies;
  While Israel doeth valiantly.
19 And out of Jacob shall one have dominion,
  And shall destroy the remnant from the city.
20 And he looked on Amalek, and took up his parable, and **said**,
  Amalek was the first of the nations;
  But his latter end shall come to destruction.
21 And he looked on the Kenite, and took up his parable, and **said**,
  Strong is thy dwelling-place,
  And thy nest is set in the rock.
22 Nevertheless Kain shall be wasted,
  Until Asshur shall carry thee away captive.
23 And he took up his parable, and said,
  Alas, who shall live when God doeth this?
24 But ships *shall come* from the coast of Kittim,

And they shall afflict Asshur, and shall afflict Eber;
And he also shall come to destruction.
25 And Balaam rose up, and went and returned to his place; and Balak also went his way.

46. IMMORALITY AND IDOLATRY WITH THE MOABITES. E47. Nu. 25$^{1b.2.4}$

1b And the people began to play the harlot with the daughters of Moab: 2 for they called the people unto the sacrifices of their gods; and the people did eat, and bowed down to their gods.

4 And Jehovah said unto Moses, Take all the chiefs of the people, and hang them up unto Jehovah before the sun, that the fierce anger of Jehovah may turn away from Israel.

47. CONQUEST OF GILEAD FROM THE AMORITES BY THE CHILDREN OF MACHIR THE SON OF MANASSEH. Jg. 1. Dt. 3$^{14-15}$ (R: Dr., Smend, Marti, St. et al.). P78. Nu. 32$^{39-42}$

39 And the children of Machir the son of Manasseh went to Gilead, and took it, and dispossessed the Amorites that were therein. 40 And Moses gave Gilead unto Machir the son of Manasseh; and he dwelt therein. 41 And Jair, the son of Manasseh went and took the towns thereof, and called them Havvoth-jair. 42 And Nobah went and took Kenath, and the villages thereof, and called it Nobah, after his own name.

48. JOSHUA'S MEETING WITH THE "PRINCE OF THE HOST." Josh. 5$^{13-15}$

13 And it came to pass, when Joshua was by Jericho, that he lifted up his eyes and looked, and, behold, there stood a man over against him with his sword drawn in his hand: and Joshua went unto him, and said unto him, Art thou for us, or for our adversaries? 14 And he said, Nay; but *as* prince of the host of Jehovah am I now come. And Joshua fell on his face to the earth, and did worship, and said unto him, What saith my lord unto his servant? 15 And the prince of Jehovah's hosts said unto Joshua, Put off thy shoe from off thy foot; for the place wherein thou standest is holy. And Joshua did so.

49. HIVITES SEEK A COVENANT WITH ISRAEL. E61. Josh. 9$^{6-7}$

6 And they went to Joshua unto the camp at Gilgal, and

---

[46] v. 1b is generally treated literally. Cf. Ho. 1-3.
[47] E: Di., St. The fragment is probably misplaced; it should come after the death of Moses (Jg. 1, Gray) or before J46 (Nu. 25^{1b}, Smend).
[48] J: Di., Ho., Ki., CH., Gr., GFM., Pr., Smend. JEs: Ku., Co., Dr., Ad. E: St.
[49] There is very little consensus among critics as to the exact amount of material in

said unto him, and to the men of Israel, We are come from a far country: now therefore make ye a covenant with us. 7 And the men of Israel said unto the Hivites, Peradventure ye dwell among us; and how shall we make a covenant with you?

50. INCOMPLETE CONQUEST OF THE GESHURITES AND MAACATHITES.

Josh. 13[13]

13 Nevertheless the children of Israel drove not out the Geshurites, nor the Maacathites: but Geshur and Maacath dwell in the midst of Israel unto this day.

51. CONQUEST OF HEBRON AND DEBIR UNDER CALEB THE JUDAHITE. Jg. 1[11-15]. J57, 60. E65. P90.

Josh. 15[13-19]

13 And unto Caleb the son of Jephunneh he gave a portion among the children of Judah, according to the commandment of Jehovah to Joshua, even Kiriath-arba, *which Arba was* the father of Anak (the same is Hebron). 14 And Caleb drove out thence the three sons of Anak: Sheshai, and Ahiman, and Talmai, the children of Anak. 15 And he went up thence against the inhabitants of Debir: now the name of Debir beforetime was Kiriath-sepher. 16 And Caleb said, He that smiteth Kiriath-sepher, and taketh it, to him will I give Achsah my daughter to wife. 17 And Othniel the son of Kenaz, the brother of Caleb, took it: and he gave him Achsah his daughter to wife. 18 And it came to pass, when she came *unto him*, that she moved him to ask of her father a field: and she alighted from off her ass; and Caleb said, What wouldest thou? 19 And she said, Give me a blessing; for that thou hast set me in the land of the South, give me also springs of water. And he gave her the upper springs and the nether springs.

52. INCOMPLETE CONQUEST OF THE JEBUSITES (IN JERUSALEM) BY THE TRIBE OF JUDAH (OR BENJAMIN). E62. P90. Cf. 2 Sam. 5[6-10].

Josh. 15[63] Jg. 1[21]

Josh. 15[63] And as for the Jebusites, the inhabitants of Jerusalem, the children of Judah could not drive them out: but

---

Joshua that is to be assigned to the various sources. J doubtless had a much longer narrative of the covenant with the Hivites than vv. 6-7. However, the present analysis will proceed very conservatively, and will include in J only those passages from Joshua with reference to which there is practical unanimity. All doubtful material is printed as E, cf. E53-73. St. has been of great aid in Joshua, because he has collated the views of many authorities with reference to the analysis.

[50] Rd: Smend only (in imitation of 15[63] 16[10] 17[12]).

[51] vv. 13-19 are verbatim the same as Jg. 1[11-15], except that Jg. reads "Caleb's younger brother" (v. 13, cf. Josh. v. 17), "Caleb said unto her" (v. 14, cf. Josh. v. 18b), "she said unto him," "and Caleb gave her" (v. 15, cf. Josh. v. 19). Thus we have two versions of the same J passage, practically identical. Josh. v. 13 R: Smend only.

the Jebusites dwell with the children of Judah at Jerusalem unto this day.

Jg. 1^{21} And the children of Benjamin did not drive out the Jebusites that inhabited Jerusalem; but the Jebusites dwell with the children of Benjamin in Jerusalem unto this day.

53. INCOMPLETE CONQUEST OF GEZER.
Josh. 16^{10} Jg. 1^{29}

Josh. 16^{10} And they drove not out the Canaanites that dwelt in Gezer: but the Canaanites dwell in the midst of Ephraim unto this day, and are become servants to do taskwork.

Jg. 1^{29} And Ephraim drove not out the Canaanites that dwelt in Gezer; but the Canaanites dwelt in Gezer among them.

54. THE LOT OF MANASSEH. J61. E66, 67.
Josh. 17$^{11-18}$ (Jg. 1$^{27-28}$)

11 And Manasseh had in Issachar and in Asher Beth-shean and its towns, and Ibleam and its towns, and the inhabitants of Dor and its towns, and the inhabitants of En-dor and its towns, and the inhabitants of Taanach and its towns, and the inhabitants of Megiddo and its towns, even the three heights. 12 Yet the children of Manasseh could not drive out *the inhabitants of* those cities; but the Canaanites would dwell in that land. 13 And it came to pass, when the children of Israel were waxed strong, that they put the Canaanites to taskwork, and did not utterly drive them out.

14 And the children of Joseph spake unto Joshua, saying, Why hast thou given me but one lot and one part for an inheritance, seeing I am a great people, forasmuch as hitherto Jehovah hath blessed me? 15 And Joshua said unto them, If thou be a great people, get thee up to the forest, and cut down for thyself there in the land of the Perizzites and of the Rephaim; since the hill-country of Ephraim is too narrow for thee. 16 And the children of Joseph said, The hill-country is not enough for us: and all the Canaanites that dwell in the land of the valley have chariots of iron, both they who are in Beth-shean and its towns, and they who are in the valley of Jezreel. 17 And Joshua spake unto the house of Joseph, even to Ephraim and to Manasseh, saying, Thou art a great people, and hast great power; thou shalt not have one lot only: 18 but the hill-country shall be thine; for though it is a forest, thou

---

[54] Parallel to vv. 11-13 is Jg. 1$^{27-28}$, as follows:
27 And Manasseh did not drive out *the inhabitants of* Beth-shean and its towns, nor *of* Taanach and its towns, nor the inhabitants of Dor and its towns, nor the inhabitants of Ibleam and its towns, nor the inhabitants of Megiddo and its towns; but the Canaanites would dwell in that land. 28 And it came to pass, when Israel was waxed strong, that they put the Canaanites to taskwork, and did not utterly drive them out.
Josh 17$^{14-15}$ E: Pr., Smend. Rd: We.

shalt cut it down, and the goings out thereof shall be thine; for thou shalt drive out the Canaanites, though they have chariots of iron, and though they are strong.

55. DAN CONQUERS LESHEM. J63. P94.

Josh. 19⁴⁷

47 And the border of the children of Dan went out beyond them; for the children of Dan went up and fought against Leshem, and took it, and smote it with the edge of the sword, and possessed it, and dwelt therein; and called Leshem, Dan, after the name of Dan their father.

56. JUDAH AND SIMEON DEFEAT ADONI-BEZEK. E62.

Jg. 1¹⁻⁷

1¹ And it came to pass after the death of Joshua, that the children of Israel asked of Jehovah, saying, Who shall go up for us first against the Canaanites, to fight against them? 2 And Jehovah said, Judah shall go up: behold, I have delivered the land into his hand. 3 And Judah said unto Simeon his brother, Come up with me into my lot, that we may fight against the Canaanites; and I likewise will go with thee into thy lot. So Simeon went with him. 4 And Judah went up; and Jehovah delivered the Canaanites and the Perizzites into their hand: and they smote of them in Bezek ten thousand men. 5 And they found Adoni-bezek in Bezek; and they fought against him, and they smote the Canaanites and the Perizzites. 6 But Adoni-bezek fled; and they pursued after him, and caught him, and cut off his thumbs and his great toes. 7 And Adoni-bezek said, Threescore and ten kings, having their thumbs and their great toes cut off, gathered *their food* under my table; as I have done, so God hath requited me. And they brought him to Jerusalem, and he died there.

57. JUDAH ATTACKS HEBRON. J51, 60; E65.

Jg. 1⁸⁻¹⁰

8 And the children of Judah fought against Jerusalem, and took it, and smote it with the edge of the sword, and set the city on fire. 9 And afterward the children of Judah went down to fight against the Canaanites that dwelt in the hill-country, and in the South, and in the lowland. 10 And Judah went against the Canaanites that dwelt in Hebron (now the name of Hebron beforetime was Kiriath-arba); and they smote Sheshai, and Ahiman, and Talmai.

58. ALLIANCE OF THE KENITE WITH JUDAH.

Jg. 1¹⁶

16 And the children of the Kenite, Moses' brother-in-law,

---

⁵⁸ For "brother-in-law," Am. Rev., margin reads "father-in-law." Cf. J24ii.

went up out of the city of palm-trees with the children of Judah into the wilderness of Judah, which is in the south of Arad; and they went and dwelt with the people.

59. VICTORIES OF JUDAH AND SIMEON.

Jg. 1$^{17-19}$

17 And Judah went with Simeon his brother, and they smote the Canaanites that inhabited Zephath, and utterly destroyed it. And the name of the city was called Hormah. 18 Also Judah took Gaza with the border thereof, and Ashkelon with the border thereof, and Ekron, with the border thereof. 19 And Jehovah was with Judah; and he drove out *the inhabitants of* the hill-country; for he could not drive out the inhabitants of the valley, because they had chariots of iron.

60. CALEB RECEIVES HEBRON. J51.

Jg. 1^{20}

20 And they gave Hebron unto Caleb, as Moses had spoken: and he drove out thence the three sons of Anak.

Jg. 1^{21}, cf. J52.

61. THE HOUSE OF JOSEPH TAKES BETHEL (Luz). J54. E66.

Jg. 1$^{22-26}$

22 And the house of Joseph, they also went up against Beth-el; and Jehovah was with them. 23 And the house of Joseph sent to spy out Beth-el. (Now the name of the city beforetime was Luz.) 24 And the watchers saw a man come forth out of the city, and they said unto him, Show us, we pray thee, the entrance into the city, and we will deal kindly with thee. 25 And he showed them the entrance into the city; and they smote the city with the edge of the sword; but they let the man go and all his family. 26 And the man went into the land of the Hittites, and built a city, and called the name thereof Luz, which is the name thereof unto this day.

Jg. 1$^{27-28}$, cf. J54.

Jg. 1^{29}, cf. J53.

62. INCOMPLETE CONQUEST OF THE CANAANITES BY ZEBULUN, ASHER, AND NAPHTALI.

Jg. 1$^{30-33}$

30 Zebulun drove not out the inhabitants of Kitron, nor the inhabitants of Nahalol; but the Canaanites dwelt among them, and became subject to taskwork.

31 Asher drove not out the inhabitants of Acco, nor the inhabitants of Sidon, nor of Ahlab, nor of Achzib, nor of Helbah, nor of Aphik, nor of Rehob; 32 but the Asherites dwelt among the Canaanites, the inhabitants of the land; for they did not drive them out.
33 Naphtali drove not out the inhabitants of Beth-shemesh, nor the inhabitants of Beth-anath; but he dwelt among the Canaanites, the inhabitants of the land: nevertheless the inhabitants of Beth-shemesh and of Beth-anath became subject to taskwork.

63. Conflict between Dan and the Amorites. J55.
Jg. 1³⁴⁻³⁶

34 And the Amorites forced the children of Dan into the hill-country; for they would not suffer them to come down to the valley; 35 but the Amorites would dwell in mount Heres, in Aijalon, and in Shaalbim: yet the hand of the house of Joseph prevailed, so that they became subject to taskwork. 36 And the border of the Amorites was from the ascent of Akrabbim, from the rock and upward.

64. Sacrifice at Bochim.
Jg. 2¹⁻⁵

1 And the angel of Jehovah came up from Gilgal to Bochim. And he said, I made you to go up out of Egypt, and have brought you unto the land which I sware unto your fathers; and I said, I will never break my covenant with you: 2 and ye shall make no covenant with the inhabitants of this land; ye shall break down their altars. But ye have not hearkened unto my voice: why have ye done this? 3 Wherefore I also said, I will not drive them out from before you; but they shall be *as thorns* in your sides, and their gods shall be a snare unto you. 4 And it came to pass, when the angel of Jehovah spake these words unto all the children of Israel, that the people lifted up their voice, and wept. 5 And they called the name of that place Bochim: and they sacrificed there unto Jehovah.

---
⁶⁴ vv. 1b-5a Rd: We., E. Meyer, Co., GFM., Bu., Ki., et al.

CHAPTER II

E : THE ELOHISTIC OR EPHRAIMITIC NARRATIVE

1. LITERARY CHARACTERISTICS.

a. Is E a Literary Unity?

The majority hold a view of E's unity analogous to their view of J (q. v.). Since Kuenen the majority have distinguished E^1 and E^2. E^1 is, on the whole, prior to the literary prophets and certainly prior to the fall of Samaria 721. But Ex. 32 seems to presuppose that event, as punishment for "the sin of Jeroboam, son of Nebat." Hence Ex. 32, the Decalogue of Ex. 20, and all allied passages (including Josh. 24) are assigned to E^2 writing probably in Judah (although Cornill locates him in Israel) in the seventh century.

But Kittel, B. Luther, and Smend stoutly defend the unity of E, and its composition by a single literary personality, "who sketched the main plan and also wrote with reference to J, revising J's standpoint" (Kittel). E is "a thoroughly unified work" (Smend); it should be noted, however, that Smend's J^2 absorbs some of the difficult passages commonly assigned to E^2. And Proksch, who recognizes a large number of secondary elements in E, is impressed by its unity; "the plan is never lost sight of, and the pious tone of an ancient prophetic narrator determines the whole mood." There is, then, rather more inclination to recognize a single dominating plan and personality back of E than back of J.

b. The Extent of E.

E is generally held to begin with the promise to Abraham, Gn. 15, and to end with the national assembly in Josh. 24 (so, e. g., Sellin). But some, as in the case of J (q. v.), trace it through Jg., Sm., and parts of K. Smend holds that E originally carried the history down to the fall of Samaria in 721.

c. The Literary Style of E.

The literary style of E is, in general,' much closer to J than

ELOHISTIC OR EPHRAIMITIC NARRATIVE 113

to Dt. or P. Indeed, so similar are J and E that critics concede that literary criteria alone would often not suffice to distinguish E from J. Nevertheless, there are certain general differences. E is less vivid and concrete; more artificial and reflective than J (so most critics, from Bacon to Eichrodt; but Driver makes J more reflective). Yet, although more artificial and polished, E is regarded as less successful from an artistic standpoint than is J, especially in the effective structure of a series of related incidents (Proksch). E is at his best in the picturing of touching, pathetic, "teary" scenes, such as the sacrifice of Isaac, the expulsion of Hagar and Ishmael, or Jacob's tenderness to his grandsons (Proksch, Gunkel, Eichrodt).

E is characterized by a "learned" or antiquarian interest. He seems to have a scholar's idea of system far more than does J, and also lays stress on minor details from antiquity. Steuernagel cites as instances of this tendency his use of the divine name, avoiding "Jehovah" prior to Ex. 3; his hints at a chronological system in Gn. 15^{13} $29^{18.27}$ $31^{38.41}$ 45^6; his appeal to literary sources in Nu. $21^{14.27}$ (cf. JE, perhaps E, Josh. 10^{13}); his familiarity with Egyptian names and local color; his mention of the names of relatively unimportant characters such as Eliezer, Deborah, Hur, Eldad, and Medad. Smend adds E's preference for Reuben (instead of Judah J) in the Joseph story; and the view that Manasseh was born before Ephraim.

d. E's Peculiarities in the Use of Proper Names.

E is guided by a definite theory that the name Jehovah was first revealed in Ex. 3. Hence he never uses that name prior to Ex. 3, but always calls the divine being simply God (Elohim). Gn. 22^{14} and 28^{21}, the only apparent exceptions, are almost universally regarded as due to the hand of Rje. After Ex. 3, E is less consistent. In many cases he still says "God"; in others "Jehovah." Many critics connect this difference in usage with the two strata, E^1 and E^2.

Other proper names used characteristically by E are Horeb (instead of Sinai J); Amorites (as equivalent to J's Canaanites, the general term for the early inhabitants of Canaan)*; Jethro

---

* Dt. follows E in using the names "Horeb" and "Amorites." There are also other signs that Dt. preferred E.

(or Jether, instead of Hobab J); and probably E always spoke of Jacob, never of Israel as a man, although the redaction makes this relatively hypothetical. Characteristic is also the expression "the man Moses." Aaron appears in E, not in J; Joshua is much more prominent in E. The Hittites are absent from E (Proksch).

e. Other Characteristic Words and Expressions.

Certain formulæ are frequent in E, such as: "and it came to pass after these things"; "and he called" (name of person addressed is usually mentioned twice), "and he answered, Here am I, or I hear" (cf. 1 Sm. 3^{10}; Is. 6^{8}); "and he rose up early in the morning"; "lead out of Egypt"; "speak with"; "angel of God"; "mount of God"; "staff of God" (the last three rarely).

E (only) mentions massebahs (pillars) which are forbidden Dt. 16^{22}; he—but not J—uses the word "prophet"* Gn. 20^{7}; Nu. 11^{29} 12^{6} and possibly Dt. 34^{10}, cf. Miriam the prophetess Ex. 15^{20}.

He employs characteristic Hebrew words for: "be afraid," "handmaid," "harden" (of Pharaoh's heart), "master" (baal, meaning also "owner" or "husband"), "sack," "younger," and a few others. See lists as in J.

2. CHARACTERISTIC IDEAS.

a. Aim of E.

E has a more specific aim than does J. Bacon, following Schrader, describes E as the "history of the theocratic succession." That God is the supreme ruler of Israel, her Lawgiver, guiding her destinies from Abraham to the promised land, is recognized as a central idea clearly distinguished from J's simpler, more nationalistic, ethical, and religious ideal. This trait is most clearly expressed in Gn. 37^{8} Nu. $23^{9.21.23}$ (Dt. 33^{5} R), etc. (So Sellin, Cornill, Eichrodt, et al.).

b. Characteristic Religious Ideas.

E's conception of God is sublime and majestic, and nearer to the "moral monotheism" of Elijah (so Eichrodt) or Amos

---

* Of the Hexateuchal sources, D is the only one to mention prophets freely; P uses the term only Ex. 7^{1}, in a special sense. J and E were written before the prophetic movement had reached its fullest expression; P after it had died away. D was a product of that movement at its height.

ELOHISTIC OR EPHRAIMITIC NARRATIVE 115

(so Smend) than was J. Like J, he is not a theoretical monotheist; that is, he does not deny the existence of other gods (cf. Baal Peor in Nu. 25). But his henotheism is for all practical purposes monotheistic in spirit. Smend holds that the very use of the name "Elohim" to designate Jehovah, God of Israel, is monotheistic—Jehovah is *the* God.

E's God is generally regarded as more spiritual, less anthropomorphic than J's. Kittel says that E tolerates no anthropomorphisms. This is extreme. Steuernagel points out that E is in a measure anthropomorphic. God speaks face to face with Moses Ex. 33^{11} Nu. 12^8. He writes the tables of the law with his own finger Ex. 31^{18}. He speaks to Balaam Nu. $22^{9,12,20}$. He is seen and heard Ex. 3 and 19, yet not in human form.

But all agree that E strives to suppress the anthropomorphic factors in the tradition as he molds it (Eerdmans alone denies this). E never has a concrete representation of God, as does J; the theophanies of E are "colorless" (Eichrodt). God is present in the pillar of cloud and fire; he is symbolized by the ark; he dwells invisible in the tent of meeting. On Horeb he is veiled in a cloud. He does not appear in physical form; a voice is heard but no form seen, angels appear frequently as God's representatives, the divine will is imparted through dreams and visions. But God himself is too exalted to walk in the garden in the cool of the day.

While E's conception is less human, more spiritual than J's, it marks at the same time in one sense a loss in religious value. E's God is more remote, distant, transcendent than J's. He is not found in the everyday course of events; he is not immanent in nature. E is philosophically a dualist and a deist. There is, truly, in E a conception of a Divine Providence, that causes all things—even man's sin—to work together for good (Cornill cites Gn. 50^{20}). But probably E thought in terms of "special providences" rather than in terms of a God "in whom we live, and move, and have our being."

E rejects the divineness of the natural, which had been J's view, in the interests of a marked supernaturalism. Cornill contrasts Gn. 12^{10-20} J with Gn. 20^{1-17} E. The former is realistic, human, natural. The latter is equipped with the full apparatus of miracle, vision and divine intervention. Instances of this supernaturalism may be multiplied; so, in E's account of the birth of Issachar and Joseph, Gn. $30^{17ff.}$; the increase of the herds of Jacob, Gn. $31^{9ff.}$; the fact that even angels sometimes speak from heaven, Gn. 21^{17} 22^{11} instead of coming down in human form to earth, as in J; the magical properties of Moses's rod; the heightening of the miraculous in the accounts of the plagues and the crossing of the Red Sea; and the writing of the tables of law by the finger of God. God intervenes, as in Abraham's sacrifice of Isaac, in Jacob's experience at Bethel, in the wrestling with the angel (or God), in Sarah's relations to Abimelech, and in the dealings of Jacob with Laban.

With reference to the cultus, E is more friendly to sacrifice and ritual than is J (cf. Gn. 22, substitution of animal for human sacrifice). The appearance of Aaron in E indicates a tendency toward the priestly conception of religion, although Smend views the mention of Aaron as an involuntary concession on E's part.

E, and especially E^2, is hostile to all forms of idolatry. E's mention of massebahs is not an exception to this; for he interprets them as mere memorial stones, not as images or cult-objects. He rejects the teraphim, and the worship of any other god than God. He condemns idolatry in general in the Decalogue, and the worship of the golden calf in Ex. 32, cf. 1K. 12^{28}. Smend points out that the serpent of Nu. 21 is not an idol, but merely a means of grace.

E's relation to prophetism (cf. the use of the word "prophet," already mentioned) is generally regarded as even closer than J's. Bacon, for instance, views E as a man of the type of Hosea. The great ideas of E are those of the prophetic movement, except that most of the prophets laid little or no stress on the miraculous. Proksch, Kittel, et al., trace the influence of Elijah; Smend of Amos and Hosea.

Characteristically prophetic is the idea of an individual relation to God Gn. $20^{7\cdot17}$ Nu. $21^{7\cdot8}$, which Proksch compares to the attitude of Micaiah ben Imlah, 1K. 22. Prophetic also is

ELOHISTIC OR EPHRAIMITIC NARRATIVE 117

E's conception of faith Ex. 3^{14}, and in particular of God as trying or testing man's faith, Gn. 22; Ex. 20^{20}; Dt. 33^8.

c. Characteristic Ethical Ideas.

E has a decidedly more keen moral sense than has J. In numerous instances E's version of a story removes or softens the morally offensive features of J. Eichrodt compares Gn. 16^6 J with Gn. $21^{11ff.}$ E; Gn. $30^{28ff.}$ J with Gn. $31^{4ff.}$ E; Gn. $12^{10ff.}$ J with Gn. 20 E. He is thus more didactic than J.

Smend sees in Hosea and E Nu. 23^9 Josh. 24 Ex. 20 the origin of the concept of heathenism—of the Gentile as opposed to the Jew. E's Abraham assumes that the heathen have no morals, Gn. 20.

Stade, Holzinger, et al. detect a tendency to pessimism, which Proksch admits in E^2 but denies in E^1.

d. Attitude toward Culture.

J's friendliness to civilization and the arts is entirely missing in E. The prohibition of all images in religion acted as a deterrent to art.

e. Attitude toward History.

For all E's moral monotheism, he thinks of God's interest as rather narrowly confined to Israel. "The idea of world-history is missing" (Proksch). The absence of a creation-narrative, of "tables of nations," etc., is significant of this tendency. Smend, however, notes that Abraham's home was in Mesopotamia Josh. $24^{2-3.14-15}$.

Sellin points out certain characteristic historical standpoints of E. He viewed the patriarchs as polytheists, Josh. $24^{2ff.}$. He lays more stress on the epoch-making work of Moses than does J, but he also introduces important subordinate figures, such as Aaron and Miriam, who play an influential part.

J had represented the conquest of Canaan as a slow and painful process. E, on the contrary, seems to hold that Canaan was conquered by the cooperating tribes under the leadership of Joshua in a few years, by the aid of divine intervention Josh. 14^{6-15}.

E's great heroes are Joseph and Joshua.

3 HOME OF AUTHOR.

We may speak with very little qualification of another assured result of criticism, namely, that E—at least in its original form—was written in the northern kingdom, not in Judah. Smend is the only advocate of the view that the home of E was in the south. He admits E's interest in north Israel, but explains it on the ground that a southern author might entertain a hope for the future restoration of north Israel. He uses Dt. 19[8] to prove that the Jews considered themselves the spiritual successors of Israel. He asserts that Abraham, "a specifically Judahite hero," plays a larger part in E than in J; and E has the patriarchs reside in Beersheba, a southern shrine. This fact he regards as especially significant of the southern origin of E, inasmuch as J makes Jacob dwell in Shechem and Bethel, conspicuous northern shrines. Smend, however, admits that a large part of the content of J and E comes from the ancient common saga-tradition; and not every detail can be traced to the special interest of the writer. It may be that the Judahite features in E come from that tradition.

Over against Smend, the overwhelming majority of scholars since Wellhausen take the position that E's home is to be found in the northern kingdom (hence Ephraimitic). But Wellhausen, Kuenen, and many others have felt that E^2, especially Ex. 32, may have been written in Judah. Cornill, Steuernagel, et al. are not convinced of this; they hold that such condemnation of the calf-worship could easily emanate from a north Israelite, like Hosea.

Let us survey the evidence for the northern origin of E. The great heroes of E are Joseph (father of the northern tribes, Ephraim and Manasseh, cf. Gn. 37[8]—and Rachel, the mother of Joseph, is Jacob's favorite wife) and Joshua, an Ephraimite, Josh. 19[49-50].

Numerous graves, all in the territory of the northern kingdom, are mentioned: of Deborah, Rachel, Joseph, Joshua, Eleazar (Gn. 35[8.19-20] 50[24-25] Josh. 24[30.33]).

E has a special interest in the shrines of the northern kingdom: as Bethel (where tithes were to be paid Gn. 28[22]), Gilgal, Ebal, Mahanaim, Penuel, and Shechem (Kittel's list). Shechem is especially important Gn. 33[19] 34. 35[4] Josh. 24[1.25-26.32].

There are plain indications of the prosperity and predominance of the northern kingdom in Gn. 48[22] and Dt. 33[13-17].
One peculiarity of E constitutes a problem for the theory of its north Israelitic origin. The principal residence of Abraham in E is Beersheba, Gn. 20[1] 21[14,31] 22[19]. E is, indeed, silent regarding Hebron, Abraham's home in J and the chief ancient sanctuary of Judah. Nevertheless, Beersheba is in the remote south of Judæan territory, and Smend cannot see why a northern writer should thus glorify this shrine. Other critics offer an explanation, which is probably satisfactory: Beersheba is proven by 1K. 19[3] Amos 5[5] 8[14] (Ho. 4[15] "swear," in Hebrew suggests Beersheba also) to have been a favorite shrine for north Israelites and the goal of their pilgrimages. It would thus be quite natural for E, the northerner, to hallow it by associating it with the name of Abraham.

4. THE DATE OF E—750.

The great majority of critics date E in its original form about 750. So Wellhausen, Kuenen, Stade, Holzinger, Cornill, Proksch, Steuernagel, B. Luther, Kittel (since 1912), George Foote Moore, McNeile, Bacon, and many others. Most of these hold that E in its present form is a revised edition, published after the fall of Samaria in 721. Smend's view of the unity of E leads him to bring the entire document down to 700-650. But it is questionable whether Ex. 32 and Josh. 24 presuppose the fall of Samaria any more than do the prophecies of Amos and Hosea. If Cornill and Steuernagel are right in holding that E[2] was a north Israelite, and Smend is right regarding the unity of E, perhaps most of the E[2] passages were written by E in 750.

The only important difference of opinion regarding the date of E comes from Sellin, who discovers an E[1] written in the reign of Solomon. But his E[2] comes down to 800, and so he does not differ substantially from the consensus; for everyone would admit that E contains material that originated at least as early as the united kingdom.

a. Evidence for the *terminus ad quem* of the Composition of E.

120 SOURCES OF THE HEXATEUCH

i. Like J, and for similar reasons, E must have been written before Dt. Contrast the law permitting worship anywhere Ex. 20^{24} E with Dt.'s centralization of worship in Jerusalem Dt. 12. E must have been written before Dt. 16^{22}, with its prohibition of massebahs (cf. Josh. 4, and Ex. 24$^{3-8}$ E).

ii. Again, E, while more prophetic than J, must have been written before the work of Amos and Hosea had exerted much influence. On this all scholars except Smend agree. The year 750 becomes our *terminus ad quem*.

iii. Its north Israelitic origin implies that E was written before 721.

b. Evidence for the *terminus a quo* of the Composition of E.

i. E's use of ancient sources proves that it is not one of the oldest of Hebrew writings. Such sources are the Song of Miriam, Ex. 15$^{20-21}$; the Book of the Wars of Jehovah Nu. 21^{14}; the parables (taunting poems) of Balaam; the "book" mentioned in Ex. 17^{17}; and the Code of the Covenant, Ex. 20^{22}-23^{33}. In this connection should be mentioned the Book of Jashar, cited Josh. 10^{13} (JE, probably E). 2Sm. 1^{18} says that David's lament in the Song of the Bow was taken from the Book of Jashar. The LXX attributes the blessing of Solomon 1K. 8$^{12-13}$, to the same source. The Book of Jashar, then, was written during or later than the reign of Solomon· and E, which quotes Jashar, must have been still later.

ii. E was probably written after the division of the kingdom in 933. Proksch cites in proof of this statement Gn. 37^8 Nu. 23^{21} Dt. 33^7—and yet none of these passages is certainly a reference to the divided kingdom.

iii. E was written after J 850, as has already been proven under J (q. v.).

iv. E's Egyptian names (such as Potiphar, Zaphenath-paneah, etc.) are found in Egyptian records as far back as the XXII. dynasty, tenth century B. C., but not earlier (so Brugsch, Steindorf, Max Müller, Barton JBL., vol. 28, p. 153). Hence E was not written before B. C. 1000-900.

c. The Closer Determination of the Date of E.

In dating E at 750 (the *terminus ad quem*), scholars take into account the following factors:

i. E's mood of theocratic-national pride and joy on the whole presupposes a period of national prosperity, such as the reign of Jeroboam II 783-743.

ii. The relation of Amos, and especially of Hosea, to the ideas of E is such that these prophets seem to stand under its immediate influence. Sellin says, "The prophet Hosea lives and moves in the Elohist, he seems to be emerging from a current that has just recently produced E." Proksch calls E "a witness to the development of prophecy between Elijah and Hosea."

We may, then, with considerable certainty ascribe E to the latter part of the reign of Jeroboam II, so about 750.

5. THE RELATION OF E TO J.

In general, J and E are parallel accounts of the same history. E adds very few new facts not found in J, but works over substantially the same material from more reflective and theological standpoints, softening the morally offensive passages in J, substituting religious for profane motives, and divine miracles for human deeds, thus spiritualizing the ancient hero-sagas (Smend, Kittel). E moves the center of gravity of Israel's history from Judah to Joseph (Sellin).

It is evident that neither J nor E composed his narrative out of his imagination. Each drew on the existing tradition. About this fact there is no question.

But there is a question whether E actually used J. There are numerous considerations that point in the direction of the use of J by E. If E were drawing on the oral tradition quite independently of J, one would naturally expect more differences between J and E, more new materials in E. Further, the differences between the two seem to be just such as would exist if E had J before him and were intentionally improving on J's version. Hence there have been several scholars that have asserted a literary dependence of E on J: so Wellhausen, Kuenen, E. Meyer, B. Luther, Smend; George Foote Moore believes that E was probably acquainted with J, but did not copy him. Dillmann, who held to the priority of E, thought that J used E as a source.

But the great majority of critics deny a literary dependence (Eichrodt, Gunkel, et al.). It is generally held (with Steuernagel) that the differences from J are too great to be explained on the theory of literary dependence. The numerous agreements between the two are explained by the actual historical facts, and by the fixed form which the oral tradition had assumed during the united kingdom.

THE TEXT OF E

1. THE STORY OF ABRAHAM. J13. P7.

1i. GOD PROMISES SEED AND THE LAND TO ABRAM. J13i.
Gn. 15¹ᵇ·³ᵃ·²ᵇ·⁵·¹²ᵃ*·¹³⁻¹⁵·¹⁶

1b . . . in a vision, saying, Fear not, Abram: I am thy shield, *and* thy exceeding great reward.

3a And Abram said, Behold, to me thou hast given no seed, 2b and he that shall be possessor of my house is Eliezer of Damascus.

5 And he brought him forth abroad, and said, Look now toward heaven, and number the stars, if thou be able to number them: and he said unto him, So shall thy seed be. 12a . . . A deep sleep fell upon Abram . . . 13 And he said unto Abram, Know of a surety that thy seed shall be sojourners in a land that is not theirs, and shall serve them; and they shall afflict them four hundred years; 14 and also that nation, whom they shall serve, will I judge: and afterward shall they come out with great substance. 15 But thou shalt go to thy fathers in peace; thou shalt be buried in a good old age. 16. And in the fourth generation they shall come hither again: for the iniquity of the Amorite is not yet full.

1ii. ABRAHAM'S DECEPTION CONCERNING SARAH IN GERAR.
J13iv, 14iv.
Gn. 20¹⁻¹⁸

1 And Abraham journeyed from thence toward the land of the South, and dwelt between Kadesh and Shur; and he sojourned in Gerar. 2 And Abraham said of Sarah his wife, She is my sister: and Abimelech king of Gerar sent, and took Sarah. 3 But God came to Abimelech in a dream of the night, and said to him, Behold, thou art but a dead man, because of the woman whom thou hast taken; for she is a man's wife. 4 Now Abimelech had not come near her: and he said, Lord, wilt thou slay even a righteous nation? 5 Said he not himself unto me, She is my sister? and she, even she herself said, He is my brother: in the integrity of my heart and the innocency of my hands have I done this. 6 And God said unto him in the dream, Yea, I know that in the integrity of thy heart thou hast done this, and I also withheld thee from sinning against me: therefore suffered I thee not to touch her. 7 Now therefore restore the man's wife; for he is a prophet, and he shall

---

¹ⁱ There is considerable difference in detail among critics with reference to the above analysis. Many admit the presence of J and E, but do not attempt to separate them. Bu., CH., Co., Gu., St., Mi., Ki., SB (13-15 a: J) agree substantially on the analysis as given. But the division is highly precarious (Sk., Eichr., Ki.). The opening words of E (perh. "God spake to Abram") were omitted by Rje in favor of J v. 1a. Tr. in 1b: "thy reward is exceeding great."

¹ⁱⁱ v. 18 Rje: so all, vs. v. 6. Eerd. finds polytheism in v. 13, on account of the use of "Elohim" with a plural verb in Hebrew.

pray for thee, and thou shalt live: and if thou restore her not, know thou that thou shalt surely die, thou, and all that are thine. 8 And Abimelech rose early in the morning, and called all his servants, and told all these things in their ears: and the men were sore afraid. 9 Then Abimelech called Abraham, and said unto him, What hast thou done unto us? and wherein have I sinned against thee, that thou hast brought on me and on my kingdom a great sin? thou hast done deeds unto me that ought not to be done. 10 And Abimelech said unto Abraham, What sawest thou, that thou hast done this thing? 11 And Abraham said, Because I thought, Surely the fear of God is not in this place; and they will slay me for my wife's sake. 12 And moreover she is indeed my sister, the daughter of my father, but not the daughter of my mother; and she became my wife: 13 and it came to pass, when God caused me to wander from my father's house, that I said unto her, This is thy kindness which thou shalt show unto me: at every place whither we shall come, say of me, He is my brother. 14 And Abimelech took sheep and oxen, and men-servants and women-servants, and gave them unto Abraham, and restored him Sarah his wife. 15 And Abimelech said, Behold, my land is before thee: dwell where it pleaseth thee. 16 And unto Sarah he said, Behold, I have given thy brother a thousand pieces of silver: behold, it is for thee a covering of the eyes to all that are with thee; and in respect of all thou art righted. 17 And Abraham prayed unto God: and God healed Abimelech, and his wife, and his maid-servants; and they bare children. 18 For Jehovah had fast closed up all the wombs of the house of Abimelech, because of Sarah, Abraham's wife.

liii. THE BIRTH OF ISAAC. J13xi.
Gn. 21^{6a}
6a And Sarah said, God hath made me to laugh.

liv. EXPULSION OF HAGAR AND ISHMAEL: PROMISE THAT ISHMAEL WILL BECOME A GREAT NATION. J13viii. P7iii, 8.
Gn. 21$^{8-21}$
8 And the child grew, and was weaned: and Abraham made a great feast on the day that Isaac was weaned. 9 And Sarah saw the son of Hagar the Egyptian, whom she had borne unto Abraham, mocking. 10 Wherefore she said unto Abraham,

---

liii In Hebrew, this verse is a pun on the name "Isaac"; the words for "Isaac" and "laugh" are very similar: "God hath made me Isaac."
liv v. 18 R: We., Smend only.

Cast out this handmaid and her son: for the son of this handmaid shall not be heir with my son, even with Isaac. 11 And the thing was very grievous in Abraham's sight on account of his son. 12 And God said unto Abraham, Let it not be grievous in thy sight because of the lad, and because of thy handmaid; in all that Sarah saith unto thee, hearken unto her voice; for in Isaac shall thy seed be called. 13 And also of the son of the handmaid will I make a nation, because he is thy seed. 14 And Abraham rose up early in the morning, and took bread and a bottle of water, and gave it unto Hagar, putting it on her shoulder, and *gave her* the child, and sent her away: and she departed, and wandered in the wilderness of Beer-sheba. 15 And the water in the bottle was spent, and she cast the child under one of the shrubs. 16 And she went, and sat her down over against him a good way off, as it were a bowshot: for she said, Let me not look upon the death of the child. And she sat over against him, and lifted up her voice, and wept. 17 And God heard the voice of the lad; and the angel of God called to Hagar out of heaven, and said unto her, What aileth thee, Hagar? fear not; for God hath heard the voice of the lad where he is. 18 Arise, lift up the lad, and hold him in thy hand; for I will make him a great nation. 19 And God opened her eyes, and she saw a well of water; and she went, and filled the bottle with water, and gave the lad drink. 20 And God was with the lad, and he grew; and he dwelt in the wilderness, and became, as he grew up, an archer. 21 And he dwelt in the wilderness of Paran: and his mother took him a wife out of the land of Egypt.

1v. TREATY WITH ABIMELECH AT BEERSHEBA. J13xii. E1ii. Gn. $21^{22\text{-}32}$

22 And it came to pass at that time, that Abimelech and Phicol the captain of his host spake unto Abraham, saying, God is with thee in all that thou doest: 23 now therefore swear unto me here by God that thou wilt not deal falsely with me, nor with my son, nor with my son's son: but according to the kindness that I have done unto thee, thou shalt do unto me, and to the land wherein thou hast sojourned. 24 And Abraham said, I will swear. 25 And Abraham reproved Abimelech because of the well of water which Abimelech's servants had violently taken way. 26 And Abimelech said, I know not who hath done this thing: neither didst thou tell me, neither yet heard I of it, but to-day. 27 And Abraham took sheep and

---

[1v] Traces of a J narrative?—in vv. 25-26.28-30 (Co., Gu., Sk., St., Pr., SB., Ki.?), v. 32 (Ku., Ba., Co., Ad., Gu., Sk., Ki.?, SB). But the passage is regarded as unified by many, including Eerd., Eichr.

oxen, and gave them unto Abimelech; and they two made a covenant. 28 And Abraham set seven ewe lambs of the flock by themselves. 29 And Abimelech said unto Abraham, What mean these seven ewe lambs which thou hast set by themselves? 30 And he said, These seven ewe lambs shalt thou take of my hand, that it may be a witness unto me, that I have digged this well. 31 Wherefore he called that place Beer-sheba; because there they sware both of them. 32 So they made a covenant at Beer-sheba: and Abimelech rose up, and Phicol the captain of his host, and they returned into the land of the Philistines.

1vi. SACRIFICE OF ISAAC. J13vii. Eli.
Gn. 22$^{1-18}$

1 And it came to pass after these things, that God did prove Abraham, and said unto him, Abraham; and he said, Here am I. 2 And he said, Take now thy son, thine only son, whom thou lovest, even Isaac, and get thee into the land of *Moriah;* and offer him there for a burnt-offering upon one of the mountains which I will tell thee of. 3 And Abraham rose early in the morning, and saddled his ass, and took two of his young men with him, and Isaac his son; and he clave the wood for burnt-offering, and rose up, and went unto the place of which God had told him. 4 On the third day Abraham lifted up his eyes, and saw the place afar off. 5 And Abraham said unto his young men, Abide ye here with the ass, and I and the lad will go yonder; and we will worship, and come again to you. 6 And Abraham took the wood of the burnt-offering, and laid it upon Isaac his son; and he took in his hand the fire and the knife; and they went both of them together. 7 And Isaac spake unto Abraham his father, and said, My father: and he said, Here am I, my son. And he said, Behold, the fire and the wood: but where is the lamb for a burnt-offering? 8 And Abraham said, God will provide himself the lamb for a burnt-offering, my son: so they went both of them together.

9 And they came to the place which God had told him of; and Abraham built the altar there, and laid the wood in order, and bound Isaac his son, and laid him on the altar, upon the wood. 10 And Abraham stretched forth his hand, and took the knife to slay his son. 11 And the angel of Jehovah called unto him out of heaven, and said, Abraham, Abraham: and he said, Here am I. 12 And he said, Lay not thy hand upon the

---

1vi The name "Moriah" in v. 2 is difficult. It appears elsewhere only in 2 Ch. 3^1, where it refers to the temple hill in Jerusalem. Almost all critics regard it as R or a textual corruption. Syr. reads "of the Amorites," which is accepted as original by Di., Gu., Dr.?, Pr., et al. Se. alone accepts "Moriah" (meaning "Jerusalem"), and hence dates the northern E prior to the division of the kingdom in 933.—Eerd. finds polytheism here: Elohim (the gods), and Jehovah (the god that saves Isaac).—Ki. compares the story of Iphigenia. —The redactional material is due to Rje; but Syr. reads "God" in v. 11, instead of "Jehovah."

lad, neither do thou anything unto him; for now I know that thou fearest God, seeing thou hast not withheld thy son, thine only son, from me. 13 And Abraham lifted up his eyes, and looked, and, behold, behind *him* a ram caught in the thicket by his horns: and Abraham went and took the ram, and offered him up for a burnt-offering in the stead of his son. 14 And Abraham called the name of that place Jehovah-jireh: as it is said to this day, In the mount of Jehovah it shall be provided. 15 And the angel of Jehovah called unto Abraham a second time out of heaven, 16 and said, By myself have I sworn, saith Jehovah, because thou hast done this thing, and hast not withheld thy son, thine only son, 17 that in blessing I will bless thee, and in multiplying I will multipy thy seed as the stars of the heavens, and as the sand which is upon the seashore; and thy seed shall possess the gate of his enemies; 18 and in thy seed shall all the nations of the earth be blessed; because thou hast obeyed my voice.

1vii. ABRAHAM AT BEERSHEBA. J11xii. E1vi.
Gn. 22^{19}

19 So Abraham returned unto his young men, and they rose up and went together to Beer-sheba; and Abraham dwelt at Beer-sheba.

2. ISAAC, JACOB, AND ESAU. J14. P9.

2i. ISAAC DECEIVED BY REBEKAH AND JACOB WITH REFERENCE TO ESAU. J14iv, v.
Gn. 27$^{1b.11-13.16.18b-19.21-23.28-29a.30b.33b-34}$

1b And said unto him, My son: and he said unto him, Here am I . . . 11 And Jacob said to Rebekah his mother, Behold, Esau my brother is a hairy man, and I am a smooth man. 12 My father peradventure will feel me, and I shall seem to him as a deceiver; and I shall bring a curse upon me, and not a blessing. 13 And his mother said unto him, Upon me be thy curse, my son; only obey my voice, and go fetch me them. 16 And she put the skins of the kids of the goats upon his hands, and upon the smooth of his neck.
18b And said, My father: and he said, Here am I; who art thou, my son? 19 And Jacob said unto his father, I am Esau thy first-born; I have done according as thou badest me: arise, I pray thee, sit and eat of my venison, that thy soul may bless me.
21 And Isaac said unto Jacob, Come near, I pray thee, that

---

[21] Rje has preserved only fragments of E in this passage. Evidently, the J and E accounts of this episode were very similar. In spite of the fragmentary character of the above reconstruction of E, critics generally are convinced that the analysis is substantially correct, except that Dr. is inclined to attribute the whole account to J. There are slight differences in analysis by Sk., Mi., Ka.—After v. 30b, E evidently told of the return of Esau.—v. 33b is spoken by Isaac to Esau.—33b-34 are assigned to J by Sk., SB.

I may feel thee, my son, whether thou be my very son Esau or not. 22 And Jacob went near unto Isaac his father; and he felt him, and said, The voice is Jacob's voice, but the hands are the hands of Esau. 23 And he discerned him not, because his hands were hairy, as his brother Esau's hands: so he blessed him;—
 28 And God give thee of the dew of heaven,
 And of the fatness of the earth,
 And plenty of grain and new wine . . .
 29a Be lord over thy brethren,
 And let thy mother's sons bow down to thee.
30b And Jacob was yet scarce gone out from the presence of Isaac his father. 33b And I have eaten of all before thou camest, and have blessed him, yea, *and* he shall be blessed. 34 When Esau heard the words of his father, he cried with an exceeding great and bitter cry, and said unto his father, Bless me, even me also, O my father.

2ii. ISAAC BLESSES ESAU. J14vi.

Gn. 27^{39}

39 And Isaac his father answered and said unto him,
Behold, of the fatness of the earth shall be thy dwelling,
And of the dew of heaven from above.

3. THE STORY OF JACOB.

3i. ANGELS APPEAR TO JACOB ON A LADDER IN A DREAM AT BETHEL. J15i. P10iii.

Gn. 28$^{11-12.17-18.20-22}$

11 And he lighted upon a certain place, and tarried there all night, because the sun was set; and he took one of the stones of the place, and put it under his head, and lay down in that place to sleep. 12 And he dreamed; and, behold, a ladder set up on the earth, and the top of it reached to heaven; and, behold, the angels of God ascending and descending on it.

17 And he was afraid, and said, How dreadful is this place! this is none other than the house of God, and this is the gate of heaven.

18 And Jacob rose up early in the morning, and took the stone that he had put under his head, and set it up for a pillar, and poured oil upon the top of it. 20 And Jacob vowed a vow, saying, If God will be with me, and will keep me in this way that I go, and will give me bread to eat, and raiment to put on,

---

[2ii] The expressions "of the fatness" and "of the dew" should be translated, as in the Am. Rev., margin, "away from the fatness," "away from the dew." As it stands above, Isaac blesses Esau; in reality he curses him, with the antithesis of Jacob's blessing Gn. 27^{28} in E2i.

[3i] v. 21b is Rje. v. 22 reflects E's view of the importance of Bethel as a sanctuary where tithes are paid. The "pillar" is the massebah, so frequent in E.

21 so that I come again to my father's house in peace, and Jehovah will be my God, 22 then this stone, which I have set up for a pillar, shall be God's house: and of all that thou shalt give me I will surely give the tenth unto thee.

3ii. JACOB GOES TO THE LAND OF THE CHILDREN OF THE EAST. J15ii.
Gn. 29¹

1 Then Jacob went on his journey, and came to the land of the children of the east.

3iii. JACOB SERVES LABAN SEVEN YEARS FOR RACHEL. J15iii. P10i.
Gn. 29¹⁵⁻²⁰

15 And Laban said unto Jacob, Because thou art my brother, shouldest thou therefore serve me for nought? tell me, what shall thy wages be? 16 And Laban had two daughters: the name of the elder was Leah, and the name of the younger was Rachel. 17 And Leah's eyes were tender; but Rachel was beautiful and well-favored. 18 And Jacob loved Rachel; and he said, I will serve thee seven years for Rachel thy younger daughter. 19 And Laban said, It is better that I give her to thee, than that I should give her to another man: abide with me. 20 And Jacob served seven years for Rachel; and they seemed unto him but a few days, for the love he had to her.

3iv. LABAN DECEIVES JACOB REGARDING LEAH AND RACHEL.
Gn. 29²¹⁻²³·²⁵

21 And Jacob said unto Laban, Give me my wife, for my days are fulfilled, that I may go in unto her. 22 And Laban gathered together all the men of the place, and made a feast. 23 And it came to pass in the evening, that he took Leah his daughter, and brought her to him; and he went in unto her. 25 And it came to pass in the morning that, behold, it was Leah: and he said to Laban, What is this thou hast done unto me? did I not serve with thee for Rachel? wherefore then hast thou beguiled me?

3v. JACOB SERVES LABAN SEVEN YEARS FOR LEAH. J15iii. P10i.
Gn. 29²⁷⁻²⁸ᵃ·³⁰

27 Fulfill the week of this one, and we will give thee the other also for the service which thou shalt serve with me yet seven other years. 28a And Jacob did so, and fulfilled her week. 30 And he went in also unto Rachel, and he loved also Rachel more than Leah, and served with him yet seven other years.

3vi. BIRTH OF JACOB'S SONS.   J15iv.   P10iv.
    Gn. 30¹⁻³ᵃ·⁶·⁸·¹⁷⁻²⁰ᵃ·²²ᵇ⁻²³

1 And when Rachel saw that she bare Jacob no children, Rachel envied her sister; and she said unto Jacob, Give me children, or else I die. 2 And Jacob's anger was kindled against Rachel: and he said, Am I in God's stead, who hath withheld from thee the fruit of the womb? 3a And she said, Behold, my maid Bilhah, go in unto her; that she may bear upon my knees.

6 And Rachel said, God hath judged me, and hath also heard my voice, and hath given me a son: therefore called she his name Dan. 8 And Rachel said, With mighty wrestlings have I wrestled with my sister, and have prevailed: and she called his name Naphtali.

17 And God hearkened unto Leah, and she conceived, and bare Jacob a fifth son. 18 And Leah said, God hath given me my hire, because I gave my handmaid to my husband: and she called his name Issachar. 19 And Leah conceived again, and bare a sixth son to Jacob. 20a And Leah said, God hath endowed me with a good dowry.

22a And God hearkened to her, and opened her womb. 23 And she conceived, and bare a son: and said, God hath taken away my reproach.

3vii. JACOB PREPARES TO LEAVE LABAN, AND SECURES HIS WAGES.   J15v.
    Gn. 30²⁶·²⁸·³²⁻³⁴ 31²·⁴⁻¹⁸ᵃ

30²⁶ Give me my wives and my children for whom I have served thee, and let me go: for thou knowest my service wherewith I have served thee.

28 And he said, Appoint me thy wages, and I will give it.

32 I will pass through all thy flock to-day, removing from thence every speckled and spotted one, and every black one among the sheep, and the spotted and speckled among the goats: and *of such* shall be my hire. 33 So shall my righteousness answer for me hereafter, when thou shalt come concerning my hire that is before thee: every one that is not speckled and spotted among the goats, and black among the sheep, that *if found* with me, shall be counted stolen.

34 And Laban said, Behold, I would it might be according to thy word.

31² And Jacob beheld the countenance of Laban, and, behold, it was not toward him as beforetime.

---

³ᵛⁱ v. 6 "he judged," in Hebr., *dan*.—v. 8 "wrestled," Hebr. *niphtal* (Naphtali)—v. 18 "hire," Hebr. *sachar* (Issachar).—In v. 22a, "her" refers to Rachel.—v. 23 is E's account of the birth of Joseph—manifestly incomplete.
³ᵛⁱⁱ 31¹⁰·¹² R: We., Di., CH., Gu., Pr., Mi., Ho., GFM., SB. E: Dr., St., Smend. In 30²⁶ Jacob speaks; v. 28, Laban; v. 32, Jacob.

4 And Jacob sent and called Rachel and Leah to the field unto his flock, 5 and said unto them, I see your father's countenance, that it is not toward me as beforetime; but the God of my father hath been with me. 6 And ye know that with all my power I have served your father. 7 And your father hath deceived me, and changed my wages ten times; but God suffered him not to hurt me. 8 If he said thus, The speckled shall be thy wages; then all the flock bare speckled: and if he said thus, The ringstreaked shall be thy wages; then bare all the flock ringstreaked. 9 Thus God hath taken away the cattle of your father, and given them to me. 10 And it came to pass at the time that the flock conceive, that I lifted up mine eyes, and saw in a dream, and, behold, the he-goats which leaped upon the flock were ringstreaked, speckled, and grizzled. 11 And the angel of God said unto me in the dream, Jacob: and I said, Here am I. 12 And he said, Lift up now thine eyes, and see: all the he-goats which leap upon the flock are ringstreaked, speckled, and grizzled: for I have seen all that Laban doeth unto thee. 13 I am the God of Beth-el, where thou anointedst a pillar, where thou vowedst a vow unto me: now arise, get thee out from this land, and return unto the land of thy nativity. 14 And Rachel and Leah answered and said unto him, Is there yet any portion or inheritance for us in our father's house? 15 Are we not accounted by him as foreigners? for he hath sold us, and hath also quite devoured our money. 16 For all the riches which God hath taken away from our father, that is ours and our children's: now then, whatsoever God hath said unto thee, do.

17 Then Jacob rose up, and set his sons and his wives upon the camels; 18a and he carried away all his cattle.

3viii. LABAN PURSUES JACOB TO GILEAD, WHERE THEY MAKE A TREATY. J15vi. P10ii.
Gn. 31[19-24.26.28-45.53b-55]

19 Now Laban was gone to shear his sheep: and Rachel stole the teraphim that were her father's. 20 And Jacob stole away unawares to Laban the Syrian, in that he told him not that he fled. 21 So he fled with all that he had; and he rose up, and passed over the River, and set his face toward the mountain of Gilead.

22 And it was told Laban on the third day that Jacob was fled. 23 And he took his brethren with him, and pursued after him seven days' journey; and he overtook him in the mountain of Gilead. 24 And God came to Laban the Syrian in a

---
[3viii] v. 21 (in part) perh. J: Co., Mi., Sk., St., SB. (19a, 21J), Gu. Majority, E. Perh. also traces of J in vv. 31, 36a, 38-40, 44: SB. et al. Smend assigns much of the "E" material to J^1 and J^2.

dream of the night, and said unto him, Take heed to thyself that thou speak not to Jacob either good or bad.

26 And Laban said to Jacob, What hast thou done, that thou hast stolen away unawares to me, and carried away my daughters as captives of the sword? 28 and didst not suffer me to kiss my sons and my daughters? now hast thou done foolishly. 29 It is in the power of my hand to do you hurt: but the God of your father spake unto me yesternight, saying, Take heed to thyself that thou speak not to Jacob either good or bad. 30 And now, *though* thou wouldest needs be gone, because thou sore longedst after thy father's house, *yet* wherefore hast thou stolen my gods? 31 And Jacob answered and said to Laban, Because I was afraid: for I said, Lest thou shouldest take thy daughters from me by force. 32 With whomsoever thou findest thy gods, he shall not live: before our brethren discern thou what is thine with me, and take it to thee. For Jacob knew not that Rachel had stolen them.

33 And Laban went into Jacob's tent, and into Leah's tent, and into the tent of the two maid-servants; but he found them not. And he went out of Leah's tent, and entered into Rachel's tent. 34 Now Rachel had taken the teraphim, and put them in the camel's saddle, and sat upon them. And Laban felt about all the tent, but found them not. 35 And she said to her father, Let not my lord be angry that I cannot rise up before thee; for the manner of women is upon me. And he searched, but found not the teraphim.

36 And Jacob was wroth, and chode with Laban: and Jacob answered and said to Laban, What is my trespass? what is my sin, that thou hast hotly pursued after me? 37 Whereas thou hast felt about all my stuff, what hast thou found of all thy household stuff? Set it here before my brethren and thy brethren, that they may judge betwixt us two. 38 These twenty years have I been with thee; thy ewes and thy she-goats have not cast their young, and the rams of thy flock have I not eaten. 39 That which was torn of beasts I brought not unto thee; I bare the loss of it; of my hand didst thou require it, whether stolen by day or stolen by night. 40 Thus I was; in the day the drought consumed me, and the frost by night; and my sleep fled from mine eyes. 41 These twenty years have I been in thy house; I served thee fourteen years for thy two daughters, and six years for thy flock: and thou hast changed my wages ten times. 42 Except the God of my father, the God of Abraham, and the Fear of Isaac, had been with me, surely now hadst thou sent me away empty. God hath seen mine affliction and the labor of my hands, and rebuked thee yesternight.

43 And Laban answered and said unto Jacob, The daughters

are my daughters, and the children are my children, and the flocks are my flocks, and all that thou seest is mine: and what can I do this day unto these my daughters, or unto their children whom they have borne? 44 And now come, let us make a covenant, I and thou; and let it be for a witness between me and thee. 45 And Jacob took a stone, and set it up for a pillar.
53b And Jacob sware by the Fear of his father Isaac. 54 And Jacob offered a sacrifice in the mountain, and called his brethren to eat bread: and they did eat bread, and tarried all night in the mountain. 55 And early in the morning Laban rose up, and kissed his sons and his daughters, and blessed them: and Laban departed and returned unto his place.

3ix. THE ANGELS AT MAHANAIM.
Gn. 32$^{1-2}$
1 And Jacob went on his way, and the angels of God met him. 2 And Jacob said when he saw them, This is God's host: and he called the name of that place Mahanaim.

3x. JACOB SUES FOR PEACE WITH ESAU. J15vii.
Gn. 32^{13b-21}
13b And took of that which he had with him a present for Esau his brother: 14 two hundred she-goats and twenty he-goats, two hundred ewes and twenty rams, 15 thirty milch camels and their colts, forty cows and ten bulls, twenty she-asses and ten foals. 16 And he delivered them into the hand of his servants, every drove by itself, and said unto his servants, Pass over before me, and put a space betwixt drove and drove. 17 And he commanded the foremost, saying, When Esau my brother meeteth thee, and asketh thee, saying, Whose art thou? and whither goest thou? and whose are these before thee? 18 then thou shalt say, *They are* thy servant Jacob's; it is a present sent unto my lord Esau: and, behold, he also is behind us. 19 And he commanded also the second, and the third, and all that followed the droves, saying, On this manner shall ye speak unto Esau, when ye find him; 20 and ye shall say, Moreover, behold, thy servant Jacob is behind us. For he said, I will appease him with the present that goeth before me, and afterward I will see his face; peradventure he will accept me. 21 So the present passed over before him: and he himself lodged that night in the company.

3xi. JACOB CROSSES "THE STREAM." J15viii.
Gn. 32^{23}
23 And he took them, and sent them over the stream, and sent over that which he had.

---
³ˣ J: Ba., CH., Mi. JE: Ka. E: all others.
³ˣⁱ Perh. partly J: Ba., Gu., Mi., Sk.

3xii. JACOB AND ESAU ARE RECONCILED (incomplete). J15x.
Gn. 33[5b.10b-11a]

5b And he said, The children whom God hath graciously given thy servant. 10b Forasmuch as I have seen thy face, as one seeth the face of God, and thou wast pleased with me, 11a take, I pray thee, my gift that is brought to thee; because God hath dealt graciously with me, and because I have enough.

3xiii. JACOB AT SHECHEM. E3xv, 72. P10ii.
Gn. 33[18b-20]

18b And encamped before the city. 19 And he bought the parcel of ground, where he had spread his tent, at the hand of the children of Hamor, Shechem's father, for a hundred pieces of money. 20 And he erected there an altar, and called it El-Elohe-Israel.

3xiv. SHECHEM AND DINAH. J15xi. E5 (Gn. 48[22]). Jg. 9,We.
Gn. 34[1-2a.4.6.8-10.13.15-18.20-24.25*.27-29]

1 And Dinah the daughter of Leah, whom she bare unto Jacob, went out to see the daughters of the land. 2a And Shechem the son of Hamor the Hivite, the prince of the land, saw her. 4 And Shechem spake unto his father Hamor, saying, Get me this damsel to wife. 6 And Hamor the father of Shechem went out unto Jacob to commune with him.

8 And Hamor communed with them, saying, The soul of my son Shechem longeth for your daughter: I pray you, give her unto him to wife. 9 And make ye marriages with us; give your daughters unto us, and take our daughters unto you. 10 And ye shall dwell with us: and the land shall be before you; dwell and trade ye therein, and get you possessions therein.

13 And the sons of Jacob answered Shechem and Hamor his father with guile, and spake, because he had defiled Dinah their sister, 15 Only on this condition will we consent unto you: if ye will be as we are, that every male of you be circumcised; 16 then will we give our daughters unto you, and we will take your daughters to us, and we will dwell with you, and we will become one people. 17 But if ye will not hearken unto us, to be circumcised; then will we take our daughter, and we will be gone.

18 And their words pleased Hamor, and Shechem Hamor's son. 20 And Hamor and Shechem his son came unto the gate of their

---

[3xii] J: Dr., CH., St. E: all others.
[3xiv] E (cf. 35[5]): most critics, as Co., Pr., Gr., et al. P: Di., Dr.; and Ki. formerly assigned to P, but now E. R: Ku. "All admit a priestly redaction." So Sk., Smend. The redactional material indicated in the text follows Sk., and the majority. vv. 27-29 Rp: Di., and cf. P77 Nu. 31, Smend.

city, and communed with the men of their city, saying, 21 These men are peaceable with us; therefore let them dwell in the land, and trade therein; for, behold, the land is large enough for them; let us take their daughters to us for wives, and let us give them our daughters. 22 Only on this condition will the men consent unto us to dwell with us, to become one people, if every male among us be circumcised, as they are circumcised. 23 Shall not their cattle and their substance and all their beasts be ours? only let us consent unto them, and they will dwell with us. 24 And unto Hamor and unto Shechem his son hearkened all that went out of the gate of his city; and every male was circumcised, all that went out of the gate of his city.

25a And it came to pass on the third day, when they were sore . . . , and came upon the city unawares, and slew all the males. 27 The sons of Jacob came upon the slain, and plundered the city, because they had defiled their sister. 28 They took their flocks and their herds and their asses, and that which was in the city, and that which was in the field; 29 and all their wealth, and all their little ones and their wives, took they captive and made a prey, even all that was in the house.

3xv. Jacob's Altar and Massebah at Bethel. J13i. E3i, ix, xiii. P10iii.
Gn. 35$^{1-5.6b-8.14}$

1 And God said unto Jacob, Arise, go up to Beth-el, and dwell there: and make there an altar unto God, who appeared unto thee when thou fleddest from the face of Esau thy brother. 2 Then Jacob said unto his household, and to all that were with him, Put away the foreign gods that are among you, and purify yourselves, and change your garments: 3 and let us arise and go up to Beth-el; and I will make there an altar unto God, who answered me in the day of my distress, and was with me in the way which I went. 4 And they gave unto Jacob all the foreign gods which were in their hand, and the rings which were in their ears; and Jacob hid them under the oak which was by Shechem.

5 And they journeyed: and a terror of God was upon the cities that were round about them, and they did not pursue after the sons of Jacob.

6b He and all the people that were with him. 7 And he built there an altar, and called the place El-beth-el; because there God was revealed unto him, when he fled from the face of his brother.

---

³ˣᵛ vv. 2, 4 Smend interprets as due to E's monotheism; while Eerd. and Eichr. regard the verses as polytheistic. Was polytheism normal in Jacob's family, and the journey to Bethel an exceptional honor to a particular god, or was the worship of the one God viewed by E as Jacob's general practice? v. 5 R: Ku., Di., Eichr. (p. 94).

8 And Deborah Rebekah's nurse died, and she was buried below Beth-el under the oak: and the name of it was called Allon-bacuth.

14 And Jacob set up a pillar in the place where he spake with him, a pillar of stone: and he poured out a drink-offering thereon, and poured oil thereon.

3xvi. Birth of Benjamin and Death of Rachel Near Ephrath: Massebah.

Gn. 35[16-20]

16 And they journeyed from Beth-el; and there was still some distance to come to Ephrath: and Rachel travailed, and she had hard labor. 17 And it came to pass, when she was in hard labor, that the midwife said unto her, Fear not; for now thou shalt have another son. 18 And it came to pass, as her soul was departing (for she died), that she called his name Ben-oni: but his father called him Benjamin. 19 And Rachel died, and was buried in the way to Ephrath (the same is Bethlehem). 20 And Jacob set up a pillar upon her grave: the same is the Pillar of Rachel's grave unto this day.

4. The Story of Joseph. J18. P12.

4i. The Dreams of Joseph.

Gn. 37[5-11]

5 And Joseph dreamed a dream, and he told it to his brethren: and they hated him yet the more. 6 And he said unto them, Hear, I pray you, this dream which I have dreamed: 7 for, behold, we were binding sheaves in the field, and, lo, my sheaf arose, and also stood upright; and, behold, your sheaves came round about, and made obeisance to my sheaf. 8 And his brethren said to him, Shalt thou indeed reign over us? or shalt thou indeed have dominion over us? And they hated him yet the more for his dreams, and for his words. 9 And he dreamed yet another dream, and told it to his brethren, and said, Behold, I have dreamed yet a dream; and, behold, the sun and the moon and eleven stars made obeisance to me. 10 And he told it to his father, and to his brethren; and his father rebuked him, and said unto him, What is this dream that thou hast dreamed? Shall I and thy mother and thy brethren indeed come to bow down ourselves to thee to the earth? 11 And his brethren envied him; but his father kept the saying in mind.

[3xvi] "Ben-oni" means in Hebr., *the son of my sorrow*; and "Benjamin," *the son of the right hand.*—v. 19, cf. E5 ,(Gn. 48[7]), 1 S. 10[2] Jer. 31[15]. Ephrath in E was north Israelitic (Smend).

[4i] v. 5b, om. LXX. The entire passage is assigned to J² by Smend.

4ii. Joseph Taken to Egypt by the Midianites. J18i.
Gn. 37[13c.14ab.15-17.18a.19-20.22.24.28*.29-31.34]

13c And he said to him, Here am I. 14ab And he said to him, Go now, see whether it is well with thy brethren, and well with the flock; and bring me word again. 15 And a certain man found him, and, behold, he was wandering in the field: and the man asked him, saying, What seekest thou? 16 And he said, I am seeking my brethren: tell me, I pray thee, where they are feeding *the flock*. 17 And the man said, They are departed hence; for I heard them say, Let us go to Dothan. And Joseph went after his brethren, and found them in Dothan. 18a And they saw him afar off. 19 And they said one to another, Behold, this dreamer cometh. 20 Come now therefore, and let us slay him, and cast him into one of the pits, and we will say, An evil beast hath devoured him: and we shall see what will become of his dreams. 22 And Reuben said unto them, Shed no blood; cast him into this pit that is in the wilderness, but lay no hand upon him: that he might deliver him out of their hand, to restore him to his father. 24 And they took him, and cast him into the pit: and the pit was empty, there was no water in it.

28 And there passed by Midianites, merchantmen; and they drew and lifted up Joseph out of the pit. . . . And they brought Joseph into Egypt.

29 And Reuben returned unto the pit; and, behold, Joseph was not in the pit; and he rent his clothes. 30 And he returned unto his brethren, and said, The child is not; and I, whither shall I go? 31 And they took Joseph's coat, and killed a he-goat, and dipped the coat in the blood. 34 And Jacob rent his garments, and put sackcloth upon his loins, and mourned for his son many days.

4iii. Joseph the Slave of Potiphar. J18ii.
Gn. 37[36] 39[4*.6a]

37[36] And the Midianites sold him into Egypt unto Potiphar, an officer of Pharaoh's, the captain of the guard. 39[4] . . . And he ministered unto him . . . 6a And he left all that he had in Joseph's hand; and he knew not aught *that was* with him, save the bread which he did eat.

4iv. Joseph, in Charge of Two Prisoners, Interprets Their Dreams. J18iii.
Gn. 40[2-3a.4-5a.6-15a.16-23]

2 And Pharaoh was wroth against his two officers, against

[4ii] vv. 15-17 J?: We., Dr., Mi., Smend, Ki., SB.—v. 20a J: Co., GFM., Sk.—v. 34b J: Co., Sk., Gu., Smend, SB.
[4iii] 39[4.6a] E: Ad., Ka., CH., Ba., Gu., Co., Sk., Pr. R: Mi. Others, J.—v. 6a J: SB.
[4iv] Even Eerd. admits that vv. 3b, 5b do not belong in this connection.

the chief of the butlers, and against the chief of the bakers. 3a And he put them in ward in the house of the captain of the guard. 4 And the captain of the guard charged Joseph with them, and he ministered unto them: and they continued a season in ward.

5a And they dreamed a dream both of them, each man his dream, in one night, each man according to the interpretation of his dream. 6 And Joseph came in unto them in the morning, and saw them, and, behold, they were sad. 7 And he asked Pharaoh's officers that were with him in ward in his master's house, saying, Wherefore look ye so sad to-day? 8 And they said unto him, We have dreamed a dream, and there is none that can interpret it. And Joseph said unto them, Do not interpretations belong to God? tell it me, I pray you.

9 And the chief butler told his dream to Joseph, and said to him, In my dream, behold, a vine was before me; 10 and in the vine were three branches: and it was as though it budded, *and* its blossoms shot forth; *and* the clusters thereof brought forth ripe grapes: 11 and Pharaoh's cup was in my hand; and I took the grapes, and pressed them into Pharaoh's cup, and I gave the cup into Pharaoh's hand. 12 And Joseph said unto him, This is the interpretation of it: the three branches are three days; 13 within yet three days shall Pharaoh lift up thy head, and restore thee unto thine office: and thou shalt give Pharaoh's cup into his hand, after the former manner when thou wast his butler. 14 But have me in thy remembrance when it shall be well with thee, and show kindness, I pray thee, unto me, and make mention of me unto Pharaoh, and bring me out of this house: 15a for indeed I was stolen away out of the land of the Hebrews.

16 When the chief baker saw that the interpretation was good, he said unto Joseph, I also was in my dream, and, behold, three baskets of white bread were on my head: 17 and in the uppermost basket there was of all manner of baked food for Pharaoh; and the birds did eat them out of the basket upon my head. 18 And Joseph answered and said, This is the interpretation thereof: the three baskets are three days; 19 within yet three days shall Pharaoh lift up thy head from off thee, and shall hang thee on a tree; and the birds shall eat thy flesh from off thee. 20 And it came to pass the third day, which was Pharaoh's birthday, that he made a feast unto all his servants: and he lifted up the head of the chief butler and the head of the chief baker among his servants. 21 And he restored the chief butler unto his butlership again; and he gave the cup into Pharaoh's hand: 22 but he hanged the

chief baker: as Joseph had interpreted to them. 23 Yet did not the chief butler remember Joseph but forgat him.

4v. JOSEPH INTERPRETS PHARAOH'S DREAMS.
Gn. 41[1-14a.15-33]

1 And it came to pass at the end of two full years, that Pharaoh dreamed: and, behold, he stood by the river. 2 And behold, there came up out of the river seven kine, well-favored and fat-fleshed; and they fed in the reed-grass. 3 And, behold, seven other kine came up after them out of the river, ill-favored and lean-fleshed, and stood by the other kine upon the brink of the river. 4 And the ill-favored and lean-fleshed kine did eat up the seven well-favored and fat kine. So Pharaoh awoke. 5 And he slept and dreamed a second time: and, behold, seven ears of grain came up upon one stalk, rank and good. 6 And, behold, seven ears, thin and blasted with the east wind, sprung up after them. 7 And the thin ears swallowed up the seven rank and full ears. And Pharaoh awoke, and, behold, it was a dream. 8 And it came to pass in the morning that his spirit was troubled; and he sent and called for all the magicians of Egypt, and all the wise men thereof: and Pharaoh told them his dream; but there was none that could interpret them unto Pharaoh.

9 Then spake the chief butler unto Pharaoh, saying, I do remember my faults this day: 10 Pharaoh was wroth with his servants, and put me in ward in the house of the captain of the guard, me and the chief baker: 11 and we dreamed a dream in one night, I and he; we dreamed each man according to the interpretation of his dream. 12 And there was with us there a young man, a Hebrew, servant to the captain of the guard; and we told him, and he interpreted to us our dreams; to each man according to his dream he did interpret. 13 And it came to pass, as he interpreted to us, so it was; me he restored unto mine office, and him he hanged.

14a Then Pharaoh sent and called Joseph. 15 And Pharaoh said unto Joseph, I have dreamed a dream, and there is none that can interpret it: and I have heard say of thee, that when thou hearest a dream thou canst interpret it. 16 And Joseph answered Pharaoh, saying, It is not in me: God will give Pharaoh an answer of peace. 17 And Pharaoh spake unto Joseph, In my dream, behold, I stood upon the brink of the river: 18 and, behold, there came up out of the river seven kine, fat-fleshed and well-favored; and they fed in the reed-grass: 19 and, behold, seven other kine came up after them, poor and very ill-favored and lean-fleshed, such as I never saw in all the land of Egypt for badness: 20 and the lean and ill-favored

kine did eat up the first seven fat kine: 21 and when they had eaten them up, it could not be known that they had eaten them; but they were still ill-favored, as at the beginning. So I awoke. 22 And I saw in my dream, and, behold, seven ears came up upon one stalk, full and good: 23 and, behold, seven ears, withered, thin, *and* blasted with the east wind, sprung up after them: 24 and the thin ears swallowed up the seven good ears: and I told it unto the magicians; but there was none that could declare it to me.
25 And Joseph said unto Pharaoh, The dream of Pharaoh is one: what God is about to do he hath declared unto Pharaoh. 26 The seven good kine are seven years; and the seven good ears are seven years: the dream is one. 27 And the seven lean and ill-favored kine that came up after them are seven years, and also the seven empty ears blasted with the east wind; they shall be seven years of famine. 28 That is the thing which I spake unto Pharaoh: what God is about to do he hath showed unto Pharaoh. 29 Behold, there come seven years of great plenty throughout all the land of Egypt: 30 and there shall arise after them seven years of famine; and all the plenty shall be forgotten in the land of Egypt; and the famine shall consume the land; 31 and the plenty shall not be known in the land by reason of that famine which followeth; for it shall be very grievous. 32 And for that the dream was doubled unto Pharaoh, it is because the thing is established by God, and God will shortly bring it to pass. 33 Now therefore let Pharaoh look out a man discreet and wise, and set him over the land of Egypt.

4vi. JOSEPH IS MADE RULER. J18iv. P12ii.
Gn. 41[37-40.42-45]

37 And the thing was good in the eyes of Pharaoh, and in the eyes of all his servants. 38 And Pharaoh said unto his servants, Can we find such a one as this, a man in whom the spirit of God is? 39 And Pharaoh said unto Joseph, Forasmuch as God hath showed thee all this, there is none so discreet and wise as thou: 40 thou shalt be over my house, and according unto thy word shall all my people be ruled: only in the throne will I be greater than thou.
42 And Pharaoh took off his signet ring from his hand, and put it upon Joseph's hand, and arrayed him in vestures of fine linen, and put a gold chain about his neck; 43 and he made him to ride in the second chariot which he had; and they cried before him, Bow the knee: and he set him over all the land of Egypt. 44 And Pharaoh said unto Joseph, I am Pharaoh, and

---

[†vi] Some uncertain traces of J: Co., Sk., Gu., Ba., Pr., Smend. Others, E.

without thee shall no man lift up his hand or his foot in all the land of Egypt. 45 And Pharaoh called Joseph's name Zaphenath-paneah; and he gave him to wife Asenath, the daughter of Poti-phera priest of On. And Joseph went out over the land of Egypt.

4vii. JOSEPH GATHERS GRAIN FOR THE FAMINE: EPHRAIM AND MANASSEH ARE BORN. J18ix.
Gn. 41[46b-47.49-57]

46b And Joseph went out from the presence of Pharaoh, and went throughout all the land of Egypt. 47 And in the seven plenteous years the earth brought forth by handfuls. 49 And Joseph laid up grain as the sand of the sea, very much, until he left off numbering; for it was without number. 50 And unto Joseph were born two sons before the year of famine came, whom Asenath, the daughter of Poti-phera priest of On bare unto him. 51 And Joseph called the name of the firstborn Manasseh: For, *said he,* God hath made me forget all my toil, and all my father's house. 52 And the name of the second called he Ephraim: For God hath made me fruitful in the land of my affliction. 53 And the seven years of plenty, that was in the land of Egypt, came to an end. 54 And the seven years of famine began to come, according as Joseph had said: and there was famine in all lands; but in all the land of Egypt there was bread. 55 And when all the land of Egypt was famished, the people cried to Pharaoh for bread: and Pharaoh said unto all the Egyptians, Go unto Joseph; what he saith to you, do. 56 And the famine was over all the face of the earth: and Joseph opened all the storehouses, and sold unto the Egyptians; and the famine was sore in the land of Egypt. 57 And all countries came into Egypt to Joseph to buy grain, because the famine was sore in all the earth.

4viii. JOSEPH'S BROTHERS SEEK GRAIN AND RETURN TO JACOB. J18v.
Gn. 42[1.3-4a.6.7*.8-26.29-35.28b.36-37] 43[14]

1 Now Jacob saw that there was grain in Egypt, and Jacob said unto his sons, Why do ye look one upon another? 3 And Joseph's ten brethren went down to buy grain from Egypt. 4a But Benjamin, Joseph's brother, Jacob sent not with his brethren.

[4vii] Several find traces of J.
[4viii] The words from 42^7 probably belonged after v. 9a in E: Di., Ba., KS., Gu., Sk., Ki., SB. Fragments of J are found in v. 6 (We., Ka., Mi., St., Smend), and vv. 9b, 10, 11a, 12 (Co., Gu., Sk., Smend, SB.); but the majority follow the analysis of the text. v. 28b is generally regarded as belonging after v. 35, only Dr. leaving it in J. In 43^{14} the word "Almighty" (Shaddai) is Rp, cf. P17; but Ba., Mi., Gu. assign it to E and Smend to J^2. The speaker in this verse is Jacob.

6 And Joseph was the governor over the land; he it was that sold to all the people of the land. And Joseph's brethren came, and bowed themselves to him with their faces to the earth. 8 And Joseph knew his brethren, but they knew not him. 9a And Joseph remembered the dreams which he dreamed of them, 7 . . . and spake roughly with them . . , 9b and said unto them, Ye are spies; to see the nakedness of the land ye are come. 10 And they said unto him, Nay, my lord, but to buy food are thy servants come. 11 We are all one man's sons; we are true men, thy servants are no spies. 12 And he said unto them, Nay, but to see the nakedness of the land ye are come. 13 And they said, We thy servants are twelve brethren, the sons of one man in the land of Canaan; and, behold, the youngest is this day with our father, and one is not. 14 And Joseph said unto them, That is it that I spake unto you, saying, Ye are spies: 15 hereby ye shall be proved: by the life of Pharaoh ye shall not go forth hence, except your youngest brother come hither. 16 Send one of you, and let him fetch your brother, and ye shall be bound, that your words may be proved, whether there be truth in you: or else by the life of Pharaoh surely ye are spies. 17 And he put them all together into ward three days.

18 And Joseph said unto them the third day, This do, and live; for I fear God: 19 if ye be true men, let one of your brethren be bound in your prison-house; but go ye, carry grain for the famine of your houses: 20 and bring your youngest brother unto me; so shall your words be verified, and ye shall not die. And they did so. 21 And they said one to another, We are verily guilty concerning our brother, in that we saw the distress of his soul, when he besought us, and we would not hear; therefore is this distress come upon us. 22 And Reuben answered them, saying, Spake I not unto you, saying, Do not sin against the child; and ye would not hear? therefore also, behold, his blood is required. 23 And they knew not that Joseph understood them; for there was an interpreter between them. 24 And he turned himself about from them, and wept; and he returned to them, and spake to them, and took Simeon from among them, and bound him before their eyes. 25 Then Joseph commanded to fill their vessels with grain, and to restore every man's money into his sack, and to give them provision for the way: and thus was it done unto them.

26 And they laded their asses with their grain, and departed thence.

29 And they came unto Jacob their father unto the land of Canaan, and told him all that had befallen them, saying, 30 The man, the lord of the land, spake roughly with us, and

took us for spies of the country. 31 And we said unto him, We are true men; we are no spies: 32 we are twelve brethren, sons of our father; one is not, and the youngest is this day with our father in the land of Canaan. 33 And the man, the lord of the land, said unto us, Hereby shall I know that ye are true men: leave one of your brethren with me, and take *grain for* the famine of your houses, and go your way; 34 and bring your youngest brother unto me: then shall I know that ye are no spies, but that ye are true men: so will I deliver you your brother, and ye shall traffic in the land.

35 And it came to pass as they emptied their sacks, that, behold, every man's bundle of money was in his sack: and when they and their father saw their bundles of money, they were afraid, 28b saying, What is this that God has done unto us? 36 And Jacob their father said unto them, Me have ye bereaved of my children: Joseph is not, and Simeon is not, and ye will take Benjamin away: all these things are against me. 37 And Reuben spake unto his father, saying, Slay my two sons, if I bring him not to thee: deliver him into my hand, and I will bring him to thee again.

43^{14} And God Almighty give you mercy before the man, that he may release unto you your other brother and Benjamin. And if I be bereaved of my children, I am bereaved.

4ix. JOSEPH REVEALS HIMSELF TO HIS BROTHERS ON THEIR SECOND VISIT. J18vi, vii.
Gn. 43^{23b} 45$^{1b-4a.5b-9.10b-12.15-18.19-21a.21b-27}$

43^{23b} And he brought Simeon out unto them.
45^{1b} And there stood no man with them, while Joseph made himself known unto his brethren. 2 And he wept aloud: and the Egyptians heard, and the house of Pharaoh heard.

3 And Joseph said unto his brethren, I am Joseph; doth my father yet live? And his brethren could not answer him; for they were troubled at his presence. 4a And Joseph said unto his brethren, Come near to me, I pray you. And they came near.

And he said, 5b For God did send me before you to preserve life. 6 For these two years hath the famine been in the land: and there are yet five years, in which there shall be neither plowing nor harvest. 7 And God sent me before you to preserve you a remnant in the earth, and to save you alive by a great deliverance. 8 So now it was not you that sent me hither, but God: and he hath made me a father to Pharaoh,

---

^{4ix} Perh. traces of J in 45^{1b} ... ^{12} (so several, Smend). The wagons of 45^{19-21a} are usually ascribed to R; but J: Gu., Co., Pr., Mi., Ki.? and E: Smend. SB. divides: 19 J, 20 E, 21a J.

and lord of all his house, and ruler over all the land of Egypt.
9 Haste ye, and go up to my father, and say unto him, Thus
saith thy son Joseph, God hath made me lord of all Egypt:
come down unto me, tarry not. 10b And thou shalt be near
unto me, thou, and thy children, and thy children's children,
and thy flocks, and thy herds, and all that thou hast: 11 and
there will I nourish thee; for there are yet five years of famine;
lest thou come to poverty, thou, and thy household, and all
that thou hast. 12 And, behold, your eyes see, and the eyes
of my brother Benjamin, that it is my mouth that speaketh
unto you. 15 And he kissed all his brethren, and wept upon
them: and after that his brethren talked with him.

16 And the report thereof was heard in Pharaoh's house,
saying, Joseph's brethren are come: and it pleased Pharaoh
well, and his servants. 17 And Pharaoh said unto Joseph,
Say unto thy brethren, This do ye: lade your beasts, and go,
get you unto the land of Canaan; 18 and take your father and
your households, and come unto me: and I will give you the
good of the land of Egypt, and ye shall eat the fat of the land.
19 Now thou art commanded, this do ye: take you wagons out of the
land of Egypt for your little ones, and for your wives, and bring your
father, and come. 20 Also regard not your stuff; for the good of all the
land of Egypt is yours.

21 And the sons of Israel did so: and Joseph gave them wagons, according to the commandment of Pharaoh, and gave them provision for
the way. 22 To all of them he gave each man changes of raiment; but to Benjamin he gave three hundred pieces of silver,
and five changes of raiment. 23 And to his father he sent
after this manner: ten asses laden with the good things of
Egypt, and ten she-asses laden with grain and bread and provision for his father by the way. 24 So he sent his brethren
away, and they departed: and he said unto them, See that ye
fall not out by the way. 25 And they went up out of Egypt,
and came into the land of Canaan unto Jacob their father. 26
And they told him, saying, Joseph is yet alive, and he is ruler
over all the land of Egypt. And his heart fainted, for he
believed them not. 27 And they told him all the words of
Joseph, which he had said unto them: and when he saw the
wagons which Joseph had sent to carry him, the spirit of Jacob
their father revived.

4x. GOD COMMANDS JACOB IN A DREAM TO JOIN JOSEPH IN
EGYPT.

Gn. 46^{1b-5}

1b And offered sacrifices unto the God of his father Isaac.
2 And God spake unto Israel in the visions of the night, and

...48¹⁶] E4ix–5 145

said, Jacob, Jacob. And he said, Here am I. 3 And he said, I am God, the God of thy father: fear not to go down into Egypt; for I will there make of thee a great nation: 4 I will go down with thee into Egypt; and I will also surely bring thee up again: and Joseph shall put his hand upon thine eyes. 5a And Jacob rose up from Beer-sheba.

5b And the sons of Israel carried Jacob their father, and their little ones, and their wives, in the wagons which Pharaoh had sent to carry them.

4xi. JOSEPH PROVIDES A HOME FOR JACOB AND HIS FAMILY IN EGYPT. J18viii. P12iii, iv.
Gn. 47¹²

12 And Joseph nourished his father, and his brethren, and all his father's household, with bread, according to their families.

5. JACOB BLESSES JOSEPH AND HIS SONS. J19. E51. P13.
Gn. 48¹⁻²ᵃ·⁷⁻⁹ᵃ·¹⁰ᵇ⁻¹²·¹⁵⁻¹⁶·²⁰⁻²²

1 And it came to pass after these things, that one said to Joseph, Behold, thy father is sick: and he took with him his two sons, Manasseh and Ephraim. 2a And one told Jacob, and said, Behold thy son Joseph cometh unto thee.

7 And as for me, when I came from Paddan, Rachel died by me in the land of Canaan in the way, when there was still some distance to come unto Ephrath: and I buried her there in the way to Ephrath (the same is Beth-lehem).

8 And Israel beheld Joseph's sons, and said, Who are these? 9a And Joseph said unto his father, They are my sons, whom God hath given me here. 10b And he brought them near unto him; and he kissed them, and embraced them. 11 And Israel said unto Joseph, I had not thought to see thy face: and, lo, God hath let me see thy seed also. 12 And Joseph brought them out from between his knees; and he bowed himself with his face to the earth.

15 And he blessed Joseph, and said, The God before whom my fathers Abraham and Isaac did walk, the God who hath fed me all my life long unto this day, 16 the angel who hath redeemed me from all evil, bless the lads; and let my name be named on them, and the name of my fathers Abraham and Isaac; and let them grow into a multitude in the midst of the earth.

---
⁴ˣⁱ J: CH., Mi. only.
⁵ v. 7 R: Hupfeld, Bu., Co.?, CH., Ba., Mi., St., Smend. E: Gu., Pr., Ka.? P: Di., Dr. Cf. E3xvi, Gn. 35¹⁹. The name "Israel" in vv. 8, 11, 21 is R: We., Ba., Ad., Mi., Ka., Pr., St., Gu., Eichr. Ki. assigns vv. 8-9a, 10b-11 largely to J. The name "Israel" in v. 20 is not R, because it refers to the Israelites rather than to Jacob; Ka. points out that this constitutes an unintentional anachronism on the part of E.

20 And he blessed them that day, saying, In thee will Israel bless, saying, God make thee as Ephraim and as Manasseh: and he set Ephraim before Manasseh. 21 And Israel said unto Joseph, Behold, I die: but God will be with you, and bring you again unto the land of your fathers. 22 Moreover I have given to thee one portion above thy brethren, which I took out of the hand of the Amorite with my sword and with my bow.

6. THE DEATH OF JACOB AND OF JOSEPH. J20, 21. E72. P14. Gn. 50^{15-26}

15 And when Joseph's brethren saw that their father was dead, they said, It may be that Joseph will hate us, and will fully requite us all the evil which we did unto him. 16 And they sent a message unto Joseph, saying, Thy father did command before he died, saying, 17 So shall ye say unto Joseph, Forgive, I pray thee now, the transgression of thy brethren, and their sin, for that they did unto thee evil. And now, we pray thee, forgive the transgression of the servants of the God of thy father. And Joseph wept when they spake unto him. 18 And his brethren also went and fell down before his face; and they said, Behold, we are thy servants. 19 And Joseph said unto them, Fear not: for am I in the place of God? 20 And as for you, ye meant evil against me; but God meant it for good, to bring to pass, as it is this day, to save much people alive. 21 Now therefore fear ye not: I will nourish you, and your little ones. And he comforted them, and spake kindly unto them.

22 And Joseph dwelt in Egypt, he, and his father's house: and Joseph lived a hundred and ten years. 23 And Joseph saw Ephraim's children of the third generation: the children also of Machir the son of Manasseh were born upon Joseph's knees. 24 And Joseph said unto his brethren, I die; but God will surely visit you, and bring you up out of this land unto the land which he sware to Abraham, to Isaac, and to Jacob. 25 And Joseph took an oath of the children of Israel, saying, God will surely visit you, and ye shall carry up my bones from hence. 26 So Joseph died, being a hundred and ten years old: and they embalmed him, and he was put in a coffin in Egypt.

7. PHARAOH COMMANDS HEBREW MIDWIVES TO KILL MALE CHILDREN.

Ex. 1^{15-16}

15 And the king of Egypt spake to the Hebrew midwives, of

---

[6] Perh. fragments of J in vv. 18, 21-22: CH., Ho., Pr., Mi., Smend, Ki.; Di. and Sk., in v. 18 only. SB. in vv. 18 and 22.
[7] J?: Co., Gr., Ki., Smend.

...Ex. 2⁹]   E5–10   147

whom the name of the one was Shiphrah, and the name of the other Puah: 16 and he said, When ye do the office of a midwife to the Hebrew women, and see them upon the birth-stool; if it be a son, then shall ye kill him; but if it be a daughter, then she shall live.

8. THE MIDWIVES OUTWIT PHARAOH.
Ex. 1¹⁷⁻²⁰ᵃ·²¹⁻²²

17 But the midwives feared God, and did not as the king of Egypt commanded them, but saved the men-children alive. 18 And the king of Egypt called for the midwives, and said unto them, Why have ye done this thing, and have saved the men-children alive? 19 And the midwives said unto Pharaoh, Because the Hebrew women are not as the Egyptian women; for they are lively, and are delivered ere the midwife come unto them. 20a And God dealt well with the midwives. 21 And it came to pass, because the midwives feared God, that he made them households. 22 And Pharaoh charged all his people, saying, Every son that is born ye shall cast into the river, and every daughter ye shall save alive.

9. THE BIRTH OF MOSES.
Ex. 2¹⁻²

1 And there went a man of the house of Levi, and took to wife a daughter of Levi. 2 And the woman conceived, and bare a son: and when she saw him that he was a goodly child, she hid him three months.

10. MOSES IN THE BULRUSHES.
Ex. 2³⁻¹⁰

3 And when she could not longer hide him, she took for him an ark of bulrushes, and daubed it with slime and with pitch; and she put the child therein, and laid it in the flags by the river's brink. 4 And his sister stood afar off, to know what would be done to him. 5 And the daughter of Pharaoh came down to bathe at the river; and her maidens walked along by the riverside; and she saw the ark among the flags, and sent her handmaid to fetch it. 6 And she opened it, and saw the child: and, behold, the babe wept. And she had compassion on him, and said, This is one of the Hebrews' children. 7 Then said his sister to Pharaoh's daughter, Shall I go and call thee a nurse of the Hebrew women, that she may nurse the child for thee? 8 And Pharaoh's daughter said to her, Go. And the maiden went and called the child's mother. 9 And Pharaoh's

---

⁸ An uncertain amount of J may be present here: Co., Gr., Smend, Ki.; and v. 22 J: We., CH., McN., Smend.

daughter said unto her, Take this child away, and nurse it for me, and I will give thee thy wages. And the woman took the child, and nursed it. 10 And the child grew, and she brought him unto Pharaoh's daughter, and he became her son. And she called his name Moses, and said, Because I drew him out of the water.

11. Moses in the Land of Midian. J24.

11i. Moses Tends the Flock of Jethro, His Father-in-Law, on Horeb. J24ii.
Ex. 3^1

1 Now Moses was keeping the flock of Jethro his father-in-law, the priest of Midian: and he led the flock to the back of the wilderness, and came to the mountain of God, unto Horeb.

11ii. Moses on Horeb Commissioned to Free the Hebrews. J24iii.
Ex. $3^{4b.6.9-12}$

4b God called unto him . . . , and said, Moses, Moses. And he said, Here am I. 6 Moreover he said, I am the God of thy father, the God of Abraham, the God of Isaac, and the God of Jacob. And Moses hid his face; for he was afraid to look upon God.

9 And now, behold, the cry of the children of Israel is come unto me: moreover I have seen the oppression wherewith the Egyptians oppress them. 10 Come now therefore, and I will send thee unto Pharaoh, that thou mayest bring forth my people the children of Israel out of Egypt. 11 And Moses said unto God, Who am I, that I should go unto Pharaoh, and that I should bring forth the children of Israel out of Egypt? 12 And he said, Certainly I will be with thee; and this shall be the token unto thee, that I have sent thee: when thou hast brought forth the people out of Egypt, ye shall serve God upon this mountain.

11iii. God Reveals to Moses His Name I AM (Jehovah). J6 (Gn. 4^{26}). P17.
Ex. 3^{13-15}

13 And Moses said unto God, Behold, when I come unto the children of Israel, and shall say unto them, The God of your fathers hath sent me unto you; and they shall say to me, What is his name? what shall I say unto them? 14 And God said unto Moses, I AM THAT I AM: and he said, Thus shalt

---
¹¹ⁱⁱⁱ v. 15 Rd: Ba. (generally recognized), Gr., Bä., or Rje: Ho., McN. But E: CH., St., Co., Smend.

thou say unto the children of Israel, I AM hath sent me unto you. 15 And God said moreover unto Moses, Thus shalt thou say unto the children of Israel, Jehovah, the God of your fathers, the God of Abraham, the God of Isaac, and the God of Jacob, hath sent me unto you: this is my name for ever, and this is my memorial unto all generations.

11iv. GOD FORETELLS THE PLAGUES. E24iii. P18, 21.

Ex. 3^{19-20}

19 And I know that the king of Egypt will not give you leave to go, no, not by a mighty hand. 20 And I will put forth my hand, and smite Egypt with all my wonders which I will do in the midst thereof: and after that he will let you go.

11v. GOD COMMANDS THE DESPOILING OF THE EGYPTIANS. E13vii.

Ex. 3^{21-22}

21 And I will give this people favor in the sight of the Egyptians: and it shall come to pass, that, when ye go, ye shall not go empty: 22 but every woman shall ask of her neighbor, and of her that sojourneth in her house, jewels of silver, and jewels of gold, and raiment: and ye shall put them upon your sons, and upon your daughters; and ye shall despoil the Egyptians.

11vi. MOSES'S ROD. E13. P22.

Ex. 4^{17}

17 And thou shalt take in thy hand this rod, wherewith thou shalt do the signs.

11vii. MOSES SECURES JETHRO'S CONSENT TO RETURN TO EGYPT.

Ex. $4^{18.20b.21}$

18 And Moses went and returned to Jethro his father-in-law, and said unto him, Let me go, I pray thee, and return unto my brethren that are in Egypt, and see whether they be yet alive. And Jethro said to Moses, Go in peace. 20b And Moses took the rod of God in his hand. 21 And Jehovah said unto Moses, When thou goest back into Egypt, see that thou do before Pharaoh all the wonders which I have put in thy hand: but I will harden his heart, and he will not let the people go.

12. AARON MEETS MOSES IN THE WILDERNESS.

Ex. 4^{27-28}

27 And Jehovah said to Aaron, Go into the wilderness to

[11iv] E: Di., Dr., Ba., Ho., Bä., Kent, SB. J: We., Co., Smend, St., Ki., E. Meyer. R: CH., GFM., Pr., Gr., McN.
[11v] We., Co., Ki., E. Meyer, Smend assign to J; others E (as SB.).
[11vii] v. 21 R: CH., Ho., Co. (Rd), Pr., Gr., Bä., Kent, St., McN., SB. E: Di. (in substance), Dr., Ba., Ad., Ki. J: Smend (with v. 20b).
[12] R: GFM., Ho., Co., Gr., SB.

meet Moses. And he went, and met him in the mountain of God, and kissed him. 28 And Moses told Aaron all the words of Jehovah wherewith he had sent him, and all the signs wherewith he had charged him.

13. Moses in Egypt. J26. E11vi. P23.

13i. Appeal to Pharaoh, and His Harsh Reply. J26i. P22.
Ex. 5$^{1-2.4}$

1 And afterward Moses and Aaron came, and said unto Pharaoh, Thus saith Jehovah, the God of Israel, Let my people go, that they may hold a feast unto me in the wilderness. 2 And Pharaoh said, Who is Jehovah, that I should hearken unto his voice to let Israel go? I know not Jehovah, and moreover I will not let Israel go. 4 And the king of Egypt said unto them, Wherefore do ye, Moses and Aaron, loose the people from their works? get you unto your burdens.

13ii. The First Plague: Nile Turns to Blood. J26ii. P23i.
Ex. 7$^{15b.17b.20b.23}$

15b And thou shalt stand by the river's brink to meet him; and the rod which was turned to a serpent shalt thou take in thy hand. 17b Behold, I will smite with the rod that is in my hand upon the waters which are in the river, and they shall be turned to blood.

20b And he lifted up the rod, and smote the waters that were in the river, in the sight of Pharaoh, and in the sight of his servants; and all the waters that were in the river were turned to blood.

23 And Pharaoh turned and went into his house, neither did he lay even this to heart.

13iii. The Second Plague: Hail. J26vi.
Ex. 9$^{22.23a.24a.25a.35}$

22 And Jehovah said unto Moses, Stretch forth thy hand toward heaven, that there may be hail in all the land of Egypt, upon man, and upon beast, and upon every herb of the field, throughout the land of Egypt. 23a And Moses stretched forth his rod toward heaven.

24a So there was hail, and fire mingled with the hail. 25a And the hail smote throughout all the land of Egypt all that was in the field, both man and beast.

35 And the heart of Pharaoh was hardened, and he did not let the children of Israel go; as Jehovah had spoken by Moses.

[13i] For "ye, Moses and Aaron," E probably read originally, "the elders." Smend and Ki. assign v. 4 to J.
[13ii] vv. 15b, 20b J: Smend only.
[13iii] Slight traces of J: Ba., Ho., St,

13iv. THE THIRD PLAGUE: LOCUSTS. J26vii.
Ex. 10[12-13a.14a.15b.20]

12 And Jehovah said unto Moses, Stretch out thy hand over the land of Egypt for the locusts, that they may come up upon the land of Egypt, and eat every herb of the land, even all that the hail hath left. 13a And Moses stretched forth his rod over the land of Egypt.

14a And the locusts went up over all the land of Egypt, 15b and they did eat every herb of the land, and all the fruit of the trees which the hail had left.

20 But Jehovah hardened Pharaoh's heart, and he did not let the children of Israel go.

13v. THE FOURTH PLAGUE: DARKNESS.
Ex. 10[21-23.27]

21 And Jehovah said unto Moses, Stretch out thy hand toward heaven, that there may be darkness over the land of Egypt, even darkness which may be felt. 22 And Moses stretched forth his hand toward heaven; and there was a thick darkness in all the land of Egypt three days; 23 they saw not one another, neither rose any one from his place for three days: but all the children of Israel had light in their dwellings.

27 But Jehovah hardened Pharaoh's heart, and he would not let them go.

13vi. THE FIFTH PLAGUE THREATENED (THE FIRST-BORN). J26viii.
Ex. 11[1]

1 And Jehovah said unto Moses, Yet one plague more will I bring upon Pharaoh, and upon Egypt; afterwards he will let you go hence: when he shall let you go, he shall surely thrust you out hence altogether.

13vii. "THE SPOILING OF THE EGYPTIANS." E11v.
Ex. 11[2-3] 12[35-36]

11[2] Speak now in the ears of the people, and let them ask every man of his neighbor, and every woman of her neighbor, jewels of silver, and jewels of gold. 3 And Jehovah gave the people favor in the sight of the Egyptians. Moreover the man Moses was very great in the land of Egypt, in the sight of Pharaoh's servants, and in the sight of the people.

12[35] And the children of Israel did according to the word of Moses; and they asked of the Egyptians jewels of silver, and jewels of gold, and raiment; 36 and Jehovah gave the people

152   SOURCES OF THE HEXATEUCH [Ex. 12³⁶

favor in the sight of the Egyptians, so that they let them have what they asked. And they despoiled the Egyptians.

13viii. THE EXODUS FROM EGYPT. J26x. P24.
Ex. 13¹⁷⁻¹⁹

17 And it came to pass, when Pharaoh had let the people go, that God led them not by the way of the land of the Philistines, although that was near; for God said, Lest peradventure the people repent when they see war, and they return to Egypt: 18 but God led the people about, by the way of the wilderness by the Red Sea: and the children of Israel went up armed out of the land of Egypt. 19 And Moses took the bones of Joseph with him: for he had straitly sworn the children of Israel, saying, God will surely visit you; and ye shall carry up my bones away hence with you.

14 ESCAPE BY CROSSING THE RED SEA. J27. E13viii.
Ex. 14³·⁷·¹⁰ᵇ·¹⁵ᵃ*·¹⁶ᵃ·¹⁹ᵃ·²⁵ᵃ

3 And Pharaoh will say of the children of Israel, They are entangled in the land, the wilderness hath shut them in. 7 And he took six hundred chosen chariots, and all the chariots of Egypt, and captains over all of them.
10b And the children of Israel cried out unto Jehovah. . . .
15a . . . Wherefore criest thou unto me?
16a And lift thou up thy rod . . . 19a And the angel of God, who went before the camp of Israel, removed and went behind them. 25a And he took off their chariot wheels, and they drove them heavily.

15. THE SONG OF MOSES. E14. J27.
Ex. 15¹⁻¹⁹

Introductory Note.—It is generally believed (except by Se.) that this psalm was not composed by Moses or a contemporary of his, but is a late expansion of the Song of Miriam, E16: Ex. 15²¹. On this view it is no original part of E, but, rather, a poetic development of E's theme by a much later hand, who had Ex. 15²¹ before him.

The poem is regarded as a unity by most scholars; but Ew., Del., Di. found a Mosaic kernel in vv. 1b-3, and Strack, Dr., in 1b-11, 18. Nourse views 1b-12 as older than 13-18.

The date of its composition cannot be determined with certainty. vv. 13, 17 presuppose the temple (so Ba., Ad., Bä.,

---

¹⁴ The account is obviously fragmentary and there is considerable difference as to E's share.—v. 3 E: Ba., Co., Bä., Ho., Gr., Kent. P: Di., Dr., CH., St., McN.—v. 10b E: Dr., CH., Ba., Pr., Stenning, Smend (cf. Josh. 24⁷). J?: Co., Di. P: Ho., Gr., Bä., St. v. 25a E: Ba., Co., Bä., Gr., Ho., Di. J: We., Dr., St., Smend, McN.—In 25a, for "took off," read "bound," as in LXX and Syr.
¹⁵ v. 19 Rp.

Gr., Co., GFM., Stärk, et al.): although 17a may refer to the whole land as a sacred habitation, and 17b may be a later addition (CH., Se.). vv. 13-17 suggest the exilic hope of restoration (CH., McN., et al.). The song is a Passover psalm, and belongs in the same general literary type as Pss. 78, 105, 106, 114 (CH., Stärk) and 68 (McN.). The *terminus ad quem* for its origin is Neh. 9^{11} (memoirs of Ezra), where Ex. 15^5 is quoted. It is then late preexilic, Bä., exilic, CH., McN., or postexilic, Bender, St., Smend.

Ex. 15 is universally regarded as one of the best productions of Hebrew poetry (Stärk).

15^1 Then sang Moses and the children of Israel this song unto Jehovah, and spake, saying,
 I will sing unto Jehovah, for he hath triumphed gloriously:
 The horse and his rider hath he thrown into the sea.
2 Jehovah is my strength and song,
 And he is become my salvation:
 This is my God, and I will praise him;
 My father's God, and I will exalt him.
3 Jehovah is a man of war:
 Jehovah is his name.
4 Pharaoh's chariots and his host hath he cast into the sea;
 And his chosen captains are sunk in the Red Sea.
5 The deeps cover them:
 They went down into the depths like a stone.
6 Thy right hand, O Jehovah, is glorious in power,
 Thy right hand, O Jehovah, dasheth in pieces the enemy.
7 And in the greatness of thine excellency thou overthrowest
   them that rise up against thee:
 Thou sendest forth thy wrath, it consumeth them as stubble.
8 And with the blast of thy nostrils the waters were piled up,
 The floods stood upright as a heap;
 The deeps were congealed in the heart of the sea.
9 The enemy said,
 I will pursue, I will overtake, I will divide the spoil;
 My desire shall be satisfied upon them;
 I will draw my sword, my hand shall destroy them.
10 Thou didst blow with thy wind, the sea covered them:
 They sank as lead in the mighty waters.
11 Who is like unto thee, O Jehovah, among the gods?
 Who is like thee, glorious in holiness,
 Fearful in praises, doing wonders?
12 Thou stretchedst out thy right hand,
 The earth swallowed them.

13 Thou in thy lovingkindness hast led the people that thou hast redeemed:
    Thou hast guided them in thy strength to thy holy habitation.
14 The peoples have heard, they tremble:
    Pangs have taken hold on the inhabitants of Philistia.
15 Then were the chiefs of Edom dismayed;
    The mighty men of Moab, trembling taketh hold upon them:
    All the inhabitants of Canaan are melted away.
16 Terror and dread falleth upon them;
    By the greatness of thine arm they are as still as a stone;
    Till thy people pass over, O Jehovah,
    Till the people pass over that thou hast purchased.
17 Thou wilt bring them in, and plant them in the mountain of thine inheritance,
    The place, O Jehovah, which thou hast made for thee to dwell in,
    The sanctuary, O Lord, which thy hands have established.
18 Jehovah shall reign for ever and ever.

19 For the horses of Pharaoh went in with his chariots and with his horsemen into the sea, and Jehovah brought back the waters of the sea upon them; but the children of Israel walked on dry land in the midst of the sea.

16. THE SONG OF MIRIAM. E15. Micah 6⁴.

Ex. 15²⁰⁻²¹

20 And Miriam the prophetess, the sister of Aaron, took a timbrel in her hand; and all the women went out after her with timbrels and with dances. 21 And Miriam answered them,
    Sing ye to Jehovah, for he hath triumphed gloriously;
    The horse and his rider hath he thrown into the sea.

17. JEHOVAH PROVES THE ISRAELITES.

Ex. 15²⁵ᵇ⁻²⁶

25b There he made for them a statute and an ordinance, and there he proved them; 26 and he said, If thou wilt diligently hearken to the voice of Jehovah thy God, and wilt do that which is right in his eyes, and wilt give ear to his commandments, and keep all his statutes, I will put none of the diseases upon thee, which I have put upon the Egyptians: for I am Jehovah that healeth thee.

---

¹⁶ Smend alone assigns this fragment to J!
¹⁷ v. 26 Rd: Ba., Co., Ho., Pr., Bä., St., Smend, and "critics generally" Ba. Rje: We., CH.

...18¹] E15–20 155

18. MOSES SMITES THE ROCK IN HOREB TO FURNISH A WATER SUPPLY. J28, 30. P66.
Ex. 17³⁻⁶

3 And the people thirsted there for water; and the people murmured against Moses, and said, Wherefore hast thou brought us up out of Egypt, to kill us and our children and our cattle with thirst? 4 And Moses cried unto Jehovah, saying, What shall I do unto this people? they are almost ready to stone me. 5 And Jehovah said unto Moses, Pass on before the people, and take with thee of the elders of Israel; and thy rod, wherewith thou smotest the river, take in thy hand, and go. 6 Behold, I will stand before thee there upon the rock in Horeb; and thou shalt smite the rock, and there shall come water out of it, that the people may drink. And Moses did so in the sight of the elders of Israel.

19. JOSHUA'S DEFEAT OF AMALEK AT REPHIDIM: AARON AND HUR STAY UP MOSES'S HANDS. E37.
Ex. 17⁸⁻¹⁶

8 Then came Amalek, and fought with Israel in Rephidim. 9 And Moses said unto Joshua, Choose us out men, and go out, fight with Amalek: to-morrow I will stand on the top of the hill with the rod of God in my hand. 10 So Joshua did as Moses had said to him, and fought with Amalek: and Moses, Aaron, and Hur went up to the top of the hill. 11 And it came to pass, when Moses held up his hand, that Israel prevailed; and when he let down his hand, Amalek prevailed. 12 But Moses' hands were heavy; and they took a stone, and put it under him, and he sat thereon; and Aaron and Hur stayed up his hands, the one on the one side, and the other on the other side; and his hands were steady until the going down of the sun. 13 And Joshua discomfited Amalek and his people with the edge of the sword. 14 And Jehovah said unto Moses, Write this for a memorial in a book, and rehearse it in the ears of Joshua: that I will utterly blot out the remembrance of Amalek from under heaven. 15 And Moses built an altar, and called the name of it Jehovah-nissi; 16 and he said, Jehovah hath sworn: Jehovah will have war with Amalek from generation to generation.

20. JETHRO VISITS THE CAMP OF ISRAEL. E11i, vii. J35.
Ex. 18¹⁻¹²

18¹ Now Jethro, the priest of Midian, Moses' father-in-

---

[18] v. 3 J: CH., GFM., McN.
[19] J: Smend! (in spite of Joshua and Aaron). vv. 14-16 J: Ki. v. 14 R: Gr. (cf. Dt. 25¹⁹), Bä., Ho., St. (E?), Smend, Kent. The narrative is regarded as unhistorical (Smend, cf. Nu. 14³⁹ᶠᶠ·).
[20] v. 2b Rje. Perh. also other traces of Rje: vv. 2-4, Dr., Gr.; or vv. 8-10, Dr., Ho., CH. Smend finds J here, also. In v. 3, "sojourner": in Hebr. is *ger*, cf. Gershom. v. 4 "Eliezer" is made up of the Hebr. words *El* (God) and *ezer* (help).

law, heard of all that God had done for Moses, and for Israel his people, how that Jehovah had brought Israel out of Egypt. 2 And Jethro, Moses' father-in-law, took Zipporah, Moses' wife, after he had sent her away, 3 and her two sons; of whom the name of the one was Gershom; for he said, I have been a sojourner in a foreign land: 4 and the name of the other was Eliezer; for *he said*, The God of my father was my help, and delivered me from the sword of Pharaoh. 5 And Jethro, Moses' father-in-law, came with his sons and his wife unto Moses into the wilderness where he was encamped, at the mount of God: 6 and he said unto Moses, I, thy father-in-law Jethro, am come unto thee, and thy wife, and her two sons with her. 7 And Moses went out to meet his father-in-law, and did obeisance, and kissed him; and they asked each other of their welfare; and they came into the tent. 8 And Moses told his father-in-law all that Jehovah had done unto Pharaoh and to the Egyptians for Israel's sake, all the travail that had come upon them by the way, and how Jehovah delivered them. 9 And Jethro rejoiced for all the goodness which Jehovah had done to Israel, in that he had delivered them out of the hand of the Egyptians. 10 And Jethro said, Blessed be Jehovah, who hath delivered you out of the hand of the Egyptians, and out of the hand of Pharaoh; who hath delivered the people from under the hand of the Egyptians. 11 Now I know that Jehovah is greater than all gods; yea, in the thing wherein they dealt proudly against them. 12 And Jethro, Moses' father-in-law, took a burnt-offering and sacrifices for God: and Aaron came, and all the elders of Israel, to eat bread with Moses' father-in-law before God.

21. MOSES'S FATHER-IN-LAW ADVISES HIM REGARDING JUDICIAL ORGANIZATION. E20, 32. Dt. 1[9-18].

Ex. 18[13-27]

13 And it came to pass on the morrow, that Moses sat to judge the people: and the people stood about Moses from the morning unto the evening. 14 And when Moses' father-in-law saw all that he did to the people, he said, What is this thing that thou doest to the people? why sittest thou thyself alone, and all the people stand about thee from morning unto even? 15 And Moses said unto his father-in-law, Because the people come unto me to inquire of God: 16 when they have a matter, they come unto me; and I judge between a man and his neighbor, and I make them know the statutes of God, and his laws.

17 And Moses' father-in-law said unto him, The thing that

---

[21] R in vv. 25-26?: Gr., Bä., St., Ho. v. 26, cf. Dt. 17[8].

thou doest is not good. 18 Thou wilt surely wear away, both thou, and this people that is with thee: for the thing is too heavy for thee; thou art not able to perform it thyself alone. 19 Hearken now unto my voice, I will give thee counsel, and God be with thee: be thou for the people to Godward, and bring thou the causes unto God: 20 and thou shalt teach them the statutes and the laws, and shalt show them the way wherein they must walk, and the work that they must do. 21 Moreover thou shalt provide out of all the people able men, such as fear God, men of truth, hating unjust gain; and place such over them, to be rulers of thousands, rulers of hundreds, rulers of fifties, and rulers of tens: 22 and let them judge the people at all seasons: and it shall be, that every great matter they shall bring unto thee, but every small matter they shall judge themselves: so shall it be easier for thyself, and they shall bear *the burden* with thee. 23 If thou shalt do this thing, and God command thee so, then thou shalt be able to endure, and all this people also shall go to their place in peace.

24 So Moses hearkened to the voice of his father-in-law, and did all that he had said. 25 And Moses chose able men out of all Israel, and made them heads over the people, rulers of thousands, rulers of hundreds, rulers of fifties, and rulers of tens. 26 And they judged the people at all seasons: the hard causes they brought unto Moses, but every small matter they judged themselves. 27 And Moses let his father-in-law depart; and he went his way into his own land.

22. Appearance of God on the Mount. J31.

Ex. 19^{2b-3a.10-11a.14-17.19} 20¹⁸⁻²¹

19^{2b} And there Israel encamped before the mount. 3a And Moses went up unto God. 10 And Jehovah said unto Moses, Go unto the people, and sanctify them to-day and to-morrow, and let them wash their garments, 11a and be ready against the third day.

14 And Moses went down from the mount unto the people, and sanctified the people; and they washed their garments. 15 And he said unto the people, Be ready against the third day: come not near a woman.

16 And it came to pass on the third day, when it was morning, that there were thunders and lightnings, and a thick cloud upon the mount, and the voice of a trumpet exceeding loud; and all the people that were in the camp trembled. 17 And Moses brought forth the people out of the camp to meet God;

---

[22] 20¹⁸⁻²¹ after 19¹⁹: We., Bu., Ku., Jül., GFM., and "generally accepted" GFM., cf. Dt. 5. Even Eerd. makes this change; but W. H. Greene, Ba., and Nourse oppose it, and favor the present place of the Decalogue.

and they stood at the nether part of the mount. 19 And when the voice of the trumpet waxed louder and louder, Moses spake, and God answered him by a voice.

20[18] And all the people perceived the thunderings, and the lightnings, and the voice of the trumpet, and the mountain smoking: and when the people saw it, they trembled, and stood afar off. 19 And they said unto Moses, Speak thou with us, and we will hear; but let not God speak with us, lest we die. 20 And Moses said unto the people, Fear not: for God is come to prove you, and that his fear may be before you, that ye sin not. 21 And the people stood afar off, and Moses drew near unto the thick darkness where God was.

23. THE E DECALOGUE. J34. Dt. 5[1-21].
Ex. 20[1-17]

Introductory Note.—All critics are agreed that the Decalogue belongs in the E literature (except St., Rp), and owes its present form to the Deuteronomic movement (700-650ff.). Practically all (except Meisner) are also agreed that the original Decalogue consisted of the ten "words" without the expansions or reasons for obedience; the biblical expression "the ten words," stylistic considerations, and comparison with Dt. 5 lead to this hypothesis (which even Eerd. holds in a modified form).

When was the original Decalogue produced? Some hold that there is no good reason to doubt that it came from Moses: so Di., B. Delitzsch, König, Ki., Dr., Lotz, Se., Pr., Eerd., Knudson, Peritz, J. P. Peters. Gr. assigns it to the time of the Judges, for commandments II and IV presuppose the settlement in Canaan. Many, however, believe that even the original form could not have come from a period antedating B. C. 700. The Decalogue as a whole is believed to reflect the prophetic movement, and commandments II, IV, and X in particular are believed to show Canaanitic influence or other late ideas. The absence of any allusions to it before Dt. is also significant. Co. dates it in the seventh century in Judah. This general view is accepted by We., Ku., Ba., Ad., Meisner, Bä., Staerk, Baudissin, Kraetzschmar, CH., McN. (after Amos and Ho.) Kent and Smend (after Amos). Ho. 4[2] seems to be either a condensed summary of part of the Decalogue, or a beginning of the movement that culminated in Ex. 20. St. holds that Ex. 20 was taken from Dt. 5, and that Dt. 5 is exilic; for the Sabbath was the only cult-requirement that exiles could observe!

It follows from the general view presented that E in its original form did not contain the Decalogue, which was inserted by a later hand between Ex. 19[19] and 20[18]. Some hold that the narrative requires an E-Decalogue, and so try to recover it; Stärk, in Ex. $22^{26\text{-}27}$ $23^{14\text{-}16,10\text{-}12}$; Meisner in Ex. $23^{14\text{-}19}$; and also Bä. McN. points out that most of the ten words can be found in an earlier, more concrete form in CC, as follows: I, $CC20^{23a}$. II, $CC20^{23b}$. III, $CC23^{1a}$. IV, $CC23^{12}$. V, $CC21^{15,17}$. VI, $CC21^{12}$. VII, om.CC; cf. $22^{16\text{-}17}$. VIII, $CC21^{16}$ $22^{1\text{-}4}$. IX, $CC23^{1b}$. X, om.CC.

1 And God spake all these words, saying, 2 I am Jehovah thy God, who brought thee out of the land of Egypt, out of the house of bondage.
I. 3 Thou shalt have no other gods before me.
II. 4 Thou shalt not make unto thee a graven image, nor any likeness *of any thing* that is in heaven above, or that is in the earth beneath, or that is in the water under the earth: 5 thou shalt not bow down thyself unto them, nor serve them; for I Jehovah thy God am a jealous God, visiting the iniquity of the fathers upon the children, upon the third and upon the fourth generation of them that hate me, 6 and showing lovingkindness unto thousands of them that love me and keep my commandments.
III. 7 Thou shalt not take the name of Jehovah thy God in vain; for Jehovah will not hold him guiltless that taketh his name in vain.
IV. 8 Remember the sabbath day, to keep it holy. 9 Six days shalt thou labor, and do all thy work; but the seventh day is a sabbath unto Jehovah thy God: *in it* thou shalt not do any work, thou, nor thy son, nor thy daughter, thy man-servant, nor thy maid-servant, nor thy cattle, nor thy stranger that is within thy gates: 11 for in six days Jehovah made heaven and earth, the sea, and all that in them is, and rested the seventh day: wherefore Jehovah blessed the sabbath day, and hallowed it.
V. 12 Honor thy father and thy mother, that thy days may be long in the land which Jehovah thy God giveth thee.
VI. 13 Thou shalt not kill.
VII. 14 Thou shalt not commit adultery.
VIII. 15 Thou shalt not steal.
IX. 16 Thou shalt not bear false witness against thy neighbor.
X. 17 Thou shalt not covet thy neighbor's house, thou shalt not covet thy neighbor's wife, nor his man-servant, nor his maid-servant, nor his ox, nor his ass, nor anything that is thy neighbor's.

24. THE CODE (OR BOOK) OF THE COVENANT (CC). J34. CODE OF HAMMURAPI.

Introductory Note.—CC is now unanimously assigned to

---

[23] All the redaction is the work of Rd, except v. 11 which is Rp. (cf. P1). Even Eerd. admits that v. 11 is R.

the E literature, and all agree that it contains groups of laws ancient, but not homogeneous, in origin.

It is recognized that the present connection of CC with the context in E is very loose (Ex. 20^{22}; 24$^{3-8}$). Many scholars think it probable that CC was not originally E's basis for the Sinaitic covenant, as Ex. 24$^{3-8}$ now implies; but, either it occupied the present place of Dt., as Moses's final legislation in Moab (cf. E49, Dt. 27^{5-7a}: so, Ku., Se., Kent, Co., Bä., McN.); or it was Joshua's recapitulation of the Mosaic law (E70, Josh. 24^{25}: so, Ho., St., Pr.). Both views are rejected by Smend.

In its present form CC shows numerous traces of the work of Rd, but, when these are eliminated, the remaining body of laws—esp. the "Judgments" E24ii, Ex. 21^{1}-22^{17}—is probably the oldest collection of Israelitic law in existence (Gr., and cf. J34). Dr. says that in CC and the Decalogue "the teaching of Moses is preserved in its least modified form." Di., Se., Eerd. accept CC as substantially Mosaic. But most agree that the type of agricultural civilization presupposed in the laws implies the settlement in Canaan. The period of the Judges or that of the United Kingdom is coming to be widely accepted as the date of the oldest laws in CC: so, Kent, Dr., Merx, Eiselen, Gr., Pr., Ki. Smend, however, dates the collection after Amos, though admitting an earlier origin for many of the laws.

Various attempts have been made to divide the laws of CC into groups of five (pentads) or ten (decads). Paton (JBL, vol. 12, pp. 79-93) has made the most important contribution to this analysis, and has made it highly probable that the laws of CC were originally grouped in ten decads. But this view has not met with general acceptance. Of recent writers, Eerd. and Smend specifically reject it.

Smend notes that the general tendency of CC is to put cultus in the background, relative to law and morals.

24i. THE LAW OF THE ALTAR.   E49.

Ex. 20$^{22-26}$

22 And Jehovah said unto Moses, Thus thou shalt say unto the children of Israel, Ye yourselves have seen that I have talked with you from heaven.   23 Ye shall not make *other gods* with me; gods of silver, or gods of gold, ye shall not make unto you.   24 An altar of earth thou shalt make unto me, and shalt sacrifice thereon thy burnt-offerings, and thy peace-offerings, thy sheep, and thine oxen: in every place where I record my name I will come unto thee and I will bless

---

[24i] This law is very important. According to critics, it permits sacrifice at any shrine, in contrast to Dt. (ch. 12, etc.), which restricts it to Jerusalem. Smend views our passage as a direct polemic against luxury in cultus and centralization of worship (Solomon's temple, Dt.).

thee. 25 And if thou make me an altar of stone, thou shalt not build it of hewn stones; for if thou lift up thy tool upon it, thou hast polluted it. 26 Neither shalt thou go up by steps unto mine altar, that thy nakedness be not uncovered thereon.

24ii. THE JUDGMENTS (MISHPATIM).
Ex. 21^1-22^{17}

21^1 Now these are the ordinances which thou shalt set before them.
2 If thou buy a Hebrew servant, six years he shall serve: and in the seventh he shall go out free for nothing. 3 If he come in by himself, he shall go out by himself: if he be married, then his wife shall go out with him. 4 If his master give him a wife, and she bear him sons or daughters; the wife and her children shall be her master's, and he shall go out by himself. 5 But if the servant shall plainly say, I love my master, my wife, and my children; I will not go out free: 6 then his master shall bring him unto God, and shall bring him to the door, or unto the door-post; and his master shall bore his ear through with an awl; and he shall serve him for ever.
7 And if a man sell his daughter to be a maid-servant, she shall not go out as the men-servants do. 8 If she please not her master, who hath espoused her to himself, then shall he let her be redeemed: to sell her unto a foreign people he shall have no power, seeing he hath dealt deceitfully with her. 9 And if he espouse her unto his son, he shall deal with her after the manner of daughters. 10 If he take him another *wife;* her food, her raiment, and her duty of marriage, shall he not diminish. 11 And if he do not these three things unto her, then shall she go out for nothing, without money.
12 He that smiteth a man, so that he dieth, shall surely be put to death. 13 And if a man lie not in wait, but God deliver *him* into his hand; then I will appoint thee a place whither he shall flee. 14 And if a man come presumptuously upon his neighbor, to slay him with guile; thou shalt take him from mine altar, that he may die.
15 And he that smiteth his father, or his mother, shall be surely put to death.
16 And he that stealeth a man, and selleth him, or if he be found in his hand, he shall surely be put to death.
17 And he that curseth his father or his mother, shall surely be put to death.
18 And if men contend, and one smite the other with a stone,

[24ii] 21^6 probably refers to the local sanctuary (as in Code Ham., Paton); or perhaps to the household gods (Eerd.).—v. 17 gloss: McN., Paton.—vv. 22-25 gloss: Paton, Smend (24-25): it is at least out of its proper connection (Bu.). Cf. PH 42vii: Lv. $24^{10\text{-}20}$.

or with his fist, and he die not, but keep his bed; 19 if he rise again, and walk abroad upon his staff, then shall he that smote him be quit: only he shall pay for the loss of his time, and shall cause him to be thoroughly healed.

20 And if a man smite his servant, or his maid, with a rod, and he die under his hand; he shall surely be punished. 21 Notwithstanding, if he continue a day or two, he shall not be punished: for he is his money.

22 And if men strive together, and hurt a woman with child, so that her fruit depart, and yet no harm follow; he shall be surely fined, according as the woman's husband shall lay upon him; and he shall pay as the judges determine. 23 But if any harm follow, then thou shalt give life for life, 24 eye for eye, tooth for tooth, hand for hand, foot for foot, 25 burning for burning, wound for wound, stripe for stripe.

26 And if a man smite the eye of his servant, or the eye of his maid, and destroy it; he shall let him go free for his eye's sake. 27 And if he smite out his man-servant's tooth, or his maid-servant's tooth; he shall let him go free for his tooth's sake.

28 And if an ox gore a man or a woman to death, the ox shall be surely stoned, and its flesh shall not be eaten; but the owner of the ox shall be quit. 29 But if the ox was wont to gore in time past, and it hath been testified to its owner, and he hath not kept it in, but it hath killed a man or a woman; the ox shall be stoned, and its owner also shall be put to death. 30 If there be laid on him a ransom, then he shall give for the redemption of his life whatsoever is laid upon him. 31 Whether it have gored a son, or have gored a daughter, according to this judgment shall it be done unto him. 32 If the ox gore a manservant or a maid-servant, there shall be given unto their master thirty shekels of silver, and the ox shall be stoned.

33 And if a man shall open a pit, or if a man shall dig a pit and not cover it, and an ox or an ass fall therein, 34 the owner of the pit shall make it good; he shall give money unto the owner thereof, and the dead *beast* shall be his.

35 And if one man's ox hurt another's, so that it dieth, then they shall sell the live ox, and divide the price of it; and the dead also they shall divide. 36 Or if it be known that the ox was wont to gore in time past, and its owner hath not kept it in; he shall surely pay ox for ox, and the dead *beast* shall be his own.

22 If a man shall steal an ox, or a sheep, and kill it, or sell it; he shall pay five oxen for an ox, and four sheep for a sheep. 2 If the thief be found breaking in, and be smitten so that he dieth, there shall be no bloodguiltiness for him. 3 If the sun be risen upon him, there shall be bloodguiltiness for him; he shall make restitution: if he have nothing, then he shall be sold for his theft. 4 If the theft be found in his hand alive, whether it be ox, or ass, or sheep; he shall pay double. 5 If a man shall cause a field or vineyard to be eaten, and shall let his beast loose, and it feed in another man's field; of the best of his own field, and of the best of his own vineyard, shall he make restitution.

6 If fire break out, and catch in thorns, so that the shocks of grain, or the standing grain, or the field are consumed; he that kindled the fire shall surely make restitution.

7 If a man shall deliver unto his neighbor money or stuff to keep, and it be stolen out of the man's house; if the thief be found, he shall pay double. 8 If the thief be not found, then the master of the house shall come near unto God, *to see* whether he have not put his hand unto his neighbor's goods. 9 For every matter of trespass, whether it be for ox, for ass, for sheep, for raiment, *or* for any manner of lost thing, whereof one saith, This is it, the cause of both parties shall come before God; he whom God shall condemn shall pay double unto his neighbor.

10 If a man deliver unto his neighbor an ass, or an ox, or a sheep, or any beast, to keep; and it die, or be hurt, or driven away, no man seeing it: 11 the oath of Jehovah shall be between them both, whether he hath not put his hand unto his neighbor's goods; and the owner thereof shall accept it, and he shall not make restitution. 12 But if it be stolen from him, he shall make restitution unto the owner thereof. 13 If it be torn in pieces, let him bring it for witness; he shall not make good that which was torn.

14 And if a man borrow aught of his neighbor, and it be hurt, or die, the owner thereof not being with it, he shall surely make restitution. 15 If the owner thereof be with it, he shall not make it good: if it be a hired thing, it came for its hire.

16 And if a man entice a virgin that is not betrothed, and lie with her, he shall surely pay a dowry for her to be his wife. 17 If her father utterly refuse to give her unto him, he shall pay money according to the dowry of virgins.

24iii. WORDS (cf. Ex. 24³): MORAL AND CEREMONIAL.
Ex. 22¹⁸-23¹⁹
22¹⁸ Thou shalt not suffer a sorceress to live.

---

²⁴ⁱⁱⁱ All redactional material except 23¹⁵⁻¹⁹ is the work of Rd. Co., St., Ho., Gr., Smend agree on all vv. so assigned. Ba., CH., et al. agree on most. Rd. is frequently characterized by Dt.'s humanitarian interest, and by a change in number from that of the context.—22²¹ contradicts 21³⁴·³⁶ 22¹¹·¹³. Co.—23⁴⁻⁵ interrupt vv. 3 and 6; R: Co., St., Bä., Gr., Smend; only out of place: Dr., Ho., Eerd. et al.—23⁷ᵃ, cf. v. 1a, Co.—23⁹ᵃ Rd: Co., Ho., Ba., Eerd., cf. 22¹ᵃ; 23¹³ R: St., CH., Ho., Eerd., Smend; but genuine, Ba., Jül., Gr.
23¹⁵⁻¹⁹ Rje, from Ex. 34¹⁴ᶠᶠ·; so all, exc. Eerd., who believes this original and Ex. 34 a postexilic copy.

19 Whosoever lieth with a beast shall surely be put to death.
20 He that sacrificeth unto any god, save unto Jehovah only, shall be utterly destroyed. 21 And a sojourner shalt thou not wrong, neither shalt thou oppress him: for ye were sojourners in the land of Egypt. 22 Ye shall not afflict any widow, or fatherless child. 23 If thou afflict them at all, and they cry at all unto me, I will surely hear their cry; 24 and my wrath shall wax hot, and I will kill you with the sword; and your wives shall be widows, and your children fatherless.

25 If thou lend money to any of my people with thee that is poor, thou shalt not be to him as a creditor; neither shall ye lay upon him interest. 26 If thou at all take thy neighbor's garment to pledge, thou shalt restore it unto him before the sun goeth down: 27 for that is his only covering, it is his garment for his skin: wherein shall he sleep? and it shall come to pass, when he crieth unto me, that I will hear; for I am gracious.

28 Thou shalt not revile God, nor curse a ruler of thy people. 29 Thou shalt not delay to offer of thy harvest, and of the outflow of thy presses. The first-born of thy sons shalt thou give unto me. 30 Likewise shalt thou do with thine oxen, *and* with thy sheep: seven days it shall be with its dam; on the eighth day thou shalt give it me. 31 And ye shall be holy men unto me: therefore ye shall not eat any flesh that is torn of beasts in the field; ye shall cast it to the dogs.

23 Thou shalt not take up a false report: put not thy hand with the wicked to be an unrighteous witness. 2 Thou shalt not follow a multitude to do evil; neither shalt thou speak in a cause to turn aside after a multitude to wrest *justice*: 3 neither shalt thou favor a poor man in his cause.

4 If thou meet thine enemy's ox or his ass going astray, thou shalt surely bring it back to him again. 5 If thou see the ass of him that hateth thee lying under his burden, thou shalt forbear to leave him, thou shalt surely release *it* with him.

6 Thou shalt not wrest the justice *due* to thy poor in his cause. 7 Keep thee far from a false matter; and the innocent and righteous slay thou not: for I will not justify the wicked. 8 And thou shalt take no bribe: for a bribe bindeth them that have sight, and perverteth the words of the righteous. 9 And a sojourner shalt thou not oppress: for ye know the heart of a sojourner, seeing ye were sojourners in the land of Egypt.

10 And six years thou shalt sow thy land, and shalt gather in the increase thereof: 11 but the seventh year thou shalt let it rest and lie fallow, that the poor of thy people may eat: and what they leave the beast of the field shall eat. In like manner thou shalt deal with thy vineyard, *and* with thy olive-yard. 12 Six days thou shalt do thy work, and on the seventh

day thou shalt rest; that thine ox and thine ass may have rest, and the son of thy handmaid, and the sojourner, may be refreshed. 13 And in all things that I have said unto you take ye heed: and make no mention of the name of other gods, neither let it be heard out of thy mouth. 14 Three times thou shalt keep a feast unto me in the year. 15 The feast of unleavened bread shalt thou keep: seven days thou shalt eat unleavened bread, as I commanded thee, at the time appointed in the month Abib (for in it thou camest out from Egypt); and none shall appear before me empty: 16 and the feast of harvest, the first-fruits of thy labors, which thou sowest in the field: and the feast of ingathering, at the end of the year, when thou gatherest in thy labors out of the field. 17 Three times in the year all thy males shall appear before the Lord Jehovah.

18 Thou shalt not offer the blood of my sacrifice with leavened bread; neither shall the fat of my feast remain all night until the morning. 19 The first of the first-fruits of thy ground thou shalt bring into the house of Jehovah thy God. Thou shalt not boil a kid in its mother's milk.

24iv. PARENETIC CONCLUSION. P42ix. Dt. 28. Ex. 23^{20-33}

20 Behold, I send an angel before thee, to keep thee by the way, and to bring thee into the place which I have prepared. 21 Take ye heed before him, and hearken unto his voice; provoke him not; for he will not pardon your transgression: for my name is in him. 22 But if thou shalt indeed hearken unto his voice, and do all that I speak; then I will be an enemy unto thine enemies, and an adversary unto thine adversaries. 23 For mine angel shall go before thee, and bring thee in unto the Amorite, and the Hittite, and the Perizzite, and the Canaanite, and the Hivite, and the Jebusite: and I will cut them off. 24 Thou shalt not bow down to their gods, nor serve them, nor do after their works; but thou shalt utterly overthrow them, and break in pieces their pillars. 25 And ye shall serve Jehovah your God, and he will bless thy bread, and thy water; and I will take sickness away from the midst of thee. 26 There shall none cast her young, nor be barren, in thy land: the number of thy days I will fulfil. 27 I will send my terror before thee, and will discomfit all the people to whom thou shalt come, and I will make all thine enemies turn their backs unto thee. 28 And I will send the hornet before thee, which shall drive out the Hivite, the Canaanite, and the Hittite, from before thee. 29 I will not drive them out from before thee in one year, lest the land become desolate, and the beasts of the field multiply against thee. 30 By little and little I will

---

[24iv] The majority regard this conclusion as E, worked over by Rd as indicated. Ho, views it as Rje (JEs) entire; McN., Rd. Eerd. also views it as post-Deuteronomic, and Smend finds both J and E, holding that the passage is not original in CC.

drive them out from before thee, until thou be increased, and inherit the land. 31 And I will set thy border from the Red Sea even unto the sea of the Philistines, and from the wilderness unto the River: for I will deliver the inhabitants of the land into your hand; and thou shalt drive them out before thee. 32 Thou shalt make no covenant with them, nor with their gods. 33 They shall not dwell in thy land, lest they make thee sin against me; for if thou serve their gods, it will surely be a snare unto thee.

25. Moses Builds an Altar and Twelve Massebahs, and Solemnizes the Covenant. J34. E55.
Ex. 24[3-8]

3 And Moses came and told the people all the words of Jehovah, and all the ordinances: and all the people answered with one voice, and said, All the words which Jehovah hath spoken will we do. 4 And Moses wrote all the words of Jehovah, and rose up early in the morning, and builded an altar under the mount, and twelve pillars, according to the twelve tribes of Israel. 5 And he sent young men of the children of Israel, who offered burnt-offerings, and sacrificed peace-offerings of oxen unto Jehovah. 6 And Moses took half of the blood, and put it in basins; and half of the blood he sprinkled on the altar. 7 And he took the book of the covenant, and read in the audience of the people: and they said, All that Jehovah hath spoken will we do, and be obedient. 8 And Moses took the blood, and sprinkled it on the people, and said, Behold the blood of the covenant, which Jehovah hath made with you concerning all these words.

26. Moses and Joshua Receive the Tables of Stone on the Mount of God. J34.
Ex. 24[12-15a.18b] 31[18]*

12 And Jehovah said unto Moses, Come up to me into the mount, and be there: and I will give thee the tables of stone, and the law and the commandment, which I have written, that thou mayest teach them. 13 And Moses rose up, and Joshua his minister: and Moses went up into the mount of God. 14 And he said unto the elders, Tarry ye here for us, until we come again unto you: and, behold, Aaron and Hur are with you; whosoever hath a cause, let him come near unto them. 15a And Moses went up into the mount, 18b and went up into the mount: and Moses was in the mount forty

---
[25] In v. 3, the words "and . . . ordinances" are regarded as R by Ho., Eerd., et al. vv. 4a (to "Jehovah"), 7 J: St. R: Bä., Ho., Kent. Smend, et al. hold that this passage originally referred back to the Decalogue.
[26] v. 15a is assigned to P by Ho., and v. 18b, to P, by McN. The threefold repetition of the fact that Moses went up into the mount, vv. 13, 15a, 18b is striking, and may perh. be unintentional.

days and forty nights. 31^{18} And he gave unto Moses . . . , the two tables of the testimony, tables of stone, written with the finger of God.

27. THE GOLDEN CALF. E41. Dt. 9^{12}. 1K. 12^{28}.
Ex. 32$^{1\text{-}35}$

1 And when the people saw that Moses delayed to come down from the mount, the people gathered themselves together unto Aaron, and said unto him, Up, make us gods, which shall go before us; for as for this Moses, the man that brought us up out of the land of Egypt, we know not what is become of him. 2 And Aaron said unto them, Break off the golden rings, which are in the ears of your wives, of your sons, and of your daughters, and bring them unto me. 3 And all the people brake off the golden rings which were in their ears, and brought them unto Aaron. 4 And he received it at their hand, and fashioned it with a graving tool, and made it a molten calf: and they said, These are thy gods, O Israel, which brought thee up out of the land of Egypt. 5 And when Aaron saw *this*, he built an altar before it; and Aaron made proclamation, and said, To-morrow shall be a feast to Jehovah. 6 And they rose up early on the morrow, and offered burnt-offerings, and brought peace-offerings; and the people sat down to eat and to drink, and rose up to play.

7 And Jehovah spake unto Moses, Go, get thee down; for thy people, that thou broughtest up out of the land of Egypt, have corrupted themselves: 8 they have turned aside quickly out of the way which I commanded them: they have made them a molten calf, and have worshipped it, and have sacrificed unto it, and said, These are thy gods, O Israel, which brought thee up out of the land of Egypt. 9 And Jehovah said unto Moses, I have seen this people, and, behold, it is a stiffnecked people: 10 now therefore let me alone, that my wrath may wax hot against them, and that I may consume them: and I will make of thee a great nation. 11 And Moses besought Jehovah his God, and said, Jehovah, why doth thy wrath wax hot against thy people, that thou hast brought forth out of the land of Egypt with great power and with a mighty hand? 12 Wherefore should the Egyptians speak, saying, For evil did he bring

---

[27] vv. 7-14 Rje: We., CH., Ho., GFM., Co. Rd: Ku., Knobel, St., Pr., McN. R: Gr., Eerd. The revision in v. 15 is Rp. There is great difference with reference to the analysis of the chapter; the majority agree that there is a J narrative, embedded in the material; but there is no consensus with regard to the division of sources, save that all agree on a fundamental E source for the narrative. Among those that find J here are: Di., Ba., Gr., Smend, McN., CH., Ki., Ho., Westphal. The last three agree on J: vv. 1-3, 5-6, 19-20, 35. All agree that vv. 21-35 are much worked over.

The chapter is taken by many to presuppose the fall of the northern kingdom and the captivity, esp. v. 34 (cf. E70, Josh. 24^{20}). Hence these critics assign Ex. 32 to E^2, writing after 721; to whom Ex. 20 would also be assigned, on account of the tables of the law in ch. 32. Josh. 24 is assigned to the same hand. Smend uses these considerations to date E entire after 721. Others find an allusion to the captivity no more remarkable in E in 750 than in Amos or Hosea at the same time.

them forth, to slay them in the mountains, and to consume them from the face of the earth? Turn from thy fierce wrath, and repent of this evil against thy people. 13 Remember Abraham, Isaac, and Israel, thy servants, to whom thou swarest by thine own self, and saidst unto them, I will multiply your seed as the stars of heaven, and all this land that I have spoken of will I give unto your seed, and they shall inherit it for ever. 14 And Jehovah repented of the evil which he said he would do unto his people.

15 And Moses turned, and went down from the mount, with the two tables of the testimony in his hand; tables that were written on both their sides; on the one side and on the other were they written. 16 And the tables were the work of God, and the writing was the writing of God, graven upon the tables. 17 And when Joshua heard the noise of the people as they shouted, he said unto Moses, There is a noise of war in the camp. 18 And he said, It is not the voice of them that shout for mastery, neither is it the voice of them that cry for being overcome; but the noise of them that sing do I hear. 19 And it came to pass, as soon as he came nigh unto the camp, that he saw the calf and the dancing: and Moses' anger waxed hot, and he cast the tables out of his hands, and brake them beneath the mount. 20 And he took the calf which they had made, and burnt it with fire, and ground it to powder, and strewed it upon the water, and made the children of Israel drink of it.

21 And Moses said unto Aaron, What did this people unto thee, that thou hast brought a great sin upon them? 22 And Aaron said, Let not the anger of my lord wax hot: thou knowest the people, that they are *set* on evil. 23 For they said unto me, Make us gods, which shall go before us; for as for this Moses, the man that brought us up out of the land of Egypt, we know not what is become of him. 24 And I said unto them, Whosoever hath any gold, let them break it off: so they gave it me; and I cast it into the fire, and there came out this calf.

25 And when Moses saw that the people were broken loose (for Aaron had let them loose for a derision among their enemies), 26 then Moses stood in the gate of the camp, and said, Whoso is on Jehovah's side, *let him come* unto me. And all the sons of Levi gathered themselves together unto him. 27 And he said unto them, Thus saith Jehovah, the God of Israel, Put ye every man his sword upon his thigh, and go to and fro from gate to gate throughout the camp, and slay every man his brother, and every man his companion, and every man his neighbor. 28 And the sons of Levi did according to the word of Moses: and there fell of the people that day about three thousand men. 29 And Moses said, Consecrate yourselves

to-day to Jehovah, yea, every man against his son, and against his brother; that he may bestow upon you a blessing this day. 30 And it came to pass on the morrow, that Moses said unto the people, Ye have sinned a great sin: and now I will go up unto Jehovah; peradventure I shall make atonement for your sin. 31 And Moses returned unto Jehovah, and said, Oh, this people have sinned a great sin, and have made them gods of gold. 32 Yet now, if thou wilt forgive their sin—; and if not, blot me, I pray thee, out of thy book which thou hast written. 33 And Jehovah said unto Moses, Whosoever hath sinned against me, him will I blot out of my book. 34 And now go, lead the people unto *the place* of which I have spoken unto thee: behold, mine angel shall go before thee; nevertheless in the day when I visit, I will visit their sin upon them. 35 And Jehovah smote the people, because they made the calf, which Aaron made.

28. THE PEOPLE COMMANDED TO PUT OFF THEIR ORNAMENTS. Ex. 33^{3b-6}

3b For I will not go up in the midst of thee; for thou art a stiffnecked people; lest I consume thee in the way. 4 And when the people heard these evil tidings, they mourned: and no man did put on him his ornaments. 5 And Jehovah said unto Moses, Say unto the children of Israel, Ye are a stiffnecked people; if I go up into the midst of thee for one moment, I shall consume thee: therefore now put off thy ornaments from thee, that I may know what to do unto thee. 6 And the children of Israel stripped themselves of their ornaments from mount Horeb onward.

29. THE TENT OF MEETING. E32, 33, 50. P32, 34. Ex. 33^{7-11}

7 Now Moses used to take the tent and to pitch it without the camp, afar off from the camp; and he called it, The tent of meeting. And it came to pass, that every one that sought Jehovah went out unto the tent of meeting, which was without the camp. 8 And it came to pass, when Moses went out unto the Tent, that all the people rose up, and stood, every man at his tent door, and looked after Moses, until he was gone into the Tent. 9 And it came to pass, when Moses entered into the Tent, the pillar of cloud descended, and stood at the door of the Tent: and *Jehovah* spake with Moses. 10 And all the

---

[28] There is an apparent contradiction in this section. v. 4b says that no man put on his ornaments; while 5b plainly presupposes that they did have them on. Dr. calls 3b-4 and 5-6 doublets; CH., Co.?, and Smend assign 3b-4 to J. The redaction in v. 5 is Rje: Di., Dr., CH., Pr., Ho., McN.
Since We. it has been generally believed that E originally described the construction of the tent of meeting after v. 6.
[29] vv. 8-11a, mostly J: Gr., Ki.

170   SOURCES OF THE HEXATEUCH   [Ex. 33¹⁰

people saw the pillar of cloud stand at the door of the Tent: and all the people rose up and worshipped, every man at his tent door. 11 And Jehovah spake unto Moses face to face, as a man speaketh unto his friend. And he turned again into the camp: but his minister Joshua, the son of Nun, a young man, departed not out of the Tent.

30. THE ARK.   P32.
   Nu. 10³³·³⁵⁻³⁶

33 And they set forward from the mount of Jehovah three days' journey; and the ark of the covenant of Jehovah went before them three days' journey, to seek out a resting-place for them.

35 And it came to pass, when the ark set forward, that Moses said, Rise up, O Jehovah, and let thine enemies be scattered; and let them that hate thee flee before thee. 36 And when it rested, he said, Return, O Jehovah, unto the ten thousands of the thousands of Israel.

31. THE FIRE OF JEHOVAH AT TABERAH.
   Nu. 11¹⁻³

1 And the people were as murmurers, *speaking* evil in the ears of Jehovah: and when Jehovah heard it, his anger was kindled; and the fire of Jehovah burnt among them, and devoured in the uttermost part of the camp. 2 And the people cried unto Moses; and Moses prayed unto Jehovah, and the fire abated. 3 And the name of that place was called Taberah, because the fire of Jehovah burnt among them.

32. MOSES'S COMPLAINT: SEVENTY ELDERS APPOINTED. J32.
   E21, 29.
   Nu. 11¹⁴·¹⁶⁻¹⁷·²⁴ᵇ⁻³⁰

14 I am not able to bear all this people alone, because it is too heavy for me.

16 And Jehovah said unto Moses, Gather unto me seventy men of the elders of Israel, whom thou knowest to be the elders of the people, and officers over them; and bring them unto the tent of meeting, that they may stand there with thee. 17 And I will come down and talk with thee there: and I will take of the Spirit which is upon thee, and will put it upon them; and they shall bear the burden of the people with thee, that thou bear it not thyself alone.

24b And he gathered seventy men of the elders of the people, and set them round about the Tent. 25 And Jehovah

---
³⁰ E: We., Ku., Ki., Di., GFM., Ba., Se., Pr., Ho., Co., St. Perh. J or JE: CH., Gr., Dr., Kent, Gray. Gloss in v. 33, We., Ku., Ho., Ki., Gray.
³² v. 25b, tr. as above: Ba., Pr., Kent, Gray. But Gr., Ho., following Sam., Targ., Vulg., emend and tr., "and could not stop."

came down in the cloud, and spake unto him, and took of the Spirit that was upon him, and put it upon the seventy elders: and it came to pass, that, when the Spirit rested upon them, they prophesied, but they did so no more. 26 But there remained two men in the camp, the name of the one was Eldad, and the name of the other Medad: and the Spirit rested upon them; and they were of them that were written, but had not gone out unto the Tent; and they prophesied in the camp. 27 And there ran a young man, and told Moses, and said, Eldad and Medad do prophesy in the camp. 28 And Joshua the son of Nun, the minister of Moses, one of his chosen men, answered and said, My lord Moses, forbid them. 29 And Moses said unto him, Art thou jealous for my sake? would that all Jehovah's people were prophets, that Jehovah would put his Spirit upon them! 30 And Moses gat him into the camp, he and the elders of Israel.

33. THE LEPROSY OF MIRIAM. E29.
Nu. 12$^{1-15}$

12^1 And Miriam and Aaron spake against Moses because of the Cushite woman whom he had married; for he had married a Cushite woman. 2 And they said, Hath Jehovah indeed spoken only with Moses? hath he not spoken also with us? And Jehovah heard it. 3 Now the man Moses was very meek, above all the men that were upon the face of the earth.

4 And Jehovah spake suddenly unto Moses, and unto Aaron, and unto Miriam, Come out ye three unto the tent of meeting. And they three came out. 5 And Jehovah came down in a pillar of cloud, and stood at the door of the Tent, and called Aaron and Miriam; and they both came forth. 6 And he said, Hear now my words: if there be a prophet among you, I Jehovah will make myself known unto him in a vision, I will speak with him in a dream. 7 My servant Moses is not so; he is faithful in all my house: 8 with him will I speak mouth to mouth, even manifestly, and not in dark speeches; and the form of Jehovah shall he behold: wherefore then were ye not afraid to speak against my servant, against Moses?

9 And the anger of Jehovah was kindled against them; and he departed. 10 And the cloud removed from over the Tent; and, behold, Miriam was leprous, as *white as* snow: and Aaron looked upon Miriam, and, behold, she was leprous. 11 And Aaron said unto Moses, Oh, my lord, lay not, I pray thee, sin upon us, for that we have done foolishly, and for that we have sinned. 12 Let her not, I pray, be as one dead, of whom the flesh is half consumed when he cometh out of his mother's

---
[33] In v. 1, Rp.

womb. 13 And Moses cried unto Jehovah, saying, Heal her, O God, I beseech thee. 14 And Jehovah said unto Moses, If her father had but spit in her face, should she not be ashamed seven days? let her be shut up without the camp seven days, and after that she shall be brought in again. 15 And Miriam was shut up without the camp seven days: and the people journeyed not till Miriam was brought in again.

34. THE COMMISSION AND REPORT OF THE SPIES. J38, 40. P55, 57.

Nu. 13$^{17c-18.20.23-24.26b.30-31.32b.33}$

17c And go up into the hill-country: 18 and see the land, what it is; and the people that dwell therein, whether they are strong or weak, whether they are few or many; 20 and what the land is, whether it is fat or lean, whether there is wood therein, or not. And be ye of good courage, and bring of the fruit of the land. Now the time was the time of the first-ripe grapes.

23 And they came unto the valley of Eshcol, and cut down from thence a branch with one cluster of grapes, and they bare it upon a staff between two; *they brought* also of the pomegranates, and of the figs. 24 That place was called the valley of Eshcol, because of the cluster which the children of Israel cut down from thence.

26b . . . to Kadesh; and brought back word unto them, and unto all the congregation, and showed them the fruit of the land.

30 And Caleb stilled the people before Moses, and said, Let us go up at once, and possess it; for we are well able to overcome it. 31 But the men that went up with him said, We are not able to go up against the people; for they are stronger than we, 32b and all the people that we saw in it are men of great stature. 33 And there we saw the Nephilim, the sons of Anak, who come of the Nephilim: and we were in our own sight as grasshoppers, and so we were in their sight.

35. THE FEAR OF THE PEOPLE. J39. E34. P56.

Nu. 14$^{1b.4}$

1b . . . And cried . . . , 4 and they said one to another, Let us make a captain, and let us return into Egypt.

36. JEHOVAH'S REBUKE OF THE PEOPLE. J41. P58.

Nu. 14$^{22-24.25}$

22 Because all those men that have seen my glory, and my signs, which I wrought in Egypt and in the wilderness, yet

---

[34] Some (e. g., Gr., Gray, Smend) find traces of J in 18, and 30-31. v. 26b is edited by Rp: Ba., Pr., Bä., et al. The gloss in v. 33 (either Rd or Rje) aims to identify the Nephilim of E with the sons of Anak of J.—vv. 32b-33, cf. A⁻. 29-10.
[35] v. 1b perh. J or JE: Ba., St., Gray.—v. 4 E: Ku., Ba., GFM., CH., Gr., Kent. JE: Dr., We., Ka., Gray. J: Co., Bä., St.?
[36] E: most critics. But Rje: CH., GFM., Gr. E²: Ku. Smend assigns to E only vv. 24-25b. 25a is a gloss: Ka., Bä., Kent, Gr., apparently contradicting E37, v. 45.

have tempted me these ten times, and have not hearkened to my voice; 23 surely they shall not see the land which I sware unto their fathers, neither shall any of them that despised me see it: 24 but my servant Caleb, because he had another spirit with him, and hath followed me fully, him will I bring into the land whereinto he went; and his seed shall possess it.

25 Now the Amalekite and the Canaanite dwell in the valley: to-morrow turn ye, and get you into the wilderness by the way to the Red Sea.

37. THE PEOPLE DISOBEY JEHOVAH AND ARE DEFEATED BY THE AMALEKITES. E19.

Nu. 14^{39-45}

39 And Moses told these words unto all the children of Israel: and the people mourned greatly. 40 And they rose up early in the morning, and gat them up to the top of the mountain, saying, Lo, we are here, and will go up unto the place which Jehovah hath promised: for we have sinned. 41 And Moses said, Wherefore now do ye transgress the commandment of Jehovah, seeing it shall not prosper? 42 Go not up, for Jehovah is not among you; that ye be not smitten down before your enemies. 43 For there the Amalekite and the Canaanite are before you, and ye shall fall by the sword: because ye are turned back from following Jehovah, therefore Jehovah will not be with you. 44 But they presumed to go up to the top of the mountain: nevertheless the ark of the covenant of Jehovah, and Moses, departed not out of the camp. 45 Then the Amalekite came down, and the Canaanite who dwelt in that mountain, and smote them and beat them down, even unto Hormah.

38. DESTRUCTION OF DATHAN AND ABIRAM. E48. P62.

Nu. $16^{1b-2a.12-15.25-26.27b-31.32a.33-34}$

Introductory Note.—It is agreed that this narrative is to be distinguished from the Korah story of P62 (cf. Dt. 11^6, Ps. 106^{17-18}, where Nu. 16^{32} is referred to, but Korah is not mentioned); and that the Dathan and Abiram story is itself composite JE. The detailed separation has not been made with any success. In general, according to We., Co., Smend, J predominates. The majority (Ku., CH., Di., Ba., Schrader, GFM., et al.) hold that E predominates. In particular, vv. 32a, 33b-34 are E: Co., Pr., CH., Ba.

1b Dathan and Abiram, the sons of Eliab, and On, the son of Peleth, sons of Reuben, took *men*. 2a And they rose up before Moses.

---

[37] Perh. traces of J, "but data seem insufficient for detailed analysis," Gray. J^2, entire: Smend.

12 And Moses sent to call Dathan and Abiram, the sons of Eliab; and they said, We will not come up: 13 is it a small thing that thou hast brought us up out of a land flowing with milk and honey, to kill us in the wilderness, but thou must needs make thyself also a prince over us? 14 Moreover thou hast not brought us into a land flowing with milk and honey, nor given us inheritance of fields and vineyards: wilt thou put out the eyes of these men? we will not come up.

15 And Moses was very wroth, and said unto Jehovah, Respect not thou their offering: I have not taken one ass from them, neither have I hurt one of them. 25 And Moses rose up and went unto Dathan and Abiram; and the elders of Israel followed him. 26 And he spake unto the congregation, saying, Depart, I pray you, from the tents of these wicked men, and touch nothing of theirs, lest ye be consumed in all their sins.

27b And Dathan and Abiram came out, and stood at the door of their tents, and their wives, and their sons, and their little ones.

28 And Moses said, Hereby ye shall know that Jehovah hath sent me to do all these works; for *I have* not *done them* of mine own mind. 29 If these men die the common death of all men, or if they be visited after the visitation of all men; then Jehovah hath not sent me. 30 But if Jehovah make a new thing, and the ground open its mouth, and swallow them up, with all that appertain unto them, and they go down alive into Sheol; then ye shall understand that these men have despised Jehovah. 31 And it came to pass, as he made an end of speaking all these words, that the ground clave asunder that was under them; 32a and the earth opened its mouth, and swallowed them up, and their households. 33 So they, and all that appertained to them, went down alive into Sheol: and the earth closed upon them, and they perished from among the assembly. 34 And all Israel that were round about them fled at the cry of them; for they said, Lest the earth swallow us up.

39. DEATH OF MIRIAM IN KADESH. J37.
Nu. 20¹ᵇ

1b And the people abode in Kadesh; and Miriam died there, and was buried there.

40. EDOM REFUSES PASSAGE TO ISRAEL.
Nu. 20¹⁴⁻²¹

14 And Moses sent messengers from Kadesh unto the king of Edom, Thus saith thy brother Israel, Thou knowest all the

---
⁴⁰ We. alone assigns to J. Some others find traces of J: CH., Pr., Gray, Gr., Ho., Smend. Most assign it to E.

travail that hath befallen us: 15 how our fathers went down into Egypt, and we dwelt in Egypt a long time; and the Egyptians dealt ill with us, and our fathers: 16 and when we cried unto Jehovah, he heard our voice, and sent an angel, and brought us forth out of Egypt: and, behold, we are in Kadesh, a city in the uttermost of thy border. 17 Let us pass, I pray thee, through thy land: we will not pass through field or through vineyard, neither will we drink of the water of the wells; we will go along the king's highway; we will not turn aside to the right hand nor to the left, until we have passed thy border. 18 And Edom said unto him, Thou shalt not pass through me, lest I come out with the sword against thee. 19 And the children of Israel said unto him, We will go up by the highway; and if we drink of thy water, I and my cattle, then will I give the price thereof: let me only, without *doing anything else*, pass through on my feet. 20 And he said, Thou shalt not pass through. And Edom came out against him with much people, and with a strong hand. 21 Thus Edom refused to give Israel passage through his border: wherefore Israel turned away from him.

41. THE SERPENT OF BRASS. E27. 2K. 18^4.
Nu. 21^{4b-9}

4b . . . by the way to the Red Sea, to compass the land of Edom: and the soul of the people was much discouraged because of the way. 5 And the people spake against God, and against Moses, Wherefore have ye brought us up out of Egypt to die in the wilderness? for there is no bread, and there is no water; and our soul loatheth this light bread. 6 And Jehovah sent fiery serpents among the people, and they bit the people; and much people of Israel died. 7 And the people came to Moses, and said, We have sinned, because we have spoken against Jehovah, and against thee; pray unto Jehovah, that he take away the serpents from us. And Moses prayed for the people. 8 And Jehovah said unto Moses, Make thee a fiery serpent, and set it upon a standard: and it shall come to pass, that every one that is bitten, when he seeth it, shall live. 9 And Moses made a serpent of brass, and set it upon the standard: and it came to pass, that if a serpent had bitten any man, when he looked unto the serpent of brass, he lived.

---

[41] Smend finds here evidence of the Judæan origin of E. E is friendly to the serpent of brass in the temple at Jerusalem, asserting its Mosaic and nonidolatrous origin; and at the same time is hostile to the idolatrous "golden calves" of Jeroboam I in Ex. 32. In reply to Smend it may be pointed out that E was a prophet, and that he was not necessarily bound by a narrow, nationalistic outlook.

42. JOURNEY FROM THE ARNON TO PISGAH: ANCIENT SONGS.
Nu. 21$^{12\text{-}20}$

12 From thence they journeyed, and encamped in the valley of Zered. 13 From thence they journeyed, and encamped on the other side of the Arnon, which is in the wilderness, that cometh out of the border of the Amorites: for the Arnon is the border of Moab, between Moab and the Amorites. 14 Wherefore it is said in the book of the Wars of Jehovah,
    Vaheb in Suphah,
    And the valleys of the Arnon,
15 And the slope of the valleys
    That inclineth toward the dwelling of Ar,
    And leaneth upon the border of Moab.
16 And from thence *they journeyed* to Beer: that is the well whereof Jehovah said unto Moses, Gather the people together, and I will give them water.
    17 Then sang Israel this song:
    Spring up, O well; sing ye unto it:
18 The well, which the princes digged,
    Which the nobles of the people delved,
    With the sceptre, *and* with their staves.
And from the wilderness *they journeyed* to Mattanah; 19 and from Mattanah to Nahaliel; and from Nahaliel to Bamoth; 20 and from Bamoth to the valley that is in the field of Moab, to the top of Pisgah, which looketh down upon the desert.

43. SIHON, KING OF HESHBON, DEFEATED: A SONG "OF THEM THAT SPEAK IN PROVERBS." Jg. 11$^{19\text{-}22}$.
Nu. 21$^{21\text{-}32}$

Introductory Note.—The song, vv. 27-30, is generally believed to come from the ninth century, and originally to reflect Omri's victories over Moab. We., Stade, Meyer, Co., Pr., Smend, et al. view it as a later insertion in E. The context is regarded as E chiefly on account of the Amorites. "No one can translate" v. 30 (Ki.).

21 And Israel sent messengers unto Sihon king of the Amorites, saying, 22 Let me pass through thy land: we will not turn aside into field, or into vineyard; we will not drink of the water of the wells: we will go by the king's highway, until we have passed thy border. 23 And Sihon would not suffer Israel to pass through his border; but Sihon gathered all his people together, and went out against Israel into the wilderness, and

---

[42] vv. 16-20 perh. J: Ba., CH., Kent.—The journey here recorded began originally with Kadesh (Smend).
[43] vv. 24b-25 seem not to belong to E (Gray); they may be Rje or perh. J: CH., Ba., GFM.?, Pr., Bä.?, Gr.?, Smend (who leaves only parts of 21, 23, 27-30 in E).

came to Jahaz; and he fought against Israel. 24 And Israel smote him with the edge of the sword, and possessed his land from the Arnon unto the Jabbok, even unto the children of Ammon; for the border of the children of Ammon was strong. 25 And Israel took all these cities: and Israel dwelt in all the cities of the Amorites, in Heshbon, and in all the towns thereof. 26 For Heshbon was the city of Sihon the king of the Amorites, who had fought against the former king of Moab, and taken all his land out of his hand, even unto the Arnon.
27 Wherefore they that speak in proverbs say,
Come ye to Heshbon;
Let the city of Sihon be built and established:
28 For a fire is gone out of Heshbon,
A flame from the city of Sihon:
It hath devoured Ar of Moab,
The lords of the high places of the Arnon.
29 Woe to thee, Moab!
Thou art undone, O people of Chemosh:
He hath given his sons as fugitives,
And his daughters into captivity,
Unto Sihon king of the Amorites.
30 We have shot at them; Heshbon is perished even unto Dibon,
And we have laid waste even unto Nophah,
Which *reacheth* unto Medeba.
31 Thus Israel dwelt in the land of the Amorites. 32 And Moses sent to spy out Jazer; and they took the towns thereof, and drove out the Amorites that were there.

44. (Rd) OG, KING OF BASHAN, DEFEATED. From Dt. 3$^{1-3}$. Nu. 21$^{33-35}$

33 And they turned and went up by the way of Bashan: and Og the king of Bashan went out against them, he and all his people, to battle at Edrei. 34 And Jehovah said unto Moses, Fear him not: for I have delivered him into thy hand, and all his people, and his land; and thou shalt do to him as thou didst unto Sihon king of the Amorites, who dwelt at Heshbon. 35 So they smote him, and his sons and all his people, until there was none left him remaining: and they possessed his land.

45. THE STORY OF BALAAM. J44. Dt. 23$^{4-5}$.
Nu. 22$^{2-4.5*.8-10.12-16.19-21.36.38.40-41}$

2 And Balak the son of Zippor saw all that Israel had done to the Amorites. 3 And Moab was sore afraid of the people, because they were many: and Moab was distressed because of the children of Israel.

---

[44] The tendency to interpolate passages from Dt. in Nu., strong in LXX, here affects MT.
[45] v. 5, Pethor: in Syria, cf. E46, Nu. 23^7, Dt. 23^4 (GFM.). The parallel in J44 locates his home in Ammon (emended text). v. 21 (and . . . ass) J: Di., Ho., Pr., Ba. Smend finds J in vv. 13-16.

4 And Moab said unto the elders of Midian, Now will this multitude lick up all that is round about us, as the ox licketh up the grass of the field. And Balak the son of Zippor was king of Moab at that time.
5 . . . To Pethor, which is by the River . . . 8 And he said unto them, Lodge here this night, and I will bring you word again, as Jehovah shall speak unto me: and the princes of Moab abode with Balaam.
9 And God came unto Balaam, and said, What men are these with thee? 10 And Balaam said unto God, Balak the son of Zippor, king of Moab, hath sent unto me, *saying*, . . .
12 And God said unto Balaam, Thou shalt not go with them; thou shalt not curse the people; for they are blessed.
13 And Balaam rose up in the morning, and said unto the princes of Balak, Get you into your land; for Jehovah refuseth to give me leave to go with you. 14 And the princes of Moab rose up, and they went unto Balak, and said, Balaam refuseth to come with us.
15 And Balak sent yet again princes, more, and more honorable than they. 16 And they came to Balaam, and said to him, Thus saith Balak, the son of Zippor, Let nothing, I pray thee, hinder thee from coming unto me.
19 Now therefore, I pray you, tarry ye also here this night, that I may know what Jehovah will speak unto me more.
20 And God came unto Balaam at night, and said unto him, If the men are come to call thee, rise up, go with them; but only the word which I speak unto thee, that shalt thou do.
21 And Balaam rose up in the morning, and saddled his ass, and went with the princes of Moab.
36 And when Balak heard that Balaam was come, he went out to meet him unto the City of Moab, which is on the border of the Arnon, which is in the utmost part of the border. 38 And Balaam said unto Balak, Lo, I am come unto thee: have I now any power at all to speak anything? the word that God putteth in my mouth, that shall I speak.
40 And Balak sacrificed oxen and sheep, and sent to Balaam, and to the princes that were with him. 41 And it came to pass in the morning, that Balak took Balaam, and brought him up into the high places of Baal; and he saw from thence the utmost part of the people.

46. THE PARABLES OF BALAAM. J45.

Nu. 23$^{1-30}$

1 And Balaam said unto Balak, Build me here seven altars,

---

[46] The section is generally regarded as E. JE: Ho., Pr. vv. 27-30: Rje. Se. interprets the parables eschatologically, cf. vv. 9, 10, 21; Co., however, finds these vv. "specifically theocratic."

and prepare me here seven bullocks and seven rams. 2 And Balak did as Balaam had spoken; and Balak and Balaam offered on every altar a bullock and a ram. 3 And Balaam said unto Balak, Stand by thy burnt-offering, and I will go: peradventure Jehovah will come to meet me; and whatsoever he showeth me I will tell thee. And he went to a bare height. 4 And God met Balaam: and he said unto him, I have prepared the seven altars, and I have offered up a bullock and a ram on every altar. 5 And Jehovah put a word in Balaam's mouth, and said, Return unto Balak, and thus thou shalt speak. 6 And he returned unto him, and, lo, he was standing by his burnt-offering, he, and all the princes of Moab. 7 And he took up his parable, and said,

From Aram hath Balak brought me,
The king of Moab from the mountains of the East:
Come, curse me Jacob,
And come, defy Israel.
8 How shall I curse, whom God hath not cursed?
And how shall I defy, whom Jehovah hath not defied?
9 For from the top of the rocks I see him,
And from the hills I behold him:
Lo, it is a people that dwelleth alone,
And shall not be reckoned among the nations.
10 Who can count the dust of Jacob,
Or number the fourth part of Israel?
Let me die the death of the righteous,
And let my last end be like his!

11 And Balak said unto Balaam, What hast thou done unto me? I took thee to curse mine enemies, and, behold, thou hast blessed them altogether. 12 And he answered and said, Must I not take heed to speak that which Jehovah putteth in my mouth?

13 And Balak said unto him, Come, I pray thee, with me unto another place, from whence thou mayest see them; thou shalt see but the utmost part of them, and shalt not see them all: and curse me them from thence. 14 And he took him into the field of Zophim, to the top of Pisgah, and built seven altars, and offered up a bullock and a ram on every altar. 15 And he said unto Balak, Stand here by thy burnt-offering, while I meet *Jehovah* yonder. 16 And Jehovah met Balaam, and put a word in his mouth, and said, Return unto Balak, and thus shalt thou speak. 17 And he came to him, and, lo, he was standing by his burnt-offering, and the princes of Moab with him. And Balak said unto him, What hath Jehovah spoken? 18 And he took up his parable, and said,

Rise up, Balak, and hear;
Hearken unto me, thou son of Zippor:
19 God is not a man, that he should lie,
Neither the son of man, that he should repent:
Hath he said, and will he not do it?
Or hath he spoken, and will he not make it good?
20 Behold, I have received *commandment* to bless:
And he hath blessed, and I cannot reverse it.
21 He hath not beheld iniquity in Jacob;
Neither hath he seen perverseness in Israel:
Jehovah his God is with him,
And the shout of a king is among them.
22 God bringeth them forth out of Egypt;
He hath as it were the strength of the wild-ox.
23 Surely there is no enchantment with Jacob;
Neither is there any divination with Israel:
Now shall it be said of Jacob and of Israel,
What hath God wrought!
24 Behold, the people riseth up as a lioness,
And as a lion doth he lift himself up:
He shall not lie down until he eat of the prey,
And drink the blood of the slain.

25 And Balak said unto Balaam, Neither curse them at all, nor bless them at all. 26 But Balaam answered and said unto Balak, Told not I thee, saying, All that Jehovah speaketh, that I must do?

27 And Balak said unto Balaam, Come now, I will take thee unto another place; peradventure it will please God that thou mayest curse me them from thence. 28 And Balak took Balaam unto the top of Peor, that looketh down upon the desert. 29 And Balaam said unto Balak, Build me here seven altars, and prepare me here seven bullocks and seven rams. 30 And Balak did as Balaam had said, and offered up a bullock and a ram on every altar.

47. IDOLATRY: BAAL-PEOR. J44. Ho. 9^{10}.

Nu. 25$^{1a.3.5}$.

1a And Israel abode in Shittim. 3 And Israel joined himself unto Baal-peor: and the anger of Jehovah was kindled against Israel. 5 And Moses said unto the judges of Israel, Slay ye every one his men that have joined themselves unto Baal-peor.

48. JOURNEY FROM BEEROTH BENE-JAAKAN TO JOTBATHAH: DEATH OF AARON. E38, 73.

Dt. 10$^{6-7}$.

6 And the children of Israel journeyed from Beeroth Bene-

---

[47] Smend attributes this to J^1 (our J46 is J^2), largely on the ground that E traces the origin of idolatry to earlier times—either at Horeb (Ex. 32) or in Mesopotamia (Josh. 24$^{2.14.15}$).

[48] Originally after Nu. 21^9 E41, Smend.

jaakan to Moserah. There Aaron died, and there he was buried; and Eleazar his son ministered in the priest's office in his stead. 7 From thence they journeyed unto Gudgodah; and from Gudgodah to Jotbathah, a land of brooks of water.

49. The Law of the Altar. E24i.
Dt. 27$^{5\text{-}7a}$

5 And there thou shalt build an altar unto Jehovah thy God, an altar of stones: thou shalt lift up no iron *tool* upon them. 6 Thou shalt build the altar of Jehovah thy God of unhewn stones; and thou shalt offer burnt-offerings thereon unto Jehovah thy God: 7a and thou shalt sacrifice peace-offerings, and shalt eat there.

50. Jehovah Appears to Moses and Joshua in the Tent of Meeting: Joshua's Charge. E29.
Dt. 31$^{14\text{-}15.23}$

14 And Jehovah said unto Moses, Behold, thy days approach that thou must die: call Joshua, and present yourselves in the tent of meeting, that I may give him a charge. And Moses and Joshua went, and presented themselves in the tent of meeting. 15 And Jehovah appeared in the Tent in a pillar of cloud: and the pillar of cloud stood over the door of the Tent. 23 And he gave Joshua the son of Nun a charge, and said, Be strong and of good courage; for thou shalt bring the children of Israel into the land which I sware unto them: and I will be with thee.

51. The Blessing of Moses. J19. P13, 84.
Dt. 33$^{1\text{-}29}$

Introductory Note.—Since Graf critics have been practically unanimous in assigning this blessing to E, and dating it in the reign of Jeroboam II. Ba. alone assigns it to J. Gr. dates it "in the relatively quiet and peaceful epoch which preceded the storm pictured in the song of Deborah" (so also in general, König, Se., Ki.). Di., Dr., Westphal place it in the reign of Jeroboam I. All recognize that Dt. 33 is younger than the blessing of Jacob J19: Gn. 49.

Significant items for the dating are (Eiselen 263ff.): the disappearance of Simeon, Reuben on the decline, Judah separated from his brethren, Levi the priestly tribe, house of Jehovah in land of Benjamin, and Joseph the most prominent among the tribes.

---

[51] vv. 2-5, 26-29 are a later framework for the ancient blessing; it is probably the work of an Rd, and may be postexilic: CH., Marti, St., Co., Gr., Ki.

1 And this is the blessing, wherewith Moses the man of God blessed the children of Israel before his death. 2 And he said,
   Jehovah came from Sinai,
   And rose from Seir unto them;
   He shined forth from mount Paran,
   And he came from the ten thousands of holy ones:
   At his right hand was a fiery law for them.
3 Yea, he loveth the people;
   All his saints are in thy hand:
   And they sat down at thy feet;
   Every one shall receive of thy words.
4 Moses commanded us a law,
   An inheritance for the assembly of Jacob.
5 And he was king in Jeshurun,
   When the heads of the people were gathered,
   All the tribes of Israel together.
6 Let Reuben live, and not die;
   Nor let his men be few.
7 And this is *the blessing* of Judah: and he said,
   Hear, Jehovah, the voice of Judah,
   And bring him in unto his people.
   With his hands he contended for himself;
   And thou shalt be a help against his adversaries.
8 And of Levi he said,
   Thy Thummim and thy Urim are with thy godly one,
   Whom thou didst prove at Massah,
   With whom thou didst strive at the waters of Meribah;
9 Who said of his father, and of his mother, I have not seen him;
   Neither did he acknowledge his brethren,
   Nor knew he his own children:
   For they have observed thy word,
   And keep thy covenant.
10 They shall teach Jacob thine ordinances,
   And Israel thy law:
   They shall put incense before thee,
   And whole burnt-offering upon thine altar.
11 Bless, Jehovah, his substance,
   And accept the work of his hands:
   Smite through the loins of them that rise up against him,
   And of them that hate him, that they rise not again.
12 Of Benjamin he said,
   The beloved of Jehovah shall dwell in safety by him;
   He covereth him all the day long,
   And he dwelleth between his shoulders.
13 And of Joseph he said,

Blessed of Jehovah be his land,
For the precious things of heaven, for the dew,
And for the deep that coucheth beneath,
14 And for the precious things of the fruits of the sun,
And for the precious things of the growth of the moons,
15 And for the chief things of the ancient mountains,
And for the precious things of the everlasting hills,
16 And for the precious things of the earth and the fulness thereof,
And the good will of him that dwelt in the bush.
Let *the blessing* come upon the head of Joseph,
And upon the crown of the head of him that was separate from his brethren.
17 The firstling of his herd, majesty is his;
And his horns are the horns of the wild-ox:
With them he shall push the peoples all of them, *even* the ends of the earth:
And they are the ten thousands of Ephraim,
And they are the thousands of Manasseh.
18 And of Zebulun he said,
Rejoice, Zebulun, in thy going out;
And, Issachar, in thy tents.
19 They shall call the peoples unto the mountain;
There shall they offer sacrifices of righteousness:
For they shall suck the abundance of the seas,
And the hidden treasures of the sand.
20 And of Gad he said,
Blessed be he that enlargeth Gad:
He dwelleth as a lioness,
And teareth the arm, yea, the crown of the head.
21 And he provided the first part for himself,
For there was the lawgiver's portion reserved;
And he came *with* the heads of the people;
He executed the righteousness of Jehovah,
And his ordinances with Israel.
22 And of Dan he said,
Dan is a lion's whelp,
That leapeth forth from Bashan.
23 And of Naphtali he said,
O Naphtali, satisfied with favor,
And full with the blessing of Jehovah,
Possess thou the west and the south.
24 And of Asher he said,
Blessed be Asher with children;
Let him be acceptable unto his brethren,
And let him dip his foot in oil.

25 Thy bars shall be iron and brass:
And as thy days, so shall thy strength be.
26 There is none like unto God, O Jeshurun,
Who rideth upon the heavens for thy help,
And in his excellency on the skies.
27 The eternal God is *thy* dwelling-place,
And underneath are the everlasting arms.
And he thrust out the enemy from before thee,
And said, Destroy.
28 And Israel dwelleth in safety,
The fountain of Jacob alone,
In a land of grain and new wine;
Yea, his heavens drop down dew.
29 Happy art thou, O Israel:
Who is like unto thee, a people saved by Jehovah,
The shield of thy help,
And the sword of thy excellency!
And thine enemies shall submit themselves unto thee;
And thou shalt tread upon their high places.

52. THE DEATH OF MOSES. P84.
Dt. $34^{1b-6.10}$

1b ... to the top of Pisgah, that is over against Jericho. And Jehovah showed him all the land of Gilead, unto Dan, 2 and all Naphtali, and the land of Ephraim and Manasseh, and all the land of Judah, unto the hinder sea, 3 and the South, and the Plain of the valley of Jericho the city of palm-trees, unto Zoar. 4 And Jehovah said unto him, This is the land which I sware unto Abraham, unto Isaac, and unto Jacob, saying, I will give it unto thy seed: I have caused thee to see it with thine eyes, but thou shalt not go over thither.

5 So Moses the servant of Jehovah died there in the land of Moab, according to the word of Jehovah. 6 And he buried him in the valley in the land of Moab over against Beth-peor: but no man knoweth of his sepulchre unto this day.

10 And there hath not arisen a prophet since in Israel like unto Moses, whom Jehovah knew face to face.

53. JE RAHAB THE SPY IN JERICHO. J49, note.
Josh. $2^{1-9a.12-23}$

Introductory Note on Sections 53-73.—These sections include unanalyzed JE material. There is general agreement that J and E are interwoven in many of the narratives (so

---
[52] There is no agreement among authorities with reference to the detailed analysis of Dt. 34. There may be J and Rd in the passage printed above. Many believe that 1b-4 and 5-6 come from different sources.
[53] Mainly J: GFM., Ki , Smend (J² and J¹). Mainly E: Albers, St., Co.

...Josh. 2¹²]   E51–52 JE53   185

Albers, Bennett, Ho., Pr., Gr., CH., Kent, GFM., Smend, et al.), but there is no consensus as to details, except in the separation of the J passages printed in J 48-55.

The unanalyzed JE material is printed with E, because E is the later document, and because We., St., et al. hold that E is the real main source of Josh. (esp. in ch. 8-11: We., Hollenberg, Meyer, Stade).

St. has collated the consensus of scholars with reference to the analysis of Josh., and the present edition owes much to him.

The analysis is rendered very difficult by the fact that Rd has worked over the older sources so thoroughly from his standpoint; and also by the uncertainty of the text. MT and LXX vary widely; often LXX is shorter and evidently aims at omitting superfluous material in MT. Apparently MT has also experienced certain glosses since LXX was translated.

1 And Joshua the son of Nun sent out of Shittim two men as spies secretly, saying, Go, view the land, and Jericho. And they went, and came into the house of a harlot whose name was Rahab, and lay there. 2 And it was told the king of Jericho, saying, Behold, there came men in hither to-night of the children of Israel to search out the land. 3 And the king of Jericho sent unto Rahab, saying, Bring forth the men that are come to thee, that are entered into thy house; for they are come to search out all the land. 4 And the woman took the two men, and hid them; and she said, Yea, the men came unto me, but I knew not whence they were: 5 and it came to pass about the time of the shutting of the gate, when it was dark, that the men went out; whither the men went I know not: pursue after them quickly; for ye will overtake them. 6 But she had brought them up to the roof, and hid them with the stalks of flax, which she had laid in order upon the roof. 7 And the men pursued after them the way to the Jordan unto the fords: and as soon as they that pursued after them were gone out, they shut the gate.

8 And before they were laid down, she came up unto them upon the roof; 9 and she said unto the men, I know that Jehovah hath given you the land, and that the fear of you is fallen upon us, and that all the inhabitants of the land melt away before you. 10 For we have heard how Jehovah dried up the water of the Red Sea before you, when ye came out of Egypt; and what ye did unto the two kings of the Amorites, that were beyond the Jordan, unto Sihon and to Og, whom ye utterly destroyed. 11 And as soon as we had heard it, our hearts did melt, neither did there remain any more spirit in any man, because of you: for Jehovah your God, he is God in heaven above, and on earth beneath. 12 Now therefore, I pray you, swear unto me by

Jehovah, since I have dealt kindly with you, that ye also will deal kindly with my father's house, and give me a true token; 13 and that ye will save alive my father, and my mother, and my brethren, and my sisters, and all that they have, and will deliver our lives from death. 14 And the men said unto her, Our life for yours, if ye utter not this our business; and it shall be, when Jehovah giveth us the land, that we will deal kindly and truly with thee.

15 Then she let them down by a cord through the window: for her house was upon the side of the wall, and she dwelt upon the wall. 16 And she said unto them, Get you to the mountain, lest the pursuers light upon you; and hide yourselves there three days, until the pursuers be returned: and afterward may ye go your way. 17 And the men said unto her, We will be guiltless of this thine oath which thou hast made us to swear. 18 Behold, when we come into the land, thou shalt bind this line of scarlet thread in the window which thou didst let us down by: and thou shalt gather unto thee into the house thy father, and thy mother, and thy brethren, and all thy father's household. 19 And it shall be, that whosoever shall go out of the doors of thy house into the street, his blood shall be upon his head, and we shall be guiltless: and whosoever shall be with thee in the house, his blood shall be on our head, if any hand be upon him. 20 But if thou utter this our business, then we shall be guiltless of thine oath which thou hast made us to swear. 21 And she said, According unto your words, so be it. And she sent them away, and they departed: and she bound the scarlet line in the window.

22 And they went, and came unto the mountain, and abode there three days, until the pursuers were returned: and the pursuers sought them throughout all the way, but found them not. 23 Then the two men returned, and descended from the mountain, and passed over, and came to Joshua the son of Nun; and they told him all that had befallen them.

54. JE The Crossing of the Jordan.   P85.
Josh. $3^{1.5.9-17}$

1 And Joshua rose up early in the morning; and they removed from Shittim, and came to the Jordan, he and all the children of Israel; and they lodged there before they passed over. 5 And Joshua said unto the people, Sanctify yourselves; for to-morrow Jehovah will do wonders among you.

9 And Joshua said unto the children of Israel, Come hither, and hear the words of Jehovah your God. 10 And Joshua said, Hereby ye shall know that the living God is among you, and that he will without fail drive out from before you the Canaan-

ite, and the Hittite, and the Hivite, and the Perizzite, and the Girgashite, and the Amorite, and the Jebusite. 11 Behold, the ark of the covenant of the Lord of all the earth passeth over before you into the Jordan. 12 Now therefore take you twelve men out of the tribes of Israel, for every tribe a man. 13 And it shall come to pass, when the soles of the feet of the priests that bear the ark of Jehovah, the Lord of all the earth, shall rest in the waters of the Jordan, that the waters of the Jordan shall be cut off, even the waters that come down from above; and they shall stand in one heap.

14 And it came to pass, when the people removed from their tents, to pass over the Jordan, the priests that bare the ark of the covenant being before the people; 15 and when they that bare the ark were come unto the Jordan, and the feet of the priests that bare the ark were dipped in the brink of the water (for the Jordan overfloweth all its banks all the time of harvest), 16 that the waters which came down from above stood, and rose up in one heap, a great way off, at Adam, the city that is beside Zarethan; and those that went down toward the sea of the Arabah, even the Salt Sea, were wholly cut off: and the people passed over right against Jericho. 17 And the priests that bare the ark of the covenant of Jehovah stood firm on dry ground in the midst of the Jordan; and all Israel passed over on dry ground, until all the nation were passed clean over the Jordan.

55. JE TWELVE STONES FROM THE JORDAN SET UP IN GILGAL. E25.

Josh. $4^{1.3.4-11.18.20}$

1 And it came to pass, when all the nation were clean passed over the Jordan, that Jehovah spake unto Joshua, saying, 3 And command ye them, saying, Take you hence out of the midst of the Jordan, out of the place where the priests' feet stood firm, twelve stones, and carry them over with you, and lay them down in the lodging-place, where ye shall lodge this night. 4 Then Joshua called the twelve men, whom he had prepared of the children of Israel, out of every tribe a man: 5 and Joshua said unto them, Pass over before the ark of Jehovah your God into the midst of the Jordan, and take you up every man of you a stone upon his shoulder, according unto the number of the tribes of the children of Israel; 6 that this may be a sign among you, that, when your children ask in time to come, saying, What mean ye by these stones? 7 then ye shall say unto them, Because the waters of the Jordan were cut off before the ark of the covenant of Jehovah; when it passed over

---

[55] Mainly E: GFM. But there is very wide difference in detail.

the Jordan, the waters of the Jordan were cut off: and these stones shall be for a memorial unto the children of Israel for ever.

8 And the children of Israel did so as Joshua commanded, and took up twelve stones out of the midst of the Jordan, as Jehovah spake unto Joshua, according to the number of the tribes of the children of Israel; and they carried them over with them unto the place where they lodged, and laid them down there. 9 And Joshua set up twelve stones in the midst of the Jordan, in the place where the feet of the priests that bare the ark of the covenant stood: and they are there unto this day. 10 For the priests that bare the ark stood in the midst of the Jordan, until everything was finished that Jehovah commanded Joshua to speak unto the people, according to all that Moses commanded Joshua: and the people hasted and passed over. 11 And it came to pass, when all the people were clean passed over, that the ark of Jehovah passed over, and the priests, in the presence of the people.

18 And it came to pass, when the priests that bare the ark of the covenant of Jehovah were come up out of the midst of the Jordan, and the soles of the priests' feet were lifted up unto the dry ground, that the waters of the Jordan returned unto their place, and went over all its banks, as aforetime.

20 And those twelve stones, which they took out of the Jordan, did Joshua set up in Gilgal.

56. E Israelites Circumcised at Gilgal. J25.
Josh. $5^{2.3.8-9}$

2 At that time Jehovah said unto Joshua, Make thee knives of flint, and circumcise again the children of Israel the second time. 3 And Joshua made him knives of flint, and circumcised the children of Israel at the hill of the foreskins. 8 And it came to pass, when they had done circumcising all the nation, that they abode in their places in the camp, till they were whole. 9 And Jehovah said unto Joshua, This day have I rolled away the reproach of Egypt from off you. Wherefore the name of that place was called Gilgal, unto this day.

57. JE Capture of Jericho.
Josh. $6^{1.3-26}$

1 Now Jericho was straitly shut up because of the children of Israel: none went out, and none came in.

3 And ye shall compass the city, all the men of war, going about the city once. Thus shalt thou do six days. 4 And seven priests shall bear seven trumpets of rams' horns before

---

[56] E: Hollenberg, Di., Ho., St., Pr., Kent, GFM., Ki. JE: Dr., Ad. J: Ku., Co., Bennett, Gr., CH., Smend (cf. E3xiv).

...6¹⁹]   E55–57 (55,57 JE)   189

the ark: and the seventh day ye shall compass the city seven times, and the priests shall blow the trumpets. 5 And it shall be, that, when they make a long blast with the ram's horn, and when ye hear the sound of the trumpet, all the people shall shout with a great shout; and the wall of the city shall fall down flat, and the people shall go up every man straight before him. 6 And Joshua the son of Nun called the priests, and said unto them, Take up the ark of the covenant, and let seven priests bear seven trumpets of rams' horns before the ark of Jehovah. 7 And they said unto the people, Pass on, and compass the city, and let the armed men pass on before the ark of Jehovah.

8 And it was so, that, when Joshua had spoken unto the people, the seven priests bearing the seven trumpets of rams' horns before Jehovah passed on, and blew the trumpets: and the ark of the covenant of Jehovah followed them. 9 And the armed men went before the priests that blew the trumpets, and the rearward went after the ark, *the priests* blowing the trumpets as they went. 10 And Joshua commanded the people, saying, Ye shall not shout, nor let your voice be heard, neither shall any word proceed out of your mouth, until the day I bid you shout; then shall ye shout. 11 So he caused the ark of Jehovah to compass the city, going about it once: and they came into the camp, and lodged in the camp.

12 And Joshua rose early in the morning, and the priests took up the ark of Jehovah. 13 And the seven priests bearing the seven trumpets of rams' horns before the ark of Jehovah went on continually, and blew the trumpets: and the armed men went before them; and the rearward came after the ark of Jehovah, *the priests* blowing the trumpets as they went. 14 And the second day they compassed the city once, and returned into the camp: so they did six days.

15 And it came to pass on the seventh day, that they rose early at the dawning of the day, and compassed the city after the same manner seven times: only on that day they compassed the city seven times. 16 And it came to pass at the seventh time, when the priests blew the trumpets, Joshua said unto the people, Shout; for Jehovah hath given you the city. 17 And the city shall be devoted, even it and all that is therein, to Jehovah: only Rahab the harlot shall live, she and all that are with her in the house, because she hid the messengers that we sent. 18 But as for you, only keep yourselves from the devoted thing, lest when ye have devoted it, ye take of the devoted thing; so would ye make the camp of Israel accursed, and trouble it. 19 But all the silver, and gold, and vessels of brass and iron, are holy unto Jehovah: they shall come into

the treasury of Jehovah. 20 So the people shouted, and *the priests* blew the trumpets: and it came to pass, when the people heard the sound of the trumpet, that the people shouted with a great shout, and the wall fell down flat, so that the people went up into the city, every man straight before him, and they took the city. 21 And they utterly destroyed all that was in the city, both man and woman, both young and old, and ox, and sheep, and ass, with the edge of the sword.

22 And Joshua said unto the two men that had spied out the land, Go into the harlot's house, and bring out thence the woman, and all that she hath, as ye sware unto her. 23 And the young men the spies went in, and brought out Rahab, and her father, and her mother, and her brethren, and all that she had; all her kindred also they brought out; and they set them without the camp of Israel. 24 And they burnt the city with fire, and all that was therein; only the silver, and the gold, and the vessels of brass and of iron, they put into the treasury of the house of Jehovah. 25 But Rahab the harlot, and her father's household, and all that she had, did Joshua save alive; and she dwelt in the midst of Israel unto this day, because she hid the messengers, whom Joshua sent to spy out Jericho. 26 And Joshua charged them with an oath at that time, saying, Cursed be the man before Jehovah, that riseth up and buildeth this city Jericho: with the loss of his first-born shall he lay the foundation thereof, and with the loss of his youngest son shall he set up the gates of it.

58. JE Israel Defeated at Ai.
Josh. 7$^{2\text{-}5}$

2 And Joshua sent men from Jericho to Ai, which is beside Beth-aven, on the east side of Beth-el, and spake unto them, saying, Go up and spy out the land. And the men went up and spied out Ai. 3 And they returned to Joshua, and said unto him, Let not all the people go up; but let about two or three thousand men go up and smite Ai; make not all the people to toil thither; for they are but few. 4 So there went up thither of the people about three thousand men: and they fled before the men of Ai. 5 And the men of Ai smote of them about thirty and six men; and they chased them *from* before the gate even unto Shebarim, and smote them at the descent: and the hearts of the people melted, and became as water.

59. JE Achan's Violation of the Ban Punished. P87.
Josh. 7$^{1.6\text{-}26}$

1 But the children of Israel committed a trespass in the devoted thing;

---
[19] v. 1: Rp.

for Achan, the son of Carmi, the son of Zabdi, the son of Zerah, of the tribe of Judah, took of the devoted thing: and the anger of Jehovah was kindled against the children of Israel.

6 And Joshua rent his clothes, and fell to the earth upon his face before the ark of Jehovah until the evening, he and the elders of Israel; and they put dust upon their heads. 7 And Joshua said, Alas, O Lord Jehovah, wherefore hast thou at all brought this people over the Jordan, to deliver us into the hand of the Amorites, to cause us to perish? would that we had been content and dwelt beyond the Jordan! 8 Oh, Lord, what shall I say, after that Israel hath turned their backs before their enemies! 9 For the Canaanites and all the inhabitants of the land will hear of it, and will compass us round, and cut off our name from the earth: and what wilt thou do for thy great name?

10 And Jehovah said unto Joshua, Get thee up; wherefore art thou thus fallen upon thy face? 11 Israel hath sinned; yea, they have even transgressed my covenant which I commanded them: yea, they have even taken of the devoted thing, and have also stolen, and dissembled also; and they have even put it among their own stuff. 12 Therefore the children of Israel cannot stand before their enemies; they turn their backs before their enemies, because they are become accursed: I will not be with you any more, except ye destroy the devoted thing from among you. 13 Up, sanctify the people, and say, Sanctify yourselves against to-morrow: for thus saith Jehovah, the God of Israel, There is a devoted thing in the midst of thee, O Israel; thou canst not stand before thine enemies, until ye take away the devoted thing from among you. 14 In the morning therefore ye shall be brought near by your tribes: and it shall be, that the tribe which Jehovah taketh shall come near by families; and the family which Jehovah shall take shall come near by households; and the household which Jehovah shall take shall come near man by man. 15 And it shall be, that he that is taken with the devoted thing shall be burnt with fire, he and all that he hath; because he hath transgressed the covenant of Jehovah, and because he hath wrought folly in Israel.

16 So Joshua rose up early in the morning, and brought Israel near by their tribes; and the tribe of Judah was taken: 17 and he brought near the family of Judah; and he took the family of the Zerahites: and he brought near the family of the Zerahites man by man; and Zabdi was taken: 18 and he brought near his household man by man; and Achan the son of Carmi, the son of Zabdi, the son of Zerah, of the tribe of Judah, was taken. 19 And Joshua said unto Achan, My son,

give, I pray thee, glory to Jehovah, the God of Israel, and make confession unto him; and tell me now what thou hast done; hide it not from me. 20 And Achan answered Joshua, and said, Of a truth I have sinned against Jehovah, the God of Israel, and thus and thus have I done: 21 when I saw among the spoil a goodly Babylonish mantle, and two hundred shekels of silver, and a wedge of gold of fifty shekels weight, then I coveted them, and took them; and, behold, they are hid in the earth in the midst of my tent, and the silver under it.

22 So Joshua sent messengers, and they ran unto the tent; and, behold, it was hid in his tent, and the silver under it. 23 And they took them from the midst of the tent, and brought them unto Joshua, and unto all the children of Israel; and they laid them down before Jehovah. 24 And Joshua, and all Israel with him, took Achan the son of Zerah, and the silver, and the mantle, and the wedge of gold, and his sons, and his daughters, and his oxen, and his asses, and his sheep, and his tent, and all that he had: and they brought them up unto the valley of Achor. 25 And Joshua said, Why hast thou troubled us? Jehovah shall trouble thee this day. And all Israel stoned him with stones; and they burned them with fire, and stoned them with stones. 26 And they raised over him a great heap of stones, unto this day; and Jehovah turned from the fierceness of his anger. Wherefore the name of that place was called, The valley of Achor, unto this day.

60. JE THE CAPTURE OF AI.
Josh. 8$^{1-29}$

1 And Jehovah said unto Joshua, Fear not, neither be thou dismayed: take all the people of war with thee, and arise, go up to Ai; see, I have given into thy hand the king of Ai, and his people, and his city, and his land; 2 and thou shalt do to Ai and her king as thou didst unto Jericho and her king: only the spoil thereof, and the cattle thereof, shall ye take for a prey unto yourselves: set thee an ambush for the city behind it.

3 So Joshua arose, and all the people of war, to go up to Ai: and Joshua chose out thirty thousand men, the mighty men of valor, and sent them forth by night. 4 And he commanded them, saying, Behold, ye shall lie in ambush against the city, behind the city; go not very far from the city, but be ye all ready: 5 and I, and all the people that are with me, will approach unto the city. And it shall come to pass, when they come out against us, as at the first, that we will flee before them; 6 and they will come out after us, till we have drawn them away from the city; for they will say, They flee before us, as at the first: so we will flee before them; 7 and ye shall

rise up from the ambush, and take possession of the city: for Jehovah your God will deliver it into your hand. 8 And it shall be, when ye have seized upon the city, that ye shall set the city on fire; according to the word of Jehovah shall ye do: see, I have commanded you. 9 And Joshua sent them forth; and they went to the ambushment, and abode between Beth-el and Ai, on the west side of Ai: but Joshua lodged that night among the people.

10 And Joshua arose up early in the morning, and mustered the people, and went up, he and the elders of Israel, before the people to Ai. 11 And all the people, *even* the *men of* war that were with him, went up, and drew nigh, and came before the city, and encamped on the north side of Ai: now there was a valley between him and Ai. 12 And he took about five thousand men, and set them in ambush between Beth-el and Ai, on the west side of the city. 13 So they set the people, even all the host that was on the north of the city, and their liers-in-wait that were on the west of the city; and Joshua went that night into the midst of the valley. 14 And it came to pass, when the king of Ai saw it, that they hasted and rose up early, and the men of the city went out against Israel to battle, he and all his people, at the time appointed, before the Arabah; but he knew not that there was an ambush against him behind the city. 15 And Joshua and all Israel made as if they were beaten before them, and fled by the way of the wilderness. 16 And all the people that were in the city were called together to pursue after them: and they pursued after Joshua, and were drawn away from the city. 17 And there was not a man left in Ai or Beth-el, that went not out after Israel: and they left the city open, and pursued after Israel.

18 And Jehovah said unto Joshua, Stretch out the javelin that is in thy hand toward Ai; for I will give it into thy hand. And Joshua stretched out the javelin that was in his hand toward the city. 19 And the ambush arose quickly out of their place, and they ran as soon as he had stretched out his hand, and entered into the city, and took it; and they hasted and set the city on fire. 20 And when the men of Ai looked behind them, they saw, and, behold, the smoke of the city ascended up to heaven, and they had no power to flee this way or that way: and the people that fled to the wilderness turned back upon the pursuers. 21 And when Joshua and all Israel saw that the ambush had taken the city, and that the smoke of the city ascended, then they turned again, and slew the men of Ai. 22 And the others came forth out of the city against them; so they were in the midst of Israel, some on this side, and some on that side: and they smote them, so that

they let none of them remain or escape. 23 And the king of Ai they took alive, and brought him to Joshua.
24 And it came to pass, when Israel had made an end of slaying all the inhabitants of Ai in the field, in the wilderness wherein they pursued them, and they were all fallen by the edge of the sword, until they were consumed, that all Israel returned unto Ai, and smote it with the edge of the sword. 25 And all that fell that day, both of men and women, were twelve thousand, even all the men of Ai. 26 For Joshua drew not back his hand, wherewith he stretched out the javelin, until he had utterly destroyed all the inhabitants of Ai. 27 Only the cattle and the spoil of that city Israel took for a prey unto themselves, according unto the word of Jehovah which he commanded Joshua. 28 So Joshua burnt Ai, and made it a heap for ever, even a desolation, unto this day. 29 And the king of Ai he hanged on a tree until the eventide: and at the going down of the sun Joshua commanded, and they took his body down from the tree, and cast it at the entrance of the gate of the city, and raised thereon a great heap of stones, unto this day.

61. JE Treaty with the Gibeonites. J49. P87.
Josh. $9^{3-5.8-9a.11-13.15a.16.22-23.26-27a}$.

3 But when the inhabitants of Gibeon heard what Joshua had done unto Jericho and to Ai, 4 they also did work wilily, and went and made as if they had been ambassadors, and took old sacks upon their asses, and wine-skins, old and rent and bound up, 5 and old and patched shoes upon their feet, and old garments upon them; and all the bread of their provision was dry and was become mouldy.

8 And they said unto Joshua, We are thy servants.
And Joshua said unto them, Who are ye? and from whence come ye?

9a And they said unto him, From a very far country thy servants are come because of the name of Jehovah thy God. 11 And our elders and all the inhabitants of our country spake to us, saying, Take provision in your hand for the journey, and go to meet them, and say unto them, We are your servants: and now make ye a covenant with us. 12 This our bread we took hot for our provision out of our houses on the day we came forth to go unto you; but now, behold, it is dry, and is become mouldy: 13 and these wine-skins, which we filled, were new; and, behold, they are rent: and these our garments and our shoes are become old by reason of the very long journey.

15a And Joshua made peace with them. 16 And it came to

---

[61] GFM. (1901) said that there was general agreement that this passage is J; while St. (1912) declared that it is generally assigned to E! Smend (1912) makes it mainly J^2.

pass at the end of three days after they had made a covenant with them, that they heard that they were their neighbors, and that they dwelt among them. 22 And Joshua called for them, and he spake unto them, saying, Wherefore have ye beguiled us, saying, We are very far from you; when ye dwell among us? 23 Now therefore ye are cursed, and there shall never fail to be of you bondmen both hewers of wood and drawers of water for the house of my God. 26 And so did he unto them, and delivered them out of the hand of the children of Israel that they slew them not. 27a And Joshua made them that day hewers of wood and drawers of water for the congregation, and for the altar of Jehovah, unto this day.

62. JE JOSHUA DEFEATS THE KINGS OF SOUTH CANAAN ALLIED WITH ADONI-ZEDEK OF JERUSALEM. J52, 56.
Josh. 10$^{1-7.9-14a.15-24.26-27}$

1 Now it came to pass, when Adoni-zedek king of Jerusalem heard how Joshua had taken Ai, and had utterly destroyed it (as he had done to Jericho and her king, so he had done to Ai and her king), and how the inhabitants of Gibeon had made peace with Israel, and were among them; 2 that they feared greatly, because Gibeon was a great city, as one of the royal cities, and because it was greater than Ai, and all the men thereof were mighty. 3 Wherefore Adoni-zedek king of Jerusalem sent unto Hoham king of Hebron, and unto Piram king of Jarmuth, and unto Japhia king of Lachish, and unto Debir king of Eglon, saying, 4 Come up unto me, and help me, and let us smite Gibeon; for it hath made peace with Joshua and with the children of Israel. 5 Therefore the five kings of the Amorites, the king of Jerusalem, the king of Hebron, the king of Jarmuth, the king of Lachish, the king of Eglon, gathered themselves together, and went up, they and all their hosts, and encamped against Gibeon, and made war against it.

6 And the men of Gibeon sent unto Joshua to the camp to Gilgal, saying, Slack not thy hand from thy servants; come up to us quickly, and save us, and help us: for all the kings of the Amorites that dwell in the hill-country are gathered together against us. 7 So Joshua went up from Gilgal, he, and all the people of war with him, and all the mighty men of valor. 9 Joshua therefore came upon them suddenly; *for* he went up from Gilgal all the night. 10 And Jehovah discomfited them before Israel, and he slew them with a great slaughter at Gibeon, and chased them by the way of the ascent of Beth-horon, and smote them to Azekah, and unto Makkedah. 11 And it came to pass, as they fled from before Israel, while they were

[62] vv. 16-27 are regarded as late by We., Smend.

at the descent of Beth-horon, that Jehovah cast down great stones from heaven upon them unto Azekah, and they died: they were more who died with the hailstones than they whom the children of Israel slew with the sword.

12 Then spake Joshua to Jehovah in the day when Jehovah delivered up the Amorites before the children of Israel; and he said in the sight of Israel,
    Sun, stand thou still upon Gibeon;
    And thou, Moon, in the valley of Aijalon.
13 And the sun stood still, and the moon stayed,
    Until the nation had avenged themselves of their enemies.
Is not this written in the book of Jashar? And the sun stayed in the midst of heaven, and hasted not to go down about a whole day. 14a And there was no day like that before it or after it, that Jehovah hearkened unto the voice of a man . . .

15 And Joshua returned, and all Israel with him, unto the camp to Gilgal.

16 And these five kings fled, and hid themselves in the cave at Makkedah. 17 And it was told Joshua, saying, The five kings are found, hidden in the cave at Makkedah. 18 And Joshua said, Roll great stones unto the mouth of the cave, and set men by it to keep them: 19 but stay not ye; pursue after your enemies, and smite the hindmost of them; suffer them not to enter into their cities: for Jehovah your God hath delivered them into your hand. 20 And it came to pass, when Joshua and the children of Israel had made an end of slaying them with a very great slaughter, till they were consumed, and the remnant which remained of them had entered into the fortified cities, 21 that all the people returned to the camp to Joshua at Makkedah in peace: none moved his tongue against any of the children of Israel.

22 Then said Joshua, Open the mouth of the cave, and bring forth those five kings unto me out of the cave. 23 And they did so, and brought forth those five kings unto him out of the cave, the king of Jerusalem, the king of Hebron, the king of Jarmuth, the king of Lachish, the king of Eglon. 24 And it came to pass, when they brought forth those kings unto Joshua, that Joshua called for all the men of Israel, and said unto the chiefs of the men of war that went with him, Come near, put your feet upon the necks of these kings. And they came near, and put their feet upon the necks of them. 25 And Joshua said unto them, Fear not, nor be dismayed; be strong and of good courage: for thus shall Jehovah do to all your enemies against whom ye fight. 26 And afterward Joshua smote them, and put them to death, and hanged them on five trees: and they were hanging upon the trees until the evening. 27 And it came to pass at the time

of the going down of the sun, that Joshua commanded, and they took them down off the trees, and cast them into the cave wherein they had hidden themselves, and laid great stones on the mouth of the cave, unto this very day.

63. JE Joshua Defeats the Kings of North Canaan Allied with Jabin of Hazor. Jg. 4, 5.
Josh. 11[1-2,4-9]

1 And it came to pass, when Jabin king of Hazor heard thereof, that he sent to Jobab king of Madon, and to the king of Shimron, and to the king of Achshaph, 2 and to the kings that were on the north, in the hill-country, and in the Arabah south of Chinneroth, and in the lowland, and in the heights of Dor on the west.

4 And they went out, they and all their hosts with them, much people, even as the sand that is upon the seashore in multitude, with horses and chariots very many. 5 And all these kings met together; and they came and encamped together at the waters of Merom, to fight with Israel.

6 And Jehovah said unto Joshua, Be not afraid because of them; for to-morrow at this time will I deliver them up all slain before Israel: thou shalt hock their horses, and burn their chariots with fire. 7 So Joshua came, and all the people of war with him, against them by the waters of Merom suddenly, and fell upon them. 8 And Jehovah delivered them into the hand of Israel, and they smote them, and chased them unto great Sidon, and unto Misrephoth-maim, and unto the valley of Mizpeh eastward; and they smote them, until they left them none remaining. 9 And Joshua did unto them as Jehovah bade him: he hocked their horses, and burnt their chariots with fire.

64. JE The Division of the Land. J54, 55. P71.
Josh. 13[1,7]

1 Now Joshua was old and well stricken in years; and Jehovah said unto him, Thou art old and well stricken in years, and there remaineth yet very much land to be possessed. 7 Now therefore divide this land for an inheritance unto the nine tribes, and the half-tribe of Manasseh.

65. E Hebron, the Lot of Caleb. J51, 57, 60.
Josh. 14[6-15]*

6 Then the children of Judah drew nigh unto Joshua in Gilgal: and Caleb the son of Jephunneh the Kenizzite said unto him, Thou knowest the thing that Jehovah spake unto Moses

---
[63] Chiefly E: Smend.
[65] E: Di., Dr., Ho., CH., Se., Pr., GFM., St., Smend (with some J²). This is one of the very few passages unanimously assigned to E in Josh.

the man of God concerning me and concerning thee in Kadesh-barnea. 7 Forty years old was I when Moses the servant of Jehovah sent me from Kadesh-barnea to spy out the land; and I brought him word again as it was in my heart. 8 Nevertheless my brethren that went up with me made the heart of the people melt; but I wholly followed Jehovah my God. 9 And Moses sware on that day, saying, Surely the land whereon thy foot hath trodden shall be an inheritance to thee and to thy children for ever, because thou hast wholly followed Jehovah my God. 10 And now, behold, Jehovah hath kept me alive, as he spake, these forty and five years, from the time that Jehovah spake this word unto Moses, while Israel walked in the wilderness: and now, lo, I am this day fourscore and five years old. 11 As yet I am as strong this day as I was in the day that Moses sent me: as my strength was then, even so is my strength now, for war, and to go out and to come in. 12 Now therefore give me this hill-country, whereof Jehovah spake in that day; for thou heardest in that day how the Anakim were there, and cities great and fortified: it may be that Jehovah will be with me, and I shall drive them out, as Jehovah spake.

13 And Joshua blessed him; and he gave Hebron unto Caleb the son of Jephunneh for an inheritance. 14 Therefore Hebron became the inheritance of Caleb the son of Jephunneh the Kenizzite unto this day; because that he wholly followed Jehovah, the God of Israel. 15* Now the name of Hebron beforetime was Kiriath-arba; *which Arba was* the greatest man among the Anakim.

66. JE THE LOT OF JOSEPH.   J61.   P91.
Josh. 16$^{1-3.9}$

1 And the lot came out for the children of Joseph from the Jordan at Jericho, at the waters of Jericho on the east, even the wilderness, going up from Jericho through the hill-country to Beth-el; 2 and it went out from Beth-el to Luz, and passed along unto the border of the Archites to Ataroth; 3 and it went down westward to the border of the Japhletites, unto the border of Beth-horon the nether, even unto Gezer; and the goings out thereof were at the sea; 9 together with the cities which were set apart for the children of Ephraim in the midst of the inheritance of the children of Manasseh, all the cities with their villages.

67. JE THE LOT OF MANASSEH.   J54.
Josh. 17$^{1b-2.8.10b}$

1b As for Machir the first-born of Manasseh, the father of

Gilead, because he was a man of war, therefore he had Gilead and Bashan. 2 So *the lot* was for the rest of the children of Manasseh according to their families: for the children of Abiezer, and for the children of Helek, and for the children of Asriel, and for the children of Shechem, and for the children of Hepher, and for the children of Shemida: these were the male children of Manasseh the son of Joseph according to their families.
8 The land of Tappuah belonged to Manasseh; but Tappuah on the border of Manasseh belonged to the children of Ephraim. 10b And they reached to Asher on the north and to Issachar on the east.

68. E THE LOTS OF SEVEN TRIBES.
Josh. 18[2-6.8-10]

2 And there remained among the children of Israel seven tribes, which had not yet divided their inheritance. 3 And Joshua said unto the children of Israel, How long are ye slack to go in to possess the land, which Jehovah, the God of your fathers, hath given you? 4 Appoint for you three men of each tribe: and I will send them, and they shall arise, and walk through the land, and describe it according to their inheritance; and they shall come unto me. 5 And they shall divide it into seven portions: Judah shall abide in his border on the south, and the house of Joseph shall abide in their border on the north. 6 And ye shall describe the land into seven portions, and bring *the description* hither to me; and I will cast lots for you here before Jehovah our God.
8 And the men arose, and went: and Joshua charged them that went to describe the land, saying, Go and walk through the land, and describe it, and come again to me; and I will cast lots for you here before Jehovah in Shiloh. 9 And the men went and passed through the land, and described it by cities into seven portions in a book; and they came to Joshua unto the camp at Shiloh. 10 And Joshua cast lots for them in Shiloh before Jehovah: and there Joshua divided the land unto the children of Israel according to their divisions.

69. E TIMNATH-SERAH OF EPHRAIM THE INHERITANCE OF JOSHUA.
Josh. 19[49-50]

49 So they made an end of distributing the land for inheritance by the borders thereof; and the children of Israel gave an inheritance to Joshua the son of Nun in the midst of

---
[68] Substantially E: Di., Ki., CH., GFM., Pr. J[2]: Kent. D[2]: St. Others: JE.
[69] E: GFM., Co., Kent, Pr. JE: Dr.?, Ka., Ad. D[2]: St. P: CH.

them: 50 according to the commandment of Jehovah they gave him the city which he asked, even Timnath-serah in the hill-country of Ephraim; and he built the city, and dwelt therein.

70. E JOSHUA'S FAREWELL ADDRESS. Josh. 24²⁸; cf. Jg. 2⁶ Rd. Josh. 24¹⁻²⁸

1 And Joshua gathered all the tribes of Israel to Shechem, and called for the elders of Israel, and for their heads, and for their judges, and for their officers; and they presented themselves before God. 2 And Joshua said unto all the people, Thus saith Jehovah, the God of Israel, Your fathers dwelt of old time beyond the River, even Terah, the father of Abraham, and the father of Nahor: and they served other gods. 3 And I took your father Abraham from beyond the River, and led him throughout all the land of Canaan, and multiplied his seed, and gave him Isaac. 4 And I gave unto Isaac Jacob and Esau: and I gave unto Esau mount Seir, to possess it; and Jacob and his children went down into Egypt. 5 And I sent Moses and Aaron, and I plagued Egypt, according to that which I did in the midst thereof: and afterward I brought you out. 6 And I brought your fathers out of Egypt: and ye came unto the sea; and the Egyptians pursued after your fathers with chariots and with horsemen unto the Red Sea. 7 And when they cried out unto Jehovah, he put darkness between you and the Egyptians, and brought the sea upon them, and covered them: and your eyes saw what I did in Egypt: and ye dwelt in the wilderness many days. 8 And I brought you into the land of the Amorites, that dwelt beyond the Jordan: and they fought with you; and I gave them into your hand, and ye possessed their land; and I destroyed them from before you. 9 Then Balak the son of Zippor, king of Moab, arose and fought against Israel: and he sent and called Balaam the son of Beor to curse you; 10 but I would not hearken unto Balaam; therefore he blessed you still: so I delivered you out of his hand. 11 And ye went over the Jordan, and came unto Jericho: and the men of Jericho fought against you, the Amorite, and the Perizzite, and the Canaanite, and the Hittite, and the Girgashite, and the Hivite, and the Jebusite; and I delivered them into your hand. 12 And I sent the hornet before you,

---

[70] Scholars are unanimous in assigning Josh. 24 to E, except that Smend finds a few traces of J.—The original scene of the giving of the laws of CC may have been just before or after v. 25 (cf. E24, Introductory Note).

Joshua's address is held by many to presuppose the fall of Samaria 721 (v. 20) as E27, q. v. This would mean that the chapter belongs to E².

We. points out that the characteristic peculiarities of E are abundant: the name "Amorites" for the early inhabitants of Palestine; Shechem as a holy place of assembly; Joshua as a second Moses; strong consciousness of the uniqueness of Israelitic religion (concept of heathendom); massebah in Shechem treated as a memorial sign.

which drove them out from before you, even the two kings of the Amorites; not with thy sword, nor with thy bow. 13 And I gave you a land whereon thou hadst not labored, and cities which ye built not, and ye dwell therein; of vineyards and oliveyards which ye planted not do ye eat.

14 Now therefore fear Jehovah, and serve him in sincerity and in truth; and put away the gods which your fathers served beyond the River, and in Egypt; and serve ye Jehovah. 15 And if it seem evil unto you to serve Jehovah, choose you this day whom ye will serve; whether the gods which your fathers served that were beyond the River, or the gods of the Amorites, in whose land ye dwell: but as for me and my house, we will serve Jehovah.

16 And the people answered and said, Far be it from us that we should forsake Jehovah, to serve other gods; 17 for Jehovah our God, he it is that brought us and our fathers up out of the land of Egypt, from the house of bondage, and that did those great signs in our sight, and preserved us in all the way wherein we went, and among all the peoples through the midst of whom we passed; 18 and Jehovah drove out from before us all the peoples, even the Amorites that dwelt in the land: therefore we also will serve Jehovah; for he is our God.

19 And Joshua said unto the people, Ye cannot serve Jehovah; for he is a holy God; he is a jealous God; he will not forgive your transgression nor your sins. 20 If ye forsake Jehovah, and serve foreign gods, then he will turn and do you evil, and consume you, after that he hath done you good. 21 And the people said unto Joshua, Nay; but we will serve Jehovah. 22 And Joshua said unto the people, Ye are witnesses against yourselves that ye have chosen you Jehovah, to serve him. And they said, We are witnesses. 23 Now therefore put away, *said he*, the foreign gods which are among you, and incline your heart unto Jehovah, the God of Israel. 24 And the people said unto Joshua, Jehovah our God will we serve, and unto his voice will we hearken. 25 So Joshua made a covenant with the people that day, and set them a statute and an ordinance in Shechem. 26 And Joshua wrote these words in the book of the law of God; and he took a great stone, and set it up there under the oak that was by the sanctuary of Jehovah. 27 And Joshua said unto all the people, Behold, this stone shall be a witness against us; for it hath heard all the words of Jehovah which he spake unto us: it shall be therefore a witness against you, lest ye deny your God. 28 So Joshua sent the people away, every man unto his inheritance.

71. E THE DEATH OF JOSHUA. Jg. $2^{8-9(7)}$ Rd.
  Josh. $24^{29-30(31)}$

29 And it came to pass after these things, that Joshua the son of Nun, the servant of Jehovah, died, being a hundred and ten years old. 30 And they buried him in the border of his inheritance in Timnath-serah, which is in the hill-country of Ephraim, on the north of the mountain of Gaash. 31 And Israel served Jehovah all the days of Joshua, and all the days of the elders that outlived Joshua, and had known all the work of Jehovah, that he had wrought for Israel.

72. E JOSEPH BURIED IN SHECHEM. E3xiii, 6 (Gn. 50^{25}).
  Josh. 24^{32}

32 And the bones of Joseph, which the children of Israel brought up out of Egypt, buried they in Shechem, in the parcel of ground which Jacob bought of the sons of Hamor the father of Shechem for a hundred pieces of money: and they became the inheritance of the children of Joseph.

73. E THE DEATH OF ELEAZAR. E48.
  Josh. 24^{33}

33 And Eleazar the son of Aaron died; and they buried him in the hill of Phinehas his son, which was given him in the hill-country of Ephraim.

CHAPTER III

P: THE PRIESTLY CODE

1. LITERARY CHARACTERISTICS.

P is far less in need of an explanatory introduction than is J or E. Its characteristics impress themselves at once on every reader. No page, no verse, of P (with few exceptions) could be taken for J or E. If any body of literature ever bore on its face the marks of belonging together, it is the priestly code. Eerdmans was strategic in his method of attack; if P can be undermined, then, indeed, modern literary and historical criticism is hopelessly in error.

a. Is P a Literary Unity?

There is great unanimity among critics with reference to the unity of P. The literature in this collection of history and laws is a unity in the spiritual sense—it embodies unified ideals and uses a unified stereotyped vocabulary; but in the sense of being written by one author or at one time, it is certainly not a unity (so all, even Driver). It is, rather, like a law book that has been amended by successive sessions of a legislature, without any indication as to when or by whom the amendments were made.

Practically all critics since Wellhausen and Kuenen distinguish at least four separate strata in P: (1) Ph or H, the Code of Holiness Lv. 17-26, and a few other passages; (2) Pg, the "Grundschrift"—the basic document—the backbone of the main structure; (3) Ps, numerous later additions to Pg; (4) Rp, the work of the final redactor of the Hexateuch, who combined JED with P in the spirit of P and made such alterations and additions as to create a final unity out of the entire composition.

In the following text the attempt is not made to distinguish the strata of Pg, Ps, and Rp; partly because of differences of opinion among critics as to the exact separation, but chiefly because such distinctions are relatively unimportant.

Recent writers are, however, tending to magnify the function of Rp. For example, the famous formula "These are the generations of," and the entire chronological scheme are made a later addition of Rp, not merely by Eerdmans, but also by Smend and Eichrodt (Sellin is also impressed by the arguments). But there is as yet no consensus regarding this hypothesis.

b. The Extent of P.

All are agreed that P begins with the creation in Gn. 1, and extends through the conquest of Canaan in Josh.

c. The Literary Style of P.

The style of P is very marked and is entirely different from that of J or E. It is formal, repetitious, precise, abstract in descriptions of Deity, yet minutely concrete in descriptions of objects, such as the tabernacle; legal, statistical, but usually dignified and elevated, and sometimes sublime, as in Gn. 1. It is characterized by interest in genealogy. "There is a tendency to describe an object in full each time that it is mentioned; a direction is followed, as a rule, by an account of its execution, usually in the same words. Sometimes the circumstantiality leads to diffuseness, as in parts of Nu. 1-4 and (an extreme case) Nu. 7" (Driver).

P is a literalist. "Metaphors, similes, etc., are eschewed (Nu. 27[17b] is an exception) and there is generally an absence of the poetical or dramatic element" (Driver).

The factor of "learned" editing, of fitting everything into a theory about the past, is far more highly developed in P than in E (Steuernagel).

d. P's Peculiarities in the Use of Proper Names.

Generally P shows himself dependent on JE where he is dealing with the same persons or places.

However, a few peculiarities may be noted. He always prefers the expression "land of Canaan" or Egypt; he speaks of Sinai (with J), not Horeb (E, D); up to Gn. 17 he uses the forms "Abram" and "Sarai"; the original home of the Hebrews he only calls Paddan Aram (vs. Aram Naharaim J). P alone

PRIESTLY CODE 205

tells us that Ur of the Chaldees was Abraham's city. With reference to the divine name, he follows the usage of E rather than J; but also frequently employs the name "God Almighty" (El Shaddai) which is in J Gn. 49^{25}, Nu. 24$^{4.16}$.

e. Characteristic Words and Expressions.

Driver lists 50 characteristic expressions of P; McNeile 33. It would be superfluous to attempt here a complete list. Some of the more important words and expressions are (following McNeile): anoint, atonement, burn, between the two evenings, congregation (of the Israel of the exodus in H and P 115 t., never elsewhere), dwell, dwelling, everlasting ordinance, families (after your or their) generations, glory of Jehovah, heave, holy, holiness, hosts, incense, offer, priest (act as a), prince, Sabbatic observance (tr. solemn rest, cf. P 29: Ex. 16^{23}), this self-same day, soul (in sense of person: in P nearly 100 t., not in J or E), strange (in sense of one who does not belong to the tribe or family of the priests; or used of things not ritually correct), swarm, testimony, tribe (literally, staff: 150 t. in P, 23 t. in 1 Ch., never in JED).

The force of these stylistic criteria is seen the more clearly when one considers that many of P's peculiar terms are found outside the Pentateuch almost wholly in Ezekiel (exilic) and Chronicles (post-exilic). For instance, Driver points out that the ancient form of the personal pronoun, first person singular —*anoki*—is to be found in P only in Gn. 23^4, and in Ez. only in 36^{28}; whereas the later form—*ani*—is found in every other instance in P and Ez., and also in the later literature in general, such as Lam., Hag., Zech. 1-8, Chron., Ezra, Neh., Esther, Eccl., Dn. In all this material *anoki* occurs only Neh. 1^6, Dn. 10^{11}, 1 Ch. 17^1 (from 2S. 7^1). The ancient form (*ani*) is always used by JE.

2. CHARACTERISTIC IDEAS.

a. Aim of P.

P has a single aim: to teach the ritual law, with its divine historical sanctions. P has, indeed, a brief outline narrative of the nation's history from the creation to Joshua; but the only function of the history is to provide the framework for the establishing of ritual and legal institutions. P "wishes to give only a history of the cultus" (Sellin).

P is distinctively the priestly code, written in the interests of the priestly class, its functions, its prerogatives, and its perquisites. P was perhaps written as a book for the people rather than for the priests (Wurster, Cornill); it was none the less dominated by priestly ideals. Bacon was right in saying that it is concerned with the hierocracy rather than with the theocracy, as in E.

b. Characteristic Religious Ideas.

P starts from the dominating idea of the absoluteness of God (Holzinger, Eichrodt). God is more transcendent, less anthropomorphic than in E. He speaks and it is done. Not only does P avoid all anthropomorphisms and all idolatry; but even all holy places (except the temple)—all sacred springs, trees, asherahs, massebahs—are excluded. Not even angels are mentioned; a fact which Steuernagel ascribes to an opposition to the cult of angels.

God "appears," but never in material form (in spite of Gn. $1^{26f.}$ $5^{1ff.}$ 9^6), not even in dreams. The theophany is a "glory," a supernatural light Ex. $24^{16f.}$ 34^{29-35}. Dillmann says that anthropopathic expressions are always scrupulously avoided by P. Gn. 2^{2-3} and Ex. 31^{17b} are P's nearest approach to anthropomorphism.

P's ideal of religion is to follow the divine commands in blind obedience (Eichrodt), fulfilling the enormously complicated requirements of the ritual law.

c. Characteristic Ethical Ideas.

P's interest lies in forms and ceremonies, not in the moral life. He may, as Steuernagel points out, insist on sin-offerings, and behind the cultus there may often be an ethical background; but it is background, not foreground.

P carries further E's tendency of eliminating the morally offensive from the stories about the patriarchs. They are represented as being models of good behavior. But P was more interested in correct deportment than he was in inner righteousness.

The wider religious and theological bearing of the ethical

life had no interest for P. Unlike J, he does not inquire about the origin of evil; unlike Jeremiah and the writer of Job, he does not pause to reflect on "the justice of the divine government of the universe" (Dillmann). "In the circles from which the priestly law book comes to us, the spirituality of ethical religion, and the idea of direct relations of God to man, seems to have died out" (Bacon).

d. Attitude toward Culture.

For P there was no culture that was not identical with his type of ceremonial religion. Historically, P performed the function of protecting Judaism from being disintegrated by the influences of foreign, especially Hellenistic, culture.

e. Attitude toward History.

P has certain very definite characteristic historical standpoints. In the main, he conceives of the sacred history as divided into four periods: from Adam to Noah, from Noah to Abraham, from Abraham to Moses, and from Moses to Joshua. Since Wellhausen it has been customary to say that P introduces each of these periods with a covenant, so that the priestly code is described as a *quattuor foedorum liber*—a book of four covenants.

But recent writers—especially Steuernagel, Eerdmans, and Eichrodt—point out that there is in P no trace of a covenant in the strict sense either at the creation or at Sinai. We must speak, then, of four periods (not of four covenants), as follows:

A. From the creation to Noah.—No covenant. God called Elohim.

B. From Noah to Abraham.—Covenant with Noah, affecting God's relation to all living creatures; the rainbow, God's covenant token Gn. 9^{12-13}. God called Elohim.

C. From Abraham to Moses.—Covenant with Abraham, affecting God's relation to Israel; circumcision, the covenant token Gn. 17^{11}. God frequently called El Shaddai (God Almighty).

D. From Moses to Joshua.—No new covenant; a period of fulfillment; the Sabbath, the characteristic sign Ex. 31^{13}. God called Jehovah.

During the first three, the pre-Mosaic, periods, P holds that there was no cultus whatever; no sacrifice,* no distinction of clean and unclean, no priesthood, no mention of the name "Jehovah." The reason for this is P's theory that the legitimate cultus begins with Moses, and the revelation on Sinai. Certain customs regarding food and circumcision were substantially the only religious institutions that existed in the pre-Mosaic period. Eichrodt points out that these involve neither cultus nor piety.

There are numerous other guiding ideas in P's interpretation of history. He conceives the earliest men as living to be nine hundred years old, or even older; whereas with the increase of sin in the world, human life becomes shorter. He magnifies the priestly element, not merely by assigning a complex ceremonial legislation to the sojourn at Sinai, but also by giving Aaron and his sons a far greater part than did the earlier records,† and by a far more complicated conception of the cultus (day of atonement, jubilees, tabernacle).

The question as to the historical truthfulness of P has been much discussed. There is no doubt that P in many instances is guided by ancient and reliable tradition, perhaps including some true data not found in J, E, or D. Driver mentions as proof that he follows tradition "the fact that even where it set antiquity in an unfavorable light he still does not shrink from recording it" (Ex. 16^2 Lv. 10^1 Nu. $20^{12.24}$ Nu. 27^{13-14}). But, on the whole, P does not tell what did happen; he tells what, in view of his ritualistic theories and practices, ought to have happened. The chronologies are plainly based, as all agree, not on fact, but on a highly artificial theory; the statistics attribute impossible numbers to the Israelites (as in Nu. 1-4); it is incredible that the beautiful and sumptuous tabernacle should have been carried about for forty years in the wilderness. Colenso's attack on the historicity of the Pentateuch touched P almost wholly, and was "pulverizing" (so Kuenen, quoted with approval by Bacon).

Bacon says that in P "all natural relations and perspectives

---

* Hence Noah offers sacrifice in the prophetic, non-ritualistic J, but not in the priestly, ritualistic P. Further, in P Noah takes but two of each kind into the ark, thus precluding sacrifice of any kind that was to be preserved; whereas in J, he takes seven of each kind.
† Aaron is missing from J; and is only incidental in E; in Dt. 9^{20} 10^6 32^{50}.

PRIESTLY CODE 209

of time and space are utterly lost from view. . . . This writer no longer has before his eyes a single remnant of historical realism and moves purely in an artificial, mechanical world of marvel." Bacon doubtless overstates the case; he neglects the possibility of certain strata of ancient, trustworthy material in P (recognized by Eerdmans, Sellin, Gunkel, Kittel, Eichrodt, et al.). But, on the whole, the resultant critical judgment of P is expressed in Gunkel's words, to the effect that P is moved by "the spirit of an orthodoxy indifferent to history."

3. HOME OF AUTHOR.

Substantially all critics agree that the home of P was in Babylonia. The priestly writer was one of the Jews that remained in Babylonia after 538, when many of the exiles returned. This follows from the critical view of the date of P as 500, and from the statements in Ezra $7^{6.10\text{-}11}$, Neh. 8^1, which seem to imply that Ezra brought the law of P with him from Babylonia.

4. THE DATE OF P—500.

The question of the date of P has been the storm-center of critical discussion. But neither Dillmann, who long held that P was pre-exilic and the earliest of the Hexateuchal sources, nor Eerdmans, who denies the existence of P as a unity, has any appreciable following. That P, in its earliest unified form, was written about 500 is an assured result of contemporary criticism.

a. Evidence for the *terminus ad quem* of the Composition of P.

The evidence is overwhelming, and is denied by no one, that the books of Ezra and Nehemiah, especially Neh. 8-10, presuppose the existence of many of the characteristic provisions of P. Neh. 8^1 is dated in the year 444. It is also generally held that Ezra 7^6 and the context presupposes that the book of the law used in 444 was brought by Ezra from Babylon in 458; but there are varying opinions regarding the detailed chronology of this period. All critics agree that P (Pg) arose not later than 458.

b. Evidence for the *terminus a quo* of the Composition of P.

i. P was not in existence before the exile.

The entire evidence of the historical books (except Chronicles, written 300, based on P) betrays no acquaintance with the characteristic institutions of P. The ritual practiced, for example, in the times of the Judges and Samuel, was very much simpler than that of P and entirely different. The attitude of the prophets toward form and ceremony could not have been so intensely bitter had the gorgeous system of P been endowed with the authority of Moses; passages like Jer. 7^{22}, Ho. 6^6, Amos 5^{25} are incompatible with the existence of P.*

ii. P is later than Dt.

Dt. shows no acquaintance with the characteristic ideas, historical conceptions, or ritual institutions of P, but draws entirely on JE, many think on E only.† On the other hand, P presupposes the centralization of worship established by Dt., and in every respect shows a more complicated organization of priesthood and ritual.‡

iii. P is later than Ez.

Lv. 17-26 is generally recognized as older than the main body of P; and H is very closely related to Ez., having been written entire, or in part, under the influence of Ezekiel.§ Vocabulary, style, religious conceptions, ideas about institutions and the priesthood in Ez. are remarkably similar in many respects to corresponding ideas in P. At the same time there is so much difference in detail that Ezekiel could not have written with P before him. (Proksch alone dissents, holding that the earliest form of P was written about 600.) Since Ezekiel's literary activity ceased about 570, that year is our *terminus a quo*.

iv. P was written after 538.

Had P been in existence in 538 it is very difficult to see why

---

* Ho. 8^{12} probably points to the existence of written laws, such as are to be found in J and E. But many translate, "Were I to write for them my laws by myriads they would be counted as a strange thing." Cf. the anti-critical case in W. Möller's book, Are the Critics Right?

† Only "three items of Dt. unnamed by JE are found in P": the seventy souls of Israel when Jacob went down into Egypt; the construction of the ark of acacia wood; and the reckoning of the spies as twelve (Carpenter and Harford, et al.). Even Dillmann admits that this would not prove the use of P by D.

‡ Carpenter and Harford compare:

Dt.	P
18^3	Lv. 7^{33} Nu. $18^{9-11.14}$
15^{19} $12^{6.17}$	Nu. $18^{17.12}$
$14^{22.28}$	Nu. $18^{21ff.26ff.}$ Lv. 27^{32}
10^9	Nu. 18^{20}, but contrast Nu. 35^{1-8}

§ See P42 H, Introductory Note.

PRIESTLY CODE 211

it was not carried back with the exiles, and used as the basis of the restored community.

c. The Closer Determination of the Date of P.

It is agreed that writers during the period 538-458 knew nothing of the laws of P (cf. Haggai, Zechariah, Malachi). Many have felt that Ezra, "the ready scribe in the law of Moses," might plausibly be viewed as the writer of P, but the great majority incline to regard this as psychologically improbable, and to date P shortly before Ezra, that is, about 500. This result of the Graf-Wellhausen school is accepted by all critics to-day. To give a list of authorities would be a work of supererogation. It would include all the authorities consulted, save Eerdmans, Dillmann (who came to doubt his own view—Smend). and Proksch (who dates his P¹ about 600).

5. RELATION OF P TO JE.

It is the almost unanimous opinion of critics that P used JE. So, for example, Budde, Holzinger, Bacon, Steuernagel, Smend, Eichrodt, and almost all others. Gunkel alone dissents, holding that P's source was "neither J nor E, but related to them." The majority opinion inclines to hold that where J and E differ, P usually prefers E, the more ritualistic and theocratic of the two, as D had also done. Proksch and Steuernagel have shown that P follows E in the use of the names "Elohim" and "Jehovah," in the prominence of Aaron and of Joshua, in such features as the tablets of the law and the tent of meeting. But P follows J in using the name "Sinai" (vs. E and D), in associating the Passover with the exodus, and in adopting the ancient name "El Shaddai" from Gn. 49^{25} (which also appears in Gn. 43^{14} Rp in E).

The majority are convinced that P used JE and no other source either oral or written (Bacon). They would say that where P adds to JE he draws on his imagination or his theories. But there is now an increasing tendency to recognize ancient material in P, based on previously existing oral or written sources (Kittel, Sellin, Eerdmans, Eichrodt, Proksch, Steuernagel).

The work of the future is the historical and religious interpretation of the documents.

THE TEXT OF P

A. From the creation to Noah (no covenant: God called Elohim).

1. THE CREATION: "THE GENERATIONS OF THE HEAVENS AND OF THE EARTH." J1.

Gn. 1¹-2⁴ᵃ

1 In the beginning God created the heavens and the earth. 2 And the earth was waste and void; and darkness was upon the face of the deep: and the Spirit of God moved upon the face of the waters. 3 And God said, Let there be light: and there was light. 4 And God saw the light, that it was good: and God divided the light from the darkness. 5 And God called the light Day, and the darkness he called Night. And there was evening and there was morning, one day.

6 And God said, Let there be a firmament in the midst of the waters, and let it divide the waters from the waters. 7 And God made the firmament, and divided the waters which were under the firmament from the waters which were above the firmament: and it was so. 8 And God called the firmament Heaven. And there was evening and there was morning, a second day.

9 And God said, Let the waters under the heavens be gathered together unto one place, and let the dry land appear: and it was so. 10 And God called the dry land Earth; and the gathering together of the waters called he Seas: and God saw that it was good. 11 And God said, Let the earth put forth grass, herbs yielding seed, *and* fruit-trees bearing fruit after their kind, wherein is the seed thereof, upon the earth: and it was so. 12 And the earth brought forth grass, herbs yielding seed after their kind, and trees bearing fruit, wherein is the seed thereof, after their kind: and God saw that it was good. 13 And there was evening and there was morning, a third day.

14 And God said, Let there be lights in the firmament of heaven to divide the day from the night; and let them be for signs, and for seasons, and for days and years: 15 and let them be for lights in the firmament of heaven to give light upon the earth: and it was so. 16 And God made the two great lights; the greater light to rule the day, and the lesser light to rule the night: *he made* the stars also. 17 And God set them in the firmament of heaven to give light upon the

---

[1] 2³: institution of the Sabbath. Cf. E23: Ex. 20¹¹ Rp. Several critics hold that 2⁴ᵃ originally preceded 1¹, as a heading, but Smend calls this more than doubtful. Some recent critics view all the references to "generations" in P as later redaction.

earth, 18 and to rule over the day and over the night, and to divide the light from the darkness: and God saw that it was good. 19 And there was evening and there was morning, a fourth day.

20 And God said, Let the waters swarm with swarms of living creatures, and let birds fly above the earth in the open firmament of heaven. 21 And God created the great seamonsters, and every living creature that moveth, wherewith the waters swarmed, after their kind, and every winged bird after its kind: and God saw that it was good. 22 And God blessed them, saying, Be fruitful, and multiply, and fill the waters in the seas, and let birds multiply on the earth. 23 And there was evening and there was morning, a fifth day.

24 And God said, Let the earth bring forth living creatures after their kind, cattle, and creeping things, and beasts of the earth after their kind: and it was so. 25 And God made the beasts of the earth after their kind, and the cattle after their kind, and everything that creepeth upon the ground after its kind: and God saw that it was good. 26 And God said, Let us make man in our image, after our likeness: and let them have dominion over the fish of the sea, and over the birds of the heavens, and over the cattle, and over all the earth, and over every creeping thing that creepeth upon the earth. 27 And God created man in his own image, in the image of God created he him; male and female created he them. 28 And God blessed them: and God said unto them, Be fruitful, and multiply, and replenish the earth, and subdue it; and have dominion over the fish of the sea, and over the birds of the heavens, and over every living thing that moveth upon the earth. 29 And God said, Behold, I have given you every herb yielding seed, which is upon the face of all the earth, and every tree, in which is the fruit of a tree yielding seed; to you it shall be for food: 30 and to every beast of the earth, and to every bird of the heavens, and to everything that creepeth upon the earth, wherein there is life, *I have given* every green herb for food: and it was so. 31 And God saw everything that he had made, and, behold, it was very good. And there was evening and there was morning, the sixth day.

2 And the heavens and the earth were finished, and all the host of them. 2 And on the seventh day God finished his work which he had made; and he rested on the seventh day from all his work which he had made. 3 And God blessed the seventh day, and hallowed it; because that in it he rested from all his work which God had created and made.

4a These are the generations of the heavens and of the earth when they were created.

2. "The Book of the Generations of Adam." J6.

Gn. 5[1-28] [30-32]

1 This is the book of the generations of Adam. In the day that God created man, in the likeness of God made he him; 2 male and female created he them, and blessed them, and called their name Adam, in the day when they were created. 3 And Adam lived a hundred and thirty years, and begat *a son* in his own likeness, after his image; and called his name Seth: 4 and the days of Adam after he begat Seth were eight hundred years: and he begat sons and daughters. 5 And all the days that Adam lived were nine hundred and thirty years: and he died.

6 And Seth lived a hundred and five years, and begat Enosh: 7 and Seth lived after he begat Enosh eight hundred and seven years, and begat sons and daughters: 8 and all the days of Seth were nine hundred and twelve years: and he died.

9 And Enosh lived ninety years, and begat Kenan: 10 and Enosh lived after he begat Kenan eight hundred and fifteen years, and begat sons and daughters: 11 and all the days of Enosh were nine hundred and five years: and he died.

12 And Kenan lived seventy years, and begat Mahalalel: 13 and Kenan lived after he begat Mahalalel eight hundred and forty years, and begat sons and daughters: 14 and all the days of Kenan were nine hundred and ten years: and he died.

15 And Mahalalel lived sixty and five years, and begat Jared: 16 and Mahalalel lived after he begat Jared eight hundred and thirty years, and begat sons and daughters: 17 and all the days of Mahalalel were eight hundred ninety and five years: and he died.

18 And Jared lived a hundred sixty and two years, and begat Enoch: 19 and Jared lived after he begat Enoch eight hundred years, and begat sons and daughters: 20 and all the days of Jared were nine hundred sixty and two years: and he died.

21 And Enoch lived sixty and five years, and begat Methuselah: 22 and Enoch walked with God after he begat Methuselah three hundred years, and begat sons and daughters: 23 and all the days of Enoch were three hundred sixty and five years: 24 and Enoch walked with God: and he was not; for God took him.

25 And Methuselah lived a hundred eighty and seven years, and begat Lamech: 26 and Methuselah lived after he begat

---

[2] vv. 22, 24 are interpreted by Eerd. as ancient polytheism. But others reject this; cf. the monotheistic passage J13ix: Gn. 18[17] (Ho., Eichr. et al.).

Lamech seven hundred eighty and two years, and begat sons and daughters: 27 and all the days of Methuselah were nine hundred sixty and nine years: and he died.
28 And Lamech lived a hundred eighty and two years, and begat a son. 30 And Lamech lived after he begat Noah five hundred ninety and five years, and begat sons and daughters: 31 And all the days of Lamech were seven hundred seventy and seven years: and he died.
32 And Noah was five hundred years old: and Noah begat Shem, Ham, and Japheth.

B. From Noah to Abraham (introduced by a covenant affecting all living creatures, with the rainbow as token: God called Elohim).

3. "The Generations of Noah."

3i. Noah and His Sons. J7.
Gn. 6⁹⁻¹⁰
9 These are the generations of Noah. Noah was a righteous man, *and* perfect in his generations: Noah walked with God. 10 And Noah begat three sons, Shem, Ham, and Japheth.

3ii. The Sinfulness of the Earth. J9.
Gn. 6¹¹⁻¹²
11 And the earth was corrupt before God, and the earth was filled with violence. 12 And God saw the earth, and, behold it was corrupt; for all flesh had corrupted their way upon the earth.

3iii. The Story of the Deluge. J9.
Gn. 6¹³⁻²² 7⁶.¹¹.¹³⁻¹⁶ᵃ.¹⁷ᵃ.¹⁸⁻²¹.²⁴ 8¹⁻²ᵃ.³ᵇ⁻⁵.¹³ᵃ.¹⁴⁻¹⁹

6¹³ And God said unto Noah, The end of all flesh is come before me; for the earth is filled with violence through them; and, behold, I will destroy them with the earth. 14 Make thee an ark of gopher wood; rooms shalt thou make in the ark, and shalt pitch it within and without with pitch. 15 And this is how thou shalt make it: the length of the ark three hundred cubits, the breadth of it fifty cubits, and the height of it thirty cubits. 16 A light shalt thou make to the ark, and to a cubit shalt thou finish it upward; and the door of the ark shalt thou set in the side thereof; with lower, second, and third stories shalt thou make it. 17 And I, behold, I do bring the flood of waters upon the earth, to destroy all flesh, wherein

---
[iii] P 3iii (and P1) are viewed by Eerd. alone as pre-exilic. Others, however, admit that the material may well come from a pre-exilic tradition, although it surely assumed its present form after the exile.

is the breath of life, from under heaven; everything that is in the earth shall die. 18 But I will establish my covenant with thee; and thou shalt come into the ark, thou, and thy sons, and thy wife, and thy sons' wives with thee. 19 And of every living thing of all flesh, two of every sort shalt thou bring into the ark, to keep them alive with thee; they shall be male and female. 20 Of the birds after their kind, and of the cattle after their kind, of every creeping thing of the ground after its kind, two of every sort shall come unto thee, to keep them alive. 21 And take thou unto thee of all food that is eaten, and gather it to thee; and it shall be for food for thee, and for them. 22 Thus did Noah; according to all that God commanded him, so did he.

7 ^{6} And Noah was six hundred years old when the flood of waters was upon the earth. 11 In the six hundredth year of Noah's life, in the second month, on the seventeenth day of the month, on the same day were all the fountains of the great deep broken up, and the windows of heaven were opened. 13 In the selfsame day entered Noah, and Shem, and Ham, and Japheth, the sons of Noah, and Noah's wife, and the three wives of his sons with them, into the ark; 14 they, and every beast after its kind, and all the cattle after their kind, and every creeping thing that creepeth upon the earth after its kind, and every bird after its kind, every bird of every sort. 15 And they went in unto Noah into the ark, two and two of all flesh wherein is the breath of life. 16a And they that went in, went in male and female of all flesh, as God commanded him.

17a And the flood was forty days upon the earth. 18 And the waters prevailed, and increased greatly upon the earth; and the ark went upon the face of the waters. 19 And the waters prevailed exceedingly upon the earth; and all the high mountains that were under the whole heaven were covered. 20 Fifteen cubits upward did the waters prevail; and the mountains were covered. 21 And all flesh died that moved upon the earth, both birds, and cattle, and beasts, and every creeping thing that creepeth upon the earth, and every man. 24 And the waters prevailed upon the earth a hundred and fifty days.

8 And God remembered Noah, and all the beasts, and all the cattle that were with him in the ark: and God made a wind to pass over the earth, and the waters assuaged; 2a the fountains also of the deep and the windows of heaven were stopped. 3b And after the end of a hundred and fifty days the waters decreased. 4 And the ark rested in the seventh month, on the seventeenth day of the month, upon the moun-

...9¹¹] P3iii–iv 217

tains of Ararat. 5 And the waters decreased continually unto the tenth month: in the tenth month, on the first day of the month, were the tops of the mountains seen. 13a And it came to pass in the six hundred and first year, in the first month, the first day of the month, the waters were dried up from off the earth. 14 And in the second month, on the seven and twentieth day of the month, was the earth dry. 15 And God spake unto Noah, saying, 16 Go forth from the ark, thou, and thy wife, and thy sons, and thy sons' wives with thee. 17 Bring forth with thee every living thing that is with thee of all flesh, both birds, and cattle, and every creeping thing that creepeth upon the earth; that they may breed abundantly in the earth, and be fruitful, and multiply upon the earth. 18 And Noah went forth, and his sons, and his wife, and his sons' wives with him: 19 every beast, every creeping thing, and every bird, whatsoever moveth upon the earth, after their families, went forth out of the ark.

3iv. COVENANT WITH NOAH: BOW OF PROMISE. J9.
Gn. 9¹⁻¹⁷

1 And God blessed Noah and his sons, and said unto them, Be fruitful, and multiply, and replenish the earth. 2 And the fear of you and the dread of you shall be upon every beast of the earth, and upon every bird of the heavens; with all wherewith the ground teemeth, and all the fishes of the sea, into your hand are they delivered. 3 Every moving thing that liveth shall be food for you; as the green herb have I given you all. 4 But flesh with the life thereof, *which is* the blood thereof, shall ye not eat. 5 And surely your blood, *the blood* of your lives, will I require; at the hand of every beast will I require it: and at the hand of man, even at the hand of every man's brother, will I require the life of man. 6 Whoso sheddeth man's blood, by man shall his blood be shed: for in the image of God made he man. 7 And you, be ye fruitful, and multiply; bring forth abundantly in the earth, and multiply therein.

8 And God spake unto Noah, and to his sons with him, saying, 9 And I, behold, I establish my covenant with you, and with your seed after you; 10 and with every living creature that is with you, the birds, the cattle, and every beast of the earth with you; of all that go out of the ark, even every beast of the earth. 11 And I will establish my covenant with you; neither shall all flesh be cut off any more by the waters of the flood; neither shall there any more be a flood to destroy the

---

³ⁱᵛ Ritual prohibition of blood, v. 4, and of murder, v. 5. v. 16 is regarded by Eerd. as polytheistic; R: Eichr.

earth. 12 And God said, This is the token of the covenant which I make between me and you and every living creature that is with you, for perpetual generations: 13 I do set my bow in the cloud, and it shall be for a token of a covenant between me and the earth. 14 And it shall come to pass, when I bring a cloud over the earth, that the bow shall be seen in the cloud, 15 and I will remember my covenant, which is between me and you and every living creature of all flesh; and the waters shall no more become a flood to destroy all flesh. 16 And the bow shall be in the cloud; and I will look upon it, that I may remember the everlasting covenant between God and every living creature of all flesh that is upon the earth. 17 And God said unto Noah, This is the token of the covenant which I have established between me and all flesh that is upon the earth.

3v. THE DEATH OF NOAH.

Gn. 9$^{28-29}$

28 And Noah lived after the flood three hundred and fifty years. 29 And all the days of Noah were nine hundred and fifty years: and he died.

4. "THE GENERATIONS OF THE SONS OF NOAH." J11.

Gn. 10$^{1-7.20.22-23.31-32}$

1 Now these are the generations of the sons of Noah, *namely*, of Shem, Ham, and Japheth: and unto them were sons born after the flood.

2 The sons of Japheth: Gomer, and Magog, and Madai, and Javan, and Tubal, and Meshech, and Tiras. 3 And the sons of Gomer: Ashkenaz, and Riphath, and Togarmah. 4 And the sons of Javan: Elishah, and Tarshish, Kittim, and Dodanim. 5 Of these were the isles of the nations divided in their lands, every one after his tongue, after their families, in their nations.

6 And the sons of Ham: Cush, and Mizraim, and Put, and Canaan. 7 And the sons of Cush: Seba, and Havilah, and Sabtah, and Raamah, and Sabteca; and the sons of Raamah:

---

[4] The descendants of Noah are largely the names of cities, tribes, and nations that can be identified as such. The following identifications are from Sk.: Gomer is the Cimmerians (Assyrian Gamir); Magog, the Scythians, cf. Ez. 38^2 39^6; Madai, the Medes—Media; Javan, Greece (Ionia); Tubal and Meshech (cf. Ez. 27^{13} 32^{26} 38$^{2-3}$ 39^1) are the Tibarenoi and Moschoi of Herodotus iii. 94; Tiras, the Etruscans?; Ashkenaz, the Scythians? (Herod. i. 103, 106, Jer.); Riphath, the Paphlagonians (Josephus); Togarmah, the Phrygians? or Armenians? (cf. Ez. 38^6 27^{14}); Elishah, Carthage? or Cyprus? (cf. Ez. 27^7); Tarshish, Tartesos (in South Spain); Kittim, Cyprus or South Italy? (cf. Dn. 11^{30}); Dodanim, the Dardanians?; Cush, Nubia; Mizraim, Egypt; Put, the Lybians?; Canaan; Seba, Saba, on the Red Sea; Havilah?; Sabtah?; Raamah, Ragmat; Sabteca?; Sheba, the Sabæans of SW. Arabia; Dedan, the Dedanites of N. Arabia, cf. Ez. 25^{13} 27^{20} 38^{13}; Elam, Elamites; Asshur, Assyria; Arpachshad, province of Assyria next to Armenia?; Lud, the Lydians?; Aram, the Aramæans; Uz? (cf. Gn. 22^{21} 36^{20} Job 1^1); Hul?; Gether?; Mash?. The absence of Babylonia is remarkable.

Sheba, and Dedan. 20 These are the sons of Ham, after their families, after their tongues, in their lands, in their nations.
22 The sons of Shem: Elam, and Asshur, and Arpachshad, and Lud, and Aram. 23 And the sons of Aram: Uz, and Hul, and Gether, and Mash. 31 These are the sons of Shem, after their families, after their tongues, in their lands, after their nations.
32 These are the families of the sons of Noah, after their generations, in their nations: and of these were the nations divided in the earth after the flood.

5. "THE GENERATIONS OF SHEM." J11.
   Gn. 11$^{10\text{-}26}$
10 These are the generations of Shem. Shem was a hundred years old, and begat Arpachshad two years after the flood: 11 and Shem lived after he begat Arpachshad five hundred years, and begat sons and daughters.
12 And Arpachshad lived five and thirty years, and begat Shelah: 13 and Arpachshad lived after he begat Shelah four hundred and three years, and begat sons and daughters.
14 And Shelah lived thirty years, and begat Eber: 15 and Shelah lived after he begat Eber four hundred and three years, and begat sons and daughters.
16 And Eber lived four and thirty years, and begat Peleg: 17 and Eber lived after he begat Peleg four hundred and thirty years, and begat sons and daughters.
18 And Peleg lived thirty years, and begat Reu: 19 and Peleg lived after he begat Reu two hundred and nine years, and begat sons and daughters.
20 And Reu lived two and thirty years, and begat Serug: 21 and Reu lived after he begat Serug two hundred and seven years, and begat sons and daughters.
22 And Serug lived thirty years, and begat Nahor: 23 and Serug lived after he begat Nahor two hundred years, and begat sons and daughters.
24 And Nahor lived nine and twenty years, and begat Terah: 25 and Nahor lived after he begat Terah a hundred and nineteen years, and begat sons and daughters.
26 And Terah lived seventy years, and begat Abram, Nahor, and Haran.

6. "THE GENERATIONS OF TERAH."
   Gn. 11$^{27.31\text{-}32}$
27 Now these are the generations of Terah. Terah begat Abram, Nahor, and Haran; and Haran begat Lot. 31 And Terah took Abram his son, and Lot the son of Haran, his son's

son, and Sarai his daughter-in-law, his son Abram's wife; and they went forth with them from Ur of the Chaldees, to go into the land of Canaan; and they came unto Haran, and dwelt there. 32 And the days of Terah were two hundred and five years: and Terah died in Haran.

C. From Abraham to Moses (introduced by a covenant affecting Israel only, with circumcision as token: God called El Shaddai).

7. THE STORY OF ABRAHAM. J13. E1.

7i. MIGRATION TO CANAAN. J13iii.
Gn. 12^{4b-5}
4b And Abram was seventy and five years old when he departed out of Haran. 5 And Abram took Sarai his wife, and Lot his brother's son, and all their substance that they had gathered, and the souls that they had gotten in Haran; and they went to go forth into the land of Canaan; and into the land of Canaan they came.

7ii. SEPARATION OF ABRAM AND LOT. J13v.
Gn. 13$^{6.11b-12a}$
6 And the land was not able to bear them, that they might dwell together: for their substance was great, so that they could not dwell together. 11b And they separated themselves the one from the other. 12a Abram dwelt in the land of Canaan, and Lot dwelt in the cities of the Plain.

7iii. THE BIRTH OF ISHMAEL. J13vii. E1iv.
Gn. 16$^{1a.3.15-16}$
1a Now Sarai, Abram's wife, bare him no children. 3 And Sarai, Abram's wife, took Hagar the Egyptian, her handmaid, after Abram had dwelt ten years in the land of Canaan, and gave her to Abram her husband to be his wife.
15 And Hagar bare Abram a son: and Abram called the name of his son, whom Hagar bare, Ishmael. 16 And Abram was fourscore and six years old, when Hagar bare Ishmael to Abram.

7iv. COVENANT OF EL SHADDAI WITH ABRAM (ABRAHAM). J13ii. E1i. P17.
Gn. 17$^{1-21}$
1 And when Abram was ninety years old and nine, Jehovah

7iv v. 1, the name "Jehovah" is Rp; here, Gn. 21^{1b} are the only cases of its occurrence before Ex. 6 in a P context. Name "God Almighty," in Hebr., *El Shaddai*, a designation of Deity characteristic of P, but found also in E4viii: Gn. 43^{14}, where it is probably Rp; and in J19: Gn. 49^{25} and J45: Nu. 24^{4,16}. *El Shaddai* is probably original in the J passages,

appeared to Abram, and said unto him, I am God Almighty; walk before me, and be thou perfect. 2 And I will make my covenant between me and thee, and will multiply thee exceedingly. 3 And Abram fell on his face: and God talked with him, saying, 4 As for me, behold, my covenant is with thee, and thou shalt be the father of a multitude of nations. 5 Neither shall thy name any more be called Abram, but thy name shall be Abraham; for the father of a multitude of nations have I made thee. 6 And I will make thee exceeding fruitful, and I will make nations of thee, and kings shall come out of thee. 7 And I will establish my covenant between me and thee and thy seed after thee throughout their generations for an everlasting covenant, to be a God unto thee and to thy seed after thee. 8 And I will give unto thee, and to thy seed after thee, the land of thy sojournings, all the land of Canaan, for an everlasting possession; and I will be their God.

9 And God said unto Abraham, And as for thee, thou shalt keep my covenant, thou, and thy seed after thee throughout their generations. 10 This is my covenant, which ye shall keep, between me and you and thy seed after thee: every male among you shall be circumcised. 11 And ye shall be circumcised in the flesh of your foreskin; and it shall be a token of a covenant betwixt me and you. 12 And he that is eight days old shall be circumcised among you, every male throughout your generations, he that is born in the house, or bought with money of any foreigner that is not of thy seed. 13 He that is born in thy house, and he that is bought with thy money, must needs be circumcised: and my covenant shall be in your flesh for an everlasting covenant. 14 And the uncircumcised male who is not circumcised in the flesh of his foreskin, that soul shall be cut off from his people; he hath broken my covenant.

15 And God said unto Abraham, As for Sarai thy wife, thou shalt not call her name Sarai, but Sarah shall her name be. 16 And I will bless her, and moreover I will give thee a son of her: yea, I will bless her, and she shall be *a mother of* nations; kings of peoples shall be of her. 17 Then Abraham fell upon his face, and laughed, and said in his heart, Shall a child be born unto him that is a hundred years old? and shall Sarah, that is ninety years old, bear? 18 And Abraham said unto God, Oh that Ishmael might live before thee! 19 And God said, Nay, but Sarah thy wife shall bear thee a son; and thou shalt call his name Isaac: and I will establish my covenant with him for an everlasting covenant for his seed after him.

P appropriating and extending the use of the ancient name recorded in the oracles of the past.
 v. 5 "Abram," in Hebr., *exalted father;* "Abraham," *father of a multitude.* v. 15 Sarah, in Hebr., *princess.*

20 And as for Ishmael, I have heard thee: behold, I have blessed him, and will make him fruitful, and will multiply him exceedingly; twelve princes shall he beget, and I will make him a great nation. 21 But my covenant will I establish with Isaac, whom Sarah shall bear unto thee at this set time in the next year.

7v. ABRAHAM'S HOUSEHOLD IS CIRCUMCISED. J25.

Gn. 17^{22-27}

22 And he left off talking with him, and God went up from Abraham. 23 And Abraham took Ishmael his son, and all that were born in his house, and all that were bought with his money, every male among the men of Abraham's house, and circumcised the flesh of their foreskin in the selfsame day, as God had said unto him. 24 And Abraham was ninety years old and nine, when he was circumcised in the flesh of his foreskin. 25 And Ishmael his son was thirteen years old, when he was circumcised in the flesh of his foreskin. 26 In the selfsame day was Abraham circumcised, and Ishmael his son. 27 And all the men of his house, those born in the house, and those bought with money of a foreigner, were circumcised with him.

7vi. LOT RESCUED FROM SODOM. J13ix.

Gn. 19^{29}

29 And it came to pass, when God destroyed the cities of the Plain, that God remembered Abraham, and sent Lot out of the midst of the overthrow, when he overthrew the cities in which Lot dwelt.

7vii. BIRTH AND CIRCUMCISION OF ISAAC. J13xi. E1iii.

Gn. $21^{1b.2b-5}$

1b And Jehovah did unto Sarah as he had spoken, 2b at the set time of which God had spoken to him. 3 And Abraham called the name of his son that was born unto him, whom Sarah bare to him, Isaac. 4 And Abraham circumcised his son Isaac when he was eight days old, as God had commanded him. 5 And Abraham was a hundred years old, when his son Isaac was born unto him.

7viii. DEATH OF SARAH, AND BURIAL NEAR HEBRON, IN A FIELD PURCHASED FROM THE HITTITES. P9ii. Ez. $16^{3.45}$.

Gn. 23^{1-20}

1 And the life of Sarah was a hundred and seven and twenty

[7vi] Placed by We., and many, after 13^{12} (Smend).
[7viii] There is a difference of opinion as to whether this section (so much fuller of concrete detail than any other narrative in P) is an original part of P, a later expansion (so

years: these were the years of the life of Sarah. 2 And Sarah died in Kiriatharba (the same is Hebron), in the land of Canaan: and Abraham came to mourn for Sarah, and to weep for her. 3 And Abraham rose up from before his dead, and spake unto the children of Heth, saying, 4 I am a stranger and a sojourner with you: give me a possession of a buryingplace with you, that I may bury my dead out of my sight. 5 And the children of Heth answered Abraham, saying unto him, 6 Hear us, my lord; thou art a prince of God among us: in the choice of our sepulchres bury thy dead; none of us shall withhold from thee his sepulchre, but that thou mayest bury thy dead. 7 And Abraham rose up, and bowed himself to the people of the land, even to the children of Heth. 8 And he communed with them, saying, If it be your mind that I should bury my dead out of my sight, hear me, and entreat for me to Ephron the son of Zohar, 9 that he may give me the cave of Machpelah, which he hath, which is in the end of his field; for the full price let him give it to me in the midst of you for a possession of a burying-place. 10 Now Ephron was sitting in the midst of the children of Heth: and Ephron the Hittite answered Abraham in the audience of the children of Heth, even of all that went in at the gate of his city, saying, 11 Nay, my lord, hear me: the field give I thee, and the cave that is therein, I give it thee; in the presence of the children of my people give I it thee: bury thy dead. 12 And Abraham bowed himself down before the people of the land. 13 And he spake unto Ephron in the audience of the people of the land, saying, But if thou wilt, I pray thee, hear me: I will give the price of the field; take it of me, and I will bury my dead there. 14 And Ephron answered Abraham, saying unto him, 15 My lord, hearken unto me: a piece of land worth four hundred shekels of silver, what is that betwixt me and thee? bury therefore thy dead. 16 And Abraham hearkened unto Ephron; and Abraham weighed to Ephron the silver which he had named in the audience of the children of Heth, four hundred shekels of silver, current *money* with the merchant.

17 So the field of Ephron, which was in Machpelah, which was before Mamre, the field, and the cave which was therein, and all the trees that were in the field, that were in all the border thereof round about, were made sure 18 unto Abraham for a possession in the presence of the children of Heth, before all that went in at the gate of his city. 19 And after

---

most critics, cf. Ho., Smend, et al.) or a relatively ancient, at least pre-exilic, narrative (Eerd.). It seems to Eerd., Smend, to betray an interest in ancestor-worship that is foreign to P (cf. Is. 65⁴ 63¹⁶). A "field of Abram," cf. v. 20, is mentioned in an inscription of Shishak I.—The conception that the Hittites were the ancient inhabitants of Canaan rests on reliable tradition, cf. P9ii.

this, Abraham buried Sarah his wife in the cave of the field of Machpelah before Mamre (the same is Hebron), in the land of Canaan. 20 And the field, and the cave that is therein, were made sure unto Abraham for a possession of a burying-place by the children of Heth.

7ix. DEATH AND BURIAL OF ABRAHAM NEAR HEBRON. P7viii.
Gn. 25^{7-11a}

7 And these are the days of the years of Abraham's life which he lived, a hundred threescore and fifteen years. 8 And Abraham gave up the ghost, and died in a good old age, an old man, and full *of years*, and was gathered to his people. 9 And Isaac and Ishmael his sons buried him in the cave of Machpelah, in the field of Ephron the son of Zohar the Hittite, which is before Mamre; 10 the field which Abraham purchased of the children of Heth: there was Abraham buried, and Sarah his wife. 11a And it came to pass after the death of Abraham, that God blessed Isaac his son.

8. "THE GENERATIONS OF ISHMAEL." Eliv.
Gn. 25$^{12-17}$

12 Now these are the generations of Ishmael, Abraham's son, whom Hagar the Egyptian, Sarah's handmaid, bare unto Abraham: 13 and these are the names of the sons of Ishmael, by their names, according to their generations: the first-born of Ishmael, Nebaioth; and Kedar, and Adbeel, and Mibsam, 14 and Mishma, and Dumah, and Massa, 15 Hadad, and Tema, Jetur, Naphish, and Kedemah: 16 these are the sons of Ishmael, and these are their names, by their villages, and by their encampments; twelve princes according to their nations. 17 And these are the years of the life of Ishmael, a hundred and thirty and seven years: and he gave up the ghost and died, and was gathered unto his people.

9. "THE GENERATIONS OF ISAAC." J14. E2.

9i. ISAAC MARRIES REBEKAH. J13xv.
Gn. 25$^{19-20.26b}$

19 And these are the generations of Isaac, Abraham's son: Abraham begat Isaac: 20 and Isaac was forty years old when he took Rebekah, the daughter of Bethuel the Syrian of Paddan-aram, the sister of Laban the Syrian, to be his wife.

26b . . . And Isaac was threescore years old when she bare them.

9ii. ESAU MARRIES TWO HITTITE WOMEN. P7viii.
Gn. 26$^{34-35}$

34 And when Esau was forty years old he took to wife Judith

the daughter of Beeri the Hittite, and Basemath the daughter of Elon the Hittite: 35 and they were a grief of mind unto Isaac and to Rebekah.

9iii. ISAAC BLESSES JACOB IN THE NAME OF EL SHADDAI, AND SENDS HIM TO LABAN FOR A WIFE.
Gn. 27^{46}-28^5
46 And Rebekah said to Isaac, I am weary of my life because of the daughters of Heth: if Jacob take a wife of the daughters of Heth, such as these, of the daughters of the land, what good shall my life do me? 28^1 And Isaac called Jacob, and blessed him, and charged him, and said unto him, Thou shalt not take a wife of the daughters of Canaan. 2 Arise, go to Paddan-aram, to the house of Bethuel thy mother's father; and take thee a wife from thence of the daughters of Laban thy mother's brother. 3 And God Almighty bless thee, and make thee fruitful, and multiply thee, that thou mayest be a company of peoples; 4 and give thee the blessing of Abraham, to thee, and to thy seed with thee; that thou mayest inherit the land of thy sojournings, which God gave unto Abraham. 5 And Isaac sent away Jacob: and he went to Paddan-aram unto Laban, son of Bethuel the Syrian, the brother of Rebekah, Jacob's and Esau's mother.

9iv. ESAU MARRIES MAHALATH, DAUGHTER OF ISHMAEL.
Gn. 28^{6-9}
6 Now Esau saw that Isaac had blessed Jacob and sent him away to Paddan-aram, to take him a wife from thence; and that as he blessed him he gave him a charge, saying, Thou shalt not take a wife of the daughters of Canaan; 7 and that Jacob obeyed his father and his mother, and was gone to Paddan-aram: 8 and Esau saw that the daughters of Canaan pleased not Isaac his father; 9 and Esau went unto Ishmael, and took, besides the wives that he had, Mahalath the daughter of Ishmael Abraham's son, the sister of Nebaioth, to be his wife.

10. "THE GENERATIONS OF JACOB." J15. E3.

10i. JACOB'S FAMILY IN PADDAN-ARAM. J15iii, iv. P3iii-vi.
Gn. $29^{24.28b-29}$ 30^{22a}
24 And Laban gave Zilpah his handmaid unto his daughter Leah for a handmaid. 28b And he gave him Rachel his daughter to wife. 29 And Laban gave to Rachel his daughter Bilhah his handmaid to be her handmaid. 30^{22a} And God remembered Rachel.

10ii. JACOB RETURNS FROM PADDAN-ARAM TO SHECHEM.
J15vff. E3viiff., xiii.
Gn. 31^{18b} 33^{18a}

31^{18b} . . . and all his substance which he had gathered, the cattle of his getting, which he had gathered in Paddan-aram, to go to Isaac his father unto the land of Canaan. 33^{18a} And Jacob came in peace to the city of Shechem, which is in the land of Canaan, when he came from Paddan-aram.

10iii. EL SHADDAI APPEARS TO JACOB AT BETHEL. J15i. E3i, xv. P9iii.
Gn. 35$^{6a.9-13.15}$

6a So Jacob came to Luz, which is in the land of Canaan (the same is Beth-el).

9 And God appeared unto Jacob again, when he came from Paddan-aram, and blessed him. 10 And God said unto him, Thy name is Jacob: thy name shall not be called any more Jacob, but Israel shall be thy name: and he called his name Israel. 11 And God said unto him, I am God Almighty: be fruitful and multiply; a nation and a company of nations shall be of thee, and kings shall come out of thy loins; 12 and the land which I gave unto Abraham and Isaac, to thee I will give it, and to thy seed after thee will I give the land. 13 And God went up from him in the place where he spake with him. 15 And Jacob called the name of the place where God spake with him, Beth-el.

10iv. THE TWELVE SONS OF JACOB. J15iv. E3vi.
Gn. 35^{22b-26}

22b Now the sons of Jacob were twelve: 23 the sons of Leah: Reuben, Jacob's first-born, and Simeon, and Levi, and Judah, and Issachar, and Zebulun; 24 the sons of Rachel: Joseph and Benjamin; 25 and the sons of Bilhah, Rachel's handmaid: Dan and Naphtali; 26 and the sons of Zilpah, Leah's handmaid: Gad and Asher: these are the sons of Jacob, that were born to him in Paddan-aram.

10v. DEATH OF ISAAC.
Gn. 35$^{27-29}$

27 And Jacob came unto Isaac his father to Mamre, to Kiriath-arba (the same is Hebron), where Abraham and Isaac sojourned.

28 And the days of Isaac were a hundred and fourscore years. 29 And Isaac gave up the ghost, and died, and was gathered unto his people, old and full of days: and Esau and Jacob his sons buried him.

10iv (and v)—late R: Eerd., Dahse.

Gn. 36, cf. P11.

10vi. JACOB IN CANAAN.
Gn. 37^{1-2a}
1 And Jacob dwelt in the land of his father's sojournings, in the land of Canaan. 2a These are the generations of Jacob.

11. "THE GENERATIONS OF ESAU." J16.
Gn. 36$^{1-30.40-43}$
1 Now these are the generations of Esau (the same is Edom). 2 Esau took his wives of the daughters of Canaan: Adah the daughter of Elon the Hittite, and Oholibamah the daughter of Anah, the daughter of Zibeon the Hivite, 3 and Basemath Ishmael's daughter, sister of Nebaioth. 4 And Adah bare to Esau Eliphaz; and Basemath bare Reuel; 5 and Oholibamah bare Jeush, and Jalam, and Korah: these are the sons of Esau, that were born unto him in the land of Canaan. 6 And Esau took his wives, and his sons, and his daughters, and all the souls of his house, and his cattle, and all his beasts, and all his possessions, which he had gathered in the land of Canaan; and went into a land away from his brother Jacob. 7 For their substance was too great for them to dwell together; and the land of their sojournings could not bear them because of their cattle. 8 And Esau dwelt in mount Seir: Esau is Edom.

9 And these are the generations of Esau the father of the Edomites in mount Seir: 10 these are the names of Esau's sons: Eliphaz the son of Adah the wife of Esau, Reuel the son of Basemath the wife of Esau. 11 And the sons of Eliphaz were Teman, Omar, Zepho, and Gatam, and Kenaz. 12 And Timna was concubine to Eliphaz Esau's son; and she bare to Eliphaz Amalek: these are the sons of Adah, Esau's wife. 13 And these are the sons of Reuel: Nahath, and Zerah, Shammah, and Mizzah: these were the sons of Basemath, Esau's wife. 14 And these were the sons of Oholibamah the daughter of Anah, the daughter of Zibeon, Esau's wife: and she bare to Esau Jeush, and Jalam, and Korah.

15 These are the chiefs of the sons of Esau: the sons of Eliphaz the first-born of Esau: chief Teman, chief Omar, chief Zepho, chief Kenaz, 16 chief Korah, chief Gatam, chief Amalek: these are the chiefs that came of Eliphaz in the land of Edom; these are the sons of Adah. 17 And these are the sons of Reuel, Esau's son: chief Nahath, chief Zerah, chief Shammah, chief Mizzah: these are the chiefs that came of Reuel in the land of Edom; these are the sons of Basemath, Esau's wife. 18 And these are the sons of Oholibamah, Esau's

---

[11] vv. 1-30 include an uncertain amount of older material that has been subjected to considerable revision, cf. Co., Ka., Dr., et al. All agree that vv. 40-43 are P.

wife: chief Jeush, chief Jalam, chief Korah: these are the chiefs that came of Oholibamah the daughter of Anah, Esau's wife. 19 These are the sons of Esau, and these are their chiefs: the same is Edom.
20 These are the sons of Seir the Horite, the inhabitants of the land: Lotan and Shobal and Zibeon and Anah, 21 and Dishon and Ezer and Dishan: these are the chiefs that came of the Horites, the children of Seir in the land of Edom. 22 And the children of Lotan were Hori and Heman; and Lotan's sister was Timna. 23 And these are the children of Shobal: Alvan and Manahath and Ebal, Shepho and Onam. 24 And these are the children of Zibeon: Aiah and Anah; this is Anah who found the hot springs in the wilderness, as he fed the asses of Zibeon his father. 25 And these are the children of Anah: Dishon and Oholibamah the daughter of Anah. 26 And these are the children of Dishon: Hemdan and Eshban and Ithran and Cheran. 27 These are the children of Ezer: Bilhan and Zaavan and Akan. 28 These are the children of Dishan: Uz and Aran. 29 These are the chiefs that came of the Horites: chief Lotan, chief Shobal, chief Zibeon, chief Anah, 30 chief Dishon, chief Ezer, chief Dishan: these are the chiefs that came of the Horites, according to their chiefs in the land of Seir.
40 And these are the names of the chiefs that came of Esau, according to their families, after their places, by their names: chief Timna, chief Alvah, chief Jetheth, 41 chief Oholibamah, chief Elah, chief Pinon, 42 chief Kenaz, chief Teman, chief Mibzar, 43 chief Magdiel, chief Iram: these are the chiefs of Edom, according to their habitations in the land of their possession. This is Esau, the father of the Edomites.

12. THE STORY OF JOSEPH. J18. E4.

12i. JOSEPH THE TALEBEARER.

Gn. 37[2b]

2b Joseph, being seventeen years old, was feeding the flock with his brethren; and he was a lad with the sons of Bilhah, and with the sons of Zilpah, his father's wives: and Joseph brought the evil report of them unto their father.

12ii. HIS HONORS IN EGYPT. J18iv. E4vi.

Gn. 41[46a]

46a And Joseph was thirty years old when he stood before Pharaoh king of Egypt.

[12i] P: most critics. J: Di., Dr. (or E), Ba., St., Ki.

12iii. JACOB'S HOUSEHOLD MOVES TO EGYPT. J18viii. E4xi.
Gn. 46⁶⁻²⁷

6 And they took their cattle and their goods, which they had gotten in the land of Canaan, and came into Egypt, Jacob, and all his seed with him: 7 his sons, and his sons' sons with him, his daughters, and his sons' daughters, and all his seed brought he with him into Egypt. 8 And these are the names of the children of Israel, who came into Egypt, Jacob and his sons: Reuben, Jacob's first-born. 9 And the sons of Reuben: Hanoch, and Pallu, and Hezron, and Carmi. 10 And the sons of Simeon: Jemuel, and Jamin, and Ohad, and Jachin, and Zohar, and Shaul the son of a Canaanitish woman. 11 And the sons of Levi: Gershon, Kohath, and Merari. 12 And the sons of Judah: Er, and Onan, and Shelah, and Perez, and Zerah; but Er and Onan died in the land of Canaan. And the sons of Perez were Hezron and Hamul. 13 And the sons of Issachar: Tola, and Puvah, and Iob, and Shimron. 14 And the sons of Zebulun: Sered, and Elon, and Jahleel. 15 These are the sons of Leah, whom she bare unto Jacob in Paddan-aram, with his daughter Dinah: all the souls of his sons and his daughters were thirty and three. 16 And the sons of Gad: Ziphion, and Haggi, Shuni, and Ezbon, Eri, and Arodi, and Areli. 17 And the sons of Asher: Imnah, and Ishvah, and Ishvi, and Beriah, and Serah their sister; and the sons of Beriah: Heber, and Malchiel. 18 These are the sons of Zilpah, whom Laban gave to Leah his daughter; and these she bare unto Jacob, even sixteen souls. 19 The sons of Rachel Jacob's wife: Joseph and Benjamin. 20 And unto Joseph in the land of Egypt were born Manasseh and Ephraim, whom Asenath, the daughter of Poti-phera priest of On, bare unto him. 21 And the sons of Benjamin: Bela, and Becher, and Ashbel, Gera, and Naaman, Ehi, and Rosh, Muppim, and Huppim, and Ard. 22 These are the sons of Rachel, who were born to Jacob: all the souls were fourteen. 23 And the sons of Dan: Hushim. 24 And the sons of Naphtali: Jahzeel, and Guni, and Jezer, and Shillem. 25 These are the sons of Bilhah, whom Laban gave unto Rachel his daughter, and these she bare unto Jacob: all the souls were seven. 26 All the souls that came with Jacob into Egypt, that came out of his loins, besides Jacob's sons' wives, all the souls were threescore and six; 27 and the sons of Joseph, who were born to him in Egypt, were two souls: all the souls of the house of Jacob, that came into Egypt, were threescore and ten.

12iv. PHARAOH SHOWS FAVOR TO JACOB. E4xi.
Gn. 47⁵ᵇ⁻⁶ᵃ·⁷⁻¹¹·²⁷ᵇ⁻²⁸

5b Thy father and thy brethren are come unto thee: 6a the land of Egypt is before thee; in the best of the land make thy father and thy brethren to dwell. 7 And Joseph brought in

---
¹²ⁱⁱⁱ vv. 8-27 are generally regarded as a later addition of Ps. So, e. g., Ka., Gu., CH., St., Co.?, Kayser, Pr., Smend (based on P15: Ex. 1¹⁻⁵).

Jacob his father, and set him before Pharaoh: and Jacob blessed Pharaoh.

8 And Pharaoh said unto Jacob, How many are the days of the years of thy life? 9 And Jacob said unto Pharaoh, The days of the years of my pilgrimage are a hundred and thirty years: few and evil have been the days of the years of my life, and they have not attained unto the days of the years of the life of my fathers in the days of their pilgrimage. 10 And Jacob blessed Pharaoh, and went out from the presence of Pharaoh.

11 And Joseph placed his father and his brethren, and gave them a possession in the land of Egypt, in the best of the land, in the land of Rameses, as Pharaoh had commanded. 27b And they gat them possessions therein, and were fruitful, and multiplied exceedingly.

28 And Jacob lived in the land of Egypt seventeen years: so the days of Jacob, the years of his life, were a hundred forty and seven years.

12v. JACOB TELLS JOSEPH OF THE PROMISE OF EL SHADDAI. P10iii.

Gn. 48$^{3-6}$

3 And Jacob said unto Joseph, God Almighty appeared unto me at Luz in the land of Canaan, and blessed me, 4 and said unto me, Behold, I will make thee fruitful, and multiply thee, and I will make of thee a company of peoples, and will give this land to thy seed after thee for an everlasting possession. 5 And now thy two sons, who were born unto thee in the land of Egypt before I came unto thee into Egypt, are mine; Ephraim and Manasseh, even as Reuben and Simeon, shall be mine. 6 And thy issue, that thou begettest after them, shall be thine; they shall be called after the name of their brethren in their inheritance.

13. JACOB BLESSES HIS SONS. J19. E5, 51. P7viii.

Gn. 49$^{1a.28b-32}$

1a And Jacob called unto his sons, and said . . . , 28b every one according to his blessing he blessed them. 28 And he charged them, and said unto them, I am to be gathered unto my people: bury me with my fathers in the cave that is in the field of Ephron the Hittite, 30 in the cave that is in the field of Machpelah, which is before Mamre, in the land of Canaan, which Abraham bought with the field from Ephron the Hittite for a possession of a burying-place. 31 There they buried Abraham and Sarah his wife; there they buried Isaac and

---

[12v] Eerd. and Dahse regard this as late R.

...Ex. 2^{25}] P12iv–16 231

Rebekah his wife; and there I buried Leah— 32 the field and the cave that is therein, which was purchased from the children of Heth.

14. The Death and Burial of Jacob. J20. E6.
Gn. 49^{33} $50^{12\text{-}13}$

33 And when Jacob made an end of charging his sons, . . . yielded up the ghost, and was gathered unto his people. 50^{12} And his sons did unto him according as he commanded them: 13 for his sons carried him into the land of Canaan, and buried him in the cave of the field of Machpelah, which Abraham bought with the field, for a possession of a buryingplace, of Ephron the Hittite, before Mamre.

D. From Moses to the conquest of Canaan: the fulfillment of the covenant (Sabbath, the sign: God called Jehovah).

15. The Increase of the Israelites in Egypt. P12iii.
Ex. $1^{1\text{-}5.7}$

1 Now these are the names of the sons of Israel, who came into Egypt (every man and his household came with Jacob): 2 Reuben, Simeon, Levi, and Judah, 3 Issachar, Zebulun, and Benjamin, 4 Dan and Naphtali, Gad and Asher. 5 And all the souls that came out of the loins of Jacob were seventy souls: and Joseph was in Egypt already. 7 And the children of Israel were fruitful, and increased abundantly, and multiplied, and waxed exceeding mighty; and the land was filled with them.

16. The Israelites Oppressed by the Egyptians. J22.
Ex. $1^{13\text{-}14}$ $2^{23\text{b}\text{-}25}$

13 And the Egyptians made the children of Israel to serve with rigor: 14 and they made their lives bitter with hard service, in mortar and in brick, and in all manner of service in the field, all their service, wherein they made them serve with rigor.

$2^{23\text{b}}$ And the children of Israel sighed by reason of the bondage, and they cried, and their cry came up unto God by reason of the bondage. 24 And God heard their groaning, and God remembered his covenant with Abraham, with Isaac, and with Jacob. 25 And God saw the children of Israel, and God took knowledge *of them*.

---

[16] 1^{14}: redundant and probably composite.

232 SOURCES OF THE HEXATEUCH [Ex. 6²

17. GOD REVEALS TO MOSES HIS NAME JEHOVAH. J6 (Gn. 4²⁶). E4viii, 11iii. P7iv.

Ex. 6²⁻³

2 And God spake unto Moses, and said unto him, I am Jehovah: 3 and I appeared unto Abraham, unto Isaac, and unto Jacob, as God Almighty; but by my name Jehovah I was not known to them.

18. GOD PROMISES RELEASE TO THE ISRAELITES. J24iii. E11iv.

Ex. 6⁴⁻¹³

4 And I have also established my covenant with them, to give them the land of Canaan, the land of their sojournings, wherein they sojourned. 5 And moreover I have heard the groaning of the children of Israel, whom the Egyptians keep in bondage; and I have remembered my covenant. 6 Wherefore say unto the children of Israel, I am Jehovah, and I will bring you out from under the burdens of the Egyptians, and I will rid you out of their bondage, and I will redeem you with an outstretched arm, and with great judgments: 7 and I will take you to me for a people, and I will be to you a God; and ye shall know that I am Jehovah your God, who bringeth you out from under the burdens of the Egyptians. 8 And I will bring you in unto the land which I sware to give to Abraham, to Isaac, and to Jacob; and I will give it you for a heritage: I am Jehovah. 9 And Moses spake so unto the children of Israel: but they hearkened not unto Moses for anguish of spirit, and for cruel bondage.

10 And Jehovah spake unto Moses, saying, 11 Go in, speak unto Pharaoh king of Egypt, that he let the children of Israel go out of his land. 12 And Moses spake before Jehovah, saying, Behold, the children of Israel have not hearkened unto me; how then shall Pharaoh hear me, who am of uncircumcised lips? 13 And Jehovah spake unto Moses and unto Aaron, and gave them a charge unto the children of Israel, and unto Pharaoh king of Egypt, to bring the children of Israel out of the land of Egypt.

19. LIST OF ISRAELITE FAMILIES. P12iii, 15.

Ex. 6¹⁴⁻²⁷

14 These are the heads of their fathers' houses. The sons of Reuben the first-born of Israel: Hanoch, and Pallu, Hezron, and Carmi; these are the families of Reuben. 15 And the

---
[17] "God Almighty," in Hebr., *El Shaddai*.
[18] vv. 6-8 interrupt the connection and are perh. secondary, Pr. Kayser. Dr. connects with H.
[19] Probably secondary.

sons of Simeon: Jemuel, and Jamin, and Ohad, and Jachin, and Zohar, and Shaul the son of a Canaanitish woman; these are the families of Simeon. 16 And these are the names of the sons of Levi according to their generations: Gershon, and Kohath, and Merari; and the years of the life of Levi were a hundred thirty and seven years. 17 The sons of Gershon: Libni and Shimei, according to their families. 18 And the sons of Kohath: Amram, and Izhar, and Hebron, and Uzziel; and the years of the life of Kohath were a hundred thirty and three years. 19 And the sons of Merari: Mahli and Mushi. These are the families of the Levites according to their generations. 20 And Amram took him Jochebed his father's sister to wife; and she bare him Aaron and Moses: and the years of the life of Amram were a hundred and thirty and seven years. 21 And the sons of Izhar: Korah, and Nepheg, and Zichri. 22 And the sons of Uzziel: Mishael, and Elzaphan, and Sithri. 23 And Aaron took him Elisheba, the daughter of Amminadab, the sister of Nahshon, to wife; and she bare him Nadab and Abihu, Eleazar and Ithamar. 24 And the sons of Korah: Assir, and Elkanah, and Abiasaph; these are the families of the Korahites. 25 And Eleazar Aaron's son took him one of the daughters of Putiel to wife; and she bare him Phinehas. These are the heads of the fathers' *houses* of the Levites according to their families. 26 These are that Aaron and Moses, to whom Jehovah said, Bring out the children of Israel from the land of Egypt according to their hosts. 27 These are they that spake to Pharaoh king of Egypt, to bring out the children of Israel from Egypt: these are that Moses and Aaron.

20. AARON AS MOSES'S "PROPHET." J26i.
Ex. 6^{28}-7^2
28 And it came to pass on the day when Jehovah spake unto Moses in the land of Egypt, 29 that Jehovah spake unto Moses, saying, I am Jehovah: speak thou unto Pharaoh king of Egypt all that I speak unto thee. 30 And Moses said before Jehovah, Behold, I am of uncircumcised lips, and how shall Pharaoh hearken unto me? 7^1 And Jehovah said unto Moses, See, I have made thee as God to Pharaoh; and Aaron thy brother shall be thy prophet. 2 Thou shalt speak all that I command thee; and Aaron thy brother shall speak unto Pharaoh, that he let the children of Israel go out of his land.

21. GOD FORETELLS THE PLAGUES. E11iv.
Ex. 7^{3-7}
3 And I will harden Pharaoh's heart, and multiply my signs and my wonders in the land of Egypt. 4 But Pharaoh will

not hearken unto you, and I will lay my hand upon Egypt, and bring forth my hosts, my people the children of Israel, out of the land of Egypt by great judgments. 5 And the Egyptians shall know that I am Jehovah, when I stretch forth my hand upon Egypt, and bring out the children of Israel from among them. 6 And Moses and Aaron did so; as Jehovah commanded them, so did they. 7 And Moses was fourscore years old, and Aaron fourscore and three years old when they spake unto Pharaoh.

22. APPEAL TO PHARAOH: RODS MADE REPTILES. J26i. E11vi, 13i. P63.

Ex. 7⁸⁻¹³

8 And Jehovah spake unto Moses and unto Aaron, saying, 9 When Pharaoh shall speak unto you, saying, Show a wonder for you; then thou shalt say unto Aaron, Take thy rod, and cast it down before Pharaoh, that it become a serpent. 10 And Moses and Aaron went in unto Pharaoh, and they did so, as Jehovah had commanded: and Aaron cast down his rod before Pharaoh and before his servants, and it became a serpent. 11 Then Pharaoh also called for the wise men and the sorcerers: and they also, the magicians of Egypt, did in like manner with their enchantments. 12 For they cast down every man his rod, and they became serpents: but Aaron's rod swallowed up their rods. 13 And Pharaoh's heart was hardened, and he hearkened not unto them; as Jehovah had spoken.

23. THE PLAGUES. J26. E13.

23i. THE FIRST PLAGUE: WATERS TURN TO BLOOD. J26ii. E13ii.

Ex. 7¹⁹⁻²⁰ᵃ·²¹ᵇ⁻²²

19 And Jehovah said unto Moses, Say unto Aaron, Take thy rod, and stretch out thy hand over the waters of Egypt, over their rivers, over their streams, and over their pools, and over all their ponds of water, that they may become blood; and there shall be blood throughout all the land of Egypt, both in vessels of wood and in vessels of stone. 20a And Moses and Aaron did so, as Jehovah commanded.

21b And the blood was throughout all the land of Egypt. 22 And the magicians of Egypt did in like manner with their enchantments: and Pharaoh's heart was hardened, and he hearkened not unto them; as Jehovah had spoken.

---

²² The word tr. "serpent" means *any large reptile* (Am. Rev., margin). So vv. 9, 10, 11 and all references in P to the "serpent."

23ii. THE SECOND PLAGUE: FROGS.   J26iii.
Ex. 8⁵⁻⁷·¹⁵ᵇ

5 And Jehovah said unto Moses, Say unto Aaron, Stretch forth thy hand with thy rod over the rivers, over the streams, and over the pools, and cause frogs to come up upon the land of Egypt. 6 And Aaron stretched out his hand over the waters of Egypt. And the frogs came up, and covered the land of Egypt. 7 And the magicians did in like manner with their enchantments, and brought up frogs upon the land of Egypt, 15b . . . and hearkened not unto them; as Jehovah had spoken.

23iii. THE THIRD PLAGUE: LICE.   Not in J or E.
Ex. 8¹⁶⁻¹⁹

16 And Jehovah said unto Moses, Say unto Aaron, Stretch out thy rod, and smite the dust of the earth, that it may become lice throughout all the land of Egypt. 17 And they did so.

And Aaron stretched out his hand with his rod, and smote the dust of the earth, and there were lice upon man, and upon beast; all the dust of the earth became lice throughout all the land of Egypt. 18 And the magicians did so with their enchantments to bring forth lice, but they could not: and there were lice upon man, and upon beast. 19 Then the magicians said unto Pharaoh, This is the finger of God: and Pharaoh's heart was hardened, and he hearkened not unto them; as Jehovah had spoken.

23iv. THE FOURTH PLAGUE: BOILS.   Not in J or E.
Ex. 9⁸⁻¹² 11⁹⁻¹⁰

8 And Jehovah said unto Moses and unto Aaron, Take to you handfuls of ashes of the furnace, and let Moses sprinkle it toward heaven in the sight of Pharaoh. 9 And it shall become small dust over all the land of Egypt, and there shall be a boil breaking forth with blains upon man and upon beast.

11 And the magicians could not stand before Moses because of the boils; for the boils were upon the magicians, and upon all the Egyptians. 12 And Jehovah hardened the heart of Pharaoh, and he hearkened not unto them; as Jehovah had spoken unto Moses.

9 And Jehovah said unto Moses, Pharaoh will not hearken unto you; that my wonders may be multiplied in the land of Egypt. 10 And Moses and Aaron did all these wonders before Pharaoh: and Jehovah hardened Pharaoh's heart, and he did not let the children of Israel go out of his land.

---
²³ⁱⁱ The subject of v. 15b is Pharaoh, cf. P23i, v. 22.
²³ⁱᵛ 11⁹⁻¹⁰: Rp. Smend and McN. find Rje.

23v. JEHOVAH COMMANDS THE INSTITUTION OF THE PASSOVER IN CONNECTION WITH THE FIFTH PLAGUE: THE FIRST-BORN. J26ix. P51.

Ex. 12$^{1-20.28}$

1 And Jehovah spake unto Moses and Aaron in the land of Egypt, saying, 2 This month shall be unto you the beginning of months: it shall be the first month of the year to you. 3 Speak ye unto all the congregation of Israel, saying, In the tenth *day* of this month they shall take to them every man a lamb, according to their fathers' houses, a lamb for a household: 4 and if the household be too little for a lamb, then shall he and his neighbor next unto his house take one according to the number of the souls; according to every man's eating ye shall make your count for the lamb. 5 Your lamb shall be without blemish, a male a year old: ye shall take it from the sheep, or from the goats: 6 and ye shall keep it until the fourteenth day of the same month; and the whole assembly of the congregation of Israel shall kill it at even. 7 And they shall take of the blood, and put it on the two side-posts and on the lintel, upon the houses wherein they shall eat it. 8 And they shall eat the flesh in that night, roast with fire, and unleavened bread; with bitter herbs they shall eat it. 9 Eat not of it raw, nor boiled at all with water, but roast with fire; its head with its legs and with the inwards thereof. 10 And ye shall let nothing of it remain until the morning; but that which remaineth of it until the morning ye shall burn with fire. 11 And thus shall ye eat it: with your loins girded, your shoes on your feet, and your staff in your hand; and ye shall eat it in haste: it is Jehovah's passover. 12 For I will go through the land of Egypt in that night, and will smite all the first-born in the land of Egypt, both man and beast; and against all the gods of Egypt I will execute judgments: I am Jehovah. 13 And the blood shall be to you for a token upon the houses where ye are: and when I see the blood, I will pass over you, and there shall no plague be upon you to destroy you, when I smite the land of Egypt. 14 And this day shall be unto you for a memorial, and ye shall keep it a feast to Jehovah: throughout your generations ye shall keep it a feast by an ordinance for ever.

15 Seven days shall ye eat unleavened bread; even the first day ye shall put away leaven out of your houses: for whosoever eateth leavened bread from the first day until the seventh day, that soul shall be cut off from Israel. 16 And in the first day there shall be to you a holy convocation, and in the seventh

---

[23v] There is some question as to the unity of vv. 1-20, Pr., Bä. Eerd. regards vv. 1-14 as pre-exilic and pre-Deuteronomic (contrasting Ezra 6^{19ff}. 2 Ch. 30^{5ff}. 35^{10ff}.).

day a holy convocation; no manner of work shall be done in them, save that which every man must eat, that only may be done by you. 17 And ye shall observe the *feast of* unleavened bread; for in this selfsame day have I brought your hosts out of the land of Egypt: therefore shall ye observe this day throughout your generations by an ordinance for ever. 18 In the first *month*, on the fourteenth day of the month at even, ye shall eat unleavened bread, until the one and twentieth day of the month at even. 19 Seven days shall there be no leaven found in your houses: for whosoever eateth that which is leavened, that soul shall be cut off from the congregation of Israel, whether he be a sojourner, or one that is born in the land. 20 Ye shall eat nothing leavened; in all your habitations shall ye eat unleavened bread. 28 And the children of Israel went and did so; as Jehovah had commanded Moses and Aaron, so did they.

24. DEPARTURE OF THE ISRAELITES FROM RAMESES TO SUCCOTH. J23x. E13viii. P79.
Ex. $12^{37a.40-41.42}$

37a And the children of Israel journeyed from Rameses to Succoth.

40 Now the time that the children of Israel dwelt in Egypt was four hundred and thirty years. 41 And it came to pass at the end of four hundred and thirty years, even the selfsame day it came to pass, that all the hosts of Jehovah went out from the land of Egypt. 42 It is a night to be much observed unto Jehovah for bringing them out from the land of Egypt: this is that night of Jehovah, to be much observed of all the children of Israel throughout their generations.

25. THE LAW OF THE PASSOVER: SOJOURNERS.
Ex. 12^{43-51}

43 And Jehovah said unto Moses and Aaron, This is the ordinance of the passover: there shall no foreigner eat thereof; 44 but every man's servant that is bought for money, when thou hast circumcised him, then shall he eat thereof. 45 A sojourner and a hired servant shall not eat thereof. 46 In one house shall it be eaten; thou shalt not carry forth aught of the flesh abroad out of the house; neither shall ye break a bone thereof. 47 All the congregation of Israel shall keep it. 48 And when a stranger shall sojourn with thee, and will keep the passover to Jehovah, let all his males be circumcised, and then let him come near and keep it; and he shall be as one that is born in the land: but no uncircumcised person shall eat

---
[24] v. 42 is difficult; both the translation and the analysis of this verse are very uncertain.

thereof. 49 One law shall be to him that is home-born, and unto the stranger that sojourneth among you. 50 Thus did all the children of Israel; as Jehovah commanded Moses and Aaron, so did they. 51 And it came to pass the selfsame day, that Jehovah did bring the children of Israel out of the land of Egypt by their hosts.

26. THE LAW OF THE FIRST-BORN. J34.
Ex. 13$^{1-2}$
1 And Jehovah spake unto Moses, saying, 2 Sanctify unto me all the first-born, whatsoever openeth the womb among the children of Israel, both of man and of beast: it is mine.

27. JOURNEY FROM SUCCOTH TO PI-HAHIROTH. P79.
Ex. 13^{20} 14$^{1-2}$
20 And they took their journey from Succoth, and encamped in Etham, in the edge of the wilderness.
14^{1} And Jehovah spake unto Moses, saying, 2 Speak unto the children of Israel, that they turn back and encamp before Pi-hahiroth, between Migdol and the sea, before Baal-zephon: over against it shall ye encamp by the sea.

28. JEHOVAH CAUSES PHARAOH TO PURSUE THE ISRAELITES, WHO ESCAPE THROUGH THE RED SEA. J27. E14.
Ex. 14$^{4.8-9.15*.16b-18.21*.22-23.26-27a.28a.29}$
4 And I will harden Pharaoh's heart, and he shall follow after them; and I will get me honor upon Pharaoh, and upon all his host; and the Egyptians shall know that I am Jehovah. And they did so. 8 And Jehovah hardened the heart of Pharaoh king of Egypt, and he pursued after the children of Israel: for the children of Israel went out with a high hand. 9 And the Egyptians pursued after them, all the horses *and* chariots of Pharaoh, and his horsemen, and his army, and overtook them encamping by the sea, beside Pi-hahiroth, before Baal-zephon.
15* And Jehovah said unto Moses, . . . Speak unto the children of Israel, that they go forward. 16b And stretch out thy hand over the sea, and divide it: and the children of Israel shall go into the midst of the sea on dry ground. 17 And I, behold, I will harden the hearts of the Egyptians, and they shall go in after them: and I will get me honor upon Pharaoh, and upon all his host, upon his chariots, and upon his horsemen. 18 And the Egyptians shall know that I am Jehovah, when I have gotten me honor upon Pharaoh, upon his chariots, and upon his horsemen.
21* And Moses stretched out his hand over the sea, . . .

and the waters were divided. 22 And the children of Israel went into the midst of the sea upon the dry ground: and the waters were a wall unto them on their right hand, and on their left. 23 And the Egyptians pursued, and went in after them into the midst of the sea, all Pharaoh's horses, his chariots, and his horsemen.
26 And Jehovah said unto Moses, Stretch out thy hand over the sea, that the waters may come again upon the Egyptians, upon their chariots, and upon their horsemen. 27a And Moses stretched forth his hand over the sea.
28a And the waters returned, and covered the chariots, and the horsemen, even all the host of Pharaoh that went in after them into the sea. 29 But the children of Israel walked upon dry land in the midst of the sea; and the waters were a wall unto them on their right hand, and on their left.

29. ISRAELITES ARE FED WITH QUAILS AND BREAD. J29, 36.
Ex. 16$^{1-3.6-13a.15b-20.22-36}$

1 And they took their journey from Elim, and all the congregation of the children of Israel came unto the wilderness of Sin, which is between Elim and Sinai, on the fifteenth day of the second month after their departing out of the land of Egypt. 2 And the whole congregation of the children of Israel murmured against Moses and against Aaron in the wilderness: 3 and the children of Israel said unto them, Would that we had died by the hand of Jehovah in the land of Egypt, when we sat by the flesh-pots, when we did eat bread to the full; for ye have brought us forth into this wilderness, to kill this whole assembly with hunger.
6 And Moses and Aaron said unto all the children of Israel, At even, then ye shall know that Jehovah hath brought you out from the land of Egypt; 7 and in the morning, then ye shall see the glory of Jehovah; for that he heareth your murmurings against Jehovah: and what are we, that ye murmur against us? 8 And Moses said, *This shall be,* when Jehovah shall give you in the evening flesh to eat, and in the morning bread to the full; for that Jehovah heareth your murmurings which ye murmur against him: and what are we? your murmurings are not against us, but against Jehovah. 9 And Moses said unto Aaron, Say unto all the congregation of the children of Israel, Come near before Jehovah; for he hath heard your murmurings. 10 And it came to pass, as Aaron spake unto the whole congregation of the children of Israel, that they looked toward the wilderness, and, behold, the glory

---

[29] There is no consensus regarding the details of analysis in this chapter. E. g., Smend finds no P in vv. 16-36.

of Jehovah appeared in the cloud. 11 And Jehovah spake unto Moses, saying, 12 I have heard the murmurings of the children of Israel: speak unto them, saying, At even ye shall eat flesh, and in the morning ye shall be filled with bread; and ye shall know that I am Jehovah your God.

13 And it came to pass at even, that the quails came up, and covered the camp.

15b And Moses said unto them, It is the bread which Jehovah hath given you to eat. 16 This is the thing which Jehovah hath commanded. Gather ye of it every man according to his eating; an omer a head, according to the number of your persons, shall ye take it, every man for them that are in his tent. 17 And the children of Israel did so, and gathered some more, some less. 18 And when they measured it with an omer, he that gathered much had nothing over, and he that gathered little had no lack; they gathered every man according to his eating. 19 And Moses said unto them, Let no man leave of it till the morning. 20 Notwithstanding they hearkened not unto Moses; but some of them left of it until the morning, and it bred worms, and became foul: and Moses was wroth with them.

22 And it came to pass, that on the sixth day they gathered twice as much bread, two omers for each one: and all the rulers of the congregation came and told Moses. 23 And he said unto them, This is that which Jehovah hath spoken, To-morrow is a solemn rest, a holy sabbath unto Jehovah: bake that which ye will bake, and boil that which ye will boil; and all that remaineth over lay up for you to be kept until the morning. 24 And they laid it up till the morning, as Moses bade: and it did not become foul, neither was there any worm therein. 25 And Moses said, Eat that to-day; for to-day is a sabbath unto Jehovah: to-day ye shall not find it in the field. 26 Six days ye shall gather it; but on the seventh day is the sabbath, in it there shall be none. 27 And it came to pass on the seventh day, that there went out some of the people to gather, and they found none. 28 And Jehovah said unto Moses, How long refuse ye to keep my commandments and my laws? 29 See, for that Jehovah hath given you the sabbath, therefore he giveth you on the sixth day the bread of two days; abide ye every man in his place, let no man go out of his place on the seventh day. 30 So the people rested on the seventh day.

31 And the house of Israel called the name thereof Manna: and it was like coriander seed, white; and the taste of it was like wafers *made* with honey. 32 And Moses said, This is the thing which Jehovah hath commanded, Let an omerful of it

be kept throughout your generations, that they may see the bread wherewith I fed you in the wilderness, when I brought you forth from the land of Egypt. 33 And Moses said unto Aaron, Take a pot, and put an omerful of manna therein, and lay it up before Jehovah, to be kept throughout your generations. 34 As Jehovah commanded Moses, so Aaron laid it up before the Testimony, to be kept. 35 And the children of Israel did eat the manna forty years, until they came to a land inhabited; they did eat the manna, until they came unto the borders of the land of Canaan. 36 Now an omer is the tenth part of an ephah.

30. JOURNEY FROM THE WILDERNESS OF SIN TO THE WILDERNESS OF SINAI. P54, 79.

Ex. 17^{1a} 19^{2a-1}

1a And all the congregation of the children of Israel journeyed from the wilderness of Sin, by their journeys, according to the commandment of Jehovah, and encamped in Rephidim. 19^{2a} And when they were departed from Rephidim, and were come to the wilderness of Sinai, they encamped in the wilderness. 1 In the third month after the children of Israel were gone forth out of the land of Egypt, the same day came they into the wilderness of Sinai.

31. APPEARANCE OF JEHOVAH ON SINAI. J31. E22.

Ex. $24^{15b-18a}$

15b And the cloud covered the mount. 16 And the glory of Jehovah abode upon mount Sinai, and the cloud covered it six days: and the seventh day he called unto Moses out of the midst of the cloud. 17 And the appearance of the glory of Jehovah was like devouring fire on the top of the mount in the eyes of the children of Israel. 18a And Moses entered into the midst of the cloud.

32. INSTRUCTIONS FOR BUILDING THE TABERNACLE AND THE ARK. E28, 29.

Ex. 25^1-31^{11}

25 And Jehovah spake unto Moses, saying, 2 Speak unto the children of Israel, that they take for me an offering: of every man whose heart maketh him willing ye shall take my offering. 3 And this is the offering which ye shall take of them: gold, and silver, and brass, 4 and blue, and purple, and scarlet, and fine linen, and goats' *hair*, 5 and rams' skins dyed red, and sealskins, and acacia wood, 6 oil for the light, spices for the anointing oil, and for the sweet incense, 7 onyx stones, and stones to be set, for the ephod, and for the breast-

plate. 8 And let them make me a sanctuary, that I may dwell among them. 9 According to all that I show thee, the pattern of the tabernacle, and the pattern of all the furniture thereof, even so shall ye make it.

10 And they shall make an ark of acacia wood: two cubits and a half shall be the length thereof, and a cubit and a half the breadth thereof, and a cubit and a half the height thereof. 11 And thou shalt overlay it with pure gold, within and without shalt thou overlay it, and shalt make upon it a crown of gold round about. 12 And thou shalt cast four rings of gold for it, and put them in the four feet thereof; and two rings shall be on the one side of it, and two rings on the other side of it. 13 And thou shalt make staves of acacia wood, and overlay them with gold. 14 And thou shalt put the staves into the rings on the sides of the ark, wherewith to bear the ark. 15 The staves shall be in the rings of the ark: they shall not be taken from it. 16 And thou shalt put into the ark the testimony which I shall give thee. 17 And thou shalt make a mercy-seat of pure gold: two cubits and a half *shall be* the length thereof, and a cubit and a half the breadth thereof. 18 And thou shalt make two cherubim of gold; of beaten work shalt thou make them, at the two ends of the mercy-seat. 19 And make one cherub at the one end, and one cherub at the other end: of one piece with the mercy-seat shall ye make the cherubim on the two ends thereof. 20 And the cherubim shall spread out their wings on high, covering the mercy-seat with their wings, with their faces one to another; toward the mercy-seat shall the faces of the cherubim be. 21 And thou shalt put the mercy-seat above upon the ark; and in the ark thou shalt put the testimony that I shall give thee. 22 And there I will meet with thee, and I will commune with thee from above the mercy-seat, from between the two cherubim which are upon the ark of the testimony, of all things which I will give thee in commandment unto the children of Israel.

23 And thou shalt make a table of acacia wood: two cubits *shall be* the length thereof, and a cubit the breadth thereof, and a cubit and a half the height thereof. 24 And thou shalt overlay it with pure gold, and make thereto a crown of gold round about. 25 And thou shalt make unto it a border of a handbreadth round about; and thou shalt make a golden crown to the border thereof round about. 26 And thou shalt make for it four rings of gold, and put the rings in the four corners that are on the four feet thereof. 27 Close by the border shall the rings be, for places for the staves to bear the table. 28 And thou shalt make the staves of acacia wood, and overlay them with gold, that the table may be borne with them. 29 And

thou shalt make the dishes thereof, and the spoons thereof, and the flagons thereof, and the bowls thereof, wherewith to pour out: of pure gold shalt thou make them. 30 And thou shalt set upon the table showbread before me alway. 31 And thou shalt make a candlestick of pure gold: of beaten work shall the candlestick be made, even its base, and its shaft; its cups, its knops, and its flowers, shall be of one piece with it: 32 and there shall be six branches going out of the sides thereof; three branches of the candlestick out of the one side thereof, and three branches of the candlestick out of the other side thereof: 33 three cups made like almond-blossoms in one branch, a knop and a flower; and three cups made like almond-blossoms in the other branch, a knop and a flower: so for the six branches going out of the candlestick: 34 and in the candlestick four cups made like almond-blossoms, the knops thereof, and the flowers thereof; 35 and a knop under two branches of one piece with it, and a knop under two branches of one piece with it, and a knop under two branches of one piece with it, for the six branches going out of the candlestick. 36 Their knops and their branches shall be of one piece with it; the whole of it one beaten work of pure gold. 37 And thou shalt make the lamps thereof, seven: and they shall light the lamps thereof, to give light over against it. 38 And the snuffers thereof, and the snuffdishes thereof, shall be of pure gold. 39 Of a talent of pure gold shall it be made, with all these vessels. 40 And see that thou make them after their pattern, which hath been showed thee in the mount.

26 Moreover thou shalt make the tabernacle with ten curtains; of fine twined linen, and blue, and purple, and scarlet, with cherubim the work of the skilful workman shalt thou make them. 2 The length of each curtain shall be eight and twenty cubits, and the breadth of each curtain four cubits: all the curtains shall have one measure. 3 Five curtains shall be coupled together one to another; and *the other* five curtains shall be coupled one to another. 4 And thou shalt make loops of blue upon the edge of the one curtain from the selvedge in the coupling; and likewise shalt thou make in the edge of the curtain that is outmost in the second coupling. 5 Fifty loops shalt thou make in the one curtain, and fifty loops shalt thou make in the edge of the curtain that is in the second coupling; the loops shall be opposite one to another. 6 And thou shalt make fifty clasps of gold, and couple the curtains one to another with the clasps: and the tabernacle shall be one *whole*.

7 And thou shalt make curtains of goats' *hair* for a tent over the tabernacle: eleven curtains shalt thou make them. 8 The length of each curtain shall be thirty cubits, and the breadth

of each curtain four cubits: the eleven curtains shall have one measure. 9 And thou shalt couple five curtains by themselves, and six curtains by themselves, and shalt double over the sixth curtain in the forefront of the tent. 10 And thou shalt make fifty loops on the edge of the one curtain that is outmost in the coupling, and fifty loops upon the edge of the curtain which is *outmost in* the second coupling. 11 And thou shalt make fifty clasps of brass, and put the clasps into the loops, and couple the tent together, that it may be one. 12 And the overhanging part that remaineth of the curtains of the tent, the half curtain that remaineth, shall hang over the back of the tabernacle. 13 And the cubit on the one side, and the cubit on the other side, of that which remaineth in the length of the curtains of the tent, shall hang over the sides of the tabernacle on this side and on that side, to cover it. 14 And thou shalt make a covering for the tent of rams' skins dyed red, and a covering of sealskins above.

15 And thou shalt make the boards for the tabernacle of acacia wood, standing up. 16 Ten cubits shall be the length of a board, and a cubit and a half the breadth of each board. 17 Two tenons shall there be in each board, joined one to another: thus shalt thou make for all the boards of the tabernacle. 18 And thou shalt make the boards for the tabernacle, twenty boards for the south side southward. 19 And thou shalt make forty sockets of silver under the twenty boards; two sockets under one board for its two tenons, and two sockets under another board for its two tenons: 20 and for the second side of the tabernacle, on the north side, twenty boards, 21 and their forty sockets of silver; two sockets under one board, and two sockets under another board. 22 And for the hinder part of the tabernacle westward thou shalt make six boards. 23 And two boards shalt thou make for the corners of the tabernacle in the hinder part. 24 And they shall be double beneath, and in like manner they shall be entire unto the top thereof unto one ring: thus shall it be for them both; they shall be for the two corners. 25 And there shall be eight boards, and their sockets of silver, sixteen sockets; two sockets under one board, and two sockets under another board.

26 And thou shalt make bars of acacia wood; five for the boards of the one side of the tabernacle, 27 and five bars for the boards of the other side of the tabernacle, and five bars for the boards of the side of the tabernacle, for the hinder part westward. 28 And the middle bar in the midst of the boards shall pass through from end to end. 29 And thou shalt overlay the boards with gold, and make their rings of gold for places for the bars: and thou shalt overlay the bars with gold. 30 And

thou shalt rear up the tabernacle according to the fashion thereof which hath been showed thee in the mount.
31 And thou shalt make a veil of blue, and purple, and scarlet, and fine twined linen: with cherubim the work of the skilful workman shall it be made: 32 and thou shalt hang it upon four pillars of acacia overlaid with gold; their hooks *shall be* of gold, upon four sockets of silver. 33 And thou shalt hang up the veil under the clasps, and shalt bring in thither within the veil the ark of the testimony: and the veil shall separate unto you between the holy place and the most holy. 34 And thou shalt put the mercy-seat upon the ark of the testimony in the most holy place. 35 And thou shalt set the table without the veil, and the candlestick over against the table on the side of the tabernacle toward the south: and thou shalt put the table on the north side.
36 And thou shalt make a screen for the door of the Tent, of blue, and purple, and scarlet, and fine twined linen, the work of the embroiderer. 37 And thou shalt make for the screen five pillars of acacia, and overlay them with gold; their hooks shall be of gold: and thou shalt cast five sockets of brass for them.

27 And thou shalt make the altar of acacia wood, five cubits long, and five cubits broad; the altar shall be foursquare: and the height thereof shall be three cubits. 2 And thou shalt make the horns of it upon the four corners thereof; the horns thereof shall be of one piece with it: and thou shalt overlay it with brass. 3 And thou shalt make its pots to take away its ashes, and its shovels, and its basins, and its flesh-hooks, and its firepans: all the vessels thereof thou shalt make of brass. 4 And thou shalt make for it a grating of network of brass; and upon the net shalt thou make four brazen rings in the four corners thereof. 5 And thou shalt put it under the ledge round the altar beneath, that the net may reach halfway up the altar. 6 And thou shalt make staves for the altar, staves of acacia wood, and overlay them with brass. 7 And the staves thereof shall be put into the rings, and the staves shall be upon the two sides of the altar, in bearing it. 8 Hollow with planks shalt thou make it: as it hath been showed thee in the mount, so shall they make it.
9 And thou shalt make the court of the tabernacle: for the south side southward there shall be hangings for the court of fine twined linen a hundred cubits long for one side: 10 and the pillars thereof shall be twenty, and their sockets twenty, of brass; the hooks of the pillars and their fillets *shall be* of silver. 11 And likewise for the north side in length there shall be hangings a hundred cubits long, and the pillars thereof

twenty, and their sockets twenty, of brass; the hooks of the pillars, and their fillets, of silver. 12 And for the breadth of the court on the west side shall be hangings of fifty cubits; their pillars ten, and their sockets ten. 13 And the breadth of the court on the east side eastward shall be fifty cubits. 14 The hangings for the one side *of the gate* shall be fifteen cubits; their pillars three, and their sockets three. 15 And for the other side shall be hangings of fifteen cubits; their pillars three, and their sockets three. 16 And for the gate of the court shall be a screen of twenty cubits, of blue, and purple, and scarlet, and fine twined linen, the work of the embroiderer; their pillars four, and their sockets four. 17 All the pillars of the court round about shall be filleted with silver; their hooks of silver, and their sockets of brass. 18 The length of the court shall be a hundred cubits, and the breadth fifty every where, and the height five cubits, of fine twined linen, and their sockets of brass. 19 All the instruments of the tabernacle in all the service thereof, and all the pins thereof, and all the pins of the court, shall be of brass.

20 And thou shalt command the children of Israel, that they bring unto thee pure olive oil beaten for the light, to cause a lamp to burn continually. 21 In the tent of meeting, without the veil which is before the testimony, Aaron and his sons shall keep it in order from evening to morning before Jehovah: it shall be a statute for ever throughout their generations on the behalf of the children of Israel.

28 And bring thou near unto thee Aaron thy brother, and his sons with him, from among the children of Israel, that he may minister unto me in the priest's office, even Aaron, Nadab and Abihu, Eleazar and Ithamar, Aaron's sons. 2 And thou shalt make holy garments for Aaron thy brother, for glory and for beauty. 3 And thou shalt speak unto all that are wise-hearted, whom I have filled with the spirit of wisdom, that they make Aaron's garments to sanctify him, that he may minister unto me in the priest's office. 4 And these are the garments which they shall make: a breastplate, and an ephod, and a robe, and a coat of checker work, a mitre, and a girdle: and they shall make holy garments for Aaron thy brother, and his sons, that he may minister unto me in the priest's office. 5 And they shall take the gold, and the blue, and the purple, and the scarlet, and the fine linen.

6 And they shall make the ephod of gold, of blue, and purple, scarlet, and fine twined linen, the work of the skilful workman. 7 It shall have two shoulder-pieces joined to the two ends thereof, that it may be joined together. 8 And the skilfully woven band, which is upon it, wherewith to gird it on, shall be

like the work thereof *and* of the same piece; of gold, of blue, and purple, and scarlet, and fine twined linen. 9 And thou shalt take two onyx stones, and grave on them the names of the children of Israel: 10 six of their names on the one stone, and the names of the six that remain on the other stone, according to their birth. 11 With the work of an engraver in stone, like the engravings of a signet, shalt thou engrave the two stones, according to the names of the children of Israel: thou shalt make them to be inclosed in settings of gold. 12 And thou shalt put the two stones upon the shoulder-pieces of the ephod, to be stones of memorial for the children of Israel: and Aaron shall bear their names before Jehovah upon his two shoulders for a memorial. 13 And thou shalt make settings of gold, 14 and two chains of pure gold; like cords shalt thou make them of wreathen work: and thou shalt put the wreathen chains on the settings.

15 And thou shalt make a breastplate of judgment, the work of the skilful workman; like the work of the ephod thou shalt make it; of gold, of blue, and purple, and scarlet, and fine twined linen, shalt thou make it. 16 Foursquare it shall be *and* double; a span shall be the length thereof, and a span the breadth thereof. 17 And thou shalt set in it settings of stones, four rows of stones: a row of sardius, topaz, and carbuncle shall be the first row; 18 and the second row an emerald, a sapphire, and a diamond; 19 and the third row a jacinth, an agate, and an amethyst; 20 and the fourth row a beryl, and an onyx, and a jasper: they shall be inclosed in gold in their settings. 21 And the stones shall be according to the names of the children of Israel, twelve, according to their names; like the engravings of a signet, every one according to his name, they shall be for the twelve tribes. 22 And thou shalt make upon the breastplate chains like cords, of wreathen work of pure gold. 23 And thou shalt make upon the breastplate two rings of gold, and shalt put the two rings on the two ends of the breastplate. 24 And thou shalt put the two wreathen chains of gold in the two rings at the ends of the breastplate. 25 And the *other* two ends of the two wreathen chains thou shalt put on the two settings, and put them on the shoulder-pieces of the ephod in the forepart thereof. 26 And thou shalt make two rings of gold, and thou shalt put them upon the two ends of the breastplate, upon the edge thereof, which is toward the side of the ephod inward. 27 And thou shalt make two rings of gold, and shalt put them on the two shoulder-pieces of the ephod underneath, in the forepart thereof, close by the coupling thereof, above the skilfully woven band of the ephod. 28 And they shall bind the breastplate by the rings

thereof unto the rings of the ephod with a lace of blue, that it may be upon the skilfully woven band of the ephod, and that the breastplate be not loosed from the ephod. 29 And Aaron shall bear the names of the children of Israel in the breastplate of judgment upon his heart, when he goeth in unto the holy place, for a memorial before Jehovah continually. 30 And thou shalt put in the breastplate of judgment the Urim and the Thummim; and they shall be upon Aaron's heart, when he goeth in before Jehovah: and Aaron shall bear the judgment of the children of Israel upon his heart before Jehovah continually.
  31 And thou shalt make the robe of the ephod all of blue. 32 And it shall have a hole for the head in the midst thereof: it shall have a binding of woven work round about the hole of it, as it were the hole of a coat of mail, that it be not rent. 33 And upon the skirts of it thou shalt make pomegranates of blue, and of purple, and of scarlet, round about the skirts thereof; and bells of gold between them round about: 34 a golden bell and a pomegranate, a golden bell and a pomegranate, upon the skirts of the robe round about. 35 And it shall be upon Aaron to minister: and the sound thereof shall be heard when he goeth in unto the holy place before Jehovah, and when he cometh out, that he die not.
  36 And thou shalt make a plate of pure gold, and grave upon it, like the engravings of a signet, HOLY TO JEHOVAH. 37 And thou shalt put it on a lace of blue, and it shall be upon the mitre; upon the forefront of the mitre it shall be. 38 And it shall be upon Aaron's forehead, and Aaron shall bear the iniquity of the holy things, which the children of Israel shall hallow in all their holy gifts; and it shall be always upon his forehead, that they may be accepted before Jehovah. 39 And thou shalt weave the coat in checker work of fine linen, and thou shalt make a mitre of fine linen, and thou shalt make a girdle, the work of the embroiderer.
  40 And for Aaron's sons thou shalt make coats, and thou shalt make for them girdles, and head-tires shalt thou make for them, for glory and for beauty. 41 And thou shalt put them upon Aaron thy brother, and upon his sons with him, and shalt anoint them, and consecrate them, and sanctify them, that they may minister unto me in the priest's office. 42 And thou shalt make them linen breeches to cover the flesh of their nakedness; from the loins even unto the thighs they shall reach: 43 and they shall be upon Aaron, and upon his sons, when they go in unto the tent of meeting, or when they come near unto the altar to minister in the holy place; that they bear not iniquity, and die: it shall be a statute for ever unto him and unto his seed after him.

29 And this is the thing that thou shalt do unto them to hallow them, to minister unto me in the priest's office: take one young bullock and two rams without blemish, 2 and unleavened bread, and cakes unleavened mingled with oil, and wafers unleavened anointed with oil: of fine wheaten flour shalt thou make them. 3 And thou shalt put them into one basket, and bring them in the basket, with the bullock and the two rams. 4 And Aaron and his sons thou shalt bring unto the door of the tent of meeting, and shalt wash them with water. 5 And thou shalt take the garments, and put upon Aaron the coat, and the robe of the ephod, and the ephod, and the breastplate, and gird him with the skilfully woven band of the ephod; 6 and thou shalt set the mitre upon his head, and put the holy crown upon the mitre. 7 Then shalt thou take the anointing oil, and pour it upon his head, and anoint him. 8 And thou shalt bring his sons, and put coats upon them. 9 And thou shalt gird them with girdles, Aaron and his sons, and bind headtires on them: and they shall have the priesthood by a perpetual statute: and thou shalt consecrate Aaron and his sons.

10 And thou shalt bring the bullock before the tent of meeting: and Aaron and his sons shall lay their hands upon the head of the bullock. 11 And thou shalt kill the bullock before Jehovah, at the door of the tent of meeting. 12 And thou shalt take of the blood of the bullock, and put it upon the horns of the altar with thy finger; and thou shalt pour out all the blood at the base of the altar. 13 And thou shalt take all the fat that covereth the inwards, and the caul upon the liver, and the two kidneys, and the fat that is upon them, and burn them upon the altar. 14 But the flesh of the bullock, and its skin, and its dung, shalt thou burn with fire without the camp: it is a sin-offering.

15 Thou shalt also take the one ram; and Aaron and his sons shall lay their hands upon the head of the ram. 16 And thou shalt slay the ram, and thou shalt take its blood, and sprinkle it round about upon the altar. 17 And thou shalt cut the ram into its pieces, and wash its inwards, and its legs, and put them with its pieces, and with its head. 18 And thou shalt burn the whole ram upon the altar: it is a burnt-offering unto Jehovah; it is a sweet savor, an offering made by fire unto Jehovah.

19 And thou shalt take the other ram; and Aaron and his sons shall lay their hands upon the head of the ram. 20 Then shalt thou kill the ram, and take of its blood, and put it upon the tip of the right ear of Aaron, and upon the tip of the right ear of his sons, and upon the thumb of their right hand, and upon the great toe of their right foot, and sprinkle the blood upon the altar round about. 21 And thou shalt take of the

blood that is upon the altar, and of the anointing oil, and sprinkle it upon Aaron, and upon his garments, and upon his sons, and upon the garments of his sons with him: and he shall be hallowed, and his garments, and his sons, and his sons' garments with him. 22 Also thou shalt take of the ram the fat, and the fat tail, and the fat that covereth the inwards, and the caul of the liver, and the two kidneys, and the fat that is upon them, and the right thigh (for it is a ram of consecration), 23 and one loaf of bread, and one cake of oiled bread, and one wafer, out of the basket of unleavened bread that is before Jehovah: 24 and thou shalt put the whole upon the hands of Aaron, and upon the hands of his sons, and shalt wave them for a wave-offering before Jehovah. 25 And thou shalt take them from their hands, and burn them on the altar upon the burnt-offering, for a sweet savor before Jehovah: it is an offering made by fire unto Jehovah.

26 And thou shalt take the breast of Aaron's ram of consecration, and wave it for a wave-offering before Jehovah: and it shall be thy portion. 27 And thou shalt sanctify the breast of the wave-offering, and the thigh of the heave-offering, which is waved, and which is heaved up, of the ram of consecration, even of that which is for Aaron, and of that which is for his sons: 28 and it shall be for Aaron and his sons as *their* portion for ever from the children of Israel; for it is a heave-offering: and it shall be a heave-offering from the children of Israel of the sacrifices of their peace-offerings, even their heave-offering unto Jehovah.

29 And the holy garments of Aaron shall be for his sons after him, to be anointed in them, and to be consecrated in them. 30 Seven days shall the son that is priest in his stead put them on, when he cometh into the tent of meeting to minister in the holy place.

31 And thou shalt take the ram of consecration, and boil its flesh in a holy place. 32 And Aaron and his sons shall eat the flesh of the ram, and the bread that is in the basket, at the door of the tent of meeting. 33 And they shall eat those things wherewith atonement was made, to consecrate *and* to sanctify them: but a stranger shall not eat thereof, because they are holy. 34 And if aught of the flesh of the consecration, or of the bread, remain unto the morning, then thou shalt burn the remainder with fire: it shall not be eaten, because it is holy.

35 And thus shalt thou do unto Aaron, and to his sons, according to all that I have commanded thee: seven days shalt thou consecrate them. 36 And every day shalt thou offer the bullock of sin-offering for atonement: and thou shalt cleanse the altar, when thou makest atonement for it; and thou shalt

anoint it, to sanctify it. 37 Seven days thou shalt make atonement for the altar, and sanctify it: and the altar shall be most holy; whatsoever toucheth the altar shall be holy. 38 Now this is that which thou shalt offer upon the altar: two lambs a year old day by day continually. 39 The one lamb thou shalt offer in the morning; and the other lamb thou shalt offer at even: 40 and with the one lamb a tenth part *of an ephah* of fine flour mingled with the fourth part of a hin of beaten oil; and the fourth part of a hin of wine for a drink-offering. 41 And the other lamb thou shalt offer at even, and shalt do thereto according to the meal-offering of the morning, and according to the drink-offering thereof, for a sweet savor, an offering made by fire unto Jehovah. 42 It shall be a continual burnt-offering throughout your generations at the door of the tent of meeting before Jehovah, where I will meet with you, to speak there unto thee. 43 And there I will meet with the children of Israel; and *the Tent* shall be sanctified by my glory. 44 And I will sanctify the tent of meeting, and the altar: Aaron also and his sons will I sanctify, to minister to me in the priest's office. 45 And I will dwell among the children of Israel, and will be their God. 46 And they shall know that I am Jehovah their God, that brought them forth out of the land of Egypt, that I might dwell among them: I am Jehovah their God.

30 And thou shalt make an altar to burn incense upon: of acacia wood shalt thou make it. 2 A cubit shall be the length thereof, and a cubit the breadth thereof; foursquare shall it be; and two cubits shall be the height thereof: the horns thereof shall be of one piece with it. 3 And thou shalt overlay it with pure gold, the top thereof, and the sides thereof round about, and the horns thereof; and thou shalt make unto it a crown of gold round about. 4 And two golden rings shalt thou make for it under the crown thereof; upon the two ribs thereof, upon the two sides of it shalt thou make them; and they shall be for places for staves wherewith to bear it. 5 And thou shalt make the staves of acacia wood, and overlay them with gold. 6 And thou shalt put it before the veil that is by the ark of the testimony, before the mercy-seat that is over the testimony, where I will meet with thee. 7 And Aaron shall burn thereof incense of sweet spices: every morning, when he dresseth the lamps, he shall burn it. 8 And when Aaron lighteth the lamps at even, he shall burn it, a perpetual incense before Jehovah throughout your generations. 9 Ye shall offer no strange incense thereon, nor burnt-offering, nor meal-offering; and ye shall pour no drink-offering thereon. 10 And Aaron shall make atonement upon the horns of it once in the

year; with the blood of the sin-offering of atonement once in the year shall he make atonement for it throughout your generations: it is most holy unto Jehovah.

11 And Jehovah spake unto Moses, saying, 12 When thou takest the sum of the children of Israel, according to those that are numbered of them, then shall they give every man a ransom for his soul unto Jehovah, when thou numberest them; that there be no plague among them, when thou numberest them. 13 This they shall give, every one that passeth over unto them that are numbered: half a shekel after the shekel of the sanctuary (the shekel is twenty gerahs), half a shekel for an offering to Jehovah. 14 Every one that passeth over unto them that are numbered, from twenty years old and upward, shall give the offering of Jehovah. 15 The rich shall not give more, and the poor shall not give less, than the half shekel, when they give the offering of Jehovah, to make atonement for your souls. 16 And thou shalt take the atonement money from the children of Israel, and shalt appoint it for the service of the tent of meeting; that it may be a memorial for the children of Israel before Jehovah, to make atonement for your souls.

17 And Jehovah spake unto Moses, saying, 18 Thou shalt also make a laver of brass, and the base thereof of brass, whereat to wash. And thou shalt put it between the tent of meeting and the altar, and thou shalt put water therein. 19 And Aaron and his sons shall wash their hands and their feet thereat: 20 when they go into the tent of meeting, they shall wash with water, that they die not; or when they come near to the altar to minister, to burn an offering made by fire unto Jehovah. 21 So they shall wash their hands and their feet, that they die not: and it shall be a statute for ever to them, even to him and to his seed throughout their generations.

22 Moreover Jehovah spake unto Moses, saying, 23 Take thou also unto thee the chief spices: of flowing myrrh five hundred *shekels*, and of sweet cinnamon half so much, even two hundred and fifty, and of sweet calamus two hundred and fifty, 24 and of cassia five hundred, after the shekel of the sanctuary, and of olive oil a hin; 25 and thou shalt make it a holy anointing oil, a perfume compounded after the art of the perfumer: it shall be a holy anointing oil. 26 And thou shalt anoint therewith the tent of meeting, and the ark of the testimony, 27 and the table and all the vessels thereof, and the candlestick and the vessels thereof, and the altar of incense, 28 and the altar of burnt-offering with all the vessels thereof, and the laver and the base thereof. 29 And thou shalt sanctify them, that they may be most holy: whatsoever toucheth

them shall be holy. 30 And thou shalt anoint Aaron and his sons, and sanctify them, that they may minister unto me in the priest's office. 31 And thou shalt speak unto the children of Israel, saying, This shall be a holy anointing oil unto me throughout your generations. 32 Upon the flesh of man shall it not be poured, neither shall ye make any like it, according to the composition thereof: it is holy, *and* it shall be holy unto you. 33 Whosoever compoundeth any like it, or whosoever putteth any of it upon a stranger, he shall be cut off from his people.

34 And Jehovah said unto Moses, Take unto thee sweet spices, stacte, and onycha, and galbanum; sweet spices with pure frankincense: of each shall there be a like weight; 35 and thou shalt make of it incense, a perfume after the art of the perfumer, seasoned with salt, pure *and* holy: 36 and thou shalt beat some of it very small, and put of it before the testimony in the tent of meeting, where I will meet with thee: it shall be unto you most holy. 37 And the incense which thou shalt make, according to the composition thereof ye shall not make for yourselves: it shall be unto thee holy for Jehovah. 38 Whosoever shall make like unto that, to smell thereof, he shall be cut off from his people.

31 And Jehovah spake unto Moses, saying, 2 See, I have called by name Bezalel the son of Uri, the son of Hur, of the tribe of Judah: 3 and I have filled him with the Spirit of God, in wisdom, and in understanding, and in knowledge, and in all manner of workmanship, 4 to devise skilful works, to work in gold, and in silver, and in brass, 5 and in cutting of stones for setting, and in carving of wood, to work in all manner of workmanship. 6 And I, behold, I have appointed with him Oholiab, the son of Ahisamach, of the tribe of Dan; and in the hearts of all that are wise-hearted I have put wisdom, that they may make all that I have commanded thee: 7 the tent of meeting, and the ark of the testimony, and the mercy-seat that is thereupon, and all the furniture of the Tent, 8 and the table and its vessels, and the pure candlestick with all its vessels, and the altar of incense, 9 and the altar of burnt-offering with all its vessels, and the laver and its base, 10 and the finely wrought garments, and the holy garments for Aaron the priest, and the garments of his sons, to minister in the priest's office, 11 and the anointing oil, and the incense of sweet spices for the holy place: according to all that I have commanded thee shall they do.

33. THE LAW OF THE SABBATH. P1, 60.
Ex. 31^{12-17}

12 And Jehovah spake unto Moses, saying, 13 Speak thou

also unto the children of Israel, saying, Verily ye shall keep my sabbaths: for it is a sign between me and you throughout your generations; that ye may know that I am Jehovah who sanctifieth you. 14 Ye shall keep the sabbath therefore; for it is holy unto you: every one that profaneth it shall surely be put to death; for whosoever doeth any work therein, that soul shall be cut off from among his people. 15 Six days shall work be done; but on the seventh day is a sabbath of solemn rest, holy to Jehovah; whosoever doeth any work on the sabbath day, he shall surely be put to death. 16 Wherefore the children of Israel shall keep the sabbath, to observe the sabbath throughout their generations, for a perpetual covenant. 17 It is a sign between me and the children of Israel for ever: for in six days Jehovah made heaven and earth, and on the seventh day he rested, and was refreshed.

34. How Moses Communed with God. E29.

Ex. 31^{18*} 34^{29-35}

31^{18*} ... When he had made an end of communing with him upon mount Sinai ..., 34^{29} and it came to pass, when Moses came down from mount Sinai with the two tables of the testimony in Moses' hand, when he came down from the mount, that Moses knew not that the skin of his face shone by reason of his speaking with him. 30 And when Aaron and all the children of Israel saw Moses, behold, the skin of his face shone; and they were afraid to come nigh him. 31 And Moses called unto them; and Aaron and all the rulers of the congregation returned unto him: and Moses spake to them. 32 And afterward all the children of Israel came nigh: and he gave them in commandment all that Jehovah had spoken with him in mount Sinai. 33 And when Moses had done speaking with them, he put a veil on his face. 34 But when Moses went in before Jehovah to speak with him, he took the veil off, until he came out; and he came out, and spake unto the children of Israel that which he was commanded. 35 And the children of Israel saw the face of Moses, that the skin of Moses' face shone; and Moses put the veil upon his face again, until he went in to speak with him.

35. Moses Carries Out the Divine Commands Regarding the Sabbath, the Tabernacle, and the Ark. P32, 33.

Ex. 35^1-40^{33}

35 And Moses assembled all the congregation of the children of Israel, and said unto them, These are the words which Jehovah hath commanded, that ye should do them.

---

[35] Largely a verbatim repetition of P32, 33. It is generally recognized as secondary (Ps).

2 Six days shall work be done; but on the seventh day there shall be to you a holy day, a sabbath of solemn rest to Jehovah: whosoever doeth any work therein shall be put to death. 3 Ye shall kindle no fire throughout your habitations upon the sabbath day.

4 And Moses spake unto all the congregation of the children of Israel, saying, This is the thing which Jehovah commanded, saying, 5 Take ye from among you an offering unto Jehovah; whosoever is of a willing heart, let him bring it, Jehovah's offering: gold, and silver, and brass, 6 and blue, and purple, and scarlet, and fine linen, and goats' *hair*, 7 and rams' skins dyed red, and sealskins, and acacia wood, 8 and oil for the light, and spices for the anointing oil, and for the sweet incense, 9 and onyx stones, and stones to be set, for the ephod, and for the breastplate.

10 And let every wise-hearted man among you come, and make all that Jehovah hath commanded: 11 the tabernacle, its tent, and its covering, its clasps, and its boards, its bars, its pillars, and its sockets; 12 the ark, and the staves thereof, the mercy-seat, and the veil of the screen; 13 the table, and its staves, and all its vessels, and the showbread; 14 the candlestick also for the light, and its vessels, and its lamps, and the oil for the light; 15 and the altar of incense, and its staves, and the anointing oil, and the sweet incense, and the screen for the door, at the door of the tabernacle; 16 the altar of burnt-offering, with its grating of brass, its staves, and all its vessels, the laver and its base; 17 the hangings of the court, the pillars thereof, and their sockets, and the screen for the gate of the court; 18 the pins of the tabernacle, and the pins of the court, and their cords; 19 the finely wrought garments, for ministering in the holy place, the holy garments for Aaron the priest, and the garments of his sons, to minister in the priest's office.

20 And all the congregation of the children of Israel departed from the presence of Moses. 21 And they came, every one whose heart stirred him up, and every one whom his spirit made willing, *and* brought Jehovah's offering, for the work of the tent of meeting, and for all the service thereof, and for the holy garments. 22 And they came, both men and women, as many as were willing-hearted, *and* brought brooches, and earrings, and signet-rings, and armlets, all jewels of gold; even every man that offered an offering of gold unto Jehovah. 23 And every man, with whom was found blue, and purple, and scarlet, and fine linen, and goats' *hair*, and rams' skins dyed red, and sealskins, brought them. 24 Every one that did offer an offering of silver and brass brought Jehovah's

offering; and every man, with whom was found acacia wood for any work of the service, brought it. 25 And all the women that were wise-hearted did spin with their hands, and brought that which they had spun, the blue, and the purple, the scarlet, and the fine linen. 26 And all the women whose heart stirred them up in wisdom spun the goats' *hair*. 27 And the rulers brought the onyx stones, and the stones to be set, for the ephod, and for the breastplate; 28 and the spice, and the oil; for the light, and for the anointing oil, and for the sweet incense. 29 The children of Israel brought a freewill-offering unto Jehovah; every man and woman, whose heart made them willing to bring for all the work, which Jehovah had commanded to be made by Moses.

30 And Moses said unto the children of Israel, See, Jehovah hath called by name Bezalel the son of Uri, the son of Hur, of the tribe of Judah; 31 and he hath filled him with the Spirit of God, in wisdom, in understanding, and in knowledge, and in all manner of workmanship; 32 and to devise skilful works, to work in gold, and in silver, and in brass, 33 and in cutting of stones for setting, and in carving of wood, to work in all manner of skilful workmanship. 34 And he hath put in his heart that he may teach, both he, and Oholiab, the son of Ahisamach, of the tribe of Dan. 35 Them hath he filled with wisdom of heart, to work all manner of workmanship, of the engraver, and of the skilful workman, and of the embroiderer, in blue, and in purple, in scarlet, and in fine linen, and of the weaver, even of them that do any workmanship, and of those that devise skilful works.

36 And Bezalel and Oholiab shall work, and every wise-hearted man, in whom Jehovah hath put wisdom and understanding to know how to work all the work for the service of the sanctuary, according to all that Jehovah hath commanded.

2 And Moses called Bezalel and Oholiab, and every wise-hearted man, in whose heart Jehovah had put wisdom, even every one whose heart stirred him up to come unto the work to do it: 3 and they received of Moses all the offering which the children of Israel had brought for the work of the service of the sanctuary, wherewith to make it. And they brought yet unto him freewill-offerings every morning. 4 And all the wise men that wrought all the work of the sanctuary, came every man from his work which they wrought; 5 and they spake unto Moses, saying, The people bring much more than enough for the service of the work which Jehovah commanded to make. 6 And Moses gave commandment, and they caused it to be proclaimed throughout the camp, saying, Let neither

man nor woman make any more work for the offering of the sanctuary. So the people were restrained from bringing. 7 For the stuff they had was sufficient for all the work to make it, and too much.

8 And all the wise-hearted men among them that wrought the work made the tabernacle with ten curtains; of fine twined linen, and blue, and purple, and scarlet, with cherubim, the work of the skilful workman, *Bezalel* made them. 9 The length of each curtain was eight and twenty cubits, and the breadth of each curtain four cubits: all the curtains had one measure. 10 And he coupled five curtains one to another: and *the other* five curtains he coupled one to another. 11 And he made loops of blue upon the edge of the one curtain from the selvedge in the coupling: likewise he made in the edge of the curtain that was outmost in the second coupling. 12 Fifty loops made he in the one curtain, and fifty loops made he in the edge of the curtain that was in the second coupling: the loops were opposite one to another. 13 And he made fifty clasps of gold, and coupled the curtains one to another with the clasps: so the tabernacle was one.

14 And he made curtains of goats' *hair* for a tent over the tabernacle: eleven curtains he made them. 15 The length of each curtain was thirty cubits, and four cubits the breadth of each curtain: the eleven curtains had one measure. 16 And he coupled five curtains by themselves, and six curtains by themselves. 17 And he made fifty loops on the edge of the curtain that was outmost in the coupling, and fifty loops made he upon the edge of the curtain which was *outmost in* the second coupling. 18 And he made fifty clasps of brass to couple the tent together, that it might be one. 19 And he made a covering for the tent of rams' skins dyed red, and a covering of sealskins above.

20 And he made the boards for the tabernacle, of acacia wood, standing up. 21 Ten cubits was the length of a board, and a cubit and a half the breadth of each board. 22 Each board had two tenons, joined one to another: thus did he make for all the boards of the tabernacle. 23 And he made the boards for the tabernacle: twenty boards for the south side southward; 24 and he made forty sockets of silver under the twenty boards; two sockets under one board for its two tenons, and two sockets under another board for its two tenons. 25 And for the second side of the tabernacle, on the north side, he made twenty boards, 26 and their forty sockets of silver; two sockets under one board, and two sockets under another board. 27 And for the hinder part of the tabernacle westward he made six boards. 28 And two boards made he for the cor-

ners of the tabernacle in the hinder part. 29 And they were double beneath; and in like manner they were entire unto the top thereof unto one ring: thus he did to both of them in the two corners. 30 And there were eight boards, and their sockets of silver, sixteen sockets; under every board two sockets.

31 And he made bars of acacia wood; five for the boards of the one side of the tabernacle, 32 and five bars for the boards of the other side of the tabernacle, and five bars for the boards of the tabernacle for the hinder part westward. 33 And he made the middle bar to pass through in the midst of the boards from the one end to the other. 34 And he overlaid the boards with gold, and made their rings of gold for places for the bars, and overlaid the bars with gold.

35 And he made the veil of blue, and purple, and scarlet, and fine twined linen: with cherubim, the work of the skilful workman, made he it. 36 And he made thereunto four pillars of acacia, and overlaid them with gold: their hooks were of gold; and he cast for them four sockets of silver. 37 And he made a screen for the door of the Tent, of blue, and purple, and scarlet, and fine twined linen, the work of the embroiderer; 38 and the five pillars of it with their hooks: and he overlaid their capitals and their fillets with gold; and their five sockets were of brass.

37 And Bezalel made the ark of acacia wood: two cubits and a half was the length of it, and a cubit and a half the breadth of it, and a cubit and a half the height of it. 2 And he overlaid it with pure gold within and without, and made a crown of gold to it round about. 3 And he cast for it four rings of gold, in the four feet thereof; even two rings on the one side of it, and two rings on the other side of it. 4 And he made staves of acacia wood, and overlaid them with gold. 5 And he put the staves into the rings on the sides of the ark, to bear the ark. 6 And he made a mercy-seat of pure gold: two cubits and a half *was* the length thereof, and a cubit and a half the breadth thereof. 7 And he made two cherubim of gold; of beaten work made he them, at the two ends of the mercy-seat; 8 one cherub at the one end, and one cherub at the other end: of one piece with the mercy-seat made he the cherubim at the two ends thereof. 9 And the cherubim spread out their wings on high, covering the mercy-seat with their wings, with their faces one to another; toward the mercy-seat were the faces of the cherubim.

10 And he made the table of acacia wood: two cubits *was* the length thereof, and a cubit the breadth thereof, and a cubit and a half the height thereof. 11 And he overlaid it with pure gold, and made thereto a crown of gold round about.

12 And he made unto it a border of a handbreadth round about, and made a golden crown to the border thereof round about. 13 And he cast for it four rings of gold, and put the rings in the four corners that were on the four feet thereof. 14 Close by the border were the rings, the places for the staves to bear the table. 15 And he made the staves of acacia wood, and overlaid them with gold, to bear the table. 16 And he made the vessels which were upon the table, the dishes thereof, and the spoons thereof, and the bowls thereof, and the flagons thereof, wherewith to pour out, of pure gold.

17 And he made the candlestick of pure gold: of beaten work made he the candlestick, even its base, and its shaft; its cups, its knops, and its flowers, were of one piece with it. 18 And there were six branches going out of the sides thereof; three branches of the candlestick out of the one side thereof, and three branches of the candlestick out of the other side thereof: 19 three cups made like almond-blossoms in one branch, a knop and a flower; and three cups made like almond-blossoms in the other branch, a knop and a flower: so for the six branches going out of the candlestick. 20 And in the candlestick were four cups made like almond-blossoms, the knops thereof, and the flowers thereof; 21 and a knop under two branches of one piece with it, and a knop under two branches of one piece with it, and a knop under two branches of one piece with it, for the six branches going out of it. 22 Their knops and their branches were of one piece with it: the whole of it was one beaten work of pure gold. 23 And he made the lamps thereof, seven, and the snuffers thereof, and the snuff-dishes thereof, of pure gold. 24 Of a talent of pure gold made he it, and all the vessels thereof.

25 And he made the altar of incense of acacia wood: a cubit was the length thereof, and a cubit the breadth thereof, four-square; and two cubits was the height thereof; the horns thereof were of one piece with it. 26 And he overlaid it with pure gold, the top thereof, and the sides thereof round about, and the horns of it: and he made unto it a crown of gold round about. 27 And he made for it two golden rings under the crown thereof, upon the two ribs thereof, upon the two sides of it, for places for staves wherewith to bear it. 28 And he made the staves of acacia wood, and overlaid them with gold. 29 And he made the holy anointing oil, and the pure incense of sweet spices, after the art of the perfumer.

38 And he made the altar of burnt-offering of acacia wood: five cubits was the length thereof, and five cubits the breadth thereof, foursquare; and three cubits the height thereof. 2 And he made the horns thereof upon the four corners of it; the horns thereof were of one piece with it: and he overlaid it with brass. 3 And he made all the vessels of the altar, the pots, and the shovels, and the basins, the flesh-hooks, and the firepans: all the vessels thereof made he of brass. 4 And he made for the altar a grating of network of brass, under the ledge round it beneath, reaching halfway up. 5 And he cast four rings for the four ends of the grating of brass, to be places for the staves. 6 And he made the staves of acacia wood, and overlaid them with brass. 7 And he put the staves into the rings on the sides of the altar, wherewith to bear it; he made it hollow with planks.

8 And he made the laver of brass, and the base thereof of brass, of the mirrors of the ministering women that ministered at the door of the tent of meeting.

9 And he made the court: for the south side southward the hangings of the court were of fine twined linen, a hundred cubits; 10 their pillars were twenty, and their sockets twenty, of brass; the hooks of the pillars and their fillets were of silver. 11 And for the north side a hundred cubits, their pillars twenty, and their sockets twenty, of brass; the hooks of the pillars, and their fillets, of silver. 12 And for the west side were hangings of fifty cubits, their pillars ten, and their sockets ten; the hooks of the pillars, and their fillets, of silver. 13 And for the east side eastward fifty cubits. 14 The hangings for the one side *of the gate* were fifteen cubits; their pillars three, and their sockets three; 15 and so for the other side: on this hand and that hand by the gate of the court were hangings of fifteen cubits; their pillars three, and their sockets three. 16 All the hangings of the court round about were of fine twined linen. 17 And the sockets for the pillars were of brass; the hooks of the pillars, and their fillets, of silver; and the overlaying of their capitals, of silver; and all the pillars of the court were filleted with silver. 18 And the screen for the gate of the court was the work of the embroiderer, of blue, and purple, and scarlet, and fine twined linen: and twenty cubits was the length, and the height in the breadth was five cubits, answerable to the hangings of the court. 19 And their pillars were four, and their sockets four, of brass; their hooks of silver, and the overlaying of their capitals, and their fillets, of silver. 20 And all the pins of the tabernacle, and of the court round about, were of brass.

21 This is the sum of *the things for* the tabernacle, even the tabernacle of the testimony, as they were counted, according to the commandment of Moses, for the service of the Levites, by the hand of Ithamar, the son of Aaron the priest. 22 And Bezalel the son of Uri, the son of Hur, of the tribe of Judah,

made all that Jehovah commanded Moses. 23 And with him was Oholiab, the son of Ahisamach, of the tribe of Dan, an engraver, and a skilful workman, and an embroiderer in blue, and in purple, and in scarlet, and in fine linen.

24 All the gold that was used for the work in all the work of the sanctuary, even the gold of the offering, was twenty and nine talents, and seven hundred and thirty shekels, after the shekel of the sanctuary. 25 And the silver of them that were numbered of the congregation was a hundred talents, and a thousand seven hundred and threescore and fifteen shekels, after the shekel of the sanctuary: 26 a beka a head, *that is*, half a shekel, after the shekel of the sanctuary, for every one that passed over to them that were numbered, from twenty years old and upward, for six hundred thousand and three thousand and five hundred and fifty men. 27 And the hundred talents of silver were for casting the sockets of the sanctuary, and the sockets of the veil; a hundred sockets for the hundred talents, a talent for a socket. 28 And of the thousand seven hundred seventy and five *shekels* he made hooks for the pillars, and overlaid their capitals, and made fillets for them. 29 And the brass of the offering was seventy talents, and two thousand and four hundred shekels. 30 And therewith he made the sockets to the door of the tent of meeting, and the brazen altar, and the brazen grating for it, and all the vessels of the altar, 31 and the sockets of the court round about, and the sockets of the gate of the court, and all the pins of the tabernacle, and all the pins of the court round about.

39 And of the blue, and purple, and scarlet, they made finely wrought garments, for ministering in the holy place, and made the holy garments for Aaron; as Jehovah commanded Moses.

2 And he made the ephod of gold, blue, and purple, and scarlet, and fine twined linen. 3 And they did beat the gold into thin plates, and cut it into wires, to work it in the blue, and in the purple, and in the scarlet, and in the fine linen, the work of the skilful workman. 4 They made shoulder-pieces for it, joined together; at the two ends was it joined together. 5 And the skilfully woven band, that was upon it, wherewith to gird it on, was of the same piece *and* like the work thereof; of gold, of blue, and purple, and scarlet, and fine twined linen; as Jehovah commanded Moses.

6 And they wrought the onyx stones, inclosed in settings of gold, graven with the engravings of a signet, according to the names of the children of Israel. 7 And he put them on the shoulder-pieces of the ephod, to be stones of memorial for the children of Israel; as Jehovah commanded Moses.

8 And he made the breastplate, the work of the skilful workman, like the work of the ephod; of gold, of blue, and purple, and scarlet, and fine twined linen. 9 It was foursquare; they made the breastplate double: a span was the length thereof, and a span the breadth thereof, being double. 10 And they set in it four rows of stones. A row of sardius, topaz, and carbuncle was the first row; 11 and the second row, an emerald, a sapphire, and a diamond; 12 and the third row, a jacinth, an agate, and an amethyst; 13 and the fourth row, a beryl, an onyx, and a jasper: they were inclosed in inclosings of gold in their settings. 14 And the stones were according to the names of the children of Israel, twelve, according to their names; like the engravings of a signet, every one according to his name, for the twelve tribes. 15 And they made upon the breastplate chains like cords, of wreathen work of pure gold. 16 And they made two settings of gold, and two gold rings, and put the two rings on the two ends of the breastplate. 17 And they put the two wreathen chains of gold in the two rings at the ends of the breastplate. 18 And the *other* two ends of the two wreathen chains they put on the two settings, and put them on the shoulder-pieces of the ephod, in the forepart thereof. 19 And they made two rings of gold, and put them upon the two ends of the breastplate, upon the edge thereof, which was toward the side of the ephod inward. 20 And they made two rings of gold, and put them on the two shoulder-pieces of the ephod underneath, in the forepart thereof, close by the coupling thereof, above the skilfully woven band of the ephod. 21 And they did bind the breastplate by the rings thereof unto the rings of the ephod with a lace of blue, that it might be upon the skilfully woven band of the ephod, and that the breastplate might not be loosed from the ephod; as Jehovah commanded Moses.

22 And he made the robe of the ephod of woven work, all of blue; 23 and the hole of the robe in the midst thereof, as the hole of a coat of mail, with a binding round about the hole of it, that it should not be rent. 24 And they made upon the skirts of the robe pomegranates of blue, and purple, and scarlet, *and* twined *linen,* 25 And they made bells of pure gold, and put the bells between the pomegranates upon the skirts of the robe around about, between the pomegranates; 26 a bell and a pomegranate, a bell and a pomegranate, upon the skirts of the robe round about, to minister in; as Jehovah commanded Moses.

27 And they made the coats of fine linen of woven work for Aaron, and for his sons, 28 and the mitre of fine linen, and the goodly head-tires of fine linen, and the linen breeches of

fine twined linen, 29 and the girdle of fine twined linen, and blue, and purple, and scarlet, the work of the embroiderer; as Jehovah commanded Moses. 30 And they made the plate of the holy crown of pure gold, and wrote upon it a writing, like the engravings of a signet, HOLY TO JEHOVAH. 31 And they tied unto it a lace of blue, to fasten it upon the mitre above; as Jehovah commanded Moses.

32 Thus was finished all the work of the tabernacle of the tent of meeting: and the children of Israel did according to all that Jehovah commanded Moses; so did they. 33 And they brought the tabernacle unto Moses, the Tent, and all its furniture, its clasps, its boards, its bars, and its pillars, and its sockets; 34 and the covering of rams' skins dyed red, and the covering of sealskins, and the veil of the screen; 35 the ark of the testimony, and the staves thereof, and the mercy-seat; 36 the table, all the vessels thereof, and the showbread; 37 the pure candlestick, the lamps thereof, even the lamps to be set in order, and all the vessels thereof, and the oil for the light; 38 and the golden altar, and the anointing oil, and the sweet incense, and the screen for the door of the Tent; 39 the brazen altar, and its grating of brass, its staves, and all its vessels, the laver and its base; 40 the hangings of the court, its pillars, and its sockets, and the screen for the gate of the court, the cords thereof, and the pins thereof, and all the instruments of the service of the tabernacle, for the tent of meeting; 41 the finely wrought garments for ministering in the holy place, and the holy garments for Aaron the priest, and the garments of his sons, to minister in the priest's office. 42 According to all that Jehovah commanded Moses, so the children of Israel did all the work. 43 And Moses saw all the work, and, behold, they had done it; as Jehovah had commanded, even so had they done it: and Moses blessed them.

40 And Jehovah spake unto Moses, saying, 2 On the first day of the first month shalt thou rear up the tabernacle of the tent of meeting. 3 And thou shalt put therein the ark of the testimony, and thou shalt screen the ark with the veil. 4 And thou shalt bring in the table, and set in order the things that are upon it; and thou shalt bring in the candlestick, and light the lamps thereof. 5 And thou shalt set the golden altar for incense before the ark of the testimony, and put the screen of the door to the tabernacle. 6 And thou shalt set the altar of burnt-offering before the door of the tabernacle of the tent of meeting. 7 And thou shalt set the laver between the tent of meeting and the altar, and shalt put water therein. 8 And thou shalt set up the court round about, and hang up the screen of the gate of the court. 9 And thou shalt take the anointing oil, and anoint the tabernacle, and all that is therein, and shalt hallow it, and all the furniture thereof: and it shall be holy. 10 And thou shalt anoint the altar of burnt-offering, and all its vessels, and sanctify the altar: and the altar shall be most holy. 11 And thou shalt anoint the laver and its base, and sanctify it. 12 And thou shalt bring Aaron and his sons unto the door of the tent of meeting, and shalt wash them with water. 13 And thou shalt put upon Aaron the holy garments; and thou shalt anoint him, and sanctify him, that he may minister unto me in the priest's office. 14 And thou shalt bring his sons, and put coats upon them; 15 and thou shalt anoint them, as thou didst anoint their father, that they may minister unto me in the priest's office: and their anointing shall be to them for an everlasting priesthood throughout their generations. 16 Thus did Moses: according to all that Jehovah commanded him, so did he.

17 And it came to pass in the first month in the second year, on the first day of the month, that the tabernacle was reared up. 18 And Moses reared up the tabernacle, and laid its sockets, and set up the boards thereof, and put in the bars thereof, and reared up its pillars. 19 And he spread the tent over the tabernacle, and put the covering of the tent above upon it; as Jehovah commanded Moses. 20 And he took and put the testimony into the ark, and set the staves on the ark, and put the mercy-seat above upon the ark: 21 and he brought the ark into the tabernacle, and set up the veil of the screen, and screened the ark of the testimony; as Jehovah commanded Moses. 22 And he put the table in the tent of meeting, upon the side of the tabernacle northward, without the veil. 23 And he set the bread in order upon it before Jehovah; as Jehovah commanded Moses. 24 And he put the candlestick in the tent of meeting, over against the table, on the side of the tabernacle southward. 25 And he lighted the lamps before Jehovah; as Jehovah commanded Moses. 26 And he put the golden altar in the tent of meeting before the veil: 27 and he burnt thereon incense of sweet spices; as Jehovah commanded Moses. 28 And he put the screen of the door to the tabernacle. 29 And he set the altar of burnt-offering at the door of the tabernacle of the tent of meeting, and offered upon it the burnt-offering and the meal-offering; as Jehovah commanded Moses. 30 And he set the laver between the tent of meeting and the altar, and put water therein, wherewith to wash. 31 And Moses and Aaron and his sons washed their hands and their feet thereat; 32 when they went into the tent of meeting, and when they came near unto the altar, they

washed; as Jehovah commanded Moses. 33 And he reared up the court round about the tabernacle and the altar, and set up the screen of the gate of the court. So Moses finished the work.

36. THE CLOUD OF JEHOVAH. P52, 38.
Ex. 40^{34-38}

34 Then the cloud covered the tent of meeting, and the glory of Jehovah filled the tabernacle. 35 And Moses was not able to enter into the tent of meeting, because the cloud abode thereon, and the glory of Jehovah filled the tabernacle. 36 And when the cloud was taken up from over the tabernacle, the children of Israel went onward, throughout all their journeys: 37 but if the cloud was not taken up, then they journeyed not till the day that it was taken up. 38 For the cloud of Jehovah was upon the tabernacle by day, and there was fire therein by night, in the sight of all the house of Israel, throughout all their journeys.

37. THE LAW OF OFFERINGS.
Lv. 1-7

37i. BURNT-OFERINGS.
Lv. 1^{1-17}

1 And Jehovah called unto Moses, and spake unto him out of the tent of meeting, saying, 2 Speak unto the children of Israel, and say unto them, When any man of you offereth an oblation unto Jehovah, ye shall offer your oblation of the cattle, *even* of the herd and of the flock.
3 If his oblation be a burnt-offering of the herd, he shall offer it a male without blemish: he shall offer it at the door of the tent of meeting, that he may be accepted before Jehovah. 4 And he shall lay his hand upon the head of the burnt-offering; and it shall be accepted for him to make atonement for him. 5 And he shall kill the bullock before Jehovah: and Aaron's sons, the priests, shall present the blood, and sprinkle the blood round about upon the altar that is at the door of the tent of meeting. 6 And he shall flay the burnt-offering, and cut it into its pieces. 7 And the sons of Aaron the priest shall put fire upon the altar, and lay wood in order upon the fire; 8 and Aaron's sons, the priests, shall lay the pieces, the head, and the fat, in order upon the wood that is on the fire which is upon the altar: 9 but its inwards and its legs shall he wash with water. And the priest shall burn the whole on the altar, for a burnt-offering, an offering made by fire, of a sweet savor unto Jehovah.

10 And if his oblation be of the flock, of the sheep, or of the goats, for a burnt-offering; he shall offer it a male without blemish. 11 And he shall kill it on the side of the altar northward before Jehovah: and Aaron's sons, the priests, shall sprinkle its blood upon the altar round about. 12 And he shall cut it into its pieces, with its head and its fat; and the priest shall lay them in order on the wood that is on the fire which is upon the altar: 13 but the inwards and the legs shall he wash with water. And the priest shall offer the whole, and burn it upon the altar: it is a burnt-offering, an offering made by fire, of a sweet savor unto Jehovah.

14 And if his oblation to Jehovah be a burnt-offering of birds, then he shall offer his oblation of turtle-doves, or of young pigeons. 15 And the priest shall bring it unto the altar, and wring off its head, and burn it on the altar; and the blood thereof shall be drained out on the side of the altar; 16 and he shall take away its crop with the filth thereof, and cast it beside the altar on the east part, in the place of the ashes: 17 and he shall rend it by the wings thereof, *but* shall not divide it asunder. And the priest shall burn it upon the altar, upon the wood that is upon the fire: it is a burnt-offering, an offering made by fire, of a sweet savor unto Jehovah.

37ii. MEAL-OFFERINGS.

Lv. 2^{1-16}

1 And when any one offereth an oblation of a meal-offering unto Jehovah, his oblation shall be of fine flour; and he shall pour oil upon it, and put frankincense thereon: 2 and he shall bring it to Aaron's sons the priests; and he shall take thereout his handful of the fine flour thereof, and of the oil thereof, with all the frankincense thereof. And the priest shall burn *it as* the memorial thereof upon the altar, an offering made by fire, of a sweet savor unto Jehovah: 3 and that which is left of the meal-offering shall be Aaron's and his sons': it is a thing most holy of the offerings of Jehovah made by fire.

4 And when thou offerest an oblation of a meal-offering baken in the oven, it shall be unleavened cakes of fine flour mingled with oil, or unleavened wafers anointed with oil. 5 And if thy oblation be a meal-offering of the baking-pan, it shall be of fine flour unleavened, mingled with oil. 6 Thou shalt part it in pieces, and pour oil thereon: it is a meal-offering. 7 And if thy oblation be a meal-offering of the frying-pan, it shall be made of fine flour with oil. 8 And thou shalt bring the meal-offering that is made of these things unto Jehovah: and it shall be presented unto the priest, and he shall bring it unto the altar. 9 And the priest shall take up from the meal-offering

the memorial thereof, and shall burn it upon the altar, an offering made by fire, of a sweet savor unto Jehovah. 10 And that which is left of the meal-offering shall be Aaron's and his sons': it is a thing most holy of the offerings of Jehovah made by fire. 11 No meal-offering, which ye shall offer unto Jehovah, shall be made with leaven; for ye shall burn no leaven, nor any honey, as an offering made by fire unto Jehovah. 12 As an oblation of first-*fruits* ye shall offer them unto Jehovah: but they shall not come up for a sweet savor on the altar. 13 And every oblation of thy meal-offering shalt thou season with salt; neither shalt thou suffer the salt of the covenant of thy God to be lacking from thy meal-offering: with all thine oblations thou shalt offer salt.

14 And if thou offer a meal-offering of first-fruits unto Jehovah, thou shalt offer for the meal-offering of thy first-fruits grain in the ear parched with fire, bruised grain of the fresh ear. 15 And thou shalt put oil upon it, and lay frankincense thereon: it is a meal-offering. 16 And the priest shall burn the memorial of it, part of the bruised grain thereof, and part of the oil thereof, with all the frankincense thereof: it is an offering made by fire unto Jehovah.

37iii. PEACE-OFFERINGS.

Lv. 3$^{1-17}$

1 And if his oblation be a sacrifice of peace-offerings; if he offer of the herd, whether male or female, he shall offer it without blemish before Jehovah. 2 And he shall lay his hand upon the head of his oblation, and kill it at the door of the tent of meeting: and Aaron's sons the priests shall sprinkle the blood upon the altar round about. 3 And he shall offer of the sacrifice of peace-offerings an offering made by fire unto Jehovah; the fat that covereth the inwards, and all the fat that is upon the inwards, 4 and the two kidneys, and the fat that is on them, which is by the loins, and the caul upon the liver, with the kidneys, shall he take away. 5 And Aaron's sons shall burn it on the altar upon the burnt-offering, which is upon the wood that is on the fire: it is an offering made by fire, of a sweet savor unto Jehovah.

6 And if his oblation for a sacrifice of peace-offerings unto Jehovah be of the flock; male or female, he shall offer it without blemish. 7 If he offer a lamb for his oblation, then shall he offer it before Jehovah; 8 and he shall lay his hand upon the head of his oblation, and kill it before the tent of meeting: and Aaron's sons shall sprinkle the blood thereof upon the altar round about. 9 And he shall offer of the sacrifice of peace-offerings an offering made by fire unto Jehovah; the fat thereof,

the fat tail entire, he shall take away hard by the backbone; and the fat that covereth the inwards, and all the fat that is upon the inwards, 10 and the two kidneys, and the fat that is upon them, which is by the loins, and the caul upon the liver, with the kidneys, shall he take away. 11 And the priest shall burn it upon the altar: it is the food of the offering made by fire unto Jehovah.

12 And if his oblation be a goat, then he shall offer it before Jehovah: 13 and he shall lay his hand upon the head of it, and kill it before the tent of meeting; and the sons of Aaron shall sprinkle the blood thereof upon the altar round about. 14 And he shall offer thereof his oblation, *even* an offering made by fire unto Jehovah; the fat that covereth the inwards, and all the fat that is upon the inwards, 15 and the two kidneys, and the fat that is upon them, which is by the loins, and the caul upon the liver, with the kidneys, shall he take away. 16 And the priest shall burn them upon the altar: it is the food of the offering made by fire, for a sweet savor; all the fat is Jehovah's. 17 It shall be a perpetual statute throughout your generations in all your dwellings, that ye shall eat neither fat nor blood.

37iv. SIN-OFFERINGS.   P32: Ex. 29.
Lv. 4^1-5^{13}

1 And Jehovah spake unto Moses, saying, 2 Speak unto the children of Israel, saying, If any one shall sin unwittingly, in any of the things which Jehovah hath commanded not to be done, and shall do any one of them: 3 if the anointed priest shall sin so as to bring guilt on the people, then let him offer for his sin, which he hath sinned, a young bullock without blemish unto Jehovah for a sin-offering. 4 And he shall bring the bullock unto the door of the tent of meeting before Jehovah; and he shall lay his hand upon the head of the bullock, and kill the bullock before Jehovah. 5 And the anointed priest shall take of the blood of the bullock, and bring it to the tent of meeting: 6 and the priest shall dip his finger in the blood, and sprinkle of the blood seven times before Jehovah, before the veil of the sanctuary. 7 And the priest shall put of the blood upon the horns of the altar of sweet incense before Jehovah, which is in the tent of meeting; and all the blood of the bullock shall he pour out at the base of the altar of burnt-offering, which is at the door of the tent of meeting. 8 And all the fat of the bullock of the sin-offering he shall take off from it; the fat that covereth the inwards, and all the fat that is upon the inwards, 9 and the two kidneys, and the fat that is upon them, which is by the loins, and the caul upon the liver,

with the kidneys, shall he take away, 10 as it is taken off from the ox of the sacrifice of peace-offerings: and the priest shall burn them upon the altar of burnt-offering. 11 And the skin of the bullock, and all its flesh, with its head, and with its legs, and its inwards, and its dung, 12 even the whole bullock shall he carry forth without the camp unto a clean place, where the ashes are poured out, and burn it on wood with fire: where the ashes are poured out shall it be burnt.

13 And if the whole congregation of Israel err, and the thing be hid from the eyes of the assembly, and they have done any of the things which Jehovah hath commanded not to be done, and are guilty; 14 when the sin wherein they have sinned is known, then the assembly shall offer a young bullock for a sin-offering, and bring it before the tent of meeting. 15 And the elders of the congregation shall lay their hands upon the head of the bullock before Jehovah; and the bullock shall be killed before Jehovah. 16 And the anointed priest shall bring of the blood of the bullock to the tent of meeting: 17 and the priest shall dip his finger in the blood, and sprinkle it seven times before Jehovah, before the veil. 18 And he shall put of the blood upon the horns of the altar which is before Jehovah, that is in the tent of meeting; and all the blood shall he pour out at the base of the altar of burnt-offering, which is at the door of the tent of meeting. 19 And all the fat thereof shall he take off from it, and burn it upon the altar. 20 Thus shall he do with the bullock; as he did with the bullock of the sin-offering, so shall he do with this; and the priest shall make atonement for them, and they shall be forgiven. 21 And he shall carry forth the bullock without the camp, and burn it as he burned the first bullock: it is the sin-offering for the assembly.

22 When a ruler sinneth, and doeth unwittingly any one of all the things which Jehovah his God hath commanded not to be done, and is guilty; 23 if his sin, wherein he hath sinned, be made known to him, he shall bring for his oblation a goat, a male without blemish. 24 And he shall lay his hand upon the head of the goat, and kill it in the place where they kill the burnt-offering before Jehovah: it is a sin-offering. 25 And the priest shall take of the blood of the sin-offering with his finger, and put it upon the horns of the altar of burnt-offering; and the blood thereof shall he pour out at the base of the altar of burnt-offering. 26 And all the fat thereof shall he burn upon the altar, as the fat of the sacrifice of peace-offerings; and the priest shall make atonement for him as concerning his sin, and he shall be forgiven.

27 And if any one of the common people sin unwittingly, in

doing any of the things which Jehovah hath commanded not to be done, and be guilty; 28 if his sin, which he hath sinned, be made known to him, then he shall bring for his oblation a goat, a female without blemish, for his sin which he hath sinned. 29 And he shall lay his hand upon the head of the sin-offering, and kill the sin-offering in the place of burnt-offering. 30 And the priest shall take of the blood thereof with his finger, and put it upon the horns of the altar of burnt-offering; and all the blood thereof shall he pour out at the base of the altar. 31 And all the fat thereof shall he take away, as the fat is taken away from off the sacrifice of peace-offerings; and the priest shall burn it upon the altar for a sweet savor unto Jehovah; and the priest shall make atonement for him, and he shall be forgiven.

32 And if he bring a lamb as his oblation for a sin-offering, he shall bring it a female without blemish. 33 And he shall lay his hand upon the head of the sin-offering, and kill it for a sin-offering in the place where they kill the burnt-offering. 34 And the priest shall take of the blood of the sin-offering with his finger, and put it upon the horns of the altar of burnt-offering; and all the blood thereof shall he pour out at the base of the altar. 35 And all the fat thereof shall he take away, as the fat of the lamb is taken away from the sacrifice of peace-offerings; and the priest shall burn them on the altar, upon the offerings of Jehovah made by fire; and the priest shall make atonement for him as touching his sin that he hath sinned, and he shall be forgiven.

5 And if any one sin, in that he heareth the voice of adjuration, he being a witness, whether he hath seen or known, if he do not utter *it*, then he shall bear his iniquity. 2 Or if any one touch any unclean thing, whether it be the carcass of an unclean beast, or the carcass of unclean cattle, or the carcass of unclean creeping things, and it be hidden from him, and he be unclean, then he shall be guilty. 3 Or if he touch the uncleanness of man, whatsoever his uncleanness be wherewith he is unclean, and it be hid from him; when he knoweth of it, then he shall be guilty. 4 Or if any one swear rashly with his lips to do evil, or to do good, whatsoever it be that a man shall utter rashly with an oath, and it be hid from him; when he knoweth of it, then he shall be guilty in one of these *things*. 5 And it shall be, when he shall be guilty in one of these *things*, that he shall confess that wherein he hath sinned: 6 and he shall bring his trespass-offering unto Jehovah for his sin which he hath sinned, a female from the flock, a lamb or a goat, for a sin-offering; and the priest shall make atonement for him as concerning his sin.

7 And if his means suffice not for a lamb, then he shall bring his trespass-offering for that wherein he hath sinned, two turtle-doves, or two young pigeons, unto Jehovah; one for a sin-offering, and the other for a burnt-offering. 8 And he shall bring them unto the priest, who shall offer that which is for the sin-offering first, and wring off its head from its neck, but shall not divide it asunder: 9 and he shall sprinkle of the blood of the sin-offering upon the side of the altar; and the rest of the blood shall be drained out at the base of the altar: it is a sin-offering. 10 And he shall offer the second for a burnt-offering, according to the ordinance; and the priest shall make atonement for him as concerning his sin which he hath sinned, and he shall be forgiven.

11 But if his means suffice not for two turtle-doves, or two young pigeons, then he shall bring his oblation for that wherein he hath sinned, the tenth part of an ephah of fine flour for a sin-offering: he shall put no oil upon it, neither shall he put any frankincense thereon; for it is a sin-offering. 12 And he shall bring it to the priest, and the priest shall take his handful of it as the memorial thereof, and burn it on the altar, upon the offerings of Jehovah made by fire: it is a sin-offering. 13 And the priest shall make atonement for him as touching his sin that he hath sinned in any of these things, and he shall be forgiven: and *the remnant* shall be the priest's, as the meal-offering.

37v. TRESPASS-OFFERINGS (OR GUILT-OFFERINGS).
Lv. 5^{14}-6^7.

14 And Jehovah spake unto Moses, saying, 15 If any one commit a trespass, and sin unwittingly, in the holy things of Jehovah; then he shall bring his trespass-offering unto Jehovah, a ram without blemish out of the flock, according to thy estimation in silver by shekels, after the shekel of the sanctuary, for a trespass-offering: 16 and he shall make restitution for that which he hath done amiss in the holy thing, and shall add the fifth part thereto, and give it unto the priest; and the priest shall make atonement for him with the ram of the trespass-offering, and he shall be forgiven.

17 And if any one sin, and do any of the things which Jehovah hath commanded not to be done; though he knew it not, yet is he guilty, and shall bear his iniquity. 18 And he shall bring a ram without blemish out of the flock, according to thy estimation, for a trespass-offering, unto the priest; and the priest shall make atonement for him concerning the thing wherein he erred unwittingly and knew it not, and he shall be forgiven. 19 It is a trespass-offering: he is certainly guilty before Jehovah.

6 And Jehovah spake unto Moses, saying, 2 If any one sin, and commit a trespass against Jehovah, and deal falsely with his neighbor in a matter of deposit, or of bargain, or of robbery, or have oppressed his neighbor, 3 or have found that which was lost, and deal falsely therein, and swear to a lie; in any of all these things that a man doeth, sinning therein; 4 then it shall be, if he hath sinned, and is guilty, that he shall restore that which he took by robbery, or the thing which he hath gotten by oppression, or the deposit which was committed to him, or the lost thing which he found, 5 or anything about which he hath sworn falsely; he shall even restore it in full, and shall add the fifth part more thereto; unto him to whom it appertaineth shall he give it, in the day of his being found guilty. 6 And he shall bring his trespass-offering unto Jehovah, a ram without blemish out of the flock, according to thy estimation, for a trespass-offering, unto the priest: 7 and the priest shall make atonement for him before Jehovah; and he shall be forgiven concerning whatsoever he doeth so as to be guilty thereby.

37vi. PRESCRIPTIONS FOR THE PRIESTS WITH REFERENCE TO OFFERINGS. P42iii H.

Lv. 6^8-7^{38}

8 And Jehovah spake unto Moses, saying, 9 Command Aaron and his sons, saying, This is the law of the burnt-offering: the burnt-offering shall be on the hearth upon the altar all night unto the morning; and the fire of the altar shall be kept burning thereon. 10 And the priest shall put on his linen garment, and his linen breeches shall he put upon his flesh; and he shall take up the ashes whereto the fire hath consumed the burnt-offering on the altar, and he shall put them beside the altar. 11 And he shall put off his garments, and put on other garments, and carry forth the ashes without the camp unto a clean place. 12 And the fire upon the altar shall be kept burning thereon, it shall not go out; and the priest shall burn wood on it every morning: and he shall lay the burnt-offering in order upon it, and shall burn thereon the fat of the peace-offerings. 13 Fire shall be kept burning upon the altar continually; it shall not go out.

14 And this is the law of the meal-offering: the sons of Aaron shall offer it before Jehovah, before the altar. 15 And he shall take up therefrom his handful, of the fine flour of the meal-offering, and of the oil thereof, and all the frankincense which is upon the meal-offering, and shall burn it upon the altar for a sweet savor, as the memorial thereof, unto Jehovah. 16 And that which is left thereof shall Aaron and his sons eat:

it shall be eaten without leaven in a holy place; in the court of the tent of meeting they shall eat it. 17 It shall not be baken with leaven. I have given it as their portion of my offerings made by fire; it is most holy, as the sin-offering, and as the trespass-offering. 18 Every male among the children of Aaron shall eat of it, as *his* portion for ever throughout your generations, from the offerings of Jehovah made by fire: whosoever toucheth them shall be holy.

19 And Jehovah spake unto Moses, saying, 20 This is the oblation of Aaron and of his sons, which they shall offer unto Jehovah in the day when he is anointed: the tenth part of an ephah of fine flour for a meal-offering perpetually, half of it in the morning, and half thereof in the evening. 21 On a baking-pan it shall be made with oil; when it is soaked, thou shalt bring it in: in baken pieces shalt thou offer the meal-offering for a sweet savor unto Jehovah. 22 And the anointed priest that shall be in his stead from among his sons shall offer it: by a statute for ever it shall be wholly burnt unto Jehovah. 23 And every meal-offering of the priest shall be wholly burnt: it shall not be eaten.

24 And Jehovah spake unto Moses, saying, 25 Speak unto Aaron and to his sons, saying, This is the law of the sin-offering: in the place where the burnt-offering is killed shall the sin-offering be killed before Jehovah: it is most holy. 26 The priest that offereth it for sin shall eat it: in a holy place shall it be eaten, in the court of the tent of meeting. 27 Whatsoever shall touch the flesh thereof shall be holy; and when there is sprinkled of the blood thereof upon any garment, thou shalt wash that whereon it was sprinkled in a holy place. 28 But the earthen vessel wherein it is boiled shall be broken; and if it be boiled in a brazen vessel, it shall be scoured, and rinsed in water. 29 Every male among the priests shall eat thereof: it is most holy. 30 And no sin-offering, whereof any of the blood is brought into the tent of meeting to make atonement in the holy place, shall be eaten: it shall be burnt with fire.

7 And this is the law of the trespass-offering: it is most holy. 2 In the place where they kill the burnt-offering shall they kill the trespass-offering; and the blood thereof shall he sprinkle upon the altar round about. 3 And he shall offer of it all the fat thereof: the fat tail, and the fat that covereth the inwards, 4 and the two kidneys, and the fat that is on them, which is by the loins, and the caul upon the liver, with the kidneys, shall he take away; 5 and the priest shall burn them upon the altar for an offering made by fire unto Jehovah: it is a trespass-offering. 6 Every male among the priests shall eat thereof: it shall be eaten in a holy place: it is **most holy.**

7 As is the sin-offering, so is the trespass-offering; there is one law for them: the priest that maketh atonement therewith, he shall have it. 8 And the priest that offereth any man's burnt-offering, even the priest shall have to himself the skin of the burnt-offering which he hath offered. 9 And every meal-offering that is baken in the oven, and all that is dressed in the frying-pan, and on the baking-pan, shall be the priest's that offereth it. 10 And every meal-offering, mingled with oil, or dry, shall all the sons of Aaron have, one as well as another.
11 And this is the law of the sacrifice of peace-offerings, which one shall offer unto Jehovah. 12 If he offer it for a thanksgiving, then he shall offer with the sacrifice of thanksgiving unleavened cakes mingled with oil, and unleavened wafers anointed with oil, and cakes mingled with oil, of fine flour soaked. 13 With cakes of leavened bread he shall offer his oblation with the sacrifice of his peace-offerings for thanksgiving. 14 And of it he shall offer one out of each oblation for a heave-offering unto Jehovah; it shall be the priest's that sprinkleth the blood of the peace-offerings.
15 And the flesh of the sacrifice of his peace-offerings for thanksgiving shall be eaten on the day of his oblation; he shall not leave any of it until the morning. 16 But if the sacrifice of his oblation be a vow, or a freewill-offering, it shall be eaten on the day that he offereth his sacrifice; and on the morrow that which remaineth of it shall be eaten: 17 but that which remaineth of the flesh of the sacrifice on the third day shall be burnt with fire. 18 And if any of the flesh of the sacrifice of his peace-offerings be eaten on the third day, it shall not be accepted, neither shall it be imputed unto him that offereth it: it shall be an abomination, and the soul that eateth of it shall bear his iniquity.
19 And the flesh that toucheth any unclean thing shall not be eaten; it shall be burnt with fire. And as for the flesh, every one that is clean shall eat thereof: 20 but the soul that eateth of the flesh of the sacrifice of peace-offerings, that pertain unto Jehovah, having his uncleanness upon him, that soul shall be cut off from his people. 21 And when any one shall touch any unclean thing, the uncleanness of man, or an unclean beast, or any unclean abomination, and eat of the flesh of the sacrifice of peace-offerings, which pertain unto Jehovah, that soul shall be cut off from his people.
22 And Jehovah spake unto Moses, saying, 23 Speak unto the children of Israel, saying, Ye shall eat no fat, of ox, or sheep, or goat. 24 And the fat of that which dieth of itself, and the fat of that which is torn of beasts, may be used for any other service; but ye shall in no wise eat of it. 25 For whosoever

eateth the fat of the beast, of which men offer an offering made by fire unto Jehovah, even the soul that eateth it shall be cut off from his people. 26 And ye shall eat no manner of blood, whether it be of bird or of beast, in any of your dwellings. 27 Whosoever it be that eateth any blood, that soul shall be cut off from his people.

28 And Jehovah spake unto Moses, saying, 29 Speak unto the children of Israel, saying, He that offereth the sacrifice of his peace-offerings unto Jehovah shall bring his oblation unto Jehovah out of the sacrifice of his peace-offerings: 30 his own hands shall bring the offerings of Jehovah made by fire; the fat with the breast shall he bring, that the breast may be waved for a wave-offering before Jehovah. 31 And the priest shall burn the fat upon the altar; but the breast shall be Aaron's and his sons'. 32 And the right thigh shall ye give unto the priest for a heave-offering out of the sacrifices of your peace-offerings. 33 He among the sons of Aaron that offereth the blood of the peace-offerings, and the fat, shall have the right thigh for a portion. 34 For the wave-breast and the heave-thigh have I taken of the children of Israel out of the sacrifices of their peace-offerings, and have given them unto Aaron the priest and unto his sons as *their* portion for ever from the children of Israel.

35 This is the anointing-portion of Aaron, and the anointing-portion of his sons, out of the offerings of Jehovah made by fire, in the day when he presented them to minister unto Jehovah in the priest's office; 36 which Jehovah commanded to be given them of the children of Israel, in the day that he anointed them. It is *their* portion for ever throughout their generations.

37 This is the law of the burnt-offering, of the meal-offering, and of the sin-offering, and of the trespass-offering, and of the consecration, and of the sacrifice of peace-offerings; 38 which Jehovah commanded Moses in mount Sinai, in the day that he commanded the children of Israel to offer their oblations unto Jehovah, in the wilderness of Sinai.

38. CONSECRATION OF AARON AND HIS SONS AND OF OFFERINGS. P35, 36.

Lv. 8^1-9^{24}

8 And Jehovah spake unto Moses, saying, 2 Take Aaron and his sons with him, and the garments, and the anointing oil, and the bullock of the sin-offering, and the two rams, and the basket of unleavened bread; 3 and assemble thou all the congregation at the door of the tent of meeting. 4 And Moses did as Jehovah commanded him; and the congregation was assembled at the door of the tent of meeting. 5 And Moses said

unto the congregation, This is the thing which Jehovah hath commanded to be done.

6 And Moses brought Aaron and his sons, and washed them with water. 7 And he put upon him the coat, and girded him with the girdle, and clothed him with the robe, and put the ephod upon him, and he girded him with the skilfully woven band of the ephod, and bound it unto him therewith. 8 And he placed the breastplate upon him: and in the breastplate he put the Urim and the Thummim. 9 And he set the mitre upon his head; and upon the mitre, in front, did he set the golden plate, the holy crown; as Jehovah commanded Moses.

10 And Moses took the anointing oil, and anointed the tabernacle and all that was therein, and sanctified them. 11 And he sprinkled thereof upon the altar seven times, and anointed the altar and all its vessels, and the laver and its base, to sanctify them. 12 And he poured of the anointing oil upon Aaron's head, and anointed him, to sanctify him. 13 And Moses brought Aaron's sons, and clothed them with coats, and girded them with girdles, and bound head-tires upon them; as Jehovah commanded Moses.

14 And he brought the bullock of the sin-offering: and Aaron and his sons laid their hands upon the head of the bullock of the sin-offering. 15 And he slew it; and Moses took the blood, and put it upon the horns of the altar round about with his finger, and purified the altar, and poured out the blood at the base of the altar, and sanctified it, to make atonement for it. 16 And he took all the fat that was upon the inwards, and the caul of the liver, and the two kidneys, and their fat; and Moses burned it upon the altar. 17 But the bullock, and its skin, and its flesh, and its dung, he burnt with fire without the camp; as Jehovah commanded Moses.

18 And he presented the ram of the burnt-offering: and Aaron and his sons laid their hands upon the head of the ram. 19 And he killed it; and Moses sprinkled the blood upon the altar round about. 20 And he cut the ram into its pieces; and Moses burnt the head, and the pieces, and the fat. 21 And he washed the inwards and the legs with water; and Moses burnt the whole ram upon the altar: it was a burnt-offering for a sweet savor: it was an offering made by fire unto Jehovah; as Jehovah commanded Moses.

22 And he presented the other ram, the ram of consecration: and Aaron and his sons laid their hands upon the head of the ram. 23 And he slew it; and Moses took of the blood thereof, and put it upon the tip of Aaron's right ear, and upon the thumb of his right hand, and upon the great toe of his right foot. 24 And he brought Aaron's sons; and Moses put of the

blood upon the tip of their right ear, and upon the thumb of their right hand, and upon the great toe of their right foot: and Moses sprinkled the blood upon the altar round about. 25 And he took the fat, and the fat tail, and all the fat that was upon the inwards, and the caul of the liver, and the two kidneys, and their fat, and the right thigh: 26 and out of the basket of unleavened bread, that was before Jehovah, he took one unleavened cake, and one cake of oiled bread, and one wafer, and placed them on the fat, and upon the right thigh: 27 and he put the whole upon the hands of Aaron, and upon the hands of his sons, and waved them for a wave-offering before Jehovah. 28 And Moses took them from off their hands, and burnt them on the altar upon the burnt-offering: they were a consecration for a sweet savor: it was an offering made by fire unto Jehovah. 29 And Moses took the breast, and waved it for a wave-offering before Jehovah: it was Moses' portion of the ram of consecration; as Jehovah commanded Moses.

30 And Moses took of the anointing oil, and of the blood which was upon the altar, and sprinkled it upon Aaron, upon his garments, and upon his sons, and upon his sons' garments with him, and sanctified Aaron, his garments, and his sons, and his sons' garments with him.

31 And Moses said unto Aaron and to his sons, Boil the flesh at the door of the tent of meeting: and there eat it and the bread that is in the basket of consecration, as I commanded, saying, Aaron and his sons shall eat it. 32 And that which remaineth of the flesh and of the bread shall ye burn with fire. 33 And ye shall not go out from the door of the tent of meeting seven days, until the days of your consecration be fulfilled: for he shall consecrate you seven days. 34 As hath been done this day, so Jehovah hath commanded to do, to make atonement for you. 35 And at the door of the tent of meeting shall ye abide day and night seven days, and keep the charge of Jehovah, that ye die not: for so I am commanded. 36 And Aaron and his sons did all the things which Jehovah commanded by Moses.

9 And it came to pass on the eighth day, that Moses called Aaron and his sons, and the elders of Israel; 2 and he said unto Aaron, Take thee a calf of the herd for a sin-offering, and a ram for a burnt-offering, without blemish, and offer them before Jehovah. 3 And unto the children of Israel thou shalt speak, saying, Take ye a he-goat for a sin-offering; and a calf and a lamb, both a year old, without blemish, for a burnt-offering; 4 and an ox and a ram for peace-offerings, to sacrifice before Jehovah; and a meal-offering mingled with oil: for

to-day Jehovah appeareth unto you. 5 And they brought that which Moses commanded before the tent of meeting: and all the congregation drew near and stood before Jehovah. 6 And Moses said, This is the thing which Jehovah commanded that ye should do: and the glory of Jehovah shall appear unto you. 7 And Moses said unto Aaron, Draw near unto the altar, and offer thy sin-offering, and thy burnt-offering, and make atonement for thyself, and for the people; and offer the oblation of the people, and make atonement for them; as Jehovah commanded.

8 So Aaron drew near unto the altar, and slew the calf of the sin-offering, which was for himself. 9 And the sons of Aaron presented the blood unto him; and he dipped his finger in the blood, and put it upon the horns of the altar, and poured out the blood at the base of the altar: 10 but the fat, and the kidneys, and the caul from the liver of the sin-offering, he burnt upon the altar; as Jehovah commanded Moses. 11 And the flesh and the skin he burnt with fire without the camp.

12 And he slew the burnt-offering; and Aaron's sons delivered unto him the blood, and he sprinkled it upon the altar round about. 13 And they delivered the burnt-offering unto him, piece by piece, and the head: and he burnt them upon the altar. 14 And he washed the inwards and the legs, and burnt them upon the burnt-offering on the altar.

15 And he presented the people's oblation, and took the goat of the sin-offering which was for the people, and slew it, and offered it for sin, as the first. 16 And he presented the burnt-offering, and offered it according to the ordinance. 17 And he presented the meal-offering, and filled his hand therefrom, and burnt it upon the altar, besides the burnt-offering of the morning.

18 He slew also the ox and the ram, the sacrifice of peace-offerings, which was for the people: and Aaron's sons delivered unto him the blood, which he sprinkled upon the altar round about, 19 and the fat of the ox and of the ram, the fat tail, and that which covereth *the inwards*, and the kidneys, and the caul of the liver: 20 and they put the fat upon the breasts, and he burnt the fat upon the altar: 21 and the breasts and the right thigh Aaron waved for a wave-offering before Jehovah; as Moses commanded.

22 And Aaron lifted up his hands toward the people, and blessed them; and he came down from offering the sin-offering, and the burnt-offering, and the peace-offerings. 23 And Moses and Aaron went into the tent of meeting, and came out, and blessed the people: and the glory of Jehovah appeared unto all the people. 24 And there came forth fire from before Jeho-

vah, and consumed upon the altar the burnt-offering and the fat: and when all the people saw it, they shouted, and fell on their faces.

39. THE SIN OF NADAB AND ABIHU.
Lv. 10$^{1\text{-}20}$

1 And Nadab and Abihu, the sons of Aaron, took each of them his censer, and put fire therein, and laid incense thereon, and offered strange fire before Jehovah, which he had not commanded them. 2 And there came forth fire from before Jehovah, and devoured them, and they died before Jehovah. 3 Then Moses said unto Aaron, This is it that Jehovah spake, saying, I will be sanctified in them that come nigh me, and before all the people I will be glorified. And Aaron held his peace. 4 And Moses called Mishael and Elzaphan, the sons of Uzziel, the uncle of Aaron, and said unto them, Draw near, carry your brethren from before the sanctuary out of the camp. 5 So they drew near, and carried them in their coats out of the camp, as Moses had said. 6 And Moses said unto Aaron, and unto Eleazar and unto Ithamar, his sons, Let not the hair of your heads go loose, neither rend your clothes; that ye die not, and that he be not wroth with all the congregation: but let your brethren, the whole house of Israel, bewail the burning which Jehovah hath kindled. 7 And ye shall not go out from the door of the tent of meeting, lest ye die; for the anointing oil of Jehovah is upon you. And they did according to the word of Moses.

8 And Jehovah spake unto Aaron, saying, 9 Drink no wine nor strong drink, thou, nor thy sons with thee, when ye go into the tent of meeting, that ye die not: it shall be a statute for ever throughout your generations: 10 and that ye may make a distinction between the holy and the common, and between the unclean and the clean; 11 and that ye may teach the children of Israel all the statutes which Jehovah hath spoken unto them by Moses.

12 And Moses spake unto Aaron, and unto Eleazar and unto Ithamar, his sons that were left, Take the meal-offering that remaineth of the offerings of Jehovah made by fire, and eat it without leaven beside the altar; for it is most holy; 13 and ye shall eat it in a holy place, because it is thy portion, and thy sons' portion, of the offerings of Jehovah made by fire: for so I am commanded. 14 And the wave-breast and the heave-thigh shall ye eat in a clean place, thou, and thy sons, and thy daughters with thee: for they are given as thy portion, and thy sons' portion, out of the sacrifices of the peace-offerings of the children of Israel. 15 The heave-thigh and the wave-breast

shall they bring with the offerings made by fire of the fat, to wave it for a wave-offering before Jehovah: and it shall be thine, and thy sons' with thee, as a portion for ever; as Jehovah hath commanded. 16 And Moses diligently sought the goat of the sin-offering, and, behold, it was burnt: and he was angry with Eleazar and with Ithamar, the sons of Aaron that were left, saying, 17 Wherefore have ye not eaten the sin-offering in the place of the sanctuary, seeing it is most holy, and he hath given it you to bear the iniquity of the congregation, to make atonement for them before Jehovah? 18 Behold, the blood of it was not brought into the sanctuary within: ye should certainly have eaten it in the sanctuary, as I commanded. 19 And Aaron spake unto Moses, Behold, this day have they offered their sin-offering and their burnt-offering before Jehovah; and there have befallen me such things as these: and if I had eaten the sin-offering to-day, would it have been well-pleasing in the sight of Jehovah? 20 And when Moses heard *that*, it was well-pleasing in his sight.

40. THE LAW OF THE CLEAN AND UNCLEAN. P40H.
Lv. 11-15

40i. ANIMALS.

Lv. 11$^{1\text{-}47}$ (exc. vv. 43-45, cf. P42iv H)

1 And Jehovah spake unto Moses and to Aaron, saying unto them, 2 Speak unto the children of Israel, saying, These are the living things which ye may eat among all the beasts that are on the earth. 3 Whatsoever parteth the hoof, and is clovenfooted, *and* cheweth the cud, among the beasts, that may ye eat. 4 Nevertheless these shall ye not eat of them that chew the cud, or of them that part the hoof: the camel, because he cheweth the cud but parteth not the hoof, he is unclean unto you. 5 And the coney, because he cheweth the cud but parteth not the hoof, he is unclean unto you. 6 And the hare, because she cheweth the cud but parteth not the hoof, she is unclean unto you. 7 And the swine, because he parteth the hoof, and is cloven-footed, but cheweth not the cud, he is unclean unto you. 8 Of their flesh ye shall not eat, and their carcasses ye shall not touch; they are unclean unto you.

9 These may ye eat of all that are in the waters: whatsoever hath fins and scales in the waters, in the seas, and in the rivers, that may ye eat. 10 And all that have not fins and scales in the seas, and in the rivers, of all that move in the waters, and of all the living creatures that are in the waters,

they are an abomination unto you, 11 and they shall be an abomination unto you; ye shall not eat of their flesh, and their carcasses ye shall have in abomination. 12 Whatsoever hath no fins nor scales in the waters, that is an abomination unto you.

13 And these ye shall have in abomination among the birds; they shall not be eaten, they are an abomination: the eagle, and the gier-eagle, and ospray, 14 and the kite, and the falcon after its kind, 15 every raven after its kind, 16 and the ostrich, and the night-hawk, and the sea-mew, and the hawk after its kind, 17 and the little owl, and the cormorant, and the great owl, 18 and the horned owl, and the pelican, and the vulture, 19 and the stork, the heron after its kind, and the hoopoe, and the bat.

20 All winged creeping things that go upon all fours are an abomination unto you. 21 Yet these may ye eat of all winged creeping things that go upon all fours, which have legs above their feet, wherewith to leap upon the earth; 22 even these of them ye may eat: the locust after its kind, and the bald locust after its kind, and the cricket after its kind, and the grasshopper after its kind. 23 But all winged creeping things, which have four feet, are an abomination unto you.

24 And by these ye shall become unclean: whosoever toucheth the carcass of them shall be unclean until the even; 25 and whosoever beareth *aught* of the carcass of them shall wash his clothes, and be unclean until the even. 26 Every beast which parteth the hoof, and is not clovenfooted, nor cheweth the cud, is unclean unto you: every one that toucheth them shall be unclean. 27 And whatsoever goeth upon its paws, among all beasts that go on all fours, they are unclean unto you: whoso toucheth their carcass shall be unclean until the even. 28 And he that beareth the carcass of them shall wash his clothes, and be unclean until the even: they are unclean unto you.

29 And these are they which are unclean unto you among the creeping things that creep upon the earth: the weasel, and the mouse, and the great lizard after its kind, 30 and the gecko, and the land-crocodile, and the lizard, and the sand-lizard, and the chameleon. 31 These are they which are unclean to you among all that creep: whosoever doth touch them, when they are dead, shall be unclean until the even. 32 And upon whatsoever any of them, when they are dead, doth fall, it shall be unclean; whether it be any vessel of wood, or raiment, or skin, or sack, whatsoever vessel it be, wherewith any work is done, it must be put into water, and it shall be unclean until the even; then shall it be clean. 33 And every earthen vessel, whereinto any of them falleth, whatsoever is in it shall

be unclean, and it ye shall break. 34 All food *therein* which may be eaten, that on which water cometh, shall be unclean; and all drink that may be drunk in every *such* vessel shall be unclean. 35 And everything whereupon *any part* of their carcass falleth shall be unclean; whether oven, or range for pots, it shall be broken in pieces: they are unclean, and shall be unclean unto you. 36 Nevertheless a fountain or a pit wherein is a gathering of water shall be clean: but that which toucheth their carcass shall be unclean. 37 And if *aught* of their carcass fall upon any sowing seed which is to be sown, it is clean. 38 But if water be put upon the seed, and *aught* of their carcass fall thereon, it is unclean unto you.

39 And if any beast, of which ye may eat, die; he that toucheth the carcass thereof shall be unclean until the even. 40 And he that eateth of the carcass of it shall wash his clothes, and be unclean until the even: he also that beareth the carcass of it shall wash his clothes, and be unclean until the even.

41 And every creeping thing that creepeth upon the earth is an abomination; it shall not be eaten. 42 Whatsoever goeth upon the belly, and whatsoever goeth upon all fours, or whatsoever hath many feet, even all creeping things that creep upon the earth, them ye shall not eat; for they are an abomination.

46 This is the law of the beast, and of the bird, and of every living creature that moveth in the waters, and of every creature that creepeth upon the earth; 47 to make a distinction between the unclean and the clean, and between the living thing that may be eaten and the living thing that may not be eaten.

40ii. MOTHERS.

Lv. 12$^{1-8}$

1 And Jehovah spake unto Moses, saying, 2 Speak unto the children of Israel, saying, If a woman conceive seed, and bear a man-child, then she shall be unclean seven days; as in the days of the impurity of her sickness shall she be unclean. 3 And in the eighth day the flesh of his foreskin shall be circumcised. 4 And she shall continue in the blood of *her* purifying three and thirty days; she shall touch no hallowed thing, nor come into the sanctuary, until the days of her purifying be fulfilled. 5 But if she bear a maid-child, then she shall be unclean two weeks, as in her impurity; and she shall continue in the blood of *her* purifying threescore and six days.

6 And when the days of her purifying are fulfilled, for a son, or for a daughter, she shall bring a lamb a year old for a burnt-offering, and a young pigeon, or a turtle-dove, for a sin-offering,

unto the door of the tent of meeting, unto the priest: 7 and he shall offer it before Jehovah, and make atonement for her; and she shall be cleansed from the fountain of her blood. This is the law for her that beareth, whether a male or a female. 8 And if her means suffice not for a lamb, then she shall take two turtle-doves, or two young pigeons; the one for a burnt-offering, and the other for a sin-offering: and the priest shall make atonement for her, and she shall be clean.

40iii. LEPROSY.
Lv. 13^1-14^{57}

13^1 And Jehovah spake unto Moses and unto Aaron, saying, 2 When a man shall have in the skin of his flesh a rising, or a scab, or a bright spot, and it become in the skin of his flesh the plague of leprosy, then he shall be brought unto Aaron the priest, or unto one of his sons the priests: 3 and the priest shall look on the plague in the skin of the flesh: and if the hair in the plague be turned white, and the appearance of the plague be deeper than the skin of his flesh, it is the plague of leprosy; and the priest shall look on him, and pronounce him unclean. 4 And if the bright spot be white in the skin of his flesh, and the appearance thereof be not deeper than the skin, and the hair thereof be not turned white, then the priest shall shut up *him that hath* the plague seven days: 5 and the priest shall look on him the seventh day: and, behold, if in his eyes the plague be at a stay, and the plague be not spread in the skin, then the priest shall shut him up seven days more: 6 and the priest shall look on him again the seventh day; and, behold, if the plague be dim, and the plague be not spread in the skin, then the priest shall pronounce him clean: it is a scab: and he shall wash his clothes, and be clean. 7 But if the scab spread abroad in the skin, after that he hath showed himself to the priest for his cleansing, he shall show himself to the priest again: 8 and the priest shall look; and, behold, if the scab be spread in the skin, then the priest shall pronounce him unclean: it is leprosy.

9 When the plague of leprosy is in a man, then he shall be brought unto the priest; 10 and the priest shall look; and, behold, if there be a white rising in the skin, and it have turned the hair white, and there be quick raw flesh in the rising, 11 it is an old leprosy in the skin of his flesh, and the priest shall pronounce him unclean: he shall not shut him up; for he is unclean. 12 And if the leprosy break out abroad in the skin, and the leprosy cover all the skin of *him that hath* the plague from his head even to his feet, as far as appeareth to the priest: 13 then the priest shall look; and, behold, if the leprosy have

covered all his flesh, he shall pronounce *him* clean *that hath* the plague: it is all turned white: he is clean. 14 But whensoever raw flesh appeareth in him, he shall be unclean. 15 And the priest shall look on the raw flesh, and pronounce him unclean: the raw flesh is unclean: it is leprosy. 16 Or if the raw flesh turn again, and be changed unto white, then he shall come unto the priest; 17 and the priest shall look on him; and, behold, if the plague be turned into white, then the priest shall pronounce *him* clean *that hath* the plague: he is clean.

18 And when the flesh hath in the skin thereof a boil, and it is healed, 19 and in the place of the boil there is a white rising, or a bright spot, reddish-white, then it shall be showed to the priest; 20 and the priest shall look; and, behold, if the appearance thereof be lower than the skin, and the hair thereof be turned white, then the priest shall pronounce him unclean: it is the plague of leprosy, it hath broken out in the boil. 21 But if the priest look on it, and, behold, there be no white hairs therein, and it be not lower than the skin, but be dim; then the priest shall shut him up seven days: 22 and if it spread abroad in the skin, then the priest shall pronounce him unclean: it is a plague. 23 But if the bright spot stay in its place, and be not spread, it is the scar of the boil; and the priest shall pronounce him clean.

24 Or when the flesh hath in the skin thereof a burning by fire, and the quick *flesh* of the burning become a bright spot, reddish-white, or white; 25 then the priest shall look upon it; and, behold, if the hair in the bright spot be turned white, and the appearance thereof be deeper than the skin; it is leprosy, it hath broken out in the burning: and the priest shall pronounce him unclean: it is the plague of leprosy. 26 But if the priest look on it, and, behold, there be no white hair in the bright spot, and it be no lower than the skin, but be dim; then the priest shall shut him up seven days: 27 and the priest shall look upon him the seventh day: if it spread abroad in the skin, then the priest shall pronounce him unclean: it is the plague of leprosy. 28 And if the bright spot stay in its place, and be not spread in the skin, but be dim; it is the rising of the burning, and the priest shall pronounce him clean: for it is the scar of the burning.

29 And when a man or woman hath a plague upon the head or upon the beard, 30 then the priest shall look on the plague; and, behold, if the appearance thereof be deeper than the skin, and there be in it yellow thin hair, then the priest shall pronounce him unclean: it is a scall, it is leprosy of the head or of the beard. 31 And if the priest look on the plague of the scall, and, behold, the appearance thereof be not deeper than

the skin, and there be no black hair in it, then the priest shall shut up *him that hath* the plague of the scall seven days: 32 and in the seventh day the priest shall look on the plague; and, behold, if the scall be not spread, and there be in it no yellow hair, and the appearance of the scall be not deeper than the skin, 33 then he shall be shaven, but the scall shall he not shave; and the priest shall shut up *him that hath* the scall seven days more: 34 and in the seventh day the priest shall look on the scall; and, behold, if the scall be not spread in the skin, and the appearance thereof be not deeper than the skin; then the priest shall pronounce him clean: and he shall wash his clothes, and be clean. 35 But if the scall spread abroad in the skin after his cleansing, 36 then the priest shall look on him; and, behold, if the scall be spread in the skin, the priest shall not seek for the yellow hair; he is unclean. 37 But if in his eyes the scall be at a stay, and black hair be grown up therein; the scall is healed, he is clean: and the priest shall pronounce him clean.

38 And when a man or a woman hath in the skin of the flesh bright spots, even white bright spots; 39 then the priest shall look; and, behold, if the bright spots in the skin of their flesh be of a dull white, it is a tetter, it hath broken out in the skin; he is clean.

40 And if a man's hair be fallen off his head, he is bald; *yet* is he clean. 41 And if his hair be fallen off from the front part of his head, he is forehead bald; *yet* is he clean. 42 But if there be in the bald head, or the bald forehead, a reddish-white plague; it is leprosy breaking out in his bald head, or his bald forehead. 43 Then the priest shall look upon him; and, behold, if the rising of the plague be reddish-white in his bald head, or in his bald forehead, as the appearance of leprosy in the skin of the flesh; 44 he is a leprous man, he is unclean; the priest shall surely pronounce him unclean; his plague is in his head.

45 And the leper in whom the plague is, his clothes shall be rent, and the hair of his head shall go loose, and he shall cover his upper lip, and shall cry, Unclean, unclean. 46 All the days wherein the plague is in him he shall be unclean; he is unclean: he shall dwell alone; without the camp shall his dwelling be.

47 The garment also that the plague of leprosy is in, whether it be a woollen garment, or a linen garment; 48 whether it be in warp, or woof; of linen, or of woollen; whether in a skin, or in anything made of skin; 49 if the plague be greenish or reddish in the garment, or in the skin, or in the warp, or in the woof, or in anything of skin; it is the plague of leprosy, and shall be showed unto the priest. 50 And the priest shall look

upon the plague, and shut up *that which hath* the plague seven days: 51 and he shall look on the plague on the seventh day: if the plague be spread in the garment, either in the warp, or in the woof, or in the skin, whatever service skin is used for; the plague is a fretting leprosy; it is unclean. 52 And he shall burn the garment, whether the warp or the woof, in woollen or in linen, or anything of skin, wherein the plague is: for it is a fretting leprosy; it shall be burnt in the fire.

53 And if the priest shall look, and, behold, the plague be not spread in the garment, either in the warp, or in the woof, or in anything of skin; 54 then the priest shall command that they wash the thing wherein the plague is, and he shall shut it up seven days more: 55 and the priest shall look, after that the plague is washed; and, behold, if the plague have not changed its color, and the plague be not spread, it is unclean; thou shalt burn it in the fire: it is a fret, whether the bareness be within or without.

56 And if the priest look, and, behold, the plague be dim after the washing thereof, then he shall rend it out of the garment, or out of the skin, or out of the warp, or out of the woof: 57 and if it appear still in the garment, either in the warp, or in the woof, or in anything of skin, it is breaking out: thou shalt burn that wherein the plague is with fire. 58 And the garment, either the warp, or the woof, or whatsoever thing of skin it be, which thou shalt wash, if the plague be departed from them, then it shall be washed the second time, and shall be clean.

59 This is the law of the plague of leprosy in a garment of woollen or linen, either in the warp, or the woof, or anything of skin, to pronounce it clean, or to pronounce it unclean.

14 And Jehovah spake unto Moses, saying, 2 This shall be the law of the leper in the day of his cleansing: he shall be brought unto the priest: 3 and the priest shall go forth out of the camp; and the priest shall look; and, behold, if the plague of leprosy be healed in the leper, 4 then shall the priest command to take for him that is to be cleansed two living clean birds, and cedar-wood, and scarlet, and hyssop: 5 and the priest shall command to kill one of the birds in an earthen vessel over running water. 6 As for the living bird, he shall take it, and the cedar-wood, and the scarlet, and the hyssop, and shall dip them and the living bird in the blood of the bird that was killed over the running water: 7 and he shall sprinkle upon him that is to be cleansed from the leprosy seven times, and shall pronounce him clean, and shall let go the living bird into the open field. 8 And he that is to be cleansed shall wash his clothes, and shave off all his hair, and bathe himself in water; and he shall be clean: and after that he shall come into the camp, but shall dwell outside his tent seven days. 9 And it shall be on the seventh day, that he shall shave all his hair off his head and his beard and his eyebrows, even all his hair he shall shave off: and he shall wash his clothes, and he shall bathe his flesh in water, and he shall be clean.

10 And on the eighth day he shall take two he-lambs without blemish, and one ewe-lamb a year old without blemish, and three tenth parts *of an ephah* of fine flour for a meal-offering, mingled with oil, and one log of oil. 11 And the priest that cleanseth him shall set the man that is to be cleansed, and those things, before Jehovah, at the door of the tent of meeting. 12 And the priest shall take one of the he-lambs, and offer him for a trespass-offering, and the log of oil, and wave them for a wave-offering before Jehovah: 13 and he shall kill the he-lamb in the place where they kill the sin-offering and the burnt-offering, in the place of the sanctuary: for as the sin-offering is the priest's, so is the trespass-offering: it is most holy. 14 And the priest shall take of the blood of the trespass-offering, and the priest shall put it upon the tip of the right ear of him that is to be cleansed, and upon the thumb of his right hand, and upon the great toe of his right foot. 15 And the priest shall take of the log of oil, and pour it into the palm of his own left hand; 16 and the priest shall dip his right finger in the oil that is in his left hand, and shall sprinkle of the oil with his finger seven times before Jehovah. 17 And of the rest of the oil that is in his hand shall the priest put upon the tip of the right ear of him that is to be cleansed, and upon the thumb of his right hand, and upon the great toe of his right foot, upon the blood of the trespass-offering: 18 and the rest of the oil that is in the priest's hand he shall put upon the head of him that is to be cleansed: and the priest shall make atonement for him before Jehovah. 19 And the priest shall offer the sin-offering, and make atonement for him that is to be cleansed because of his uncleanness: and afterward he shall kill the burnt-offering; 20 and the priest shall offer the burnt-offering and the meal-offering upon the altar: and the priest shall make atonement for him, and he shall be clean.

21 And if he be poor, and cannot get so much, then he shall take one he-lamb for a trespass-offering to be waved, to make atonement for him, and one tenth part *of an ephah* of fine flour mingled with oil for a meal-offering, and a log of oil; 22 and two turtle-doves, or two young pigeons, such as he is able to get; and the one shall be a sin-offering, and the other a burnt-offering. 23 And on the eighth day he shall bring them for

his cleansing unto the priest, unto the door of the tent of meeting, before Jehovah: 24 and the priest shall take the lamb of the trespass-offering, and the log of oil, and the priest shall wave them for a wave-offering before Jehovah. 25 And he shall kill the lamb of the trespass-offering; and the priest shall take of the blood of the trespass-offering, and put it upon the tip of the right ear of him that is to be cleansed, and upon the thumb of his right hand, and upon the great toe of his right foot. 26 And the priest shall pour of the oil into the palm of his own left hand; 27 and the priest shall sprinkle with his right finger some of the oil that is in his left hand seven times before Jehovah: 28 and the priest shall put of the oil that is in his hand upon the tip of the right ear of him that is to be cleansed, and upon the thumb of his right hand, and upon the great toe of his right foot, upon the place of the blood of the trespass-offering: 29 and the rest of the oil that is in the priest's hand he shall put upon the head of him that is to be cleansed, to make atonement for him before Jehovah. 30 And he shall offer one of the turtle-doves, or of the young pigeons, such as he is able to get, 31 even such as he is able to get, the one for a sin-offering, and the other for a burnt-offering, with the meal-offering: and the priest shall make atonement for him that is to be cleansed before Jehovah. 32 This is the law of him in whom is the plague of leprosy, who is not able to get *that which pertaineth* to his cleansing.

33 And Jehovah spake unto Moses and unto Aaron, saying, 34 When ye are come into the land of Canaan, which I give to you for a possession, and I put the plague of leprosy in a house of the land of your possession; 35 then he that owneth the house shall come and tell the priest, saying, There seemeth to me to be as it were a plague in the house. 36 And the priest shall command that they empty the house, before the priest goeth in to see the plague, that all that is in the house be not made unclean: and afterward the priest shall go in to see the house: 37 and he shall look on the plague; and, behold, if the plague be in the walls of the house with hollow streaks, greenish or reddish, and the appearance thereof be lower than the wall; 38 then the priest shall go out of the house to the door of the house, and shut up the house seven days. 39 And the priest shall come again the seventh day, and shall look; and, behold, if the plague be spread in the walls of the house; 40 then the priest shall command that they take out the stones in which the plague is, and cast them into an unclean place without the city: 41 and he shall cause the house to be scraped within round about, and they shall pour out the mortar, that they scrape off, without the city into an unclean place: 42 and

they shall take other stones, and put them in the place of those stones; and he shall take other mortar, and shall plaster the house. 43 And if the plague come again, and break out in the house, after that he hath taken out the stones, and after he hath scraped the house, and after it is plastered; 44 then the priest shall come in and look; and, behold, if the plague be spread in the house, it is a fretting leprosy in the house: it is unclean. 45 And he shall break down the house, the stones of it, and the timber thereof, and all the mortar of the house; and he shall carry them forth out of the city into an unclean place. 46 Moreover he that goeth into the house all the while that it is shut up shall be unclean until the even. 47 And he that lieth in the house shall wash his clothes; and he that eateth in the house shall wash his clothes.

48 And if the priest shall come in, and look, and, behold, the plague hath not spread in the house, after the house was plastered; then the priest shall pronounce the house clean, because the plague is healed. 49 And he shall take to cleanse the house two birds, and cedar-wood, and scarlet, and hyssop: 50 and he shall kill one of the birds in an earthen vessel over running water: 51 and he shall take the cedar-wood, and the hyssop, and the scarlet, and the living bird, and dip them in the blood of the slain bird, and in the running water, and sprinkle the house seven times: 52 and he shall cleanse the house with the blood of the bird, and with the running water, and with the living bird, and with the cedar-wood, and with the hyssop, and with the scarlet: 53 but he shall let go the living bird out of the city into the open field: so shall he make atonement for the house; and it shall be clean.

54 This is the law for all manner of plague of leprosy, and for a scall, 55 and for the leprosy of a garment, and for a house, 56 and for a rising, and for a scab, and for a bright spot; 57 to teach when it is unclean, and when it is clean: this is the law of leprosy.

40iv. SEXUAL UNCLEANNESS. P42iiH.
Lv. 15$^{1-33}$

1 And Jehovah spake unto Moses and to Aaron, saying, 2 Speak unto the children of Israel and say unto them, When any man hath an issue out of his flesh, because of his issue he is unclean. 3 And this shall be his uncleanness in his issue: whether his flesh run with his issue, or his flesh be stopped from his issue, it is his uncleanness. 4 Every bed whereon he that hath the issue lieth shall be unclean; and everything whereon he sitteth shall be unclean. 5 And whosoever touch-

eth his bed shall wash his clothes, and bathe himself in water, and be unclean until the even. 6 And he that sitteth on anything whereon he that hath the issue sat shall wash his clothes, and bathe himself in water, and be unclean until the even. 7 And he that toucheth the flesh of him that hath the issue shall wash his clothes, and bathe himself in water, and be unclean until the even. 8 And if he that hath an issue spit upon him that is clean, then he shall wash his clothes, and bathe himself in water, and be unclean until the even. 9 And what saddle soever he that hath the issue rideth upon shall be unclean. 10 And whosoever toucheth anything that was under him shall be unclean until the even: and he that beareth those things shall wash his clothes, and bathe himself in water, and be unclean until the even. 11 And whomsoever he that hath the issue toucheth, without having rinsed his hands in water, he shall wash his clothes, and bathe himself in water, and be unclean until the even. 12 And the earthen vessel, which he that hath the issue toucheth, shall be broken; and every vessel of wood shall be rinsed in water.

13 And when he that hath an issue is cleansed of his issue, then he shall number to himself seven days for his cleansing, and wash his clothes; and he shall bathe his flesh in running water, and shall be clean. 14 And on the eighth day he shall take to him two turtle-doves, or two young pigeons, and come before Jehovah unto the door of the tent of meeting, and give them unto the priest: 15 and the priest shall offer them, the one for a sin-offering, and the other for a burnt-offering; and the priest shall make atonement for him before Jehovah for his issue.

16 And if any man's seed of copulation go out from him, then he shall bathe all his flesh in water, and be unclean until the even. 17 And every garment, and every skin, whereon is the seed of copulation, shall be washed with water, and be unclean until the even. 18 The woman also with whom a man shall lie with seed of copulation, they shall both bathe themselves in water, and be unclean until the even.

19 And if a woman have an issue, *and* her issue in her flesh be blood, she shall be in her impurity seven days: and whosoever toucheth her shall be unclean until the even. 20 And everything that she lieth upon in her impurity shall be unclean: everything also that she sitteth upon shall be unclean. 21 And whosoever toucheth her bed shall wash his clothes, and bathe himself in water, and be unclean until the even. 22 And whosoever toucheth anything that she sitteth upon shall wash his clothes, and bathe himself in water, and be unclean until the even. 23 And if it be on the bed, or on anything whereon

she sitteth, when he toucheth it, he shall be unclean until the even. 24 And if any man lie with her, and her impurity be upon him, he shall be unclean seven days; and every bed whereon he lieth shall be unclean. 25 And if a woman have an issue of her blood many days not in the time of her impurity, or if she have an issue beyond the time of her impurity; all the days of the issue of her uncleanness she shall be as in the days of her impurity: she is unclean. 26 Every bed whereon she lieth all the days of her issue shall be unto her as the bed of her impurity: and everything whereon she sitteth shall be unclean, as the uncleanness of her impurity. 27 And whosoever toucheth those things shall be unclean, and shall wash his clothes, and bathe himself in water, and be unclean until the even. 28 But if she be cleansed of her issue, then she shall number to herself seven days, and after that she shall be clean. 29 And on the eighth day she shall take unto her two turtle-doves, or two young pigeons, and bring them unto the priest, to the door of the tent of meeting. 30 And the priest shall offer the one for a sin-offering, and the other for a burnt-offering; and the priest shall make atonement for her before Jehovah for the issue of her uncleanness.

31 Thus shall ye separate the children of Israel from their uncleanness, that they die not in their uncleanness, when they defile my tabernacle that is in the midst of them.

32 This is the law of him that hath an issue, and of him whose seed of copulation goeth from him, so that he is unclean thereby; 33 and of her that is sick with her impurity, and of him that hath an issue, of the man, and of the woman, and of him that lieth with her that is unclean.

41. THE DAY OF ATONEMENT.
Lv. 16$^{1-34}$

1 And Jehovah spake unto Moses, after the death of the two sons of Aaron, when they drew near before Jehovah, and died; 2 and Jehovah said unto Moses, Speak unto Aaron thy brother, that he come not at all times into the holy place within the veil, before the mercy-seat which is upon the ark; that he die not: for I will appear in the cloud upon the mercy-seat. 3 Herewith shall Aaron come into the holy place: with a young bullock for a sin-offering, and a ram for a burnt-offering. 4 He shall put on the holy linen coat, and he shall have the linen breeches upon his flesh, and shall be girded with the linen girdle, and with the linen mitre shall he be attired: they are the holy garments; and he shall bathe his flesh in water, and put them on. 5 And he shall take of the congre-

gation of the children of Israel two he-goats for a sin-offering, and one ram for a burnt-offering.

6 And Aaron shall present the bullock of the sin-offering, which is for himself, and make atonement for himself, and for his house. 7 And he shall take the two goats, and set them before Jehovah at the door of the tent of meeting. 8 And Aaron shall cast lots upon the two goats; one lot for Jehovah, and the other lot for Azazel. 9 And Aaron shall present the goat upon which the lot fell for Jehovah, and offer him for a sin-offering. 10 But the goat, on which the lot fell for Azazel, shall be set alive before Jehovah, to make atonement for him, to send him away for Azazel into the wilderness.

11 And Aaron shall present the bullock of the sin-offering, which is for himself, and shall make atonement for himself, and for his house, and shall kill the bullock of the sin-offering which is for himself. 12 And he shall take a censer full of coals of fire from off the altar before Jehovah, and his hands full of sweet incense beaten small, and bring it within the veil: 13 and he shall put the incense upon the fire before Jehovah, that the cloud of the incense may cover the mercy-seat that is upon the testimony, that he die not: 14 and he shall take of the blood of the bullock, and sprinkle it with his finger upon the mercy-seat on the east; and before the mercy-seat shall he sprinkle of the blood with his finger seven times.

15 Then shall he kill the goat of the sin-offering, that is for the people, and bring his blood within the veil, and do with his blood as he did with the blood of the bullock, and sprinkle it upon the mercy-seat, and before the mercy-seat: 16 and he shall make atonement for the holy place, because of the uncleannesses of the children of Israel, and because of their transgressions, even all their sins: and so shall he do for the tent of meeting, that dwelleth with them in the midst of their uncleannesses. 17 And there shall be no man in the tent of meeting when he goeth in to make atonement in the holy place, until he come out, and have made atonement for himself, and for his household, and for all the assembly of Israel. 18 And he shall go out unto the altar that is before Jehovah, and make atonement for it, and shall take of the blood of the bullock, and of the blood of the goat, and put it upon the horns of the altar round about. 19 And he shall sprinkle of the blood upon it with his finger seven times, and cleanse it, and hallow it from the uncleannesses of the children of Israel.

20 And when he hath made an end of atoning for the holy place, and the tent of meeting, and the altar, he shall present the live goat: 21 and Aaron shall lay both his hands upon the head of the live goat, and confess over him all the iniquities of

the children of Israel, and all their transgressions, even all their sins; and he shall put them upon the head of the goat, and shall send him away by the hand of a man that is in readiness into the wilderness: 22 and the goat shall bear upon him all their iniquities unto a solitary land: and he shall let go the goat in the wilderness.

23 And Aaron shall come into the tent of meeting, and shall put off the linen garments, which he put on when he went into the holy place, and shall leave them there: 24 and he shall bathe his flesh in water in a holy place, and put on his garments, and come forth, and offer his burnt-offering and the burnt-offering of the people, and make atonement for himself and for the people. 25 And the fat of the sin-offering shall he burn upon the altar. 26 And he that letteth go the goat for Azazel shall wash his clothes, and bathe his flesh in water, and afterward he shall come into the camp. 27 And the bullock of the sin-offering, and the goat of the sin-offering, whose blood was brought in to make atonement in the holy place, shall be carried forth without the camp; and they shall burn in the fire their skins, and their flesh, and their dung. 28 And he that burneth them shall wash his clothes, and bathe his flesh in water, and afterward he shall come into the camp.

29 And it shall be a statute for ever unto you: in the seventh month, on the tenth day of the month, ye shall afflict your souls, and shall do no manner of work, the home-born, or the stranger that sojourneth among you: 30 for on this day shall atonement be made for you, to cleanse you; from all your sins shall ye be clean before Jehovah. 31 It is a sabbath of solemn rest unto you, and ye shall afflict your souls; it is a statute for ever. 32 And the priest, who shall be anointed and who shall be consecrated to be priest in his father's stead, shall make the atonement, and shall put on the linen garments, even the holy garments: 33 and he shall make atonement for the holy sanctuary; and he shall make atonement for the tent of meeting and for the altar; and he shall make atonement for the priests and for all the people of the assembly. 34 And this shall be an everlasting statute unto you, to make atonement for the children of Israel because of all their sins once in the year. And he did as Jehovah commanded Moses.

42. H THE CODE OF HOLINESS.
Lv. 17-26

Introductory Note.—H (the code or law of Holiness—a name suggested by Klostermann) is universally recognized as a separate body of laws, incorporated in P by an Rp (who revised H extensively) and representing an earlier practice than the main legislation of P. It has marked affinities with Ez. 40-48 (cf. Dr. LOT. 145-149), and some have held that Ez. was the author of H; but this view is now rejected by all. H is generally regarded as later than the publication of Dt., 621 (except by Di., Se.).

There is difference of opinion as to the chronological relation between H and Ez. In any event, H contains some, probably much, old, pre-exilic material. Hence it is dated before Ez. by Dr., GFM., Kent, Eiselen, et al. But ch. 26 shows so plainly the influence of Ez. that the majority are inclined to date it 570-550: so We., Ku., Ka., Co., Stärk, Benzinger, Smend, Stade, St., Bä. (the last two emphasizing particularly the presence of pre-exilic material in H).

In various articles, Paton has shown that the original form of H, as of CC, probably consisted of pentads and decads, each decad ending with the formula, "I am Jehovah" (cf. artt. in JBL., vols. 16, 17, 18, and in *Hebraica* April-July 1894).

The main body of the following text is H: the passages in smaller type are generally assigned to P or Rp.

42i. H LAWS CONCERNING SLAUGHTER AND SACRIFICE. Lv. 17$^{1-16}$

1 And Jehovah spake unto Moses, saying, 2 Speak unto Aaron, and unto his sons, and unto all the children of Israel, and say unto them: This is the thing which Jehovah hath commanded, saying, 3 What man soever there be of the house of Israel, that killeth an ox, or lamb, or goat, in the camp, or that killeth it without the camp, 4 and hath not brought it unto the door of the tent of meeting, to offer it as an oblation unto Jehovah before the tabernacle of Jehovah: blood shall be imputed unto that man; he hath shed blood; and that man shall be cut off from among his people: 5 to the end that the children of Israel may bring their sacrifices, which they sacrifice in the open field, even that they may bring them unto Jehovah, unto the door of the tent of meeting, unto the priest, and sacrifice them for sacrifices of peace-offerings unto Jehovah. 6 And the priest shall sprinkle the blood upon the altar of Jehovah at the door of the tent of meeting, and burn the fat for a sweet savor unto Jehovah. 7 And they shall no more sacrifice their sacrifices unto the he-goats, after which they play the harlot. This shall be a statute for ever unto them throughout their generations.

8 And thou shalt say unto them, Whatsoever man there be of the house of Israel, or of the strangers that sojourn among them, that offereth a burnt-offering or sacrifice, 9 and bring-

---

[42i] vv. 15-16: P. The redaction is Rp. So Paton, Dr., Co., Bä., St., et al., in the main. vv. 3, 8, 10, 13, 15 cf. Ez. 14^{4,7,8} 44^{10,12}.

eth it not unto the door of the tent of meeting, to sacrifice it unto Jehovah; that man shall be cut off from his people. 10 And whatsoever man there be of the house of Israel, or of the strangers that sojourn among them, that eateth any manner of blood, I will set my face against that soul that eateth blood, and will cut him off from among his people. 11 For the life of the flesh is in the blood; and I have given it to you upon the altar to make atonement for your souls: for it is the blood that maketh atonement by reason of the life. 12 Therefore I said unto the children of Israel, No soul of you shall eat blood, neither shall any stranger that sojourneth among you eat blood. 13 And whatsoever man there be of the children of Israel, or of the strangers that sojourn among them, who taketh in hunting any beast or bird that may be eaten; he shall pour out the blood thereof, and cover it with dust.

14 For as to the life of all flesh, the blood thereof is *all one* with the life thereof: therefore I said unto the children of Israel, Ye shall eat the blood of no manner of flesh; for the life of all flesh is the blood thereof: whosoever eateth it shall be cut off. 15 And every soul that eateth that which dieth of itself, or that which is torn of beasts, whether he be home-born or a sojourner, he shall wash his clothes, and bathe himself in water, and be unclean until the even: then shall he be clean. 16 But if he wash them not, nor bathe his flesh, then he shall bear his iniquity.

42ii. H LAWS CONCERNING SEXUAL IMPURITIES. P40iv.
Lv. 18^{1-30}

1 And Jehovah spake unto Moses, saying, 2 Speak unto the children of Israel, and say unto them, I am Jehovah your God. 3 After the doings of the land of Egypt, wherein ye dwelt, shall ye not do: and after the doings of the land of Canaan, whither I bring you, shall ye not do; neither shall ye walk in their statutes. 4 Mine ordinances shall ye do, and my statutes shall ye keep, to walk therein: I am Jehovah your God. 5 Ye shall therefore keep my statutes, and mine ordinances; which if a man do, he shall live in them: I am Jehovah.

6 None of you shall approach to any that are near of kin to him, to uncover *their* nakedness: I am Jehovah. 7 The nakedness of thy father, even the nakedness of thy mother, shalt thou not uncover: she is thy mother; thou shalt not uncover her nakedness. 8 The nakedness of thy father's wife shalt thou not uncover; it is thy father's nakedness. 9 The nakedness of thy sister, the daughter of thy father, or the daughter of thy mother, whether born at home, or born abroad, even

---

[42ii] Dr. notes that the laws are in the second person singular, while the parenetic framework vv. 1-5, 24-30 is plural.—Cf. Ez. $18^{6-7,11,15}$ $22^{10,11}$ (Kent).

their nakedness thou shalt not uncover. 10 The nakedness of thy son's daughter, or of thy daughter's daughter, even their nakedness thou shalt not uncover: for theirs is thine own nakedness. 11 The nakedness of thy father's wife's daughter, begotten of thy father, she is thy sister, thou shalt not uncover her nakedness. 12 Thou shalt not uncover the nakedness of thy father's sister: she is thy father's near kinswoman. 13 Thou shalt not uncover the nakedness of thy mother's sister: for she is thy mother's near kinswoman. 14 Thou shalt not uncover the nakedness of thy father's brother, thou shalt not approach to his wife: she is thine aunt. 15 Thou shalt not uncover the nakedness of thy daughter-in-law: she is thy son's wife; thou shalt not uncover her nakedness. 16 Thou shalt not uncover the nakedness of thy brother's wife: it is thy brother's nakedness. 17 Thou shalt not uncover the nakedness of a woman and her daughter; thou shalt not take her son's daughter, or her daughter's daughter, to uncover her nakedness; they are near kinswomen: it is wickedness. 18 And thou shalt not take a wife to her sister, to be a rival *to her*, to uncover her nakedness, besides the other in her life-time.

19 And thou shalt not approach unto a woman to uncover her nakedness, as long as she is impure by her uncleanness. 20 And thou shalt not lie carnally with thy neighbor's wife, to defile thyself with her. 21 And thou shalt not give any of thy seed to make them pass through *the fire* to Molech; neither shalt thou profane the name of thy God: I am Jehovah. 22 Thou shalt not lie with mankind, as with womankind: it is abomination. 23 And thou shalt not lie with any beast to defile thyself therewith; neither shall any woman stand before a beast, to lie down thereto: it is confusion.

24 Defile not ye yourselves in any of these things: for in all these the nations are defiled which I cast out from before you; 25 and the land is defiled: therefore I do visit the iniquity thereof upon it, and the land vomiteth out her inhabitants. 26 Ye therefore shall keep my statutes and mine ordinances, and shall not do any of these abominations; neither the home-born, nor the stranger that sojourneth among you 27 (for all these abominations have the men of the land done, that were before you, and the land is defiled); 28 that the land vomit not you out also, when ye defile it, as it vomited out the nation that was before you. 29 For whosoever shall do any of these abominations, even the souls that do them shall be cut off from among their people. 30 Therefore shall ye keep my charge, that ye practise not any of these abominable customs, which were practised before you, and that ye defile not yourselves therein: I am Jehovah your God.

42iii. H SUNDRY LAWS CHIEFLY MORAL IN CHARACTER. E23, 24. J34 (parallels suggested by Sellin).
Lv. 19$^{1\text{-}37}$ Nu. 15$^{37\text{-}41}$

1 And Jehovah spake unto Moses, saying, 2 Speak unto all the congregation of the children of Israel, and say unto them, Ye shall be holy; for I Jehovah your God am holy. 3 Ye shall fear every man his mother, and his father; and ye shall keep my sabbaths: I am Jehovah your God. 4 Turn ye not unto idols, nor make to yourselves molten gods: I am Jehovah your God.
5 And when ye offer a sacrifice of peace-offerings unto Jehovah, ye shall offer it that ye may be accepted. 6 It shall be eaten the same day ye offer it, and on the morrow: and if aught remain until the third day, it shall be burnt with fire. 7 And if it be eaten at all on the third day, it is an abomination; it shall not be accepted: 8 but every one that eateth it shall bear his iniquity, because he hath profaned the holy thing of Jehovah: and that soul shall be cut off from his people.
9 And when ye reap the harvest of your land, thou shalt not wholly reap the corners of thy field, neither shalt thou gather the gleaning of thy harvest. 10 And thou shalt not glean thy vineyard, neither shalt thou gather the fallen fruit of thy vineyard; thou shalt leave them for the poor and for the sojourner: I am Jehovah your God.
11 Ye shall not steal; neither shall ye deal falsely, nor lie one to another. 12 And ye shall not swear by my name falsely, and profane the name of thy God: I am Jehovah.
13 Thou shalt not oppress thy neighbor, nor rob him: the wages of a hired servant shall not abide with thee all night until the morning. 14 Thou shalt not curse the deaf, nor put a stumblingblock before the blind; but thou shalt fear thy God: I am Jehovah.
15 Ye shall do no unrighteousness in judgment: thou shalt not respect the person of the poor, nor honor the person of the mighty; but in righteousness shalt thou judge thy neighbor. 16 Thou shalt not go up and down as a talebearer among thy people: neither shalt thou stand against the blood of thy neighbor: I am Jehovah.
17 Thou shalt not hate thy brother in thy heart: thou shalt surely rebuke thy neighbor, and not bear sin because of him. 18 Thou shalt not take vengeance, nor bear any grudge against the children of thy people; but thou shalt love thy neighbor as thyself: I am Jehovah.

42iii vv. 5-8, cf. P37vi: Lv. 7$^{15\text{-}18}$. v. 18b, cf. Mk. 12^{31}. v. 30, cf. 20^3; 21$^{12.23}$ 26^2 and Ez. 5^{11} 8^6 23$^{38.39}$ (Kent). Nu. 15$^{37\text{-}41}$ H: Horst, Delitzsch, Di., Ku., Ka.?, Bä., St., Eiselen. (P61).

19 Ye shall keep my statutes. Thou shalt not let thy cattle gender with a diverse kind: thou shalt not sow thy field with two kinds of seed: neither shall there come upon thee a garment of two kinds of stuff mingled together. 20 And whosoever lieth carnally with a woman, that is a bondmaid, betrothed to a husband, and not at all redeemed, nor freedom given her; they shall be punished; they shall not be put to death, because she was not free. 21 And he shall bring his trespass-offering unto Jehovah, unto the door of the tent of meeting, even a ram for a trespass-offering. 22 And the priest shall make atonement for him with the ram of the trespass-offering before Jehovah for his sin which he hath sinned: and the sin which he hath sinned shall be forgiven him.

23 And when ye shall come into the land, and shall have planted all manner of trees for food, then ye shall count the fruit thereof as their uncircumcision: three years shall they be as uncircumcised unto you; it shall not be eaten. 24 But in the fourth year all the fruit thereof shall be holy, for giving praise unto Jehovah. 25 And in the fifth year shall ye eat of the fruit thereof, that it may yield unto you the increase thereof: I am Jehovah your God.

26 Ye shall not eat anything with the blood: neither shall ye use enchantments, nor practise augury. 27 Ye shall not round the corners of your heads, neither shalt thou mar the corners of thy beard. 28 Ye shall not make any cuttings in your flesh for the dead, nor print any marks upon you: I am Jehovah.

29 Profane not thy daughter, to make her a harlot; lest the land fall to whoredom, and the land become full of wickedness. 30 Ye shall keep my sabbaths, and reverence my sanctuary: I am Jehovah.

31 Turn ye not unto them that have familiar spirits, nor unto the wizards; seek them not out, to be defiled by them: I am Jehovah your God.

32 Thou shalt rise up before the hoary head, and honor the face of the old man, and thou shalt fear thy God: I am Jehovah.

33 And if a stranger sojourn with thee in your land, ye shall not do him wrong. 34 The stranger that sojourneth with you shall be unto you as the home-born among you, and thou shalt love him as thyself; for ye were sojourners in the land of Egypt: I am Jehovah your God.

35 Ye shall do no unrighteousness in judgment, in measures of length, of weight, or of quantity. 36 Just balances, just weights, a just ephah, and a just hin, shall ye have: I am Jehovah your God, who brought you out of the land of Egypt.

37 And ye shall observe all my statutes, and all mine ordinances, and do them: I am Jehovah.
Nu. 15^{37} And Jehovah spake unto Moses, saying, 38 Speak unto the children of Israel, and bid them that they make them fringes in the borders of their garments throughout their generations, and that they put upon the fringe of each border a cord of blue: 39 and it shall be unto you for a fringe, that ye may look upon it, and remember all the commandments of Jehovah, and do them; and that ye follow not after your own heart and your own eyes, after which ye use to play the harlot; 40 that ye may remember and do all my commandments, and be holy unto your God. 41 I am Jehovah your God, who brought you out of the land of Egypt, to be your God: I am Jehovah your God.

42iv. H "PENALTIES INFLICTED FOR CERTAIN OFFENSES SPECIFIED IN 18 AND 19$^{30-31}$" (DR.).
Lv. 20$^{1-24}$ 11$^{43-45}$ 20$^{25-27}$

1 And Jehovah spake unto Moses, saying, 2 Moreover, thou shalt say to the children of Israel, Whosoever he be of the children of Israel, or of the strangers that sojourn in Israel, that giveth of his seed unto Molech; he shall surely be put to death: the people of the land shall stone him with stones. 3 I also will set my face against that man, and will cut him off from among his people; because he hath given of his seed unto Molech, to defile my sanctuary, and to profane my holy name. 4 And if the people of the land do at all hide their eyes from that man, when he giveth of his seed unto Molech, and put him not to death; 5 then I will set my face against that man, and against his family, and will cut him off, and all that play the harlot after him, to play the harlot with Molech, from among their people.

6 And the soul that turneth unto them that have familiar spirits, and unto the wizards, to play the harlot after them, I will even set my face against that soul, and will cut him off from among his people. 7 Sanctify yourselves therefore, and be ye holy; for I am Jehovah your God. 8 And ye shall keep my statutes, and do them: I am Jehovah who sanctifieth you. 9 For every one that curseth his father or his mother shall surely be put to death: he hath cursed his father or his mother; his blood shall be upon him.

10 And the man that committeth adultery with another man's wife, even he that committeth adultery with his neigh-

---

^{42iv} Ch. 20 covers many of the same subjects as are discussed in 18-19; but Paton believes that 20 is the work of the same early non-priestly redactor that edited the laws of 18-19 before H was united with P.—Lv. 11$^{43-45}$ H: Di., Dr., Horst, Ku., Bä., St., Eiselen, et al. All agree that it connects with 20^{24b-26}, and Bä. locates it after v. 24, as above.

bor's wife, the adulterer and the adulteress shall surely be put to death. 11 And the man that lieth with his father's wife hath uncovered his father's nakedness: both of them shall surely be put to death; their blood shall be upon them. 12 And if a man lie with his daughter-in-law, both of them shall surely be put to death: they have wrought confusion; their blood shall be upon them. 13 And if a man lie with mankind, as with womankind, both of them have committed abomination: they shall surely be put to death; their blood shall be upon them. 14 And if a man take a wife and her mother, it is wickedness: they shall be burnt with fire, both he and they; that there be no wickedness among you. 15 And if a man lie with a beast, he shall surely be put to death: and ye shall slay the beast. 16 And if a woman approach unto any beast, and lie down thereto, thou shalt kill the woman, and the beast: they shall surely be put to death; their blood shall be upon them.

17 And if a man shall take his sister, his father's daughter, or his mother's daughter, and see her nakedness, and she see his nakedness; it is a shameful thing; and they shall be cut off in the sight of the children of their people: he hath uncovered his sister's nakedness; he shall bear his iniquity. 18 And if a man shall lie with a woman having her sickness, and shall uncover her nakedness; he hath made naked her fountain, and she hath uncovered the fountain of her blood: and both of them shall be cut off from among their people. 19 And thou shalt not uncover the nakedness of thy mother's sister, nor of thy father's sister; for he hath made naked his near kin: they shall bear their iniquity. 20 And if a man shall lie with his uncle's wife, he hath uncovered his uncle's nakedness: they shall bear their sin; they shall die childless. 21 And if a man shall take his brother's wife, it is impurity: he hath uncovered his brother's nakedness; they shall be childless.

22 Ye shall therefore keep all my statutes, and all mine ordinances, and do them; that the land, whither I bring you to dwell therein, vomit you not out. 23 And ye shall not walk in the customs of the nation, which I cast out before you: for they did all these things, and therefore I abhorred them. 24 But I have said unto you, Ye shall inherit their land, and I will give it unto you to possess it, a land flowing with milk and honey: I am Jehovah your God, who hath separated you from the peoples.

11^{43} Ye shall not make yourselves abominable with any creeping thing that creepeth, neither shall ye make yourselves unclean with them, that ye should be defiled thereby. 44 For I am Jehovah your God: sanctify yourselves therefore, and be ye holy; for I am holy: neither shall ye defile yourselves with any manner of creeping thing that moveth upon the earth. 45 For I am Jehovah that brought you up out of the land of Egypt, to be your God: ye shall therefore be holy, for I am holy. 20²⁵ Ye shall therefore make a distinction between the clean beast and the unclean, and between the unclean fowl and the clean: and ye shall not make your souls abominable by beast, or by bird, or by anything wherewith the ground teemeth, which I have separated from you as unclean. 26 And ye shall be holy unto me: for I, Jehovah, am holy, and have set you apart from the peoples, that ye should be mine.

27 A man also or a woman that hath a familiar spirit, or that is a wizard, shall surely be put to death: they shall stone them with stones; their blood shall be upon them.

42v. H RULES FOR THE PRIESTS.

Lv. 21¹-22³³

21 And Jehovah said unto Moses, Speak unto the priests, the sons of Aaron, and say unto them, There shall none defile himself for the dead among his people; 2 except for his kin, that is near unto him, for his mother, and for his father, and for his son, and for his daughter, and for his brother, 3 and for his sister a virgin, that is near unto him, that hath had no husband; for her may he defile himself. 4 He shall not defile himself, *being* a chief man among his people, to profane himself. 5 They shall not make baldness upon their head, neither shall they shave off the corner of their beard, nor make any cuttings in their flesh. 6 They shall be holy unto their God, and not profane the name of their God; for the offerings of Jehovah made by fire, the bread of their God, they do offer: therefore they shall be holy. 7 They shall not take a woman that is a harlot, or profane; neither shall they take a woman put away from her husband: for he is holy unto his God. 8 Thou shalt sanctify him therefore; for he offereth the bread of thy God: he shall be holy unto thee; for I Jehovah, who sanctify you, am holy. 9 And the daughter of any priest, if she profane herself by playing the harlot, she profaneth her father: she shall be burnt with fire.

10 And he that is the high priest among his brethren, upon whose head the anointing oil is poured, and that is consecrated to put on the garments, shall not let the hair of his head go loose, nor rend his clothes; 11 neither shall he go in to any dead body, nor defile himself for his father, or for his mother; 12 neither shall he go out of the sanctuary, nor profane the sanctuary of his God; for the crown of the anointing oil of his God is upon him: I am Jehovah. 13 And he shall take a wife in her virginity.

14 A widow, or one divorced, or a profane woman, a harlot, these shall he not take: but a virgin of his own people shall he take to wife. 15 And he shall not profane his seed among his people: for I am Jehovah who sanctifieth him.

16 And Jehovah spake unto Moses, saying, 17 Speak unto Aaron, saying, Whosoever he be of thy seed throughout their generations that hath a blemish, let him not approach to offer the bread of his God. 18 For whatsoever man he be that hath a blemish, he shall not approach: a blind man, or a lame, or he that hath a flat nose, or anything superfluous, 19 or a man that is broken-footed, or broken-handed, 20 or crook-backed, or a dwarf, or that hath a blemish in his eye, or is scurvy, or scabbed, or hath his stones broken; 21 no man of the seed of Aaron the priest, that hath a blemish, shall come nigh to offer the offerings of Jehovah made by fire: he hath a blemish; he shall not come nigh to offer the bread of his God. 22 He shall eat the bread of his God, both of the most holy, and of the holy: 23 only he shall not go in unto the veil, nor come nigh unto the altar, because he hath a blemish; that he profane not my sanctuaries: for I am Jehovah who sanctifieth them. 24 So Moses spake unto Aaron, and to his sons, and unto all the children of Israel.

22 And Jehovah spake unto Moses, saying, 2 Speak unto Aaron and to his sons, that they separate themselves from the holy things of the children of Israel, which they hallow unto me, and that they profane not my holy name: I am Jehovah. 3 Say unto them, Whosoever he be of all your seed throughout your generations, that approacheth unto the holy things, which the children of Israel hallow unto Jehovah, having his uncleanness upon him, that soul shall be cut off from before me: I am Jehovah. 4 What man soever of the seed of Aaron is a leper, or hath an issue; he shall not eat of the holy things, until he be clean. And whoso toucheth anything that is unclean by the dead, or a man whose seed goeth from him; 5 or whosoever toucheth any creeping thing, whereby he may be made unclean, or a man of whom he may take uncleanness, whatsoever uncleanness he hath; 6 the soul that toucheth any such shall be unclean until the even, and shall not eat of the holy things unless he bathe his flesh in water. 7 And when the sun is down, he shall be clean; and afterward he shall eat of the holy things, because it is his bread. 8 That which dieth of itself, or is torn of beasts, he shall not eat, to defile himself therewith: I am Jehovah. 9 They shall therefore keep my charge, lest they bear sin for it, and die therein, if they profane it: I am Jehovah who sanctifieth them.

10 There shall no stranger eat of the holy thing: a sojourner

of the priest's, or a hired servant, shall not eat of the holy thing. 11 But if a priest buy any soul, the purchase of his money, he shall eat of it; and such as are born in his house, they shall eat of his bread. 12 And if a priest's daughter be married unto a stranger, she shall not eat of the heave-offering of the holy things. 13 But if a priest's daughter be a widow, or divorced, and have no child, and be returned unto her father's house, as in her youth, she shall eat of her father's bread: but there shall no stranger eat thereof. 14 And if a man eat of the holy thing unwittingly, then he shall put the fifth part thereof unto it, and shall give unto the priest the holy thing. 15 And they shall not profane the holy things of the children of Israel, which they offer unto Jehovah, 16 and so cause them to bear the iniquity that bringeth guilt, when they eat their holy things: for I am Jehovah who sanctifieth them.

17 And Jehovah spake unto Moses, saying, 18 Speak unto Aaron, and to his sons, and unto all the children of Israel, and say unto them, Whosoever he be of the house of Israel, or of the sojourners in Israel, that offereth his oblation, whether it be any of their vows, or any of their freewill-offerings, which they offer unto Jehovah for a burnt-offering; 19 that ye may be accepted, *ye shall offer* a male without blemish, of the bullocks, of the sheep, or of the goats. 20 But whatsoever hath a blemish, that shall ye not offer: for it shall not be acceptable for you. 21 And whosoever offereth a sacrifice of peace-offerings unto Jehovah to accomplish a vow, or for a freewill-offering, of the herd or of the flock, it shall be perfect to be accepted; there shall be no blemish therein. 22 Blind, or broken, or maimed, or having a wen, or scurvy, or scabbed, ye shall not offer these unto Jehovah, nor make an offering by fire of them upon the altar unto Jehovah. 23 Either a bullock or a lamb that hath anything superfluous or lacking in his parts, that mayest thou offer for a freewill-offering; but for a vow it shall not be accepted. 24 That which hath its stones bruised, or crushed, or broken, or cut, ye shall not offer unto Jehovah; neither shall ye do *thus* in your land. 25 Neither from the hand of a foreigner shall ye offer the bread of your God of any of these; because their corruption is in them, there is a blemish in them: they shall not be accepted for you.

26 And Jehovah spake unto Moses, saying, 27 When a bullock, or a sheep, or a goat, is brought forth, then it shall be seven days under the dam; and from the eighth day and thenceforth it shall be accepted for the oblation of an offering made by fire unto Jehovah. 28 And whether it be cow or ewe, ye shall not kill it and its young both in one day. 29 And when ye

sacrifice a sacrifice of thanksgiving unto Jehovah, ye shall sacrifice it that ye may be accepted. 30 On the same day it shall be eaten; ye shall leave none of it until the morning: I am Jehovah. 31 Therefore shall ye keep my commandments, and do them: I am Jehovah. 32 And ye shall not profane my holy name; but I will be hallowed among the children of Israel: I am Jehovah who halloweth you, 33 who brought you out of the land of Egypt, to be your God: I am Jehovah.

42vi. H CALENDAR OF FEASTS. P75.
Lv. 23$^{1\text{-}44}$

1 And Jehovah spake unto Moses, saying, 2 Speak unto the children of Israel, and say unto them, The set feasts of Jehovah, which ye shall proclaim to be holy convocations, even these are my set feasts. 3 Six days shall work be done: but on the seventh day is a sabbath of solemn rest, a holy convocation; ye shall do no manner of work: it is a sabbath unto Jehovah in all your dwellings.

4 These are the set feasts of Jehovah, even holy convocations, which ye shall proclaim in their appointed season. 5 In the first month, on the fourteenth day of the month at even, is Jehovah's passover. 6 And on the fifteenth day of the same month is the feast of unleavened bread unto Jehovah: seven days ye shall eat unleavened bread. 7 In the first day ye shall have a holy convocation: ye shall do no servile work. 8 But ye shall offer an offering made by fire unto Jehovah seven days: in the seventh day is a holy convocation; ye shall do no servile work.

9 And Jehovah spake unto Moses, saying, 10 Speak unto the children of Israel, and say unto them, When ye are come into the land which I give unto you, and shall reap the harvest thereof, then ye shall bring the sheaf of the first-fruits of your harvest unto the priest: 11 and he shall wave the sheaf before Jehovah, to be accepted for you: on the morrow after the sabbath the priest shall wave it. 12 And in the day when ye wave the sheaf, ye shall offer a he-lamb without blemish a year old for a burnt-offering unto Jehovah. 13 And the meal-offering thereof shall be two tenth parts *of an ephah* of fine flour mingled with oil, an offering made by fire unto Jehovah for a sweet savor; and the drink-offering thereof shall be of wine, the fourth part of a hin. 14 And ye shall eat neither bread, nor parched grain, nor fresh ears, until this selfsame day, until ye have brought the oblation of your God: it is a statute for ever throughout your generations in all your dwellings.

15 And ye shall count unto you from the morrow after the sabbath, from the day that ye brought the sheaf of the wave-offering; seven sabbaths shall there be complete: 16 even unto the morrow after the seventh sabbath shall ye number fifty days; and ye shall offer a new meal-offering unto Jehovah. 17 Ye

---

42vi The material in smaller type is P: Ka., Dr., St., CH., Bä., Delitzsch, Co., et al.

shall bring out of your habitations two wave-loaves of two tenth parts *of an ephah:* they shall be of fine flour, they shall be baken with leaven, for first-fruits unto Jehovah. 18 And ye shall present with the bread seven lambs without blemish a year old, and one young bullock, and two rams: they shall be a burnt-offering unto Jehovah, with their meal-offering, and their drink-offerings, even an offering made by fire, of a sweet savor unto Jehovah. 19 And ye shall offer one he-goat for a sin-offering, and two he-lambs a year old for a sacrifice of peace-offerings. 20 And the priest shall wave them with the bread of the first-fruits for a wave-offering before Jehovah, with the two lambs: they shall be holy to Jehovah for the priest. 21 And ye shall make proclamation on the selfsame day; there shall be a holy convocation unto you; ye shall do no servile work: it is a statute for ever in all your dwellings throughout your generations.

22 And when ye reap the harvest of your land, thou shalt not wholly reap the corners of thy field, neither shalt thou gather the gleaning of thy harvest: thou shalt leave them for the poor, and for the sojourner: I am Jehovah your God.

23 And Jehovah spake unto Moses, saying, 24 Speak unto the children of Israel, saying, In the seventh month, on the first day of the month, shall be a solemn rest unto you, a memorial of blowing of trumpets, a holy convocation. 25 Ye shall do no servile work; and ye shall offer an offering made by fire unto Jehovah.

26 And Jehovah spake unto Moses, saying, 27 Howbeit on the tenth day of this seventh month is the day of atonement: it shall be a holy convocation unto you, and ye shall afflict your souls; and ye shall offer an offering made by fire unto Jehovah. 28 And ye shall do no manner of work in that same day; for it is a day of atonement, to make atonement for you before Jehovah your God. 29 For whatsoever soul it be that shall not be afflicted in that same day; he shall be cut off from his people. 30 And whatsoever soul it be that doeth any manner of work in that same day, that soul will I destroy from among his people. 31 Ye shall do no manner of work: it is a statute for ever throughout your generations in all your dwellings. 32 It shall be unto you a sabbath of solemn rest, and ye shall afflict your souls: in the ninth day of the month at even, from even unto even, shall ye keep your sabbath.

33 And Jehovah spake unto Moses, saying, 34 Speak unto the children of Israel, saying, On the fifteenth day of this seventh month is the feast of tabernacles for seven days unto Jehovah. 35 On the first day shall be a holy convocation: ye shall do no servile work. 36 Seven days ye shall offer an offering made by fire unto Jehovah: on the eighth day shall be a holy convocation unto you; and ye shall offer an offering made by fire unto Jehovah: it is a solemn assembly; ye shall do no servile work.

37 These are the set feasts of Jehovah, which ye shall proclaim to be holy convocations, to offer an offering made by fire unto Jehovah, a burnt-

offering, and a meal-offering, a sacrifice, and drink-offerings, each on its own day; 38 besides the sabbaths of Jehovah, and besides your gifts, and besides all your vows, and besides all your freewill-offerings, which ye give unto Jehovah.

39 Howbeit on the fifteenth day of the seventh month, when ye have gathered in the fruits of the land, ye shall keep the feast of Jehovah seven days: on the first day shall be a solemn rest, and on the eighth day shall be a solemn rest. 40 And ye shall take you on the first day the fruit of goodly trees, branches of palm-trees, and boughs of thick trees, and willows of the brook; and ye shall rejoice before Jehovah your God seven days. 41 And ye shall keep it a feast unto Jehovah seven days in the year: it is a statute for ever throughout your generations; ye shall keep it in the seventh month. 42 Ye shall dwell in booths seven days; all that are home-born in Israel shall dwell in booths; 43 that your generations may know that I made the children of Israel to dwell in booths, when I brought them out of the land of Egypt: I am Jehovah your God. 44 And Moses declared unto the children of Israel the set feasts of Jehovah.

42vii. P PUNISHMENT OF BLASPHEMY, AND THE *lex talionis.*
E24ii: Ex. 21$^{23-25}$.

Lv. 24$^{1-23}$

1 And Jehovah spake unto Moses, saying, 2 Command the children of Israel, that they bring unto thee pure olive oil beaten for the light, to cause a lamp to burn continually. 3 Without the veil of the testimony, in the tent of meeting, shall Aaron keep it in order from evening to morning before Jehovah continually: it shall be a statute for ever throughout your generations. 4 He shall keep in order the lamps upon the pure candlestick before Jehovah continually.

5 And thou shalt take fine flour, and bake twelve cakes thereof: two tenth parts ¦*of an ephah* shall be in one cake. 6 And thou shalt set them in two rows, six on a row, upon the pure table before Jehovah. 7 And thou shalt put pure frankincense upon each row, that it may be to the bread for a memorial, even an offering made by fire unto Jehovah. 8 Every sabbath day he shall set it in order before Jehovah continually; it is on the behalf of the children of Israel, an everlasting covenant. 9 And it shall be for Aaron and his sons; and they shall eat it in a holy place: for it is most holy unto him of the offerings of Jehovah made by fire by a perpetual statute.

10 And the son of an Israelitish woman, whose father was an Egyptian, went out among the children of Israel; and the son of the Israelitish woman and a man of Israel strove together in the camp: 11 and the son of the Israelitish woman blasphemed the Name, and cursed; and they brought him unto Moses. And his mother's name was Shelomith, the

---
42vii Lv. 24 is almost wholly P; but vv. 15-22 are from H.

daughter of Dibri, of the tribe of Dan. 12 And they put him in ward, that it might be declared unto them at the mouth of Jehovah. 13 And Jehovah spake unto Moses, saying, 14 Bring forth him that hath cursed without the camp; and let all that heard him lay their hands upon his head, and let all the congregation stone him. 15 And thou shalt speak unto the children of Israel, saying, Whosoever curseth his God shall bear his sin. 16 And he that blasphemeth the name of Jehovah, he shall surely be put to death; all the congregation shall certainly stone him: as well the sojourner, as the home-born, when he blasphemeth the name *of Jehovah*, shall be put to death. 17 And he that smiteth any man mortally shall surely be put to death. 18 And he that smiteth a beast mortally shall make it good, life for life. 19 And if a man cause a blemish in his neighbor; as he hath done, so shall it be done to him: 20 breach for breach, eye for eye, tooth for tooth; as he hath caused a blemish in a man, so shall it be rendered unto him. 21 And he that killeth a beast shall make it good: and he that killeth a man shall be put to death.   22 Ye shall have one manner of law, as well for the sojourner, as for the home-born: for I am Jehovah your God.   23 And Moses spake to the children of Israel; and they brought forth him that had cursed out of the camp, and stoned him with stones. And the children of Israel did as Jehovah commanded Moses.

42viii. H THE SABBATICAL YEAR, AND THE YEAR OF JUBILEE. Lv. 25$^{1\text{-}55}$

1 And Jehovah spake unto Moses in mount Sinai, saying, 2 Speak unto the children of Israel, and say unto them, When ye come into the land which I give you, then shall the land keep a sabbath unto Jehovah. 3 Six years thou shalt sow thy field, and six years thou shalt prune thy vineyard, and gather in the fruits thereof; 4 but in the seventh year shall be a sabbath of solemn rest for the land, a sabbath unto Jehovah: thou shalt neither sow thy field, nor prune thy vineyard. 5 That which groweth of itself of thy harvest thou shalt not reap, and the grapes of thy undressed vine thou shalt not gather: it shall be a year of solemn rest for the land. 6 And the sabbath of the land shall be for food for you; for thee, and for thy servant and for thy maid, and for thy hired servant and for thy stranger, who sojourn with thee. 7 And for thy cattle, and for the beasts that are in thy land, shall all the increase thereof be for food.

8 And thou shalt number seven sabbaths of years unto thee, seven times seven years; and there shall be unto thee the days

---

[42viii] The material in small print is chiefly P (or Rp). There is some difference regarding the analysis; all would, however, assign to H the verses so assigned above, save for possible minor touches by Rp. Haupt, Dr., Kent, CH., Ka. agree substantially, while St., Paton give more to H. Paton says that 23a is generally regarded as H.

of seven sabbaths of years, even forty and nine years. 9 Then shalt thou send abroad the loud trumpet on the tenth day of the seventh month; in the day of atonement shall ye send abroad the trumpet throughout all your land. 10 And ye shall hallow the fiftieth year, and proclaim liberty throughout the land unto all the inhabitants thereof: it shall be a jubilee unto you; and ye shall return every man unto his possession, and ye shall return every man unto his family. 11 A jubilee shall that fiftieth year be unto you: ye shall not sow, neither reap that which groweth of itself in it, nor gather *the grapes* in it of the undressed vines. 12 For it is a jubilee; it shall be holy unto you: ye shall eat the increase thereof out of the field.

13 In this year of jubilee ye shall return every man unto his possession. 14 And if thou sell aught unto thy neighbor, or buy of thy neighbor's hand, ye shall not wrong one another. 15 According to the number of years after the jubilee thou shalt buy of thy neighbor, *and* according unto the number of years of the crops he shall sell unto thee. 16 According to the multitude of the years thou shalt increase the price thereof, and according to the fewness of the years thou shalt diminish the price of it; for the number of the crops doth he sell unto thee. 17 And ye shall not wrong one another; but thou shalt fear thy God: for I am Jehovah your God.

18 Wherefore ye shall do my statutes, and keep mine ordinances and do them; and ye shall dwell in the land in safety. 19 And the land shall yield its fruit, and ye shall eat your fill, and dwell therein in safety. 20 And if ye shall say, What shall we eat the seventh year? behold, we shall not sow, nor gather in our increase; 21 then I will command my blessing upon you in the sixth year, and it shall bring forth fruit for the three years. 22 And ye shall sow the eighth year, and eat of the fruits, the old store; until the ninth year, until its fruits come in, ye shall eat the old store.

23 And the land shall not be sold in perpetuity; for the land is mine: for ye are strangers and sojourners with me. 24 And in all the land of your possession ye shall grant a redemption for the land. 25 If thy brother be waxed poor, and sell some of his possession, then shall his kinsman that is next unto him come, and shall redeem that which his brother hath sold. 26 And if a man have no one to redeem it, and he be waxed rich and find sufficient to redeem it; 27 then let him reckon the years of the sale thereof, and restore the overplus unto the man to whom he sold it; and he shall return unto his possession. 28 But if he be not able to get it back for himself, then that which he hath sold shall remain in the hand of him that hath bought it until the year of jubilee: and in the jubilee it shall go out, and he shall return unto his possession.

29 And if a man sell a dwelling-house in a walled city, then he may

redeem it within a whole year after it is sold; for a full year shall he have the right of redemption. 30 And if it be not redeemed within the space of a full year, then the house that is in the walled city shall be made sure in perpetuity to him that bought it, throughout his generations: it shall not go out in the jubilee. 31 But the houses of the villages which have no wall round about them shall be reckoned with the fields of the country: they may be redeemed, and they shall go out in the jubilee. 32 Nevertheless the cities of the Levites, the houses of the cities of their possession, may the Levites redeem at any time. 33 And if one of the Levites redeem, then the house that was sold, and the city of his possession, shall go out in the jubilee; for the houses of the cities of the Levites are their possession among the children of Israel. 34 But the field of the suburbs of their cities may not be sold; for it is their perpetual possession.

35 And if thy brother be waxed poor, and his hand fail with thee; then thou shalt uphold him: *as* a stranger and a sojourner shall he live with thee. 36 Take thou no interest of him or increase, but fear thy God; that thy brother may live with thee. 37 Thou shalt not give him thy money upon interest, nor give him thy victuals for increase. 38 I am Jehovah your God, who brought you forth out of the land of Egypt, to give you the land of Canaan, *and* to be your God.

39 And if thy brother be waxed poor with thee, and sell himself unto thee; thou shalt not make him to serve as a bondservant. 40 As a hired servant, and as a sojourner, he shall be with thee; he shall serve with thee unto the year of jubilee: 41 then shall he go out from thee, he and his children with him, and shall return unto his own family, and unto the possession of his fathers shall he return. 42 For they are my servants, whom I brought forth out of the land of Egypt: they shall not be sold as bondmen. 43 Thou shalt not rule over him with rigor, but shalt fear thy God. 44 And as for thy bondmen, and thy bondmaids, whom thou shalt have; of the nations that are round about you, of them shall ye buy bondmen and bondmaids. 45 Moreover of the children of the strangers that sojourn among you, of them shall ye buy, and of their families that are with you, which they have begotten in your land: and they shall be your possession. 46 And ye shall make them an inheritance for your children after you, to hold for a possession; of them shall ye take your bondmen for ever: but over your brethren the children of Israel ye shall not rule, one over another, with rigor.

47 And if a stranger or sojourner with thee be waxed rich, and thy brother be waxed poor beside him, and sell himself unto the stranger *or* sojourner with thee, or to the stock of the stranger's family; 48 after that he is sold he may be redeemed: one of his brethren may redeem him; 49 or his uncle, or his uncle's son, may redeem him, or any that is nigh of kin unto him of his family may redeem him;

or if he be waxed rich, he may redeem himself. 50 And he shall reckon with him that bought him from the year that he sold himself to him unto the year of jubilee: and the price of his sale shall be according unto the number of years; according to the time of a hired servant shall he be with him. 51 If there be yet many years, according unto them he shall give back the price of his redemption out of the money that he was bought for. 52 And if there remain but few years unto the year of jubilee, then he shall reckon with him; according unto his years shall he give back the price of his redemption. 53 As a servant hired year by year shall he be with him: he shall not rule with rigor over him in thy sight. 54 And if he be not redeemed by these *means*, then he shall go out in the year of jubilee, he, and his children with him. 55 For unto me the children of Israel are servants; they are my servants whom I brought forth out of the land of Egypt: I am Jehovah your God.

42ix. H PARENETIC CONCLUSION. E24iv. Dt. 28. Lv. 26$^{1-46}$.

1 Ye shall make you no idols, neither shall ye rear you up a graven image, or a pillar, neither shall ye place any figured stone in your land, to bow down unto it: for I am Jehovah your God. 2 Ye shall keep my sabbaths, and reverence my sanctuary: I am Jehovah.

3 If ye walk in my statutes, and keep my commandments, and do them; 4 then I will give your rains in their season, and the land shall yield its increase, and the trees of the field shall yield their fruit. 5 And your threshing shall reach unto the vintage, and the vintage shall reach unto the sowing time; and ye shall eat your bread to the full, and dwell in your land safely. 6 And I will give peace in the land, and ye shall lie down, and none shall make you afraid: and I will cause evil beasts to cease out of the land, neither shall the sword go through your land. 7 And ye shall chase your enemies, and they shall fall before you by the sword. 8 And five of you shall chase a hundred, and a hundred of you shall chase ten thousand; and your enemies shall fall before you by the sword. 9 And I will have respect unto you, and make you fruitful, and multiply you, and will establish my covenant with you. 10 And ye shall eat old store long kept, and ye shall bring forth the old because of the new. 11 And I will set my tabernacle among you: and my soul shall not abhor you. 12 And I will walk among you, and will be your God, and ye shall be my people. 13 I am Jehovah your God, who brought you forth out of the land of Egypt, that ye should not be their

---

[42ix] It is generally believed that the author of this section is the original compiler of H. vv. 1-2 (v. 2, cf. 19^{30}) are "fundamental commands of the theocracy" Ka. vv. 31-34, 38, 44 plainly presuppose the exile. v. 34 is cited 2 Ch. 36$^{21-22}$ as a word of Jeremiah (a confirmation of the exilic dating). v. 46 is Rp's conclusion to 17-26.

bondmen; and I have broken the bars of your yoke, and made you go upright.
14 But if ye will not hearken unto me, and will not do all these commandments; 15 and if ye shall reject my statutes, and if your soul abhor mine ordinances, so that ye will not do all my commandments, but break my covenant; 16 I also will do this unto you: I will appoint terror over you, even consumption and fever, that shall consume the eyes, and make the soul to pine away; and ye shall sow your seed in vain, for your enemies shall eat it. 17 And I will set my face against you, and ye shall be smitten before your enemies: they that hate you shall rule over you; and ye shall flee when none pursueth you. 18 And if ye will not yet for these things hearken unto me, then I will chastise you seven times more for your sins. 19 And I will break the pride of your power: and I will make your heaven as iron, and your earth as brass; 20 and your strength shall be spent in vain; for your land shall not yield its increase, neither shall the trees of the land yield their fruit.
21 And if ye walk contrary unto me, and will not hearken unto me, I will bring seven times more plagues upon you according to your sins. 22 And I will send the beast of the field among you, which shall rob you of your children, and destroy your cattle, and make you few in number; and your ways shall become desolate.
23 And if by these things ye will not be reformed unto me, but will walk contrary unto me; 24 then will I also walk contrary unto you; and I will smite you, even I, seven times for your sins. 25 And I will bring a sword upon you, that shall execute the vengeance of the covenant; and ye shall be gathered together within your cities: and I will send the pestilence among you; and ye shall be delivered into the hand of the enemy. 26 When I break your staff of bread, ten women shall bake your bread in one oven, and they shall deliver your bread again by weight: and ye shall eat, and not be satisfied.
27 And if ye will not for all this hearken unto me, but walk contrary unto me; 28 then I will walk contrary unto you in wrath; and I also will chastise you seven times for your sins. 29 And ye shall eat the flesh of your sons, and the flesh of your daughters shall ye eat. 30 And I will destroy your high places, and cut down your sun-images, and cast your dead bodies upon the bodies of your idols; and my soul shall abhor you. 31 And I will make your cities a waste, and will bring your sanctuaries unto desolation, and I will not smell the savor of your sweet odors. 32 And I will bring the land into desolation; and your enemies that dwell therein shall be astonished at it. 33 And you will I scatter among the nations, and I will draw out the

sword after you: and your land shall be a desolation, and your cities shall be a waste. 34 Then shall the land enjoy its sabbaths, as long as it lieth desolate, and ye are in your enemies' land; even then shall the land rest, and enjoy its sabbaths. 35 As long as it lieth desolate it shall have rest, even the rest which it had not in your sabbaths, when ye dwelt upon it. 36 And as for them that are left of you, I will send a faintness into their heart in the lands of their enemies: and the sound of a driven leaf shall chase them; and they shall flee, as one fleeth from the sword; and they shall fall when none pursueth. 37 And they shall stumble one upon another, as it were before the sword, when none pursueth: and ye shall have no power to stand before your enemies. 38 And ye shall perish among the nations, and the land of your enemies shall eat you up. 39 And they that are left of you shall pine away in their iniquity in your enemies' lands; and also in the iniquities of their fathers shall they pine away with them.

40 And they shall confess their iniquity, and the iniquity of their fathers, in their trespass which they trespassed against me, and also that, because they walked contrary unto me, 41 I also walked contrary unto them, and brought them into the land of their enemies: if then their uncircumcised heart be humbled, and they then accept of the punishment of their iniquity; 42 then will I remember my covenant with Jacob; and also my covenant with Isaac, and also my covenant with Abraham will I remember; and I will remember the land. 43 The land also shall be left by them, and shall enjoy its sabbaths, while it lieth desolate without them: and they shall accept of the punishment of their iniquity; because, even because they rejected mine ordinances, and their soul abhorred my statutes. 44 And yet for all that, when they are in the land of their enemies, I will not reject them, neither will I abhor them, to destroy them utterly, and to break my covenant with them; for I am Jehovah their God; 45 but I will for their sakes remember the covenant of their ancestors, whom I brought forth out of the land of Egypt in the sight of the nations, that I might be their God: I am Jehovah.

46 These are the statutes and ordinances and laws, which Jehovah made between him and the children of Israel in mount Sinai by Moses.

43. VOWS, DEVOTED THINGS, AND TITHES. P47iv, 76.
Lv. 27¹⁻³⁴

1 And Jehovah spake unto Moses, saying, 2 Speak unto

---
⁴³ The chapter is regarded as a late element in P (Ps). vv. 32-33: contrast Neh. 10³⁷⁻³⁸ 12⁴⁴ 13⁵,¹² and 2 Ch. 31⁵⁻⁶ (HDB., art. "Tithe").

the children of Israel, and say unto them, When a man shall accomplish a vow, the persons shall be for Jehovah by thy estimation. 3 And thy estimation shall be of the male from twenty years old even unto sixty years old, even thy estimation shall be fifty shekels of silver, after the shekel of the sanctuary. 4 And if it be a female, then thy estimation shall be thirty shekels. 5 And if it be from five years old even unto twenty years old, then thy estimation shall be of the male twenty shekels, and for the female ten shekels. 6 And if it be from a month old even unto five years old, then thy estimation shall be of the male five shekels of silver, and for the female thy estimation shall be three shekels of silver. 7 And if it be from sixty years old and upward; if it be a male, then thy estimation shall be fifteen shekels, and for the female ten shekels. 8 But if he be poorer than thy estimation, then he shall be set before the priest, and the priest shall value him; according to the ability of him that vowed shall the priest value him.

9 And if it be a beast, whereof men offer an oblation unto Jehovah, all that any man giveth of such unto Jehovah shall be holy. 10 He shall not alter it, nor change it, a good for a bad, or a bad for a good: and if he shall at all change beast for beast, then both it and that for which it is changed shall be holy. 11 And if it be any unclean beast, of which they do not offer an oblation unto Jehovah, then he shall set the beast before the priest; 12 and the priest shall value it, whether it be good or bad: as thou the priest valuest it, so shall it be. 13 But if he will indeed redeem it, then he shall add the fifth part thereof unto thy estimation.

14 And when a man shall sanctify his house to be holy unto Jehovah, then the priest shall estimate it, whether it be good or bad: as the priest shall estimate it, so shall it stand. 15 And if he that sanctified it will redeem his house, then he shall add the fifth part of the money of thy estimation unto it, and it shall be his.

16 And if a man shall sanctify unto Jehovah part of the field of his possession, then thy estimation shall be according to the sowing thereof: the sowing of a homer of barley *shall be valued* at fifty shekels of silver. 17 If he sanctify his field from the year of jubilee, according to thy estimation it shall stand. 18 But if he sanctify his field after the jubilee, then the priest shall reckon unto him the money according to the years that remain unto the year of jubilee; and an abatement shall be made from thy estimation. 19 And if he that sanctified the field will indeed redeem it, then he shall add the fifth part of the money of thy estimation unto it, and it shall be assured to him. 20 And if he will not redeem the field, or if he have sold

the field to another man, it shall not be redeemed any more: 21 but the field, when it goeth out in the jubilee, shall be holy unto Jehovah, as a field devoted; the possession thereof shall be the priest's. 22 And if he sanctify unto Jehovah a field which he hath bought, which is not of the field of his possession; 23 then the priest shall reckon unto him the worth of thy estimation unto the year of jubilee: and he shall give thine estimation in that day, as a holy thing unto Jehovah. 24 In the year of jubilee the field shall return unto him of whom it was bought, even to him to whom the possession of the land belongeth. 25 And all thy estimations shall be according to the shekel of the sanctuary: twenty gerahs shall be the shekel.

26 Only the firstling among beasts, which is made a firstling to Jehovah, no man shall sanctify it; whether it be ox or sheep, it is Jehovah's. 27 And if it be of an unclean beast, then he shall ransom it according to thine estimation, and shall add unto it the fifth part thereof: or if it be not redeemed, then it shall be sold according to thy estimation.

28 Notwithstanding, no devoted thing, that a man shall devote unto Jehovah of all that he hath, whether of man or beast, or of the field of his possession, shall be sold or redeemed: every devoted thing is most holy unto Jehovah. 29 No one devoted, that shall be devoted from among men, shall be ransomed; he shall surely be put to death.

30 And all the tithe of the land, whether of the seed of the land, or of the fruit of the tree, is Jehovah's: it is holy unto Jehovah. 31 And if a man will redeem aught of his tithe, he shall add unto it the fifth part thereof. 32 And all the tithe of the herd or the flock, whatsoever passeth under the rod, the tenth shall be holy unto Jehovah. 33 He shall not search whether it be good or bad, neither shall he change it: and if he change it at all, then both it and that for which it is changed shall be holy; it shall not be redeemed.

34 These are the commandments, which Jehovah commanded Moses for the children of Israel in mount Sinai.

44. THE CENSUS OF THE CHILDREN OF ISRAEL. P70.

Nu. 1[1-54]

1 And Jehovah spake unto Moses in the wilderness of Sinai, in the tent of meeting, on the first day of the second month, in the second year after they were come out of the land of Egypt, saying, 2 Take ye the sum of all the congregation of the children of Israel, by their families, by their fathers' houses, according to the number of the names, every male, by their polls; 3 from twenty years old and upward, all that are able to go forth to war in Israel, thou and Aaron shall number them by

their hosts. 4 And with you there shall be a man of every tribe; every one head of his father's house. 5 And these are the names of the men that shall stand with you. Of Reuben: Elizur the son of Shedeur. 6 Of Simeon: Shelumiel the son of Zurishaddai. 7 Of Judah: Nahshon the son of Amminadab. 8 Of Issachar: Nethanel the son of Zuar. 9 Of Zebulun: Eliab the son of Helon. 10 Of the children of Joseph: Of Ephraim: Elishama the son of Ammihud. Of Manasseh: Gamaliel the son of Pedahzur. 11 Of Benjamin: Abidan the son of Gideoni. 12 Of Dan: Ahiezer the son of Ammishaddai. 13 Of Asher: Pagiel the son of Ochran. 14 Of Gad: Eliasaph the son of Deuel. 15 Of Naphtali: Ahira the son of Enan. 16 These are they that were called of the congregation, the princes of the tribes of their fathers; they were the heads of the thousands of Israel. 17 And Moses and Aaron took these men that are mentioned by name: 18 and they assembled all the congregation together on the first day of the second month; and they declared their pedigrees after their families, by their fathers' houses, according to the number of the names, from twenty years old and upward, by their polls. 19 As Jehovah commanded Moses, so he numbered them in the wilderness of Sinai.

20 And the children of Reuben, Israel's first-born, their generations, by their families, by their fathers' houses, according to the number of the names, by their polls, every male from twenty years old and upward, all that were able to go forth to war; 21 those that were numbered of them, of the tribe of Reuben, were forty and six thousand and five hundred.

22 Of the children of Simeon, their generations, by their families, by their fathers' houses, those that were numbered thereof according to the number of the names, by their polls, every male from twenty years old and upward, all that were able to go forth to war; 23 those that were numbered of them, of the tribe of Simeon, were fifty and nine thousand and three hundred.

24 Of the children of Gad, their generations, by their families, by their fathers' houses, according to the number of the names, from twenty years old and upward, all that were able to go forth to war; 25 those that were numbered of them, of the tribe of Gad, were forty and five thousand six hundred and fifty.

26 Of the children of Judah, their generations, by their families, by their fathers' houses, according to the number of the names, from twenty years old and upward, all that were able to go forth to war; 27 those that were numbered of them, of the tribe of Judah, were threescore and fourteen thousand and six hundred.

28 Of the children of Issachar, their generations, by their families, by their fathers' houses, according to the number of the names, from twenty years old and upward, all that were able to go forth to war; 29 those that were numbered of them, of the tribe of Issachar, were fifty and four thousand and four hundred.

30 Of the children of Zebulun, their generations, by their families, by their fathers' houses, according to the number of the names, from twenty years old and upward, all that were able to go forth to war; 31 those that were numbered of them, of the tribe of Zebulun, were fifty and seven thousand and four hundred.

32 Of the children of Joseph, *namely*, of the children of Ephraim, their generations, by their families, by their fathers' houses, according to the number of the names, from twenty years old and upward, all that were able to go forth to war; 33 those that were numbered of them, of the tribe of Ephraim, were forty thousand and five hundred.

34 Of the children of Manasseh, their generations, by their families, by their fathers' houses, according to the number of the names, from twenty years old and upward, all that were able to go forth to war; 35 those that were numbered of them, of the tribe of Manasseh, were thirty and two thousand and two hundred.

36 Of the children of Benjamin, their generations, by their families, by their fathers' houses, according to the number of the names, from twenty years old and upward, all that were able to go forth to war; 37 those that were numbered of them, of the tribe of Benjamin, were thirty and five thousand and four hundred.

38 Of the children of Dan, their generations, by their families, by their fathers' houses, according to the number of the names, from twenty years old and upward, all that were able to go forth to war; 39 those that were numbered of them, of the tribe of Dan, were threescore and two thousand and seven hundred.

40 Of the children of Asher, their generations, by their families, by their fathers' houses, according to the number of the names, from twenty years old and upward, all that were able to go forth to war; 41 those that were numbered of them, of the tribe of Asher, were forty and one thousand and five hundred.

42 Of the children of Naphtali, their generations, by their families, by their fathers' houses, according to the number of the names, from twenty years old and upward, all that were able to go forth to war; 43 those that were numbered of them, of the

tribe of Naphtali, were fifty and three thousand and four hundred.

44 These are they that were numbered, whom Moses and Aaron numbered, and the princes of Israel, being twelve men; they were each one for his fathers' house. 45 So all they that were numbered of the children of Israel by their fathers' houses, from twenty years old and upward, all that were able to go forth to war in Israel; 46 even all they that were numbered were six hundred thousand and three thousand and five hundred and fifty.

47 But the Levites after the tribe of their fathers were not numbered among them. 48 For Jehovah spake unto Moses, saying, 49 Only the tribe of Levi thou shalt not number, neither shalt thou take the sum of them among the children of Israel: 50 but appoint thou the Levites over the tabernacle of the testimony, and over all the furniture thereof, and over all that belongeth to it: they shall bear the tabernacle, and all the furniture thereof; and they shall minister unto it, and shall encamp round about the tabernacle. 51 And when the tabernacle setteth forward, the Levites shall take it down; and when the tabernacle is to be pitched, the Levites shall set it up: and the stranger that cometh nigh shall be put to death. 52 And the children of Israel shall pitch their tents, every man by his own camp, and every man by his own standard, according to their hosts. 53 But the Levites shall encamp round about the tabernacle of the testimony, that there be no wrath upon the congregation of the children of Israel: and the Levites shall keep the charge of the tabernacle of the testimony. 54 Thus did the children of Israel; according to all that Jehovah commanded Moses, so did they.

45. THE CAMP.
Nu. 2$^{1-34}$

1 And Jehovah spake unto Moses and unto Aaron, saying, 2 The children of Israel shall encamp every man by his own standard, with the ensigns of their fathers' houses: over against the tent of meeting shall they encamp round about. 3 And those that encamp on the east side toward the sunrising shall be they of the standard of the camp of Judah, according to their hosts: and the prince of the children of Judah shall be Nahshon the son of Amminadab. 4 And his host, and those that were numbered of them, were three score and fourteen thousand and six hundred. 5 And those that encamp next unto him shall be the tribe of Issachar: and the prince of the children of Issachar shall be Nethanel the son of Zuar. 6 And his host, and those that were numbered thereof, were

fifty and four thousand and four hundred. 7 *And* the tribe of Zebulun: and the prince of the children of Zebulun shall be Eliab the son of Helon. 8 And his host, and those that were numbered thereof, were fifty and seven thousand and four hundred. 9 All that were numbered of the camp of Judah were a hundred thousand and fourscore thousand and six thousand and four hundred, according to their hosts. They shall set forth first.

10 On the south side shall be the standard of the camp of Reuben according to their hosts: and the prince of the children of Reuben shall be Elizur the son of Shedeur. 11 And his host, and those that were numbered thereof, were forty and six thousand and five hundred. 12 And those that encamp next unto him shall be the tribe of Simeon: and the prince of the children of Simeon shall be Shelumiel the son of Zurishaddai. 13 And his host, and those that were numbered of them, were fifty and nine thousand and three hundred. 14 And the tribe of Gad: and the prince of the children of Gad shall be Eliasaph the son of Reuel. 15 And his host, and those that were numbered of them, were forty and five thousand and six hundred and fifty. 16 All that were numbered of the camp of Reuben were a hundred thousand and fifty and one thousand and four hundred and fifty, according to their hosts. And they shall set forth second.

17 Then the tent of meeting shall set forward, with the camp of the Levites in the midst of the camps: as they encamp, so shall they set forward, every man in his place, by their standards.

18 On the west side shall be the standard of the camp of Ephraim according to their hosts: and the prince of the children of Ephraim shall be Elishama the son of Ammihud. 19 And his host, and those that were numbered of them, were forty thousand and five hundred. 20 And next unto him shall be the tribe of Manasseh: and the prince of the children of Manasseh shall be Gamaliel the son of Pedahzur. 21 And his host, and those that were numbered of them, were thirty and two thousand and two hundred. 22 And the tribe of Benjamin: and the prince of the children of Benjamin shall be Abidan the son of Gideoni. 23 And his host, and those that were numbered of them, were thirty and five thousand and four hundred. 24 All that were numbered of the camp of Ephraim were a hundred thousand and eight thousand and a hundred, according to their hosts. And they shall set forth third.

25 On the north side shall be the standard of the camp of Dan according to their hosts: and the prince of the children of Dan shall be Ahiezer the son of Ammishaddai. 26 And his

host, and those that were numbered of them, were threescore and two thousand and seven hundred. 27 And those that encamp next unto him shall be the tribe of Asher: and the prince of the children of Asher shall be Pagiel the son of Ochran. 28 And his host, and those that were numbered of them, were forty and one thousand and five hundred. 29 And the tribe of Naphtali: and the prince of the children of Naphtali shall be Ahira the son of Enan. 30 And his host, and those that were numbered of them, were fifty and three thousand and four hundred. 31 All that were numbered of the camp of Dan were a hundred thousand and fifty and seven thousand and six hundred. They shall set forth hindmost by their standards.

32 These are they that were numbered of the children of Israel by their fathers' houses: all that were numbered of the camps according to their hosts were six hundred thousand and three thousand and five hundred and fifty. 33 But the Levites were not numbered among the children of Israel; as Jehovah commanded Moses. 34 Thus did the children of Israel; according to all that Jehovah commanded Moses, so they encamped by their standards, and so they set forward, every one by their families, according to their fathers' houses.

46. "THE GENERATIONS OF AARON AND MOSES": THE SONS OF AARON AND THE LEVITES—THEIR DUTIES. P50, 64, 1, 39.
Nu. 3^1-4^{49}

3 Now these are the generations of Aaron and Moses in the day that Jehovah spake with Moses in mount Sinai. 2 And these are the names of the sons of Aaron: Nadab the firstborn, and Abihu, Eleazar, and Ithamar. 3 These are the names of the sons of Aaron, the priests that were anointed, whom he consecrated to minister in the priest's office. 4 And Nadab and Abihu died before Jehovah, when they offered strange fire before Jehovah, in the wilderness of Sinai, and they had no children; and Eleazar and Ithamar ministered in the priest's office in the presence of Aaron their father.

5 And Jehovah spake unto Moses, saying, 6 Bring the tribe of Levi near, and set them before Aaron the priest, that they may minister unto him. 7 And they shall keep his charge, and the charge of the whole congregation before the tent of meeting, to do the service of the tabernacle. 8 And they shall keep all the furniture of the tent of meeting, and the charge of the children of Israel, to do the service of the tabernacle. 9 And thou shalt give the Levites unto Aaron and to his sons: they are wholly given unto him on the behalf of the children of Israel.

10 And thou shalt appoint Aaron and his sons, and they shall keep their priesthood: and the stranger that cometh nigh shall be put to death.

11 And Jehovah spake unto Moses, saying, 12 And I, behold, I have taken the Levites from among the children of Israel instead of all the first-born that openeth the womb among the children of Israel; and the Levites shall be mine: 13 for all the first-born are mine; on the day that I smote all the first-born in the land of Egypt I hallowed unto me all the first-born in Israel, both man and beast; mine they shall be: I am Jehovah.

14 And Jehovah spake unto Moses in the wilderness of Sinai, saying, 15 Number the children of Levi by their fathers' houses, by their families: every male from a month old and upward shalt thou number them. 16 And Moses numbered them according to the word of Jehovah, as he was commanded. 17 And these were the sons of Levi by their names: Gershon, and Kohath, and Merari. 18 And these are the names of the sons of Gershon by their families: Libni and Shimei. 19 And the sons of Kohath by their families: Amram, and Izhar, Hebron, and Uzziel. 20 And the sons of Merari by their families: Mahli and Mushi. These are the families of the Levites according to their fathers' houses.

21 Of Gershon was the family of the Libnites, and the family of the Shimeites: these are the families of the Gershonites. 22 Those that were numbered of them, according to the number of all the males, from a month old and upward, even those that were numbered of them were seven thousand and five hundred. 23 The families of the Gershonites shall encamp behind the tabernacle westward. 24 And the prince of the fathers' house of the Gershonites shall be Eliasaph the son of Lael. 25 And the charge of the sons of Gershon in the tent of meeting shall be the tabernacle, and the Tent, the covering thereof, and the screen for the door of the tent of meeting, 26 and the hangings of the court, and the screen for the door of the court, which is by the tabernacle, and by the altar round about, and the cords of it for all the service thereof.

27 And of Kohath was the family of the Amramites, and the family of the Izharites, and the family of the Hebronites, and the family of the Uzzielites: these are the families of the Kohathites. 28 According to the number of all the males, from a month old and upward, there were eight thousand and six hundred, keeping the charge of the sanctuary. 29 The families of the sons of Kohath shall encamp on the side of the tabernacle southward. 30 And the prince of the fathers' house of the families of the Kohathites shall be Elizaphan the son of Uzziel. 31 And

their charge shall be the ark, and the table, and the candlestick, and the altars, and the vessels of the sanctuary wherewith they minister, and the screen, and all the service thereof. 32 And Eleazar the son of Aaron the priest shall be prince of the princes of the Levites, *and have* the oversight of them that keep the charge of the sanctuary.

33 Of Merari was the family of the Mahlites, and the family of the Mushites: these are the families of Merari. 34 And those that were numbered of them, according to the number of all the males, from a month old and upward, were six thousand and two hundred. 35 And the prince of the fathers' house of the families of Merari was Zuriel the son of Abihail: they shall encamp on the side of the tabernacle northward. 36 And the appointed charge of the sons of Merari shall be the boards of the tabernacle, and the bars thereof, and the pillars thereof, and the sockets thereof, and all the instruments thereof, and all the service thereof, 37 and the pillars of the court round about, and their sockets, and their pins, and their cords.

38 And those that encamp before the tabernacle eastward, before the tent of meeting toward the sunrising, shall be Moses, and Aaron and his sons, keeping the charge of the sanctuary for the charge of the children of Israel; and the stranger that cometh nigh shall be put to death. 39 All that were numbered of the Levites, whom Moses and Aaron numbered at the commandment of Jehovah, by their families, all the males from a month old and upward, were twenty and two thousand.

40 And Jehovah said unto Moses, Number all the first-born males of the children of Israel from a month old and upward, and take the number of their names. 41 And thou shalt take the Levites for me (I am Jehovah) instead of all the first-born among the children of Israel; and the cattle of the Levites instead of all the firstlings among the cattle of the children of Israel. 42 And Moses numbered, as Jehovah commanded him, all the first-born among the children of Israel. 43 And all the first-born males according to the number of names, from a month old and upward, of those that were numbered of them, were twenty and two thousand two hundred and threescore and thirteen.

44 And Jehovah spake unto Moses, saying, 45 Take the Levites instead of all the first-born among the children of Israel, and the cattle of the Levites instead of their cattle; and the Levites shall be mine: I am Jehovah. 46 And for the redemption of the two hundred and threescore and thirteen of the first-born of the children of Israel, that are over and above *the number of* the Levites, 47 thou shalt take five shekels apiece by the poll; after the shekel of the sanctuary shalt thou take

them (the shekel is twenty gerahs): 48 and thou shalt give the money, wherewith the odd number of them is redeemed, unto Aaron and to his sons. 49 And Moses took the redemption-money from them that were over and above them that were redeemed by the Levites; 50 from the first-born of the children of Israel took he the money, a thousand three hundred and threescore and five *shekels*, after the shekel of the sanctuary: 51 and Moses gave the redemption-money unto Aaron and to his sons, according to the word of Jehovah, as Jehovah commanded Moses.

4 And Jehovah spake unto Moses and unto Aaron, saying, 2 Take the sum of the sons of Kohath from among the sons of Levi, by their families, by their fathers' houses, 3 from thirty years old and upward even until fifty years old, all that enter upon the service, to do the work in the tent of meeting. 4 This is the service of the sons of Kohath in the tent of meeting, *about* the most holy things: 5 when the camp setteth forward, Aaron shall go in, and his sons, and they shall take down the veil of the screen, and cover the ark of the testimony with it, 6 and shall put thereon a covering of sealskin, and shall spread over it a cloth all of blue, and shall put in the staves thereof. 7 And upon the table of showbread they shall spread a cloth of blue, and put thereon the dishes, and the spoons, and the bowls and the cups wherewith to pour out; and the continual bread shall be thereon: 8 and they shall spread upon them a cloth of scarlet, and cover the same with a covering of sealskin, and shall put in the staves thereof. 9 And they shall take a cloth of blue, and cover the candlestick of the light, and its lamps, and its snuffers, and its snuffdishes, and all the oil vessels thereof, wherewith they minister unto it: 10 and they shall put it and all the vessels thereof within a covering of sealskin, and shall put it upon the frame. 11 And upon the golden altar they shall spread a cloth of blue, and cover it with a covering of sealskin, and shall put in the staves thereof: 12 and they shall take all the vessels of ministry, wherewith they minister in the sanctuary, and put them in a cloth of blue, and cover them with a covering of sealskin, and shall put them on the frame. 13 And they shall take away the ashes from the altar, and spread a purple cloth thereon: 14 And they shall put upon it all the vessels thereof, wherewith they minister about it, the firepans, the flesh-hooks, and the shovels, and the basins, all the vessels of the altar; and they shall spread upon it a covering of sealskin, and put in the staves thereof. 15 And when Aaron and his sons have made an end of covering the sanctuary, and all the furniture of the sanctuary, as the camp is to set forward; after that, the sons of Kohath shall come to bear it: but they shall not touch the sanctuary, lest they die. These things are the bur-

den of the sons of Kohath in the tent of meeting. 16 And the charge of Eleazar the son of Aaron the priest shall be the oil for the light, and the sweet incense, and the continual meal-offering, and the anointing oil, the charge of all the tabernacle, and of all that therein is, the sanctuary, and the furniture thereof.

17 And Jehovah spake unto Moses and unto Aaron, saying, 18 Cut ye not off the tribe of the families of the Kohathites from among the Levites; 19 but thus do unto them, that they may live, and not die, when they approach unto the most holy things: Aaron and his sons shall go in, and appoint them every one to his service and to his burden; 20 but they shall not go in to see the sanctuary even for a moment, lest they die.

21 And Jehovah spake unto Moses, saying, 22 Take the sum of the sons of Gershon also, by their fathers' houses, by their families; 23 from thirty years old and upward until fifty years old shalt thou number them; all that enter in to wait upon the service, to do the work in the tent of meeting. 24 This is the service of the families of the Gershonites, in serving and in bearing burdens: 25 they shall bear the curtains of the tabernacle, and the tent of meeting, its covering, and the covering of sealskin that is above upon it, and the screen for the door of the tent of meeting, 26 and the hangings of the court, and the screen for the door of the gate of the court, which is by the tabernacle and by the altar round about, and their cords, and all the instruments of their service, and whatsoever shall be done with them: therein shall they serve. 27 At the commandment of Aaron and his sons shall be all the service of the sons of the Gershonites, in all their burden, and in all their service; and ye shall appoint unto them in charge all their burden. 28 This is the service of the families of the sons of the Gershonites in the tent of meeting: and their charge shall be under the hand of Ithamar the son of Aaron the priest.

29 As for the sons of Merari, thou shalt number them by their families, by their fathers' houses; 30 from thirty years old and upward even unto fifty years old shalt thou number them, every one that entereth upon the service, to do the work of the tent of meeting. 31 And this is the charge of their burden, according to all their service in the tent of meeting: the boards of the tabernacle, and the bars thereof, and the pillars thereof, and the sockets thereof, 32 and the pillars of the court round about, and their sockets, and their pins, and their cords, with all their instruments, and with all their service: and by name ye shall appoint the instruments of the charge of their burden. 33 This is the service of the families of the sons of Merari, according to all their service, in the tent of meeting, under the hand of Ithamar the son of Aaron the priest.

34 And Moses and Aaron and the princes of the congregation numbered the sons of the Kohathites by their families, and by their fathers' houses, 35 from thirty years old and upward even unto fifty years old, every one that entered upon the service, for work in the tent of meeting: 36 and those that were numbered of them by their families were two thousand seven hundred and fifty. 37 These are they that were numbered of the families of the Kohathites, all that did serve in the tent of meeting, whom Moses and Aaron numbered according to the commandment of Jehovah by Moses.

38 And those that were numbered of the sons of Gershon, their families, and by their fathers' houses, 39 from thirty years old and upward even unto fifty years old, every one that entered upon the service, for work in the tent of meeting, 40 even those that were numbered of them, by their families, by their fathers' houses, were two thousand and six hundred and thirty. 41 These are they that were numbered of the families of the sons of Gershon, all that did serve in the tent of meeting, whom Moses and Aaron numbered according to the commandment of Jehovah.

42 And those that were numbered of the families of the sons of Merari, by their families, by their fathers' houses, 43 from thirty years old and upward even unto fifty years old, every one that entered upon the service, for work in the tent of meeting, 44 even those that were numbered of them by their families, were three thousand and two hundred. 45 These are they that were numbered of the families of the sons of Merari, whom Moses and Aaron numbered according to the commandment of Jehovah by Moses.

46 All those that were numbered of the Levites, whom Moses and Aaron and the princes of Israel numbered, by their families, and by their fathers' houses, 47 from thirty years old and upward even unto fifty years old, every one that entered in to do the work of service, and the work of bearing burdens in the tent of meeting, 48 even those that were numbered of them, were eight thousand and five hundred and fourscore. 49 According to the commandment of Jehovah they were numbered by Moses, every one according to his service, and according to his burden: thus were they numbered of him, as Jehovah commanded Moses.

47. MISCELLANEOUS LAWS.
Nu. 5^1-6^{21}

47i. THE UNCLEAN WITHOUT THE CAMP. P40.
Nu. 5^{1-4}

1 And Jehovah spake unto Moses, saying, 2 Command the

children of Israel, that they put out of the camp every leper, and every one that hath an issue, and whosoever is unclean by the dead: 3 both male and female shall ye put out, without the camp shall ye put them; that they defile not their camp, in the midst whereof I dwell. 4 And the children of Israel did so, and put them out without the camp; as Jehovah spake unto Moses, so did the children of Israel.

47ii. RESTITUTION AND ATONEMENT FOR TRESPASS.
Nu. 5^{5-10}

5 And Jehovah spake unto Moses, saying, 6 Speak unto the children of Israel, When a man or woman shall commit any sin that men commit, so as to trespass against Jehovah, and that soul shall be guilty; 7 then he shall confess his sin which he hath done: and he shall make restitution for his guilt in full, and add unto it the fifth part thereof, and give it unto him in respect of whom he hath been guilty. 8 But if the man have no kinsman to whom restitution may be made for the guilt, the restitution for guilt which is made unto Jehovah shall be the priest's; besides the ram of the atonement, whereby atonement shall be made for him. 9 And every heave-offering of all the holy things of the children of Israel, which they present unto the priest, shall be his. 10 And every man's hallowed things shall be his: whatsoever any man giveth the priest, it shall be his.

47iii. ADULTERY.
Nu. 5^{11-31}

11 And Jehovah spake unto Moses, saying, 12 Speak unto the children of Israel, and say unto them, If any man's wife go aside, and commit a trespass against him, 13 and a man lie with her carnally, and it be hid from the eyes of her husband, and be kept close, and she be defiled, and there be no witness against her, and she be not taken in the act; 14 and the spirit of jealousy come upon him, and he be jealous of his wife, and she be defiled: or if the spirit of jealousy come upon him, and he be jealous of his wife, and she be not defiled: 15 then shall the man bring his wife unto the priest, and shall bring her oblation for her, the tenth part of an ephah of barley meal; he shall pour no oil upon it, nor put frankincense thereon; for it is a meal-offering of jealousy, a meal-offering of memorial, bringing iniquity to remembrance.

16 And the priest shall bring her near, and set her before Jehovah: 17 and the priest shall take holy water in an earthen vessel; and of the dust that is on the floor of the tabernacle the priest shall take, and put it into the water. 18 And the

priest shall set the woman before Jehovah, and let the hair of the woman's head go loose, and put the meal-offering of memorial in her hands, which is the meal-offering of jealousy: and the priest shall have in his hand the water of bitterness that causeth the curse. 19 And the priest shall cause her to swear, and shall say unto the woman, If no man have lain with thee, and if thou have not gone aside to uncleanness, being under thy husband, be thou free from this water of bitterness that causeth the curse. 20 But if thou have gone aside, being under thy husband, and if thou be defiled, and some man have lain with thee besides thy husband: 21 then the priest shall cause the woman to swear with the oath of cursing, and the priest shall say unto the woman, Jehovah make thee a curse and an oath among thy people, when Jehovah doth make thy thigh to fall away, and thy body to swell; 22 and this water that causeth the curse shall go into thy bowels, and make thy body to swell, and thy thigh to fall away. And the woman shall say, Amen, Amen.

23 And the priest shall write these curses in a book, and he shall blot them out into the water of bitterness: 24 and he shall make the woman drink the water of bitterness that causeth the curse; and the water that causeth the curse shall enter into her *and become* bitter. 25 And the priest shall take the meal-offering of jealousy out of the woman's hand, and shall wave the meal-offering before Jehovah, and bring it unto the altar: 26 and the priest shall take a handful of the meal-offering, as the memorial thereof, and burn it upon the altar, and afterward shall make the woman drink the water. 27 And when he hath made her drink the water, then it shall come to pass, if she be defiled, and have committed a trespass against her husband, that the water that causeth the curse shall enter into her *and become* bitter, and her body shall swell, and her thigh shall fall away: and the woman shall be a curse among her people. 28 And if the woman be not defiled, but be clean; then she shall be free, and shall conceive seed.

29 This is the law of jealousy, when a wife, being under her husband, goeth aside, and is defiled; 30 or when the spirit of jealousy cometh upon a man, and he is jealous of his wife; then shall he set the woman before Jehovah, and the priest shall execute upon her all this law. 31 And the man shall be free from iniquity, and that woman shall bear her iniquity.

47iv. THE NAZIRITE VOW. Jg. 13$^{5.7}$ 16^{17}. Am. 2$^{11-12}$. Lam. 4^7. Nu. 6$^{1-21}$

1 And Jehovah spake unto Moses, saying, 2 Speak unto the children of Israel, and say unto them, When either man or woman shall make a special vow, the vow of a Nazirite, to sep-

arate himself unto Jehovah, 3 he shall separate himself from wine and strong drink; he shall drink no vinegar of wine, or vinegar of strong drink, neither shall he drink any juice of grapes, nor eat fresh grapes or dried. 4 All the days of his separation shall he eat nothing that is made of the grape-vine, from the kernels even to the husk.

5 All the days of his vow of separation there shall no razor come upon his head: until the days be fulfilled, in which he separateth himself unto Jehovah, he shall be holy; he shall let the locks of the hair of his head grow long.

6 All the days that he separateth himself unto Jehovah he shall not come near to a dead body. 7 He shall not make himself unclean for his father, or for his mother, for his brother, or for his sister, when they die; because his separation unto God is upon his head. 8 All the days of his separation he is holy unto Jehovah.

9 And if any man die very suddenly beside him, and he defile the head of his separation; then he shall shave his head in the day of his cleansing, on the seventh day shall he shave it. 10 And on the eighth day he shall bring two turtle-doves, or two young pigeons, to the priest, to the door of the tent of meeting: 11 and the priest shall offer one for a sin-offering, and the other for a burnt-offering, and make atonement for him, for that he sinned by reason of the dead, and shall hallow his head that same day. 12 And he shall separate unto Jehovah the days of his separation, and shall bring a he-lamb a year old for a trespass-offering: but the former days shall be void, because his separation was defiled.

13 And this is the law of the Nazirite, when the days of his separation are fulfilled: he shall be brought unto the door of the tent of meeting: 14 and he shall offer his oblation unto Jehovah, one he-lamb a year old without blemish for a burnt-offering, and one ewe-lamb a year old without blemish for a sin-offering, and one ram without blemish for peace-offerings, 15 and a basket of unleavened bread, cakes of fine flour mingled with oil, and unleavened wafers anointed with oil, and their meal-offering, and their drink-offerings. 16 And the priest shall present them before Jehovah, and shall offer his sin-offering, and his burnt-offering: 17 and he shall offer the ram for a sacrifice of peace-offerings unto Jehovah, with the basket of unleavened bread: the priest shall offer also the meal-offering thereof, and the drink-offering thereof. 18 And the Nazirite shall shave the head of his separation at the door of the tent of meeting, and shall take the hair of the head of his separation, and put it on the fire which is under the sacrifice of peace-offerings. 19 And the priest shall take the boiled shoulder

of the ram, and one unleavened cake out of the basket, and one unleavened wafer, and shall put them upon the hands of the Nazirite, after he hath shaven *the head of* his separation; 20 and the priest shall wave them for a wave-offering before Jehovah; this is holy for the priest, together with the wave-breast and heave-thigh: and after that the Nazirite may drink wine.

21 This is the law of the Nazirite who voweth, *and of* his oblation unto Jehovah for his separation, besides that which he is able to get: according to his vow which he voweth, so he must do after the law of his separation.

48. THE AARONIC BLESSING.
Nu. 6$^{22-27}$

22 And Jehovah spake unto Moses, saying, 23 Speak unto Aaron and unto his sons, saying, On this wise ye shall bless the children of Israel: ye shall say unto them,

24 Jehovah bless thee, and keep thee:

25 Jehovah make his face to shine upon thee, and be gracious unto thee:

26 Jehovah lift up his countenance upon thee, and give thee peace.

27 So shall they put my name upon the children of Israel; and I will bless them.

49. THE OFFERING OF THE PRINCES OF ISRAEL.
Nu. 7$^{1-88}$

1 And it came to pass on the day that Moses had made an end of setting up the tabernacle, and had anointed it and sanctified it, and all the furniture thereof, and the altar and all the vessels thereof, and had anointed them and sanctified them; 2 that the princes of Israel, the heads of their fathers' houses, offered. These were the princes of the tribes, these are they that were over them that were numbered: 3 and they brought their oblation before Jehovah, six covered wagons, and twelve oxen; a wagon for every two of the princes, and for each one an ox: and they presented them before the tabernacle. 4 And Jehovah spake unto Moses, saying, 5 Take it of them, that they may be *used* in doing the service of the tent of meeting; and thou shalt give them unto the Levites, to every man according to his service. 6 And Moses took the wagons and the oxen, and gave them unto the Levites. 7 Two wagons and four oxen he gave unto the sons of Gershon, according to their service: 8 and four wagons and eight oxen he gave unto the sons of Merari, according unto their service, under the hand of Ithamar the son of Aaron the priest. 9 But unto the sons of Kohath he gave none, because the service of the sanctuary belonged unto

them; they bare it upon their shoulders. 10 And the princes offered for the dedication of the altar in the day that it was anointed, even the princes offered their oblation before the altar. 11 And Jehovah said unto Moses, They shall offer their oblation, each prince on his day, for the dedication of the altar. 12 And he that offered his oblation the first day was Nahshon the son of Amminadab, of the tribe of Judah: 13 and his oblation was one silver platter, the weight whereof was a hundred and thirty *shekels*, one silver bowl of seventy shekels, after the shekel of the sanctuary; both of them full of fine flour mingled with oil for a meal-offering; 14 one golden spoon of ten *shekels*, full of incense; 15 one young bullock, one ram, one he-lamb a year old, for a burnt-offering; 16 one male of the goats for a sin-offering; 17 and for the sacrifice of peace offerings, two oxen, five rams, five he-goats, five he-lambs a year old: this was the oblation of Nahshon the son of Amminadab.

18 On the second day Nethanel the son of Zuar, prince of Issachar, did offer: 19 he offered for his oblation one silver platter, the weight whereof was a hundred and thirty *shekels*, one silver bowl of seventy shekels, after the shekel of the sanctuary; both of them full of fine flour mingled with oil for a meal-offering; 20 one golden spoon of ten *shekels*, full of incense; 21 one young bullock, one ram, one he-lamb a year old, for a burnt-offering; 22 one male of the goats for a sin-offering; 23 and for the sacrifice of peace-offerings, two oxen, five rams, five he-goats, five he-lambs a year old: this was the oblation of Nethanel the son of Zuar.

24 On the third day Eliab the son of Helon, prince of the children of Zebulun: 25 his oblation was one silver platter, the weight whereof was a hundred and thirty *shekels*, one silver bowl of seventy shekels, after the shekel of the sanctuary; both of them full of fine flour mingled with oil for a meal-offering; 26 one golden spoon of ten *shekels*, full of incense; 27 one young bullock, one ram, one he-lamb a year old, for a burnt-offering; 28 one male of the goats for a sin-offering; 29 and for the sacrifice of peace-offerings, two oxen, five rams, five he-goats, five he-lambs a year old: this was the oblation of Eliab the son of Helon.

30 On the fourth day Elizur the son of Shedeur, prince of the children of Reuben; 31 his oblation was one silver platter, the weight whereof was a hundred and thirty *shekels*, one silver bowl of seventy shekels, after the shekel of the sanctuary; both of them full of fine flour mingled with oil for a meal-offering; 32 one golden spoon of ten *shekels*, full of incense; 33 one young bullock, one ram, one he-lamb a year old, for a burnt-

offering; 34 one male of the goats for a sin-offering; 35 and for the sacrifice of peace-offerings, two oxen, five rams, five he-goats, five he-lambs a year old: this was the oblation of Elizur the son of Shedeur.

36 On the fifth day Shelumiel the son of Zurishaddai, prince of the children of Simeon: 37 his oblation was one silver platter, the weight whereof was a hundred and thirty *shekels*, one silver bowl of seventy shekels, after the shekel of the sanctuary; both of them full of fine flour mingled with oil for a meal-offering; 38 one golden spoon of ten *shekels*, full of incense; 39 one young bullock, one ram, one he-lamb a year old, for a burnt-offering; 40 one male of the goats for a sin-offering; 41 and for the sacrifice of peace-offerings, two oxen, five rams, five he-goats, five he-lambs a year old: this was the oblation of Shelumiel the son of Zurishaddai.

42 On the sixth day Eliasaph the son of Deuel, prince of the children of Gad: 43 his oblation was one silver platter, the weight whereof was a hundred and thirty *shekels*, one silver bowl of seventy shekels, after the shekel of the sanctuary; both of them full of fine flour mingled with oil for a meal-offering; 44 one golden spoon of ten *shekels*, full of incense; 45 one young bullock, one ram, one he-lamb a year old, for a burnt-offering; 46 one male of the goats for a sin-offering; 47 and for the sacrifice of peace-offerings, two oxen, five rams, five he-goats, five he-lambs a year old: this was the oblation of Eliasaph the son of Deuel.

48 On the seventh day Elishama the son of Ammihud, prince of the children of Ephraim: 49 his oblation was one silver platter, the weight whereof was a hundred and thirty *shekels*, one silver bowl of seventy shekels, after the shekel of the sanctuary; both of them full of fine flour mingled with oil for a meal-offering; 50 one golden spoon of ten *shekels*, full of incense; 51 one young bullock, one ram, one he-lamb a year old, for a burnt-offering; 52 one male of the goats for a sin-offering; 53 and for the sacrifice of peace offerings, two oxen, five rams, five he-goats, five he-lambs a year old: this was the oblation of Elishama the son of Ammihud.

54 On the eighth day Gamaliel the son of Pedahzur, prince of the children of Manasseh: 55 his oblation was one silver platter, the weight whereof was a hundred and thirty *shekels*, one silver bowl of seventy shekels, after the shekel of the sanctuary; both of them full of fine flour mingled with oil for a meal-offering; 56 one golden spoon of ten *shekels*, full of incense; 57 one young bullock, one ram, one he-lamb, a year old, for a burnt-offering; 58 one male of the goats for a sin-offering; 59 and for the sacrifice of peace-offerings, two oxen, five rams,

five he-goats, five he-lambs a year old: this was the oblation of Gamaliel the son of Pedahzur.

60 On the ninth day Abidan the son of Gideoni, prince of the children of Benjamin: 61 his oblation was one silver platter, the weight whereof was a hundred and thirty *shekels*, one silver bowl of seventy shekels, after the shekel of the sanctuary; both of them full of fine flour mingled with oil for a meal-offering; 62 one golden spoon of ten *shekels*, full of incense; 63 one young bullock, one ram, one he-lamb a year old, for a burnt-offering; 64 one male of the goats for a sin offering; 65 and for the sacrifice of peace-offerings, two oxen, five rams, five he-goats, five he-lambs a year old: this was the oblation of Abidan the son of Gideoni.

66 On the tenth day Ahiezer the son of Ammishaddai, prince of the children of Dan: 67 his oblation was one silver platter, the weight whereof was a hundred and thirty *shekels*, one silver bowl of seventy shekels, after the shekel of the sanctuary; both of them full of fine flour mingled with oil for a meal-offering; 68 one golden spoon of ten *shekels*, full of incense; 69 one young bullock, one ram, one he-lamb a year old, for a burnt-offering; 70 one male of the goats for a sin-offering; 71 and for the sacrifice of peace-offerings, two oxen, five rams, five he-goats, five he-lambs a year old: this was the oblation of Ahiezer the son of Ammishaddai.

72 On the eleventh day Pagiel the son of Ochran, prince of the children of Asher: 73 his oblation was one silver platter, the weight whereof was a hundred and thirty *shekels*, one silver bowl of seventy shekels, after the shekel of the sanctuary; both of them full of fine flour mingled with oil for a meal-offering; 74 one golden spoon of ten *shekels*, full of incense; 75 one young bullock, one ram, one he-lamb a year old, for a burnt-offering; 76 one male of the goats for a sin-offering; 77 and for the sacrifice of peace-offerings, two oxen, five rams, five he-goats, five he-lambs a year old: this was the oblation of Pagiel the son of Ochran.

78 On the twelfth day Ahira the son of Enan, prince of the children of Naphtali: 79 his oblation was one silver platter, the weight whereof was a hundred and thirty *shekels*, one silver bowl of seventy shekels, after the shekel of the sanctuary; both of them full of fine flour mingled with oil for a meal-offering; 80 one golden spoon of ten *shekels*, full of incense; 81 one young bullock, one ram, one he-lamb a year old, for a burnt-offering; 82 one male of the goats for a sin-offering; 83 and for the sacrifice of peace-offerings, two oxen, five rams, five he-goats, five he-lambs a year old: this was the oblation of Ahira the son of Enan.

84 This was the dedication of the altar, in the day when it was anointed, by the princes of Israel: twelve silver platters, twelve silver bowls, twelve golden spoons; 85 each silver platter *weighing* a hundred and thirty *shekels*, and each bowl seventy; all the silver of the vessels two thousand and four hundred *shekels*, after the shekel of the sanctuary; 86 the twelve golden spoons, full of incense, *weighing* ten *shekels* apiece, after the shekel of the sanctuary; all the gold of the spoons a hundred and twenty *shekels*; 87 all the oxen for the burnt-offering twelve bullocks, the rams twelve, the he-lambs a year old twelve, and their meal-offering; and the males of the goats for a sin-offering twelve; 88 and all the oxen for the sacrifice of peace-offerings twenty and four bullocks, the rams sixty, the he-goats sixty, the he-lambs a year old sixty. This was the dedication of the altar, after that it was anointed.

50. Purification of the Levites. P46.
Nu. 7^{89}-8^{26}

7^{89} And when Moses went into the tent of meeting to speak with him, then he heard the Voice speaking unto him from above the mercy-seat that was upon the ark of the testimony, from between the two cherubim: and he spake unto him.

8^1 And Jehovah spake unto Moses, saying, 2 Speak unto Aaron, and say unto him, When thou lightest the lamps, the seven lamps shall give light in front of the candlestick. 3 And Aaron did so; he lighted the lamps thereof *so as to give light* in front of the candlestick, as Jehovah commanded Moses. 4 And this was the work of the candlestick, beaten work of gold; unto the base thereof, *and* unto the flowers thereof, it was beaten work: according unto the pattern which Jehovah had showed Moses, so he made the candlestick.

5 And Jehovah spake unto Moses, saying, 6 Take the Levites from among the children of Israel, and cleanse them. 7 And thus shalt thou do unto them, to cleanse them: sprinkle the water of expiation upon them, and let them cause a razor to pass over all their flesh, and let them wash their clothes, and cleanse themselves. 8 Then let them take a young bullock, and its meal-offering, fine flour mingled with oil; and another young bullock shalt thou take for a sin-offering. 9 And thou shalt present the Levites before the tent of meeting: and thou shalt assemble the whole congregation of the children of Israel: 10 and thou shalt present the Levites before Jehovah. And the children of Israel shall lay their hands upon the Levites: 11 and Aaron shall offer the Levites before Jehovah for a wave-offering, on the behalf of the children of Israel, that it may be theirs to do the service of Jehovah. 12 And the Levites shall

lay their hands upon the heads of the bullocks: and offer thou the one for a sin-offering, and the other for a burnt-offering, unto Jehovah, to make atonement for the Levites. 13 And thou shalt set the Levites before Aaron, and before his sons, and offer them for a wave-offering unto Jehovah. 14 Thus shalt thou separate the Levites from among the children of Israel; and the Levites shall be mine. 15 And after that shall the Levites go in to do the service of the tent of meeting: and thou shalt cleanse them, and offer them for a wave-offering. 16 For they are wholly given unto me from among the children of Israel; instead of all that openeth the womb, even the first-born of all the children of Israel, have I taken them unto me. 17 For all the first-born among the children of Israel are mine, both man and beast: on the day that I smote all the first-born in the land of Egypt I sanctified them for myself. 18 And I have taken the Levites instead of all the first-born among the children of Israel. 19 And I have given the Levites as a gift to Aaron and to his sons from among the children of Israel, to do the service of the children of Israel in the tent of meeting, and to make atonement for the children of Israel; that there be no plague among the children of Israel, when the children of Israel come nigh unto the sanctuary.

20 Thus did Moses, and Aaron, and all the congregation of the children of Israel, unto the Levites: according unto all that Jehovah commanded Moses touching the Levites, so did the children of Israel unto them. 21 And the Levites purified themselves from sin, and they washed their clothes: and Aaron offered them for a wave-offering before Jehovah; and Aaron made atonement for them to cleanse them. 22 And after that went the Levites in to do their service in the tent of meeting before Aaron, and before his sons: as Jehovah had commanded Moses concerning the Levites, so did they unto them.

23 And Jehovah spake unto Moses, saying, 24 This is that which belongeth unto the Levites: from twenty and five years old and upward they shall go in to wait upon the service in the work of the tent of meeting: 25 and from the age of fifty years they shall cease waiting upon the work, and shall serve no more, 26 but shall minister with their brethren in the tent of meeting, to keep the charge, and shall do no service. Thus shalt thou do unto the Levites touching their charges.

51. THE LAW OF THE PASSOVER. J26ix. P23v.
Nu. 9^{1-14}

1 And Jehovah spake unto Moses in the wilderness of Sinai, in the first month of the second year after they were come out of the land of Egypt, saying, 2 Moreover let the children of

Israel keep the passover in its appointed season. 3 In the fourteenth day of this month, at even, ye shall keep it in its appointed season: according to all the statutes of it, and according to all the ordinances thereof, shall ye keep it. 4 And Moses spake unto the children of Israel, that they should keep the passover. 5 And they kept the passover in the first *month*, on the fourteenth day of the month, at even, in the wilderness of Sinai: according to all that Jehovah commanded Moses, so did the children of Israel. 6 And there were certain men, who were unclean by reason of the dead body of a man, so that they could not keep the passover on that day: and they came before Moses and before Aaron on that day: 7 and those men said unto him, We are unclean by reason of the dead body of a man: wherefore are we kept back, that we may not offer the oblation of Jehovah in its appointed season among the children of Israel? 8 And Moses said unto them, Stay ye, that I may hear what Jehovah will command concerning you.

9 And Jehovah spake unto Moses, saying, 10 Speak unto the children of Israel, saying, If any man of you or of your generations shall be unclean by reason of a dead body, or be on a journey afar off, yet he shall keep the passover unto Jehovah. 11 In the second month on the fourteenth day at even they shall keep it; they shall eat it with unleavened bread and bitter herbs: 12 they shall leave none of it unto the morning, nor break a bone thereof: according to all the statute of the passover they shall keep it. 13 But the man that is clean, and is not on a journey, and forbeareth to keep the passover, that soul shall be cut off from his people; because he offered not the oblation of Jehovah in its appointed season, that man shall bear his sin. 14 And if a stranger shall sojourn among you, and will keep the passover unto Jehovah; according to the statute of the passover, and according to the ordinance thereof, so shall he do: ye shall have one statute, both for the sojourner, and for him that is born in the land.

52. THE CLOUD ON THE TABERNACLE. P36.
Nu. 9^{15-23}

15 And on the day that the tabernacle was reared up the cloud covered the tabernacle, even the tent of the testimony: and at even it was upon the tabernacle as it were the appearance of fire, until morning. 16 So it was alway: the cloud covered it, and the appearance of fire by night. 17 And whenever the cloud was taken up from over the Tent, then after that the children of Israel journeyed: and in the place where the cloud abode, there the children of Israel encamped. 18 At the com-

mandment of Jehovah the children of Israel journeyed, and at the commandment of Jehovah they encamped: as long as the cloud abode upon the tabernacle they remained encamped. 19 And when the cloud tarried upon the tabernacle many days, then the children of Israel kept the charge of Jehovah, and journeyed not. 20 And sometimes the cloud was a few days upon the tabernacle; then according to the commandment of Jehovah they remained encamped, and according to the commandment of Jehovah they journeyed. 21 And sometimes the cloud was from evening until morning; and when the cloud was taken up in the morning, they journeyed: or *if it continued* by day and by night, when the cloud was taken up, they journeyed. 22 Whether it were two days, or a month, or a year, that the cloud tarried upon the tabernacle, abiding thereon, the children of Israel remained encamped, and journeyed not; but when it was taken up, they journeyed. 23 At the commandment of Jehovah they encamped, and at the commandment of Jehovah they journeyed: they kept the charge of Jehovah, at the commandment of Jehovah by Moses.

53. THE SILVER TRUMPETS.
Nu. 10$^{1-10}$

1 And Jehovah spake unto Moses, saying, 2 Make thee two trumpets of silver; of beaten work shalt thou make them: and thou shalt use them for the calling of the congregation, and for the journeying of the camps. 3 And when they shall blow them, all the congregation shall gather themselves unto thee at the door of the tent of meeting. 4 And if they blow but one, then the princes, the heads of the thousands of Israel, shall gather themselves unto thee. 5 And when ye blow an alarm, the camps that lie on the east side shall take their journey. 6 And when ye blow an alarm the second time, the camps that lie on the south side shall take their journey: they shall blow an alarm for their journeys. 7 But when the assembly is to be gathered together, ye shall blow, but ye shall not sound an alarm. 8 And the sons of Aaron, the priests, shall blow the trumpets; and they shall be to you for a statute for ever throughout your generations. 9 And when ye go to war in your land against the adversary that oppresseth you, then ye shall sound an alarm with the trumpets; and ye shall be remembered before Jehovah your God, and ye shall be saved from your enemies. 10 Also in the day of your gladness, and in your set feasts, and in the beginnings of your months, ye shall blow the trumpets over your burnt-offerings, and over the sacrifices of your peace-offerings; and they shall be to you for a memorial before your God: I am Jehovah your God.

54. THE DEPARTURE FROM THE WILDERNESS OF SINAI. P30, 79.
Nu. 10¹¹⁻²⁸·³⁴

11 And it came to pass in the second year, in the second month, on the twentieth day of the month, that the cloud was taken up from over the tabernacle of the testimony. 12 And the children of Israel set forward according to their journeys out of the wilderness of Sinai; and the cloud abode in the wilderness of Paran. 13 And they first took their journey according to the commandment of Jehovah by Moses. 14 And in the first *place* the standard of the camp of the children of Judah set forward according to their hosts: and over his host was Nahshon the son of Amminadab. 15 And over the host of the tribe of the children of Issachar was Nethanel the son of Zuar. 16 And over the host of the tribe of the children of Zebulun was Eliab the son of Helon.

17 And the tabernacle was taken down; and the sons of Gershon and the sons of Merari, who bare the tabernacle, set forward. 18 And the standard of the camp of Reuben set forward according to their hosts: and over his host was Elizur the son of Shedeur. 19 And over the host of the tribe of the children of Simeon was Shelumiel the son of Zurishaddai. 20 And over the host of the tribe of the children of Gad was Eliasaph the son of Deuel.

21 And the Kohathites set forward, bearing the sanctuary: and *the others* did set up the tabernacle against their coming. 22 And the standard of the camp of the children of Ephraim set forward according to their hosts: and over his host was Elishama the son of Ammihud. 23 And over the host of the tribe of the children of Manasseh was Gamaliel the son of Pedahzur. 24 And over the host of the tribe of the children of Benjamin was Abidan the son of Gideoni.

25 And the standard of the camp of the children of Dan, which was the rearward of all the camps, set forward according to their hosts: and over his host was Ahiezer the son of Ammishaddai. 26 And over the host of the tribe of the children of Asher was Pagiel the son of Ochran. 27 And over the host of the tribe of the children of Naphtali was Ahira the son of Enan. 28 Thus were the journeyings of the children of Israel according to their hosts; and they set forward.

34 And the cloud of Jehovah was over them by day, when they set forward from the camp.

55. THE COMMISSION AND REPORT OF THE SPIES. J38, 40. E34.

Nu. 13¹⁻¹⁷ᵃ·²¹·²⁵⁻²⁶ᵃ·³²ᵃ

1 And Jehovah spake unto Moses, saying, 2 Send thou

men, that they may spy out the land of Canaan, which I give unto the children of Israel: of every tribe of their fathers shall ye send a man, every one a prince among them. 3 And Moses sent them from the wilderness of Paran according to the commandment of Jehovah: all of them men who were heads of the children of Israel. 4 And these were their names: Of the tribe of Reuben, Shammua the son of Zaccur. 5 Of the tribe of Simeon, Shaphat the son of Hori. 6 Of the tribe of Judah, Caleb the son of Jephunneh. 7 Of the tribe of Issachar, Igal the son of Joseph. 8 Of the tribe of Ephraim, Hoshea the son of Nun. 9 Of the tribe of Benjamin, Palti the son of Raphu. 10 Of the tribe of Zebulun, Gaddiel the son of Sodi. 11 Of the tribe of Joseph, *namely*, of the tribe of Manasseh, Gaddi the son of Susi. 12 Of the tribe of Dan, Ammiel the son of Gemalli. 13 Of the tribe of Asher, Sethur the son of Michael. 14 Of the tribe of Naphtali, Nahbi the son of Vophsi. 15 Of the tribe of Gad, Geuel the son of Machi. 16 These are the names of the men that Moses sent to spy out the land. And Moses called Hoshea the sun of Nun Joshua.

17a And Moses sent them to spy out the land of Canaan.

21 So they went up, and spied out the land from the wilderness of Zin unto Rehob, to the entrance of Hamath.

25 And they returned from spying out the land at the end of forty days. 26a And they went and came to Moses, and to Aaron, and to all the congregation of the children of Israel, unto the wilderness of Paran. 32a And they brought up an evil report of the land which they had spied out unto the children of Israel, saying, The land, through which we have gone to spy it out, is a land that eateth up the inhabitants thereof.

56. THE COMPLAINT OF THE PEOPLE. J39. E35.
Nu. $14^{1a.2}$

1a And all the congregation lifted up their voice, 2 and all the children of Israel murmured against Moses and against Aaron: and the whole congregation said unto them, Would that we had died in the land of Egypt! or would that we had died in this wilderness!

57. THE ANSWER OF JOSHUA AND CALEB. J40. E34.
Nu. $14^{5-7.10}$

5 Then Moses and Aaron fell on their faces before all the assembly of the congregation of the children of Israel. 6 And Joshua the son of Nun and Caleb the son of Jephunneh, who were of them that spied out the land, rent their clothes: 7 and they spake unto all the congregation of the children of Israel,

saying, The land, which we passed through to spy it out, is an exceeding good land.
10 But all the congregation bade stone them with stones. And the glory of Jehovah appeared in the tent of meeting unto all the children of Israel.

58. JEHOVAH'S REBUKE OF THE PEOPLE. J41. E36.
Nu. 14$^{26-30.34-38}$

26 And Jehovah spake unto Moses and unto Aaron, saying, 27 How long *shall I bear* with this evil congregation, that murmur against me? I have heard the murmurings of the children of Israel, which they murmur against me. 28 Say unto them, As I live, saith Jehovah, surely as ye have spoken in mine ears, so will I do to you: 29 your dead bodies shall fall in this wilderness; and all that were numbered of you, according to your whole number, from twenty years old and upward, that have murmured against me, 30 surely ye shall not come into the land, concerning which I sware that I would make you dwell therein, save Caleb the son of Jephunneh, and Joshua the son of Nun.
34 After the number of the days in which ye spied out the land, even forty days, for every day a year, shall ye bear your iniquities, even forty years, and ye shall know my alienation. 35 I, Jehovah, have spoken, surely this will I do unto all this evil congregation, that are gathered together against me: in this wilderness they shall be consumed, and there they shall die.
36 And the men, whom Moses sent to spy out the land, who returned, and made all the congregation to murmur against him, by bringing up an evil report against the land, 37 even those men that did bring up an evil report of the land, died by the plague before Jehovah. 38 But Joshua the son of Nun, and Caleb the son of Jephunneh, remained alive of those men that went to spy out the land.

59. LAWS CONCERNING OFFERINGS. P37.
Nu. 15$^{1-31}$

1 And Jehovah spake unto Moses, saying, 2 Speak unto the children of Israel, and say unto them, When ye are come into the land of your habitations, which I give unto you, 3 and will make an offering by fire unto Jehovah, a burnt-offering, or a sacrifice, to accomplish a vow, or as a freewill-offering, or in your set feasts, to make a sweet savor unto Jehovah, of the herd, or of the flock; 4 then shall he that offereth his oblation offer unto Jehovah a meal-offering of a tenth part *of an ephah* of fine

---
[58] v. 30 P: most scholars. But E: St. JE: Ho.

flour mingled with the fourth part of a hin of oil: 5 and wine for the drink-offering, the fourth part of a hin, shalt thou prepare with the burnt-offering, or for the sacrifice, for each lamb. 6 Or for a ram, thou shalt prepare for a meal-offering two tenth parts *of an ephah* of fine flour mingled with the third part of a hin of oil: 7 and for the drink-offering thou shalt offer the third part of a hin of wine, of a sweet savor unto Jehovah. 8 And when thou preparest a bullock for a burnt-offering, or for a sacrifice, to accomplish a vow, or for peace-offerings unto Jehovah; 9 then shall he offer with the bullock a meal-offering of three tenth parts *of an ephah* of fine flour mingled with half a hin of oil: 10 and thou shalt offer for the drink-offering half a hin of wine, for an offering made by fire, of a sweet savor unto Jehovah.

11 Thus shall it be done for each bullock, or for each ram, or for each of the he-lambs, or of the kids. 12 According to the number that ye shall prepare, so shall ye do to every one according to their number. 13 All that are home-born shall do these things after this manner, in offering an offering made by fire, of a sweet savor unto Jehovah. 14 And if a stranger sojourn with you, or whosoever may be among you throughout your generations, and will offer an offering made by fire, of a sweet savor unto Jehovah; as ye do, so he shall do. 15 For the assembly, there shall be one statute for you, and for the stranger that sojourneth *with you*, a statute for ever throughout your generations: as ye are, so shall the sojourner be before Jehovah. 16 One law and one ordinance shall be for you, and for the stranger that sojourneth with you.

17 And Jehovah spake unto Moses, saying, 18 Speak unto the children of Israel, and say unto them, When ye come into the land whither I bring you, 19 then it shall be, that, when ye eat of the bread of the land, ye shall offer up a heave-offering unto Jehovah. 20 Of the first of your dough ye shall offer up a cake for a heave-offering: as the heave-offering of the threshing-floor, so shall ye heave it. 21 Of the first of your dough ye shall give unto Jehovah a heave-offering throughout your generations.

22 And when ye shall err, and not observe all these commandments, which Jehovah hath spoken unto Moses, 23 even all that Jehovah hath commanded you by Moses, from the day that Jehovah gave commandment, and onward throughout your generations; 24 then it shall be, if it be done unwittingly, without the knowledge of the congregation, that all the congregation shall offer one young bullock for a burnt-offering, for a sweet savor unto Jehovah, with the meal-offering thereof, and the drink-offering thereof, acording to the ordinance, and

one he-goat for a sin-offering. 25 And the priest shall make atonement for all the congregation of the children of Israel, and they shall be forgiven; for it was an error, and they have brought their oblation, an offering made by fire unto Jehovah, and their sin-offering before Jehovah, for their error: 26 and all the congregation of the children of Israel shall be forgiven, and the stranger that sojourneth among them; for in respect of all the people it was done unwittingly.

27 And if one person sin unwittingly, then he shall offer a she-goat a year old for a sin-offering. 28 And the priest shall make atonement for the soul that erreth, when he sinneth unwittingly, before Jehovah, to make atonement for him; and he shall be forgiven. 29 Ye shall have one law for him that doeth aught unwittingly, for him that is home-born among the children of Israel, and for the stranger that sojourneth among them. 30 But the soul that doeth aught with a high hand, whether he be home-born or a sojourner, the same blasphemeth Jehovah; and that soul shall be cut off from among his people. 31 Because he hath despised the word of Jehovah, and hath broken his commandment, that soul shall utterly be cut off; his iniquity shall be upon him.

60. SABBATH-BREAKING PUNISHED. P33. Is. 56^{2-7} 58^{13-14}. Neh. 13^{15-22}.

Nu. 15^{32-36}

32 And while the children of Israel were in the wilderness, they found a man gathering sticks upon the sabbath day. 33 And they that found him gathering sticks brought him unto Moses and Aaron, and unto all the congregation. 34 And they put him in ward, because it had not been declared what should be done to him. 35 And Jehovah said unto Moses, The man shall surely be put to death: all the congregation shall stone him with stones without the camp. 36 And all the congregation brought him without the camp, and stoned him to death with stones; as Jehovah commanded Moses.

61. THE LAW OF FRINGES. Cf. P42iiiH.

Nu. 15^{37-41}

62. THE REBELLION OF KORAH AGAINST MOSES AND AARON. E38.

Nu. $16^{1a.2-11.16-24.27a.35-50}$

1a Now Korah, the son of Izhar, the son of Kohath, the son of Levi, 2 . . . with certain of the children of Israel, two hun-

---

[60] This incident, like numerous others in P, has the character of a legal precedent.
[62] At least vv. 7b-11, 36-40 are secondary (Ps).

dred and fifty princes of the congregation, called to the assembly, men of renown; 3 and they assembled themselves together against Moses and against Aaron, and said unto them, Ye take too much upon you, seeing all the congregation are holy, every one of them, and Jehovah is among them: wherefore then lift ye up yourselves above the assembly of Jehovah?
4 And when Moses heard it, he fell upon his face: 5 and he spake unto Korah and unto all his company, saying, In the morning Jehovah will show who are his, and who is holy, and will cause him to come near unto him: even him whom he shall choose will he cause to come near unto him. 6 This do: take you censers, Korah, and all his company; 7 and put fire in them, and put incense upon them before Jehovah to-morrow: and it shall be that the man whom Jehovah doth choose, he *shall be* holy: ye take too much upon you, ye sons of Levi. 8 And Moses said unto Korah, Hear now, ye sons of Levi: 9 *seemeth it but* a small thing unto you, that the God of Israel hath separated you from the congregation of Israel, to bring you near to himself, to do the service of the tabernacle of Jehovah, and to stand before the congregation to minister unto them; 10 and that he hath brought thee near, and all thy brethren the sons of Levi with thee? and seek ye the priesthood also? 11 Therefore thou and all thy company are gathered together against Jehovah: and Aaron, what is he that ye murmur against him?
16 And Moses said unto Korah, Be thou and all thy company before Jehovah, thou, and they, and Aaron, to-morrow: 17 and take ye every man his censer, and put incense upon them, and bring ye before Jehovah every man his censer, two hundred and fifty censers; thou also, and Aaron, each his censer. 18 And they took every man his censer, and put fire in them, and laid incense thereon, and stood at the door of the tent of meeting with Moses and Aaron. 19 And Korah assembled all the congregation against them unto the door of the tent of meeting: and the glory of Jehovah appeared unto all the congregation.
20 And Jehovah spake unto Moses and unto Aaron, saying, 21 Separate yourselves from among this congregation, that I may consume them in a moment. 22 And they fell upon their faces, and said, O God, the God of the spirits of all flesh, shall one man sin, and wilt thou be wroth with all the congregation? 23 And Jehovah spake unto Moses, saying, 24 Speak unto the congregation, saying, Get you up from about the tabernacle of Korah, Dathan, and Abiram.
27a So they gat them up from the tabernacle of Korah, Dathan, and Abiram, on every side.

35 And fire came forth from Jehovah, and devoured the two hundred and fifty men that offered the incense.

36 And Jehovah spake unto Moses, saying, 37 Speak unto Eleazar the son of Aaron the priest, that he take up the censers out of the burning, and scatter thou the fire yonder; for they are holy, 38 even the censers of the sinners against their own lives; and let them be made beaten plates for a covering of the altar: for they offered them before Jehovah; therefore they are holy; and they shall be a sign unto the children of Israel. 39 And Eleazar the priest took the brazen censers, which they that were burnt had offered; and they beat them out for a covering of the altar, 40 to be a memorial unto the children of Israel, to the end that no stranger, that is not of the seed of Aaron, come near to burn incense before Jehovah; that he be not as Korah, and as his company: as Jehovah spake unto him by Moses.

41 But on the morrow all the congregation of the children of Israel murmured against Moses and against Aaron, saying, Ye have killed the people of Jehovah. 42 And it came to pass, when the congregation was assembled against Moses and against Aaron, that they looked toward the tent of meeting: and, behold, the cloud covered it, and the glory of Jehovah appeared. 43 And Moses and Aaron came to the front of the tent of meeting. 44 And Jehovah spake unto Moses, saying, 45 Get you up from among this congregation, that I may consume them in a moment. And they fell upon their faces. 46 And Moses said unto Aaron, Take thy censer, and put fire therein from off the altar, and lay incense thereon, and carry it quickly unto the congregation, and make atonement for them: for there is wrath gone out from Jehovah; the plague is begun. 47 And Aaron took as Moses spake, and ran into the midst of the assembly; and, behold, the plague was begun among the people: and he put on the incense, and made atonement for the people. 48 And he stood between the dead and the living; and the plague was stayed. 49 Now they that died by the plague were fourteen thousand and seven hundred, besides them that died about the matter of Korah. 50 And Aaron returned unto Moses unto the door of the tent of meeting: and the plague was stayed.

63. THE BUDDING OF AARON'S ROD. P22.
Nu. 17$^{1-13}$

1 And Jehovah spake unto Moses, saying, 2 Speak unto the children of Israel, and take of them rods, one for each fathers' house, of all their princes according to their fathers' houses, twelve rods: write thou every man's name upon his rod.

3 And thou shalt write Aaron's name upon the rod of Levi; for there shall be one rod for each head of their fathers' houses. 4 And thou shalt lay them up in the tent of meeting before the testimony, where I meet with you. 5 And it shall come to pass, that the rod of the man whom I shall choose shall bud: and I will make to cease from me the murmurings of the children of Israel, which they murmur against you. 6 And Moses spake unto the children of Israel; and all their princes gave him rods, for each prince one, according to their fathers' houses, even twelve rods: and the rod of Aaron was among their rods. 7 And Moses laid up the rods before Jehovah in the tent of the testimony.

8 And it came to pass on the morrow, that Moses went into the tent of the testimony; and, behold, the rod of Aaron for the house of Levi was budded, and put forth buds, and produced blossoms, and bare ripe almonds. 9 And Moses brought out all the rods from before Jehovah unto all the children of Israel: and they looked, and took every man his rod. 10 And Jehovah said unto Moses, Put back the rod of Aaron before the testimony, to be kept for a token against the children of rebellion; that thou mayest make an end of their murmurings against me, that they die not. 11 Thus did Moses: as Jehovah commanded him, so did he.

12 And the children of Israel spake unto Moses, saying, Behold, we perish, we are undone, we are all undone. 13 Every one that cometh near, that cometh near unto the tabernacle of Jehovah, dieth: shall we perish all of us?

64. THE DUTIES AND PERQUISITES OF THE SONS OF AARON (PRIESTS) AND LEVITES. P46.

Nu. 18$^{1-32}$

1 And Jehovah said unto Aaron, Thou and thy sons and thy father's house with thee shall bear the iniquity of the sanctuary; and thou and thy sons with thee shall bear the iniquity of your priesthood. 2 And thy brethren also, the tribe of Levi, the tribe of thy father, bring thou near with thee, that they may be joined unto thee, and minister unto thee: but thou and thy sons with thee shall be before the tent of the testimony. 3 And they shall keep thy charge, and the charge of all the Tent: only they shall not come nigh unto the vessels of the sanctuary and unto the altar, that they die not, neither they, nor ye. 4 And they shall be joined unto thee, and keep the charge of the tent of meeting, for all the service of the Tent: and a stranger shall not come nigh unto you. 5 And ye shall keep the charge of the sanctuary, and the charge of the altar; that there be wrath no more upon the children of Israel. 6 And I,

behold, I have taken your brethren the Levites from among the children of Israel: to you they are a gift, given unto Jehovah, to do the service of the tent of meeting. 7 And thou and thy sons with thee shall keep your priesthood for everything of the altar, and for that within the veil; and ye shall serve: I give you the priesthood as a service of gift: and the stranger that cometh nigh shall be put to death.

8 And Jehovah spake unto Aaron, And I, behold, I have given thee the charge of my heave-offerings, even all the hallowed things of the children of Israel; unto thee have I given them by reason of the anointing, and to thy sons, as a portion for ever. 9 This shall be thine of the most holy things, *reserved* from the fire: every oblation of theirs, even every meal-offering of theirs, and every sin-offering of theirs, and every trespass-offering of theirs, which they shall render unto me, shall be most holy for thee and for thy sons. 10 As the most holy things shalt thou eat thereof; every male shall eat thereof: it shall be holy unto thee. 11 And this is thine: the heave-offering of their gift, even all the wave-offerings of the children of Israel; I have given them unto thee, and to thy sons and to thy daughters with thee, as a portion for ever; every one that is clean in thy house shall eat thereof. 12 All the best of the oil, and all the best of the vintage, and of the grain, the first-fruits of them which they give unto Jehovah, to thee have I given them. 13 The first-ripe fruits of all that is in their land, which they bring unto Jehovah, shall be thine; every one that is clean in thy house shall eat thereof. 14 Everything devoted in Israel shall be thine. 15 Everything that openeth the womb, of all flesh which they offer unto Jehovah, both of man and beast shall be thine: nevertheless the first-born of man shalt thou surely redeem, and the firstling of unclean beasts shalt thou redeem. 16 And those that are to be redeemed of them from a month old shalt thou redeem, according to thine estimation, for the money of five shekels, after the shekel of the sanctuary (the same is twenty gerahs). 17 But the firstling of a cow, or the firstling of a sheep, or the firstling of a goat, thou shalt not redeem; they are holy: thou shalt sprinkle their blood upon the altar, and shalt burn their fat for an offering made by fire, for a sweet savor unto Jehovah. 18 And the flesh of them shall be thine, as the wave-breast and as the right thigh, it shall be thine. 19 All the heave-offerings of the holy things, which the children of Israel offer unto Jehovah, have I given thee, and thy sons and daughters with thee, as a portion for ever: it is a covenant of salt for ever before Jehovah unto thee and to thy seed with thee. 20 And Jehovah said unto Aaron, Thou shalt have no inheritance in their land, neither shalt thou have

any portion among them: I am thy portion and thine inheritance among the children of Israel.

21 And unto the children of Levi, behold, I have given all the tithe in Israel for an inheritance, in return for their service which they serve, even the service of the tent of meeting. 22 And henceforth the children of Israel shall not come nigh the tent of meeting, lest they bear sin, and die. 23 But the Levites shall do the service of the tent of meeting, and they shall bear their iniquity: it shall be a statute for ever throughout your generations; and among the children of Israel they shall have no inheritance. 24 For the tithe of the children of Israel, which they offer as a heave-offering unto Jehovah, I have given to the Levites for an inheritance: therefore I have said unto them, Among the children of Israel they shall have no inheritance.

25 And Jehovah spake unto Moses, saying, 26 Moreover thou shalt speak unto the Levites, and say unto them, When ye take of the children of Israel the tithe which I have given you from them for your inheritance, then ye shall offer up a heave-offering of it for Jehovah, a tithe of the tithe. 27 And your heave-offering shall be reckoned unto you, as though it were the grain of the threshing-floor, and as the fulness of the winepress. 28 Thus ye also shall offer a heave-offering unto Jehovah of all your tithes, which ye receive of the children of Israel; and thereof ye shall give Jehovah's heave-offering to Aaron the priest. 29 Out of all your gifts ye shall offer every heave-offering of Jehovah, of all the best thereof, even the hallowed part thereof out of it. 30 Therefore thou shalt say unto them, When ye heave the best thereof from it, then it shall be reckoned unto the Levites as the increase of the threshing-floor, and as the increase of the winepress. 31 And ye shall eat it in every place, ye and your households: for it is your reward in return for your service in the tent of meeting. 32 And ye shall bear no sin by reason of it, when ye have heaved from it the best thereof: and ye shall not profane the holy things of the children of Israel, that ye die not.

65. LAW OF PURIFICATION FROM UNCLEANNESS DUE TO CONTACT WITH THE DEAD. P40.

Nu. $19^{1\text{-}22}$

1 And Jehovah spake unto Moses and unto Aaron, saying, 2 This is the statute of the law which Jehovah hath commanded, saying, Speak unto the children of Israel, that they bring thee a red heifer without spot, wherein is no blemish, *and* upon which never came yoke. 3 And ye shall give her unto Eleazar the priest, and he shall bring her forth without the

camp, and one shall slay her before his face: 4 and Eleazar the priest shall take of her blood with his finger, and sprinkle of her blood toward the front of the tent of meeting seven times. 5 And one shall burn the heifer in his sight; her skin, and her flesh, and her blood, with her dung, shall he burn: 6 and the priest shall take cedar-wood, and hyssop, and scarlet, and cast it into the midst of the burning of the heifer. 7 Then the priest shall wash his clothes, and he shall bathe his flesh in water, and afterward he shall come into the camp, and the priest shall be unclean until the even. 8 And he that burneth her shall wash his clothes in water, and bathe his flesh in water, and shall be unclean until the even. 9 And a man that is clean shall gather up the ashes of the heifer, and lay them up without the camp in a clean place; and it shall be kept for the congregation of the children of Israel for a water for impurity: it is a sin-offering. 10 And he that gathereth the ashes of the heifer shall wash his clothes, and be unclean until the even: and it shall be unto the children of Israel, and unto the stranger that sojourneth among them, for a statute for ever.

11 He that toucheth the dead body of any man shall be unclean seven days: 12 the same shall purify himself therewith on the third day, and on the seventh day he shall be clean: but if he purify not himself the third day, then the seventh day he shall not be clean. 13 Whosoever toucheth a dead person, the body of a man that hath died, and purifieth not himself, defileth the tabernacle of Jehovah; and that soul shall be cut off from Israel: because the water for impurity was not sprinkled upon him, he shall be unclean; his uncleanness is yet upon him.

14 This is the law when a man dieth in a tent: every one that cometh into the tent, and every one that is in the tent, shall be unclean seven days. 15 And every open vessel, which hath no covering bound upon it, is unclean. 16 And whosoever in the open field toucheth one that is slain with a sword, or a dead body, or a bone of a man, or a grave, shall be unclean seven days. 17 And for the unclean they shall take of the ashes of the burning of the sin-offering; and running water shall be put thereto in a vessel: 18 and a clean person shall take hyssop, and dip it in the water, and sprinkle it upon the tent, and upon all the vessels, and upon the persons that were there, and upon him that touched the bone, or the slain, or the dead, or the grave: 19 and the clean person shall sprinkle upon the unclean on the third day, and on the seventh day: and on the seventh day he shall purify him; and he shall wash his clothes, and bathe himself in water, and shall be clean at even.

20 But the man that shall be unclean, and shall not purify himself, that soul shall be cut off from the midst of the assembly,

because he hath defiled the sanctuary of Jehovah: the water for impurity hath not been sprinkled upon him; he is unclean. 21 And it shall be a perpetual statute unto them: and he that sprinkleth the water for impurity shall wash his clothes; and he that toucheth the water for impurity shall be unclean until even. 22 And whatsoever the unclean person toucheth shall be unclean; and the soul that toucheth it shall be unclean until even.

66. WATER FROM THE ROCK AT MERIBAH IN THE WILDERNESS OF ZIN (KADESH). J30. E18. Ps. 106$^{32\text{-}33}$.
Nu. 20$^{1a.2.3b\text{-}4.6\text{-}13}$

1a And the children of Israel, even the whole congregation, came into the wilderness of Zin in the first month.

2 And there was no water for the congregation: and they assembled themselves together against Moses and against Aaron.— 3b. . . Would that we had died when our brethren died before Jehovah! 4 And why have ye brought the assembly of Jehovah into this wilderness, that we should die there, we and our beasts?

6 And Moses and Aaron went from the presence of the assembly unto the door of the tent of meeting, and fell upon their faces: and the glory of Jehovah appeared unto them. 7 And Jehovah spake unto Moses, saying, 8 Take the rod, and assemble the congregation, thou, and Aaron thy brother, and speak ye unto the rock before their eyes, that it give forth its water; and thou shalt bring forth to them water out of the rock; so thou shalt give the congregation and their cattle drink. 9 And Moses took the rod from before Jehovah, as he commanded him.

10 And Moses and Aaron gathered the assembly together before the rock, and he said unto them, Hear now, ye rebels; shall we bring you forth water out of this rock? 11 And Moses lifted up his hand, and smote the rock with his rod twice: and water came forth abundantly, and the congregation drank, and their cattle. 12 And Jehovah said unto Moses and Aaron, Because ye believed not in me, to sanctify me in the eyes of the children of Israel, therefore ye shall not bring this assembly into the land which I have given them. 13 These are the waters of Meribah; because the children of Israel strove with Jehovah, and he was sanctified in them.

67. DEATH OF AARON ON MOUNT HOR. P66, 79: Nu. 33$^{38\text{-}39}$.
Nu. 20$^{22\text{-}29}$

22 And they journeyed from Kadesh: and the children of

---

[66] vv. 7-13 contain more or less E or JE: Gr., St., Ka., et al., or J: Smend. There is doubtless considerable revision by Rp (Smend).—Meribah is at Kadesh, cf. Ez. 47^{19} 48^{28} Dt. 32^{51} GFM.

Israel, even the whole congregation, came unto mount Hor. 23 And Jehovah spake unto Moses and Aaron in mount Hor, by the border of the land of Edom, saying, 24 Aaron shall be gathered unto his people; for he shall not enter into the land which I have given unto the children of Israel, because ye rebelled against my word at the waters of Meribah. 25 Take Aaron and Eleazar his son, and bring them up unto mount Hor; 26 and strip Aaron of his garments, and put them upon Eleazar his son: and Aaron shall be gathered *unto his people*, and shall die there. 27 And Moses did as Jehovah commanded: and they went up into mount Hor in the sight of all the congregation. 28 And Moses stripped Aaron of his garments, and put them upon Eleazar his son; and Aaron died there on the top of the mount: and Moses and Eleazar came down from the mount. 29 And when all the congregation saw that Aaron was dead, they wept for Aaron thirty days, even all the house of Israel.

68. JOURNEY FROM MOUNT HOR TO THE PLAINS OF MOAB. P79. Nu. 21$^{4a.10\text{-}11}$ 22^1

4a And they journeyed from mount Hor. 10 And the children of Israel journeyed, and encamped in Oboth. 11 And they journeyed from Oboth, and encamped at Iye-abarim, in the wilderness which is before Moab, toward the sunrising. 22^1 And the children of Israel journeyed, and encamped in the plains of Moab beyond the Jordan at Jericho.

69. AN ISRAELITE WHO MARRIES A MIDIANITE IS KILLED. J13iv: Gn.25^2, 24, 44. E45. P60, 77. Ezra 9^1-10^{44}. Neh. 13$^{23\text{-}27}$. Vs. Ruth.

Nu. 25$^{6\text{-}18}$

6 And, behold, one of the children of Israel came and brought unto his brethren a Midianitish woman in the sight of Moses, and in the sight of all the congregation of the children of Israel, while they were weeping at the door of the tent of meeting. 7 And when Phinehas, the son of Eleazar, the son of Aaron the priest, saw it, he rose up from the midst of the congregation, and took a spear in his hand; 8 and he went after the man of Israel into the pavilion, and thrust both of them through, the man of Israel, and the woman through her body. So the plague

---

[68] After 22^1 there is an omission in P (Dr.).
[69] The reff. to the "plague" vv. 8-9, 16-18 (latter Rp?), cf. also P62: Nu. 16$^{48\text{-}50}$, indicate that Rp has omitted P's account of the occasion of the plague, and has substituted J46 and E47, q.v. P "may have related that Balaam, a soothsayer resident among the Midianites, suggested to the Midianites that they should seduce the Hebrews into intermarrying with them, and thus involve Yahweh's destructive anger on their enemies; and that the stratagem so far succeeded that Yahweh plagued Israel" (Gray 384; so Di., Ki., Ra., Dr., We.).

was stayed from the children of Israel. 9 And those that died by the plague were twenty and four thousand. 10 And Jehovah spake unto Moses, saying, 11 Phinehas, the son of Eleazar, the son of Aaron the priest, hath turned my wrath away from the children of Israel, in that he was jealous with my jealousy among them, so that I consumed not the children of Israel in my jealousy. 12 Wherefore say, Behold, I give unto him my covenant of peace: 13 and it shall be unto him, and to his seed after him, the covenant of an everlasting priesthood; because he was jealous for his God, and made atonement for the children of Israel.

14 Now the name of the man of Israel that was slain, who was slain with the Midianitish woman, was Zimri, the son of Salu, a prince of a fathers' house among the Simeonites. 15 And the name of the Midianitish woman that was slain was Cozbi, the daughter of Zur; he was head of the people of a fathers' house in Midian.

16 And Jehovah spake unto Moses, saying, 17 Vex the Midianites, and smite them; 18 for they vex you with their wiles, wherewith they have beguiled you in the matter of Peor, and in the matter of Cozbi, the daughter of the prince of Midian, their sister, who was slain on the day of the plague in the matter of Peor.

70. CENSUS OF THE MEN OF WAR.   P44.   2 S.24.   1Ch.21.

Nu. 26^{1-51}

1 And it came to pass after the plague, that Jehovah spake unto Moses and unto Eleazar the son of Aaron the priest, saying, 2 Take the sum of all the congregation of the children of Israel, from twenty years old and upward, by their fathers' houses, all that are able to go forth to war in Israel. 3 And Moses and Eleazar the priest spake with them in the plains of Moab by the Jordan at Jericho, saying, 4 *Take the sum of the people*, from twenty years old and upward; as Jehovah commanded Moses and the children of Israel, that came forth out of the land of Egypt.

5 Reuben, the first-born of Israel; the sons of Reuben: *of* Hanoch, the family of the Hanochites; of Pallu, the family of the Palluites; 6 of Hezron, the family of the Hezronites; of Carmi, the family of the Carmites. 7 These are the families of the Reubenites; and they that were numbered of them were forty and three thousand and seven hundred and thirty. 8 And the sons of Pallu: Eliab. 9 And the sons of Eliab: Nemuel, and Dathan, and Abiram. These are that Dathan and Abiram, who were called of the congregation, who strove against Moses and against Aaron in the company of Korah, when they strove against Jehovah, 10 and the

earth opened its mouth, and swallowed them up together with Korah, when that company died; what time the fire devoured two hundred and fifty men, and they became a sign. 11 Notwithstanding the sons of Korah died not.

12 The sons of Simeon after their families: of Nemuel, the family of the Nemuelites; of Jamin, the family of the Jaminites; of Jachin, the family of the Jachinites; 13 of Zerah, the family of the Zerahites; of Shaul, the family of the Shaulites. 14 These are the families of the Simeonites, twenty and two thousand and two hundred.

15 The sons of Gad after their families: of Zephon, the family of the Zephonites; of Haggi, the family of the Haggites; of Shuni, the family of the Shunites; 16 of Ozni, the family of the Oznites; of Eri, the family of the Erites; 17 of Arod, the family of the Arodites; of Areli, the family of the Arelites. 18 These are the families of the sons of Gad according to those that were numbered of them, forty thousand and five hundred.

19 The sons of Judah: Er and Onan; and Er and Onan died in the land of Canaan. 20 And the sons of Judah after their families were: of Shelah, the family of the Shelanites; of Perez, the family of the Perezites; of Zerah, the family of the Zerahites. 21 And the sons of Perez were: of Hezron, the family of the Hezronites; of Hamul, the family of the Hamulites. 22 These are the families of Judah according to those that were numbered of them, threescore and sixteen thousand and five hundred.

23 The sons of Issachar after their families: *of* Tola, the family of the Tolaites; of Puvah, the family of the Punites; 24 of Jashub, the family of the Jashubites; of Shimron, the family of the Shimronites. 25 These are the families of Issachar according to those that were numbered of them, threescore and four thousand and three hundred.

26 The sons of Zebulun after their families: of Sered, the family of the Seredites; of Elon, the family of the Elonites; of Jahleel, the family of the Jahleelites. 27 These are the families of the Zebulunites according to those that were numbered of them, threescore thousand and five hundred.

28 The sons of Joseph after their families: Manasseh and Ephraim. 29 The sons of Manasseh: of Machir, the family of the Machirites; and Machir begat Gilead: of Gilead, the family of the Gileadites. 30 These are the sons of Gilead: *of* Iezer, the family of the Iezerites; of Helek, the family of the Helekites; 31 and *of* Asriel, the family of the Asrielites; and *of* Shechem, the family of the Shechemites; 32 and *of* Shemida, the family of the Shemidaites; and *of* Hepher, the family of

the Hepherites. 33 And Zelophehad the son of Hepher had no sons, but daughters: and the names of the daughters of Zelophehad were Mahlah, and Noah, Hoglah, Milcah, and Tirzah. 34 These are the families of Manasseh; and they that were numbered of them were fifty and two thousand and seven hundred.

35 These are the sons of Ephraim after their families: of Shuthelah, the family of the Shuthelahites; of Becher, the family of the Becherites; of Tahan, the family of the Tahanites. 36 And these are the sons of Shuthelah: of Eran, the family of the Eranites. 37 These are the families of the sons of Ephraim according to those that were numbered of them, thirty and two thousand and five hundred. These are the sons of Joseph after their families.

38 The sons of Benjamin after their families: of Bela, the family of the Belaites; of Ashbel, the family of the Ashbelites; of Ahiram, the family of the Ahiramites; 39 of Shephupham, the family of the Shuphamites; of Hupham, the family of the Huphamites. 40 And the sons of Bela were Ard and Naaman: *of Ard*, the family of the Ardites; of Naaman, the family of the Naamites. 41 These are the sons of Benjamin after their families; and they that were numbered of them were forty and five thousand and six hundred.

42 These are the sons of Dan after their families: of Shuham, the family of the Shuhamites. These are the families of Dan after their families. 43 All the families of the Shuhamites, according to those that were numbered of them, were threescore and four thousand and four hundred.

44 The sons of Asher after their families: of Imnah, the family of the Imnites; of Ishvi, the family of the Ishvites; of Beriah, the family of the Beriites. 45 Of the sons of Beriah: of Heber, the family of the Heberites; of Malchiel, the family of the Malchielites. 46 And the name of the daughter of Asher was Serah. 47 These are the families of the sons of Asher according to those that were numbered of them, fifty and three thousand and four hundred.

48 The sons of Naphtali after their families: of Jahzeel, the family of the Jahzeelites; of Guni, the family of the Gunites; 49 of Jezer, the family of the Jezerites; of Shillem, the family of the Shillemites. 50 These are the families of Naphtali according to their families; and they that were numbered of them were forty and five thousand and four hundred.

51 These are they that were numbered of the children of Israel, six hundred thousand and a thousand seven hundred and thirty.

71. COMMAND TO DIVIDE CANAAN BY LOT. J53, 54. E64. P80.

Nu. 26⁵²⁻⁵⁶

52 And Jehovah spake unto Moses, saying, 53 Unto these the land shall be divided for an inheritance according to the number of names. 54 To the more thou shalt give the more inheritance, and to the fewer thou shalt give the less inheritance: to every one according to those that were numbered of him shall his inheritance be given. 55 Notwithstanding, the land shall be divided by lot: according to the names of the tribes of their fathers they shall inherit. 56 According to the lot shall their inheritance be divided between the more and the fewer.

72. CENSUS OF THE LEVITES.

Nu. 26⁵⁷⁻⁶⁵

57 And these are they that were numbered of the Levites after their families: of Gershon, the family of the Gershonites; of Kohath, the family of the Kohathites; of Merari, the family of the Merarites. 58 These are the families of Levi: the family of the Libnites, the family of the Hebronites, the family of the Mahlites, the family of the Mushites, the family of the Korahites. And Kohath begat Amram. 59 And the name of Amram's wife was Jochebed, the daughter of Levi, who was born to Levi in Egypt: and she bare unto Amram Aaron and Moses, and Miriam their sister. 60 And unto Aaron were born Nadab and Abihu, Eleazar and Ithamar. 61 And Nadab and Abihu died, when they offered strange fire before Jehovah. 62 And they that were numbered of them were twenty and three thousand, every male from a month old and upward: for they were not numbered among the children of Israel, because there was no inheritance given them among the children of Israel.

63 These are they that were numbered by Moses and Eleazar the priest, who numbered the children of Israel in the plains of Moab by the Jordan at Jericho. 64 But among these there was not a man of them that were numbered by Moses and Aaron the priest, who numbered the children of Israel in the wilderness of Sinai. 65 For Jehovah had said of them, They shall surely die in the wilderness. And there was not left a man of them, save Caleb the son of Jephunneh, and Joshua the son of Nun.

73. THE INHERITANCE OF THE DAUGHTERS OF ZELOPHEHAD. P71, 82.

Nu. 27¹⁻¹¹

1 Then drew near the daughters of Zelophehad, the son

---

⁷³ Another legal precedent.

of Hepher, the son of Gilead, the son of Machir, the son of Manasseh, of the families of Manasseh the son of Joseph; and these are the names of his daughters: Mahlah, Noah, and Hoglah, and Milcah, and Tirzah. 2 And they stood before Moses, and before Eleazar the priest, and before the princes and all the congregation, at the door of the tent of meeting, saying, 3 Our father died in the wilderness, and he was not among the company of them that gathered themselves together against Jehovah in the company of Korah: but he died in his own sin; and he had no sons. 4 Why should the name of our father be taken away from among his family, because he had no son? Give unto us a possession among the brethren of our father. 5 And Moses brought their cause before Jehovah.

6 And Jehovah spake unto Moses, saying, 7 The daughters of Zelophehad speak right: thou shalt surely give them a possession of an inheritance among their father's brethren; and thou shalt cause the inheritance of their father to pass unto them. 8 And thou shalt speak unto the children of Israel, saying, If a man die, and have no son, then ye shall cause his inheritance to pass unto his daughter. 9 And if he have no daughter, then ye shall give his inheritance unto his brethren. 10 And if he have no brethren, then ye shall give his inheritance unto his father's brethren. 11 And if his father have no brethren, then ye shall give his inheritance unto his kinsman that is next to him of his family, and he shall possess it: and it shall be unto the children of Israel a statute *and* ordinance, as Jehovah commanded Moses.

74. MOSES SEES CANAAN FROM MOUNT ABARIM AND APPOINTS JOSHUA AS HIS SUCCESSOR. P67, 83, 84.

Nu. $27^{12\text{-}23}$

12 And Jehovah said unto Moses, Get thee up into this mountain of Abarim, and behold the land which I have given unto the children of Israel. 13 And when thou hast seen it, thou also shalt be gathered unto thy people, as Aaron thy brother was gathered; 14 because ye rebelled against my word in the wilderness of Zin, in the strife of the congregation, to sanctify me at the waters before their eyes. (These are the waters of Meribah of Kadesh in the wilderness of Zin.)

15 And Moses spake unto Jehovah, saying, 16 Let Jehovah the God of the spirits of all flesh, appoint a man over the congregation, 17 who may go out before them, and who may come in before them, and who may lead them out, and who may bring them in; that the congregation of Jehovah be not as sheep which have no shepherd. 18 And Jehovah said unto Moses, Take thee Joshua the son of Nun, a man in whom is

the Spirit, and lay thy hand upon him; 19 and set him before Eleazar the priest, and before all the congregation; and give him a charge in their sight. 20 And thou shalt put of thine honor upon him, that all the congregation of the children of Israel may obey. 21 And he shall stand before Eleazar the priest, who shall inquire for him by the judgment of the Urim before Jehovah: at his word shall they go out, and at his word they shall come in, both he, and all the children of Israel with him, even all the congregation. 22 And Moses did as Jehovah commanded him; and he took Joshua, and set him before Eleazar the priest, and before all the congregation: 23 and he laid his hands upon him, and gave him a charge, as Jehovah spake by Moses.

75. LAWS FOR VARIOUS OFFERINGS ON SPECIAL DAYS. P37. P42viH.
Nu. 28¹–29⁴⁰

28 And Jehovah spake unto Moses, saying, 2 Command the children of Israel, and say unto them, My oblation, my food for my offerings made by fire, of a sweet savor unto me, shall ye observe to offer unto me in their due season. 3 And thou shalt say unto them, This is the offering made by fire which ye shall offer unto Jehovah: he-lambs a year old without blemish, two day by day, for a continual burnt-offering. 4 The one lamb shalt thou offer in the morning, and the other lamb shalt thou offer at even; 5 and the tenth part of an ephah of fine flour for a meal-offering, mingled with the fourth part of a hin of beaten oil. 6 It is a continual burnt-offering, which was ordained in mount Sinai for a sweet savor, an offering made by fire unto Jehovah. 7 And the drink-offering thereof shall be the fourth part of a hin for the one lamb: in the holy place shalt thou pour out a drink-offering of strong drink unto Jehovah. 8 And the other lamb shalt thou offer at even: as the meal-offering of the morning, and as the drink-offering thereof, thou shalt offer it, an offering made by fire, of a sweet savor unto Jehovah.

9 And on the Sabbath day two he-lambs a year old without blemish, and two tenth parts *of an ephah* of fine flour for a meal-offering, mingled with oil, and the drink-offering thereof: 10 this is the burnt-offering of every sabbath, besides the continual burnt-offering, and the drink-offering thereof.

11 And in the beginnings of your months ye shall offer a burnt-offering unto Jehovah: two young bullocks and one ram, seven he-lambs a year old without blemish; 12 and three tenth

---

[75] Nu. 28 supplements Lv. 23. 28³⁻⁸ is substantially the same as P32: Ex. 29³⁸⁻⁴²; 29³⁹⁻⁴⁰ is a subscription.

parts *of an ephah* of fine flour for a meal-offering, mingled with oil, for each bullock; and two tenth parts of fine flour for a meal-offering, mingled with oil, for the one ram; 13 and a tenth part of fine flour mingled with oil for a meal-offering unto every lamb; for a burnt-offering of a sweet savor, an offering made by fire unto Jehovah. 14 And their drink-offerings shall be half a hin of wine for a bullock, and the third part of a hin for the ram, and the fourth part of a hin for a lamb: this is the burnt-offering of every month throughout the months of the year. 15 And one he-goat for a sin-offering unto Jehovah; it shall be offered beside the continual burnt-offering, and the drink-offering thereof.

16 And in the first month, on the fourteenth day of the month, is Jehovah's passover. 17 And on the fifteenth day of this month shall be a feast: seven days shall unleavened bread be eaten. 18 In the first day shall be a holy convocation; ye shall do no servile work; 19 but ye shall offer an offering made by fire, a burnt-offering unto Jehovah: two young bullocks, and one ram, and seven he-lambs a year old; they shall be unto you without blemish; 20 and their meal-offering, fine flour mingled with oil: three tenth parts shall ye offer for a bullock, and two tenth parts for the ram; 21 a tenth part shalt thou offer for every lamb of the seven lambs; 22 and one he-goat for a sin-offering, to make atonement for you. 23 Ye shall offer these besides the burnt-offering of the morning, which is for a continual burnt-offering. 24 After this manner ye shall offer daily, for seven days, the food of the offering made by fire, of a sweet savor unto Jehovah: it shall be offered beside the continual burnt-offering, and the drink-offering thereof. 25 And on the seventh day ye shall have a holy convocation; ye shall do no servile work.

26 Also in the day of the first-fruits, when ye offer a new meal-offering unto Jehovah in your *feast of* weeks, ye shall have a holy convocation; ye shall do no servile work; 27 but ye shall offer a burnt-offering for a sweet savor unto Jehovah: two young bullocks, one ram, seven he-lambs a year old; 28 and their meal-offering, fine flour mingled with oil, three tenth parts for each bullock, two tenth parts for the one ram, 29 a tenth part for every lamb of the seven lambs; 30 one he-goat, to make atonement for you. 31 Besides the continual burnt-offering, and the meal-offering thereof, ye shall offer them (they shall be unto you without blemish), and their drink-offerings.

29 And in the seventh month, on the first day of the month, ye shall have a holy convocation; ye shall do no servile work: it is a day of blowing of trumpets unto you. 2 And

ye shall offer a burnt-offering for a sweet savor unto Jehovah: one young bullock, one ram, seven he-lambs a year old without blemish; 3 and their meal-offering, fine flour mingled with oil, three tenth parts for the bullock, two tenth parts for the ram, 4 and one tenth part for every lamb of the seven lambs; 5 and one he-goat for a sin-offering, to make atonement for you; 6 besides the burnt offering of the new moon, and the meal-offering thereof, and the continual burnt-offering and the meal-offering thereof, and their drink-offerings, according unto their ordinance, for a sweet savor, an offering made by fire unto Jehovah.

7 And on the tenth day of this seventh month ye shall have a holy convocation; and ye shall afflict your souls: ye shall do no manner of work; 8 but ye shall offer a burnt-offering unto Jehovah for a sweet savor: one young bullock, one ram, seven he-lambs a year old; they shall be unto you without blemish; 9 and their meal-offering, fine flour mingled with oil, three tenth parts for the bullock, two tenth parts for the one ram, 10 a tenth part for every lamb of the seven lambs: 11 one he-goat for a sin-offering; besides the sin-offering of atonement, and the continual burnt-offering, and the meal-offering thereof, and their drink-offerings.

12 And on the fifteenth day of the seventh month ye shall have a holy convocation; ye shall do no servile work, and ye shall keep a feast unto Jehovah seven days: 13 and ye shall offer a burnt-offering, an offering made by fire, of a sweet savor unto Jehovah; thirteen young bullocks, two rams, fourteen he-lambs a year old; they shall be without blemish; 14 and their meal-offering, fine flour mingled with oil, three tenth parts for every bullock of the thirteen bullocks, two tenth parts for each ram of the two rams, 15 and a tenth part for every lamb of the fourteen lambs; 16 and one he-goat for a sin-offering; besides the continual burnt-offering, the meal-offering thereof, and the drink-offering thereof.

17 And on the second day *ye shall offer* twelve young bullocks, two rams, fourteen he-lambs a year old without blemish; 18 and their meal-offering and their drink-offerings for the bullocks, for the rams, and for the lambs, according to their number, after the ordinance; 19 and one he-goat for a sin-offering; besides the continual burnt-offering, and the meal-offering thereof, and their drink-offerings.

20 And on the third day eleven bullocks, two rams, fourteen he-lambs a year old without blemish; 21 and their meal-offering and their drink-offerings for the bullocks, for the rams, and for the lambs, according to their number, after the ordinance; 22 and one he-goat for a sin-offering; besides the continual

burnt-offering, and the meal-offering thereof, and the drink-offering thereof.

23 And on the fourth day ten bullocks, two rams, fourteen he-lambs a year old without blemish; 24 their meal-offering and their drink-offerings for the bullocks, for the rams, and for the lambs, according to their number, after the ordinance; 25 and one he-goat for a sin-offering; besides the continual burnt-offering, the meal-offering thereof, and the drink-offering thereof.

26 And on the fifth day nine bullocks, two rams, fourteen he-lambs a year old without blemish; 27 and their meal-offering and their drink-offerings for the bullocks, for the rams, and for the lambs, according to their number, after the ordinance; 28 and one he-goat for a sin-offering; besides the continual burnt-offering, and the meal-offering thereof, and the drink-offering thereof.

29 And on the sixth day eight bullocks, two rams, fourteen he-lambs a year old without blemish; 30 and their meal-offering and their drink-offerings for the bullocks, for the rams, and for the lambs according to their number, after the ordinance; 31 and one he-goat for a sin-offering; besides the continual burnt-offering, the meal-offering thereof, and the drink-offerings thereof.

32 And on the seventh day seven bullocks, two rams, fourteen he-lambs a year old without blemish; 33 and their meal-offering and their drink-offerings for the bullocks, for the rams, and for the lambs, according to their number, after the ordinance; 34 and one he-goat for a sin-offering; besides the continual burnt-offering, the meal-offering thereof, and the drink-offering thereof.

35 On the eighth day ye shall have a solemn assembly: ye shall do no servile work; 36 but ye shall offer a burnt-offering, an offering made by fire, of a sweet savor unto Jehovah: one bullock, one ram, seven he-lambs a year old without blemish; 37 their meal-offering and their drink-offerings for the bullock, for the ram, and for the lambs, shall be according to their number, after the ordinance: 38 and one he-goat for a sin-offering; besides the continual burnt-offering, and the meal-offering thereof, and the drink-offering thereof.

39 These ye shall offer unto Jehovah in your set feasts, besides your vows, and your freewill-offerings, for your burnt-offerings, and for your meal-offerings, and for your drink-offerings, and for your peace-offerings. 40 And Moses told the children of Israel according to all that Jehovah commanded Moses.

76. Laws Governing Vows. P43.

Nu. 30:1-16

1 And Moses spake unto the heads of the tribes of the children of Israel, saying, This is the thing which Jehovah hath commanded. 2 When a man voweth a vow unto Jehovah, or sweareth an oath to bind his soul with a bond, he shall not break his word; he shall do according to all that proceedeth out of his mouth. 3 Also when a woman voweth a vow unto Jehovah, and bindeth herself by a bond, being in her father's house, in her youth, 4 and her father heareth her vow, and her bond wherewith she hath bound her soul, and her father holdeth his peace at her; then all her vows shall stand, and every bond wherewith she hath bound her soul shall stand. 5 But if her father disallow her in the day that he heareth, none of her vows, or of her bonds wherewith she hath bound her soul, shall stand: and Jehovah will forgive her, because her father disallowed her.

6 And if she be *married* to a husband, while her vows are upon her, or the rash utterance of her lips, wherewith she hath bound her soul, 7 and her husband hear it, and hold his peace at her in the day that he heareth it; then her vows shall stand, and her bonds wherewith she hath bound her soul shall stand. 8 But if her husband disallow her in the day that he heareth it, then he shall make void her vow which is upon her, and the rash utterance of her lips, wherewith she hath bound her soul: and Jehovah will forgive her.

9 But the vow of a widow, or of her that is divorced, *even* everything wherewith she hath bound her soul, shall stand against her. 10 And if she vowed in her husband's house, or bound her soul by a bond with an oath, 11 and her husband heard it, and held his peace at her, and disallowed her not; then all her vows shall stand, and every bond wherewith she bound her soul shall stand. 12 But if her husband made them null and void in the day that he heard them, then whatsoever proceeded out of her lips concerning her vows, or concerning the bond of her soul, shall not stand: her husband hath made them void; and Jehovah will forgive her.

13 Every vow, and every binding oath to afflict the soul, her husband may establish it, or her husband may make it void. 14 But if her husband altogether hold his peace at her from day to day, then he establisheth all her vows, or all her bonds, which are upon her: he hath established them, because he held his peace at her in the day that he heard them. 15 But if he shall make them null and void after that he hath heard them, then he shall bear her iniquity. 16 These are the statutes, which Jehovah commanded Moses, between a man and his wife,

between a father and his daughter, being in her youth, in her father's house.

77. THE WAR AGAINST MIDIAN. J24. P69. Jg. 6–8. Is. 9^4 10^{26}. Ps. 83^{9-12}.

Nu. 31^{1-54}

1 And Jehovah spake unto Moses, saying, 2 Avenge the children of Israel of the Midianites: afterward shalt thou be gathered unto thy people. 3 And Moses spake unto the people, saying, Arm ye men from among you for the war, that they may go against Midian, to execute Jehovah's vengeance on Midian. 4 Of every tribe a thousand, throughout all the tribes of Israel, shall ye send to the war. 5 So there were delivered, out of the thousands of Israel, a thousand of every tribe, twelve thousand armed for war. 6 And Moses sent them, a thousand of every tribe, to the war, them and Phinehas the son of Eleazar the priest, to the war, with the vessels of the sanctuary and the trumpets for the alarm in his hand. 7 And they warred against Midian, as Jehovah commanded Moses; and they slew every male. 8 And they slew the kings of Midian with the rest of their slain: Evi, and Rekem, and Zur, and Hur, and Reba, the five kings of Midian: Balaam also the son of Beor they slew with the sword. 9 And the children of Israel took captive the women of Midian and their little ones; and all their cattle, and all their flocks, and all their goods, they took for a prey. 10 And all their cities in the places wherein they dwelt, and all their encampments, they burnt with fire. 11 And they took all the spoil, and all the prey, both of man and of beast. 12 And they brought the captives, and the prey, and the spoil, unto Moses, and unto Eleazar the priest, and unto the congregation of the children of Israel, unto the camp at the plains of Moab, which are by the Jordan at Jericho.

13 And Moses, and Eleazar the priest, and all the princes of the congregation, went forth to meet them without the camp. 14 And Moses was wroth with the officers of the host, the captains of thousands and the captains of hundreds, who came from the service of the war. 15 And Moses said unto them, Have ye saved all the women alive? 16 Behold, these caused the children of Israel, through the counsel of Balaam, to commit trespass against Jehovah in the matter of Peor, and so the plague was among the congregation of Jehovah. 17 Now therefore kill every male among the little ones, and kill every woman that hath known man by lying with him. 18 But all the women-children, that have not known man by lying with him, keep alive for yourselves. 19 And encamp ye without the camp seven days: whosoever hath killed any person, and whosoever

hath touched any slain, purify yourselves on the third day and on the seventh day, ye and your captives. 20 And as to every garment, and all that is made of skin, and all work of goats' *hair*, and all things made of wood, ye shall purify yourselves.

21 And Eleazar the priest said unto the men of war that went to the battle, This is the statute of the law which Jehovah hath commanded Moses: 22 howbeit the gold, and the silver, the brass, the iron, the tin, and the lead, 23 everything that may abide the fire, ye shall make to go through the fire, and it shall be clean; nevertheless it shall be purified with the water for impurity: and all that abideth not the fire ye shall make to go through the water. 24 And ye shall wash your clothes on the seventh day, and ye shall be clean; and afterward ye shall come into the camp.

25 And Jehovah spake unto Moses, saying, 26 Take the sum of the prey that was taken, both of man and of beast, thou, and Eleazar the priest, and the heads of the fathers' *houses* of the congregation; 27 and divide the prey into two parts: between the men skilled in war, that went out to battle, and all the congregation. 28 And levy a tribute unto Jehovah of the men of war that went out to battle: one soul of five hundred, *both* of the persons, and of the oxen, and of the asses, and of the flocks: 29 take it of their half, and give it unto Eleazar the priest, for Jehovah's heave-offering. 30 And of the children of Israel's half, thou shalt take one drawn out of every fifty, of the persons, of the oxen, of the asses, and of the flocks, *even* of all the cattle, and give them unto the Levites, that keep the charge of the tabernacle of Jehovah. 31 And Moses and Eleazar the priest did as Jehovah commanded Moses.

32 Now the prey, over and above the booty which the men of war took, was six hundred thousand and seventy thousand and five thousand sheep, 33 and threescore and twelve thousand oxen, 34 and threescore and one thousand asses, 35 and thirty and two thousand persons in all, of the women that had not known man by lying with him. 36 And the half, which was the portion of them that went out to war, was in number three hundred thousand and thirty thousand and seven thousand and five hundred sheep: 37 and Jehovah's tribute of the sheep was six hundred and threescore and fifteen. 38 And the oxen were thirty and six thousand; of which Jehovah's tribute was threescore and twelve. 39 And the asses were thirty thousand and five hundred; of which Jehovah's tribute was threescore and one. 40 And the persons were sixteen thousand; of whom Jehovah's tribute was thirty and two persons. 41 And Moses gave the tribute, which was Jehovah's heave-offering, unto Eleazar the priest, as Jehovah commanded Moses.

42 And of the children of Israel's half, which Moses divided off from the men that warred 43 (now the congregation's half was three hundred thousand and thirty thousand, seven thousand and five hundred sheep, 44 and thirty and six thousand oxen, 45 and thirty thousand and five hundred asses, 46 and sixteen thousand persons), 47 even of the children of Israel's half, Moses took one drawn out of every fifty, both of man and of beast, and gave them unto the Levites, that kept the charge of the tabernacle of Jehovah; as Jehovah commanded Moses.

48 And the officers that were over the thousands of the host, the captains of thousands, and the captains of hundreds, came near unto Moses; 49 and they said unto Moses, Thy servants have taken the sum of the men of war that are under our charge, and there lacketh not one man of us. 50 And we have brought Jehovah's oblation, what every man hath gotten, of jewels of gold, ankle-chains, and bracelets, signet-rings, ear-rings, and armlets, to make atonement for our souls before Jehovah. 51 And Moses and Eleazar the priest took the gold of them, even all wrought jewels. 52 And all the gold of the heave-offering that they offered up to Jehovah, of the captains of thousands, and of the captains of hundreds, was sixteen thousand seven hundred and fifty shekels. 53 (*For* the men of war had taken booty, every man for himself.) 54 And Moses and Eleazar the priest took the gold of the captains of thousands and of hundreds, and brought it into the tent of meeting, for a memorial for the children of Israel before Jehovah.

78. THE LOTS OF REUBEN, GAD, AND MANASSEH. J47. P73, 88, 92.

Nu. 32[1-38]

1 Now the children of Reuben and the children of Gad had a very great multitude of cattle: and when they saw the land of Jazer, and the land of Gilead, that, behold, the place was a place for cattle; 2 the children of Gad and the children of Reuben came and spake unto Moses, and to Eleazar the priest, and unto the princes of the congregation, saying, 3 Ataroth, and Dibon, and Jazer, and Nimrah, and Heshbon, and Elealeh, and Sebam, and Nebo, and Beon, 4 the land which Jehovah smote before the congregation of Israel, is a land for cattle; and thy servants have cattle. 5 And they said, If we have found favor in thy sight, let this land be given unto thy servants for a possession; bring us not over the Jordan.

---

[78] There is wide difference among critics as to the analysis of this chapter in detail. All recognize that it is composite—JEP—and that its present form is due to Rp. vv. 39–42 are printed as J; further separation of sources is at present impracticable.

6 And Moses said unto the children of Gad and to the children of Reuben, Shall your brethren go to the war, and shall ye sit here? 7 And wherefore discourage ye the heart of the children of Israel from going over into the land which Jehovah hath given them? 8 Thus did your fathers, when I sent them from Kadesh-barnea to see the land. 9 For when they went up unto the valley of Eshcol, and saw the land, they discouraged the heart of the children of Israel, that they should not go into the land which Jehovah had given them. 10 And Jehovah's anger was kindled in that day, and he sware, saying, 11 Surely none of the men that came up out of Egypt, from twenty years old and upward, shall see the land which I sware unto Abraham, unto Isaac, and unto Jacob; because they have not wholly followed me: 12 save Caleb the son of Jephunneh the Kenizzite, and Joshua the son of Nun; because they have wholly followed Jehovah. 13 And Jehovah's anger was kindled against Israel, and he made them wander to and fro in the wilderness forty years, until all the generation, that had done evil in the sight of Jehovah, was consumed. 14 And, behold, ye are risen up in your fathers' stead, an increase of sinful men, to augment yet the fierce anger of Jehovah toward Israel. 15 For if ye turn away from after him, he will yet again leave them in the wilderness; and ye will destroy all this people.

16 And they came near unto him, and said, We will build sheepfolds here for our cattle, and cities for our little ones: 17 but we ourselves will be ready armed to go before the children of Israel, until we have brought them unto their place: and our little ones shall dwell in the fortified cities because of the inhabitants of the land. 18 We will not return unto our houses, until the children of Israel have inherited every man his inheritance. 19 For we will not inherit with them on the other side of the Jordan, and forward; because our inheritance is fallen to us on this side of the Jordan eastward.

20 And Moses said unto them, If ye will do this thing, if ye will arm yourselves to go before Jehovah to the war, 21 and every armed man of you will pass over the Jordan before Jehovah, until he hath driven out his enemies from before him, 22 and the land is subdued before Jehovah; then afterward ye shall return, and be guiltless towards Jehovah, and towards Israel; and this land shall be unto you for a possession before Jehovah. 23 But if ye will not do so, behold, ye have sinned against Jehovah; and be sure your sin will find you out. 24 Build you cities for your little ones, and folds for your sheep; and do that which hath proceeded out of your mouth. 25 And the children of Gad and the children of Reuben spake unto Moses, saying, Thy servants will do as my lord command-

eth. 26 Our little ones, our wives, our flocks, and all our cattle, shall be there in the cities of Gilead; 27 but thy servants will pass over, every man that is armed for war, before Jehovah to battle, as my lord saith.

28 So Moses gave charge concerning them to Eleazar the priest, and to Joshua the son of Nun, and to the heads of the fathers' *houses* of the tribes of the children of Israel. 29 And Moses said unto them, If the children of Gad and the children of Reuben will pass with you over the Jordan, every man that is armed to battle, before Jehovah, and the land shall be subdued before you; then ye shall give them the land of Gilead for a possession: 30 but if they will not pass over with you armed, they shall have possessions among you in the land of Canaan. 31 And the children of Gad and the children of Reuben answered, saying, As Jehovah hath said unto thy servants, so will we do. 32 We will pass over armed before Jehovah into the land of Canaan, and the possession of our inheritance *shall remain* with us beyond the Jordan.

33 And Moses gave unto them, even to the children of Gad, and to the children of Reuben, and unto the half-tribe of Manasseh the son of Joseph, the kingdom of Sihon king of the Amorites, and the kingdom of Og king of Bashan, the land, according to the cities thereof with *their* borders, even the cities of the land round about. 34 And the children of Gad built Dibon, and Ataroth, and Aroer, 35 and Atroth-shophan, and Jazer, and Jogbehah, 36 and Beth-nimrah, and Beth-haran: fortified cities, and folds for sheep. 37 And the children of Reuben built Heshbon, and Elealeh, and Kiriathaim, 38 and Nebo, and Baal-meon, (their names being changed,) and Sibmah: and they gave other names unto the cities which they builded.

79. A LIST OF THE JOURNEYS FROM RAMESES IN EGYPT TO ABEL-SHITTIM IN MOAB. P24, 27, 30, 34, 68.

Nu. 33[1-49]

1 These are the journeys of the children of Israel, when they went forth out of the land of Egypt by their hosts under the hand of Moses and Aaron. 2 And Moses wrote their goings out according to their journeys by the commandment of Jehovah: and these are their journeys according to their goings out. 3 And they journeyed from Rameses in the first month, on the fifteenth day of the first month; on the morrow after the passover the children of Israel went out with a high hand in the sight of all the Egyptians, 4 while the Egyptians were

---

[79] The chapter presupposes JEP (Ka.) and must therefore be the work of an Rp. (or Ps). vv. 38-39, cf. P67.

burying all their first-born, whom Jehovah had smitten among them: upon their gods also Jehovah executed judgments. 5 And the children of Israel journeyed from Rameses, and encamped in Succoth. 6 And they journeyed from Succoth, and encamped in Etham, which is in the edge of the wilderness. 7 And they journeyed from Etham, and turned back unto Pi-hahiroth, which is before Baal-zephon: and they encamped before Migdol. 8 And they journeyed from before Hahiroth, and passed through the midst of the sea into the wilderness: and they went three days' journey in the wilderness of Etham, and encamped in Marah. 9 And they journeyed from Marah, and came unto Elim: and in Elim were twelve springs of water, and threescore and ten palm-trees; and they encamped there. 10 And they journeyed from Elim, and encamped by the Red Sea. 11 And they journeyed from the Red Sea, and encamped in the wilderness of Sin. 12 And they journeyed from the wilderness of Sin, and encamped in Dophkah. 13 And they journeyed from Dophkah, and encamped in Alush. 14 And they journeyed from Alush, and encamped in Rephidim, where was no water for the people to drink. 15 And they journeyed from Rephidim, and encamped in the wilderness of Sinai. 16 And they journeyed from the wilderness of Sinai, and encamped in Kibroth-hattaavah. 17 And they journeyed from Kibroth-hattaavah, and encamped in Hazeroth. 18 And they journeyed from Hazeroth, and encamped in Rithmah. 19 And they journeyed from Rithmah, and encamped in Rimmon-perez. 20 And they journeyed from Rimmon-perez, and encamped in Libnah. 21 And they journeyed from Libnah, and encamped in Rissah. 22 And they journeyed from Rissah and encamped in Kehelathah. 23 And they journeyed from Kehelathah, and encamped in mount Shepher. 24 And they journeyed from mount Shepher, and encamped in Haradah. 25 And they journeyed from Haradah, and encamped in Makheloth. 26 And they journeyed from Makheloth, and encamped in Tahath. 27 And they journeyed from Tahath, and encamped in Terah. 28 And they journeyed from Terah, and encamped in Mithkah. 29 And they journeyed from Mithkah, and encamped in Hashmonah. 30 And they journeyed from Hashmonah, and encamped in Moseroth. 31 And they journeyed from Moseroth, and encamped in Bene-jaakan. 32 And they journeyed from Bene-jaakan, and encamped in Hor-haggidgad. 33 And they journeyed from Hor-haggidgad, and encamped in Jotbathah. 34 And they journeyed from Jotbathah, and encamped in Abronah. 35 And they journeyed from Abronah, and encamped in Ezion-geber. 36 And they journeyed from Ezion-

geber, and encamped in the wilderness of Zin (the same is Kadesh). 37 And they journeyed from Kadesh, and encamped in mount Hor, in the edge of the land of Edom.
38 And Aaron the priest went up into mount Hor at the commandment of Jehovah, and died there, in the fortieth year after the children of Israel were come out of the land of Egypt, in the fifth month, on the first day of the month. 39 And Aaron was a hundred and twenty and three years old when he died in mount Hor.
40 And the Canaanite, the king of Arad, who dwelt in the South in the land of Canaan, heard of the coming of the children of Israel.
41 And they journeyed from mount Hor, and encamped in Zalmonah. 42 And they journeyed from Zalmonah, and encamped in Punon. 43 And they journeyed from Punon, and encamped in Oboth. 44 And they journeyed from Oboth, and encamped in Iye-abarim, in the border of Moab. 45 And they journeyed from Iyim, and encamped in Dibon-gad. 46 And they journeyed from Dibon-gad, and encamped in Almon-diblathaim. 47 And they journeyed from Almon-diblathaim, and encamped in the mountains of Abarim, before Nebo. 48 And they journeyed from the mountains of Abarim, and encamped in the plains of Moab by the Jordan at Jericho. 49 And they encamped by the Jordan, from Beth-jeshimoth even unto Abel-shittim in the plains of Moab.

80. COMMAND TO CONQUER CANAAN AND DIVIDE IT BY LOT AMONG THE TRIBES AND THE LEVITES. P71, 89, 96.
Nu. 33^{50}–35^{8}

33^{50} And Jehovah spake unto Moses in the plains of Moab by the Jordan at Jericho, saying, 51 Speak unto the children of Israel, and say unto them, When ye pass over the Jordan into the land of Canaan, 52 then ye shall drive out all the inhabitants of the land from before you, and destroy all their figured *stones*, and destroy all their molten images, and demolish all their high places: 53 and ye shall take possession of the land, and dwell therein; for unto you have I given the land to possess it. 54 And ye shall inherit the land by lot according to your families; to the more ye shall give the more inheritance, and to the fewer thou shalt give the less inheritance: wheresoever the lot falleth to any man, that shall be his; according to the tribes of your fathers shall ye inherit. 55 But if ye will not drive out the inhabitants of the land from before you, then shall those that ye let remain of them be as pricks in your eyes, and as thorns in your sides, and they shall vex you in the land wherein ye dwell. 56 And it shall come to pass, that, as I thought to do unto them, so will I do unto you.

34 And Jehovah spake unto Moses, saying, 2 Command the children of Israel and say unto them, When ye come into the land of Canaan (this is the land that shall fall unto you for an inheritance, even the land of Canaan according to the borders thereof), 3 then your south quarter shall be from the wilderness of Zin along by the side of Edom, and your south border shall be from the end of the Salt Sea eastward; 4 and your border shall turn about southward of the ascent of Akrabbim, and pass along to Zin; and the goings out thereof shall be southward of Kadesh-barnea; and it shall go forth to Hazar-addar, and pass along to Azmon; 5 and the border shall turn about from Azmon unto the brook of Egypt, and the goings out thereof shall be at the sea.

6 And for the western border, ye shall have the great sea and the border *thereof*: this shall be your west border.

7 And this shall be your north border: from the great sea ye shall mark out for you mount Hor; 8 from mount Hor ye shall mark out unto the entrance of Hamath; and the goings out of the border shall be at Zedad; 9 and the border shall go forth to Ziphron, and the goings out thereof shall be at Hazar-enan: this shall be your north border.

10 And ye shall mark out your east border from Hazar-enan to Shepham; 11 and the border shall go down from Shepham to Riblah, on the east side of Ain; and the border shall go down, and shall reach unto the side of the sea of Chinnereth eastward; 12 and the border shall go down to the Jordan, and the goings out thereof shall be at the Salt Sea. This shall be your land according to the borders thereof round about.

13 And Moses commanded the children of Israel, saying, This is the land which ye shall inherit by lot, which Jehovah hath commanded to give unto the nine tribes, and to the half-tribe: 14 for the tribe of the children of Reuben according to their fathers' houses, and the tribe of the children of Gad according to their fathers' houses, have received, and the half-tribe of Manasseh have received, their inheritance: 15 the two tribes and the half-tribe have received their inheritance beyond the Jordan at Jericho eastward, toward the sunrising.

16 And Jehovah spake unto Moses, saying, 17 These are the names of the men that shall divide the land unto you for inheritance: Eleazar the priest, and Joshua the son of Nun. 18 And ye shall take one prince of every tribe, to divide the land for inheritance. 19 And these are the names of the men: Of the tribe of Judah, Caleb the son of Jephunneh. 20 And of the tribe of the children of Simeon, Shemuel the son of Ammihud. 21 Of the tribe of Benjamin, Elidad the son of Chislon. 22 And of the tribe of the children of Dan a prince, Bukki the son of

Jogli. 23 Of the children of Joseph: of the tribe of the children of Manasseh a prince, Hanniel the son of Ephod. 24 And of the tribe of the children of Ephraim a prince, Kemuel the son of Shiphtan. 25 And of the tribe of the children of Zebulun a prince, Elizaphan the son of Parnach. 26 And of the tribe of the children of Issachar a prince, Paltiel the son of Azzan. 27 And of the tribe of the children of Asher a prince, Ahihud the son of Shelomi. 28 And of the tribe of the children of Naphtali a prince, Pedahel the son of Ammihud. 29 These are they whom Jehovah commanded to divide the inheritance unto the children of Israel in the land of Canaan.

35 And Jehovah spake unto Moses in the plains of Moab by the Jordan at Jericho, saying, 2 Command the children of Israel, that they give unto the Levites of the inheritance of their possession cities to dwell in; and suburbs for the cities round about them shall ye give unto the Levites. 3 And the cities shall they have to dwell in; and their suburbs shall be for their cattle, and for their substance, and for all their beasts. 4 And the suburbs of the cities, which ye shall give unto the Levites, shall be from the wall of the city and outward a thousand cubits round about. 5 And ye shall measure without the city for the east side two thousand cubits, and for the south side two thousand cubits, and for the west side two thousand cubits, and for the north side two thousand cubits, the city being in the midst. This shall be to them the suburbs of the cities. 6 And the cities which ye shall give unto the Levites, they shall be the six cities of refuge, which ye shall give for the manslayer to flee unto: and besides them ye shall give forty and two cities. 7 All the cities which ye shall give to the Levites shall be forty and eight cities; them *shall ye give* with their suburbs. 8 And concerning the cities which ye shall give of the possession of the children of Israel, from the many ye shall take many; and from the few ye shall take few: every one according to his inheritance which he inheriteth shall give of his cities unto the Levites.

81. CITIES OF REFUGE. P80: Nu. 35^6, P95.
Nu. 35$^{9\text{-}34}$

9 And Jehovah spake unto Moses, saying, 10 Speak unto the children of Israel, and say unto them, When ye pass over the Jordan into the land of Canaan, 11 then ye shall appoint you cities to be cities of refuge for you, that the manslayer that killeth any person unwittingly may flee thither. 12 And the cities shall be unto you for refuge from the avenger, that the manslayer die not, until he stand before the congregation for judgment. 13 And the cities which ye shall give shall be for

you six cities of refuge. 14 Ye shall give three cities beyond the Jordan, and three cities shall ye give in the land of Canaan; they shall be cities of refuge. 15 For the children of Israel, and for the stranger and for the sojourner among them, shall these six cities be for refuge; that every one that killeth any person unwittingly may flee thither.
16 But if he smote him with an instrument of iron, so that he died, he is a murderer: the murderer shall surely be put to death. 17 And if he smote him with a stone in the hand, whereby a man may die, and he died, he is a murderer: the murderer shall surely be put to death. 18 Or if he smote him with a weapon of wood in the hand, whereby a man may die, and he died, he is a murderer: the murderer shall surely be put to death. 19 The avenger of blood shall himself put the murderer to death: when he meeteth him, he shall put him to death. 20 And if he thrust him of hatred, or hurled at him, lying in wait, so that he died, 21 or in enmity smote him with his hand, so that he died; he that smote him shall surely be put to death; he is a murderer: the avenger of blood shall put the murderer to death, when he meeteth him.
22 But if he thrust him suddenly without enmity, or hurled upon him anything without lying in wait, 23 or with any stone, whereby a man may die, seeing him not, and cast it upon him, so that he died, and he was not his enemy, neither sought his harm; 24 then the congregation shall judge between the smiter and the avenger of blood according to these ordinances; 25 and the congregation shall deliver the manslayer out of the hand of the avenger of blood, and the congregation shall restore him to his city of refuge, whither he was fled: and he shall dwell therein until the death of the high priest, who was anointed with the holy oil. 26 But if the manslayer shall at any time go beyond the border of his city of refuge, whither he fleeth, 27 and the avenger of blood find him without the border of his city of refuge, and the avenger of blood slay the manslayer; he shall not be guilty of blood, 28 because he should have remained in his city of refuge until the death of the high priest: but after the death of the high priest the manslayer shall return into the land of his possession.
29 And these things shall be for a statute *and* ordinance unto you throughout your generations in all your dwellings. 30 Whoso killeth any person, the murderer shall be slain at the mouth of witnesses: but one witness shall not testify against any person that he die. 31 Moreover ye shall take no ransom for the life of a murderer, that is guilty of death; but he shall surely be put to death. 32 And ye shall take no ransom for him that is fled to his city of refuge, that he may come again

to dwell in the land, until the death of the priest. 33 So ye shall not pollute the land wherein ye are: for blood, it polluteth the land; and no expiation can be made for the land for the blood that is shed therein, but by the blood of him that shed it. 34 And thou shalt not defile the land which ye inhabit, in the midst of which I dwell: for I, Jehovah, dwell in the midst of the children of Israel.

82. FURTHER LAWS REGARDING THE INHERITANCE OF THE DAUGHTERS OF ZELOPHEHAD. P73.
Nu. 36^{1-13}

1 And the heads of the fathers' *houses* of the family of the children of Gilead, the son of Machir, the son of Manasseh, of the families of the sons of Joseph, came near, and spake before Moses, and before the princes, the heads of the fathers' *houses* of the children of Israel: 2 and they said, Jehovah commanded my lord to give the land for inheritance by lot to the children of Israel: and my lord was commanded by Jehovah to give the inheritance of Zelophehad our brother unto his daughters. 3 And if they be married to any of the sons of the *other* tribes of the children of Israel, then will their inheritance be taken away from the inheritance of our fathers, and will be added to the inheritance of the tribe whereunto they shall belong: so will it be taken away from the lot of our inheritance. 4 And when the jubilee of the children of Israel shall be, then will their inheritance be added unto the inheritance of the tribe whereunto they shall belong: so will their inheritance be taken away from the inheritance of the tribe of our fathers.

5 And Moses commanded the children of Israel according to the word of Jehovah, saying, The tribe of the sons of Joseph speaketh right. 6 This is the thing which Jehovah doth command concerning the daughters of Zelophehad, saying, Let them be married to whom they think best; only into the family of the tribe of their father shall they be married. 7 So shall no inheritance of the children of Israel remove from tribe to tribe; for the children of Israel shall cleave every one to the inheritance of the tribe of his fathers. 8 And every daughter, that possesseth an inheritance in any tribe of the children of Israel, shall be wife unto one of the family of the tribe of her father, that the children of Israel may possess every man the inheritance of his fathers. 9 So shall no inheritance remove from one tribe to another tribe; for the tribes of the children of Israel shall cleave every one to his own inheritance.

10 Even as Jehovah commanded Moses, so did the daughters of Zelophehad: 11 for Mahlah, Tirzah, and Hoglah, and Milcah, and Noah, the daughters of Zelophehad, were married

unto their father's brothers' sons. 12 They were married into the families of the sons of Manasseh the son of Joseph; and their inheritance remained in the tribe of the family of their father.

13 These are the commandments and the ordinances which Jehovah commanded by Moses unto the children of Israel in the plains of Moab by the Jordan at Jericho.

83. Moses Commanded to Go Up into Mount Abarim (Nebo) to View Canaan, and Die. P74, 84.
Dt. 32$^{48\text{-}52}$

48 And Jehovah spake unto Moses that selfsame day, saying, 49 Get thee up into this mountain of Abarim, unto mount Nebo, which is in the land of Moab, that is over against Jericho; and behold the land of Canaan, which I give unto the children of Israel for a possession; 50 and die in the mount whither thou goest up, and be gathered unto thy people, as Aaron thy brother died in mount Hor, and was gathered unto his people: 51 because ye trespassed against me in the midst of the children of Israel at the waters of Meribah of Kadesh, in the wilderness of Zin; because ye sanctified me not in the midst of the children of Israel. 52 For thou shalt see the land before thee; but thou shalt not go thither into the land which I give the children of Israel.

84. Moses Dies in Mount Nebo, and is Succeeded by Joshua. E52. P83.
Dt. 34$^{1a.7\text{-}9}$

1a And Moses went up from the plains of Moab unto mount Nebo. 7 And Moses was a hundred and twenty years old when he died: his eye was not dim, nor his natural force abated. 8 And the children of Israel wept for Moses in the plains of Moab thirty days: so the days of weeping in the mourning for Moses were ended.

9 And Joshua the son of Nun was full of the spirit of wisdom; for Moses had laid his hands upon him: and the children of Israel hearkened unto him, and did as Jehovah commanded Moses.

85. The Crossing of the Jordan. E54.
Josh. 4$^{13.15\text{-}17.19}$

13 About forty thousand ready armed for war passed over before Jehovah unto battle, to the plains of Jericho.

15 And Jehovah spake unto Joshua, saying, 16 Command

---

[85] vv. 13, 15-17 are perh. Deuteronomic: St.

the priests that bear the ark of the testimony, that they come up out of the Jordan.

17 Joshua therefore commanded the priests, saying, Come ye up out of the Jordan.

19 And the people came up out of the Jordan on the tenth day of the first month, and encamped in Gilgal, on the east border of Jericho.

86. First Passover in Canaan: the Manna Ceases.
Josh. $5^{10\text{-}12}$

10 And the children of Israel encamped in Gilgal; and they kept the passover on the fourteenth day of the month at even in the plains of Jericho. 11 And they did eat of the produce of the land on the morrow after the passover, unleavened cakes and parched grain, in the selfsame day. 12 And the manna ceased on the morrow, after they had eaten of the produce of the land; neither had the children of Israel manna any more; but they did eat of the fruit of the land of Canaan that year.

87. The Covenant with the Gibeonites is Kept. J49. E61.
Josh. $9^{15b.17\text{-}21}$

15b And the princes of the congregation sware unto them. 17 And the children of Israel journeyed, and came unto their cities on the third day. Now their cities were Gibeon and Chephirah and Beeroth, and Kiriath-jearim. 18 And the children of Israel smote them not, because the princes of the congregation had sworn unto them by Jehovah, the God of Israel. And all the congregation murmured against the princes. 19 But all the princes said unto all the congregation, We have sworn unto them by Jehovah, the God of Israel: now therefore we may not touch them. 20 This we will do to them, and let them live; lest wrath be upon us, because of the oath which we sware unto them. 21 And the princes said unto them, Let them live: so they became hewers of wood and drawers of water unto all the congregation, as the princes had spoken unto them.

88. The Lots of Reuben, Gad, and Manasseh. P78. Josh. 18^1, cf. 1S. 4^{3ff}.
Josh. 18^1 $13^{15\text{-}33}$

18^1 And the whole congregation of the children of Israel assembled themselves together at Shiloh, and set up the tent of meeting there: and the land was subdued before them.

13^{15} And Moses gave unto the tribe of the children of Reuben

---
[87] v. 17 gloss, om. LXX.
[88] 18^1 should be either here or before 14^1: We., Ku., St., Ka., Di., Dr., Pr. Vs. Smend: 18^1 Rp. $13^{29\text{-}31}$ worked over by Rp: Dr., St., Ho., Bennett, Pr.

according to their families. 16 And their border was from
Aroer, that is on the edge of the valley of the Arnon, and the
city that is in the middle of the valley, and all the plain by
Medeba; 17 Heshbon, and all its cities that are in the plain;
Dibon, and Bamoth-baal, and Beth-baal-meon, 18 and Jahaz,
and Kedemoth, and Mephaath, 19 and Kiriathaim, and Sibmah, and Zereth-shahar in the mount of the valley, 20 and
Beth-peor, and the slopes of Pisgah, and Beth-jeshimoth, 21 and
all the cities of the plain, and all the kingdom of Sihon king of
the Amorites, who reigned in Heshbon, whom Moses smote
with the chiefs of Midian, Evi, and Rekem, and Zur, and Hur,
and Reba, the princes of Sihon, that dwelt in the land. 22 Balaam also the son of Beor, the soothsayer, did the children of
Israel slay with the sword among the rest of their slain. 23 And
the border of the children of Reuben was the Jordan, and the border *thereof*. This was the inheritance of the children of Reuben
according to their families, the cities and the villages thereof.

24 And Moses gave unto the tribe of Gad, unto the children
of Gad, according to their families. 25 And their border was
Jazer, and all the cities of Gilead, and half the land of the children of Ammon, unto Aroer that is before Rabbah; 26 and from
Heshbon unto Ramath-mizpeh, and Betonim; and from Mahanaim unto the border of Debir; 27 and in the valley, Beth-
haram, and Beth-nimrah, and Succoth, and Zaphon, the rest
of the kingdom of Sihon king of Heshbon, the Jordan and the
border *thereof*, unto the uttermost part of the sea of Chinnereth
beyond the Jordan eastward. 28 This is the inheritance of the
children of Gad according to their families, the cities and the
villages thereof.

29 And Moses gave *inheritance* unto the half-tribe of Manasseh: and it was for the half-tribe of the children of Manasseh
according to their families. 30 And their border was from
Mahanaim, all Bashan, all the kingdom of Og king of Bashan,
and all the towns of Jair, which are in Bashan, threescore cities:
31 and half Gilead, and Ashtaroth, and Edrei, the cities of
the kingdom of Og in Bashan, were for the children of Machir
the son of Manasseh, even for the half of the children of Machir
according to their families.

32 These are the inheritances which Moses distributed in the
plains of Moab, beyond the Jordan at Jericho, eastward. 33 But
unto the tribe of Levi Moses gave no inheritance: Jehovah, the
God of Israel, is their inheritance, as he spake unto them.

89. THE PLAN OF ALLOTMENT OF THE LAND. P80, 71.
Josh. 14$^{1\text{-}5}$

14^1 And these are the inheritances which the children of

Israel took in the land of Canaan, which Eleazar the priest, and Joshua the son of Nun, and the heads of the fathers' *houses* of the tribes of the children of Israel, distributed unto them, 2 by the lot of their inheritance, as Jehovah commanded by Moses, for the nine tribes, and for the half-tribe. 3 For Moses had given the inheritance of the two tribes and the half-tribe beyond the Jordan: but unto the Levites he gave no inheritance among them. 4 For the children of Joseph were two tribes, Manasseh and Ephraim: and they gave no portion unto the Levites in the land, save cities to dwell in, with the suburbs thereof for their cattle and for their substance. 5 As Jehovah commanded Moses, so the children of Israel did; and they divided the land.

90. THE LOT OF JUDAH. J51, 52.
Josh. $15^{1-12.20-62}$

1 And the lot for the tribe of the children of Judah according to their families was unto the border of Edom, even to the wilderness of Zin southward, at the uttermost part of the south. 2 And their south border was from the uttermost part of the Salt Sea, from the bay that looketh southward; 3 and it went out southward of the ascent of Akrabbim, and passed along to Zin, and went up by the south of Kadesh-barnea, and passed along by Hezron, and went up to Addar, and turned about to Karka; 4 and it passed along to Azmon, and went out at the brook of Egypt; and the goings out at the border were at the sea: this shall be your south border. 5 And the east border was the Salt Sea, even unto the end of the Jordan. And the border of the north quarter was from the bay of the sea at the end of the Jordan; 6 and the border went up to Beth-hoglah, and passed along by the north of Beth-arabah; and the border went up to the stone of Bohan the son of Reuben; 7 and the border went up to Debir from the valley of Achor, and so northward, looking toward Gilgal, that is over against the ascent of Adummim, which is on the south side of the river; and the border passed along to the waters of En-shemesh, and the goings out thereof were at En-rogel; 8 and the border went up by the valley of the son of Hinnom unto the side of the Jebusite southward (the same is Jerusalem); and the border went up to the top of the mountain that lieth before the valley of Hinnom westward, which is at the uttermost part of the vale of Rephaim northward; 9 and the border extended from the top of the mountain unto the fountain of the waters of Nephtoah, and went out to the cities of mount Ephron; and the border extended to Baalah (the same is Kiriath-jearim); 10 and the

---
[90] Pr. calls vv. 2-12 E.

border turned about from Baalah westward unto mount Seir, and passed along unto the side of mount Jearim on the north (the same is Chesalon), and went down to Beth-shemesh, and passed along by Timnah; 11 and the border went out unto the side of Ekron northward; and the border extended to Shikkeron, and passed along to mount Baalah, and went out at Jabneel; and the goings out of the border were at the sea. 12 And the west border was to the great sea, and the border *thereof*. This is the border of the children of Judah round about according to their families.

20 This is the inheritance of the tribe of the children of Judah according to their families.

21 And the uttermost cities of the tribe of the children of Judah toward the border of Edom in the South were Kabzeel, and Eder, and Jagur, 22 and Kinah, and Dimonah, and Adadah, 23 and Kedesh, and Hazor, and Ithnan, 24 Ziph, and Telem, and Bealoth, 25 and Hazor-hadattah, and Keriothhezron (the same is Hazor), 26 Amam, and Shema, and Moladah, 27 and Hazar-gaddah, and Heshmon, and Beth-pelet, 28 and Hazar-shual, and Beer-sheba, and Biziothiah, 29 Baalah, and Iim, and Ezem, 30 and Eltolad, and Chesil, and Hormah, 31 and Ziklag, and Madmannah, and Sansannah, 32 and Lebaoth, and Shilhim, and Ain, and Rimmon: all the cities are twenty and nine, with their villages.

33 In the lowland, Eshtaol, and Zorah, and Ashnah, 34 and Zanoah, and En-gannim, Tappuah, and Enam, 35 Jarmuth, and Adullam, Socoh, and Azekah, 36 and Shaaraim, and Adithaim, and Gederah, and Gederothaim; fourteen cities with their villages.

37 Zenan, and Hadashah, and Migdal-gad, 38 and Dilean, and Mizpeh, and Joktheel, 39 Lachish, and Bozkath, and Eglon, 40 and Cabbon, and Lahmam, and Chitlish, 41 and Gederoth, Beth-dagon, and Naamah, and Makkedah; sixteen cities with their villages.

42 Libnah, and Ether, and Ashan, 43 and Iphtah, and Ashnah, and Nezib, 44 and Keilah, and Achzib, and Mareshah; nine cities with their villages.

45 Ekron, with its towns and its villages; 46 from Ekron even unto the sea, all that were by the side of Ashdod, with their villages.

47 Ashdod, its towns and its villages; Gaza, its towns and its villages; unto the brook of Egypt, and the great sea, and the border *thereof*.

48 And in the hill-country, Shamir, and Jattir, and Socoh, 49 and Dannah, and Kiriath-sannah (the same is Debir), 50 and Anab, and Eshtemoh, and Anim, 51 and Goshen, and Holon, and Giloh; eleven cities with their villages.

52 Arab, and Dumah, and Eshan, 53 and Janim, and Beth-tappuah, and Aphekah, 54 and Humtah, and Kiriath-arba (the same is Hebron), and Zior; nine cities with their villages.

55 Maon, Carmel, and Ziph, and Jutah, 56 and Jezreel, and Jokdeam, and Zanoah, 57 Kain, Gibeah, and Timnah; ten cities with their villages.

58 Halhul, Beth-zur, and Gedor, 59 and Maarath, and Beth-anoth, and Eltekon; six cities with their villages.

60 Kiriath-baal (the same is Kiriath-jearim), and Rabbah; two cities with their villages.

61 In the wilderness, Beth-arabah, Middin, and Secacah, 62 and Nibshan, and the City of Salt, and Engedi; six cities with their villages.

91. THE LOT OF EPHRAIM. E66.

Josh. 16$^{4-8}$

4 And the children of Joseph, Manasseh and Ephriam, took their inheritance.

5 And the border of the children of Ephraim according to their families was *thus*: the border of their inheritance eastward was Ataroth-addar, unto Beth-horon the upper; 6 and the border went out westward at Michmethath on the north; and the border turned about eastward unto Taanath-shiloh, and passed along it on the east of Janoah; 7 and it went down from Janoah to Ataroth, and to Naarah, and reached unto Jericho, and went out at the Jordan. 8 From Tappuah the border went along westward to the brook of Kanah; and the goings out thereof were at the sea. This is the inheritance of the tribe of the children of Ephraim according to their families.

92. THE LOT OF MANASSEH. J54. E67. P78, 88.

Josh. 17$^{1a.3-4.7.9.10a}$

1a And *this* was the lot for the tribe of Manasseh; for he was the first-born of Joseph.

3 But Zelophehad, the son of Hepher, the son of Gilead, the son of Machir, the son of Manasseh, had no sons, but daughters: and these are the names of his daughters: Mahlah, and Noah, Hoglah, Milcah, and Tirzah. 4 And they came near before Eleazar the priest, and before Joshua the son of Nun, and before the princes, saying, Jehovah commanded Moses to give us an inheritance among our brethren: therefore according to the commandment of Jehovah he gave them an inheritance among the brethren of their father.

7 And the border of Manasseh was from Asher to Michmethath, which is before Shechem; and the border went along to the right hand, unto the inhabitants of En-tappuah. 9 And

the border went down unto the brook of Kanah, southward of the brook: . . . and the border of Manasseh was on the north side of the brook, and the goings out thereof were at the sea. 10a Southward it was Ephraim's, and northward it was Manasseh's, and the sea was his border.

Josh. 18^{11}, cf. P88.

93. THE LOT OF BENJAMIN.
Josh. 18$^{11\text{-}28}$

11 And the lot of the tribe of the children of Benjamin came up according to their families: and the border of their lot went out between the children of Judah and the children of Joseph. 12 And their border on the north quarter was from the Jordan; and the border went up to the side of Jericho on the north, and went up through the hill-country westward; and the goings out thereof were at the wilderness of Beth-aven. 13 And the border passed along from thence to Luz, to the side of Luz (the same is Beth-el), southward; and the border went down to Ataroth-addar, by the mountain that lieth on the south of Beth-horon the nether. 14 And the border extended *thence*, and turned about on the west quarter southward, from the mountain that lieth before Beth-horon southward; and the goings out thereof were at Kiriath-baal (the same is Kiriath-jearim), a city of the children of Judah: this was the west quarter. 15 And the south quarter was from the uttermost part of Kiriath-jearim; and the border went out westward, and went out to the fountain of the waters of Nephtoah; 16 and the border went down to the uttermost part of the mountain that lieth before the valley of the son of Hinnom, which is in the vale of Rephaim northward; and it went down to the valley of Hinnom, to the side of the Jebusite southward, and went down to En-rogel; 17 and it extended northward, and went out at En-shemesh, and went out to Geliloth, which is over against the ascent of Adummim; and it went down to the stone of Bohan the son of Reuben; 18 and it passed along to the side over against the Arabah northward, and went down unto the Arabah; 19 and the border passed along to the side of Beth-hoglah northward; and the goings out of the border were at the north bay of the Salt Sea, at the south end of the Jordan: this was the south border. 20 And the Jordan was the border of it on the east quarter. This was the inheritance of the children of Benjamin, by the borders thereof round about, according to their families.

21 Now the cities of the tribe of the children of Benjamin according to their families were Jericho, and Beth-hoglah, and Emek-keziz, 22 and Beth-arabah, and Zemaraim, and Beth-el,

23 and Avvim, and Parah, and Ophrah, 24 and Chephar-ammoni, and Ophni, and Geba; twelve cities with their villages: 25 Gibeon, and Ramah, and Beeroth, 26 and Mizpeh, and Chephirah, and Mozah, 27 and Rekem, and Irpeel, and Tara-lah, 28 and Zelah, Eleph, and the Jebusite (the same is Jerusalem), Gibeath, *and* Kiriath; fourteen cities with their villages. This is the inheritance of the children of Benjamin according to their families.

94. THE LOTS OF SIMEON, ZEBULUN, ISSACHAR, NAPHTALI, AND DAN. J55.
Josh. 19$^{1-8.10-46.48.51}$

1 And the second lot came out for Simeon, even for the tribe of the children of Simeon according to their families: and their inheritance was in the midst of the inheritance of the children of Judah. 2 And they had for their inheritance Beer-sheba, or Sheba, and Moladah, 3 and Hazar-shual, and Balah, and Ezem, 4 and Eltolad, and Bethul, and Hormah, 5 and Ziklag, and Beth-marcaboth, and Hazar-susah, 6 and Beth-lebaoth, and Sharuhen; thirteen cities with their villages: 7 Ain, Rimmon, and Ether, and Ashan; four cities with their villages: 8 and all the villages that were round about these cities to Baalath-beer, Ramah of the South. This is the inheritance of the tribe of the children of Simeon according to their families.

10 And the third lot came up for the children of Zebulun, according to their families. And the border of their inheritance was unto Sarid; 11 and their border went up westward, even to Maralah, and reached to Dabbesheth; and it reached to the brook that is before Jokneam; 12 and it turned from Sarid eastward toward the sunrising unto the border of Chisloth-tabor; and it went out to Daberath, and went up to Japhia; 13 and from thence it passed along eastward to Gath-hepher, to Eth-kazin; and it went out at Rimmon, which stretcheth unto Neah; 14 and the border turned about it on the north to Hannathon; and the goings out thereof were at the valley of Iphtah-el; 15 and Kattath, and Nahalal, and Shimron, and Idalah, and Bethlehem: twelve cities with their villages. 16 This is the inheritance of the children of Zebulun according to their families, these cities with their villages.

17 The fourth lot came out for Issachar, even for the children of Issachar according to their families. 18 And their border was unto Jezreel, and Chesulloth, and Shunem, 19 and Hapharaim, and Shion, and Anaharath, 20 and Rabbith, and Kishion, and Ebez, 21 and Remeth, and En-gannim, and En-haddah, and Beth-pazzez, 22 and the border reached to Tabor,

---
[94] Lists of cities in 19$^{13-38}$ are JE: We., Smend,

and Shahazumah, and Beth-shemesh; and the goings out of their border were at the Jordan: sixteen cities with their villages. 23 This is the inheritance of the tribe of the children of Issachar according to their families, the cities with their villages.
24 And the fifth lot came out for the tribe of the children of Asher according to their families. 25 And their border was Helkath, and Hali, and Beten, and Achshaph, 26 and Allammelech, and Amad, and Mishal; and it reached to Carmel westward, and to Shihor-libnath; 27 and it turned toward the sunrising to Beth-dagon, and reached to Zebulun, and to the valley of Iphtah-el northward to Beth-emek and Neiel; and it went out to Cabul on the left hand, 28 and Ebron, and Rehob, and Hammon, and Kanah, even unto great Sidon; 29 and the border turned to Ramah, and to the fortified city of Tyre; and the border turned to Hosah; and the goings out thereof were at the sea by the region of Achzib; 30 Ummah also, and Aphek, and Rehob: twenty and two cities with their villages. 31 This is the inheritance of the tribe of the children of Asher according to their families, these cities with their villages.
32 The sixth lot came out for the children of Naphtali, even for the children of Naphtali according to their families. 33 And their border was from Heleph, from the oak in Zaanannim, and Adam-inekeb, and Jabneel, unto Lakkum; and the goings out thereof were at the Jordan; 34 and the border turned westward to Aznoth-tabor, and went out from thence to Hukkok; and it reached to Zebulun on the south, and reached to Asher on the west, and to Judah at the Jordan toward the sunrising. 35 And the fortified cities were Ziddim, Zer, and Hammath, Rakkath, and Chinnereth, 36 and Adamah, and Ramah, and Hazor, 37 and Kedesh, and Edrei, and En-hazor, 38 and Iron, and Migdal-el, Horem, and Beth-anath, and Beth-shemesh; nineteen cities with their villages. 39 This is the inheritance of the tribe of the children of Naphtali according to their families, the cities with their villages.
40 The seventh lot came out for the tribe of the children of Dan according to their families. 41 And the border of their inheritance was Zorah, and Eshtaol, and Irshemesh, 42 and Shaalabbin, and Aijalon, and Ithlah, 43 and Elon, and Timnah, and Ekron, 44 and Eltekeh, and Gibbethon, and Baalath, 45 and Jehud, and Bene-berak, and Gath-rimmon, 46 and Me-jarkon, and Rakkon, with the border over against Joppa. 48 This is the inheritance of the tribe of the children of Dan according to their families, these cities with their villages.
51 These are the inheritances, which Eleazar the priest, and Joshua the son of Nun, and the heads of the fathers' *houses* of the tribes of the children of Israel, distributed for inheritance

by lot in Shiloh before Jehovah, at the door of the tent of meeting. So they made an end of dividing the land.

95. CITIES OF REFUGE. P81.
Josh. 20[1-6a, 7-9]

1 And Jehovah spake unto Joshua, saying, 2 Speak to the children of Israel, saying, Assign you the cities of refuge, whereof I spake unto you by Moses, 3 that the manslayer that killeth any person unwittingly *and* unawares may flee thither: and they shall be unto you for a refuge from the avenger of blood. 4 And he shall flee unto one of those cities, and shall stand at the entrance of the gate of the city, and declare his cause in the ears of the elders of that city; and they shall take him into the city unto them, and give him a place, that he may dwell among them. 5 And if the avenger of blood pursue after him, then they shall not deliver up the manslayer into his hand; because he smote his neighbor unawares, and hated him not beforetime. 6 And he shall dwell in that city, until he stand before the congregation for judgment, until the death of the high priest that shall be in those days: then shall the manslayer return, and come unto his own city, and unto his own house, unto the city from whence he fled.

7 And they set apart Kedesh in Galilee in the hill-country of Naphtali, and Shechem in the hill-country of Ephraim, and Kiriath-arba (the same is Hebron) in the hill-country of Judah. 8 And beyond the Jordan at Jericho eastward, they assigned Bezer in the wilderness in the plain out of the tribe of Reuben, and Ramoth in Gilead out of the tribe of Gad, and Golan in Bashan out of the tribe of Manasseh. 9 These were the appointed cities for all the children of Israel, and for the stranger that sojourneth among them, that whosoever killeth any person unwittingly might flee thither, and not die by the hand of the avenger of blood, until he stood before the congregation.

96. CITIES FOR THE LEVITES. P80.
Josh. 21[1-42]

1 Then came near the heads of fathers' *houses* of the Levites unto Eleazar the priest, and unto Joshua the son of Nun, and unto the heads of fathers' *houses* of the tribes of the children of Israel; 2 and they spake unto them at Shiloh in the land of Canaan, saying, Jehovah commanded by Moses to give us cities to dwell in, with the suburbs thereof for our cattle. 3 And the children of Israel gave unto the Levites out of their inheritance, according to the commandment of Jehovah, these cities with their suburbs.

¶⁶ vv. 4-6 (except "until . . . judgment" in v. 6) are R: om. LXX.

4 And the lot came out for the families of the Kohathites: and the children of Aaron the priest, who were of the Levites, had by lot out of the tribe of Judah, and out of the tribe of the Simeonites, and out of the tribe of Benjamin, thirteen cities.

5 And the rest of the children of Kohath had by lot out of the families of the tribe of Ephraim, and out of the tribe of Dan, and out of the half-tribe of Manasseh, ten cities.

6 And the children of Gershon had by lot out of the families of the tribe of Issachar, and out of the tribe of Asher, and out of the tribe of Naphtali, and out of the half-tribe of Manasseh in Bashan, thirteen cities.

7 The children of Merari according to their families had out of the tribe of Reuben, and out of the tribe of Gad, and out of the tribe of Zebulun, twelve cities.

8 And the children of Israel gave by lot unto the Levites these cities with their suburbs, as Jehovah commanded by Moses. 9 And they gave out of the tribe of the children of Judah, and out of the tribe of the children of Simeon, these cities which are *here* mentioned by name: 10 and they were for the children of Aaron, of the families of the Kohathites, who were of the children of Levi; for theirs was the first lot. 11 And they gave them Kiriath-arba, *which Arba was* the father of Anak (the same is Hebron), in the hill-country of Judah; with the suburbs thereof round about it. 12 But the fields of the city, and the villages thereof, gave they to Caleb the son of Jephunneh for his possession.

13 And unto the children of Aaron the priest they gave Hebron with its suburbs, the city of refuge for the manslayer, and Libnah with its suburbs, 14 and Jattir with its suburbs, and Eshtemoa with its suburbs, 15 and Holon with its suburbs, and Debir with its suburbs, 16 and Ain with its suburbs, and Juttah with its suburbs, *and* Beth-shemesh with its suburbs; nine cities out of those two tribes. 17 And out of the tribe of Benjamin, Gibeon with its suburbs, Geba with its suburbs, 18 Anathoth with its suburbs, and Almon with its suburbs; four cities. 19 All the cities of the children of Aaron, the priests, were thirteen cities with their suburbs.

20 And the families of the children of Kohath, the Levites, even the rest of the children of Kohath, they had the cities of their lot out of the tribe of Ephraim. 21 And they gave them Shechem with its suburbs in the hill-country of Ephraim, the city of refuge for the manslayer, and Gezer with its suburbs, 22 and Kibzaim with its suburbs, and Beth-horon with its suburbs; four cities. 23 And out of the tribe of Dan, Elteke with its suburbs, Gibbethon with its suburbs. 24 Aijalon

with its suburbs, Gath-rimmon with its suburbs; four cities. 25 And out of the half-tribe of Manasseh, Taanach with its suburbs, and Gath-rimmon with its suburbs; two cities. 26 All the cities of the families of the rest of the children of Kohath were ten with their suburbs.

27 And unto the children of Gershon, of the families of the Levites, out of the half-tribe of Manasseh *they gave* Golan in Bashan with its suburbs, the city of refuge for the manslayer, and Be-eshterah with its suburbs; two cities. 28 And out of the tribe of Issachar, Kishion with its suburbs, Daberath with its suburbs, 29 Jarmuth with its suburbs, En-gannim with its suburbs; four cities. 30 And out of the tribe of Asher, Mishal with its suburbs, Abdon with its suburbs, 31 Helkath with its suburbs, and Rehob with its suburbs; four cities. 32 And out of the tribe of Naphtali, Kedesh in Galilee with its suburbs, the city of refuge for the manslayer, and Hammoth-dor with its suburbs, and Kartan with its suburbs; three cities. 33 All the cities of the Gershonites according to their families were thirteen cities with their suburbs.

34 And unto the families of the children of Merari, the rest of the Levites, out of the tribe of Zebulun, Jokneam with its suburbs, and Kartah with its suburbs, 35 Dimnah with its suburbs, Nahalal with its suburbs; four cities. 36 And out of the tribe of Reuben, Bezer with its suburbs, and Jahaz with its suburbs, 37 Kedemoth with its suburbs, and Mephaath with its suburbs; four cities. 38 And out of the tribe of Gad, Ramoth in Gilead with its suburbs, the city of refuge for the manslayer, and Mahanaim with its suburbs, 39 Heshbon with its suburbs, Jazer with its suburbs; four cities in all. 40 All *these were* the cities of the children of Merari according to their families, even the rest of the families of the Levites; and their lot was twelve cities.

41 All the cities of the Levites in the midst of the possession of the children of Israel were forty and eight cities with their suburbs. 42 These cities were every one with their suburbs round about them: thus it was with all these cities.

97. Reuben, Gad, and Manasseh Build an Altar in Gilead, but Agree Not to Sacrifice on It. P78, 88.

Josh. 22$^{9-34}$

9 And the children of Reuben and the children of Gad and the half-tribe of Manasseh returned, and departed from the children of Israel out of Shiloh, which is in the land of Canaan, to go unto the land of Gilead, to the land of their possession,

---

⁹⁷ v. 34, "*Ed,*" in Hebr., witness.

whereof they were possessed, according to the commandment of Jehovah by Moses.

10 And when they came unto the region about the Jordan, that is in the land of Canaan, the children of Reuben and the children of Gad and the half-tribe of Manasseh built there an altar by the Jordan, a great altar to look upon. 11 And the children of Israel heard say, Behold, the children of Reuben and the children of Gad and the half-tribe of Manasseh have built an altar in the forefront of the land of Canaan, in the region about the Jordan, on the side that pertaineth to the children of Israel. 12 And when the children of Israel heard of it, the whole congregation of the children of Israel gathered themselves together at Shiloh, to go up against them to war.

13 And the children of Israel sent unto the children of Reuben, and to the children of Gad, and to the half-tribe of Manasseh, into the land of Gilead, Phinehas the son of Eleazar the priest, 14 and with him ten princes, one prince of a fathers' house for each of the tribes of Israel; and they were every one of them head of their fathers' houses among the thousands of Israel. 15 And they came unto the children of Reuben, and to the children of Gad, and to the half-tribe of Manasseh, unto the land of Gilead, and they spake with them, saying, 16 Thus saith the whole congregation of Jehovah, What trespass is this that ye have committed against the God of Israel, to turn away this day from following Jehovah, in that ye have builded you an altar, to rebel this day against Jehovah? 17 Is the iniquity of Peor too little for us, from which we have not cleansed ourselves unto this day, although there came a plague upon the congregation of Jehovah, 18 that ye must turn away this day from following Jehovah? and it will be, seeing ye rebel to-day against Jehovah, that to-morrow he will be wroth with the whole congregation of Israel. 19 Howbeit, if the land of your possession be unclean, then pass ye over unto the land of the possession of Jehovah, wherein Jehovah's tabernacle dwelleth, and take possession among us: but rebel not against Jehovah, nor rebel against us, in building you an altar besides the altar of Jehovah our God. 20 Did not Achan the son of Zerah commit a trespass in the devoted thing, and wrath fell upon all the congregation of Israel? and that man perished not alone in his iniquity.

21 Then the children of Reuben and the children of Gad and the half-tribe of Manasseh answered, and spake unto the heads of the thousands of Israel, 22 The Mighty One, God, Jehovah, the Mighty One, God, Jehovah, he knoweth; and Israel he shall know: if it be in rebellion, or if in trespass

against Jehovah (save thou us not this day), 23 that we have built us an altar to turn away from following Jehovah; or if to offer thereon burnt-offering or meal-offering, or if to offer sacrifices of peace-offerings thereon, let Jehovah himself require it; 24 and if we have not *rather* out of carefulness done this, *and* of purpose, saying, In time to come your children might speak unto our children, saying, What have ye to do with Jehovah, the God of Israel? 25 for Jehovah hath made the Jordan a border between us and you, ye children of Reuben and children of Gad; ye have no portion in Jehovah: so might your children make our children cease from fearing Jehovah. 26 Therefore we said, Let us now prepare to build us an altar, not for burnt-offering, nor for sacrifice: 27 but it shall be a witness between us and you, and between our generations after us, that we may do the service of Jehovah before him with our burnt-offerings, and with our sacrifices, and with our peace-offerings; that your children may not say to our children in time to come, Ye have no portion in Jehovah. 28 Therefore said we, It shall be, when they so say to us or to our generations in time to come, that we shall say, Behold the pattern of the altar of Jehovah, which our fathers made, not for burnt-offering, nor for sacrifice; but it is a witness between us and you. 29 Far be it from us that we should rebel against Jehovah, and turn away this day from following Jehovah, to build an altar for burnt-offering, for meal-offering, or for sacrifice, besides the altar of Jehovah our God that is before his tabernacle.

30 And when Phinehas the priest, and the princes of the congregation, even the heads of the thousands of Israel that were with him, heard the words that the children of Reuben and the children of Gad and the children of Manasseh spake, it pleased them well. 31 And Phinehas the son of Eleazar the priest said unto the children of Reuben, and to the children of Gad, and to the children of Manasseh, This day we know that Jehovah is in the midst of us, because ye have not committed this trespass against Jehovah: now have ye delivered the children of Israel out of the hand of Jehovah. 32 And Phinehas the son of Eleazar the priest, and the princes, returned from the children of Reuben, and from the children of Gad, out of the land of Gilead, unto the land of Canaan, to the children of Israel, and brought them word again. 33 And the thing pleased the children of Israel; and the children of Israel blessed God, and spake no more of going up against them to war, to destroy the land wherein the children of Reuben and the children of Gad dwelt. 34 And the children of Reuben and the children of Gad called the altar *Ed*: For, *said they,* it is a witness between us that Jehovah is God.

LATE R ABRAM RESCUES LOT FROM THE KINGS OF ELAM, GOIIM, SHINAR, AND ELLASAR, AND IS BLESSED BY MELCHIZEDEK.

Gn. 14$^{1\text{-}24}$

Introductory Note.—Gn. 14 is universally recognized to belong in none of the Pentateuchal sources (Di., however, thought that it had a groundwork from E worked over by R or Rd).

There is difference of opinion among critics as to the origin and historicity of this chapter. Some hold that it is an independent ancient tradition: so Kittel, who holds that it was written by a north-Israelite for the Canaanites about the time of David. Se. advances the theory that it was an ancient cuneiform inscription in the Jebusite archives in Jerusalem (cf. the glosses in vv. 2, 3, 7, etc.; Se. makes vv. 17, 20–24 R). Paton finds here an ancient Palestinian document. Hommel regards it as historical.

Most critics admit that a certain measure of ancient tradition may be embodied in the chapter, as in the names of the kings (Amraphel—Hammurapi; Arioch—Eri-Agu; Chedorlaomer—Kudur-lagamar, Sk.) But the majority regard it as late (post-exilic) and as an unhistorical midrash, so far as the details and its present form are concerned. So: We., Ku., Nöldeke, Co., Bu., St., Ba., Briggs, Gu., Dr., GFM., CH., Wildeboer, Sk., Barton. Even Ki. regards vv 14–17 as unhistorical, and refers to the Sinuhe story (Gr. TB., 210-217), although vv. 18-20, from Canaanite sources, are, in his opinion, trustworthy. On the whole discussion see Barton's valuable article "Abraham and Archæology," JBL. vol. 28, pp. 152-168.

1 And it came to pass in the days of Amraphel king of Shinar, Arioch king of Ellasar, Chedorlaomer king of Elam, and Tidal king of Goiim, 2 that they made war with Bera king of Sodom, and with Birsha king of Gomorrah, Shinab king of Admah, and Shemeber king of Zeboiim, and the king of Bela (the same is Zoar). 3 All these joined together in the vale of Siddim (the same is the Salt Sea). 4 Twelve years they served Chedorlaomer, and in the thirteenth year they rebelled. 5 And in the fourteenth year came Chedorlaomer, and the kings that were with him, and smote the Rephaim in Ashterothkarnaim, and the Zuzim in Ham, and the Emin in Shavehkiriathaim, 6 and the Horites in their mount Seir, unto El-paran, which is by the wilderness. 7 And they returned, and came to Enmishpat (the same is Kadesh), and smote all the country of the Amalekites, and also the Amorites, that dwelt in Hazazon-

---

Late R "God Most High" in v. 18ff. is in Hebr. *El Elyon.*

tamar. 8 And there went out the king of Sodom, and the king of Gomorrah, and the king of Admah, and the king of Zeboiim, and the king of Bela (the same is Zoar); and they set the battle in array against them in the vale of Siddim; 9 against Chedorlaomer king of Elam, and Tidal king of Goiim, and Amraphel king of Shinar, and Arioch king of Ellasar; four kings against the five. 10 Now the vale of Siddim was full of slime pits; and the kings of Sodom and Gomorrah fled, and they fell there, and they that remained fled to the mountain. 11 And they took all the goods of Sodom and Gomorrah, and all their victuals, and went their way. 12 And they took Lot, Abram's brother's son, who dwelt in Sodom, and his goods, and departed.

13 And there came one that had escaped, and told Abram the Hebrew: now he dwelt by the oaks of Mamre, the Amorite, brother of Eshcol, and brother of Aner; and these were confederate with Abram. 14 And when Abram heard that his brother was taken captive, he led forth his trained men, born in his house, three hundred and eighteen, and pursued as far as Dan. 15 And he divided himself against them by night, he and his servants, and smote them, and pursued them unto Hobah, which is on the left hand of Damascus. 16 And he brought back all the goods, and also brought back his brother Lot, and his goods, and the women also, and the people.

17 And the king of Sodom went out to meet him, after his return from the slaughter of Chedorlaomer and the kings that were with him, at the vale of Shaveh (the same is the King's Vale). 18 And Melchizedek king of Salem brought forth bread and wine: and he was priest of God Most High. 19 And he blessed him, and said, Blessed be Abram of God Most High, possessor of heaven and earth; 20 and blessed be God Most High, who hath delivered thine enemies into thy hand. And he gave him a tenth of all. 21 And the king of Sodom said unto Abram, Give me the persons, and take the goods to thyself. 22 And Abram said to the king of Sodom, I have lifted up my hand unto Jehovah, God Most High, possessor of heaven and earth, 23 that I will not take a thread nor a shoe-latchet nor aught that is thine, lest thou shouldest say, I have made Abram rich: 24 save only that which the young men have eaten, and the portion of the men that went with me, Aner, Eshcol, and Mamre; let them take their portion.

BIBLIOGRAPHY

Note.—This bibliography lays no claim to completeness. It includes almost exclusively such books as have been actually used in the preparation of the present volume. Abbreviations employed in the text for the name of each critic are printed before his name.

- (Ad.) Addis, W. E., The Documents of the Hexateuch. 2 parts. New York and London, 1893.
  ....., art., "Aaron," Enc. Bib.
- (Ba.) Bacon, B. W., The Genesis of Genesis. Hartford, 1892.
  ....., The Triple Tradition of the Exodus. Hartford, 1894.
- (Bä.) Bäntsch, B., Exodus-Leviticus. Göttingen, 1900.
  ...., Numeri. Göttingen, 1903.
  (Both of the above volumes are in the Handkommentar zum Alten Testament.)
  Barton, G. A., art., "Abraham and Archæology," JBL., vol. 28.
- (Bu.) Budde, K., Das nomadische Ideal. Preuss. Jahrb., 1896.
  Briggs, C. A., The Higher Criticism of the Hexateuch. New York, 1893.
  Carpenter, J. E., and Harford-Battersby, G., The Hexateuch according to the Revised Version. London, 1900. "The Oxford Hexateuch."
- (CH.) ...., ..., and Harford G., The Composition of the Hexateuch. London, 1902.
- (Co.) Cornill, C. H., Einleitung in die kanonischen Bücher des Alten Testaments. 6th ed. Tübingen, 1908.
  ...., Zur Einleitung in das Alte Testament. Tübingen, 1912.
  Cook, S. A., art., "Aaron," Encyclopædia Britannica.
  Dahse, J., Textkritische Materialien zur Hexateuchfrage. I. Giessen, 1912.
- (Del.) Delitzsch.
- (Di.) Dillmann, A. (ed. R. Kittel), Handbuch der alttestamentlichen Theologie. Leipzig, 1895.
  ...., Kurzgefasstes exegetisches Handbuch zum Alten Testament. Genesis. 5th ed. Leipzig, 1886. Exodus und Leviticus. 2d ed. Leipzig, 1880. Numeri, Deuteronomium, und Josua. 2d ed. Leipzig, 1886.
- (Dr.) Driver, S. R., Introduction to the Literature of the Old Testament. Revised ed. New York, 1913.
  ......, The Book of Genesis. London, 1904.
  ......, Exodus, in the Cambridge Bible. 1911.
  ......, The Book of Leviticus, in Holy Bible, Polychrome ed. New York, 1898.

388 SOURCES OF THE HEXATEUCH

(Eerd.) Eerdmans, B., Alttestamentliche Studien. 3 parts. Giessen, 1908-1910.

Eiselen, F. C., The Books of the Pentateuch. New York, 1916.

(Enc. Bib.) Encyclopædia Biblica. 4 vols. Ed. T. K. Cheyne. London, 1899-1903.

(Ew.) Ewald.

(GFM.) See Moore, George Foote.

Gray, G. B., Studies in Hebrew Proper Names. London, 1896.

....., A Critical and Exegetical Commentary on Numbers. New York, 1903.

(Gr.) Gressmann, H., Der Ursprung der Israelitisch-jüdischen Eschatologie. Göttingen, 1905.

........., Die Schriften des Alten Testaments, I. 2. Die Anfänge Israels. Göttingen, 1914.

........., ... , II. 1. Die älteste Geschichtsschreibung und Prophetie Israels. Göttingen, 1910.

(Gr.TB.) ...., Altorientalische Texte und Bilder. Tübingen, 1909.

(Gu.) Gunkel, H., Die Schriften des Alten Testaments, I. 1. Die Urgeschichte und die Patriarchen. Göttingen, 1911.

......, Genesis. 3d ed. In Handkommentar zum Alten Testament. Göttingen, 1910.

(HDB.) Hastings, J., ed., A Dictionary of the Bible. 5 vols. Edinburgh and New York, 1903-1904.

(Ho.) Holzinger, H., Einleitung in den Hexateuch. Freiburg und Leipzig, 1893. (With tables showing the analysis of Di., We., Ku., Co., Bu., Jül., etc.).

International Standard Bible Encyclopædia, ed. J. Orr. 5 vols. Chicago, 1915.

(JBL.) Journal of Biblical Literature.

(Ka.) Kautzsch, E., Die Heilige Schrift des Alten Testaments. 3d ed. Tübingen, 1909. (Gn.-Nu., and Josh. by Ka. and Ho. Dt. by Marti.).

Kent, C. F., The Beginnings of Hebrew History, in Student's Old Testament. New York, 1904.

....., Israel's Laws and Legal Precedents, in same. New York, 1907.

(Ki.) Kittel, R., Geschichte des Volkes Israel. 2 vols. 2d ed. Gotha, 1912.

Knudson, A. C., The So-called J-Decalogue, in JBL., vol. 27, pt. 1, 1909.

König, E., Die moderne Pentateuchkritik und ihre neueste Bekämpfung, 1914.

BIBLIOGRAPHY 389

(Ku.) Kuenen, A., An Historical-critical Inquiry into the Origin and Composition of the Hexateuch. Tr., London, 1886.

Luther, B., Die Persönlichkeit des Jahvisten, in Meyer, q.v., pp. 105-173.

(McN.) McNeile, A. H., The Book of Exodus, with Introduction and Notes. London, 1908.

(Mi.) Mitchell, H. G., Genesis, in Bible for Home and School. New York, 1909.

Meinhold, R., Sabbat und Woche. Göttingen, 1905.

Meissner, B., Der Dekalog. 1893.

Meyer, E., Die Israeliten und ihre Nachbarstämme. Halle, 1906.

(GFM.) Moore, G. F., Tatian's Diatessaron and the Pentateuch, in JBL. 1890, Pt. II.

....., artt., "Genesis," "Exodus," "Leviticus," "Numbers," "Deuteronomy," and "Joshua," in Enc. Bib.

....., The Literature of the Old Testament. New York and London, 1913.

Naville, E., The Text of the Old Testament. British Academy, 1917.

Paton, L. B., The Original Form of the Book of the Covenant, in JBL. vols. 12, 16.

....., The Original Form of Lv. xxi, xxii, in JBL. 17.

....., The Original Form of Lv. xxiii, xxv, in JBL. 18.

Peritz, I. J., Old Testament History. New York, 1915.

(Pr.) Proksch, O., Das nordhebräische Sagenbuch, die Elohimquelle übersetzt und untersucht. Leipzig, 1906.

Rogers, R. W., A History of Babylonia and Assyria. 3d ed. New York, 1916.

....., Cuneiform Parallels to the Old Testament. New York, 1912.

(SB.) La Sainte Bible (La Bible du Centenaire). First installment, Gn. 1^1-Ex. 9^{16}. General editor, Adolphe Lods (Sorbonne). Genesis, Louis Aubert (Neuchatel). Exodus, Henri Trabaud (Geneva). Société Biblique de Paris, 1916ff.

(Se.) Sellin, E., Einleitung in das Alte Testament. Leipzig, 1910.

....., Zur Einleitung in das Alte Testament. Leipzig, 1912.

(Sk.) Skinner, J. A., A critical and exegetical Commentary on Genesis. New York, 1910.

Smend, R., Die Erzählung des Hexateuch auf ihre Quellen untersucht. Berlin, 1912.

Stade, B., Biblische Theologie des Alten Testaments. Tübingen, 1905.

(Sten.) Stenning, J. F., art., "Exodus," in Encyclopædia Britannica.

SOURCES OF THE HEXATEUCH

(St.) Steuernagel, C., Einleitung in das Alte Testament. Tübingen, 1912.

............, Deuteronomium, Josua, Einleitung in den Hexateuch, in Handkommentar zum Alten Testament. Göttingen, 1900.

(We.) Wellhausen, J., Die Komposition des Hexateuchs und der historischen Bücher des Alten Testaments. 3d ed. Berlin, 1899.

White, H. A., art., "Aaron," in HDB.

Woods, F. H., art., "Hexateuch," in HDB.

Wood, I. F., and Grant, E., The Bible as Literature. New York, 1914.

ABBREVIATIONS

Note.—For abbreviations of names of critics and books of reference, see the preceding bibliography.

Am. Rev.—American Standard Version of the Bible.
art., artt.—article, articles.
cf.—compare.
E—The Elohistic document.
ed.—editor, edition, edited by, etc.
esp.—especially.
et al.—and others.
exc.—except.
Hebr.—Hebrew.
J—the Jahvistic document.
LXX—the Septuagint, or Greek tr. of the OT.
marg.—margin.
om.—omit, omits.
OT.—Old Testament.
P—the Priestly code.
perh.—perhaps.
q.v.—which see.
R—Redactor or reviser.
Rd, Rje, Rp—Redactor of the school of Dt., JE, or P.
ref., reff.—reference, references.
Sam. Pent.—Samaritan Pentateuch.
Syr.—Syriac tr.
Targ. Onk.—Targum of Onkelos.
tr.—translate, translation, etc.
v., vv.—verse, verses.
Vulg.—Vulgate (Latin) translation.
. . .—indicates some omission, as $6^{7\cdots15}$, meaning, chapter 6, verses 7 to 15, with some omissions.
*—indicates that only a portion of the passage in question is intended.

INDEX

NOTE.—No attempt is made in this index to distinguish the various Rs. Reference to the text will show the extent of the redaction.—* indicates that the verse or passage belongs to the source mentioned only in part.—Reff. are to sections of the various documents.

Genesis

1^1-2^{4a}	P1
2^{4b}-4^{26}	J1-6
5^{1-28}	P2
5^{29}	J7
5^{30-32}	P2
6^{1-8}	J8-9
6^{9-22}	P3i-iii
7^{1-5}	J9
7^6	P3iii
7^{7-10}	J9
7^{11}	P3iii
7^{12}	J9
7^{13-16a}	P3iii
7^{16b}	J9
7^{17a}	P3iii
7^{17b}	J9
7^{18-21}	P3iii
7^{22-23}	J9
7^{24}-8^{2a}	P3iii
8^{2b-3a}	J9
8^{3b-5}	P3iii
8^{6-12}	J9
8^{13a}	P3iii
8^{13b}	J9
8^{14-19}	P3iii
8^{20-22}	J9
9^{1-17}	P3iv
9^{18-19}	J11
9^{20-27}	J10
10^{1-7}	P4
10^{8-19}	J11
10^{20}	P4
10^{21}	J11
10^{22-23}	P4
10^{24-30}	J11
10^{31-32}	P4
11^{1-9}	J12
11^{10-26}	P5
11^{27}	P6
11^{28-30}	J13i
11^{31-32}	P6
12^{1-4a}	J13ii
12^{4b-5}	P7i
12^{6-13^5}	J13iii-v
13^6	P7ii
13^{7-11a}	J13v
$13^{11b-12a}$	P7ii
13^{12b-18}	J13v
14^{1-24}	Late R
15^{1a}	J13vi
15^{1b}	E1i
15^{2a}	J13vi
15^{2b-3a}	E1i
15^{3b-4}	J13vi
15^5	E1i
15^{6-11}	J13vi
15^{12*}	J13vi
15^{12*}	E1i
15^{13-16}	E1i
15^{17-21}	J13vi
16^{1a}	P7iii
16^{1b-2}	J13vii
16^3	P7iii
16^{4-14}	J13vii
16^{15}-17^{27}	P7iii-v
18^1-19^{28}	J13viii-ix
19^{29}	P7vi
19^{30-38}	J13x
20^{1-18}	E1ii
21^{1a}	J13xi
21^{1b}	P7vii
21^{2a}	J13xi
21^{2b-5}	P7vii
21^{6a}	E1iii
21^{6b-7}	J13xi
21^{8-32}	E1iv-v
21^{33-34}	J13xii
22^{1-19}	E1vi-vii
22^{20-24}	J13xiii
23^{1-20}	P7viii
24^1-25^6	J13xiv-xv
25^{7-11a}	P7ix
25^{11b}	J14i
25^{12-17}	P8
25^{18}	J13xv
25^{19-20}	P9i
25^{21-26a}	J14ii
25^{26b}	P9i
25^{27}-26^{33}	J14iii-iv
26^{34-35}	P9ii
27^{1a}	J14v
27^{1b}	E2i
27^{2-10}	J14v
27^{11-13}	E2i
27^{14-15}	J14v
27^{16}	E2i
27^{17-18a}	J14v
27^{18b-19}	E2i
27^{20}	J14v
27^{21-23}	E2i
27^{24-27}	J14v
27^{28}	E2i
$27^{29a,c}$	J14v
27^{29b}	E2i
27^{30a}	J14v
27^{30b}	E2i
$27^{30c-33a}$	J14v
27^{33b-34}	E2i
27^{35-38}	J14v-vi
27^{39}	E2ii
27^{40-45}	J14vi
27^{46}-28^9	P9iii-iv
28^{10}	J15i
28^{11-12}	E3i
28^{13-16}	J15i
28^{17-18}	E3i
28^{19}	J15i
28^{20}-29^1	E3i-ii

392 SOURCES OF THE HEXATEUCH

Reference	Source	Reference	Source
29$^{2-14}$	J15ii	37^{2b}	P12i
29$^{15-23}$	E3iii-iv	37$^{3-4}$	J18i
29^{24}	P10i	37$^{5-11}$	E4i
29^{25}	E3iv	37$^{12-13ab}$	J18i
29^{26}	J15iii	37$^{13c-14ab}$	E4ii
29^{27-28a}	E3v	37^{14c}	J18i
29^{28b-29}	P10i	37^{15-18a}	E4ii
29^{30}	E3v	37^{18b}	J18i
29$^{31-35}$	J15iii-iv	37$^{19-20}$	E4ii
30^{1-3a}	E3vi	37^{21}	J18i
30^{3b-5}	J15iv	37^{22}	E4ii
30^{6}	E3vi	37^{23}	J18i
30^{7}	J15iv	37^{24}	E4ii
30^{8}	E3vi	37$^{25-27}$	J18i
30$^{9-16}$	J15iv	37^{28a}	E4ii
30^{17-20a}	E3vi	37^{28b}	J18i
30^{20b-21}	J15iv	37^{28c-31}	E4ii
30^{22a}	P10i	37$^{32-33}$	J18i
30^{22b-23}	E3vi	37^{34}	E4ii
30$^{24-25}$	J15iv-v	37^{35}	J18i
30^{26}	E3vii	37^{36}	E4iii
30^{27}	J15v	38$^{1-30}$	J17
30^{28}	E3vii	39^{1-4a}*	J18ii
30$^{29-31}$	J15v	39^{4a}*	E4iii
30$^{32-34}$	E3vii	39^{4b-5}	J18ii
30$^{35-31^1}$	J15v	39^{5a}	E4iii
31^{2}	E3vii	39^{5b-19}	J18ii
31^{3}	J15v	39^{20}–40^{1}	J18ii-iii
31^{4-18a}	E3vii	40^{2-3a}	E4iv
31^{18b}	P10ii	40^{3b}	J18iii
31$^{19-24}$	E3viii	40^{4-5a}	E4iv
31^{25}	J15vi	40^{5b}	J18iii
31^{26}	E3viii	40^{6-15a}	E4iv
31^{27}	J15vi	40^{15b}	J18iii
31$^{28-45}$	E3viii	40^{16}–41^{14a}	E4iv-v
31^{46-53a}	J15vi	41^{14b}	J18iv
31^{53b}–32^{2}	E3viii-ix	41$^{15-33}$	E4v
32^{3-13a}	J15vii	41$^{34-36}$	J18iv
32^{13b-21}	E3x	41$^{37-40}$	E4vi
32^{22}	J15viii	41^{41}	J18iv
32^{23}	E3xi	41$^{42-45}$	E4vi
32^{24}–33^{5a}	J15ix-x	41^{46a}	P12ii
33^{5b}	E3xii	41^{46b-47}	E4vii
33^{6-10a}	J15x	41^{48}	J18iv
33$^{10b-11a}$	E3xii	41$^{49-57}$	E4vii
33^{11b-17}	J13x	42^{1}	E4viii
33^{18a}	P10ii	42^{2}	J18v
33^{18b}–34^{2a}	E3xiii	42^{3-4a}	E4viii
34^{2b-3}	J15xi	42^{4b-5}	J18v
34^{4}	E3xiv	42^{6}	E4viii
34^{5}	J15xi	42^{7}*	J18v
34^{6}	E3xiv	42^{7}*	E4viii
34^{7}	J15xi	42$^{8-26}$	E4viii
34$^{8-10}$	E3xiv	42$^{27-28}$	J18v
34$^{11-12}$	J15xi	42$^{29-37}$	E4viii
34^{13}	E3xiv	42^{38}–43^{13}	J18v-vi
34^{14}	J15xi	43^{14}	E4viii
34$^{15-18}$	E3xiv	43^{15-23a}	J18vi
34^{19}	J15xi	43^{23b}	E4ix
34^{20-25a}	E3xiv	43^{24}–44^{34}	J18vi
34^{25b-26}	J15xi	45^{1a}	J18vii
34$^{27-29}$	E3xiv	45^{1b-4a}	E4ix
34$^{30-31}$	J15xi	45^{4b-5a}	J18vii
35$^{1-5}$	E3xv	45^{5b-9}	E4ix
35^{6a}	P10iii	45^{10a}	J18vii
35^{6b-8}	E3xv	45^{10b-12}	E4ix
35$^{9-13}$	P10iii	45$^{13-14}$	J18vii
35^{14}	E3xv	45$^{15-27}$	E4ix
35^{15}	P10iii	45^{28}	J18vii
35$^{16-20}$	E3xvi	46^{1a}	J18viii
35^{21-22a}	J15xii	46^{1b-5}	E4x
35^{22b-29}	P10iv-v	46$^{6-27}$	P12iii
36$^{1-30}$	P11	46^{28}–47^{5a}	J18viii
36$^{31-39}$	J16	47^{5b-6a}	P12iv
36$^{40-43}$	P11	47^{6b}	J18viii
37^{1-2a}	P10vi	47$^{7-11}$	P12iv

INDEX 393

47^{12}	E4xi
47^{12-26}	J18
47^{27a}	J19
47^{27b-29}	P12v
47^{29-31}	J19
48^{1-2a}	E5
48^{2b}	J19
48^{3-6}	P12v
48^{7-9a}	E5
48^{9b-10a}	J19
48^{10b-12}	E5
48^{13-14}	J19
48^{15-16}	E5
48^{17-19}	J19
48^{20-22}	E5
49^{1a}	P13
49^{1b-25a}	J19
49^{25b-32}	P13
49^{33a*}	J20
$49^{33#}$	P13
50^{1-11}	J20
50^{12-13}	P14
50^{14}	J20
50^{15-26}	E6

Exodus

1^{1-5}	P15
1^6	J21
1^7	P15
1^{8-12}	J22
1^{13-14}	P16
1^{15-20a}	E7-8
1^{20b}	J22
1^{21-22}	E8
2^{1-10}	E9-10
2^{11-22}	J23-24ii
2^{23a}	J24iii
2^{23b-25}	P16
3^1	E11i
3^{2-4a}	J24iii
3^{4b}	E11ii
3^5	J24iii
3^6	E11ii
3^{7-8}	J24iii
3^{9-15}	E11ii-iii
3^{16-18}	J24iii
3^{19-22}	E11iv-v
4^{1-16}	J24iii
4^{17-18}	E11vi-vii
4^{19-20a}	J24iii
4^{20b-21}	E11vii
4^{22-23}	J24iii
4^{24-26}	J25
4^{27-28}	E12
4^{29-31}	J26i
5^{1-2}	E13i
5^3	J26i
5^4	E13i
5^{5-6^1}	J26i
$6^{2-7^{13}}$	P17-22
7^{14-15a}	J26ii
7^{15b}	E13i
7^{16-17a}	J26ii
7^{17b}	E13iii
7^{18}	J26ii
7^{19-20a}	P23i
7^{20b}	E13ii
7^{21a}	J26ii
7^{21b-22}	P23i
7^{23}	E13ii
7^{24-25}	J26ii
8^{1-4}	J26iii
8^{5-7}	P23ii
8^{8-15a}	J26iii
8^{15b-19}	P23ii-iii
8^{20-32}	J26iv
9^{1-7}	J26v
9^{8-12}	P23iv
9^{13-21}	J26vi
9^{22-28a}	E13iii
9^{28b}	J26vi
9^{24a}	E13iii
9^{24b}	J26vi
9^{25a}	E13iii
9^{25b-34}	J26vi
9^{35}	E13iii
10^{1-11}	J26vii
10^{12-12a}	E13iv
10^{13b}	J26vii
10^{14a}	E13iv
$10^{14b-15a}$	J26vii
10^{15b}	E13iv
10^{15c-19}	J26vii
10^{20-23}	E13iv-v
10^{24-26}	J26viii
10^{27}	E13v
10^{28-29}	J26viii
11^{1-3}	E13vi-vii
11^{4-8}	J26viii
11^{9-10}	P23iv
12^{1-20}	P23v
12^{21-27}	J26ix
12^{28}	P23v
12^{29-34}	J26ix
12^{35-36}	E13vii
12^{37a}	P24
12^{37b-39}	J26x
12^{40-13^2}	P24-26
13^{3-16}	J26x
13^{17-19}	E13viii
13^{20}	P27
13^{21-22}	J26x
14^{1-2}	P27
14^3	E14
14^4	P28
14^{5-6}	J27
14^7	E14
14^{8-9}	P28
14^{10a}	J27
14^{10b}	E14
14^{11-14}	J27
14^{15}	P28
14^{16a}	E14
14^{16b-18}	P28
14^{19a}	E14
14^{19b-20}	J27
14^{21a}	P28
14^{21b}	J27
14^{22-23}	P28
14^{24}	J27
14^{25a}	E14
14^{25b}	J27
14^{26-27a}	P28
14^{27b}	J27
14^{28a}	P28
14^{28b}	J27
14^{29}	P28
14^{30-31}	J27
15^{1-21}	E15-16
15^{22-25a}	J28
15^{25b-26}	E17
15^{27}	J28
16^{1-3}	P29
16^{4-5}	J29
16^{6-13a}	P29
$16^{13b-15a}$	J29
16^{15b-20}	P29
16^{21}	J29
16^{22-36}	P29
17^{1a}	P30
17^{1b-2}	J30

394 SOURCES OF THE HEXATEUCH

17^{3-6}	E18
17^7	J30
17^{8}-18^{27}	E19-21
19^{1-2a}	P30
19^{2b-3a}	E22
19^{3b-9}	J31
19^{10-11a}	E22
19^{11b-13}	J31
19^{14-17}	E22
19^{18}	J31
19^{19}	E22
19^{20-25}	J31
20^{1-17}	E23
20^{18-21}	E22
20^{22}-23^{33}	E24
24^{1-2}	J32
24^{3-8}	E25
24^{9-11}	J32
24^{12-15a}	E26
$24^{15b-18a}$	P31
24^{18b}	E26
25^1-31^{17}	P32-33
$31^{18a\cdot b}$	P34
31^{18c}	E26
32^{1-35}	E27
33^{1-3a}	J33
33^{3b-11}	E28-29
33^{12-23}	J33
34^{1-28}	J34
34^{29-35}	P34
35^1-40^{38}	P35-36

Leviticus

1^1-16^{34}	P37-41
17^1-26^{46}	P42H
27^{1-34}	P43

Numbers

1^1-10^{28}	P44-54
10^{29-32}	J35
10^{33}	E30
10^{34}	P54
10^{35-36}	E30
11^{1-3}	E31
11^{4-10}	J36
11^{11-12}	J33
11^{13}	J36
11^{14}	E32
11^{15}	J33
11^{16-17}	E32
11^{18-24a}	J36
11^{24b-30}	E32
11^{31-35}	J36-37
12^{1-15}	E33
12^{16}	J37
13^{1-17a}	P55
13^{17b}	J38
13^{17c-18}	E34
13^{19}	J38
13^{20}	E34
13^{21}	P55
13^{22}	J38
13^{23-24}	E34
13^{25-26a}	P55
13^{26b}	E34
13^{27-29}	J38
13^{30-31}	E34
13^{32a}	P55
13^{32b-33}	E34
14^{1a}	P56
14^{1b}	E35
14^{1c}	J39
14^2	P56
14^3	J39
14^4	E35
14^{5-7}	P57
14^{8-9}	J40
14^{10}	P57
14^{11-21}	J41
14^{22-25}	E36
14^{26-30}	P58
14^{31-33}	J41
14^{34-38}	P58
14^{39-45}	E37
15^{1-41}	P59-61
16^{1a}	P62
16^{1b}	E38
16^{2-11}	P62
16^{12-15}	E38
16^{16-24}	P62
16^{25-26}	E38
16^{27a}	P62
$16^{27b-32a}$	E38
16^{32b}	P62
16^{33-34}	E38
16^{35-50}	P62
17^1-19^{22}	P63-65
20^{1a}	P66
20^{1b}	E39
20^2	P66
20^{3a}	J42
20^{3b-4}	P66
20^5	J42
20^{6-13}	P66
20^{14-21}	E40
20^{22-29}	P67
21^{1-3}	J43
21^{4a}	P68
21^{4b-9}	E41
21^{10-11}	P68
21^{12-35}	E42-44
22^1	P68
22^{2-5a}	E45
22^{5b}	J44
22^{6-7}	J44
22^{8-10}	E45
22^{11}	J44
22^{12-16}	E45
22^{17-18}	J44
22^{19-21}	E45
22^{22-35}	J44
22^{36}	E45
22^{37}	J44
22^{38}	E45
22^{39}	J44
22^{40-41}	E45
23^{1-30}	E46
24^{1-2}	J44
24^{3-25}	J45
25^{1a}	E47
25^{1b-2}	J46
25^3	E47
25^4	J46
25^5	E47
25^6-32^{36}	P69-78
32^{39-42}	J47
33^1-36^{13}	P79-82

Deuteronomy

(Passages from E and P only)

10^{6-7}	E48
27^{5-7a}	E49
$31^{14-15, 23}$	E50
32^{48-52}	P83
33^{1-29}	E51
34^{1a}	P84
34^{1b-6}	E52
34^{7-9}	P84
34^{10}	E52

INDEX

Joshua

(The analysis here is much less certain than in the previous books. There is, however, practically unanimous agreement on the verses assigned below to J, E, and P. Uncertainty is indicated by the use of the symbol JE. Substantially all sections not assigned come from Rd or, in a few cases, from Rp.)

$2^{1-9a.12-23}$ E53JE
$3^{1.5.9-17}$ E54JE
$4^{1.3.4-11}$ E55JE
$4^{12.15-17}$ P85
4^{13} E55JE
4^{19} P85
4^{20} E55JE
$5^{2-3.8-9}$ E56
5^{10-12} P86
5^{13-15} J48
$6^{1.2-26}$ E57JE
7^{2-5} E58JE
7^{6-26} E59JE
8^{1-29} E60JE
9^{3-5} E61JE
9^{6-7} J49
$9^{8-9a.11-13.15a}$ E61JE
9^{15b} P87
9^{16} E61JE
9^{17-21} P87
$9^{22-23.26-27a}$ E61JE
$10^{1-7.9-14a.15-27*}$ E62JE
$11^{1-2.4-9}$ E63JE
$13^{1.7}$ E64JE
13^{13} J50
13^{15-33} P88
14^{1-5} P89
14^{6-15} E65
15^{1-12} P90
15^{13-19} J51
15^{20-62} P90
15^{63} J52
16^{1-3} E66JE
16^{4-8} P91
16^{9} E66JE
16^{10} J53
17^{1a} P92
17^{1b-2} E67JE
$17^{3-4.7}$ P92
17^{5} E67JE
17^{9-10a} P92
17^{10b} E67JE
17^{11-18} J54
18^{1} P88
$18^{2-6.8-10}$ E68
18^{11-28} P93
$19^{1-8.10-46}$ P94
19^{47} J55
19^{48} P94
19^{49-50} E69
19^{51} P94
20^{1-9} P95
21^{1-42} P96
22^{9-34} P97
24^{1-33} E70-73

Judges

1^{1-10} J56-57
1^{11-15} J51
1^{16-20} J58-60
1^{21} J52
1^{22-26} J61
1^{27-28} J54
1^{29} J53
1^{30-36} J62-63
2^{1-5} J64

www.ingramcontent.com/pod-product-compliance
Lightning Source LLC
Chambersburg PA
CBHW071225230426
43668CB00011B/1303